Capturing Caste in Law

This book is about the legal regulation of caste discrimination. It highlights the difficulty of capturing caste in international and domestic law and suggests solutions. Its aim is to contribute to the task of understanding how to secure effective legal protection from and prevention of discrimination on grounds of caste, and why this is important and necessary. It does this by examining the legal conceptualisation and regulation of caste as a social category and as a ground of discrimination, in international law and in two national jurisdictions (India and the UK), identifying their complexities, strengths, limitations and potential. Adopting a broadly chronological approach, the book aims to present an account of the role of law in the construction of caste inequality and discrimination, and the subsequent legal efforts to dismantle it. The book will be of value to lawyers and non-lawyers, academics and students of human rights, international law, equalities and discrimination, descent-based and caste-based discrimination, minority rights and South Asia and its diaspora. It will be a resource for legal practitioners and those in the public and non-governmental sectors involved in the implementation, interpretation and enforcement of equality law in the UK – the first European country to introduce the word caste into domestic equality legislation – and in other countries with South Asian diasporas such as the USA.

Annapurna Waughray is Professor of Human Rights Law at Manchester Metropolitan University, UK.

Routledge Research in Human Rights Law

For more information about this series, please visit: www.routledge.com/Routledge-Research-in-Human-Rights-Law/book-series/HUMRIGHTSLAW

Capturing Caste in Law

The Legal Regulation
of Caste Discrimination

Annapurna Waughray

LONDON AND NEW YORK

First published 2022
by Routledge
4 Park Square, Milton Park, Abingdon, Oxon OX14 4RN

and by Routledge
605 Third Avenue, New York, NY 10158

Routledge is an imprint of the Taylor & Francis Group, an informa business

British Library Cataloguing-in-Publication Data
A catalogue record for this book is available from the British Library

Library of Congress Cataloging-in-Publication Data
Names: Waughray, Annapurna, 1960– author.
Title: Capturing caste in law : the legal regulation of caste discrimination / Annapurna Waughray.
Description: Abingdon, Oxon [UK] ; New York, NY : Routledge, 2022. | Series: Routledge research in human rights law | Includes bibliographical references and index.
Identifiers: LCCN 2021043819 (print) | LCCN 2021043820 (ebook) | ISBN 9781138807761 (hardback) | ISBN 9781032009735 (paperback) | ISBN 9781315750934 (ebook)
Subjects: LCSH: Caste—Law and legislation—India—History. | India—Scheduled tribes—Legal status, laws, etc. | Dalits—Legal status, laws, etc.—India. | Caste-based discrimination—India. | Caste—Law and legislation—Great Britian—History. | Great Britain. Equality Act 2010. | Minorities—Legal status, laws, etc.—Great Britain. | International law and human rights. | International Convention on the Elimination of All Forms of Racial Discrimination (1965 December 21)
Classification: LCC KNS2107.C37 W38 2022 (print) | LCC KNS2107.C37 (ebook) | DDC 342.5408/7—dc23/eng/20211105
LC record available at https://lccn.loc.gov/2021043819
LC ebook record available at https://lccn.loc.gov/2021043820

ISBN: 978-1-138-80776-1 (hbk)
ISBN: 978-1-032-00973-5 (pbk)
ISBN: 978-1-315-75093-4 (ebk)

DOI: 10.4324/9781315750934

Typeset in Galliard
by Apex CoVantage, LLC

Contents

Abbreviations

AC	Appeal Cases
ACDA	Anti Caste Discrimination Alliance
AIR	All India Reporter
All ER	All England Law Reports
AWC	Allahabad Weekly Cases
BAWS	Babasaheb Ambedkar Writings and Speeches
BCCA	British Columbia Court of Appeal
BCHRT	British Columbia Human Rights Tribunal
CAD	Constituent Assembly Debates (India)
CEDAW	UN Convention on the Elimination of All Forms of Discrimination Against Women 1979
CEDAW/CUN	Committee on the Elimination of Discrimination Against Women
CERD	UN Committee on the Elimination of Racial Discrimination
CESCR	UN Committee on Economic, Social and Cultural Rights
CMLR	Common Market Law Reports
COI	Constitution of India 1950
CRC	UN Convention on the Rights of the Child
CRC/C	UN Committee on the Rights of the Child
CRE	Commission for Racial Equality
CRPD	Convention on the Rights of Persons with Disabilities
DCLG	Department for Communities and Local Government
DDPA	Durban Declaration and Programme of Action
DHE	Department of Higher Education (India)
DLR	Discrimination Law Review
DPA	Draft Programme of Action (Durban)
DPGs	UN Draft Principles and Guidelines
DRC	Durban Review Conference
DSN-UK	Dalit Solidarity Network UK
DWD	discrimination based on work and descent
EAIA	Equality Act Impact Assessment
EA	Equality Act 2010
EAT	employment appeals tribunal
ECOSOC	UN Economic and Social Council
ECHR	European Convention on Human Rights
EHRC	Equality and Human Rights Commission
EHRR	European Human Rights Reports

EPW	Economic and Political Weekly (India)
ET	employment tribunal
EU	European Union
EWCA	England and Wales Court of Appeal
EWHC	High Court of England and Wales
GEO	Government Equalities Office
GOI	Government of India
HC	House of Commons
HCUK	Hindu Council UK
HFB	Hindu Forum of Britain
HL	House of Lords
HRC	Human Rights Committee
IACtHR	Inter-American Court of Human Rights
ICCPR	International Covenant on Civil and Political Rights 1966
ICERD	International Convention on the Elimination of All Forms of Racial Discrimination 1965
ICESCR	International Covenant on Economic, Social and Cultural Rights 1966
ICJ	International Court of Justice
ICR	Industrial Cases Reports
ICTR	International Criminal Tribunal for Rwanda
IDSN	International Dalit Solidarity Network
ILO	International Labour Organisation
IRLR	Industrial Relations Law Reports
ISCR	India Supreme Court Reports
MHRD	Ministry of Human Resource Development (India)
MJSE	Ministry of Justice and Social Empowerment (India)
NCRB	National Crime Records Bureau (India)
NCSC	National Commission for Scheduled Castes (India)
NGO	non-governmental organisation
NHRC	National Human Rights Commission (India)
NIESR	National Institute for Economic and Social Research
NZLR	New Zealand Law Reports
OBC	other backward classes
OHCHR	Office of the UN High Commissioner for Human Rights
QB	Queen's Bench
SC	Scheduled Caste
SCUK	Sikh Council UK
SR	Summary Records
SRR	UN Special Rapporteur on Racism
ST	Scheduled Tribe
TFEU	Treaty on the Functioning of the European Union
UDHR	Universal Declaration of Human Rights 1948
UKEAT	United Kingdom Employment Appeals Tribunal
UKSC	United Kingdom Supreme Court
UN	United Nations
UNGA	UN General Assembly
UNTS	United Nations Treaty Series

UPR	Universal Periodic Review
VCLT	Vienna Convention on the Law of Treaties 1969
VODI	Voice of Dalit International
WCAR	UN World Conference Against Racism, Racial Discrimination, Xenophobia and Related Intolerance 2001
WLR	Weekly Law Reports

Cases and Decisions

Legislation

United Kingdom Statutes
Administration of Justice Regulation 1781
Anti-social Behaviour, Crime and Policing Act 2014 c 12
Caste Disabilities Removal Act 1850 Act XXI of 1850
Education and Inspections Act 2006   c 40
Equality Act 2006 c 3
Equality Act 2010 c 15
Family Law Act 1996 c 27
Forced Marriage (Civil Protection) Act 2007 c 20
Government of India Act 1833 3 & 4 Will. 4 c 85
Government of India Act 1858 21 & 22 Vict. c 106
Government of India Act 1935 26 Geo. 5 c 2
Human Rights Act 1998 c 42
Marriage Act 1949 c 76
Race Relations Act 1965 c 73
Race Relations Act 1968 c 71
Race Relations Act 1976 c 74
Race Relations (Amendment) Act 2000 c 34
Sex Discrimination Act 1975 c 65

United Kingdom Statutory Instruments
Employment Equality (Religion or Belief) Regulations 2003 SI 2003/1660
Employment Equality (Sexual Orientation) Regulations 2003 SI 2003/1661
Race Relations Act 1976 (Amendment) Regulations 2003 SI 2003/1626
Equality Act (Sexual Orientation) Regulations 2007 SI 2007/126

European Union
Council Directive 2000/43/EC of 29 June 2000 implementing the principle of equal treatment between persons irrespective of racial or ethnic origin OJ 2000/L180/22
Council Directive 2000/78/EC of 27 November 2000 establishing a general framework
for equal treatment in employment and occupation OJ 2000/L303/1

Australia
Racial Discrimination Act 1975, Act No. 2 of 1975

Canada
British Columbia Human Rights Code 1996

India
Andhra Pradesh Devadasi (Prohibition of Dedication) Act 1988, Act No. 10 of 1988
Bonded Labour System (Abolition) Act 1976
Child Labour (Prohibition and Regulation) Act 1986
Constitution (Forty-second) Amendment Act 1976
Constitution of India 1950 at www.lawmin.nic.in/coi.htm
Constitution (Scheduled Castes) Order 1950 (C.O. 19)
Constitution (Scheduled Castes) Orders (Amendment) Act 1990
Employment of Manual Scavengers and Construction of Dry Latrines (Prohibition) Act 1993
Karnataka Devadasis (Prohibition of Dedication) Act 1992
Prohibition of Employment as Manual Scavengers and Their Rehabilitation Act 2013
Protection of Civil Rights Act 1955, Act No. 22 of 1955 (previously the Untouchability (Offences) Act 1955)
Scheduled Castes and Scheduled Tribes Orders (Amendment) Act 1956
Scheduled Castes and Scheduled Tribes (Prevention of Atrocities) Act 1989
Scheduled Castes and Scheduled Tribes (Prevention of Atrocities) Amendment Act 2015
Scheduled Castes and Scheduled Tribes (Prevention of Atrocities) Amendment Rules 2016
Sexual Harassment of Women at Workplace (Prevention, Prohibition and Redressal) Act 2013

Nepal
Nepali Royal Law Code 1854 (Muluki Ain)
The Caste-based Discrimination and Untouchability Act, 2068 (2011)

Sri Lanka
Prevention of Social Disabilities Act 1957 (Ceylon)

South Africa
Asiatic Land Tenure and Indian Representation Act 1946, No. 28

Treaties and Instruments

Charter of the United Nations, 24 October 1945. 1 UNTS XVI

Convention on the Prevention and Punishment of the Crime of Genocide 1948. Adopted 9 December 1948. In force 12 January 1951. 78 UNTS 277

Universal Declaration of Human Rights 1948. General Assembly Resolution 217 (III), 10 December 1948. A/RES/217 A (III)

European Convention for the Protection of Human Rights and Fundamental Freedoms, as amended by Protocols Nos. 11 and 14, 1950. Treaty Series No. 071/1953: Cm 8969

ILO Discrimination (Employment and Occupation) Convention 1958 (No. 111)

ILO Abolition of Forced Labour Convention (No. 105) 1957

Convention on Consent to Marriage, Minimum Age for Marriage and Registration of Marriages 1962. Adopted 10 December 1962. In force 9 December 1964. 521 UNTS 231

United Nations Declaration on the Elimination of Racial Discrimination 1963. General Assembly Resolution 1904 (XVIII), 20 November 1963. A/RES/18/1904

International Convention on the Elimination of All Forms of Racial Discrimination 1965. Adopted 21 December 1965. In force 4 January 1969. 660 UNTS 195

International Covenant on Economic, Social and Cultural Rights 1966. Adopted 16 December 1966. In force 3 January 1976. 999 UNTS 3

Vienna Convention on the Law of Treaties 1969. Adopted 23 May 1969. In force 27 January 1980. 1155 UNTS 331

International Covenant on Civil and Political Rights 1966. Adopted 16 December 1966. In force 23 March 1976. 999 UNTS 171

ILO Minimum Age Convention 1973 (No.138)

Convention for the Elimination of All Forms of Discrimination Against Women. Adopted 18 December 1979. In force 3 September 1981. 1249 UNTS 13

Convention Against Torture and Other Cruel, Inhuman or Degrading Treatment or Punishment 1984. Adopted 10 December 1984. In force 26 June 1987. 1465 UNTS 85

Convention on the Rights of the Child. Adopted 20 November 1989. In force 2 September 1990. 1577 UNTS 3

United Nations Declaration on the Rights of Persons Belonging to National or Ethnic, Religious and Linguistic Minorities. General Assembly Resolution 47/135, 18 December 1992. A/RES/47/135

ILO Worst Forms of Child Labour Convention 1999 (No. 182)

Convention on the Rights of Persons with Disabilities. Adopted 13 December 2006. In force 3 May 2008. 2515 UNTS 3

UN Declaration on the Rights of Indigenous Peoples. 2 October 2007. A/RES/61/295

Treaty on the Functioning of the European Union (consolidated version 2012) OJ 2012/C 326/01

Foreword

Perhaps as many as a quarter of the world's population lives in countries, mostly South Asian, in which inherited caste is a significant aspect of social organisation and identity, shaping opportunity and the experience of discrimination. Although readily overlooked, the influence of caste has become truly global through population mobility and in diaspora communities outside South Asia. Finding a way to view caste in its modern and transnational form is a challenge. This book is a response to that challenge.

By examining caste in terms of the history of its legal conceptualisation and regulation in two national jurisdictions (India and the UK) and in international law, Annapurna Waughray provides an immensely valuable perspective on caste and caste-based discrimination commensurate with its contemporary reach and historical depth. This is the first extended discussion of caste in its historically and socially varied forms from a legal perspective and as such is a major contribution for and from legal scholarship, equipping lawyers worldwide with the most sophisticated understanding of caste available, informed by a balanced appraisal of the wide range of historical, sociological and religious perspectives that are today likely to be drawn into legal as well as scholarly arguments.

This analysis of caste and law not only opens up a neglected perspective on caste but also shows us that the law provides insight into a range of social, political and institutional responses to caste and its discriminatory effects. Indeed, the manner in which caste is conceived in law, how legal regulation of caste is sought or resisted and the judicial processes involved are today inseparably part of this complex institution. Moreover, through the book's treatment of social regulation, in the long view we come to a broader understanding of law itself, encompassing, for example, Dalit leader Dr Ambedkar's view of Hinduism as an apparatus of law rather than religion, and crucially his recognition that it is as law (rather than as religion) that the rules, regulations and prescriptions of caste could be challenged and changed. Hence the centrality of law to historical movements against caste hierarchy and oppression. *Capturing Caste in Law* is not then a specialist legal analysis of caste; it provides what is now a necessary element in the study of caste and its transformation for any discipline, opening to understanding the key aspects of this most complex and elusive of global social institutions.

I would go further, and suggest that *Capturing Caste in Law* aligns thinking on caste to the contemporary reality in which the sociological facts of caste are inseparable from its life in law and litigation, whether in India or internationally. Of course, the concern of law is not the social scientific description of caste but the mitigation of its potentially negative effects – inequality and discrimination – and the conception and definition of these so as to allow legal protection. But the social experience of caste, its political meaning as a basis for mobilisation, is today intimately bound up with these legal definitions and debates. This means that this book provides a window on the modern social life of caste as much as an education on how caste is circumscribed by law.

Certainly, caste is not adequately grasped in the terms of a specifically Indian cultural or Hindu religious system. As a form of social capital, inherited status, a structure of exclusion and of advantage, caste bears comparison with race, ethnicity or other social systems founded on the differential valuation of human beings against which anti-discrimination, affirmative action, equality law and other legislative instruments have been marshalled. Legal thought is able to illuminate aspects of caste in its emerging international form, precisely because debates on caste have often taken place within the framework of law. By tracing contemporary lawmaking around caste, Waughray is able further to demonstrate what has long been clear from histories of colonial and postcolonial India, namely that caste is an institution formed through the interaction of a social system with the manner of its representation and regulation in legal and administrative terms.

It is not only law in theory but also law in practice that underpins the insights of *Capturing Caste in Law*. Indeed, the intellectual project contained in this book has been developed and refined through engagement in the policy and politics of caste. The unparalleled acuity of conceptualisations, observations and grasp of the subtleties of caste is owed in part to this practical engagement in the UK alongside keen awareness of the legal landscape in India and internationally.

Waughray is a keen participant observer of contemporary processes of caste, especially in the UK. She has a close-up and engaged grasp of how legal representations and social responses to them continue to shape caste at different scales and in different contexts. Equally at ease in the contemporary worlds of legal practice and of NGOs, community organisations turning to the law for redress for hurtful discrimination, Waughray is able to mark and bridge the legal and non-legal usage of terms such as discrimination, ethnicity, ethnic origins, race and descent that have come to surround caste. In short, this book brings uncommon insight to the interaction of legislative and social processes because of Waughray's understanding of these processes by being there, and playing a role as the leading expert on caste and law in the UK. This provides a unique grasp of the politics of legislation on caste in the first country outside South Asia to recognise caste prejudice and discrimination.

The attempt to introduce legislation on caste-based discrimination in the UK has stalled, as the Conservative Government shamefully becomes the first to repeal an element of equality law before it has even been implemented. The controversy over this legislation is no parochial matter: it speaks to wider issues in the reframing of caste in non-Indian, non-exceptionalist terms, and to the significance of law in the struggle between those who seek legal redress for a type of identity-based discrimination which others seek to keep outside of law. The controversy, carefully described in the book, demonstrates the capacity of law to invoke caste as a social category as a means to protect people inescapably marked by inferiorised identities and who suffer invisible judgments about their worth. But it also reveals the strength of resistance to the word "caste" entering legal discourse, where it is conceived as an incursion into inner community spaces of a religious minority; in short, a contest provoked by law between claims to freedom from caste discrimination and claims to the freedom of caste association in the name of religion.

The UK controversy over anti-caste discrimination law has a wider significance. As forms of caste association, networking, opportunity hoarding and exclusion become more diverse and dispersed, and as simple classical models of caste as a ritual and religious system are discredited, the beneficiaries of the caste-networked society and economy increasingly silence, disguise and deny caste and its effects. This book is thus important in holding the realities of caste inequality and discrimination to account.

Waughray is not only rigorous in her attention to empirical evidence but also consistent in her ethical stance. She brings an activist's deep appreciation of the significance of caste discrimination in the UK and of law in its prevention, a sophisticated practising lawyer's sensibility to the implications for judicial practice and a scholarly grasp of the context and comparative importance of the unfolding events in which she plays a significant part. With growing public debate on varied kinds of identity-based discrimination, the profound impact of caste and its judgments and the need for recognition of harm and the means for redress, this is a book whose time is now.

David Mosse
London, October 2021

Preface and acknowledgements

This book is about the legal regulation of caste discrimination. It highlights the difficulty of capturing caste in international and domestic law and suggests some solutions. Its aim is to contribute to the task of understanding how to secure effective legal protection from and prevention of discrimination on grounds of caste, and why this is important and necessary. It does this by examining the legal capture of caste as a social category and as a ground of discrimination, and the legal frameworks for combating caste-based discrimination, in international law and in two national jurisdictions, India and the UK, identifying their complexities, strengths, limitations and potential.

This book, and the doctoral research on which it is based, would not have been possible without the help, support and encouragement of many people. I am deeply indebted to my doctoral supervisors Professor Dominic McGoldrick and Anne Morris at the University of Liverpool for their wise guidance, advice, recommendations, patience and support, and for the time, energy and care which they invested in the original PhD research. My thanks also to Emeritus Professor Patrick Thornberry (Keele University) for his comments as external supervisor on the international law chapters. I thank Routledge, my publisher, for their extraordinary patience with me and with the project. I am grateful to the University of Liverpool for a PhD partial fees grant and Manchester Metropolitan University for matching it, and the Modern Law Review for awarding me a Modern Law Review scholarship. My thanks to Mark James, Diana Massey, Damian Mather, Kay Lalor and all my colleagues at Manchester Metropolitan University for their support and encouragement, and to the Manchester Metropolitan University library staff for their professionalism, patience and helpfulness over the years. I thank my extended family in Hyderabad and Bengaluru for their generosity, kindness and support and for looking after me during my visits to India. I am grateful to my late great-uncle, Justice Upendralal Waghray and the late Justice O Chinnappa Reddy, his friend, for generous and wide-ranging discussions in Hyderabad on caste, discrimination, India, social justice and the law. I am grateful to the following for all that I have learned from them: the late Shekur Bagul, Upendra Baxi, Joshua Castellino, Raj Chand, the late Bhagwan Das, Santosh Das, Raj Chand, Paul Diwaker, S Japhet, Ravi-varma Kumar, Medha Kotwal Lele, PL Mimroth, Satpal Muman, Manjula Pradeep, Avatthi Ramaiah, Vidya Bhushan Rawat, DN Sandanshiv, the late Bojja Tarakam, SK Thorat, Meena Varma and the late Eleanor Zelliot. Thank you to the Manchester Metropolitan University Ambedkar Memorial Lecture Committee for the opportunities that membership of the Committee has provided for discussion and learning.

I owe a very special debt of gratitude to the following friends and colleagues who have shaped and challenged my ideas and thinking on caste and the law through conversation, discussion and debate over the years, many of whom have contributed to this book by their generous reading and comments on various drafts of different chapters: the late Burjor Avari, Meena Dhanda, Nuno Ferreira, Erica Howard, Ann Hynes, David Keane, Corinne Lennox, Aase Mygind Madsen, David Mosse, Eleanor Nesbitt, Javaid Rehman, Murali Shanmugave-lan, Surya Subedi, Nicole Weickgennant Thiara and Stephen Whittle. I thank Sheila Seal, Helena Kettleborough, Annabel Latham, Catherine Lecourtois and Jean-Luc Touboulie for their friendship, support and encouragement during the writing process. I thank my brother Dominic Kailashnath Waughray. I thank my dear friends Rachel Cooper and Mark Robin-son for their constant support, encouragement and advice since the idea for this research was first conceived with them in New Delhi almost two decades ago. I thank Julian Long Howison without whose contribution, support, help and advice over many years this research and this book would not have been possible. Finally, my thanks go to my children Indra, Silas and Beatrix Howison Waughray for their love, patience and forbearance and for the love and joy they bring me.

Manchester, October 2021

Introduction

Context

Caste is a complex social phenomenon characterised by its historical fluidity, adaptability and resilience regardless of changing social, economic and political conditions. As a system of social organisation and stratification, and as a form of inherited social identity, its origins and the mechanisms of its survival are contested, but its history extends back into the ancient past. It is generally accepted that caste is inherited (acquired by birth) and is maintained by endogamy, whereby marriage is restricted to individuals of the same caste.[1]

Caste is associated predominantly with South Asia, in particular India, where it has been embedded for centuries as a form of social differentiation and a mechanism for inequality.[2] Discrimination, subordination and oppression on grounds of caste affect almost 201 million Dalits (formerly known as "untouchables") in India alone, where they comprise over 16% of the population.[3] Significantly, caste also occurs among South Asian diaspora communities, including in the United Kingdom (where estimates of the numbers of people of Dalit origin range from 50,000 to 200,000 or more) and the United States of America.[4] In 2013, the UK Parliament became the first non-South Asian legislature to require caste to be added to equality legislation as a ground of discrimination; however, in the face of vigorous opposition, primarily from religious groups, successive governments have declined to amend the Equality Act 2010. The work of anti-caste and Dalit activists in the UK to secure statutory protection from caste discrimination, and the opposition this has engendered, is examined in Part 3 of this book.

Caste is distinguished from other forms of social stratification based on inherited status by its textual underpinnings in certain strands of Hinduism[5] and by the dehumanising concept and practice of untouchability, whereby certain humans are deemed, by birth and lineage, to be intrinsically, permanently and irredeemably "polluted." Although caste is associated

---

1 M Dhanda, A Waughray, D Keane, and D Mosse, 'Caste in Britain: Socio-Legal Review', *Equality and Human Rights Commission Research Report 91* (Manchester: Equality and Human Rights Commission, 2014) 3. Parts of this book contain material which appeared in limited form in 'Caste in Britain: Socio-Legal Review'.
2 Ibid.
3 See B Natrajan, *The Culturalization of Caste in India: Identity and Inequality in a Multicultural Age* (Abingdon and New York: Routledge, 2012). Dalit is a South-Asian political term of self-identification meaning "crushed" or " 'broken" in Marathi, a regional language of western India; see Chapter 1.
4 See H Metcalfe and H Rolfe, *Caste Discrimination and Harassment in Great Britain* (London: GEO, 2010) 20; T Soundararajan, 'A New Lawsuit Shines a Light on Caste Discrimination in the U.S. and Around the World', *The Washington Post*, 13 July 2020.
5 On Hinduism as a nineteenth-century neologism, see Chapter 1 and Chapter 9.

DOI: 10.4324/9781315750934-1

textually and doctrinally only with Hinduism, it is not and never has been strictly or solely a religious, or a religion-specific, phenomenon. Distinctions and discrimination based on caste are found among South Asian followers of Islam and Christianity, despite the absence of a doctrinal basis for caste in these religions, and among some followers of Sikhism despite Sikhism's doctrinal renunciation of caste, as well as among adherents of other religions and none. India's Ministry of Minority Affairs has described caste as a 'general social characteristic' regardless of whether it is recognised or not by the philosophy and teachings of any particular religion.[6]

Dalits in contemporary South Asia suffer from systemic and widespread marginalisation; physical and social exclusion; and discrimination and violation of their economic, social, cultural, civil and political rights, ranging from discriminatory and oppressive behaviour in the public, social and private spheres, and humiliation and lack of civility in day-to-day life, through to severe deprivation and extreme violence.[7] Amid ongoing debate in India about the changing nature of caste, institutionalised caste-based inequality persists despite constitutional and legislative prohibitions of caste discrimination and caste-based violence, the criminalisation of the practice of untouchability and constitutional affirmative action policies in favour of Dalits. Despite being unlawful in India since 1950, and despite examples of its "suspension" in some urban public spaces, untouchability continues to manifest in practices such as the avoidance of physical contact or even physical proximity (for example, avoiding sitting next to a Dalit pupil or student in class), taboos on inter-dining and the taking of water from castes considered "polluting," residential segregation and taboos and restrictions on Dalits' use of facilities such as roads, wells, shops and restaurants.[8] More extreme is the use of systemic violence or "atrocities," frequently of a highly gendered nature, as a means of maintaining Dalits' subordinated social and economic status. For many Dalits, the social and economic impacts of India's post-1991 economic liberalisation have acted to reinforce rather than to overturn their historically subordinate social and economic position in the social order, while serious discriminatory barriers remain in the formal urban labour market, even for highly qualified Dalits.[9] The political equality for Dalits, introduced on independence in the Constitution of 1950, has not led to economic equality. Since the 1990s, Dalit activists have brought the existence of political, social and economic discrimination, exclusion, deprivation and mistreatment on grounds of caste in India and elsewhere to the attention of United Nations (UN) human rights bodies, the European Union (EU) and, latterly, the British Parliament. Using the language of human rights, they have reframed caste discrimination as a domestic and international human rights issue. In the UN arena and in the UK, their demand has been inter alia for the legal regulation of caste discrimination via treaty law and domestic legislation, while in India their demand has been for the effective

---

6 *Report of the National Commission for Religious and Linguistic Minorities* (New Delhi: Ministry of Minority Affairs, 2009) 153–154.

7 Historically, under the dominant social and value systems, the Dalits were completely 'outside the fold' and did not even have the right to have rights: '[t]he Untouchables have no rights against the Touchables; they must not insist on rights'; BR Ambedkar, 'Outside the Fold', in V Rodrigues (ed.), *The Essential Writings of BR Ambedkar* (New Delhi: Oxford University Press, 2002) 330–331.

8 Navsarjan Trust and Robert F Kennedy Centre for Justice and Human Rights, 'Understanding Untouchability: A Comprehensive Study of Practices and Conditions in 1589 Villages' (2010) 17–20, at https://archive.crin.org/en/docs/Untouchability_Report_Navsarjan_2010.pdf.

9 See, for example, SK Thorat and K Newman, *Blocked by Caste: Economic Discrimination in Modern India* (New Delhi: Oxford University Press, 2012).

implementation and enforcement of existing laws and for new strategies and policies to remedy ongoing economic and social inequality in all its forms.

Given that caste is such a complex phenomenon, it is not surprising that law, both national and international, has found it difficult to capture caste adequately or to address caste-based discrimination. The pre-eminent scholar of caste, Dr BR Ambedkar (1891–1956), one of India's greatest political thinkers and leaders, a lawyer and an economist by training, a drafter of India's 1950 Constitution, a campaigner for social justice and human rights and for the eradication of caste and himself a Dalit, was the first person to study caste in a comprehensive, holistic and interdisciplinary way. Since his death, caste has been the subject of extensive academic study by South Asian and Western scholars alike. Initially, these scholars were predominantly sociologists and anthropologists. Only later did caste become a subject of study for historians, political scientists, political theorists and economists, as well as scholars from disciplines such as religious studies, education, philosophy, psychology and cultural studies. There is now a vast body of knowledge on all aspects of caste in modern India and, increasingly, the South Asian diaspora, across a wide range of disciplines. However, with some notable exceptions, caste and caste discrimination have attracted limited attention from legal scholars and lawyers,[10] which has resulted in an imbalance in the understanding of this complex area. There is a need for more thinking about how law does, or might, address the phenomenon of caste and caste discrimination, including in the diaspora, a gap this book seeks to address by highlighting the challenges of capturing the concept in international and domestic law, and suggesting some solutions.

This book, then, looks at caste and caste discrimination through the prism of law, and is the first to do so across three jurisdictions. Specifically, it is concerned with the legal regulation of caste discrimination in Indian law,[11] in international human rights law and in British law. The engagement of European law and the legal systems of other states, including those with South Asian diasporas, with caste as a ground of discrimination, is beyond the scope of the present book. Adopting a broadly chronological approach, it provides an account of the evolution of legal conceptualisations and the legal regulation of caste and caste discrimination over centuries in India, since the mid-1980s in the UN and since the mid-2000s in the UK. Over the course of the book, the interrelationship between these three legal arenas as sites of political power and contestation, and the way in which they are kept notionally separate, or brought together, by political action, is revealed. Caste discrimination is a contemporary human rights violation which blights hundreds of millions of lives every day across South Asia and the diaspora, 'albeit one which remains insufficiently recognised'.[12] It is thus imperative that states in which caste discrimination occurs make use of the full range of available tools – i.e. international human rights treaty law, bodies and mechanisms, domestic legislation, economic and social policies, equality duties, affirmative action and civic education – to acknowledge and tackle it.

The book is, first, intended for academic lawyers and law students, especially those interested in international and domestic human rights law, as well as lawyers and activists in the

---

10 Exceptions include Upendra Baxi, Joshua Castellino, Marc Galanter, KG Kannabiran, David Keane, Krishna Iyer, Suresh Mane, Smita Narula, Patrick Thornberry.

11 For present purposes, "Indian law" is used to mean secular state law, including constitutional law, statute law (civil and criminal), and common law (case law), but not customary or personal law.

12 A Waughray and D Keane, 'CERD and Caste-Based Discrimination', in *Fifty Years of the International Convention on the Elimination of All Forms of Racial Discrimination: A Living Instrument* (Manchester: Manchester University Press, 2017) 121–149, 146.

public, non-governmental organisation (NGO) and inter-governmental organisation (IGO) sectors involved in the implementation and enforcement of equality law, to provide them with an understanding of caste as a ground of discrimination in a historical and a comparative context. It also aims to provide campaigners, regardless of their stance, with legal arguments for more informed discussion. Second, it is written for scholars of social science disciplines, religious studies and social policy who are less familiar with legal analysis and practice, whether in a hybrid legal system such as India, a common law system such as the UK or the international human rights legal regime under the auspices of the United Nations. Terms such as "discrimination," "ethnicity," "ethnic origins," "race" and "descent" have legal and non-legal meanings and are interpreted and used differently by lawyers and non-lawyers. The book seeks to bridge the divide between lawyers and non-lawyers by providing a clear and accessible historical and comparative account of the role of law in the construction of caste inequality and discrimination in South Asia and its diaspora, as well as domestic and international legal efforts to remedy and eradicate such discrimination. It also speaks to the relationship between legal and other forms of knowledge about society in a way that is accessible to lawyers and non-lawyers alike.

The book addresses four principal questions. First, how has the concept of caste and the phenomenon of discrimination and inequality on grounds of caste been defined, constructed and addressed by law? Second, what has been the trajectory of caste discrimination, of the religious, social and legal rationales for such discrimination *and* for its elimination, and what has been the evolution of legal remedies? Third, what are the benefits and limitations of existing legal analyses of and strategies for addressing caste discrimination in India, in international law and in the UK? Fourth, what factors have influenced – and acted as obstacles to – the development of new legal analyses and strategies for the elimination of caste discrimination? What lessons can be learned from the answers to these questions, and what recommendations can be made for the future shaping of law and policy?[13]

Conceptual approach

The book adopts a holistic approach to the problem of how caste can be captured in law and how we can deal with caste discrimination through law, by bringing different perspectives to bear. It combines elements of "doctrinal" research (providing a systematic exposition and critique of the legal rules under examination) with 'problem, policy and law reform-based non-doctrinal research'.[14] The work is historical and comparative, socio-legal and interdisciplinary. It examines the interface and interlinkage between national and international legal orders, straddling human rights law, minority rights and national discrimination and criminal law, across two geographical jurisdictions, namely India and the United Kingdom.

---

13   Iyola Solanke reminds us not to conflate "law" and "policy": policies 'do not by themselves confer actionable legal rights' and do not have to include legal measures; 'policy recognition' of a problem or issue does not necessarily lead to a commitment to legislate and thence to 'legal definition' i.e. formal legal prohibition; I Solanke, *Making Anti-Racial Discrimination Law: A Comparative History of Social Action and Anti-Racial Discrimination Law* (Abingdon: Routledge, 2009) xiv–xv.

14   M Pendleton, 'Non-Empirical Discovery in Legal Scholarship – Choosing, Researching and Writing a Traditional Scholarly Article', in M McConville and W Hong Chui (eds.), *Research Methods for Law* (Edinburgh: Edinburgh University Press, 2007) 159–180, 159. Pendleton interprets the term "research" in the context of legal scholarship to cover 'a whole range of investigative, analytical, critical, theoretical and/or synthesising intellectual activity by academic lawyers'; ibid., 161.

Methods and sources

The book takes India and the UK as "case studies" in a loose sense. India is the paradigmatic example of the longevity of caste, and the country with the world's largest Dalit population and the greatest experience of the use of law to tackle caste discrimination. The UK is the first country outside South Asia to recognise officially the existence of caste prejudice and discrimination on its shores and whose legislature has mandated the amendment of equality legislation to prohibit caste discrimination. However, successive administrations have not only lacked 'an active commitment to legislate' (to borrow Iyiola Solanke's term), but they have increasingly displayed an active aversion to legislating, culminating in an announcement in July 2018 by the then Conservative Government of their intention to repeal the statutory duty imposed by Parliament in 2013 to legislate against caste discrimination.[15]

The book draws on written sources consisting of UN documents; UK and Indian legislation and case law; government publications and official statistics from the UK and India; UK parliamentary records; India's Constituent Assembly Debates; press and other media material (relied on for its contemporaneous capture of events and the public mood, rather than its objectivity); material produced by non-governmental organisations and inter-governmental organisations (NGOs and IGOs) (so-called grey literature); correspondence produced by a variety of actors, which depicts these actors' views of events; and the author's contemporaneous records of meetings and discussions. Government and NGO websites were also widely used, as was peer-reviewed scholarly work (academic journals and books). The author has had access to sources such as contemporaneous documents, correspondence and materials, as well as opportunities for discussion and debate and the sharing of views which have informed the research on which this book is based.[16] The problems this book identifies and seeks to address 'may not necessarily all be legal but the focus for analysis is the law, whether it is a focus on reasoning internal to the law or on law in context'.[17] There is a strong argument that the 'ethical premises' underpinning scholarly research and writing should be transparent;[18] in this case, it is the premise that caste discrimination, as a form of discrimination prohibited by international human rights law, should be subject to effective legal regulation domestically as well as internationally.

Organisation of the book

The book is in three parts. Part 1 (*The Making and Remaking of Caste*) spans Chapters 1 to 3, Part 2 (*Caste and International Human Rights Law*) spans Chapters 4 and 5 and Part 3 (*Legal Regulation of Caste Discrimination in the UK*) spans Chapters 6 to 9. Caste is complicated to understand and theorise, and so the book starts by explaining how it can be understood in sociological, historical, religious, cultural, economic, material, psychological and ideological terms. Part 1 explores, in Chapters 1 and 2, the socio-historical framework of caste and introduces some of the issues relating to its complexity. The paradox of its

---

15 See Chapter 9.
16 The book draws on Professor David Feldman's definition of scholarship as 'an action informed by a distinctive attitude of mind', and legal scholarship as 'a conception which results from the application of the concept of scholarship to the special kinds of problems that are discovered in the study of laws and legal systems'; see D Feldman, 'The Nature of Legal Scholarship', 52(4) *Modern Law Review* (1989) 498–517, 502.
17 E Fisher and others, 'Maturity and Methodology: Starting a Debate About Environmental Law Scholarship', 21(2) *Journal of Environmental Law* (2009) 213–250, 216.
18 See Pendleton (n 14) 164–165.

persistence and tenacity, albeit in changing form, is also addressed. What emerges from these chapters is an understanding that historically the most significant divide has been, and remains, between Dalits and non-Dalits.

Chapter 3 sets out the nature of caste discrimination in contemporary India, explores its historical, political, social and economic features and examines and critiques the legal responses introduced by India to combat it. Chapter 3 also examines the contradictions inherent in India's legal categorisation of the Dalits, specifically the exclusion of non-Indic religionists, principally Muslims and Christians, from the Scheduled Caste legal category, and argues why and how the law should be reformed to remove these contradictions.[19]

Part 2 focuses on the engagement of international human rights law and UN human rights mechanisms with caste discrimination. It examines the "internationalisation" of caste by Dalit activists from the 1980s onwards and the value of this strategy for Dalit advocacy, given that positive provisions on caste discrimination in India's constitution and domestic legislation had already been in place for forty years. Chapter 4 examines the evolution, from the mid-1990s onwards, of the conceptualisation of caste by the UN Committee on the Elimination of Racial Discrimination (CERD) as a form of discrimination based on descent – and hence a form of racial discrimination prohibited by Article 1 of the International Convention on the Elimination of Racial Discrimination (ICERD).[20] Chapter 4 also briefly evaluates the engagement of other treaty bodies with the issue of caste and caste discrimination. Dalits have also pursued non-treaty approaches, including minority rights and indigenous people's approaches, before UN forums. Chapter 5 provides an evaluation of the value and success of these approaches.[21]

Part 3 of the book focuses on the UK and the challenge involved in countering caste discrimination with law in the diaspora. It identifies and explores the limitations and problems of relying on the protected characteristics of race and religion or belief for capturing caste. Chapter 6 contextualises the problem, outlining the history of the Dalit presence in the UK, caste divisions and the caste-based discrimination encountered by Dalits within South Asian communities. Chapter 7 examines the British discrimination law model and analyses the possibilities of the protected characteristics of race and religion or belief as "legal homes" for caste.

Chapter 8 analyses the debates on the inclusion of an express prohibition of caste discrimination in the Equality Act 2010 during the passage of the Equality Bill through Parliament in 2009–2010, which resulted in caste being introduced at the margins of that law.

Chapter 9 is concerned with legal and political developments, from the enactment of the Equality Act in April 2010 until the Conservative Government's announcement in July 2018 of its intention to repeal the statutory duty to introduce caste discrimination legislation.

Caste discrimination is an egregious violation of international human rights law affecting millions of people globally every day. It is an affront to civilised society and has no place in twenty-first-century democracies. Non-legal approaches to tackling it as a global issue are

---

19 See A Waughray, 'Caste Discrimination and Minority Rights: The Case of India's Dalits', 17(2) *International Journal on Minority and Group Rights* (2010) 327–353.
20 Adopted 21 December 1965. In force 4 January 1969. 660 UNTS 195. Indian ratification 3 December 1968. UK ratification 7 March 1969. Racial discrimination is defined in Article 1(1) of ICERD by reference to any distinction, exclusion, restriction or preference based on race, colour, descent or national or ethnic origin.
21 A lengthier treatment of Dalit rights as minority rights in international law, as well as Dalits and minorities in Indian constitutional law, can be found in Waughray, 'Caste Discrimination and Minority Rights: The Case of India's Dalits' (n 19).

essential, but so is the effective use of domestic and international human rights law. The difficulties of capturing caste in law are examined in this book. They are not insurmountable; rather, the challenge lies in securing political and social commitment in those states where caste discrimination occurs to caste discrimination legislation and its enforcement, because the progressive elimination of caste discrimination is essential to a flourishing twenty-first-century democracy.

Part I

The making and remaking of caste

1 What is caste?*

Caste is a multifaceted and complex social phenomenon which has to be understood in historical, sociological, cultural, psychological, economic, religious and ideological as well as legal terms. This chapter introduces the concept of caste and examines what is meant by caste, both sociologically and legally. It identifies and explains the operative features of caste as a social and ideological construct, and describes the ways in which it has been conceptualised, theorised and analysed as a sociological and legal phenomenon. The chapter is in three sections. Section 1 starts by introducing the key concepts associated with caste and some of its key features, including a discussion of the concept and practice of untouchability. Section 2 sets out the historical and textual origins of a caste society, while Section 3 summarises the principal sociological theories and interpretations of caste.

1.1 Introductory concepts

Caste is commonly associated with India, where it has existed as a social identifier and as a system of social relations and social stratification for several thousand years,[1] but it also exists in other South Asian countries (Nepal, Pakistan, Bangladesh and Sri Lanka) and the South Asian diaspora, including in the UK and the USA, while communities suffering from discrimination based on descent and "work and descent" – wider international categories of which caste discrimination is a subcategory – exist worldwide.[2] Discrimination, exploitation, subordination and oppression on the grounds of caste affect over 201 million Dalits in India alone, where they account for over 16% of the population.[3] In the UK, a government-commissioned report in 2010 estimated the size of what it termed the

---

* Parts of this chapter appeared in *Modern Law Review* Vol. 72(2) in 'Caste Discrimination: A Twenty-First Century Challenge for UK Discrimination Law?'

1 S Bayly, *Caste, Society and Politics in Modern India from the Eighteenth Century to the Modern Age* (Cambridge: Cambridge University Press, 1999) 13; GS Ghurye, *Caste and Race in India* (Mumbai: Popular Prakashan Pvt. Ltd., 1969).

2 See A Eide and Y Yokota, expanded Working Paper on discrimination based on work and descent (DWD), UN Commission on Human Rights, Sub-Commission on the Promotion and Protection of Human Rights (UN Sub-Commission); UN Doc. E/CN.4/Sub.2/2003/24, 26 June 2003, paras 10–43; Y Yokota and C Chung, final report on DWD; Human Rights Council; A/HRC/11/CRP.3, 18 May 2009. See also UN Sub-Commission, Resolution 2000/4, Discrimination based on work and descent, 11 August 2000; UN Doc. E/CN.4/Sub.2/2000/46, 23 November 2000, 25.

3 Census of India 2011, Total Population, Population of Scheduled Castes and Scheduled Tribes and their proportions to the total population.

'low-caste' (meaning Dalit) population as ranging between 'a minimum of 50,000 to 200,000 or more'.[4]

1.1.1 Caste

The word "caste" comes from the Portuguese *casta*, meaning species, race or pure breed. It was first used in India in the sixteenth century by Portuguese traders to distinguish between Moors (Muslims) and non-Muslims, and to denote the system of communities based on birth groups which the Europeans encountered in India.[5] As scholars such as Galanter and Ballard show, while caste is by no means the only feature of South Asian social organisation on the subcontinent or in its diaspora – individuals have multiple overlapping affiliations of kinship, language, region and religion as well as caste – nevertheless, in a traditionally highly compartmentalised social order, caste remains significant as an identifier and as a mechanism for and a source of social stratification, stigmatisation, social exclusion, inequality and discrimination on the subcontinent as well as the diaspora.[6]

1.1.2 Descent

Descent is an international legal category which includes but is not limited to caste. Legal usage of the term originates in the 1833 Government of India Act, which prohibited discrimination against Indians ("natives") in employment with the British East India Company on grounds of religion, place of birth, descent or colour.[7] Indians were distinguished from Europeans by virtue of their "descent," meaning their racial and ethnic origins. As a ground of discrimination, it was included in the Government of India (GOI) Act 1935 and subsequently in the Constitution of India (COI) 1950. In 1965, it was included (at India's behest) as one of five limbs in the definition of racial discrimination in the UN International Convention on the Elimination of All Forms of Racial Discrimination (ICERD),[8] prompted in part by India's concern to address discrimination against persons of Indian origin in apartheid South Africa. The UN Committee on the Elimination of Racial Discrimination (CERD) – ICERD's monitoring body[9] – has affirmed that discrimination based on descent

---

4 H Metcalfe and H Rolfe, *Caste Discrimination and Harassment in Great Britain* (London: Government Equalities Office, 2010) 3, 20. Estimates of the size of the UK Dalit population vary considerably. There are no official statistics on this population.

5 Bayly (n 1) 105–107; U Sharma, *Caste* (New Delhi: Viva Books, 2002) 1; M Galanter, *Competing Equalities: Law and the Backward Classes in India* (Berkeley and Los Angeles: University of California Press, 1984) 7; S Guha, *Beyond Caste: Identity and Power in South Asia, Past and Present* (Leiden: Brill, 2013) 19–30.

6 R Ballard, 'The Emergence of Desh Pardesh', in R Ballard (ed.), *Desh Pardesh: The South Asian Presence in Britain* (London: Hurst & Co, 1994) 5–9; Galanter (1984), ibid., 7–17; O Mendelsohn and M Vicziany, *The Untouchables: Subordination, Poverty and the State in Modern India* (Cambridge: Cambridge University Press, 1998). On caste as a meaningful concept in the UK see Howat et al., 'Measuring caste discrimination in Britain – a feasibility study' (March 2017) para 4.1. For a critique of the position that caste is a figment of the Western imagination see D Sutton, '"So-Called Caste": SN Balagangadhara, the Ghent School and the Politics of Grievance', 26(3) *Contemporary South Asia* (2018) 336–349.

7 A Lester and G Bindman, *Race and Law* (Harmondsworth: Penguin, 1972) 383; S Wolpert, *A New History of India* (Oxford: Oxford University Press, 2009, 8th edition) 219–220. See also Chapter 4.

8 Adopted 21 December 1965. In force 4 January 1969. 660 UNTS 195. "Racial discrimination" is defined in Article 1(1) as discrimination based on race, colour, descent or national or ethnic origin.

9 See https://www.ohchr.org/en/hrbodies/cerd/pages/cerdindex.aspx (visited 5 January 2022).

includes discrimination 'on the basis of caste and analogous systems of inherited status'.[10] In 2000, the former UN Sub-Commission on the Promotion and Protection of Human Rights declared caste discrimination prohibited by international human rights law, as a subset of a new international legal category, namely discrimination based on work and descent.[11]

There is no agreed sociological or legal definition of caste, in South Asia or beyond. Castes are typically described as closed, endogamous,[12] hereditary-membership status groups, traditionally related to occupation, characterised by separation and ranked within a strict hierarchical framework 'in which status is usually privileged over power and wealth'.[13] Traditionally, marriage between castes and the sharing of food and drink (commensality), in particular the taking of water by so-called high castes from so-called lower castes, are prohibited.

According to the Explanatory Notes to the UK's Equality Act 2010,

> [t]he term "caste" denotes a hereditary, endogamous (marrying within the group) community associated with a traditional occupation and ranked accordingly on a per-ceived scale of ritual purity. It is generally (but not exclusively) associated with South Asia, particularly India, and its diaspora. It can encompass the four classes (varnas) of Hindu tradition (the Brahman, Kshatriya, Vaishya and Shudra communities); the thou-sands of regional Hindu, Sikh, Christian, Muslim or other religious groups known as jatis; and groups amongst South Asian Muslims called biradaris. Some jatis regarded as below the varna hierarchy (once termed "untouchable") are known as Dalit.[14]

1.1.3 Varna

Whilst caste is not – and never has been – solely a religious phenomenon, ideological ration-alisation for caste can be found in orthodox Hindu creation mythology and its hierarchical division of ancient Indian society into four broad hereditary groups, or classes, known as *varnas*, traditionally linked to occupation or social function: Brahmans (priests), Kshatriyas (warriors and rulers), Vaisyas (traders, artisans and producers) and Shudras (servants and

---

10 CERD, General Recommendation 29 on Article 1, Paragraph 1 (Descent), 22 August 2002, UN Doc. A/57/18 (2002) 111. CERD first affirmed that caste falls within the ambit of descent in 1996 in its concluding observations on India's ninth to fourteenth state reports; see CERD, Concluding Observa-tions – India; UN Doc. A/51/18 (1996) paras 339–373.

11 UN Sub-Commission, Resolution 2000/4, Discrimination based on work and descent; see (n 2).

12 Endogamy is the practice of marrying within a specific social group, by custom or by law; it 'confines the ties of kinship and marriage within a small and defined group and thereby enables it to maintain clear social boundaries with other groups of the same kind'; A Beteille, 'The Peculiar Tenacity of Caste', *EPW* (31 March 2012) 41–48, 44.

13 H Gorringe and I Rafanell, 'The Embodiment of Caste: Oppression, Protest and Social Change', 41 *Sociol-ogy* (2007) 97–114, 102. See also S Jodhka, *Oxford India Short Introductions: Caste* (New Delhi: Oxford University Press, 2012). In the leading Indian case of *Indra Sawhney v Union of India*, AIR 1993 SC 477 para 82, the Indian Supreme Court defined caste as a socially homogenous class and also as an occupa-tional grouping, membership of which is involuntary and hereditary: 'Lowlier the hereditary occupation, lowlier the social standing of the class in the graded hierarchy'. Even where the individual does not follow that occupation, 'still the label remains and his [sic] identity is not changed'.

14 Equality Act 2010 Explanatory Notes, 10 August 2010, para 49, drafted by the Government Equalities Office (GEO). The Sikh Council UK (SCUK) and the Sikh Federation UK cited the reference to Sikhs in the Explanatory Notes as the reason for their opposition to the inclusion of caste in the Equality Act 2010.

labourers).[15] The first three groups comprise the "twice-born" castes (in Sanskrit, *dvija* castes) forming roughly 25% of India's population, so called because male children of these groups are eligible to undergo an initiation ceremony symbolising a second, spiritual rebirth which marks them as entitled to study and recite the ancient Hindu scriptures, or Vedas (see Section 2 of this chapter).[16] The fourth group, the Shudras (over half the Indian population), consists of the so-called lower castes, known in Indian constitutional, legal and administrative terminology as 'other backward classes' (OBCs).[17] Within the four-fold *varna* (*chatur-varna*) system, a distinction can thus be drawn between the three *dvija* groups, on the one hand, and the *non-dvijas* or Shudras, on the other.

1.1.4 *Dalits: outside the* varna *system*

Outside the *varna* system, comprising a fifth group at the very bottom of the social hierarchy, are the Dalits. They have traditionally been considered by non-Dalits to be irredeemably and permanently polluted, hence "untouchable," people with whom all physical and social contact is to be avoided for fear of defilement.[18] A fundamental structural division thus exists between Dalits, on the one hand, and non-Dalits (or "dominant" castes) on the other.

"Dalit" is a South Asian political term of self-identification meaning "crushed" or "broken" in Marathi, a regional language of western India. It was first used by Jotirao Phule, a nineteenth-century anti-caste radical and campaigner against caste oppression.[19] The term was popularised in India in the 1970s as a militant, assertive category by the Dalit Panther Party (a leftist political organisation inspired by the Black Panthers in the USA) and the Dalit literary movement in Maharashtra.[20] It replaced Gandhi's term "Harijan," adopted in 1931 and meaning "children of God," now widely considered as condescending and demeaning.[21]

15 G Flood, *An Introduction to Hinduism* (Cambridge: Cambridge University Press, 1998) 11–12, 48–49, 58–61. Flood explains that *varna* means colour, referring not to skin colour or racial characteristics but to a system of colour symbolism, reflecting the social hierarchy.

16 "Twice-born" status is conferred by an initiation ceremony, *upanayana*, where the male child is invested with a "sacred thread" worn permanently across the body except when bathing. According to McGee, '[N]owadays the sacred thread has "largely become a hallmark of Brahmin-hood" and "a mark of social status rather than of religious knowledge"'; M McGee, 'Samskara', in S Mittal and G Thursby (eds.), *The Hindu World* (Abingdon: Routledge, 2004) 332–356, 345.

17 The OBCs are groups designated as less severely socially and educationally disadvantaged than the Dalits, which do not suffer from the stigma of untouchability; see Chapter 3.

18 See Mendelsohn and Vicziany (n 6); J Leslie, *Authority and Meaning in Indian Religions: Hinduism and the Case of Valmiki* (Aldershot: Ashgate, 2003) 2–40; M Marriot, 'Varna and Jati', in Mittal and Thursby (eds.) (n 16) 379–382.

19 E Zelliot, 'Dalit – New Cultural Context for an Old Marathi Word', in E Zelliot (ed.), *From Untouchable to Dalit: Essays on the Ambedkar Movement* (New Delhi: Manohar, 1998) 267–292, 271. On Phule see R O'Hanlon, *Caste, Conflict and Ideology: Mahatma Jotirao Phule and Low Caste Protest in Nineteenth Century Western India* (Cambridge: Cambridge University Press, 1985); G Deshpande (ed.), *Selected Writings of Jotirao Phule* (New Delhi: LeftWord Books, 2002).

20 S Paik, 'Mahar-Dalit-Buddhist: The History and Politics of Naming in Maharasthra', 45(2) *Contributions to Indian Sociology* (2011) 217–241, 218, fn 1, 228; Zelliot (1998), ibid. See also J Gokhale-Turner, 'The Dalit Panthers and the Radicalisation of the Untouchables', 17(1) *The Journal of Commonwealth & Comparative Politics* (1979) 77–93, 77; U Khobragade, 'The Revolutionary Journey of Dalit Literature', *HuffPost Blog*, 15 February 2017; Y Maitreya, 'Maharashtra's Dalit Literature Visionary: How Baburao Bagul's Words Exposed a Casteist Society', *FirstPost*, 21 October 2017.

21 The term "Harijan" was coined in the nineteenth century by the Brahmin saint and poet Nasingh Mehta. It was adopted by Gandhi in lieu of the label "untouchable," replacing "Young India" as the title of his

The term "Dalit" is now closely associated with Dr Bhimrao Ramji ("Babasaheb") Ambedkar (1891–1956). Ambedkar was a deeply radical thinker, a US-trained economist and British-trained lawyer, a jurist, scholar, writer, chairman of the Drafting Committee of independent India's Constitution of 1950, himself a Dalit (a Mahar – a Dalit caste from the state of Maharashtra in western India) and one of India's greatest political leaders and campaigners for human rights, the rights of the "untouchables" and the eradication of caste.[22] "Dalit" captures the particular stigmatisation, exploitation and economic, social, cultural, political and psychological oppression which is central to caste "as form of institutionalised domination,"[23] but it also captures strength and resistance to inequality and oppression: 'To call oneself Dalit . . . is to convert a negative description into a confrontational identity'.[24]

Dalit is not official terminology; in post-independence India the constitutional, legal and administrative term is "Scheduled Caste" (SC), meaning those castes listed in a Schedule to the Constitution. Originally drawn up by the British in 1936, the Schedule lists those disadvantaged and socially excluded castes previously known as "Depressed Classes" and subsequently as "untouchables."[25] Scheduled Caste status is established by a caste certificate issued by the authorities attesting to membership of a Scheduled Caste and entitling the holder to the benefit of constitutional affirmative action policies (reservations) and other legal and administrative protections and measures. The Scheduled Caste constitutional category does not include Dalit Muslims and Christians; it is restricted on religious grounds to followers of Indic religions, i.e. Hinduism, Sikhism or Buddhism.[26]

A similar mechanism is used to establish Scheduled Tribe (ST) and OBC status.[27] The Scheduled Tribes, comprising over 84 million people, or 8.2% of India's population, are a distinct legal and administrative category, embracing groups from India's forests and hills, traditionally distinguished by tribal (indigenous) characteristics and cultural and spatial isolation from the mainstream population.[28] Although external to the caste system and not

journal; S Charsley, '"Untouchable": What Is in a Name?' 2(1) *Journal of the Royal Anthropological Institute* (1996) 1–23, 8.

22 For a biography of Ambedkar, see C Jaffrelot, *Dr Ambedkar and Untouchability: Analysing and Fighting Caste* (New Delhi: Permanent Black, 2005). Ambedkar mostly used the word "untouchable" 'for those castes lowest in the Hindu scale of pollution'; see E Zelliot, 'The Leadership of Babasaheb Ambedkar', in Zelliot (n 19) 53–78, 74, fn 1. Ambedkar used the term "Dalit" for the first time in his journal *Outcaste India* in 1928, 'where he characterised being Dalit as the experience of deprivation, marginalisation and stigmatisation'; A Rao, *The Caste Question: Dalits and the Politics of Modern India* (Berkeley: University of California Press, 2009) 15. Ambedkar used the term "Hindu" to refer to non-Dalits, but he distinguished between the Shudras and the *dvija* varnas.

23 H Gorringe, 'Afterword: Gendering Caste: Honor, Patriarchy and Violence', 19(3) *South Asia Multidisciplinary Academic Journal* (2018) 1–10; Paik (n 20) 228; According to Zelliot. the word "Dalit" indicates that outside factors determine so-called "untouchable" status; E Zelliot, *Ambedkar's World: The Making of Babasaheb and the Dalit Movement* (New Delhi: Navayana/Blumoon, 2004).

24 Rao (n 22) 1.

25 Constitution of India, Article 341; The Constitution (Scheduled Castes) Order 1950 (C.O. 19). See Mendelsohn and Vicziany (n 6) 2–5. The term "SC" is also used to connote Dalits in Pakistan and Bangladesh, although the Schedule mechanism is not employed there; S Jodhka and G Shah, 'Comparative Contexts of Discrimination: Caste and Untouchability in South Asia', *Economic and Political Weekly (EPW)* (27 November 2010) 99–106, 100. The Census of India 2011 lists 1,241 Scheduled Castes.

26 This religious restriction does not apply to the OBC category. See Chapter 3.

27 The constitutional term "Backward Classes" is sometimes used both to denote the OBCs alone and generically to denote the SCs, STs and OBCs combined; Galanter (n 5) 121; see Chapter 3.

28 See Total Population, Population of Scheduled Castes and Scheduled Tribes and their proportions to the total population at http://censusindia.gov.in/Tables_Published/A-Series/A-Series_links/t_00_005.aspx.

defined by untouchability or by religion, the Scheduled Tribes also experience severe inequality, marginalisation, discrimination and social segregation.[29] It has been widely argued that close interaction between certain Adivasi groups and Hindu society led to the subsuming of those groups into the "untouchable", or Dalit, category, and in fact the distinction between castes and tribes is 'to some extent arbitrary and reified by law'.[30]

In this book, the term "Dalit" is used except where the context calls for the use of historical or Indian legal/administrative terminology, while recognising that caste terminology is highly politicised. In India, Dalit is adopted by many, but not all, people of so-called "untouchable" origin,[31] whilst in Britain its use is less widespread, although this is changing. In both countries, some reject Dalit, arguing that by reinforcing notions of "broken" and "oppressed," Dalit has become yet another denigrating label; alternatively, that it is primarily associated with the new, middle-class "Dalit elite" rather than with the masses.[32] Increasingly, in both countries, those who do not self-refer as Dalit may instead assert traditional caste names[33] or self-identify by reference to religion, for example as Buddhist, Ravidassia or Valmiki. Conversely, Dalits may seek to hide rather than to assert their caste identity, while, increasingly, others reject caste-associated labels altogether.[34]

1.1.5 Jati

While the *varna* system provides an overarching ideological framework for the organisation and classification of Hindu society and its members, in concrete terms in South Asia and the diaspora, social relations are governed by an individual's membership in one of over 4,000 closed groups, or *jatis*, which are smaller-scale, local or regional endogamous kinship groups (often referred to as "communities"), hierarchically ranked within a restricted geographical locality and effectively the operational units of the caste system.[35] *Jatis* are sometimes described as subdivisions of the *varna* categories, but this is not an accurate description. Unlike *varna*,

---

In all, 705 groups are "notified" (i.e. officially recognised) by the Indian Government as Scheduled Tribes; Statistical Profile of Scheduled Tribes in India 2013, Government of India, Ministry of Tribal Affairs, at https://tribal.nic.in/ST/StatisticalProfileofSTs2013.pdf; Galanter (n 5) 147–153.

29 See A Shah, J Lerche et al., *Ground Down by Growth: Tribe, Caste, Class and Inequality in Twenty-First-Century India* (London: Pluto Press, 2018).

30 Ibid., 3; M Dhanda, A Waughray, D Keane, and D Mosse, *Caste in Britain: Socio-Legal Review' Equality and Human Rights Commission Research Report 91* (Manchester: Equality and Human Rights Commission, 2014) 3. The UK case of *Tirkey v Chandhok* (2015) involved a successful claim of caste discrimination by a claimant who described herself as an Adivasi and a Christian; see Chapter 9.

31 Dalit, alternatively Dalit-Bahujan (Bahujan meaning "majority") is also used as a *political* umbrella term encompassing SCs, OBCs and STs, together comprising around three-quarters of India's population.

32 C Dogra, 'The First Law: Sing my Name', *Outlook India*, 11 July 2011.

33 Including names the use of which in India by a non-Scheduled Caste person to refer to a Scheduled Caste person would constitute a criminal offence; see The Scheduled Castes and Scheduled Tribes (Prevention of Atrocities) Act 1989, section 3(1) x. See also 'Justified? Caste slur ONLY if made in public, in front of a public witness an offense: Bombay HC', *Sabrang India* 27 September 2019.

34 See A Waughray and N Weickgennant Thiara, 'Challenging Caste Discrimination in Britain with Literature and Law: An Interdisciplinary Study of British Dalit Writing', 21(2) *Contemporary South Asia* (2013) 116–132.

35 *Jati* (genus) indicates 'a form of existence determined by birth'; it 'describes any group of things that have generic characteristics in common'; Encyclopaedia Britannica at www.britannica.com/topic/jati-Hindu-caste; see D Killingley, 'Varna and Caste in Hindu Apologetic', in D Killingley (ed.), *The Sanskritic Tradition in the Modern World (2): Hindu Ritual and Society* (Newcastle upon Tyne: SY Killingley, 1991) 7–11, 17–18. See also 'Varna and Caste', in MN Srinivas (ed.), *Caste in Modern India* (London:

which is a Hindu concept, the concept of *jati* is a South Asian cultural concept which is not associated with any one religion.[36] Whilst a *jati* may correlate with a *varna* category, there is no complete overlap between the *varna* categories and *jati* groupings. Moreover, Dalits, who are outside the *varna* framework altogether, do not constitute a homogenous category but are themselves internally, and hierarchically, divided into different *jatis*.[37] "Caste," then, subsumes two concepts – the broad Hindu concept of *varna* and the South Asian regional concept of *jati*. Subgroupings within *jati* groups are known as "sub-castes."

1.1.6 Biraderi

The term "caste" is also used to denote a further, related concept, *biraderi*, which is a regional (largely Punjabi) term, mostly used in the UK by Muslims to denote a similar system of endogamous, hierarchically ranked groups.[38] *Biraderi* has a variety of meanings depending on context, from an extended kinship group or *zaat* (equivalent to *jati*) to a small group of intermarrying close kin, but it is generally translated as kinship group or brotherhood, with implied descent from a common male ancestor and entailing complex dynamics of support, reciprocity, obligation and control. In the UK in everyday usage, caste is used interchangeably for *varna*, *jati* and also for *biraderi*,[39] but the paradigmatic usage, in India and in the UK, is of caste as *jati*.

1.1.7 Caste membership and mobility

While there are only four *varnas*, the precise number of *jatis* cannot be known, as *jati* groups vary from region to region and are not fixed temporally but may merge or subdivide to form new groups.[40] Similarly, while the ranking of the four Hindu *varnas* is commonly

---

Asia Publishing House, 1962) 63–69. The Anthropological Survey of India 'People of India' project has identified 4,635 communities or *jatis*.

36 See J Tharamangalam, 'Caste Among Christians in India', in MN Srinivas (ed.), *Caste: Its Twentieth-Century Avatar* (New Delhi: Penguin, 1996) 263–229; D Mandelbaum, *Society in India, Volume 2: Change and Continuity* (Berkeley and Los Angeles: University of California Press, 1970) 569–571; A Eide and Y Yokota, further expanded Working Paper on DWD, UN Sub-Commission; UN Doc. E/CN.4/Sub.2/2004/31, 5 July 2004, para 46. See also R Ballard, 'Differentiation and Disjunction among the Sikhs', in Ballard (ed.) (n 6) 88–116, 91; M Banks, 'Jain Ways of Being', in Ballard (ed.) (n 6) 231–250; J Hinnells, 'Parsi Zoroastrians in London', in Ballard (ed.) (n 6) 251–271.

37 A Judge, 'Hierarchical Differentiation among Dalits', *EPW* (12 July 2003) 2990–2991. Internal differentiation between Scheduled Castes was officially recognised by the State authorities in Punjab in 1997; S Jodhka and A Kumar, 'Internal Classification of Scheduled Castes: The Punjab Story', *EPW* (27 October 2007) 20–23; T Zinkin, *Caste Today* (London: Oxford University Press, 1962) 8.

38 See Z Bhatty, 'Social Stratification Among Muslims in India', in Srinivas (n 37) 244–262; I Ahmad (ed.), *Caste and Social Stratification Among Muslims in India* (New Delhi: Manohar, 1978); A Shaw, *Kinship and Continuity: Pakistani Families in Britain* (Abingdon: Routledge, 2000) 113–135; I Din, *The New British: The Impact of Culture and Community on Young Pakistanis* (Aldershot: Ashgate, 2006) 33–34, 136–139.

39 Pakistani Muslim zaats are ranked within three broad, hierarchical categories: *ashraf* (noble), *zamindar* (landowning) and *kammi* (artisan); see P Akhtar, *British Muslim Politics: Examining Pakistani Biraderi Networks* (Basingstoke: Palgrave MacMillan, 2014) 36–38. See also "Caste System Thrives in British Asian Politics"; *Hindustan Times*, 29 December 2003.

40 For example from the adoption of new occupations by members of an existing caste or migration to a new region; A Macdonell, 'The Early History of Caste', 19(2) *American Historical Review* (1911) 230–244, 232–233.

understood to be fixed and immutable, the possibility of movement in *jati* ranking has always existed, and there is 'not always agreement as to where a particular *jati* fits'.[41] Indeed, contestation over *jati* ranking has been a feature of South Asian social organisation for hundreds of years. Crucially, though, *varna* and *jati* membership is determined by birth, that is, hereditary. Moreover, group membership, and hence social identity and status, is generally viewed as permanent (although historically this was not necessarily always, or rigidly, so).[42] Unlike class, a key feature of caste is individual 'inability or restricted ability to alter one's inherited status' (although in medieval India, at least for non-Dalits, there appears to have been more fluctuation).[43] Instead, social mobility is dependent on the re-ranking of the entire caste or *jati*: 'You are born into [your caste], you cannot choose your caste, buy it or graduate into a different caste'.[44] That said, individual *jati* mobility may sometimes occur in the context of adoption or (for women) inter-caste marriage, but this is not automatic.[45]

1.1.8 Markers for caste

In his seminal essay 'Annihilation of Caste' (1936), Ambedkar explained that, although caste has been endowed with a quasi-physical quality, it is not a physical attribute but rather 'a notion . . . a state of the mind'.[46] Accordingly, the markers identifying an individual's caste are not purely physical. *Jati* groupings are geographically defined and bounded, being local or regional rather than national. Hence, the local "caste map" is a matter of local knowledge, especially in rural areas where over 65% of India's population live; moreover, this knowledge travels with migration.[47] Non-physical markers for caste include place of origin and residence (actual or ancestral), name (although names can be changed to obscure caste status), current

---

41 E Nesbitt, *Intercultural Education: Ethnographic and Religious Approaches* (Brighton: Sussex Academic Press, 2004) 100.

42 For mythological exceptions to this rule, see Leslie (n 18) 40–45. On the suggestion of social mobility in Sanskrit texts, see U Singh, *A History of Ancient and Early Medieval India* (New Delhi: Pearson, 2015) 192. On individual (as opposed to group) social mobility in medieval India, see C Talbot, 'A Revised View of "Traditional" India: Caste, Status, and Social Mobility in Medieval Andhra', 15(1) *South Asia: Journal of South Asian Studies* (1992) 17–52. For the argument that, according to the *Mahabharata*, Brahmin status, indeed '*varna* distinctions in general', are based on the possession of qualities or virtue, not birth, see A Sharma, *Human Rights and Hinduism: A Conceptual Approach* (New Delhi: Oxford University Press, 2004) 66–69. Sharma also presents an argument that *jati* can be interpreted as referring to the entire human race, not just commensal, endogamous birth units; ibid., 71.

43 CERD (n 10) Article 1(a); Talbot, ibid., 36–46.

44 Paul Divakar, Convenor of the National Campaign on Dalit Human Rights, cited in A Waughray, 'Caste Discrimination: A Twenty-First Century Challenge for UK Discrimination Law?' 72(2) *Modern Law Review* (2009) 182–219, 187. See also *V Giri v D Suri Dora* (1960) 1SCR 42, cited in *Shrivastava v The State of Maharasthra*, Bombay High Court, Criminal Application No. 2347 (2009) para 8.

45 Galanter (n 5) 282–362; L Dudley Jenkins, *Identity and Identification in India: Defining the Disadvantaged* (New York: Routledge Curzon, 2003) 31–39, 76–79. Traditionally, it was assumed that a woman took her husband's social identity on marriage, but Indian courts have held that a Scheduled Caste woman's status does not change by virtue of her marriage to a higher caste man, nor does a "Forward Caste" woman assume her husband's status on marriage to a Scheduled Caste man; see *Urmila Ginda v Union of India* AIR 1975 Del. 115, cited in Galanter (n 5) 340; *Shrivastava v The State of Maharasthra*, ibid., paras 11–12.

46 BR Ambedkar, 'Annihilation of Caste', in V Moon (ed.), *BAWS Vol. 1* (Bombay: The Education Dept., Govt. of Maharasthra, 1989) 68.

47 'You can't hide your caste, because there is always someone from your area, and even if there is not, people make new friends. When they go to Pakistan, they visit their friends' homes and find out there'; Shaw (n 38) 125.

or ancestral occupation, religion or religious practices and education, while physical markers include appearance, body language, demeanour, speech, comportment and bodily expression.[48] Skin colour is not determinative of caste; as Taya Zinkin pointed out in 1962, while 'most upper-caste people are fairer than most lower-caste people of their region', one cannot tell caste from skin colour.[49] In the UK, while such markers may not have the same cultural resonance, name, ancestral occupation, familial place of origin, residence and religious affiliation and place of worship are used to identify caste background. For Indians, there is a further marker – official identification as a member of a Scheduled Caste (explained previously). Although context specific, the term "Scheduled Caste," has entered diaspora usage, for example on matrimonial websites.[50]

1.1.9 Caste and occupation

In classical Hindu texts, a doctrinal association exists between the four *varna*s and hereditary occupation, while *jati*s have also traditionally been associated with hereditary occupational roles. However, the link between caste and occupation has never been watertight or so rigid that individuals could not – theoretically at least – give up a hereditary occupation or enjoy occupational mobility across caste boundaries,[51] and in practice, many individuals were never employed in the occupation traditionally associated with their *varna* or *jati*. Recently, it has been argued in relation to Chamars (a Dalit caste) that the "traditional" link between caste and occupation (in this case, leather-working) was a fiction constructed in the nineteenth century.[52] However, this does not mean that caste has not dictated work and jobs, particularly for Dalits. In the "closed economy" of the village, Dalits for centuries were economically dependent on the upper castes as agricultural labourers or service providers, with little possibility of choice in employment and little or no control over the fruits of their labour.[53] Scholars have shown how, historically, slave labour, forced labour and bonded labour have been integral to the Indian economy, and how Dalits were – and still are – the principal victims of these practices. In particular, the agricultural economy, both before and after the arrival of the British in India, was dependent on unfree Dalit labour, with Dalit caste names used interchangeably with the vernacular for "slave."[54] Although slavery was

---

48 See 'Instant Indicators [of caste] in National Human Rights Commission/National Council for Teacher Education', *Addressing Discrimination Based on Sex, Caste, Religion and Disability Through Educational Interventions: A Handbook for Sensitising Teachers and Teacher Educators* (New Delhi: NCTE, 2003) 69; Gorringe and Rafanell (n 13) 97–114.

49 T Zinkin, *Caste Today* (London: Oxford University Press, 1962) 1.

50 See, for example, www.jeevansathi.com/; conversely see http://tantriclub.co.uk/asian-dating-blog-caste-system-and-dating.php. See also M Dhanda, 'Casteism Among Punjabis in Britain', *Economic and Political Weekly*, 21 January 2017.

51 Gandhi believed that in earning a living (as opposed to personal acquisition of skills or knowledge associated with another *varna*), people should follow the hereditary occupation of the *varna* into which they were born, to promote social harmony and prevent class war; see BR Ambedkar, 'What Congress and Gandhi Have Done to the Untouchables', in V Mood (ed.), *BAWS Vol. 9* (Bombay: The Education Dept., Govt. of Maharsathra, 1991) 277–278.

52 R Rawat, *Reconsidering Untouchability: Chamars and Dalit History in North India* (Bloomington: Indiana University Press, 2011).

53 Ambedkar, Annihilation of Caste (n 46) 47. See also Mendelsohn and Vicziany (n 6) 7–8; Leslie (n 18) 29–30.

54 N Gardner Cassels, *Social Legislation of the East India Company: Public Justice Versus Public Instruction* (New Delhi: Sage, 2010) 165; R Viswanath, *The Pariah Problem: Caste, Religion and the Social in Modern India* (New York: Columbia University Press, 2014) 4, 36, 38; D Kumar, *Land and Caste in South India:*

made illegal in India in 1843, this did not solve the problem of agrarian slavery for Dalits, who found themselves 'reconstituted as bonded labourers',[55] a phenomenon that persists, affecting mainly Dalits, in contemporary India.[56]

Post-independence affirmative action policies have enabled some Dalits to enter public-sector and government employment (although very few reach the highest echelons), and India's post-1991 economic liberalisation created some private-sector opportunities for some Dalits. However, the evidence shows that in the modern Indian economy, Dalits often find themselves excluded from so-called high-caste jobs, albeit now on grounds of "merit" rather than overtly because of caste (see Chapter 3).[57] Additionally, it remains the case that certain jobs, such as those considered ritually unclean – for example manual scavenging (cleaning dry latrines by hand), cleaning sewers, removal and disposal of dead animals, leather-working – are carried out almost exclusively by Dalits.[58] Global capitalism, far from transforming the working lives of Dalits (and Adivasis) in India – whether rural or urban – for the better, is instead contributing to the deepening of caste and tribe identity-based discrimination, inequality, disadvantage and exploitation.[59] Meanwhile, unlike gender, race, age, religion or other identity characteristics, caste has largely been absent from global as well as domestic debates on development policy, due to being perceived as a solely "internal," historical problem.[60]

1.1.10 Caste and religion

Although from a doctrinal point of view caste in the sense of *varna* is associated only with Hinduism,[61] caste is not solely a Hindu phenomenon; 'bounded communities', or *jatis*, have existed among non-Hindus for many hundreds of years.[62] In the UK, as in the Indian

---

Agricultural Labour in the Madras Presidency During the Nineteenth Century (Cambridge: Cambridge University Press, 1965).
55 Cassels, ibid., 209. Bonded labour refers to a long-term relationship between employee and employer which is cemented through a loan, by custom or by force, which prevents the employee from, for example, choosing his or her employer, entering into a fresh contract with the same employer or negotiating the terms and condition of her/his contract; R Srivastava, *Bonded Labour in India: Its Incidence and Pattern* (Geneva: International Labour Organisation, 2005) 2.
56 International Dalit Solidarity Network, 'Dalit, Forced and Bonded Labour', 2012, at http://idsn.org/wp-content/uploads/user_folder/pdf/New_files/Key_Issues/Bonded_Labour/DALITS_AND_BONDED_LABOUR_-_briefing_paper_2012.pdf.
57 M Panini, 'The Political Economy of Caste', in Srinivas (ed.) (n 81) 28–68; S Thorat and K Newman, *Blocked by Caste: Economic Discrimination in Modern India* (New Delhi: Oxford University Press India, 2010); A Deshpande, *The Grammar of Caste: Economic Discrimination in Contemporary India* (New Delhi: Oxford University Press India, 2011); A Subramanian, *The Caste of Merit: Engineering Education in India* (Cambridge, MA: Harvard University Press, 2019).
58 See G Shah, H Mander, S Thorat et al., *Untouchability in Rural India* (New Delhi: Sage, 2006).
59 See Shah et al. (n 29).
60 D Mosse, 'Caste and Development: Contemporary Perspectives on a Structure of Discrimination and Advantage', 110 *World Development* (2018) 422–436.
61 See Jodhka and Shah (n 25).
62 See Guha (n 5). "Hindu" was originally a Persian term for the indigenous inhabitants of the Indus Valley, subsequently used by the Muslims and the British as a religio-cultural and geographical-cultural term to denote the non-Muslim inhabitants of Hindustan – although for the argument that "Hindu" always had a distinctly religious, not just an ethno-geographical, meaning, see D Lorenzen, 'Who Invented Hinduism?' 41(4) *Comparative Studies in Society and History* (1999) 630–659, 634–635. Hindu-*ism* is a nineteenth-century term describing a "family" of religious traditions ranging from Brahminical orthodoxy to

subcontinent, caste-based identities and distinctions and discrimination on grounds of caste are also found among South Asian followers of Islam and Christianity,[63] notwithstanding the absence of a doctrinal basis for caste in Islam and Christianity's doctrinal espousal of egalitarianism, among Sikhs despite Sikhism's doctrinal rejection of caste,[64] and among those of other religions and none. Conversion from Hinduism to another religion as a means of emancipation from caste oppression has a long history in India, but in reality caste status frequently accompanies the convert into his or her new faith.[65] Caste categories are 'terminologically (and behaviourally) distinguished in all religious groups, with or without a religious designation appended (e.g. "high caste Muslim")'.[66] South Asian Christians of "untouchable" origins may be known – and may choose to self-identify – as Dalit Christians, reflecting their own or their ancestors' pre-conversion caste status, while discrimination based on caste among Christians in India and in the diaspora is well-documented.[67] Conversion to Buddhism has been a popular emancipatory strategy since Ambedkar (along with thousands of his followers) converted in 1956 to that religion, chosen for its egalitarianism and its disavowal of caste, as well as its Indic roots,[68] but this has proved an imperfect means of escaping caste oppression, since Ambedkarite Buddhists (sometimes termed "neo-Buddhists") are commonly identified as Dalits.

In 2009, India's National Commission for Religious and Linguistic Minorities noted that caste is a 'general social characteristic' regardless of 'whether the philosophy and teachings of any particular religion recognise it or not'.[69] Yet, as explained earlier, despite the cross-religious/non-religious nature of contemporary caste and associated discrimination, constitutional Scheduled Caste status in India is restricted to members of Indic religions,

---

a multiplicity of regional and local traditions; see J Lipner, *Hindus: Their Religious Beliefs and Practices* (London: Routledge, 1994) 6–9; G Flood (ed.), *The Blackwell Companion to Hinduism* (Oxford: Blackwell, 2005) 2–4. "Hindu caste system" therefore has both religious and cultural connotations. On the construction of Hinduism, see G Omvedt, *Understanding Caste: From Buddha to Ambedkar and Beyond* (Hyderabad: Orient Blackswan, 2011) x, 1–9.

63 See J Webster, 'Who Is a Dalit?' in S Michael (ed.), *Dalits in Modern India: Vision and Values* (New Delhi: Sage, 2007) 76–90; R Fell McDermott, 'From Hinduism to Christianity, from India to New York: Bondage and Exodus Experiences in the Lives of Indian Dalit Christians in the Diaspora', in K Jacobsen and S Raj (eds.), *South Asian Christian Diaspora: Invisible Diaspora in Europe and North America* (Farnham: Ashgate, 2008) 223–248; R Robinson and JM Kujur (eds.), *Margins of Faith: Dalit and Tribal Christianity in India* (New Delhi: Sage, 2010).

64 See P Judge, 'Punjabis in England: The Ad-Dharmi Experience', *EPW* (3 August 2002); K Sato, 'Divisions Among Sikh Communities in Britain and the Role of the Caste System: A Case Study of Four Gurdwaras in Multi-Ethnic Leicester', 19(1) *Journal of Punjab Studies* (2012) 1–25; R Jaspal and O Thakhar, 'Caste and Identity Processes Among British Sikhs in the Midlands', 12(1) *Sikh Formations; Religion, Culture, Theory* (2016) 187–102.

65 Zelliot (n 19) 126–127, 191, 218–221.

66 G Berreman, 'Social Categories and Social Interaction in Urban India', 74(3) *American Anthropologist* (1972) 567–586, 569.

67 See (n 63). See also P Louis, 'Dalit Christians: Betrayed by State and Church', *EPW* (21 April 2007) 1404–1408. Dalit Christian theology has been compared to Latin American "Liberation Theology", and has contributed, along with Buddhism and Ad-Dharm, to the emergence of "Dalitism" as a distinct philosophical belief and ideology which promotes an anti-caste, utopian social vision; P Rajkumar, *Dalit Theology and Dalit Liberation: Problems, Paradigms and Possibilities* (Farnham: Ashgate, 2010); G Omvedt, *Seeking Begumpura: The Social Vision of Anti-caste Intellectuals* (New Delhi: Navayana Publishing, 2008).

68 See Zelliot (n 19) 207–208. Historically, Buddhists did not unequivocally reject caste; see Y Krishan, 'Buddhism and Caste System', 48(1/2) *East and West* (1998) 41–55.

69 Government of India, *Report of the National Commission for Religious and Linguistic Minorities* (New Delhi: Ministry of Minority Affairs, 2009) 153–154.

i.e. Hindus (including Jains), Sikhs and Buddhists. Despite domestic and international calls for the Scheduled Caste category to include all Dalits irrespective of religious affiliation, Dalit Muslims and Christians are denied Scheduled Caste status and hence are ineligible to benefit from affirmative action policies for SCs (reservations) and other protections and measures available to those within the Scheduled Caste category (see Chapter 3).[70]

Conversion aside, religion has historically offered Dalits another means of escape from the psychological tyranny of caste oppression through devotion to a caste-transcending religious figure or *sant*, and the creation of distinct anti-caste or Dalit religious identities. Examples include the medieval South Indian *bhakti* movement, which challenged religious and ritual orthodoxy and the notion that so-called "untouchables" could not access the divine, producing a rich tradition of poetry and literature protesting caste inequality and envisioning alternative, anti-caste forms of social organisation,[71] and the Ad-Dharm movement, which emerged in north India in the 1920s.[72] Contemporary Ad-Dharm in India and the UK includes Valmikis and Ravidassias – anti-caste religious groupings comprising individuals from diverse religious traditions, including Hinduism and Sikhism, usually with shared Dalit origins.[73]

1.1.11 Caste as a cross-cultural concept

The question as to whether caste is a uniquely Indian or South Asian social institution, and thus is incomparable to, say, racism in the USA or class, or whether it is merely one among many versions of a universal social form involving societal inequality, has been much debated.[74] In other words, can caste be a cross-cultural as well as a geographically mobile concept? To what extent is it meaningful to talk about caste outside India (and the South Asian diaspora)? How useful is caste as a tool of analysis independent of cultural context, 'detached from any Indian anchorage'?[75] Until the late twentieth century, this debate had largely focused on the use of caste as an explanatory category for oppression in the USA

---

70 See Chapter 3; see also A Waughray, 'Caste Discrimination and Minority Rights: The Case of India's Dalits', 17 *International Journal on Minority and Group Rights* (2010) 327–353.

71 Zelliot (n 19) 270; Omvedt (n 67); Leslie (n 18) 53–64; M Wakaner, *Subalternity and Religion: The Prehistory of Dalit Empowerment in South Asia* (Abingdon: Routledge, 2010). Conversely, not all *bhakti* traditions espoused radical social change; see Flood (ed.) (n 62) 284.

72 M Juergensmeyer, *Religion as Social Vision: The Movement Against Untouchability in 20th-Century Punjab* (Berkeley: University of California Press, 1982), republished as M Juergensmeyer, *Religious Rebels in the Punjab: The Ad Dharm Challenge to Caste* (New Delhi: Navayan, 2009). The *Adi* movements (*Adi* meaning "original") of the 1920s (including Ad Dharm in north India and Adi Dravida in the south) claimed that the "untouchables" were the original inhabitants of India, with inherent traditions of a caste-less society based on notions of equality and unity.

73 Leslie (n 18) 33; E Nesbitt, *"My Dad's Hindu, My Mum's Side Are Sikhs": Issues in Religious Identity* (University of Manchester), at https://www.researchgate.net/publication/242242139_My_Dad's_Hindu_my_Mum's_side_are_Sikhs_Issues_in_Religious_Identity

74 See E Leach, 'Caste, Class and Slavery: The Taxonomic Problem', in A de Reuck and J Knight (eds.), *Caste and Race: Comparative Approaches* (London: J & A Churchill Ltd., 1967) 5–16, for whom caste and class were sociologically distinct. In contrast, Berreman and Bailey saw caste as a transferable social concept; G Berreman, *Caste and Other Inequities: Essays on Inequality* (Meerut: Folklore Institute, 1979); FG Bailey, *Caste and the Economic Frontier* (Manchester: Manchester University Press, 1964). More recently, Guha suggests caste should be understood as 'a highly involuted and politicised form of ethnic ranking'; Guha (n 5) 5–7.

75 Sharma (n 5) 17; D Keane, *Caste-Based Discrimination in International Human Rights Law* (Aldershot: Ashgate, 2007) 41–44.

based on race and colour (although JH Hutton in the 1940s used the term cross-culturally, writing of institutions analogous to caste in Africa, Japan and Burma – pre-empting international human rights law's identification of systems of inherited status "analogous" to caste some fifty years later).[76] American sociologist Oliver Cox, writing in the mid-1940s, argued that the fundamental bases of the US racial divide and caste are different, with race being based on 'physical identifiability' and caste on cultural heritage.[77] He asserted that, unlike race relations in the USA, caste 'commands a degree of collective consensus or at least compliance' from low and high castes alike[78] (a highly disputed argument). Yet, Dalit activists were long aware of what linked Dalits in India with African Americans in the USA. Jotirao Phule, the nineteenth-century anti-caste activist, dedicated his seminal 1870 essay *Gulam-giri* ('Slavery') on the enslavement of India's Dalits and Shudras to the people of America while Ambedkar wrote in 1946 to the African American intellectual and activist WEB Du Bois about African Americans' petition on racism to the UN, explaining the similarity 'between the position of the "Untouchables" in India and of the position of the Blacks in America'. In 1947, Ambedkar drafted a similar petition to the UN on behalf of India's Scheduled Castes, approved by the All-India Scheduled Castes Federation. Eventually, though, as a member of the government of the newly independent India, he decided not to send it, in order to give the Constituent Assembly and a future parliament a chance 'to deal with the matter'.[79] Latterly, American author Isobel Wilkerson has examined American society through the lens of caste, describing America as founded on a race-based caste system comparable only to the caste system in India and what she describes as the 'vanquished' 'caste system' of Nazi Germany.[80]

During the 2000s, the question was whether caste in South Asia (particularly India) can be subsumed, legally and sociologically, within the wider international concepts of racial discrimination (whether on grounds of descent or otherwise) or discrimination based on work and descent,[81] and whether "caste" in the South Asian sense has any mileage as an explanatory category for analogous forms of inherited status discrimination outside South

---

76 See L Warner, 'American Caste and Class', 42(2) *American Journal of Sociology* (1936) 234–237; G Berreman, 'Caste in India and the United States', 66(2) *American Journal of Sociology* (1960) 120–127; J Hutton, *Caste in India* (Bombay: Oxford University Press, 1963, 4th edition, first published 1946) xi. In 1888 the British Quaker Catherine Impey named her radical periodical exposing racial prejudice in the United States and the British Empire *Anti-Caste*; C Bressey, *Empire, Race and the Politics of Anti-Caste* (London: Bloomsbury, 2013) 6, 19.

77 O Cox, 'Race and Caste: A Distinction', 50(5) *American Journal of Sociology* (1945) 360–368, 362.

78 See Sharma (n 5) 17, 47–58.

79 See S Thorat and Umakant (eds.), *Caste, Race and Discrimination: Discourses in International Context* (Jaipur: Rawat/Indian Institute of Dalit Studies, 2004) xxix; V Raghavan, 'BR Ambedkar: Perspectives on International Law and Foreign Policy', paper presented to the Ambedkar International Conference, Bangalore, India, June 2017 (unpublished; copy on file with author), citing Statement by Dr BR Ambedkar in Explanation of his Resignation, reprinted in BAWS Vol. 14(2) 1317–1327. I thank Vikram Raghavan for permission to cite from his conference paper.

80 I Wilkerson, *Caste: The Lies that Divide Us* (London: Allen Lane, 2020) 17.

81 See CERD General Recommendation 29 (2002) (n 10) on caste discrimination as a subset of descent-based racial discrimination. 'Discrimination based on work and descent' includes, but is not limited to, caste. The term was adopted by the UN in 2000, in order to locate caste discrimination within a wider international human rights category as a distinct human rights violation but one of global concern, thereby avoiding a specific focus on India and Indian caste; UN Sub-Commission, Resolution 2000/4 on discrimination based on work and descent; UN Doc. E/CN.4/Sub.2/2000/46, 23 November 2000, 25; see Chapter 5.

Asia and its diaspora, for example in Japan and parts of Africa.[82] Developments in the UK since the mid-2000s have thrown up another question: whether in the context of identity-based discrimination caste has credence as a legal as well as a sociological category in the South Asian diaspora. Further, the issue of solidarity between Dalits and African Americans, in theory and in practice, is once again coming to the fore as Dalits in the USA build and consolidate links with Black, Indian and African scholars and activists on questions of caste, race and social exclusion.[83]

1.1.12 Caste in the diaspora

The South Asian diaspora exhibits examples of both the dissolution, or near-dissolution, of caste (sometimes, paradoxically, alongside the retention of caste names traditionally associated with the demarcation of caste status and continued adherence to 'pollution ideologies once associated with caste hierarchies', for example in Fiji)[84] and the persistence (or continued existence) of caste and caste consciousness, including endogamy and caste-based discrimination.[85] The picture in individual countries appears to depend in part on the history and nature of South Asian migration to the country concerned. In those countries where caste is acknowledged to exist within South Asian communities both as a form of social identity and as a source of social differentiation and discrimination, for example the UK and the USA, the question arises as to its nature and role and the possibility – or, for some, the social desirability – of its dissolution.

1.1.13 The concept and practice of untouchability

1.1.13.1 Untouchability, pollution and stigma

Two features distinguish caste discrimination from other forms of discrimination based on inherited status: first, its rationalisation and doctrinal underpinnings in certain orthodox Hindu texts and, second, the concept of untouchability.[86] Dalits have traditionally been stigmatised by discourses of pollution and untouchability labelling them as permanently

---

82 See E Obinna, 'Contesting Identity: The Osu Caste System Among Igbo of Nigeria', 10(1) *African Identities* (2012) 111–121; T Tamari, 'The Development of Caste Systems in West Africa', 32(2) *The Journal of African History* (1991) 221–250; E Su-lan Reber, 'Buraku Mondai in Japan: Historical and Modern Perspectives and Directions for the Future', 12 *Harvard Human Rights Journal* (1999) 297–360, 300, 302; T Tomotsune, 'Nakagami Kenji and the Buraku Issue in Post-War Japan', 4(2) *Inter-Asia Cultural Studies* (2003). North Korea is one of the latest countries to be identified as having a hereditary, socio-political ranking system amounting to a caste system based on family background and occupation; 'North Korea Caste System "Underpins Human Rights Abuses"', *The Telegraph*, 6 June 2012.

83 See G Lankesh, 'Dalits and African Americans: Struggles and Solidarity', *Bangalore Mirror*, 14 July 2015; S Paik, 'Building Bridges: Articulating Dalit and African American Women's Solidarity', 42(3/4) *Women's Studies Quarterly* (2014) 74–96; G Bahadur, *Ants Among Elephants: An Untouchable Family and the Making of Modern India* (New York: North Point Press, 2017).

84 S Trinka, 'Cleanliness in a Caste-Less Context: Collective Negotiations of Purity and Pollution Among Indo-Fijian Hindus', 22(1) *Anthropological Forum* (2012) 25–43.

85 For a critique of the view that caste in Mauritius is redundant, see M Claveyrolas, 'The "Land of the Vaish"? Caste Structure and Ideology in Mauritius', *South Asia Multidisciplinary Academic Journal* (2015) at http://samaj.revues.org/3886; on caste in the UK see Chapter 6.

86 The nexus between untouchability and humiliation is explored in many contemporary analyses of untouchability; see, for instance, G Guru, 'Power of Touch', 23(25) *Frontline* (2006); V Geetha,

and irredeemably polluted.[87] This 'pollution' is fictitious; Ambedkar described the concept of untouchability as a notional '*cordon sanitaire*' separating the "untouchables" from the rest of Indian society.[88] The concepts of pollution and untouchability are ritual, religious-ideological and customary in origin rather than hygiene based, with untouchability deriving ostensibly from one's own or one's ancestors' engagement in ritually "unclean" occupations (see 1.1.9 earlier in this chapter)[89] as a result of impure birth related to conduct in previous life. Despite the religious-ideological origin of this imagined "pollution," the discrimination it engenders is real and circular; many Dalits in South Asia are constrained to work in ritually polluting jobs which are also objectively dangerous, dirty and low paid, thereby reinforcing their "untouchable" status. Materially, 'untouchability has for centuries provided a convenient ideological justification for economic exploitation of a subjugated and divided labour force deprived of control of the fruits of its labour'.[90]

Despite its notional nature, caste is conceived as a physical attribute, hence permanent and immutable. The conceptualisation of untouchability in corporeal terms as a 'property of the body',[91] and its supposedly inherited and immutable nature, means that it cannot be shed by engagement in "clean" work or by professional or economic advancement. At the same time, caste, argues Rusi Jaspal, is a fundamentally psychological construct, and the concept of stigma is 'vital [to] understanding how caste identity affects the lives of South Asians'.[92] The pervasive social stigmatisation of Dalits on the subcontinent and, according to certain studies, in the diaspora means that they risk remaining stigmatised, regardless of any increase in social mobility: '[C]aste essentialism ensures that Dalits' dis-identification with the demeaning occupations traditionally associated with their group has had little or no impact on their position within the social hierarchy'.[93]

'The Humiliations of Untouchability', in G Guru (ed.), *Humiliation: Claims and Context* (New Delhi: Oxford University Press, 2011) 95–107.

87 See Mendelsohn and Vicziany (n 6); Leslie (n 18) 2–40; M Marriot, 'Varna and Jati', in Mittal and Thursby (eds.) (n 16) 379–382. Flood explains that 'the scale of purity and pollution differentiates individuals from each other on the basis of caste and gender'; Flood (n 15) 219.

88 Ambedkar (n 51) 187. Indian sociologist MN Srinivas coined the term "pollution line" to describe this division between Dalits and non-Dalits.

89 Shah et al. (n 58) 106, 106–116. Ritually unclean occupations include those associated with animal carcasses or human death, as well as objectively dirty and dangerous jobs such as cleaning sewage tanks and manual scavenging (the removal of human excrement by hand from dry latrines, unlawful in India and yet still widespread); see G Ramaswamy, *India Stinking: Manual Scavengers in Andhra Pradesh and Their Work* (Pondicherry: Navayana Publishing, 2005); Human Rights Watch, 'Cleaning Human Waste: "Manual Scavenging," Caste, and Discrimination in India' (August 2014).

90 Waughray, 'Caste Discrimination: A Twenty-First Century Challenge for UK Discrimination Law?' (n 44) 187–188.

91 Flood (n 15) 219.

92 R Jaspal, 'Caste, Social Stigma and Identity Processes', 23(1) *Psychology and Developing Societies* (2011) 27–62, 28, 33. See also Jaspal and Takhar (n 64); M Davies, *Asking the Law Question* (Sydney: Thomson Lawbook Co., 2008) 293; G Omvedt, *Ambedkar: Towards an Enlightened India* (New Delhi: Penguin Viking, 2004) 18–19.

93 Ibid., 37; B Natrajan and P Greenough (eds.), *Against Stigma: Studies in Caste, Race and Justice Since Durban* (Hyderabad: Orient Blackswan, 2009). The anthropologist Mary Douglas argues that 'the anxiety about bodily margins [pollution] expresses danger to group survival'; thus 'caste pollution represents only what it claims to be. It is *a symbolic system, based on the image of the body, whose primary concern is the ordering of a social hierarchy*' (emphasis added); M Douglas, *Purity and Danger* (London: Routledge, 2002, first published 1966) 154.

1.1.13.2 *"Touch" as a category*

Indian philosophy distinguishes between "contact" – a quality which is present in both the toucher and the touched – and "touch," which is not about contact (which is a relation), but is a quality that is inherent in the object.[94] This means that an "untouchable" person is "untouchable" – a "carrier of pollution" – whether or not they come into contact with another person; the "untouchable" can do nothing to "get rid" of his/her untouchability.[95] Thus, *'the real site of [U]ntouchability is the person who refuses to touch the untouchable'*.[96] According to Indian sociologist Gopal Guru, untouchability is a unique form of discrimination which privileges the corporeal body of the dominant caste individual (the "touchable") as "sacred" primarily in contrast to its logical counterpart, the ritually defiling or profane body (the "Un-touchable").[97] Paradoxically, this assigns a negative power to the "untouchable", whose untouchability can become a 'poison weapon' for the touchable. The "untouchable" thus presents a 'sociological danger' which must be detected and controlled. Consequently, untouchability in India is linked directly to the social, residential, educational and economic 'quarantine' (segregation) of large sections of the population.[98] According to the Indian historian V Jha, Kautilya – popularly known as the author of the ancient Hindu religio-legal text the *Arthasastra* – was 'the first lawgiver to specify touch as a penal offence'.[99] Today, Guru identifies touch as the 'primary category for caste relations'.[100]

1.1.13.3 *Untouchability, social exclusion and violence*

Untouchability is both a cause of and a mechanism for marginalisation and social exclusion.[101] Historically, many Dalits lived and laboured 'in miserable conditions, subject to violent physical discipline . . . actively prevented from absconding or owning land of their own, ideologically construed as outsiders to native society, and forced to live apart from others'.[102] Ambedkar famously recounts how, during a long journey as a child, he and his siblings were unable to get any water to drink for over twenty-four hours, because they were "untouchables".[103] In modern India, untouchability continues to manifest at the individual and structural/institutionalised level, in practices such as the avoidance of physical touch

---

94 S Sarukkai, 'Phenomenology of Untouchability', 44(37) *EPW* (12 September 2009) 39–48, 41.

95 Ambedkar (n 51) 197.

96 Sarukkai (n 94) 43 (emphasis in original). 'Untouchability is an attitude of the Hindu'; Ambedkar (n 51), ibid.

97 G Guru, 'Archaeology of Untouchability', *EPW* (12 September 2009); G Guru, 'What It Means to Be an Indian Dalit: Dalit Responses to the Durban Conference', in Natrajan and Greenough (eds.) (n 93) 168–182.

98 See UN Doc. CERD/C/IND/CO/19, 5 May 2007, para 13, on the de facto segregation of Dalits in India in a wide range of spheres.

99 V Jha, 'Candala and the Origin of Untouchability', in A Parasher-Sen (ed.), *Subordinate and Marginal Groups in Early India* (New Delhi: Oxford University Press, 2004) 157–209, 162.

100 Guru (n 97) 171.

101 See Leslie (n 18) 29–30; Shah et al. (n 58).

102 Viswanath (n 54) 3–4. For a searing account of the realities of untouchability, see BR Ambedkar, 'Outside the Fold', in V Moon (ed.), *BAWS Vol. 5* (Bombay: The Education Dept., Govt. of Maharasthra, 1989) 19–26, 21.

103 BR Ambedkar. 'On the Way to Goregaon', in V Rodrigues (ed.), *The Essential Writings of B.R. Ambedkar* (New Delhi: Oxford University Press, 2002) 47–53.

or even physical proximity (for example, avoiding sitting next to a Dalit pupil or student in class); taboos on inter-dining and the taking of water from castes considered "polluting," residential segregation;[104] taboos and restrictions on Dalits' use of facilities such as roads, wells, bathing ghats (tanks), shops, restaurants, tea rooms[105] and of certain modes of transport such as bicycles; restrictions on the clothing they can wear; occupational segregation; restrictions on choice of occupation; and the practice of endogamy.[106] Despite the abolition of untouchability and its criminalisation in the Constitution of India 1950 and in subsequent legislation,[107] and constitutional and legislative prohibitions of discrimination on grounds of caste,[108] many Dalits in contemporary India continue to be subject to severe socio-economic deprivation and exclusion and well-documented violations of their civil, political, economic and social rights,[109] their subordinated status maintained via the dual enforcement mechanisms of untouchability practices and systemic violence or 'atrocities',[110] frequently of a highly gendered nature.[111] While this type of caste-based discrimination, social exclusion and violence is not replicated in Britain, evidence from academic and government-commissioned studies, and research for the Equality and Human Rights Commission (conducted by a team including the present author), indicates the existence of caste-based prejudice, discrimination and harassment and practices of untouchability in Britain.[112]

1.1.13.4 *Is untouchability an integral aspect of caste?*

A fundamental ideological divide exists between those who believe that caste is essentially non-invidious, associational (about personal preferences) and communitarian (about social and group belonging, a source of positive personal identity and social cohesion)[113] and those who believe that as an institution it is inherently exclusionary, inegalitarian and inseparable

---

104 Ambedkar (n 102) 21; Shah et al. (n 60).
105 For example, the provision of separate cups, glasses and utensils for Dalits in roadside cafes (the "two-cup" system) which they alone are expected to use; see Shah et al. (n 58); D Karthikeyan, 'Madurai Villages Still Practicing the Two-Tumbler System', *The Hindu*, 24 May 2012.
106 Shah et al. (n 58); Navsarjan Trust and Robert F Kennedy Centre for Justice and Human Rights, 'Understanding Untouchability: A Comprehensive Study of Practices and Conditions in 1589 Villages' (2010) 17–20.
107 Article 17, Constitution of India; Protection of Civil Rights Act 1955 (originally the Untouchability (Offences) Act 1955).
108 Article 15, Constitution of India; Protection of Civil Rights Act 1955.
109 Shah et al. (n 58); S Thorat and N Kumar, *BR Ambedkar: Perspectives on Social Exclusion and Inclusive Policies* (New Delhi: Oxford University Press, 2008) 4.
110 The Scheduled Castes and Scheduled Tribes (Prevention of Atrocities) Act 1989 defines and criminalises a range of acts as 'atrocities' (hate crimes); KB Saxena, *Report on Prevention of Atrocities Against Scheduled Castes: Policy and Performance – Suggested Interventions for NHRC* (New Delhi: National Human Rights Commission, 2004). See also Chapter 3.
111 See A Irudayam s.j., J Mangubhai, and J Lee, *Dalit Women Speak Out: Violence Against Dalit Women in India, Volume I* (New Delhi: National Campaign on Dalit Human Rights, 2006). See also Rao (n 22) 6.
112 Metcalfe and Rolfe (n 4) vi; M Dhanda et al., Equality and Human Rights Commission Research Report 91 (n 30); M Dhanda, D Mosse, A Waughray et al., '*Caste in Britain: Experts' Seminar and Stakeholders Workshop, Equality and Human Rights Commission Research Report 92* (Manchester: Equality and Human Rights Commission, 2014).
113 The position espoused by Gandhi, for whom untouchability was a corruption of Hinduism and the *varna* system; see Bayly (n 1) 233–265; W Radice (ed.), *Swami Vivekananda and the Modernisation of Hinduism* (New Delhi: Oxford University Press India, 1998); Galanter (n 5) 28–29; Sharma (n 5) 52–54.

from caste-*ism* and, by extension, from discrimination.[114] Article 17 of the Constitution of India 1950 abolishes untouchability but not caste or the caste system per se. This reflects a Gandhian view of untouchability as an aberration of Hinduism and caste, with the caste system itself seen as non-objectionable – positive, even – if cleansed of untouchability.[115] In 1931, JH Hutton, India's then Census Commissioner, regarded 'the problem of Untouchability as quite separable from that of caste', disputing that it was 'a necessary condition of the survival of Hinduism' or essential to the caste system. As for the caste system itself, he warned of the 'difficulties' and 'perhaps the dangers' of getting rid of it, saying that if 'carried out at a stroke', such an undertaking would 'wreck the edifice of Hindu society'.[116]

1.1.13.5 Ambedkar, untouchability, Hinduism and caste

Ambedkar considered untouchability, Hinduism and caste as inextricably linked, and caste and untouchability to be India's 'two great social evils'.[117] To Ambedkar, caste was divisive and antisocial: a Hindu's loyalty was to his caste,[118] while to the "Untouchables",

> [H]induism is a veritable chamber of horrors. The sanctity . . . of the *Vedas, Smrtis* and *Shastras* . . . the senseless law of status by birth are to the Untouchables veritable instruments of torture which Hinduism [has forged] against the Untouchables.[119]

Ambedkar used the term "Hindus" to mean "caste Hindus," i.e. non-Dalits, as distinguished from the "Untouchables" (Dalits). Hindus observe caste, he said, 'not because they are inhuman or wrong-headed, [but] because they are deeply religious'; for Hindus, caste is a sacred institution, and 'to ask people to give up their caste is to go contrary to their fundamental religious notions' – 'a Hindu's whole life is one anxious effort to preserve his caste'.[120] Ambedkar's crucial question was how to bring about the reform of the Hindu social order, how to abolish caste. The answer lay in attacking its divine basis.[121] The difficulty, he argued, is that untouchability is not only a religious system but also an economic system which permits unmitigated economic exploitation without obligation. The system of untouchability, he wrote, 'is a gold mine to the Hindus', providing a servile class of forced labourers, sweepers and manual scavengers to do the dirty work which caste Hindus were debarred by their religion from doing; as an economic system, it was 'worse than slavery'.[122] As to whether the Hindus would 'agree to give up the economic and social advantages' which

114 The position espoused by Ambedkar, for whom caste, orthodox Hinduism, the Hindu social order and caste discrimination were inextricably linked; see Ambedkar (n 51) 274–297; V Moon (ed.), *BAWS Vol.13* (Bombay: The Education Dept., Govt. of Maharasthra, 1994) 1217. See also J Donnelly, *Universal Human Rights in Theory and Practice* (New York: Cornell University Press, 2003) 81–84.
115 See E Zelliot, 'Gandhi and Ambedkar: A Study in Leadership', in Zelliot (ed.) (n 19) 150–183.
116 Hutton (n 82).
117 BR Ambedkar, 'The Untouchables and the Pax Britannica', in V Moon (ed.), *BAWS Vol. 12* (Bombay: The Education Dept., Govt. of Maharasthra, 1993) 77–147, 132. In 2006 India's Supreme Court described the caste system as 'a curse on the nation', adding 'the sooner it is destroyed, the better'; *Lata Singh v State of UP & Another*, Writ Petition (criminal) 208 of 2004.
118 Ambedkar (n 46) 56.
119 Ambedkar (n 51) 296.
120 Ambedkar (n 46) 53, 68, 69.
121 Ibid., 67–69.
122 Ambedkar (n 51) 196, 197.

they gained from untouchability, he observed that 'vested interests have never been known to have willingly divested themselves unless there was sufficient force to compel them', hence his fear that independence would leave the "Untouchables" at the mercy of the Hindus,[123] and his determination to secure constitutional safeguards for the "Untouchables" when independence came.[124]

1.2 Religious and historical origins of a caste society

The historical and theoretical origins of caste are contested, and just as there is no universally agreed definition of caste, so there is no agreed theory of caste or its origins. This section sets out the understanding of caste as a historic religio-legal phenomenon, before turning to discuss the principal sociological theories and interpretations of caste.

1.2.1 Ancient India: Indo-Aryans, the Rg Veda *and the origins of* varna

Religious understandings of caste begin with the *Rg Veda*, India's earliest surviving religious text and the oldest text in any Indo-European language. From around 3200 BCE, northern India was home to the Bronze Age Indus Valley, or Harappan, civilisation.[125] Its demise, around 1700 BCE – probably due to environmental changes and/or natural disaster – left the way open for the Aryans (*arya* meaning "noble"). These nomadic, tribal, Indo-European-speaking peoples from Central Asia, who had migrated first into Iran and Afghanistan from around 2000 BCE, and thence into northern India, brought with them the horse, iron weaponry and worship practices centred on priestly incantations and ritual sacrifices to the gods.[126] Nineteenth-century European scholarship theorised an 'Aryan invasion' of northern India around 1500 BCE, but current scholarly consensus is of a prolonged period of intermingling and acculturation of the Aryans and the post-Harappan/-Indus peoples in the north of the country, resulting in the emergence of the Indo-Aryans.[127] *Arya* social identity was determined not racially or biologically, says the Indian historian Romila Thapar, but culturally. The Aryans were distinguished from non-Aryan indigenous groups, or *dasas/dasyus* (initially meaning "other," later "slave") and *mleccha* (foreigners or barbarians) by such characteristics as Aryan speech forms, belief systems and rituals. Although initially neither a fixed nor a homogenous category, what was fixed was the notion of a dominant group 'with the right to demand subservience from others', a notion underpinned and legitimised

---

123 Ambedkar (n 102) 26.
124 Ambedkar (n 51) 196.
125 C Maisels, *Archaeology of Politics and Power: When, Where and Why the First States Formed* (Oxford: Oxbow Books, 2010) 49. Various estimates of the span of the Indus Valley civilisation exist. It is now regarded as 'an indigenous development among peoples of mixed origin and diverse racial types who had resided in the Indus Valley for centuries'; see V Jha, 'Social Stratification in Ancient India: Some Reflections', 19(3–4) *Social Scientist* (1991) 19–40, 32–33. See also JM Kenoyer et al., 'A New Approach to Tracking Connections Between the Indus Valley and Mesopotamia', 40(5) *Journal of Archaeological Science* (2013) 2286–2297.
126 S Wolpert, *A New History of India* (Oxford: Oxford University Press, 2000, 6th edition) 21–22; R Thapar, *The Penguin History of Early India: From the Origins to AD 1300* (New Delhi: Penguin Books, 2003) 87. On the Aryans see P Heehs, *Indian Religions: A Historical Reader of Spiritual Expression and Experience* (London: Hurst & Co., 2002) 40; Wolpert, ibid., 4; L Patton, 'Veda and Upanishad', in Mittal and Thursby (eds.) (n 16) 37–51, 37.
127 Patton, ibid., 38.

by the ideology of *varna*. Subsequently, *Arya* became identified with membership of the dominant culture and superior social status, and *dasa* with subordinate status – irrespective of origins.[128]

1.2.1.1 *The* Rg Veda *and* varna

The *Rg Veda* was composed orally by the Indo-Aryans sometime between 1500 and 900 BCE,[129] although it was not written down until around 600 BCE.[130] It is the earliest of four texts known collectively as the *Vedas*, meaning (sacred) knowledge in Sanskrit.[131] The *Rg Veda* consists of 1,028 poems or mantras (incantations)[132] to the Aryan gods, grouped in ten books, or *mandalas*. The *Vedas* are considered divine revelation or *sruti*, meaning "revealed" texts seen and heard by inspired "seers" (*rsi*) who had insight into pre-existing cosmic truths. This knowledge was hereditary; it was learned by the Aryan priests, or Brahmans, at a very early age and transmitted entirely orally to children (usually boys) in Sanskrit.[133] The role of Brahmans, as 'custodians of the *Veda*',[134] was to officiate over sacrifices and other rituals and ceremonies, and to memorise and ensure the accurate oral transmission of the Vedic scriptures – on which the performance of the rituals depended – from generation to generation.[135]

1.2.1.2 Purusa-Sukta: *the Creation Myth*

In the tenth and last book of the *Rg Veda*, in verses 11–16, is found, in hymn form, the creation myth of *Purusa*, the primordial or cosmic man, from whose sacrificed and dismembered body the gods created the cosmos and society, the latter divided into the four social classes, or *varnas* (the *chaturvarna* principle):

> When they divided the Man, into how many parts did they apportion him? What do they call his mouth, his two arms and thighs and feet?
>   His mouth became the Brahman; his arms were made into the Warrior, his thighs the People, and from his feet the Servants were born.[136]

While the duties of the four social classes are not elaborated in the *Purusa* myth itself, and there is no mention of a fifth group outside the *varna* system,[137] the imagery is invoked

128 Thapar (n 126) 136.
129 Ibid., 111; Heehs (n 126) 40; Wolpert (n 7) 26.
130 Wolpert, ibid., 25; Thapar, ibid., 108.
131 M Witzl, 'Vedas and Upanishads', in Flood (ed.) (n 62) 68; Patton (n 137) 38; Flood (n 15) 35. The Vedas share a common cultural and linguistic source with the *Avesta*, the sacred text of present-day Zoroastrians (Parsees) in Iran and India; B Avari, *India: The Ancient Past* (London: Routledge, 2007) 63.
132 W Doniger, *The Hindus: An Alternative History* (Oxford: Oxford University Press, 2010) 104. Doniger and her Indian publishers Penguin Books India were subject to a lawsuit for denigration of Hinduism, resulting in the destruction of all Penguin India's copies of the book. See also V Prashad, 'Wendy Doniger's Book Is a Tribute to Hinduism's Complexity, not an Insult', *The Guardian*, 12 February 2014.
133 Patton (n 126) 39. Sanskrit evolved from Indo-European proto-Sanskrit, originating in Iran or Central Asia.
134 B Holdrege, 'Dharma', in Mittal and Thursby (eds.) (n 16) 213–248, 221.
135 The demands of memorisation gave rise to a highly developed science of mnemonics; see R Mookerji, *Ancient Indian Education: Brahmanical and Buddhist* (Chennai: Motilal Banarsidass Publishers, 2011).
136 W Doniger (trans.), *The Rig Veda* (London: Penguin Books, 1981) 31.
137 V Jha, 'Stages in the History of Untouchables', II(I) *Indian Historical Review* (1975) 14–31, 14.

in later texts, says Holdrege, to provide cosmic legitimisation for the division of labour between the *varnas* – and indeed for the hierarchical and immutable nature of the system.[138] The early Vedic texts introduce the key themes and concepts which later Hinduism would expand on and develop, and which underpin classical Hindu law – the notion of the cosmic whole[139] as holistic, ordered, balanced and governed by the principle of *rta* or cosmic order (later, *dharma*, discussed in Chapter 2), which 'ensures the integrated functioning of the natural order, the divine order, human order and sacrificial order'. *Pursusa*'s head, naval and feet are correlated with the heavens; mid-regions with the earth; and his mouth, arms, thighs and feet represent the four social classes (Brahmans, Kshatriyas, Vaishyas and Shudras).[140]

The *Purusa* hymn is important because it presents hierarchical, hereditary social groups as part of the structure of the cosmos.[141] Doniger suggests another reason: it ranks kings below priests, whereas Buddhist literature puts kings at the top. She describes this as 'one of the earliest documented theocratic takeovers'; the *Purusa* myth, she suggests, may have been the foundational myth of the Brahman class.[142] Initially, the Vedic people distinguished only two social classes, or *varnas*, namely their own (the *arya*) and that of the people they conquered (*dasas* or *dasyu*). Although the 'rigid hereditary system of the professions characteristic of the caste system was not yet in place', by the end of the Vedic period, the *varna* system was in position. By now, the important social division was not into just two classes (or groups) but four,[143] with the Shudras at the bottom.[144]

1.2.2 Origins of jati

While the origin of *varna* lies in the *Rg Veda*, the origin of *jati* is less clear. Historians have suggested that it may have originated in the clan (a similar form of social organisation) and that its roots may lie in India's pre-Aryan past, preceding *varna*;[145] floor plans in different quarters of the ancient Indus city of Mohenjo-daro, for instance, indicate a social hierarchy based on occupational status and fear of pollution through miscegenation or commensality.[146] Fear of pollution through drinking water, later associated with caste distinctions, may also have originated at this time.[147] Maisels argues that the socio-economic structure of the civilisation first encountered by the Aryans already featured economic and occupational specialisation, division of labour, economic and social stratification and endogamy (to keep craft skills within specialised groups), which he attributes to the process of urban decline.[148]

138 Holdrege (n 134) 218.
139 W Menski, *Comparative Law in a Global Context: The Legal Systems of Africa and Asia* (Cambridge: Cambridge University Press, 2006) 205.
140 Holdrege (n 134) 215, 217.
141 Flood (n 15) 49.
142 Doniger (n 132) 119.
143 Doniger, ibid., 116–118.
144 BR Ambedkar, 'Who Were the Shudras?' in Rodrigues (n 103) 385–395, 385–386.
145 Thapar (n 126) 63–64. For a detailed discussion of the origins, emergence and nature of class, kinship, *varna* and *jati* in early India, see also Singh (n 42) 291–295.
146 Wolpert (n 7) 14–16, 42. For a contrary view, see Jha (2004) in Parasher-Sen (ed.) (n 99) 206.
147 Wolpert (n 126) 16. Wolpert cites the discovery of fragments of clay drinking cups as a possible initiation of the later habit of using cups only once for fear of pollution. See also Thapar (n 126) 64. Speculation that religion underpinned Harappan social organisation is based on archaeological finds such as the Great Bath at Mohenjo Daro, which, argue scholars, was probably used by priests for ritual washing; Avari (n 131) 48–49.
148 Maisels (n 125) 51.

Recent bio-archaeological studies of Indus Valley skeletons indicate that contrary to the romanticised belief that Harappan society was unusually harmonious, egalitarian and strife-free, Indus civilisation featured 'structural violence' in the form of unequal power and access to resources, exploitation, the denial of basic needs and/or outright violence.[149]

In the later Aryan era, occupational specialisations are listed in *Brahmana* religious texts, which, as sacred books, confer a sanctity and significance to the work performed by different groups in society.[150] Nevertheless, occupation alone cannot explain the emergence of a caste social order. Wolpert suggests that fear of losing power dictated marriage within the limits of a trusted group, while the fear of losing identity, or 'racial purity', contributed to the creation of a system of thousands of *jatis*.[151] Vivekanand Jha disputes that the *varna* system came to India with the Aryans, or that untouchability originated with the Harappans. Rather, he argues, the four-fold *varna* system was an 'indigenous development' of the later Vedic period. However, Jha concurs that *varna* was 'in essence exploitative in nature and content' – sacrifices were 'consciously designed to help rulers overcome internal conflicts and to make the Vaisya and the Shudra submissive', and in this process the role of the Brahmans was crucial.[152]

1.2.3 Hierarchy, heredity, endogamy and commensality

The chief characteristics of the caste social order as it emerged in India were hierarchy (inherent in the *varna-jati* system) and hereditary occupation, essential to maintaining a division of labour. The ideological legitimisation of the system was its sanction by religion, while the principle of heredity was maintained by the twin practices of endogamy and commensality.[153] The control of women was central to the Brahmanical social order.[154] Endogamy (described by Ambedkar as the vehicle by which caste is maintained and replicated)[155] and the subordination of women are closely linked.[156] Caste hierarchy and gender hierarchy are described by Uma Chakravarti as the 'organising principles' of the Brahmanical social

---

149 G Schug et al., 'A Peaceful Realm? Trauma and Social Differentiation at Harappa' (2) *International Journal of Paleopathology* (2012) 136–147, 145.

150 The *Brahmanas* are commentaries elaborating on the four *Vedas*; Heehs (n 126) 41.

151 Wolpert (n 7) 42. See also Singh (n 42) 294.

152 Jha (n 125) 27–29.

153 A Parasher-Sen, 'Introduction', in Parasher-Sen (ed.) (n 99) 1–80, 7.

154 K Visweswaran, 'India in South Africa: Counter-Genealogies for a Subaltern Sociology?' in Natrajan and Greenough (eds.) (n 93) 326–374, 344–345. Bidner and Eswaran locate the origins of caste in the indispensability of women's contribution to the family income by supporting their husband in his occupation, and the origins of endogamy in the need to keep Brahman women within the group; see C Bidner and M Eswaran, 'A Gender-Based Theory of the Origin of the Caste System in India', 114 *Journal of Development Economics* (2015) 142–158, 154, 156.

155 See Ambedkar (n 46) 67; BR Ambedkar, 'Castes in India: Seminar Paper', Columbia University, NY, 9 May 1916 in V Moon (ed.), *Dr Babasaheb Ambedkar Writings and Speeches (BAWS) Vol. 1* (Bombay: The Education Dept., Govt. of Maharasthra, 1989) 2–22, 9. In 'Castes in India', Ambedkar described endogamy as a key to the 'mystery' of the caste system and 'the only characteristic that is peculiar to caste', ibid., 7, 9.

156 S Jaiswal, 'Studies in Early Indian Social History: Trends and Possibilities', 6(1–2) *Indian Historical Review* (1979–80) 1–63, 5, cited in Parasher-Sen (n 99) 8. Rosalind O'Hanlon notes the essential link between gender inequality in India and the maintenance of caste hierarchies, with hypergamy (women marrying their social equals or superiors) a key element for securing the caste hierarchy; R O'Hanlon, 'Caste and Its Histories in Colonial India: A Reappraisal', 51(2) *Modern Asian Studies* (2017) 432–461, 438–439.

order, with effective sexual (and social) control of women being essential in order to main-tain patrilineal succession and caste purity.[157] Traditionally, marriages (especially among the upper castes) were arranged and girls were married very young, as arranged and child mar-riages were easier to regulate according to the rules of caste.[158] Upper-caste restrictions on widow remarriage similarly served to maintain caste boundaries. While ideologies of chastity and caste purity regulated upper-caste women and girls, Dalit women were consid-ered less bound by these rules; however, they experienced (and continue to experience) the 'expropriation of manual and sexual labour',[159] including rape and sexual exploitation via the *devadasi* system (a pseudo-religious practice whereby pre-pubescent girls, usually Dalits, are dedicated to a temple or deity and condemned to a life of ritualised prostitution and sexual slavery as temple prostitutes).[160]

1.2.4 Origin of untouchability

The *Rg Veda* does not mention untouchability.[161] Hanumanthan argues that it is a "by-prod-uct" of the *varna* system, which separates the three twice-born *varnas* from the Shudras. It also separates those within the system, or *savarnas*, from those outside the system, or *ava-rnas* (the Dalits), sometimes described as *Candalas* in the later Vedic texts.[162] It is not clear why the *Candalas* became "untouchable"; they may have been so by birth or occupation, or have become "untouchable" through disapproved conduct. Buddhist and Jaina literature also refers to degraded castes (based on occupation or profession), leading Hanumanthan to attribute the growth of untouchability to taboos which existed among ancient Indians, irrespective of religion.[163] Jha considers the *Candalas* were most likely one of the indigenous tribes known to the Aryans, living on the perimeters of Aryan settlements, with whom the process of assimilation had begun;[164] they do not appear in the *Rg Veda* but are men-tioned in later Vedic literature. Jha argues that 'ideology and force were both systematically employed' to develop caste and untouchability slowly in India. Tribes 'with poor material resources' . . . 'fared badly in the unequal encounter with the Aryans', and these were the first peoples to become 'tabooed as untouchables' and relegated to the ritually lowest social position.[165]

157 U Chakravarti, 'Conceptualising Brahmanical Patriarchy in Early India: Gender, Caste, Class and State', *Economic and Political Weekly*, 3 April 1993, 579–583, 579. O'Hanlon cites the work of the Brahmin scholar Gopinatha in the late fourteenth or early fifteenth century, which describes a union between 'a high-born woman and a low-born man' as an illegitimate union, against nature; R O'Hanlon, 'Lineages of Non-Brahman Thought in Western India c. 1600–1850', Mahatma Phule Memorial Lecture, University of Calcutta, 3 December 2010, at www.academia.edu/5773846/Lineages_of_Non-Brahman_Thought.
158 Beteille (n 12) 41–48, 45.
159 A Rao, 'Introduction', in A Rao (ed.), *Gender and Caste* (New Delhi: Kali for Women, 2006) 1–47, 17–18; L Dube, 'Caste and Women', in Rao (ed.), ibid., 223–248.
160 See Chapter 3.
161 Jha (2004) in Parasher-Sen (ed.) (n 99) 158.
162 KR Hanumanthan, 'Evolution of Untouchability in Tamil Nadu Up to AD 1600', in Parasher-Sen (ed.) (n 99) 125–156, 126. See also Singh (n 42) 203–204, 294.
163 Ibid.
164 Jha (n 99) 157.
165 Jha (n 125) 29; Jha (n 99) 159–160. BR Ambedkar argued that 'the Untouchables were originally "broken men", made to live at the outskirts of villages. However, as they continued to be Buddhists and carried on with beef-eating, they came to be treated as Untouchables'; Rodrigues (n 103) 383.

1.3 Sociological theories and interpretations of caste

Sociological theories of caste[166] have fallen traditionally into two broad categories. "Essentialist" or idealist theories focus on religious and ideological factors, portraying India as a timeless society, radically and fundamentally different from European society, of which caste is the defining and essential feature. This category is associated primarily with the French sociologist Louis Dumont.[167] In contrast, secular or materialist theories focus on socio-economic and political factors.[168] However, since the 1990s, public and academic debate on caste in India has shifted from the merits and de-merits of the various theories of caste to the changing nature of the institution of caste and its relevance or irrelevance in contemporary India – whether it is dissolving in the face of democracy, modernisation and economic liberalisation, whether 'it is becoming more a political than a social category, or whether it remains as oppressive as it always has been'.[169] In the UK, caste indisputably exists as a social phenomenon. It has not been dissolved; instead, caste consciousness persists in the maintenance of caste-based identities as social/cultural identities.[170] The question thus arises whether it is possible for caste-based identities to exist independently, decoupled from the prejudice, discrimination and oppression historically associated with caste, and to become egalitarian in both theory and practice.[171]

1.3.1 Colonialism and the emergence of caste as a sociological concept

Caste as a sociological concept, writes Ursula Sharma, originated in the systematic attempts by colonial administrators and scholars to explain, theorise and interpret what was seen by many as the key feature of Indian society, and to classify Indians by caste, in order to "know," and therefore more effectively control and exploit, their subjects.[172] As a consequence, pre-existing caste norms, conventions and observances were 'expanded and sharpened', and caste language and ideology became incorporated into the structures of government, albeit some Indians 'as much as Britons . . . took the initiative in this process'.[173] Nonetheless, until the mid-nineteenth century, caste was subsidiary to race in colonial analyses of Indian society.[174] One reason, according to Gupta, for the rise of caste as a sociological category was the role of literate Brahmans who acted as interpreters of the *sastric* texts which the British authorities treated as authoritative sources of "native" law. This privileged the Brahmanical view as 'the correct interpretation of Hindu culture and custom',[175] giving Brahmans

166 For an overview of sociological theories of caste, see Sharma (n 5).

167 Sharma (n 5) 6–7.

168 SK Mitra, 'Caste, Democracy and the Politics of Community Formation in India', in U Sharma and M Searle-Chatterjee (eds.), *Contextualising Caste: Post-Dumontian Approaches* (Oxford: Blackwell, 1994).

169 P deSouza, 'Humiliation in a Crematorium', in Guru (ed.) (n 86) 124–139, 137.

170 Metcalfe and Rolfe (n 4); Dhanda (n 50).

171 Judge (n 64).

172 In seeking to classify their subjects by caste, the British were following the Mughals who categorised the Indian population on the basis of "essential" characteristics such as skin colour; Bayly (n 1) 104; Sharma (n 5) 9–10.

173 Bayly, ibid., 4.

174 S Bayly, 'Caste and "Race" in the Colonial Ethnography of India', in P Robb (ed.), *The Concept of Race in South Asia* (New Delhi: Oxford University Press, 1997) 165–218, 168, 215.

175 D Gupta, 'Caste and Politics: Identity Over System', 34 *Annual Review of Anthropology* (2005) 409–427, 413.

unprecedented influence[176] and a 'larger than legitimate role in the conception of Indian society'.[177] Another frequently cited reason for caste's emergence as a sociological category was the launch in 1871–1872 of the decennial All-India Census, through which India's British rulers sought to collect systematic information about Indian society and the economy, inter alia by classifying all Indians by religion, caste or tribal community, occupation, age and sex.[178] The colonial census was not in fact the first example of caste-wise enumeration in India (large-scale, caste-wise enumeration was carried out by the kingdom of Marwar in the seventeenth century, for example), but many writers saw the creation of caste as a census category by the British as 'not simply referential but in fact generative',[179] promoting 'identification with caste' and its transformation into a political as well as a social category,[180] and hence its emergence as a sociological category.

1.3.2 Racial theories of caste

The term "orientalism" (coined by Edward Said in 1978) describes a Western imperialist, Eurocentric, essentialising way of knowing, understanding, constructing and representing the oriental "Other."[181] Initially, race was defined by Europeans linguistically and culturally rather than in a physiological sense. Caste, nation, tribe and race were used interchangeably in the Indian context to convey ties of affinity. From the early nineteenth century, however, European ideas about race were influenced by the rise of 'race science' – evolutionary theories about the moral and biological characteristics of "civilised" (and "degenerate") races or nations and the construction of global comparative schemes of racial ranking based on physiological 'types'.[182] The idea that castes reflected *racial* differences was first mooted by Sir William Jones, the eighteenth-century scholar-official and translator, who proposed that Sanskrit and European languages were of common stock.[183] Colonial ideas of race as the basis of caste and the caste system were cemented by the colonial administrator HH Risley, the 1901 Census Commissioner of India.[184] Based on the interpretation of *varna* as colour in Hindu texts, Risley argued that the caste system was based on racial antagonism between light-skinned Aryan invaders and dark-skinned indigenous Dravidians.[185] Risley devised a hierarchical classification scheme based on anthropometric measurements which divided

---

176 Bayly (n 1) 100.
177 D Gupta, 'The Certitudes of Caste: When Identity Trumps Hierarchy', 38(1/2) *Contributions to Indian Sociology* (2004) v–xv, viii. Note, though, O'Hanlon's assertion that 'the use of Brahman expertise in Hindu textual law' did not originate with the colonial state; O'Hanlon (n 156) 440.
178 Bayly (n 1) 124. For a postcolonial history of the British India Census, see B Cohn, *An Anthropologist Among the Historians and Other Essays* (New Delhi: Oxford University Press, 2012) 231–247. See also N Peabody, 'Cents, Sense, Census: Human Inventories in Late Precolonial and Early Colonial India', 43(4) *Comparative Studies in Society and History* (2001) 819–850.
179 Peabody, ibid., 821.
180 Rao (n 22) 5.
181 E Said, *Orientalism* (London: Penguin, 2003). The term is defined in the Oxford Dictionary as 'the representation of Asia in a stereotyped way that is regarded as embodying a colonialist attitude'.
182 Bayly (n 174) 172, 173, 175, 179, 214; Bayly (n 1) 109.
183 C Bates, 'Race, Caste and Tribe in Central India: The Early Origins of Indian Anthropometry', in Robb (ed.) (n 174) 219–259, 233.
184 See Cohn (n 178) 247; H Risley, *The People of India* (1915, reprinted Delhi, Low Price Publications, 2003) 5.
185 Risley, ibid., 262, 275. See (n 15) on *varna* as meaning a system of colour symbolism reflecting the social hierarchy, not skin colour.

Indians into seven basic racial types,[186] with Dravidians considered the most primitive and
Indo-Aryans the most ethnologically advanced.[187] Caste, he believed, was an evolutionary
weapon adopted by the "superior" Aryans to preserve their purity of blood and racial stock
from the perils of miscegenation with the darker indigenous populations, i.e. castes were
races, and the distinction between high and low castes was really a distinction between peoples of supposedly "superior and inferior" racial endowment.[188]

The Indian 'non-Brahman movement' of the early twentieth century (which sought
equality of treatment for non-Brahmans, particularly in education and employment) also
espoused a racial analysis of caste, arguing that Brahmans and non-Brahmans were different
races with correspondingly divergent interests.[189] Ambedkar, however, dismissed arguments
that castes constituted separate racial groups, either in the biological or the social sciences
sense of the term:

> [T]he caste system came into being long after the different races in India had com-
> mingled in *blood and culture*. To hold that distinctions of caste are really distinctions of
> race and to treat different castes as though they were so many different races is a gross
> perversion of facts [sic].[190]

In this, he pre-empted the position of Indian Governments from the mid-1990s onwards
on the question of whether caste was the same as race (and hence whether caste discrimination was covered by international human rights provisions on racial discrimination), but for
different reasons.[191] Ambedkar's objection was to biological arguments justifying the caste
system as a mechanism for preserving the perceived racial and genetic purity – and superiority – of the dominant castes. He argued that 'men [sic] of pure race exist nowhere', that this
was especially true of the people of India and that the caste system '[did] not demarcate racial
division' but was 'a social division of people of the same race'.[192] Likewise, India since 1996,
has maintained before the UN Committee on the Elimination of Racial Discrimination
(CERD) (the monitoring body of the UN International Convention for the Elimination of

186 Bates (n 183) 242; Risley (n 184) 33–34, 276.
187 Bayly (n 1) 132. The idea that social divisions and groupings reflected innate racial characteristics of
     a moral and biological nature underpinned the notion of inherited criminality in the Criminal Tribes
     legislation, introduced in the late nineteenth century; see Bates (n 183) 248. The Criminal Tribes Act of
     1877 constructed entire tribe or caste groups as hereditarily criminal. However according to Piliavsky,
     'the stereotype [of the criminal tribe or caste] has a history stretching back far beyond British coloni-
     alism'; A Piliavsky, 'The "Criminal Tribes" in India before the British', 57(2) *Comparative Studies in
     Society and History* (2015) 323–354, 325. The role of physiognomic differences in the construction of
     caste has been the subject of much debate and contestation. Robb, for instance, argues that 'though in
     India Untouchability and indeed other concepts of Otherness were pre-eminently matters of the body,
     yet they were concerned more fundamentally with conduct than physical characteristics', noting further
     that 'in many European theories of race too, the alleged cultural and moral differences assumed greater
     importance than the physical ones'; Robb (ed.) (n 174) 9–10.
188 Bayly (n 174) 169.
189 A Beteille, 'Race and Descent as Social Categories in India', 96(2) *Daedalus* (1967) 444–463, 458. In
     the 1940s, a separatist organisation, Dravida Kazhagam, campaigned for a Dravidian state in south India
     on the grounds that the Dravidians constituted a distinct race; ibid., 459–460. On caste as racial differ-
     ence, see VT Rajshekar, *Dalit: The Black Untouchables of India* (Atlanta: Clarity Press, 1995); D Reddy,
     'The Ethnicity of Caste', 78(3) *Anthropological Quarterly* (2005) 543–584.
190 Ambedkar (n 46) 48 (emphasis added).
191 See Chapter 4.
192 Ambedkar (n 46) 49. See also Beteille (n 189) 448–449.

All Forms of Racial Discrimination) that the caste system is based on the ancient functional division of Indian society rather than distinctions based on race; however, this argument may be motivated less by ideological objections to notions of biological or genetic caste purity than by a concern to contest international scrutiny of caste-related discrimination as a form of descent-based racial discrimination under international human rights law.

1.3.3 Caste and genetics

Research by population geneticists indicates that, broadly speaking, the so-called upper castes have closer genetic affinities with West-Eurasian populations than do the so-called lower castes, who share greater similarities with Asian populations.[193] However, the existence of such genetic affinities does not mean that caste groups are genetically homogenous or distinct; indeed, the opposite has been established, in that there is 'no clear congruence of genetic and geographical or sociocultural affinities' among caste groups.[194] Moreover, 'while genes may reflect social patterns, social status is not genetic'.[195] The argument that Dalits as a whole or individual caste groups can be distinguished from each other on biological or genetic grounds was addressed by the Supreme Court of India in 2000, when a scientist tried to sue his in-laws for luring him into marrying their daughter by claiming that they came from a high-caste family, when in fact they were of low-caste origins; the court rejected his argument that the caste origins of his wife could be scientifically proven.[196]

1.3.4 Ambedkar's theory of caste

In *Castes in India* (1916), Ambedkar argued that notwithstanding its great diversity India was a country of 'deep cultural unity', which had become 'parcelled up' or subdivided into closed units, or castes. This came about when some groups within society, starting with the Brahmans (the most prestigious group), 'closed their doors', becoming self-enclosed, endogamous units, and in turn were imitated by those groups who found the door closed against them. By making themselves into a caste and closing others out, the Brahmans created 'non-Brahmans'. The codification of caste rules in Hindu religious texts invested caste with sacred authority. Ambedkar characterised the hereditary link between caste and occupation as 'not merely division of labour' but an 'unnatural division of labourers' – a 'hierarchy in which the divisions of labourers are graded one above the other', with the "Untouchables" at the bottom.[197] Moreover, untouchability justified and underpinned an economic system based on egregious exploitation of this cohort (described earlier). In *Who Were the Shudras?* (1946), Ambedkar argued that '*Chaturvarna* would have been a very

---

193 M Bamshad et al., 'Genetic Evidence on the Origins of Indian Caste Populations', 11 *Genome Research* (2001) 994–1004; A Basu et al., 'Ethnic India: A Genomic View, with Special Reference to Peopling and Structure', 13 *Genome Research* (2003) 2277–2290.

194 Basu et al., ibid., 2284; R Tahkur et al., 'Mitochondrial DNA Variation in Ranked Caste Groups of Maharashtra (India) and Its Implications on Genetic Relationships and Origins', 30(4) *Annual of Human Biology* (July–August 2003) 443–454.

195 L Jorde, transcript of conference paper presented at Anthropology, Genetic Diversity and Ethics: A Workshop at the Center for Twentieth-Century Studies, University of Wisconsin-Milwaukee, 12–13 February 1999, cited in Waughray (n 44) 208.

196 See *GV Rao v LHV Prasad & Others*, dismissal of Special Leave Petition, 6 March 2000, cited in Waughray (n 44) xxx; see also J Singh, 'Court Rules Out Caste Differences', *The Guardian*, 7 March 2000.

197 Ambedkar (n 46) 23–96, 47, 68–69; Ambedkar (n 51) 196, 170.

innocent principle if it meant no more than the mere division of society into four classes';
however, it made the principle of graded inequality 'the basis for determining the terms of
associated life between the four *varnas*'. The system of graded inequality, he said, 'is not
merely notional. It is legal and penal'. The *Shudras* are at the bottom of the gradation, but
they are subjected to 'innumerable ignominies and disabilities' and a 'legal system of pains
and penalties', which prevents them from rising above the condition fixed for them by law.
Until the fifth category of the "untouchables" came into being (referred to by Ambedkar
as the 'fifth *Varna*'), 'the *Shudras* were in the eyes of the Hindus the lowest of the low'.[198]
Ambedkar argued that Hinduism as contained in the *Vedas* and the *Smritis* was not religion
but law, being no more than a 'code of ordinances . . . invested with the character of finality
and fixity'. Crucially, he argued, if it was recognised as law rather than religion, then it could
be changed.[199]

1.3.5 Louis Dumont and his critics

In 1966, Louis Dumont, a French anthropologist, devised a theory of caste based on what
he believed to be the underlying ideological principles and values of Hindu civilisation.[200]
His influential book, *Homo Hierarchicus*, was partly a response to the ultra-empirical field-
work studies of caste in India's villages and regions in the 1950s and 1960s,[201] which he
attacked as failing to grasp India's historic essence and unique difference from the West.
Dumont identified a system of oppositions as the structure underlying the caste order, and
the opposition of the pure and the impure as the fundamental principle underlying caste (an
idea articulated earlier by Indian historian SV Ketkar).[202] Dumont viewed caste as the essence
of Indian society – a cohesive, integrated, timeless system, culturally and ideologically rooted
in Hinduism where 'each particular man [sic] in his place must contribute to the global
order' – in contrast to the atomised individualism of Western society. Despite its inherent
hierarchy and inequality, Dumont argued that caste society was not exploitative, because it
was oriented to the collective rather than to the individual, and each individual understood
and consented to their place and role; functionally, he said, the system provided social cohesion[203] (if not equality as modern human rights would understand it).

Dumont's model of caste society as a system of consensual interdependence was
widely criticised as ignoring the lived reality and the material basis of caste. "Materialists"
accused Dumont and his supporters of failing to recognise the empirical realities of caste

---

198 BR Ambedkar, 'Who Were the Shudras?' in Rodrigues (ed.) (n 103) 385–395, 385–386.
199 Ambedkar (n 46) 75–76; see also Chapter 2.
200 L Dumont, *Homo Hierarchicus: The Caste System and Its Implications* (Chicago: University of Chicago
Press, 1980, first published 1970). For a contemporaneous assessment of *Homo Hierarchicus* see 'On
the Nature of Caste in India – A Review Symposium' in *Contributions to Indian Sociology* (1971) 1–81.
See also Searle-Chatterjee and Sharma (eds.) (n 168).
201 Such as Bailey (n 74). These empirical studies were themselves a response to the text-based accounts of
Indian society produced by the "armchair" sociologists of nineteenth-century Europe.
202 Dumont (n 200) 39, 43. Ketkar identified endogamy and hierarchy as key characteristics of a system
underpinned by theological doctrine (ideology), and purity and pollution as the chief principle upon
which the entire system depends; SV Ketkar, *History of Caste in India* (New Delhi: Low Price Publications, 2010, first published 1909) 27, 29, 116, 121. Dumont cites Celestin Bouglé, *Essais sur le
régime des castes* (Cambridge: Cambridge University Press, 1971, English trans., first published 1908),
whose emphasis on the specifically Hindu/Indian nature of caste and its religious/ritual aspects, and
his holistic analysis thereof as a consensual system based on shared moral and ritual principles, predates
Dumont's analysis by almost sixty years.
203 Dumont (n 200) 9, 11, 105.

oppression,[204] i.e. caste is about power, 'institutionalised inequality, guaranteed differential access to the valued things in life'.[205] Caste systems generate 'enormous conflict'[206] and are maintained not by consensus or ideological acquiescence but through the threat or exercise of power.[207] They are marked by mobility striving, whether in the form of status emulation (termed 'Sanskritisation' by the Indian sociologist MN Srinivas)[208] or constant contestation. Dalits have overwhelmingly rejected the religious criteria and the notion of pollution by which caste is ranked; caste members 'may describe their position in the social hierarchy', but this is not necessarily 'a reflection of their own estimates of their social worth'.[209] Dalit legends and origin myths invariably portray Dalits as Brahmans or Kshatriyas in some earlier age, whose 'mythic plunge' to "untouchable" status is explained by misfortune rather than the accumulation of pollution.[210] On the one hand, as scholars recognise, rejecting one's place in the system is not the same as questioning the system itself.[211] On the other hand, there is a long history of Dalit resistance to caste oppression, Dalit caste refusal and Dalit envisioning of anti-caste, more egalitarian forms of social organisation which are only now beginning to reach a wider academic and popular audience. Consequently, the significance of the caste resistance and refusal movement for India's future cannot be overstated.[212]

In contrast to the Dumontian approach, economic and material theories of caste reject the idea of caste, and associated discrimination, as an essentially religious or ideological phenomenon. Economic and material analyses focus (1) on the link, real or symbolic, between caste and occupation (discussed earlier) and (2) on economic exploitation. It has been argued that occupational and labour differentiation and specialisation were the drivers for both endogamy and hierarchisation, involving ranking according to the prestige of the work undertaken and the status attached to the occupation according to 'ritual and/or cultural values'.[213] For Benjamin Lindt, the essential social and economic roles played by the family, and by extension caste, in the modern Indian economy reveal the economic basis of caste; caste serves as a basis for shared identity, mutual trust and solidarity, and as network for

204 See J Mencher, 'The Caste System Upside Down, or the Not-So-Mysterious East', 15(4) *Current Anthropology* (1974) 469–492; R Deliège, 'Replication and Consensus: Untouchability, Caste and Ideology in India', 27(1) *Man* (1992) 155–173; G Berreman, 'The Brahmanical View of Caste', *Contributions to Indian Sociology* (1971) 16–23.

205 Berreman (n 74) 159. By contrast, in 1979, a study was published which supported Dumont's "consensual" model of caste society; see M Moffat, *An Untouchable Community in South India* (Princeton: Princeton University Press, 1979).

206 Mitra in Searle-Chatterjee and Sharma (eds.) (n 168) 57.

207 G Berreman, 'Caste as Social Process', 23(4) *Southwestern Journal of Anthropology* (1967) 351–370, 355–356; G Berreman, 'The Study of Caste Ranking in India', 21(2) *Southwestern Journal of Anthropology* (1965) 115–129, 115; Gupta (n 175) 413.

208 Mitra in Searle-Chatterjee and Sharma (eds.) (n 168) 57.

209 Berreman (n 207) 120.

210 M Juergensmeyer, 'What If the Untouchables Don't Believe in Untouchability?' 12(1) *Bulletin of Concerned Asian Scholars* (1980) 23–28, 24.

211 R Deliège, 'The Myths of Origin of the Indian Untouchable', 28(3) *Man* (1993) 533–549, 534; D Mosse, 'Replication and Consensus among Indian Untouchable (Harijan) Castes: Comment', 29(2) *Man* (1994) 457–460, 459.

212 See Omvedt (n 67). The 'invisibilising' of Dalit analysis and vision is captured by lawyer Upendra Baxi's observation in 1995 that (in India) 'Ambedkar remains a totally forgotten figure'; U Baxi, 'Emancipation as Justice: Babasaheb's Legacy and Vision', in U Baxi and B Parekh (eds.), *Crisis and Change in Contemporary India* (New Delhi: Sage, 1995) 122–149, 122.

213 B Lindt, 'Towards a Comprehensive Model of Caste', 47(1) *Contributions to Indian Sociology* (2013) 85–112, 91–92; Maisels (n 125) 52–53.

labour recruitment in the informal economy.[214] Other economic explanations of caste point to the history of slavery in the subcontinent. Across India, writes historian Rupa Viswanath, the agrarian economy from pre-colonial times until well into the twentieth century was dependent on hereditarily unfree labour drawn from the lowest castes, namely Dalits. Historically, the caste names for these groups – for example *pariah* – were interchangeable with the regional words for "slave";[215] in parts of India in the nineteenth century, Dalit slave labourers were absolute property, attached to and sold with the land.[216] In 1974, anthropologist Joan Mencher echoed Phule and Ambedkar's analysis in describing caste as having functioned (and continuing to function) from the perspective of those at 'the lowest end', as 'a very effective system of economic exploitation', describing Dalit agrarian labourers as 'slave castes'.[217]

1.3.6 Post-Dumont: caste as orientalist "invention"

From the 1980s onwards, postcolonial scholars such as Nicholas Dirks and Ronald Inden argued that the concept of caste as we understand it today, and its perceived centrality in Indian life, is largely a product or invention of British colonial rule.[218] In 1988, Dirks wrote, '[p]aradoxically, colonialism seems to have created much of what is now accepted as Indian "tradition," including an autonomous caste structure with the Brahman clearly and unambiguously at the head'.[219] One writer, in 2011, even suggested that the 'birth of caste' is attributable solely to the colonial Census.[220] Inden, for his part, was highly critical of what he saw as Western (orientalist) representations of Indian society as static, ahistorical and defined by caste, arguing that such representations elevated the West while denigrating the Indian "Other."[221] Surinder Jodhka explains that the 'simplistic representation of caste as a uniform structure throughout the Indian subcontinent came to be viewed as the common sense about Indian society only during the British colonial period'.[222] Other scholars, whilst

---

214 Lindt, ibid., 107.
215 See Viswanath (n 54) 3, 23–24; Kumar (n 58). On slavery in South Asian history see I Chatterjee and R Eaton (eds.), *Slavery and South Asian History* (Bloomington: Indiana University Press, 2006).
216 Cassels (n 54) 186.
217 Mencher (n 204), 469–493, 469.
218 N Dirks, 'The Invention of Caste: Civil Society in Colonial India', in HL Seneviratne (ed.), *Identity, Consciousness and the Past: Forging of Caste and Community in India and Sri Lanka* (New Delhi: Oxford University Press, 1999) 120–135, 126; N Dirks, *Castes of Mind: Colonialism and the Making of Modern India* (New Delhi: Permanent Black, 2002) 5; R Inden, *Imagining India* (London: Hurst & Co, 2000). See also Said (n 198).
219 N Dirks, 'The Invention of Caste: Civil Society in Colonial India', 25 *Social Analysis* (1989) 42–52.
220 P Samarendra, 'Census in Colonial India and the Birth of Caste', *EPW* (13 August 2011) 51–58.
221 R Inden, *Imagining India* (London: Hurst & Co, 2000) 4. In recent years, an extreme version of the 'colonial invention of caste' theory has emerged, spearheaded by SN Balagangadhara at the University of Ghent, which asserts that caste and the "caste system" do not exist in India or elsewhere but are a colonial construction designed by Christians to denigrate India and Hinduism and to promote the conversion of Hindus to Christianity; furthermore, that Indians who disagree with this analysis suffer from 'colonial consciousness'. This view disregards the historical evidence of caste as a pre-colonial phenomenon, denies agency to Indian actors and is not a view shared by the present author. For a critique of the "Ghent School," see Sutton (n 6). See also Piliavsky's critique of the postcolonial history of India and what she terms the 'invention tradition' (n 187).
222 S Jodhka, *Caste* (New Delhi: Oxford University Press India, 2012) 3.

acknowledging the explicit role of the British in ensuring the continued presence of caste[223] and its "construction" as a totalising, pan-Indian concept, nonetheless assert that its roots go far deeper,[224] and although the "untouchables" as a *political* entity were indeed in one sense "constructed" or "invented" in the late colonial period, their subordination long predates the colonial era.[225] Historian Rosalind O'Hanlon has challenged the postcolonial emphasis on the colonial "construction" of caste for ignoring pre-colonial social history and vernacular critiques of caste, for wrongly assuming that vernacular, anti-Brahmin critiques of caste 'developed in colonial India as essentially derivatives of colonial discourse' and for reducing the role of Indian actors in the shaping – and critiquing – of caste in the pre-colonial and the colonial eras.[226] Chapter 2 seeks to contribute to this analysis by providing a "long view" account of the legal construction of caste inequality prior to Indian independence in 1947.

The search for an all-encompassing theory or model of caste continues to attract scholars. A "new" model (proposed by Lindt), for instance, melds the theories and interpretations just described by positing that caste is based on three elements: biological (namely endogamy and social and biological separation), economic (namely the division of labour and resulting social status differentiation and hierarchy) and ideational or rationalisation. The latter refers to the existence of a narrative which transcends the empirical facts to provide an explanation for the existence of caste, whether a religiously inspired ideology which privileges hierarchy, or a liberal approach that sees it as only related to the family, i.e. a view of caste as kinship/culture, where hierarchy is of lesser importance; either way, caste is a belief system that would not exist if the ideological element were missing. According to this model, the Dumontian approach privileges the rationalisational aspect, in contrast to the highly sophisticated Ambedkarite analysis, which emphasises the relationship between the material (economic and biological) elements, underpinned by post-hoc religious rationalisation.[227]

1.3.7 The 'tenacity of caste'

A vast body of literature exists on the persistence and tenacity of caste in post-independence India and the way in which it has survived and changed (particularly since India's 1991 economic liberalisation), adapting to democracy, capitalism, globalisation and modernisation rather than disappearing.[228] One narrative holds that the 'historical fault lines' of caste, tribe and religion have been 'aggravated in modern India', whilst a second, conversely, holds that the relevance of caste is now 'mostly limited to selection of marriage partners and has little importance in shaping material inequalities'.[229] Between these two poles lie analyses of caste as ethnic identity,[230] as cultural identity, as social organisations or communities 'in which

---

223 Sharma (n 5) 9.

224 Bayly (n 1) 3–4; Guha (n 5); O'Hanlon et al., 'Discourses of Caste Over the Longue Duree: Gopinatha and Social Classification in India, ca. 1400–1900', 6(1) *South Asian History and Culture* (2015) 102–129, 118.

225 Mendelsohn and Vicziany (n 6) 2.

226 See O'Hanlon (n 171) 443. See also Piliavsky (n 187) 324–325, for a summary of the critique of postcolonial scholarship on caste.

227 Lindt (n 213) 92, 96–97, 102.

228 Beteille (n 12); B Natrajan, *The Culturalization of Caste in India: Identity and Inequality in a Multicultural Age* (Abingdon and New York: Routledge, 2012).

229 S Desai and A Dubey, 'Caste in 21st-Century India: Competing Narratives', *EPW* (12 March 2011) 40–49, 40.

230 Reddy (n 189).

people come together to promote collective interest'[231] or as political alliances or groupings. Dipanker Gupta argues that caste *identities* have strengthened even as caste as a system has collapsed – a result of competition and caste-based political assertion consequent upon the breakdown of the closed village economy and the rise of democratic politics.[232] Andre Beteille argues that despite the decline of caste in major areas of social life (e.g. rules relating to purity and pollution, commensality, marriage and the relation between caste and occupation), caste consciousness is kept alive by politicians, political parties and the media.[233]

Where does this leave caste? It is widely acknowledged by scholars that 'the reality of caste has certainly not disappeared. . . . [C]aste is alive and kicking, not merely in the form of substantialised identities but also as a source of privileges and deprivations'.[234] Anthropologist Balmurli Natrajan identifies, and warns against, three portrayals of modern caste as 'defanged', i.e. caste as 'normal, positive and comforting'. These portrayals are (1) political: caste groups not as 'hierarchised inequalities' but as 'modern interest groups in political competition adding to the vibrancy of civil society in India's version of democracy'; (2) economic: caste as 'valorised social capital' enabling caste groups to engage productively in entrepreneurial activities and (3) cultural ('ethnicised') caste: caste groups 'simply as communities of identity seeking recognition for their cultural differences in a multicultural society . . . that celebrates such difference' (Natrajan calls this the 'culturalisation' of caste). Natrajan argues that these portrayals enable caste and casteism to 'pass' as normal, legitimate and 'everyday',[235] even as the educated middle classes express 'increasing distaste' for the values and ideology of caste.[236] Caste inequality, 'far from being regarded as invidious, continues to be seen pervasively as normal, inevitable, even "natural" '.[237] This "normalisation," i.e. the absorption of caste into the bloodstream of everyday life, he suggests, is what endows caste and casteism in India with their durability. Publicly, caste becomes reduced to its most abhorrent or violent manifestations, thus leaving everyday casteism unchallenged. Natrajan's argument is that by camouflaging caste in positive terms as 'cultural identity' or 'community', 'notions of culture and multiculturalism threaten to allow [it] to exist with impunity'.[238] This argument is explored further in Chapter 9.

Social anthropologist David Mosse identifies another limb in the conceptualisation of caste as a contemporary phenomenon – post-Dumont, post-Said/Dirks, post-Indian economic liberalisation, beyond the 'public narrative of caste either as ritual rank eroded by market relations or as identity politics deflected from everyday economic life'[239] and aside from Natrajan's ideas on the culturalisation of caste, and that is caste as an integral but concealed dimension of India's modern market economy – the very field that has been heralded as responsible for its demise and which is supposedly a "caste-free zone." Mosse argues that the effects of caste are pervasive but invisible in labour markets and the business economy, both locally and nationally. In the market economy, he stresses, caste is a resource, whether in the form of networks or 'opportunity hoarding' – advantages which are unacknowledged,

---

231 Mitra in Searle-Chatterjee and Sharma (eds.) (n 168) 67.
232 Gupta (n 175) 409.
233 Beteille (n 12) 48.
234 Jodhka (n 222) xiii–xiv.
235 Natrajan (n 228), xii–xiii, xv.
236 D Quigley, 'Is a Theory of Caste Still Possible?' in Sharma and Searle-Chatterjee (eds.) (n 168) 25–48, 37.
237 Quigley, ibid.
238 Natrajan (n 228), xv, xix.
239 D Mosse, 'The Modernity of Caste and the Market Economy', *Modern Asian Studies* (2019) (online) 1–47, 1.

and which Dalits do not share.[240] Moreover, 'Dalits are not discriminated by caste as a set of relations separate from economy, but by the very economic and market processes through which they often seek liberation'.[241] Similarly, says Mosse, the discomfort among bureaucrats and development organisations in modern India when talking about caste reflects an 'underlying message that caste is an internal matter, unique both in form and in solution to India as a post-colonial nation', outside the ambit of monitored accountability to UN human rights treaty bodies.[242]

1.4 Conclusion

Not only does caste discrimination run contrary to fundamental human rights principles of non-discrimination and equal treatment, and not only has it shown itself resistant to challenge, but also, as this chapter shows, caste itself is a slippery concept, difficult to define and categorise. As Patrick Thornberry observes, 'attempting to draw sharp lines between "race," "descent" and "caste" will not produce unambiguous results. There is an equal slippage of categories in much historical and contemporary writing on the caste question'.[243] As the understanding of terms such as caste, race and descent evolves and their meanings overlap, they become harder to disentangle. Cameron, discussing the merits of using the term "Dalit" for 'a heterogeneous group of people that shares a history of being discriminated against socially, politically, economically and religiously by those who are unlike them in social status', contends that while there is agreement on 'who the oppressors are', there is disagreement 'on what the basis of that oppression is (religious? political? economic?)' and hence difficulty in agreeing 'on means by which to eliminate the conditions of oppression'.[244] As Crispin Bates notes, 'before trying to establish "what is caste," we must first ask "who wants to define it?" ',[245] and, it could be added, 'for what purpose?'. In attempting to understand and combat caste discrimination, we must first understand how caste has survived for so long and who benefits from its continued existence.

Chapter 2 goes on to examine the formation and development of Dalit status, ideologically, materially and legally, concluding with Ambedkar's efforts to use law both to "construct" the Dalits as an oppressed minority/identity group and to "deconstruct" the oppression and discrimination from which they suffer.

---

240 Ibid. This problem was anticipated by Ambedkar in his insistence on the indivisibility of social and economic rights and civil and political rights, and the fragility of political democracy in the absence of economic (and social) democracy; see Chapters 2 and 3.

241 Mosse (n 239) 1.

242 Ibid., 13.

243 P Thornberry, 'Race, Descent and Caste Under the Convention on the Elimination of All Forms of Racial Discrimination', in K Nakano, M Yutzis, and R Onoyama (eds.), *Peoples for Human Rights Vol. 9: Descent-Based Discrimination* (Tokyo: International Movement Against All Forms of Discrimination and Racism, 2004) 119–137, 122–123.

244 M Cameron, 'Considering Dalits and Political Identity in Imagining a New Nepal', XXVII(1–2) *Himalaya* (2007) 13–26, 14.

245 Bates (n 183) 257.

2 The Dalits and the history of caste inequality

2.1 Introduction

This chapter provides a historical overview of the legal construction of caste inequality, from the Vedic period in early India (c 1500 to 500 BCE), to Dr BR Ambedkar's efforts in the first half of the twentieth century to reverse centuries of legalised caste inequality by securing legal guarantees of equality and non-discrimination for the "Untouchables" (his term), both from the British and, as independence approached, from the nationalist movement. Over a long period, caste distinctions and inequalities were constructed and maintained by law. First, we examine the rules contained in classical Hindu religio-legal literature (*dharma* literature) which underlie both discrimination on grounds of caste and also some of the contemporary difficulties in enforcing related legislation (in India) or introducing it (in the UK), and consider whether those rules – many of which were directly concerned with laying down and enforcing caste distinctions and inequalities – represented "real law" in India (at least for Hindus). During British rule, the colonial administrators, in order to give credence to "native" law, seized on Hindu religio-legal texts as the authoritative 'law of the Hindus', treating them as black letter legal codes.[1] The most well-known of these, the *Manusmrti*, or 'Law Code of Manu', became synonymous with the legal construction and maintenance of caste divisions, inequality and discrimination.[2] The chapter goes on to briefly examine the relationship between caste inequalities and law in the feudal and Islamic periods, and then the East India Company and colonial period to 1858 (when East India Company rule was transferred to the British Crown). Nepal's mid-nineteenth-century codification of caste inequality in state law as a mechanism to consolidate state control over an ethnically and culturally diverse population is then briefly discussed. Finally, the chapter turns to an overview of the 'caste reform period' of the late nineteenth and early twentieth centuries and Ambedkar's determination to secure legal guarantees of equality for Dalits as independence approached.

---

1 Plan for the Administration of Justice in Bengal 1772 (the 'Judicial Plan'), drafted by Sir Warren Hastings, Governor-General of Bengal; codified in the Administration of Justice Regulation 1781, section 93; see JM Derrett, *Religion, Law and the State in India* (London: Faber and Faber, 1968) 289.
2 See P Olivelle, *The Law Code of Manu* (Oxford: Oxford University Press, 2004) xvi–xxiii, xxxviii–xxxix; W Menski, 'The Indian Experience and Its Lessons for Britain', in B Hepple and E Szyszczak (eds.), *Discrimination: The Limits of the Law* (London: Mansell, 1993) 300–343, 302, 304.

DOI: 10.4324/9781315750934-4

2.2 The Vedic period c 1500–500 BCE: *varna,* *dharma* and *karma*

2.2.1 *The* varna *classificatory system*

In Chapter 1 we looked at the evolution of Indo-Aryan society in north India and high-lighted the importance of the *Rg Veda* as a key religio-legal text and of the *Purusa* myth for later analyses of ancient Indian society. The Vedic period saw the emergence, initially in northern India and then in the south, of a caste social order characterised by hierarchy and hereditary occupation and related social status determined by birth[3] – concepts inherent in the notion of *varna*, upon which the later caste system was 'ideologically dependent'.[4] Central to Vedism was the principle of distinctions among the orders of reality (natural, divine and human)[5] and the idea that the universe was composed of 'interconnected, but also hier-archically distinguished and ranked, components'.[6] Indian historian Romila Thapar identifies three conditions for a caste society: (1) recognised social disparities, (2) unequal access to economic resources and (3) the legitimisation of inequality through a theoretically irrevers-ible hierarchy, itself based on a supernatural authority.[7] Writing in 1965, Lingat posited that some elements of the caste system might predate the Aryans; further, as the concept of *varna* predates the caste system, it cannot be argued that the former was devised as a religious rationalisation for the latter.[8] Nevertheless, says Smith, the *varna* system allowed certain humans to 'present what was an arbitrary status claim as natural and sacred'.[9]

2.2.2 *The concepts of* dharma *and* karma

Indologist and Sanskrit scholar PV Kane defines *dharma* as

> the privileges, duties and obligations of a man, his standard of conduct as a member of the Aryan community, as a member of one of the castes, as a person in a particular stage of life.[10]

Dharma first appears in the *Rg Veda*.[11] A socio-cultural and political as well as a religious concept,[12] *dharma* is a complex concept which encompasses and also transcends a variety of

---

3 A Parasher-Sen, 'Introduction', in A Parasher-Sen (ed.), *Subordinate and Marginal Groups in Early India* (New Delhi: Oxford University Press, 2004) 1–80, 7.

4 B Smith, *Classifying the Universe: The Ancient Indian Varna System and the Origins of Caste* (New York: Oxford University Press, 1994) 8.

5 B Holdrege, 'Dharma', in S Mittal and G Thursby (eds.), *The Hindu World* (Abingdon: Routledge, 2007) 213–248, 218.

6 Smith (n 4), vii. See also U Singh, *A History of Ancient and Early Medieval India* (New Delhi: Pearson, 2015) 202–204, 291–295.

7 R Thapar, *The Penguin History of Early India: From the Origins to AD 1300* (New Delhi: Penguin Books, 2003) 63–64.

8 R Lingat, *The Classical Law of India* (Oxford: Oxford University Press, 1973) 37.

9 Smith (n 4) 7; Singh (n 6).

10 PV Kane, *History of Dharmasastra (Ancient and Medieval Religions and Civil Law), Vol. I* (Poona: Bhandarkar Oriental Research Institute, 1930) 3. See also Lingat (n 8) 4.

11 P Olivelle, *Language, Texts and Society: Explorations in Ancient Indian Culture and Religion* (Firenze: Firenze University Press, 2005) 123.

12 Holdrege (n 5) 213.

meanings, including religion, morality, rules, obligation, norms, righteousness, justice, duty and law (the term by which it is frequently translated).[13] *Dharma* applies to all elements of the cosmos – sun, water, plants, animals and humans – which must each follow their own particular *dharma* or *svadharma* (the right behaviour), in order to maintain cosmic balance. If an element 'deviates from its own *dharma* . . . the balance is disturbed'.[14] Applied to the universe, *dharma* 'signifies the eternal laws which maintain the world'.[15] Applied to humans, an individual's *dharma* is the way they should act or behave according to their status or *varna* and their stage of life (*asrama*).[16] In addition to its cosmogenic meaning, the term was connected historically to kingship and the king's duty to maintain social and moral order and to administer justice. It also had an important ritual meaning related to sacrifice.[17]

From about 500 BCE, the term underwent a 'conceptual shift' to cover socio-cultural as well as sacrificial and ritual practices:[18]

> [*Dharma*] now becomes enlarged and popularised to include all human actions. It is at first redefined as expectation of right ritual action for every Hindu, then expanded into the secular realm to include any appropriate action at any time.[19]

This expansion of *dharma* from the ritual sphere to the realm of socio-cultural norms was a political response by the Vedic elite, suggests Doniger, to alternative interpretations of *dharma* by Buddhists and Jains which were perceived to pose a threat to their power.[20] A Brahminical philosophical school, *Purva Mimamsa*, grew up, dedicated to elaborating on the expansion of *dharma*, and a new genre of literature – the *Dharmasutras* – was generated which reflected this new, expanded understanding.[21] The underlying purpose, argues Holdrege, was 'to extend Vedic legitimation beyond the ritual realm into the socio-cultural domain and thereby transform the ideological framework of Brahminical culture from a discourse of ritual to a discourse of social power'. In the process, the concept of *dharma* – despite

---

13   Holdrege, ibid.; F Edgerton, 'Dominant Ideas in the Formation of Indian Culture', 62(3) *Journal of the American Oriental Society* (1942) 151–156, 151; L Rocher, 'The Dharmasastras', in G Flood (ed.), *The Blackwell Companion to Hinduism* (Oxford: Blackwell, 2005) 102–115, 102; Lingat (n 8), x–xi. For an argument that *dharma* originally meant the maintenance of peace and security 'through law and order within the larger cosmic order' and hence is a secular and universal concept little connected to Hinduism, see S Subedi, 'Are the Principles of Human Rights "Western" Ideas? An Analysis of the Claim of the "Asian" Concept of Human Rights from the Perspectives of Hinduism', 30(1) *California Western International Law Journal* (1999) 45–69, 51–57.
14   L Rocher, 'Hindu Conceptions of Law', 29(6) *Hastings Law Journal* (1978) 1283–1305, 1285.
15   Lingat (n 8) 3.
16   Hinduism identifies four life-stages: student, householder, forest-dweller and renouncer; see Holdrege (n 5) 222.
17   Olivelle (n 11) 127. Flood describes *dharma* as the 'central ideology of orthoprax Hinduism'; G Flood, *An Introduction to Hinduism* (Cambridge: Cambridge University Press, 1998) 74. Caste is thus very much part of Hinduism's 'sociopolitical world', release from which comes from spiritual emancipation through world-renunciation.
18   Holdrege (n 5) 219–221.
19   W Menski, *Comparative Law in a Global Context: The Legal Systems of Africa and Asia* (Cambridge: Cambridge University Press, 2006) 211–212.
20   W Doniger, *The Hindus: An Alternative History* (Oxford: Oxford University Press, 2010) 278, 308–309; Holdrege (n 5) 220. Doniger's book was withdrawn in India following complaints by the Vishwa Hindu Parishad; see Chapter 1 fn 132. On Buddhism and Brahminism, see G Omvedt, *Understanding Caste: From Buddha to Ambedkar and Beyond* (Hyderabad: Orient Blackswan, 2011) 10–15.
21   Holdrege, ibid., 220; Olivelle (n 11) 132.

its supposedly transcendent nature – became bound 'linguistically, ethnically, and culturally to a specific people: the Aryans', who alone were designated as its authoritative exponents and as the custodians of the eternal language, Sanskrit, in which the *dharma* injunctions were recorded.[22]

Karma, meaning "action," is the doctrine linking conduct in this life with consequences in future lives, and conduct in previous lives with personal circumstances in this life.[23] Circumstances in this life (e.g. human or animal, caste) result directly from deeds performed in a former life, while existence in future lives is determined by deeds performed in this life. While the doctrine applies equally to all, its formulation – that circumstances in the present lifetime are the consequence of actions in past lives – means that inequality and suffering in this life cannot be changed, as they are the result of 'freely chosen behaviour in this and previous lives'.[24] It thus follows that a person's caste in this life is entirely 'of their own making'.[25]

Conformity with one's *dharma* results in improvement in status in the next life, whereas non-conformity will lead to a worse status in future lives. This idea, i.e. that people 'are fundamentally, but not unfairly, unequal,'[26] is encapsulated in the concepts of *varna*, *dharma* and *karma*. In legal terms, from c 500 BCE, this notion was reflected textually in religious and moral precepts of an increasingly "juridical" character contained in what is known as *dharma* literature, the most well-known text of which is the *Manusmrti* (described earlier).

2.2.3 *Legal nature of the early Vedic texts*

Early Vedic (Indo-Aryan) literature introduces the key themes and concepts which underpin classical Hindu law. This literature consists of the four main *Vedas* (*Rg Veda*, *Sama Veda*, *Yajur Veda* (in two versions, Black and White) and the *Atharva Veda*, each comprising a *Samhita* (core) of ritual hymns and prayers, accompanied by *Brahmanas* which interpret the rituals in the *Samhitas*, *Aranyakas*, concerned with mysticism rather than ritual, and *Upanishads*, which raise advanced philosophical and spiritual questions.[27] As to whether these texts are 'legal literature', Menski considers they were not law books but ritual manuals on the performance of sacrificial rituals executed by the Vedic priests or Brahmans.[28] Lingat, conversely, argues that the *Brahmanas*, *Aranyakas* and *Upanishads* (although not

---

22 Ibid., 221.

23 See H Tull, 'Karma', in Mittal and Thursby (eds.) (n 5) 309–331, 318, 326; Flood (n 17) 76.

24 H Coward, 'India's Constitution and Traditional Presuppositions Regarding Human Nature', in R Baird (ed.), *Religion and Law in Independent India* (New Delhi: Manohar, 1993) 24. See also BR Ambedkar, 'The Buddha and the Vedic Rishis', in V Rodrigues (ed.), *The Essential Writings of BR Ambedkar* (New Delhi: Oxford University Press, 2002) 203–216, 214.

25 R Thapar, *Ancient Indian Social History: Some Interpretations* (Hyderabad: Orient Longman, 2009, first published 1978) 28. Indian philosopher Bimal Krishna Matilal addresses what he calls the paradoxicality of caste and *karma*: 'If one's responsibility extends not only to what one does in this life but also to what one is supposed to have done in many (hypothetically construed) former lives, then the thin thread of rationality that presumably tied [merit-based] *karma* to the heredity-bound caste hierarchy becomes too elusive. And paradoxically karma becomes almost synonymous with Fate or Destiny'; see 'Caste, Karma and the *Gita*', in J Ganeri (ed.), *Ethics and Epics: The Collected Essays of Bimal Krishna Matilal Vol. 2* (New Delhi: Oxford University Press, 2015) 136–144, 138–139, 143.

26 Coward (n 24) 23.

27 L Patton, 'Veda and Upanishad', in Mittal and Thursby (eds.) (n 5) 37–51, 38; P Heehs, *Indian Religions: A Historical Reader of Spiritual Expression and Experience* (London: Hurst & Co., 2002) 41, 57.

28 Menski (n 19) 204–207.

the *Samhitas*) contain numerous rules governing behaviour,[29] while for Derrett, they are the 'earliest surviving texts containing legal rules'.[30] The *Vedas* mention the four *varnas* by name and distinguish between Aryans and non-Aryans, or *dasyu* (later to become the Shudras), with the Aryas divided into three categories which Lingat suggests are origins of the three "superior" *varnas*.[31] The *legal* relevance of the early Vedic texts lies first in the articulation of the concept of *varna*, whereby social hierarchy was presented as immutable and divinely ordained, and hence not open to challenge,[32] and secondly, the insight they provide into Vedic understanding of the universe, in particular the concept of *dharma*, integral to the development of classical Indian law.[33]

2.3 The post-Vedic and classical period: *dharma* literature c 500 BCE–700 CE

The *Veda* corpus provided the ideological underpinnings for the development of classical Hindu law teachings on caste in the *dharma* literature.[34] From the third century BCE onwards, with the expansion of *dharma* and the formulation of the *dharma* literature, according to Lingat, we see 'the appearance of something resembling legislation'.[35]

2.3.1 Dharmasutras

In addition to the *sruti* ("revealed") texts is a body of secondary sacred texts known as *smrti* (meaning "remembered" or "tradition"), composed by Vedic sages between the eighth and fourth centuries BCE. These texts include the epic poems the *Mahabharata* and the *Rama-yana*, as well as the *Dharmasutras* (c 600 BCE – 200 BCE), a set of codes concerned with 'regulating and defining social relationships within and between groups'.[36] The *Dharmas-utras* contain rules on duties, behaviour, domestic and dietary matters and family, social and sexual relationships, and they lay down religio-penal sanctions (an embryonic form of criminal law).[37] The sources of *dharma* as identified by Lingat are (1) the entire *Veda*, (2) tradition (*smrti*) and (3) "good custom" or "ideal" custom, meaning the conventions, practices and conduct of "good people" (i.e. those who know the *Veda*). In contrast to "good custom," the custom "pure and simple", as followed by everyone ("habitual practices of a group"), is identified by Lingat as a source of law but not a source of *dharma*.[38] The notion of purity and impurity (pollution) generally, including in relation to certain social groups, first appears in the *Dharmasutras*, which also lays down purificatory practices as well as penances for a range of sins, a number of which, declares Lingat, 'have all the rigour

29 Lingat (n 8) 8.
30 JM Derrett, *Dharmasastra and Juridical Literature* (Wiesbaden: Otto Harrassowitz, 1973) 7.
31 'The Iranian Aryans, closely associated with the Rig-Vedic Aryans, also practised a three-fold division of society consisting of priests, rulers and producers'; B Avari, *India: The Ancient Past* (London: Routledge, 2007) 74.
32 Smith (n 4) 7.
33 See P Olivelle, *A Dharma Reader: Classical Indian Law* (New York: Columbia University Press, 2016).
34 Smith (n 4) 28.
35 Lingat (n 8) 28.
36 Flood (n 17) 54, 55. These dates are disputed and tentative at best. See also P Olivelle, *Dharmasutras: The Law Codes of Ancient India* (New Delhi: Oxford University Press, 1999); Singh (n 6) 294.
37 Lingat (n 8) 68. The "general plan" consists of taking the Brahmin as a basis, and then 'formulating rules peculiar to the other three castes'; ibid., 52.
38 Olivelle (n 2) 23; Lingat, ibid., 6, 14.

of penal sanctions'.[39] Nevertheless, Lingat considers the treatment of legal matters in the *Dharmasutras* to be indirect, disorganised and unsystematic,[40] while for Sanskrit scholar Patrick Olivelle, they contain 'norms of correct behaviour and action'; they do not describe 'what people actually did'.[41]

2.3.2 Kautilya's Arthasasthra

This ancient treatise on law, governance and statecraft, rediscovered in the early 1900s and composed by Kautilya, likely a Brahman priest, sometime between 50 and 125 CE, was a composite of pre-existing sources which later underwent a major redaction.[42] It describes a society based on Vedic codes of conduct and ideas of social hierarchy, and a well-organised legal system with the king at the head, village tribunals in rural areas and law courts in urban centres.[43] Although not particularly focused on caste, hierarchy was clearly present; for example, says Olivelle, it provides that sons of a Brahmana wife should receive four times the inheritance than sons of a Shudra wife.[44] Additionally, it addresses the construction of caste inequality and the maintenance of caste boundaries, and it refers specifically to slaves. It was the Shudra's duty to serve the twice-born, while *Candalas* (Dalits) must live 'on the outskirts of the cemetery'.[45] Punishments were caste-based and unequal, and the severity of the punishment increased in line with the lower the caste of the offender and the higher the caste of the victim. However, the extent to which this text reflects the actual administration of justice is uncertain.[46]

2.3.3 Dharmasastras

Dharmasastra means 'the teaching or science of righteousness'.[47] The *Dharmasastras* contain legal and religious rules and a variety of dietary, hygienic and moral injunctions.[48] They differ from the *Sutras* in form and in content; for instance, they are composed in verse,

---

39 Lingat (n 8) 52–54, 63, 202; see also V Jha, 'Stages in the History of Untouchables', II(I) *Indian Historical Review* (1975) 14–31, 15.

40 Lingat (n 8) 71, 73; Olivelle (n 2), xx.

41 Olivelle, ibid., xxi–xxii; Lingat (n 8) 18. The comments of Olivelle and Lingat speak to the distinction between moral and positive law.

42 T Trautmann, *Kautilya and the Arthasastra* (Leiden: Brill, 1971) 7–8, 186; P Olivelle, *The Arthasastra: Selections from the Classic Indian Work on Statecraft* (Indianapolis: Hackett, 2012) xvi; P Olivelle, *King, Governance, and Law in Ancient India: Kautilya's Arthasastra* (New York: Oxford University Press, 2013) 29, 31. Tradition holds that Kautilya was Chanakya, chief minister of the emperor Chandragupta Maurya but Olivelle refutes this as a historical impossibility; see Olivelle (2013), 26, 34.

43 N Law, *Studies in Ancient Hindu Polity (based on the Arthasastra of Kautilya) Vol. I* (London: Longmans, Green & Co., 1914) 117.

44 Olivelle (2012) (n 42) 85.

45 Ibid., 24.

46 Given the oral nature of the culture, the absence of statutes or written law books and the regulation of everything from memory, Rocher suggests it is likely that law was administered on the basis of unwritten maxims transmitted from generation to generation in the vernacular, some of them applicable to the population of the area generally, others to specific groups, such as members of a particular caste only; see H Jones (ed.), *The Geography of Strabo* (Loeb Classical Library, Vol. 7, 1930) 86–89, cited in L Rocher, 'Law Books in an Oral Culture', 137(2) *Proceedings of the American Philosophical Society* (1993) 254–267, 260; L Rocher, 'Father Bouchet's Letter on the Administration of Hindu Law', in R Larivière (ed.), *Studies in Dharmasastra* (Calcutta: KL Mukhopadyay, 1984) 15–48, 18, cited in Rocher (1993) (n 46), ibid., 262–263.

47 Derrett (n 30) 2.

48 Rocher (2005) (n 13) 102.

include more emphasis on civil and criminal law[49] and formalise in 'law codes' *dharmic* ritual and social obligations.[50] The next two sections discuss these law codes.

2.2.3.1 Manusmrti

The oldest and most important *Dharmasastra* is the *Manavadharmasastra* (*Mdh*), or *Manusmrti*, composed sometime between 200 BCE and 200 CE,[51] a text which Olivelle states has become synonymous with caste and gender oppression.[52] It consists of twelve books in the form of a dialogue between an exalted being or teacher, Manu, his pupil or disciple, Bhrigu or Bhrgu, and a group of others wishing to learn the law of *dharma* from him. Manu is presented as the son of the primeval Lawgiver, the Creator himself, the 'Self-existent One'[53] – a device intended, notes Olivelle, to make the work more authoritative.[54] The *Purusa* myth is invoked twice in the first book[55] as legitimisation for the *varna* system and Aryan social order, becoming "almost a charter or constitution for later Brahmanical sociologists on ancient India".[56] For all social classes, but especially Brahmins (the custodians of the *Veda*), 'proper conduct' is declared 'the highest Law'.[57] On caste, Manu is very clear that there are only four 'classes' (or *varnas*): 'there is no fifth'.[58] A fifth group is named but consciously excluded from the *varna* system; these are the *Candalas*. Described as unfit for association by Brahmins,[59] they are likened to a dog or a pig (disparaged animals).[60] In a frequently quoted passage, Manu declares

> [The *Candalas*] must live outside the village; their property consists of dogs and don-keys, their garments are the clothes of the dead; they eat in broken vessels; their orna-ments are of iron, and they constantly roam about. A man who follows the Law should never seek any dealings with them. All their transactions shall be among themselves, and they must marry their own kind. They depend on others for their food, and it should be in a broken vessel. They must not go about in villages and towns at night, they may go around during the day to perform [tasks but must wear] distinguishing marks.[61]

A similar enmity is directed in the text towards Shudras, who must 'render obedient ser-vice to distinguished Brahmin householders, for a pure, obedient, soft-spoken and humble Shudra obtains a higher birth'.[62] The Shudra's role is to serve the Brahmin, from whom the Shudra is entitled to receive 'leftover food, old clothes, grain that has been cast aside, and

---

49 Holdrege (n 5) 223.
50 Ibid., 222.
51 Olivelle (2004) (n 2) xxiii; Lingat (n 8) 93. Olivelle places the earlier extreme as the first century BC.
52 Olivelle (2004) (n 2), ibid., xvii. According to Olivelle, Manu is an eponym for an unknown author, prob-ably a learned Brahmin from the north of India; ibid., xxi–xxii.
53 Olivelle (2004) (n 2), ibid., xxiii–xxv.
54 Ibid., xxi.
55 *Mdh* 1.31 and 1.87–91; see Olivelle (n 2).
56 Patrick Olivelle, personal correspondence, 2015.
57 *Mdh* 1.107–108; see Olivelle (n 2).
58 *Mdh* 10.4; ibid.
59 *Mdh* 4.79; ibid.
60 *Mdh* 12.55; ibid.
61 *Mdh*.10.51–55; ibid.
62 *Mdh* 9.334–335; ibid. On the *Shudras* and the *Candalas*, see also Singh (n 6) 203–204.

the old household items', but he must not accumulate wealth.[63] Punishments remained caste-based. For example, for physically assaulting a superior person, the low-born must lose the part of his body which caused the injury. If a low-born man attempts to occupy the same seat as a man of high rank, he should be branded on the hip or buttocks and so on.[64] The 'virulence in these injunctions'[65] reflects the very real threat, stresses Olivelle, which the lowest classes of society were perceived by the author of the text to pose to the social order and to Brahminical hegemony and privilege.[66] The later *Dharmasastra* of Yanavalkayasmriti was less harsh, writes Burjor Avari, suggesting limited social fluidity and mobility for some Shudra groups, for whom a certain weakening between caste and traditional occupation resulted in improved status; nevertheless, the position of the *Candalas* as the lowest social strata was confirmed.[67]

2.3.4 *Legal nature of the* Dharmasastras

Scholars are divided as to the legal nature of the *Dharmasastras*. Hinduism has been described as a legal tradition and Hindu theologies as 'pervaded by legal rules, legal categories and legal reasoning'.[68] In Europe, the distinction between law on the one hand and religion on the other dates only from the Enlightenment; indeed, as Davis notes, for most of history and in most of the world, religion and law overlapped.[69] For Rocher, the elements of Hindu law cannot easily be labelled as essentially religious or legal;[70] there is no 'sharp differentiation' between positive law and morality.[71] The Indian tradition, writes Larivière, 'is simply more overt . . . about the theological underpinnings of its legal system'.[72] That said, Larivière considers that the difference between the *Dharmasastras* and positive law in the Western sense has been overstated. Classical Hindu law is the law of groups, castes and regions. Its aim is neither uniformity nor neutrality; rather, it is relative to specific groups, times, places, castes and life stages.[73] Nevertheless, while the *Dharmasastras* were neither legal codes in the European sense nor legislation, Lingat suggests that there exist similarities with positive law, because they were 'based on the normative values . . . of specific groups'.[74] Corporate groups (merchants, traders, guilds, soldiers, pastoralists, farmers, castes and family

---

63 *Mdh* 10.123–125, 129; ibid.

64 *Mdh* VIII.279–283; ibid.

65 Kane (n 10) 97; Olivelle (n 2) xliv.

66 Olivelle, ibid.

67 Avari (n 31) 167.

68 D Davis, 'Hinduism as a Legal Tradition', 75(2) *Journal of the American Academy of Religion* (2007) 241–267, 241, 242.

69 Ibid., 260–261.

70 Rocher (n 14) 1286, 1289.

71 A Michaels, 'The practice of classical Hindu law', in T Lubin, D Davis and J Krishnan (eds.), *Hinduism and Law: An Introduction* (Cambridge: Cambridge University Press, 2010) 58–77, 77. Positive law is 'law whose content is clear, specific, and determinate enough to guide and coordinate human conduct, to create stable expectations, and to be enforceable in court'; JB Murphy, *The Philosophy of Positive Law: Foundations of Jurisprudence* (New Haven: Yale University Press, 2005) 4–5. Murphy explains positive law and moral law as follows: '[M]oral law forbids stealing, whereas positive law must define what counts as property, what counts as stealing, and what legal consequences flow from stealing'; ibid., 4.

72 R Larivière, 'Dharmasastra, Custom, "Real Law" and "Apocryphal" Smrtis', 32 *Journal of Indian Philosophy* (2004) 611–662, 615.

73 Michaels (n 71) 77.

74 Lingat (n 8) 141; Larivière (n 72) 613.

lineages, as well as village affiliations and temples) were among the principal legal actors in early India.[75] Individuals would have been members of several groups simultaneously, and these corporate associations administered a body of substantive laws to their own members.[76] Rocher notes that the *dharma* texts recognise a wide variety of unwritten sources of *dharma*, including custom and the laws of 'countries, castes, and families' (as long as not opposed to the sacred texts).[77] On the one hand, Olivelle points to the distinction between the *sastras* and modern-day legal codes[78] in the sense that the law on the ground was subject to any number of variables;[79] clearly, additional, 'extra-sastric' legal knowledge was required to actually judge lawsuits.[80] Indeed, for Olivelle, the *dharmasastras* are in large part ideological and political statements rather than descriptions of social reality. On the other hand, Larivière argues that although the *Dharmasastras* were general guidelines only, rather than a legal template, the *Dharmasastra* literature nonetheless 'represents in very definite terms the law of the land'.[81]

2.3.5 The feudal era c 800–1200 CE: mobility versus inequality

The period between c 800 and 1200 CE witnessed the production of a vast array of commentaries and digests on the *dharma* texts, variously seeking to interpret, construe, explain, synthesise and codify (a process which continued into the nineteenth century).[82] Derrett expresses no doubt as to the penetration of *sastric* rules into actual legal usage during this period.[83] Socially, during this period, while there was some relaxation of the *sastric* precepts on caste duties, and endogamy was less rigidly applied,[84] caste inequalities became entrenched in the north as in the south, albeit in different forms, evidenced by untouchability practices such as segregated dining and the existence of *devadasis*.[85] Yet this was also a period of tension, fluidity and change. There was a growth in sectarianism and in group attempts at social manoeuvring and 'rearrangement', given that the law in practice fostered advancement by *groups* rather than individual improvement. As society became larger and more complex, more people from outside caste society (such as tribal groups) were absorbed into the Shudra group, while those Shudras in the most menial occupations were designated as "untouchables". Social groups ("communities") possessed the power of excommunication for religious or social (caste) offences, a power perceived as promoting group/social cohesion.[86] In practical terms, law was exercised by caste and community groups, with the king as final arbiter and custodian and censor of customs, determining those repugnant to the *sastra*.[87]

75 D Davis, 'A Historical Overview of Hindu Law', in Lubin et al. (eds.) (n 71) 17–27, 17, 20–22.
76 Ibid., 19.
77 Rocher (n 14) 1298.
78 Olivelle (n 2) xl; Menski (n 19) 215.
79 'He who knows the Law should examine the *Laws of castes, regions, guilds and families*, and only then settle the Law specific to each'; *Mdh* 8.41 (emphasis added); Olivelle (n 2).
80 *Mdh* 8.1–3; Olivelle (n 2), ibid.
81 Larivière (n 72) 623, 612.
82 Lingat (n 8) 107.
83 Derrett (n 1) 196.
84 Avari (n 31) 166–167.
85 Derrett (n 1) 176, 178.
86 Ibid., 181; Avari (n 84).
87 Ibid., 162.

2.4 Medieval/Islamic India c 1206–1707

2.4.1 *The wider setting*

Turkic Muslim incursions into India began in 1000 CE, and in 1206 the Delhi Sultanate was founded in north India. In 1526, the Mughal Empire, which was to last for more than three hundred years, was established following the defeat of the Sultanate.[88] Menski explains that the Muslim political centre was too small, numerically, to impose Islamic law on India's population, the vast majority of whom remained rural Hindus.[89] Islamic law applied fully to Muslims, but to Hindus its jurisdiction extended only to crime and 'constitutional and fiscal administration'.[90] Although not equal to Muslims under Islamic law, non-Muslims were allowed to maintain their own institutions, forms of worship and personal (i.e. religious) law.[91] Hindus were allowed to settle disputes among themselves according to Hindu laws and customs,[92] which differed according to caste and locality. Writes Menski, 'the substance of Hindu law did not change as a result of Muslim domination';[93] simply, it operated as a personal law within the Mughal Empire rather than as the official law of a Hindu state.[94] During this period, as previously, administration of the law was decentralised, in that loyalty was to family, group and caste rather than to the wider community, and not at all to the state.[95] *Sastric* injunctions – whose authority was independent of the state – were enforced by moral and social sanctions,[96] operating 'in civil society as part of the general ideology of everyday life'.[97] Each village had a *panchayat*, or tribunal, which decided civil and criminal cases. In addition, each caste had its own *panchayat* issuing judgments and inflicting fines, public degradation or social exclusion by way of punishment.[98]

2.4.2 Smrti *commentarial texts and digests*

During the Islamic/medieval period, a large corpus of Brahminical commentaries and legal digests on the *smrtis* was produced. These texts reiterated the degraded and despised status of the lowest castes[99] and repeated the caste rules elaborated in the earlier *smrti* literature,[100] including the principle of punishment for the same offence on an *ascending* scale, the lower the caste of the perpetrator (although fear of popular protest may have deterred local Hindu

---

88 RC Majumdar (ed.), *The History and Culture of the Indian People, Vol. VI: The Delhi Sultanate* (Bombay: Bharatiya Vidya Bhavan, 1960) xxiii–xxv.
89 Menski (n 19) 237. See (n 1) on 'Hindu' and 'Hinduism' as neologisms.
90 Derrett (n 1) 229.
91 See AL Srivastava, 'Law and Legal Institutions', in RC Majumdar (ed.), *The History and Culture of the Indian People, Vol. VII: The Mughal Empire* (Bombay: Bharatiya Vidya Bhavan, 1974) 537–554, 538–539.
92 Derrett (n 1) 229. See also Majumdar (ed.) (n 88) 456–459.
93 Menski (n 19) 239.
94 Ibid., 237–238.
95 M Edwardes, *British India 1772–1947* (London: Sidgewick & Jackson, 1967) 2.
96 R Dhavan, 'Dharmasastra and Modern Indian Society: A Preliminary Exploration', 34(4) *Journal of the Indian Law Institute* (1992) 515–540, 516.
97 Ibid., 522, 519; Edwardes (n 95).
98 Srivastava (n 91) 537–554, 550.
99 Majumdar (ed.) (n 88) 581.
100 Majumdar attributes the large number of such texts, and the systematisation of 'the old social and religious law', as a response to the perceived threat posed by the new Sultanate; Majumdar (ed.) (n 91) 574.

rulers from imposing these punishments).[101] Indian scholar Anayana Vajpeyi has examined a body of commentarial texts (legal digests) produced between 1350 and 1700 on the topic of *Sudradharma* (the *dharma* of the *Shudra*) which, she argues, reveals the legal treatment of caste in pre-colonial India, as well as its importance.[102] The purpose of these texts was to assist courts in determining who was a Shudra; language is used 'both as a measure of lowliness and as a weapon of humiliation'. According to Vajpeyi, records of legal disputes from this period involving 'twice-born' groups and Shudras show that Shudras invariably wished to be recognised as "higher" castes rather than as Shudras. The 'centrality of caste to pre-colonial intellectual life and legal practice' is also evidenced by the existence of 'caste experts' – specialist jurists and caste scholars – who were called upon to pronounce on legal matters involving caste and to adjudicate in disputes, including, famously, the transformation of Shivaji, 'a Maratha chieftain . . . heretofore deemed a Sudra, into Chatrapati Shivaji, a Ksatriya king'.

During the same period (sometime between the 1460s and 1553), a treatise on *jatis* (specifically, a study of classes, categories and subcategories, covering descent, parentage and identity, property rights, the right to practice particular professions, prestige and ritual status, i.e. ways in which caste constituted a 'real and powerful social force in daily life') was produced by a Brahmin scholar, Gopinatha, in western India. Gopinatha's *Jativiveka* documents the emergence in the thirteenth and fourteenth centuries of 'the ranked *jatis* that we have come to think of as [modern] "caste"' as 'separated from the state and free-standing as a principle of social organisation'.[103] O'Hanlon et al. describe the *Jativiveka* as a political response to the declining influence of Hindu kings and the challenge of *bhakti*, and a defence of Brahmanical *dharma* in what Gopinatha saw as a degenerate world of mixed castes (termed the "Kaliyuga" age). It indicates that the colonial state inherited 'an order of *varna* and *jati* marked by acute and still developing tensions',[104] which had been subject to contestation over a much longer period. Pre-colonial states and local caste communities took the written *Dharmasastra* texts seriously 'as part of the apparatus of justice', a fact which later anti-caste activists were well aware of and which explains the importance they ascribed to such texts.[105]

Other scholars dispute the importance or even the existence of caste (whether *varna* or *jati*) as a form of social organisation or identity during this period. Contrary to the rigid and hierarchical social universe depicted in Brahmanical texts, medieval India was 'dynamic and expansionist', suggests Cynthia Talbot. Talbot cites data from medieval stone inscriptions in the southern Indian state of Andhra Pradesh as evidence of individual (rather than group) occupational and status mobility (i.e. occupation and status as a consequence of individual achievement, not birth), the relative unimportance of purity-pollution and caste as an ordering principle, and language and occupation rather than *varna* or *jati* as key sources of

---

101   Majumdar (ed.) (n 88) 580, 581. The principle whereby punishment diminished the "higher" the caste of the perpetrator was also frequently repeated.

102   A Vajpeyi, 'Sudradharma and legal treatments of caste', in Lubin et al. (eds.) (n 71) 154–166. Vajpeyi's spelling of "Sudra" is retained when citing directly from her work; otherwise, the spelling "Shudra" is used.

103   R O'Hanlon, G Hidas, and C Kiss, 'Discourses of Caste Over the Longue Duree: Gopinatha and Social Classification in India c. 1400–1900', 6(1) *South Asian History and Culture* (2014) 102–129, 103, 117.

104   Ibid., 118.

105   R O'Hanlon, 'Caste and Its Histories in Colonial India: A Re-Appraisal', 51(2) *Modern Asian Studies* (2017) 432–461, 443.

social identity.[106] Nevertheless, she acknowledges that social mobility was limited to certain classes of people and types of occupation. In particular, and crucially, it was not available to Dalits whose lived reality as expressed, for example, in medieval *Bhakti* literature cannot be ignored.[107]

2.5 British India, law and caste inequality 1600–1857

By the 1720s, the Mughal Empire was in terminal decline, a result of internal and external challenges to its power and authority. Although not officially defunct until 1858, its power had largely disappeared by the 1760s. Jats and Sikhs had rebelled in the north, Delhi was invaded by the Persian ruler Nadir Shah in 1739, northern India was repeatedly invaded by the Afghans and central India was attacked by the Marathas from the south. Chaos, anarchy and a breakdown in authority ensued, leaving the door open to the Europeans.[108]

2.5.1 *1600–1772: Mughal decline and the ascendancy of the British*

British rule in India originated in a Charter granted by Queen Elizabeth I in 1600 to a body of merchants, conferring on them a monopoly of trade with the East. In 1709, this became the British East India Company, whose principal object was trade for profit (backed by military force).[109] What made it unique as a commercial body was not its administrative structure but the special legislative and judicial powers of a quasi-sovereign nature, first granted in 1661, and essential to enable it to conduct trade at such long distances.[110] It exercised these powers in three autonomous "Presidencies" at Calcutta, Madras and Bombay. The 1726 Charter Act established 'Mayor's Courts' in each of the three Presidencies and vested the Company's agents with legislative powers for the first time. At this stage, British interest in India was still purely commercial,[111] but as the Mughal Empire declined, so the East India Company's political and military role in India increased.[112] In 1757, the British (i.e. East

---

106 C Talbot, 'A Revised View of 'Traditional' India: Caste, Status, and Social Mobility in Medieval Andhra', 15(1) *South Asia: Journal of South Asian Studies* (1992) 17–52, 18–24, 36–43; C Talbot, *Precolonial India in Practice; Society Region, and Identity in Medieval Andhra* (Oxford: Oxford University Press, 2001) 48, 209. See also O'Hanlon (n 105) 440, 445.

107 See, for example, E Zelliot, 'Chokhamela and Eknath: Two Bhakti Modes of Legitimacy for Modern Change', in E Zelliot (ed.), *From Untouchable to Dalit: Essays on the Ambedkar Movement* (New Delhi: Manohar, 1998) 3–32. O'Hanlon considers that 'real social marginality lay not in Shudra status but in the unfree labour of the Paraiyans'; O'Hanlon (n 105) 441.

108 B Avari, *Islamic Civilisation in South Asia: A History of Muslim Power and Presence in the Indian Sub-Continent* (London: Routledge, 2013) 131–134.

109 H Bhatia (ed.), *Origin and Development of Legal and Political System in India, Vol. II* (New Delhi: Deep and Deep Publications, 1976) viii; SV Desika Char (ed.), *Readings in the Constitutional History of India 1757–1947* (New Delhi: Oxford University Press, 1983) xxviii; B Cohn, 'From Indian Status to British Contract', in *An Anthropologist Among the Historians and Other Essays* (New Delhi: Oxford University Press, 2012) 463–482, 463.

110 Desika Char (ed.) (n 109), ibid., xxvii; N Gardner Cassels, *Social Legislation of the East India Company* (New Delhi: Sage, 2010) 5.

111 SV Desika Char, *Centralised Legislation: A History of the Legislative System of British India from 1834 to 1861* (London: Asia Publishing House, 1963) 3, citing H Cowell, *History and Constitution of the Courts and Legislative Authorities in India* (Calcutta: Thacker, Spink & Co., 1936, 6th edition) 17.

112 Avari (n 108) 150.

India Company) victory against the Nawab of Bengal at the Battle of Plassey 'started the [Company] on its great career as a territorial ruler'.[113]

When the British set foot in India, Muslim law was fairly uniform throughout the country; however, Hindu law was less so. It was contained in the ancient *smrti* treatises, in the *smrti* commentaries and digests and in custom, mostly unwritten, which varied widely according to region. Acharyya notes that there were no laws relating to public and constitutional rights, 'because such rights did not exist'.[114] Under the British, a 'haphazard'[115] legislative system developed, based on the governments of the three Presidencies. English law applied in the Presidency towns and for British-born subjects in the "mofussil" (rural) areas. Hindus and Muslims in the Presidency towns were governed by their own laws in relation to inheritance, succession, private contracts and matters relating to caste.[116] As early as 1673, the authority of local caste *panchayats* over caste disputes had been recognised, and judicial powers were gradually conferred on caste headmen, but in other matters English law applied. Anthropologist Bernard Cohn describes local areas, which he terms 'little kingdoms', as the basic jural units of India in the eighteenth and nineteenth centuries, in which the dominant castes controlled all castes beneath them. The jurisdiction of the caste *panchayats* fell entirely within the boundary of the little kingdom.[117] Outside the Presidency towns, both Muslim and Hindu criminal law applied, resulting in a multiplicity of different provisions. In civil matters, later British policy of 'non-intervention' in caste matters was presaged by the policy of the East India Company Court of Directors:

> [T]hat the Gent[ues] and other Natives be allowed to live in the full enjoyment of the privileges of their respective Casts [sic], provided they do nothing to the prejudice of the English Government.[118]

2.5.2   *1772–1857: company rule, Anglo-Hindu law and caste*[119]

Between 1765 and 1858 over half of the territorial area of India was controlled directly by a commercial entity, the East India Company, under a Charter renewed at intervals by the British Parliament. The remaining territory (owned by its Indian "allies") that the Company could not, or did not wish to, control directly was supervised by a system of indirect rule.[120] Between 1773 and 1853, the Company's Charter was renewed at twenty-year intervals. In 1858, following the Indian Rebellion and the dissolution of the East India Company, the British Government assumed the running of the direct control areas (the Presidencies and Provinces), continuing with indirect rule over the rest of India;[121] so began the period known as "the colonial Raj."

---

113 Desika Char (n 111) 3.
114 BK Acharyya, *Codification in British India* (Calcutta: SK Banerji & Sons, 1914) 78–79, cited in Desika Char (n 111) 19.
115 Desika Char, ibid., 12, 14.
116 Ibid., 18.
117 B Cohn, 'Some Notes on Law and Change in North India', in Cohn (ed.) (n 109) 554–574, 555–556.
118 'The Court of Directors on the policy towards the native inhabitants of Madras, 17 February 1726', cited in Desika Char (n 109) 17.
119 See R Rocher, 'The Creation of Anglo-Hindu Law', in Lubin et al. (eds.) (n 71) 78–88, 78.
120 See P Lawson, *The East India Company: A History* (London: Longman, 1987); S Wolpert, *A New History of India* (Oxford: Oxford University Press, 2009, 8th edition) 232.
121 The rest of India comprised principalities, or "princely states," which had not (yet) been annexed or subsumed by the Company or, after 1858, the Crown. Even at the end of British rule in 1947, there

In 1772, the Company, under Governor-General Warren Hastings, assumed direct control of Bengal. Hastings was reluctant to impose British law on Indians in the spheres of religion, caste, marriage and the family, for fear of provoking social unrest. However, if "native" law was to be applied in these spheres, the question was, where was Indian law to be found?[122] The answer was in the 'personal laws' of the Muslim and Hindu religious communities (i.e. law 'based on personal, or ascriptive, status regardless of territorial location').[123] Thus, "Anglo-Hindu" law was born. Hastings, in his 1772 Plan for the Administration of Justice, declared that 'in all suits regarding inheritance, marriage and caste and other religious usages or institutions, the laws of the *Koran* with respect to Mahomedans, and those of the *Shaster* with respect to Gentoos [Hindus], shall be invariably adhered to'.[124] The 'naive simplicity'[125] of this instruction overlooked the fact that neither Hindu nor Muslim law was contained solely in the *sastras* or the Koran but was also to be found in legal literature and customs and usages which varied from community to community, caste to caste and region to region.[126] Initially, British India courts sought assistance in the application of Hindu law from native "Law Officers" (*pandits*), elite Brahmin experts in the *sastras* who promoted the notion that, for Hindus, the *sastras* represented the law of the land as practiced in classical India. Hastings' Plan was reissued in 1793 as the Cornwallis Code.[127] In 1794, the *Manusmrti* was translated into English as the 'Institutes of Hindu Law', enabling British India courts to apply "Hindu law" directly, bypassing the opinions of the *pandits* (of whose inconsistencies and discrepancies they had become increasingly suspicious) while simultaneously confirming the impression that the *smrti* literature had the status of "black letter" law.[128]

In the period to 1857, various English translations and digests of "Hindu" law were produced to assist British judges. *Pandits* continued to be used (until their abolition in 1864), but British courts also increasingly applied unwritten custom and established usage. Consistency in legal decisions was one of the primary aims of the colonial administration, says Rosanne Rocher, and so a system of case law (central to English common law but alien to Hindu law) developed alongside a greater willingness not only to apply but also to shape Hindu law by outlawing practices deemed unacceptable, even if sanctioned by

---

were 550 "princely states" under indirect rule, with Kashmir and Hyderabad, for instance, being larger than France; Wolpert, ibid., 233, 371.

122 Rocher (n 119) 79.

123 R Sturman, 'Marriage and Family in Colonial Hindu Law', in Lubin et al. (eds.) (n 71) 89–104, 90. Colonial Hindu law applied not just to those denominated "Hindu" but also to Sikhs, Jains and Buddhists; ibid., 90.

124 Letter of 15 August 1772, cited in Desika Char (n 109) 20; Gardner Cassels (n 110) 8. These were the areas understood as being subject to *sastra* law, but they also coincided with the areas covered by English ecclesiastical law and family law; Derrett (n 1) 233; M Galanter, *Law and Society in Modern India* (Delhi: Oxford University Press, 1994) 144–145 (n 9). See also Rocher (n 119) 78–79.

125 Desika Char (n 109) 21.

126 Ibid., 20–21; Cassels (n 110) 10: 'To focus on the shastras as the source of Hindu law was to ignore that Hindu law is rooted in custom'.

127 The Cornwallis Code replaced the references to the Koran and the "Shaster" (sastras) with Mahomedan and Hindoo laws; Cassels (n 110) 10.

128 Cassels (n 110) 12; Lingat (n 8) 136. A century later, the *Manusmrti* was dismissed as a source of law by Sir Henry Maine and the administrator-historian James H Nelson (a District Judge in the Madras Presidency), among others, as a Brahmanical fantasy which did not represent a set of rules ever actually administered in India but was a purely literary work lacking any vcontact with reality; see Lingat, ibid., 139; Larivière (n 72) 626, fn 46.

the *sastra* texts.[129] For example, the Caste Disabilities Removal Act 1850 declared unlawful the forfeiture of rights or property within territories under Company rule by reason of a person renouncing, or having been excluded from the communion of, any religion, or being deprived of caste.[130] British judges were determined to distinguish between 'what was religious and what was legal'.[131] Consequently, Anglo-Hindu law came to lose much of its "Hindu" identity,[132] and "Hindu law" became reduced to "personal" (i.e. religious) law.[133] Personal law – essentially family law, (marriage, divorce, adoption, joint family matters, guardianship, minority, legitimacy, inheritance, succession, religious endowments) – was conceptualised as a 'separate legal domain' operating 'within the overarching jurisdiction of the State' but supposedly 'free from colonial intervention'.[134] As Marc Galanter explains, under "personal law," different rules were applied to members of different *varnas* – usually one rule for the Shudras and another for the three twice-born *varnas*.[135] Thus, for the colonial courts, a key issue was how to determine who was a Shudra.[136] The colonial courts developed tests, based on Hindu textual law, to determine the *varna* standing of particular castes within an overarching Hindu framework – a religious or "sacral" view of caste, says Galanter, which assumes that all groups within Hinduism can be subsumed within a *varna*. Crucially for future legal efforts to challenge caste oppression and discrimination, this view treats untouchability as a religious and ritual rather than a social or material phenomenon.[137] However, the courts accepted that textual law could be modified by custom. Where issues of caste (group) classification arose, caste groups pleaded "caste customs" before the courts, seeking to associate themselves with a 'distinctive set of cultural traits' which distinguished the caste as a 'corporate body culturally distinct from its neighbours'.[138] William McCormack argues that most alleged "caste" customs were actually regional customs, and not caste-specific. Nevertheless, he says, the courts accepted the proposition that each caste had 'a distinctive set of customs or "culture"'; in cases involving corporate actions by castes, the Bombay court applied precedents derived by analogy from the English law of clubs and religious sects.[139] Modern caste organisation in India, including what McCormack terms the 'regional integration' of castes and the notion of distinct 'caste cultures' (termed by Natrajan

---

129 Rocher (n 119) 86–87.
130 Also known as the Religious Disabilities Removal Act (Act 21 of 1850), it extended to all the East India Company's Indian subjects the protection against loss of property already guaranteed by Section 9 of the Bengal Regulation 1832 to religious groups other than Hindus and Muslims. Cassels writes that, conceived as a guarantee of civil liberties, the legislation was considered by 'Hindu memorialists' as a 'secret attack on Hindu laws', because it threatened the property customs of the caste Hindu joint family and violated the spirit of the Hastings plan; Cassels (n 110) 256–257.
131 Rocher (n 109) 87.
132 Ibid.
133 Sturman (n 123) 89.
134 Ibid., 91–92, 100. Family law in India remains separated along religious lines; see F Agnes, *Family Law Volume 1: Family Laws and Constitutional Claims* (New Delhi: Oxford University Press India, 2011); W Menski, *Modern Family Law in India* (Abingdon: Routledge, 2013).
135 Galanter (n 124) 145.
136 W McCormack, 'Caste and the British Administration of Hindu Law', 1(1) *Journal of African and Asian Studies* (1966) 25–32, 29.
137 M Galanter, *Competing Equalities: Law and the Backward Classes in India* (Berkeley: University of California Press, 1984) 318; A Rao, *The Caste Question: Dalits and the Politics of Modern India* (Berkeley: University of California Press, 2009) 4–7.
138 M Galanter, 'Changing Legal Conceptions of Caste', in M Singer and B Cohn (eds.), *Structure and Change in Indian Society* (Abingdon: Routledge, 2017) 299–336, 304.
139 McCormack (n 136) 29, 32.

the 'culturalisation' of caste and by others the 'ethnicisation' of caste),[140] has been informed, he argues, by the conceptualisation in British India courts of castes as distinct 'corporate' groups, each with their own distinct culture.[141]

The British administration became increasingly unwilling to involve itself in claims concerning caste privileges and disabilities, because these were characterised as religious matters,[142] resulting in an attitude of non-interference vis-à-vis both the maintenance and modification of the caste structure.[143] Jurisdiction was abdicated to the caste *panchayats*, whose decisions were allowed to stand with no interference (but equally no support) from the state.[144] Nevertheless, the fact that personal law fell within the jurisdiction of colonial courts (despite constituting a 'separate legal domain') meant that inevitably there was state intervention in such matters.[145] For low castes, especially women, such intervention was often not to their legal advantage; for example, 'non-elite marriage forms', which historically had recognised the economic contribution of women, were replaced by elite practices such as dowry marriage. Similarly, the 1860 Indian Penal Code criminalised lower-caste customs such as divorce and remarriage (practices which were forbidden for "high-caste" Hindu females) as bigamy or adultery.[146]

However, state intervention did not extend to challenging agrarian slavery, which was closely connected to caste (see Chapter 1).[147] Slavery was abolished in most British territories in 1833, but the East India Company refused to support its abolition in India, partly in order to avoid clashing with "native" religious and social practices, laws and customs under which slavery and servitude of various forms was lawful, but also because colonial tax income came primarily from "high-caste" landowners who depended on hereditarily unfree Dalit agricultural labour.[148] Company officials argued that unlike transatlantic slavery, the practice in India was a benign system. Moreover, as a caste custom or prerogative of the "higher castes," the use of Dalit unfree labourers was deemed a "religious" issue covered by the guarantee in the 1793 Cornwallis Code not to interfere with native religious practices and customs, and hence conveniently outside the ambit of state legal control.[149] Slavery was eventually officially abolished in India in 1843, but the legislation was poorly enforced, and Dalit agrarian slaves simply morphed into bonded labourers, their conditions little changed.[150]

---

140 See B Natrajan, *The Culturalisation of Caste in India: Identity and Inequality in a Multicultural Age* (London: Routledge, 2012).
141 McCormack (n 136) 27.
142 Derrett (n 1) 290.
143 See Cassels (n 110), Chapter 4, Civil Rights and the Policy of Religious Toleration. For example, although the Government of India Act 1833 prohibited discrimination in East India Company employment against Indians (natives) on grounds of descent, place of birth, religion or colour, it permitted the maintenance of "caste disabilities" as between Indians; see Chapter 3.
144 McCormack (n 136) 32; Galanter (n 137) 20. See also Cohn (n 109).
145 Sturman (n 123) 91.
146 Ibid., 96.
147 R Viswanath, *The Pariah Problem: Caste, Religion and the Social in Modern India* (New York: Columbia University Press, 2014) 3; D Kumar, *Land and Caste in South India: Agricultural Labour in the Madras Presidency During the Nineteenth Century* (Cambridge: Cambridge University Press, 1965) 34, 190.
148 Viswanath, ibid., 6–8; see also Cassels (n 110), Chapter 3.
149 Viswanath, ibid.
150 Ibid., 5; Kumar (n 147).

2.5.3 1858–1900: the Crown and caste inequality

Company rule, and the remnants of the Mughal Empire, ended in 1858 with British victory over the Indian Rebellion of 1857–1858. By the Government of India Act 1858, all East India Company rights and territories in the country were transferred directly to Crown control.[151] Codification and standardisation of law began with the creation of the first Law Commission and the enactment of statutes such as the Indian Penal Code in 1860. At the same time, the policy of non-interference with caste customs and religious law in personal and family matters continued.[152] In 1858, concerned to reassure native rulers and subjects of the Crown's goodwill, Queen Victoria proclaimed that that no subjects would be 'favoured, molested or disquieted, by reason of their religious faith or observances', that there should be no state interference with the religious belief or worship of any subject and that in framing and administering the law, due regard would be paid to the ancient rights, usages and customs of India. This proclamation intimated that as religious or customary 'observances', the caste-based discriminatory practices of the so-called high castes would not be challenged.[153] Fear of native sensitivity to 'religious' interference resulted in an era of 'socio-religious *laissez faire*' and a 'policy of indifference to the plight of women, [U]ntouchables and exploited children', couched in terms of religious tolerance and equality[154] and driven by concern that 'upsetting caste hierarchies amounted to interfering with the religious beliefs of Hindus'.[155] The "personal law" sphere governed by classical Hindu legal concepts and doctrines was preserved alongside the developing body of national, secular law, a situation that carried over into the post-independence era. The use of caste in general civil, criminal and commercial cases was abandoned, *sastric* and customary law was supplanted by universally applicable law in all except the personal law fields and 'British law did not recognize or try to maintain the caste order as such'.[156] Nonetheless, the law did recognise the autonomy of caste groups, in that the courts did not interfere with the 'disciplinary powers' of caste *panchayats* (tribunals) vis-à-vis 'internal' matters such as violations of caste etiquette or inter-caste relations, nor did they intervene to prevent high castes enforcing their 'prerogatives' against 'lower castes' by extra-judicial means.[157] Conversely, 'exclusionary practices' of 'high-caste' groups (i.e. practices of segregation) were upheld by the colonial courts where these related, for example, to the use of religious premises (although not secular public facilities such as roads), on the grounds that religious premises (widely defined) were private property from which Dalits were excluded by caste custom.[158] Where the 'lower castes' did have legally enforceable rights, 'they could be vindicated only by engaging in the expensive and

---

151 The 550-plus "princely states," which had never been under Company control, remained autonomous on condition of loyalty to the Crown; see Wolpert (n 120) 247.
152 Galanter (n 137) 20.
153 PI Anandan, 'The Coronation and the Depressed Classes', 24 *Hindustan Review* (1911) 529–532, 529, cited in Galanter (n 137), ibid., 20, fn 6; Viswanath (n 147) 7.
154 Wolpert (n 120), 247. See also Cassels (n 110), Chapter 4.
155 D Shyam Babu and CB Prasad, 'Six Dalit Paradoxes', *EPW* (6 June 2009) 22–25, 23.
156 Galanter (n 137) 19.
157 Ibid., 20; Rao (n 137) 86.
158 Section 21, Bombay Regulation II of 1827 restricted the colonial courts to dealing with inter-caste disputes only where they involved property or personal injury; cited by Rao (n 137) 86–87. Galanter cites cases where British India courts granted injunctions to restrain lower castes from entering temples, awarding damages in trespass to the person to higher castes for purification ceremonies necessitated by the "pollution" caused by their presence; Galanter (n 124) 147. In this way, Dalits were framed as 'the perpetrators of social violence rather than its historical victims'; Rao (n 137) 165.

uncertain process of litigation'.[159] Dominant castes were thus able to exploit colonial law (for example property law) to protect their caste status and privileges, while access to and protection of the law was effectively denied to the lower castes, notably the Dalits.[160]

2.6 Nepal: the *Muluki Ain* (Nepali Royal Law Code) 1854

Contemporaneously with British attempts to codify Indian law, Nepal produced an express codification of caste *in*equality in a national, secular law code: the Nepali Royal Law Code 1854, or *Muluki Ain* (MA), composed at the behest of Prime Minister Rana, who had seized power in 1846. The MA was a national legal code, designed to cement the territorial unification of the country in 1789. Central to the *Ain* was the concept of ascribed caste status.[161] An exercise in social and legal control, its purpose was to impose national unity on a hugely diverse and multi-ethnic society by laying down a hierarchical order based on caste. Regional laws were to discontinue and subjects punished 'uniformly according to their guilt *and caste*'.[162] The MA contains detailed rules on the identification and deprivation of caste status, positioning within the caste hierarchy, inter-caste commensality, proximity and contact, untouchability, purity rules, including transgression of the "water-line" separating pure from impure castes, the transfer of impurity and temporary impurity and inter- and intra-caste social and sexual relations.

While the Indian legal tradition required that the king respect not only *dharma* but also customary law, i.e. the "internal jurisdiction" of groups, castes, guilds and villages, his power was balanced with the spiritual power of the Brahmins, whereas under the MA, customary law and religion were only applicable if they had become *ain* law. Whatever related to caste was subject to the executive and judicial powers of the state – a level of state involvement in and regulation of caste-related behaviour and events in people's daily lives which reached deep into the private sphere.[163] Following Nepal's 1951 revolution, the MA was reissued in 1955. The 1959 Constitution declared all citizens equal before the law, and discrimination in public employment on grounds of religion, race, sex, caste and tribe was prohibited. Nonetheless, under both the reissued MA and the 1959 Constitution, social groups (meaning castes) were assured 'the right to self-determination with regard to religion, customs and social intercourse with other groups'. Discrimination against members of other social groups could thus be justified on grounds of protecting one's own religion and custom.

159 Galanter (n 137) 20.
160 Rao (n 137). Ghurye cites the example of a Mahar (Dalit) boy refused admission in 1856 to a government school which was partly privately funded, whose appeal to the Bombay Education Department was rejected because by admitting him the institution would be 'rendered practically useless to the great mass of natives', i.e. caste Hindus, who would be 'forced into association' with him. It was not until 1932 that the government declared that no grants would be paid to any state-aided educational institutions which refused admission to Depressed Class children; Ghurye, *Caste and Race in India* (Bombay: Popular Prakashan, 1969, 5th edition) 275.
161 A Hofer, *The Caste Hierarchy and the State in Nepal: A Study of the Muluki Ain of 1854* (Innsbruck: Universitatsverlag Wagner, 1979) 39.
162 Ibid., 195. Nepal was an ethnically diverse society ruled by caste-Hindu kings long before the *Ain* was introduced. See N Levine, 'Caste, State, and Ethnic Boundaries in Nepal', 46(1) *The Journal of Asian Studies* (1987) 71–88, 72.
163 Hofer (n 161) 197, 199. Notwithstanding these extensive powers, a certain amount of local autonomy was granted to local population groups who followed their own traditions and customary law regulating marriage, inheritance, etc., while remote areas inaccessible to public administration remained little affected by the caste hierarchy of the MA.

For instance, should a Dalit enter a 'cult place' used hitherto only by Brahmins, such an act could be interpreted 'as an infringement of the Brahmin's religion and customs'. Under the MA, caste was the chief factor determining an individual's juridical status; it "interfered" in marriage, inheritance and occupation, in the relationship between patient and healer and between an individual and the state. It is therefore clear that caste in the subcontinent was not merely a creation of British census compilers.[164]

2.7 Direct British rule and caste reform: 1858–1947

Direct British rule commenced in 1858. This period saw the introduction of the decennial All India Census in 1871 which sought to categorise people inter alia by caste, leading to 'a hardening of caste boundaries' as people sought to 'reshape and exploit' caste differences in order to secure, defend or gain advantages in times of immense social, economic and political change.[165] British rule – and law – also opened up new opportunities for education and advancement, mostly for the Indian elite but also, in theory at least, for a small fraction of the 'lower castes'.[166] New ideas were introduced by Indian and European intellectuals, European missionaries and Indian religious reformers and anti-caste activists such as the radical campaigners Jotirao and Savitribai Phule. Alongside the growth of nationalism, nineteenth-century India saw the emergence of various reform issues in Indian society, including social issues such as caste, and the advent of regional and region-wide caste organisations, Hindu reform groups and "non-Brahmin" movements and organisations.[167] Initially, caste reform was associated with "lower-caste" self-improvement and advancement, often measured in terms of improved status via the adoption of "upper-caste" practices (a phenomenon later termed "Sanskritisation" by Indian sociologist MN Srinivas, ironically sometimes the very practices opposed by "high caste" social reformers, such as child marriage or the ban on widows remarrying) and the achievement of a more prestigious Census entry. It was not until the end of the nineteenth century that 'mainstream reformers saw caste hierarchy and inequality as problems in their own right'.[168]

Galanter identifies two approaches to the eradication of caste inequality in the first half of the twentieth century, namely the "evangelical" and the "secular." The evangelical approach, personified by Mohandas Karamchand ("Mahatma") Gandhi (1869–1948), involved

---

164 Ibid., 206, 211. In 2011, Nepal introduced new legislation criminalising caste discrimination and untouchability.

165 S Bayly, *Caste, Society and Politics in Modern India from the Eighteenth Century to the Modern Age* (Cambridge: Cambridge University Press, 1999) 189.

166 As Galanter points out, the law did not actively support the 'lower castes to use these opportunities', yet it was used by the dominant castes to 'protect their claims to precedence' or even to 'tighten their hold on valued resources to the exclusion of lower castes [sic]'; Galanter (n 137) 21.

167 Galanter (n 137), ibid., 22–23; Zelliot (n 107) 33–50; Rao (n 137), Chapter 1. If European missionaries saw conversion to Christianity as the solution to the religious or spiritual degradation which they associated with caste, this did not necessarily equate to ideological opposition to its structural or material aspects or the social institution of caste per se; see Viswanath (n 147) 16, 43–56; D Mosse, *The Saint in the Banyan Tree: Christianity and Caste Society in India* (Berkeley: University of California Press, 2012). Missionary condemnation of caste and of the lot of the Dalits often went hand in hand with condemnation of Hinduism generally; see C Jaffrelot, *Dr Ambedkar and Untouchability: Analysing and Fighting Caste* (New Delhi: Permanent Black, 2004) 13.

168 Galanter (n 137), ibid., 23, 24. From the 1870s, the caste reform movement used the label "Depressed Classes" to refer to those at the bottom of the caste hierarchy; see S Charsley, 'Untouchable: What Is in a Name?' 23(1) *Journal of the Royal Anthropological Institute* (1996) 1–23, 6.

the uplift of untouchables to higher Hindu standards and the penance of caste Hindus for untouchability, which is seen not as an integral part of Hinduism but as some external impurity. Uplifted untouchables and repentant Hindus will join together in a purified and redeemed Hinduism.

In contrast, writes Galanter, the secular approach, personified in the first half of the twentieth century by Dr Bhimrao Ramji Ambedkar (1891–1956), attacked the denial of civil, economic and social rights to Dalits, which it sought to combat through legal and policy intervention, achieved through political action.[169]

Gandhi and Ambedkar were both London-trained barristers from western India, but from very different caste and social backgrounds and intellectual traditions, divided by 'ideological differences and by the different solutions they advocated' for the eradication of caste inequality. Although both fought for the abolition of untouchability, they were 'at odds in their programs'.[170] Gandhi, leader of the Indian National Congress from 1921–1947, was 'a dominant group leader working for a national goal [freedom from colonial rule] who was concerned, both from a moral standpoint and from a realisation of the need for unity, about injustices to a low status group within the nation'.[171] Although he condemned untouchability, Gandhi believed fervently in the Hindu social order, i.e. the *varna* system, with its traditional division of roles, occupations and duties, as a divine and harmonious ordering of society, but on the basis that the *varnas* were of equal status, and untouchability a corruption of Hinduism. Occupations were inherited but were all 'equally honourable'; thus, the manual scavenger should continue to work as a scavenger, and his or her work should be considered as worthy as that of a Brahmin.[172] According to Gandhi, the "untouchables" should be fully recognised as being integrated within Hinduism (as *Shudras*), and he was opposed to all attempts to characterise them as excluded from the Hindu fold.

Ambedkar was a Dalit, educated in the UK and the US, one of India's greatest statesmen and political leaders, a jurist/lawyer, scholar, writer, activist and campaigner for rights of Dalits. Unlike Gandhi, a "caste" Hindu, Ambedkar experienced first-hand from a young age the burden of untouchability and of caste-based discrimination and humiliation.[173] In the 1920s, he had been involved in the temple entry movement aimed at reforming Hinduism by forcing Hindu temples to admit Dalits. In 1927, he organised a conference in Mahad, western India, in protest at upper-caste Hindus' denial to Dalits of access to public water facilities, at which the *Manusmrti* (the Laws of Manu) was symbolically burnt.[174] By the

---

169 Galanter (n 137), ibid., 28, 29. In the nineteenth century, these approaches – the evangelical and the secular – were exemplified respectively by the Hindu reformers of the Arya Samaj and by the radical anti-caste leaders Jotirao Phule (1827–1890) and his wife Savitribai Phule (1831–1897); see R O'Hanlon, *Caste, Conflict and Ideology: Mahatma Jotirao Phule and Low Caste Protest in Nineteenth-Century Western India* (Cambridge: Cambridge University Press, 1985); Rao (n 137), Chapter 1; E Zelliot, 'The Nineteenth-Century Background of the Mahar and Non-Brahman Movements in Mahar', in Zelliot (ed.) (n 107) 33–50; G Deshpande (ed.), *Selected Writings of Jotirao Phule* (New Delhi: LeftWord, 2002).
170 E Zelliot, 'Gandhi and Ambedkar: A Study in Leadership', in Zelliot (ed.) (n 107) 150–183, 151, 155.
171 Ibid.; G Omvedt, *Ambedkar: Towards an Enlightened India* (New Delhi: Penguin India, 2004), xv.
172 Zelliot, ibid., 145, 158. Manual scavenging is the removal of human excrement by hand from dry latrines; see Human Rights Watch, 'Cleaning Human Waste: "Manual Scavenging," Caste, and Discrimination in India' (Report, 25 August 2014).
173 See BR Ambedkar, 'Waiting for a Visa', in V Moon (ed.), *Dr Babasaheb Ambedkar Writings and Speeches (BAWS) Vol. 12* (Bombay: Education Dept., Government of Maharasthra, 1993) 663–681; Omvedt (n 171) 5–15, 18–19. See also Jaffrelot (n 167).
174 See Jaffrelot, ibid., 48.

1930s, he had abandoned the reform of Hinduism as a strategy, instead calling on Dalits to sever all associations with Hinduism and to convert to any other religion, in order to achieve liberation from caste oppression. In 1935, at a conference in Yeola, western India, he famously declared that, although born a Hindu "Untouchable", he would not die a Hindu.[175] His use of the word "Hindu" in his subsequent writings to refer to caste Hindus reflected his position that Dalits should be considered separate from the Hindus, outside Hinduism rather than part of the Hindu fold, that Hinduism was fundamentally hierarchical, that caste was integral to Hinduism and that Hindus could not destroy the caste system without also destroying their religion.[176]

Ambedkar was not anti-religion per se; on the contrary, he declared himself 'convinced of the necessity of Religion' as long as its doctrinal basis was 'in consonance with Liberty, Equality and Fraternity, in short, Democracy'. In the last years of his life, disillusioned by the slow pace of legal and political change, he turned to Buddhism.[177] His critique of Hinduism was that it was not really religion but 'a mass of sacrificial, social, political and sanitary rules and regulations, all mixed up'; in short, 'what the Hindus call Religion is really Law or at best legalised class-ethics' – law 'misnamed' as religion.[178] These rules were iniquitous, he argued, because they were not the same for one class as for another; they governed the lives of those at the periphery, maintaining their marginalised and subordinated status in very tangible ways:

> In every village the Touchables have a code which the Untouchables are required to follow. This code lays down the omissions and commissions which the Touchables treat as offences . . . these offences are not to be found in the Penal Code enacted by the British Government. Nonetheless so far as Untouchables are concerned, they are real. A breach of any of them involves sure punishment for the Untouchables.[179]

Understanding Hinduism as law, not religion, meant that change was possible. As Ambedkar described, the idea of religion is not generally associated with the idea of change, whereas 'people know and accept that the law can be changed'.[180]

2.7.1 Ambedkar and the Untouchables

The early twentieth century also saw the emergence of anti-caste "Adi" movements (*Adi* meaning "first" or "original"), first in south India and then in the north, the most well-known example being the north Indian Ad-Dharm religious movement.[181] However, it was Ambedkar who was primarily responsible, in the two decades before independence, for the construction of the "Untouchables" as a pan-Indian social and political minority, distinct from the Hindus. While Gandhi urged voluntary individual action on the part of caste Hindus to reject and combat untouchability, Ambedkar advocated legal solutions in the form of

175 Omvedt (n 171) 61; E Zelliot, 'The Revival of Buddhism in India', in Zelliot (ed.) (n 107) 187–196, 192–194; Jaffrelot, ibid., 120–121.
176 BR Ambedkar, 'Annihilation of Caste', in *BAWS Vol 1* (Bombay: Education Dept., Govt. of Maharasthra, 1989) 23–96, 69.
177 Ibid., 76–77.
178 Ibid., 75.
179 BR Ambedkar, 'Outside the Fold', in Rodrigues (ed.) (n 24) 325–327.
180 Ambedkar (n 176) 76.
181 See M Juergensmeyer, *Religion as Social Vision: The Movement Against Untouchability in 20th-Century Punjab* (Berkeley: University of California Press, 1982).

legislative change and affirmative action quotas for the "untouchables" *qua* minority group separate from the Hindus, initially in the fields of political representation and employment and then, on independence, in political representation, public sector employment and education through the Constitution of independent India (of which he was 'one of the principal architects').[182] Until the early twentieth century, the Dalits were not conceptualised as a pan-Indian category, nor was the extent of their oppression a matter of public or national concern except to caste reform activists.[183] The rhetorical potential of the term "untouchability" – coined around 1909 to describe the particular, ritual discrimination suffered by the Dalits – was identified by Ambedkar, who transformed it from a description into a name designating an all-India political identity and a new social and legal category.[184] In the two decades prior to independence, Ambedkar ensured that the concept of "untouchability" became 'embedded in Indian understanding of the structure of their society' and ultimately embodied in the Constitution of India 1950 (COI).[185]

2.7.2 The "Scheduled Castes"

The term "Scheduled Castes" originates in the Government of India Act 1935, which identified by means of an official list those socially excluded castes – previously termed "Depressed Classes" or "untouchables" – eligible for preferential electoral treatment under the Act.[186] The Schedule was incorporated into the COI and has remained in use ever since. COI Article 366(24) defines Scheduled Castes as those castes notified as such by Presidential Order pursuant to COI Article 341.[187] Thereafter, they can be de-listed only by Parliament.[188] Currently, over 1,200 castes are Scheduled nationally.[189] Scheduled status is established by a caste certificate issued by the authorities to members of Scheduled Castes.[190] The list has changed little since the original Schedule was drawn up by the British in 1936, the basis for

---

182 Galanter (n 137) 37. For a detailed discussion of the contrast, and conflict, between Ambedkar and Gandhi, see Zelliot (n 107); Jaffrelot (n 167); Omvedt (n 171). See also Arundhati Roy, 'Introduction to "The Annihilation of Caste"', in S Anand (ed.), *The Annihilation of Caste* (London: Verso, 2014). Omvedt points out: 'while Gandhi fought for freedom from colonial rule, Ambedkar fought for a broader liberation from exploitation and oppression'; Omvedt, ibid., xiv–xvi.

183 See O Mendelsohn and M Vicziany, *The Untouchables: Subordination, Poverty and the State in Modern India* (Cambridge: Cambridge University Press, 1998) 2.

184 Charsley (n 168) 7, 9. Although the existence of the "untouchables" was not new, notes Charsley, "something new" was "constructed" in the category of Untouchable; see also Mendelsohn and Vicziany, ibid., 1–21.

185 Ibid.

186 Galanter (n 137) 130; L Dudley Jenkins, *Identity and Identification in India; Defining the Disadvantaged* (New York: Routledge Curzon, 2003) 14.

187 See Constitution of India (COI) Articles 341(1) and (2); Constitution (Scheduled Castes) Order 1950 (C.O. 19). Castes are scheduled by state; a caste may be "scheduled" in one State but not in another, such that migrant workers scheduled in their home state may be ineligible for SC reservation benefits in other states. Crucially, Scheduled Caste status in India is restricted to members of "Indic" religions, i.e. Hindus (including Jains), Sikhs and Buddhists. Muslim and Christian Dalits are not entitled to SC status or its associated benefits.

188 COI, Article 341(2).

189 See State-wise list of notified scheduled castes, 2011 Census of India, at https://censusindia.gov.in/tables_published/scst/SC%20Lists.pdf.

190 A similar mechanism is used in India to establish Scheduled Tribe and Other Backward Class status. Given the value of these benefits, a significant body of 'identity adjudication' jurisprudence has developed in India concerning claims or disputes pertaining to Scheduled status; Dudley Jenkins (n 186).

inclusion in which was untouchability – measured not according to "secular" disadvantages such as poverty or illiteracy but according to the extent of social disabilities accruing from low social and ritual status in the traditional Hindu social hierarchy (although almost total synchronicity existed between ritual disabilities and socio-economic deprivation).[191] In 1931, the Census Commissioner, JH Hutton, attempted to specify the criteria by which "untouchable" groups could be identified, but it proved impossible to devise an all-India test, due to different regional practices.[192] The Constituent Assembly – the body charged with drafting independent India's new Constitution – abolished but did not define untouchability.[193] However, the understanding was of a ritual, status-based characteristic grossly damaging to both the individual and to society, thereby giving rise to a unique type of social stigma and discrimination which was distinct from discrimination on other grounds, for example religion.[194] Crucially, untouchability was seen by the Constituent Assembly as a function of caste alone: an amendment by a Muslim member that 'no-one shall on account of his *religion or caste* be treated or regarded as an 'untouchable"' was rejected by the Assembly.[195]

Ambedkar linked the emancipation of the Dalits from caste inequality and oppression with India's emancipation from the British.[196] Central to his strategy was the assertion that the "Untouchables" were a minority group, 'distinct and separate from the Hindus',[197] entitled to recognition 'as a separate entity for political and constitutional purposes'.[198] Gandhi, by contrast, insisted that "untouchables" should not be separated politically from the Hindu fold, a prospect which he viewed as damaging to Hindu unity and therefore to the nationalist movement and *swaraj* (the struggle for independence). In 1932, the British Government had promised Dalits one vote in the general electorate and another vote in a Depressed Classes-only electorate, where only Dalits could vote for Dalit candidates – the so-called Communal Award. Gandhi went on hunger strike in protest at the promise of separate electorates for Dalits, demanding that the British Government withdraw the plan, until Ambedkar agreed, in what became known as the "Poona Pact," to reject the Communal Award in return for an increase in the number of reserved seats for the Depressed Classes in provincial legislatures and a system of primary elections for Depressed Classes alone in lieu of communal (Depressed Class only) electorates.[199]

In 1946, with independence approaching, a Constituent Assembly was established by the British to draft India's new Constitution and to act as an interim government pending its adoption. Assembly members were to be elected from the three main "communities" recognised by the British – Muslim, Sikh and "general," the latter to include all persons

191 Galanter (n 137) 122, 135.
192 Ibid., 127–128. In 1932, Ambedkar pointed out the futility of insisting on the application of uniform tests for untouchability across India, given that India was 'not a single homogenous country' but a continent; H Narke (ed.), *BAWS Vol. 2* (Bombay: Education Dept., Govt. of Maharasthra, 2005) 491.
193 See Constituent Assembly Debates of India (CAD) Vol. III, 29 April 1947 (New Delhi: Lok Sabha Secretariat); CAD Vol. VII, 29–30 November 1948, 664–669.
194 Dr Monomohon Das; CAD Vol. VII, 29 November 1948, 666.
195 Mr Ahmad; CAD Vol. VII, 29 November 1948, 669 (emphasis added).
196 D Keane, *Caste-Based Discrimination in International Human Rights Law* (Aldershot: Ashgate, 2007) 2.
197 BR Ambedkar, 'What Congress and Gandhi Have Done to the Untouchables', in *BAWS Vol. 9* (Bombay: The Education Dept., Govt. of Maharasthra, 1991) 181. Galanter notes that, as late as 1910, caste Hindu political opinion was still divided as to whether the "untouchables" should 'count' as Hindus or not; Galanter (n 137) 26, fn 24.
198 Ambedkar, *BAWS Vol. 9*, ibid., 54.
199 See E Zelliot, 'Gandhi and Ambedkar: A Study in Leadership', in Zelliot (ed.) (n 107) 150–183, 166–168; E Zelliot, *Ambedkar's World: The Making of Babasaheb Ambedkar and the Dalit Movement* (New Delhi: Navayana/Blumoom Books, 2004) 134–139; Jaffrelot (n 167) 59–67.

who were not Muslims or Sikhs – with an Advisory Committee on Minorities and Fundamental Rights (the "Minorities Committee") to report on measures for the protection of minorities.[200] Ambedkar, concerned to ensure "untouchable" representation in the Assembly and on the Minorities Committee as a separate political minority rather than as a subgroup within the Hindus, sought, unsuccessfully, a declaration from the British that "minorities" included the Scheduled Castes. Clement Atlee, the British prime minister, wrote privately to Ambedkar, saying, 'We ourselves consider the Scheduled Castes to be an important minority which should be represented on the Minority Advisory Committee', but he was unwilling to dictate to the Assembly the composition of the Minorities Committee.[201] In the event, the Scheduled Castes, as well as Christians, Parsis, Anglo-Indians and women, were brought into the Constituent Assembly by the Indian National Congress under the "general" category.[202] Ambedkar was elected to the Assembly as a member of the "general" category and appointed to the Constitution's Drafting Committee (of which he was elected Chair), the Minorities Committee and the Minorities Sub-Committee. In 1935, Ambedkar famously declared that although he was born in the Hindu religion, he would not die in the Hindu religion. Twenty years later, in October 1956, two months before his death, he led a mass conversion of half a million Dalits to Buddhism in Nagpur, Maharasthra.[203] Since then, "Ambedkarite Buddhist" has become commonplace as a term of reference and self-reference for Dalit converts to Buddhism.[204]

2.8 Conclusion

In 1945, Ambedkar described the caste system as 'a legal system maintained at the point of a bayonet'.[205] Historically, law has been used in India not only to define and categorise the Dalits but also to lay down the very parameters of their existence. It is only since the Constitution of 1950 that the principle of non-discrimination has applied de jure to the Dalits. Prior to 1950, the reverse was the case, whereby Dalits were explicitly subject, de jure and de facto, to the principle of discrimination on grounds of caste.[206] Inequality is about 'ideas, values and meanings', or ideology, as much as 'unequal distribution of material resources';[207] for Rajeev Dhavan, one of India's foremost progressive lawyers and jurists, the *sastra* corpus

> was calculated to achieve what we might call a kind of in-egalitarian harmony between races and in support of a particular view of the relationship between various groups. . . .
> *As a testament on race relations, the sastra presents a hierarchical solution to the problems*

200 B Shiva Rao, *The Framing of India's Constitution: Selected Documents, Vol. 1* (New Delhi: The Indian Institute of Public Administration, 1966) 209–224, 214, 216.

201 S Ajnat (ed.), *Letters of Ambedkar* (Jalandhar: Bheem Patrika Publications, 1993) 154, 157.

202 G Austin, *The Indian Constitution: Cornerstone of a Nation* (New Delhi: Oxford University Press, 1966) 12. In January 1947, the Muslim League announced their withdrawal from the Assembly; Wolpert (n 120) 361–363.

203 See Jaffrelot (n 167) 134–136.

204 Zelliot (n 107) 133–134, 136–140, 187–196, 207–211. Ambedkar had already developed a theory that the "untouchables" were formerly Buddhists persecuted by Vedic Hindus. Conversion was thus an escape from untouchability and a "return" to Buddhism as an egalitarian, Indic religion.

205 Ambedkar (n 197) 289.

206 Menski (n 2) 302.

207 M Schwartz, 'Indian Untouchable Texts of Resistance: Symbolic Domination and Historical Knowledge', in HL Seneviratne (ed.), *Identity, Consciousness and the Past: Forging of Caste and Community in India and Sri Lanka* (New Delhi: Oxford University Press, 1999) 177.

of race and group differentiation. Awkward though this may seem to our contemporary images of an egalitarian society, this hierarchical view was founded on a cosmological understanding of the order of things.[208]

Dhavan's argument is that the *sastra* in contemporary Indian society comprises 'a second-order reservoir of ideas and beliefs' which people draw on to make decisions and which influence how they view themselves and their relationship with others and things around them; yet, too little attention is paid to this 'ideology of everyday life, which is concerned with what we believe and our reasons for action or inaction'. After Indian independence, argues Dhavan, 'it was assumed that the unit of interpretive concern was the individual who must, *prima facie*, be treated as equal to other individuals unless the purpose of the law suggested otherwise'. However, this fundamental principle, on which modern law was founded, was at variance with the *sastra*.[209] Now, though, the defence of Hinduism is not a defence of the *sastric* way of life but is more amorphous and general, the aim being to bring Hindus together (cohesion). Thus, in India, challenges to affirmative action policies for Dalits are based not on religious arguments but on arguments that such policies are 'unworkable, unfair, inegalitarian and contrary to public interest'[210] – an analysis which resonates with some of the grounds of opposition in the UK to legislating against caste discrimination.

The ideas and beliefs underlying caste and caste discrimination are deeply rooted in rules and practices that have developed over centuries and continue to influence contemporary attitudes and behaviours, whether directly or indirectly, consciously or unconsciously. Breaking down such deeply held beliefs and practices cannot be achieved solely by legal regulation; corresponding social and political action is also required.[211] Nevertheless, legal regulation *is* essential, in that it provides a means of redress and also makes an important ideological statement.

---

208 R Dhavan, 'Dharmasastra and Modern Indian Society: A Preliminary Exploration', 34(4) *Journal of the Indian Law Institute* (1992) 515–540, 519, 525 (emphasis added).
209 Ibid., 515, 516, 536. For a debate on human rights, Hinduism and *dharma*, see S Subedi, 'Are the Principles of Human Rights "Western" Ideas? An Analysis of the Claim of the "Asian" Concept of Human Rights from the Perspectives of Hinduism', 30 *California Western International Law Journal* (1999) 45–69; M Ritter, 'Human Rights: The Universalist Controversy, a Response to Surya Subedi', 30 *California Western International Law Journal* (1999) 71–90.
210 Dhavan (n 208) 539.
211 See UN Special Rapporteur on Racism, Interim Report; UN Doc. A/66/313, 19 August 2011, paras 68–76; Special Rapporteur on Racism, Report; UN Doc. A/HRC/17/40, 24 May 2011, paras 86–92.

3 The legal regulation of caste discrimination

Lessons from India[1]

3.1 Introduction

In 1968 – over twenty years after India won her independence and eighteen years after the adoption, in 1950, of a Constitution heralding a society free from poverty, inequality and discrimination on grounds of religion, race, caste, sex or place of birth[2] – CS Dube described caste in India as an octopus 'with its tentacles in every aspect of Indian life':

> It bedevils carefully drawn plans of economic development. It defeats legislative effort to bring about social reform. It assumes a dominant role in power processes and imparts its distinctive flavour to Indian politics. Even the administrative and the academic elites are not free from its over-powering influence.

So how, he asked, 'can it be ignored as a social force?'[3]

Dube's 1968 description was echoed some thirty-five years later at the turn of the new millennium in Myron Weiner's observation that caste was still very much alive as a lived-in social reality, even though its ideological grip had somewhat weakened.[4] Dr BR Ambedkar's seminal essay 'The Annihilation of Caste', calling for an end to the caste system and the oppression associated with it, was published in 1936, but eighty-five years later, caste has not been annihilated in India, and neither has untouchability despite its abolition in the 1950 Constitution.[5] Far from becoming a caste-less society, India – notwithstanding its huge regional, linguistic and religious diversity – remains a society where caste matters. Caste as a social institution has shown a remarkable capacity over the centuries to modify and adapt to changing economic, political and social contexts. Paradoxically, '[w]hat is emerging in India is a social and political system which institutionalises and transforms but does not abolish

---

1 An earlier version of this chapter appeared in *European Yearbook of Minority Issues* Vol. 8 as 'India and the Paradox of Caste Discrimination'.
2 India became independent at midnight on 14–15 August 1947; D Lapierre and L Collins, *Freedom at Midnight* (New Delhi: Vikas Publishing House Pvt Ltd, 1997); Constitution of India 1950 (COI), in force 26 January 1950. See Article 15: Prohibition of Discrimination.
3 CS Dube, *Foreword* in Y Atal, *The Changing Frontiers of Caste* (New Delhi: National Publishing House, 1968) vii.
4 M Weiner, 'The Struggle for Equality: Caste in Indian Politics', in A Kohli (ed.), *The Success of India's Democracy* (Cambridge: Cambridge University Press, 2001) 193–225, 195.
5 BR Ambedkar, 'The Annihilation of Caste', in V Moon (ed.), *Babasaheb Ambedkar Writings and Speeches (BAWS) Vol. 1* (Bombay: The Education Dept., Govt. of Maharashtra, 1989); Constitution of India 1950, Article 17: Abolition of untouchability.

DOI: 10.4324/9781315750934-5

caste'.[6] In the past two decades, the historical-traditional link between caste/ *jati* and occupation has declined, due to economic liberalisation, globalisation, modernisation, urbanisation and the emergence of new types of jobs, resulting in greater occupational mobility and leading some commentators to conclude that caste has all but disappeared except in the social, private and intimate spheres.[7] Yet, conversely, recent research shows that for many Dalits (and Adivasis) modern global capitalism is deepening discrimination, inequality, disadvantage and exploitation based on caste and tribe identity.[8] So-called polluting jobs, i.e. those considered ritually unclean such as sanitation work (manual scavenging – described later – and cleaning sewers), removing and disposing of animal carcasses and leather-working, are still done exclusively by Dalits, and so-called upper castes still predominate in white collar jobs, while labour and capital market discrimination against Dalits presents a real barrier to Dalit economic, occupational and social mobility;[9] hence, while for upper-caste urban Indians caste identity may be of little or no consequence, or 'completely overwritten by modern professional identities of choice', Dalit identity is 'indelibly engraved', overwriting and rendering illegible all other identities.[10]

Other commentators assert that, rather than disappearing, caste understood as a relational, hierarchical system has given way to a view of caste as "difference" rather than hierarchy, where caste groups operate as free-standing, identity-based groups, and caste is seen as a form of cultural or "community" identity to be asserted and celebrated with pride, contributing to the diversity of a multicultural society, rather than as an ascribed, inherited status involving privilege for some and inequality and discrimination for others.[11] Natrajan calls this the 'culturalisation of caste' (meaning the conceptualisation of caste in terms of cultural difference or cultural identity), and it is problematic, he says, precisely because it masks the reality of caste as 'socioculturally constructed relations of ascribed status and antagonism' involving inequality and exploitation.[12]

India has extensive experience of caste as a feature of social organisation, and the oldest and most extensive legal framework for addressing discrimination on this ground, and yet

---

6 Weiner (n 4) 196.

7 For a summary of this argument, see B Natrajan, *The Culturalisation of Caste in India: Identity and Inequality in a Multicultural Age* (Abingdon: Routledge, 2012) 10–11.

8 See, for example, A Shah, J Lerche et al., *Ground Down by Growth: Tribe, Caste, Class and Inequality in Twenty-First-Century India* (London: Pluto Press, 2018). This chapter uses the terminologies "Dalit" and "Adivasi" except when referring to documents or contexts in which the constitutional, legislative and administrative terms "Scheduled Caste" (SC) and "Scheduled Tribe" (ST) are used. On these terms and terminology generally, see Chapters 1 and 2.

9 See A Subramanian, *The Caste of Merit: Engineering Education in India* (Cambridge, MA; Harvard University Press, 2019); A Deshpande, *The Grammar of Caste: Economic Discrimination in Contemporary India* (New Delhi: Oxford University Press India, 2011); SK Thorat and K Newman, *Blocked by Caste: Economic Discrimination in Modern India* (New Delhi: Oxford University Press, 2012); On the existence of caste discrimination in the urban labour market as identified in the early 1980s, see B Banerjee and JB Knight, 'Caste Discrimination in the Indian Urban Labour Market', 17 *Journal of Development Economics* (1985) 277–307, 277.

10 S Deshpande, 'Caste and Castelessness', *Economic and Political Weekly (EPW)* (13 April 2013) 32–39, 32. See also A Rao, *The Caste Question: Dalits and the Politics of Modern India* (Berkeley: University of California Press, 2009) 168; H Gorringe, 'Dalit Politics: Untouchability, Identity and Assertion', in A Kohli and P Singh (eds.), *Routledge Handbook of Indian Politics* (Abingdon: Routledge, 2013) 119–128, 122–123.

11 For a summary of this view, see Natrajan (n 7).

12 Natrajan (n 7) 4–5. See also B Natrajan, 'Cultural Identity and Beef Festivals: Toward a "Multiculturalism Against Caste"', 26(3) *Contemporary South Asia* (2018) 287–304.

there is a glaring disconnect between the country's legal and policy framework and the de facto situation on the ground. This chapter explains and assesses India's law and policies for eliminating discrimination on grounds of caste, and asks what lessons can be learned. It identifies the strengths of India's approach and also its weaknesses and limitations, and it suggests how India's experience might inform law and policy in the diaspora, for example in the UK. The chapter first identifies and explains the contemporary context and manifestations of caste discrimination in India today and then turns to India's legal framework for the elimination of discrimination on grounds of caste, including a discussion of the country's affirmative actions, or "reservation policies," before assessing their impact and the factors influencing their effectiveness. A widely focused legislative strategy for eliminating caste discrimination is now needed, coupled with a much broader approach to equality and non-discrimination underpinned by reliable policy monitoring and auditing, aligned with renewed civic and political vision, in order to overcome age-old inequalities and discrimination based on caste.

3.2 Caste discrimination in India: contemporary context

3.2.1 Caste and poverty

Despite India's rapid economic growth rate over recent decades, poverty still persists. In a country where 176 million people live in extreme poverty by international standards, and 659 million people (50.4% of the population) are poor by the international standard for similar countries, India's Dalits (together with Scheduled Tribes, or Adivasis) suffer disproportionately from socio-economic deprivation and economic exploitation.[13] According to India's National Commission for Scheduled Castes, Dalits (amounting to over 201 million people, or 16.6% of the total population) comprise over 18% of India's rural population but hold only 8.6% of the country's land. In rural areas, 52% of Dalits work as casual labourers compared to 21.6% of the total population, whilst in urban areas the figures are 21% and 5.9%, respectively. Fewer than 0.5% of Dalit households have private-sector jobs compared to 3.5% of all households. Of households without electricity, almost 38% are Dalits. Furthermore, 12.6% of Dalits have no access to drinking water, and only 24% have access to toilet facilities, compared to 42% for all India. Dalit infant mortality stands at 50.7 per one thousand births compared to 41.5 per one thousand for all India.[14] A recent review of caste and development suggests that the proportion of people in poverty increases as one descends the caste hierarchy, while 'capital wealth (land, buildings, finance etc.) is largely in the hands of the "upper" castes, and the "lowest" castes participate in the economy primarily as wage labourers'.[15]

---

13 According to World Bank 2018 data, 176 million Indians live below the international poverty line of $1.90 a day; World Bank data for 2011–2012 put the number of Indians living in extreme poverty at 21.6% of the population. In 2012, the World Bank described 659 million Indians (half the population) as poor, based on the lower-middle-income country poverty line of $3.20 per day. Members of India's SC/ST communities comprise 28% of the population but 43% of the poor. See also Shah et al. (n 8). On India's poor in the decade following 1991's economic liberalisation, see P Sainath, *Everyone Loves a Good Drought: Stories from India's Poorest Districts* (London: Review, 1996); H Mander, *Unheard Voices: Stories of Forgotten Lives* (New Delhi: Penguin, 2001).

14 *National Commission for Scheduled Castes (NCSC) Annual Report 2015–16* (New Delhi: Government of India (GOI), 2016) 26–27, 231–232, 242. According to the World Bank, only 21% of poor Indians have access to latrines, only 6% have access to tap water and 61% have access to electricity.

15 D Mosse, 'Caste and Development: Contemporary Perspectives on a Structure of Discrimination and Advantage', 110 *World Development* (2018) 422–436, 423.

3.2.2 Caste and untouchability

However, material poverty is neither unique to Dalits nor the only source of their oppression; rather, despite regional, linguistic, cultural and religious differences, they are distinguished by a shared experience of untouchability-based exclusion, discrimination and violence.[16] Although untouchability (the practice of caste-based social ostracism, segregation and exclusion) has 'changed character and lost intensity since independence',[17] and despite a decline in some of the most blatant practices,[18] a 2006 study of rural untouchability in eleven states found 'almost universal residential segregation in villages' and untouchability practiced in various forms in almost 80% of the 565 villages studied, in spite of its constitutional abolition. In one out of ten villages studied, Dalits were not allowed to wear new clothes or sandals, use umbrellas or ride bicycles, in almost half of the villages Dalit marriage processions were prohibited on public roads, and in three out of four villages Dalits were not permitted to enter *savarna* ("upper caste") homes, let alone eat with so-called upper castes.[19] A study in 2010 of untouchability in over fifteen hundred villages in the state of Gujarat reached similar conclusions. In almost all of the villages surveyed, Dalits were prohibited from renting accommodation in non-Dalit areas, Dalit labourers were served lunch separately from other workers and Dalits were forbidden from hiring cooking pots for wedding ceremonies. In the majority of villages, Dalits were denied the services of local barbers and tailors. In almost a third of the villages, they were denied access to public drinking water, and in over two-thirds of villages there was no water tap in the Dalit area.[20] The study also found evidence of 'horizontal untouchability' (Dalit-on-Dalit untouchability, i.e. the practice of untouchability by certain Dalit sub-castes against other Dalit sub-castes), particularly in terms of food- and water-related restrictions and discrimination such as lower sub-caste Dalits being prevented from eating with "higher" sub-caste Dalits.[21] India's National Commission on Scheduled Castes Annual Report 2015–2016 cites cases of Dalit schoolchildren being asked to eat their midday meal separately, and cases of "upper caste" children being asked to boycott school midday meals cooked by Dalit employees.[22] Data published in 2015, collected from over 42,000 households in 2011–2012, found that 30% of rural households compared to 20% of urban households practiced untouchability.[23] Studies indicate that untouchability is less present in urban areas where, at least in public spaces, the touchable–"untouchable" barrier is impossible to maintain and caste anonymity is easier to achieve. However, some commentators argue that this simply reflects a combination of

16 O Mendelsohn and M Vicziany, *The Untouchables: Poverty, Subordination and the State in Modern India* (Cambridge: Cambridge University Press, 1998) 12; BR Ambedkar, 'Outside the Fold', in V Moon (ed.), *BAWS Vol. 5* (Bombay: The Education Dept., Govt. of Maharashtra, 1989) 19–26.

17 Mendelsohn and Vicziany, ibid., 36. See also G Shah, 'Dalit Politics: Has It Reached an Impasse?' in N Jayal and S Pai (eds.), *Democratic Governance in India: Challenges of Poverty, Development and Identity* (New Delhi: Sage, 2001) 221–231, 227.

18 G Shah, H Mander, S Thorat et al., *Untouchability in Rural India* (New Delhi: Sage, 2006) 166.

19 Ibid., 166–167. See also B Bhatia, 'Dalit Rebellion Against Untouchability in Chakwada, Rajasthan', 40 *Contributions to Indian Sociology* (2006) 29–61.

20 Navsarjan Trust and Robert F Kennedy Centre for Justice and Human Rights, 'Understanding Untouchability: A Comprehensive Study of Practices and Conditions in 1589 Villages' (2010) 17–20.

21 Ibid., 25–26.

22 NCSC, 2015–16 (n 14) 284.

23 A Thorat and O Joshi, 'The Continuing Practice of Untouchability in India: Patterns and Mitigating Influences', India Human Development Survey Working Paper No. 2015–2, National Council of Applied Economic Research and University of Maryland, 13.

pragmatism, avoidance strategies and "compartmentalisation" by higher-status Indians who remain occupationally, residentially and socially separated from Dalits.[24] Says Deshpande, the invisibility of caste from the lives of the higher castes is a luxury of the urban elite.[25]

3.2.3 Economic and occupational inequality

Caste has long regulated economic life in India,[26] and economic activity remains skewed along caste lines, with sharp disparities in occupational mobility, status and income between non-Dalits and Dalits.[27] Bonded labour, child labour, subsistence-level agricultural day labour and low-level or menial jobs (whether in the private or public sector) are all associated with the lowest castes, in particular Dalits, who make up the vast majority of India's forty million bonded labourers (including fifteen million children), alongside Adivasis and Muslims.[28] Occupational discrimination (unequal access to jobs) accounts for a large part of the earnings differential in the salaried private-sector urban labour market between Dalits and Adivasis and the rest of the population. Since independence, constitutional affirmative action policies (discussed later) have enabled many Dalits to take up service and administrative jobs previously barred to them. However, such policies are restricted to the public sector, where Dalits are under-represented in senior posts and over-represented in the lowest grade posts. Moreover, this sector has been shrinking since the 1990s in the face of globalisation and India's economic liberalisation programme, and yet Dalits struggle to secure anything other than menial or low-status positions in the rapidly expanding formal private sector. Thorat, Jodhka and Newman attribute Dalit occupational immobility to fixed economic rights defined by caste which make it very difficult for young Dalits to accumulate the necessary social and cultural capital, namely education, social networks, cultural exposure, personal skills and confidence, financial security and fluency in the English language, to compete on a level playing field.[29] Far from disappearing as the economy modernises, argue Thorat and Newman, the formal, urban labour market shows 'continued discriminatory barriers even for highly qualified [D]alits'.[30] The view that recruitment in modern corporate India is governed strictly by merit (itself a contested concept)[31] is not supported by the

---

24 G Guru, 'Power of Touch', 23(25) *Frontline* (2006); T Vithayathil and G Singh, 'Spaces of Discrimination: Residential Segregation in Indian Cities', *EPW* (15 September 2012) 60–66; Mendelsohn and Vicziany (n 16) 40–41; H Gorringe and I Rafanell, 'The Embodiment of Caste: Oppression, Protest and Social Change', 41 *Sociology* (2007) 97–114, 106–107.

25 A Deshpande, 'The Eternal Debate', in SK Thorat and N Kumar (eds.), *In Search of Inclusive Policy: Addressing Graded Inequality* (Jaipur: Rawat Publications, 2008) 67–74, 68.

26 S Thorat and K Newman, 'Caste and Economic Discrimination: Causes, Consequences and Remedies', *EPW* (13 October 2007) 4121–4124, at 4122.

27 Ibid.; S Jodhka and K Newman, 'In the Name of Globalisation: Meritocracy, Productivity and the Hidden Language of Caste', *EPW* (13 October 2007) 4125–4132, 4127–4128; M Mohanty, 'Social Inequality, Labour Market Dynamics and Reservation', *EPW* (2 September 2006) 3777–3789; Thorat and Newman (n 9); A Deshpande (n 9).

28 S Baruah, 'Slavery & Casteism in India: No Road to Freedom', *OxHRH Blog*, 9 October 2017 at http://ohrh.law.ox.ac.uk/slavery-casteism-in-india-no-road-to-freedom; R Srivastava, *Bonded Labour in India: Its Incidence and Pattern* (Geneva: International Labour Organisation, 2005). See also Report of the UN Special Rapporteur on contemporary forms of slavery, UN Doc. A/HRC/33/46, 4 July 2016, paras 15–21.

29 Thorat and Newman (n 26) 4122; Jodhka and Newman (n 27) 4127–4128; Mohanty (n 27).

30 Ibid., 4123. Muslims were found to suffer similar discrimination.

31 A Deshpande, *Affirmative Action in India* (New Delhi: Oxford University Press, 2013) 144–148; S Fredman, 'Reversing Discrimination', 113 *Law Quarterly Review* (1997) 575–600, 580.

research.[32] Despite claims that recruitment is 'caste-blind', interviewees are frequently questioned about "family background" – a euphemism for caste. Further, a study of employer responses to written job applications found that applicants with a distinctively Dalit name (the only aspect of "family background" communicated in the application) had significantly lower odds of being contacted for an interview than equivalently qualified applicants with a stereotypically high-caste Hindu name.[33] The accumulated 'cultural capital deprivation' of many Dalits presents a major hurdle to occupational, as well as social, mobility.[34] In addition, far from being a 'caste-free zone', i.e. a domain where 'caste identity and hierarchy are absent or eroded by market processes', India's modern market economy is pervaded by caste, albeit its effects are invisiblised, denied or 'concealed from actors' frames of reference'.[35]

For Dalit entrepreneurs, ascribed social identity has not lost its significance, but remains a source of discrimination even in the context of a modern, capitalist, market-driven economy.[36] In 2009, only 10% of rural private enterprises and just under 7% of urban private enterprises were owned by Dalits, a consequence of their historical lack of access to land, capital, credit and restrictions on property owning; moreover, Dalit-owned businesses tended to be low-income-generating 'own account enterprises' run by single households without hired labour, resulting in high poverty compared to non-Dalit self-employed households, particularly in urban areas.[37] The under-representation of Dalits in business ownership, and the smaller than average size of Dalit firms, is reiterated in a 2013 study which found that for Dalits 'political gains have not manifested themselves in greater entrepreneurial prowess'.[38] This suggests that starting and growing a business is closely linked to having strong and influential networks, which Dalits often lack.[39] A 2010 study found that Dalit business owners experience caste discrimination in both their personal and their business lives and vastly more Dalits believed that caste negatively affected their businesses than felt it was a positive influence.[40] A Dalit millionaire interviewed in 2011 concluded that although economic growth has benefitted some Dalits, bias against Dalit entrepreneurs still prevails: '[w] hen there are profits to be made, then everything [about his caste] is OK. But in their mind, they're thinking, "He is a Dalit" '. Therefore, for Dalits, says Mosse, going into business 'is not just an enterprise, it is a social assertion'.[41]

32 Deshpande (n 9); S Thorat and P Attewell, 'The Legacy of Social Exclusion: A Correspondence Study of Job Discrimination in India', 42(41) *EPW* (13 October 2007) 4141–4145; Jodhka and Newman (n 27). See also Subramanian (n 9).

33 Thorat and Attewell (n 32) 4141–4145.

34 T Weisskopf, 'Impact of Reservations on Admissions to Higher Education in India', *EPW* (25 September 2004) 4339–4349.

35 D Mosse, 'The Modernity of Caste and the Market Economy' (2019) *Modern Asian Studies* (online) 1–47, 37.

36 See L Iyer, T Khanna, and A Varshney, 'Caste and Entrepreneurship in India', *Economic and Political Weekly* (9 February 2013) 52–60; D Ajit, H Donker, and R Saxena, 'Corporate Boards in India: Blocked by Caste?' *EPW* (11 August 2012) 39–43; Thorat and Newman (n 9); Deshpande (n 9); Caste discrimination in the urban labour market predates independence; see Banerjee and Knight (n 9).

37 S Thorat and N Sadana, 'Caste and Ownership in Private Enterprises', *EPW* (6 June 2009) 13–16.

38 L Iyer, T Khanna, and A Varshney, 'Caste and Entrepreneurship in India', *EPW* (9 February 2013) 52–60.

39 Ibid., 53.

40 S Jodhka, 'Dalits in Business: Self-Employed Scheduled Castes in Northwest India', *Economic & Political Weekly* (13 March 2010) 41–48, 46, 48.

41 'I was one of India's unclean Dalits . . . now I am a millionaire'; *The National*, 27 December 2011; Mosse (n 15) 429.

3.2.4 Caste and educational inequality

Article 46 of India's Constitution provides that the state 'shall promote with special care the educational and economic interests of the weaker sections of the people, and in particular of the Scheduled Castes and Scheduled Tribes and protect them from social injustice and all forms of exploitation'. However, since independence, state elementary education has been largely neglected, especially in rural areas where the majority of the population, and the majority of Dalits, live. Free compulsory education for six- to fourteen-year-old children became a fundamental constitutional right only in 2002.[42] Although Dalit literacy levels improved markedly between 1961 (10%) and 2015 (66%), they remain below the national level of 73%, and there are significant regional and gender disparities.[43] Recent research on Dalit educational attainment indicates that while the gap between Dalits and others at primary level is converging, in post-primary and higher education, disparities between Dalits and others have persisted.[44] Dalit secondary school enrolment rates are lower and drop-out rates higher than for the general population[45] (and the figures are worse for girls), due partly to the high direct costs of schooling and the need for Dalit children to work.[46] Consequently, Dalits have traditionally been significantly under-represented in the ranks of higher degree graduates.[47] Research published in 2008 shows that they formed around 23% of the urban population but just 3.6% of urban non-technical subject graduates and under 2% of urban medical graduates.[48] Dalit children are more likely to attend state-run, poor-quality, rural, non-English-medium secondary schools, which means that they are less likely to meet college admissions requirements,[49] they are less likely to have an English-medium language background (65%) than dominant caste students (43%) and more likely (52%) to come from a rural background than dominant caste students (34%).[50] In 2000, the representation of Dalits in higher education was still only half their representation in the population as a whole, and research showed that two-thirds of such students were enrolled in low-prestige programmes and were disproportionately under-represented in Masters and PhD programmes.[51] However, by 2008, 13.5% of higher education students were Dalits[52] (although the gross enrolment ratio in higher studies is reducing, according to India's National Commission for Scheduled Castes in 2015).[53] Nonetheless, access to education is not the whole story, since Dalit pupils and students suffer from discrimination *within* their schools and places of learning, which in turn affects their education outcomes (termed "pre-market discrimination"

---

42 COI Article 21-A, inserted by the Constitution (Eighty-Sixth) Amendment Act 2002, section 2.
43 NCSC, 2015–16 (n 14) 26.
44 A Deshpande, 'Contours of Caste Disadvantage', *The Hindu* (25 September 2014).
45 Government of India (GOI), Ministry of Human Resource Development (MHRD), Department of Higher Education (DHE), New Delhi; Selected Educational Statistics (SES) 2005–6, Gross Enrolment Rates.
46 GOI, National Commission for Scheduled Castes (NCSC), New Delhi, Report 2004–5, 16.
47 H Jain and CS Venkata Ratnam, 'Affirmative Action in Employment for the Scheduled Castes and the Scheduled Tribes in India', 15(7) *International Journal of Manpower* (1994) 6–25, 22.
48 S Deshpande, 'Exclusive Inequalities', in SK Thorat and N Kumar (eds.), *In Search of Inclusive Policy: Addressing Graded Inequality* (Jaipur: Rawat Publications, 2008) 323–324.
49 R Hasan and A Mehta, 'Under-Representation of Disadvantaged Classes in Colleges: What Do the Data Tell Us?' *EPW* (2 September 2006) 3791–3796; Mohanty (n 27) 3788.
50 SK Thorat, 'Discrimination on the Campus', *The Hindu* (26 January 2016).
51 Weisskopf (n 34) 4339.
52 Thorat (n 50).
53 NCSC, 2015–16 (n 14) 307.

by economists).[54] Untouchability practices in schools have already been mentioned. The suicide of a Dalit student, Rohith Vemula, at the University of Hyderabad in January 2016, sparked national and international concern and shone a spotlight on discriminatory practices and institutionalised discrimination in universities, both overt and hidden, faced by Dalit students.[55] A government committee, established in 2007 to enquire into discrimination against SC/ST students in India's premier medical school (New Delhi's All-India Institute of Medical Sciences – AIIMS), found that institutional authorities failed to recognise or to prevent the growth of a significant caste divide on campus, leading the committee's chairman, SK Thorat (a former Chairman of India's University Grants Commission), to conclude that 'ensuring admission for the socially discriminated is meaningless' if government-funded institutions fail to take 'even the most basic steps to make this access meaningful'.[56]

3.2.5 Violence

Violence against Dalits operates at both structural and individual levels, from the dehumanising, violent nature of the caste social order itself, through to the everyday violence of "small" acts of prejudice, discrimination, humiliation and stigmatisation, to untouchability practices (albeit now criminalised) and criminal acts of individual or collective violence (hate crimes). Known as "atrocities," the latter are often committed with the knowledge and acquiescence – or even at the hands – of the law enforcement agencies.[57] Non-governmental monitoring groups and statutory bodies link atrocities to greater competition between Dalits and non-Dalits for scarce resources such as land and water,[58] as well as to attempts by intermediate- and higher-caste groups to protect their status in the face of Dalit economic mobility and political mobilisation, or to punish Dalits perceived to have transgressed social or economic boundaries.[59] A 2015 study found that where the economic gap between Dalits and non-Dalits narrows, there is an increase in violent crimes (atrocities) committed by non-Dalits against Dalits.[60] Other studies have found that perpetrators of anti-Dalit violence

---

54 S Madheswaran, 'Caste Discrimination in the Indian Urban Labour Market: An Econometric Analysis', 53(3) *Rivista Internazionale di Scienze Economiche e Commerciali* (2006) 349–372.
55 See S Ovichegen, *Faces of Discrimination in Higher Education in India: Quota Policy, Social Justice and the Dalits* (London: Routledge, 2015); M Sitlhou, 'India's Universities are Falling Terribly Short on Addressing Caste Discrimination', *The Wire*, 21 November 2017; V Kumar, 'Discrimination on Campuses of Higher Learning: A Perspective from Below', *EPW* (6 February 2016) 12–15.
56 Editorial, 'Thorat Committee Report: Caste Discrimination in AIIMS', *EPW* (2 June 2007) 2032; SK Thorat et al., 'Report of the Committee to Enquire into the Allegation of Differential Treatment of SC/ST Students in AIIMS, New Delhi', at www.nlhmb.in/Reports%20AIIMS.pdf.
57 On violence against Dalits and the role of law enforcement agencies, see Human Rights Watch, Broken People: Caste Violence Against India's Untouchables, 1999; KB Saxena, *Report on Prevention of Atrocities Against Scheduled Castes: Policy and Performance – Suggested Interventions and Initiatives for NHRC* (New Delhi: National Human Rights Commission, India, 2004); H Gorringe, '*Banal Violence?* The Everyday Underpinnings of Collective Violence', 13 *Identities: Global Studies in Culture and Power* (2006) 237–260. On untouchability as violence, see Rao (n 11); Human Rights Watch, *Caste Discrimination: A Global Concern*, 2001.
58 See Sakshi Human Rights Watch, Secunderabad, *Dalit Human Rights Monitor, Andhra Pradesh 2000–2003*, 3–4.
59 A Teltumbde, *Khairlanji: A Strange and Bitter Crop* (New Delhi: Navayana Publishing, 2008) 15–16; R Kothari, 'Rise of the Dalits and the Renewed Debate on Caste', *EPW* (25 June 1994) 1589–1594, 1593. See also NCSC, 2015–16 (n 14) 265.
60 S Sharma, 'Caste-based crimes and economic status: evidence from India', 43(1) *Journal of Comparative Economics* (2015) 204–226.

are frequently "other backward classes" (OBCs), i.e. those castes just above the Dalits in the social hierarchy, the 2006 Khairlanji atrocity in Maharashtra (in which four members of a Dalit family were tortured and murdered by an OBC mob) being a well-publicised example.[61]

India is a party to the Convention on the Elimination of All Forms of Racial Discrimination 1965 (ICERD), and the International Covenant on Economic, Social and Cultural Rights 1966 (ICESCR) (see Chapter 4). The monitoring bodies of these treaties, namely the UN Committee on the Elimination of Racial Discrimination (CERD) and the UN Committee on Economic, Social and Cultural Rights (CESCR), have noted allegations of police failure to register, investigate and properly assist victims of atrocities and caste discrimination.[62] Paradoxically, untouchability offers no protection against caste-based sexual violence. Punitive or coercive violence against Dalits is often characterised by its highly gendered nature, with women and girls the deliberate targets of gendered untouchability practices and sexual violence, and rape and sexual torture are an integral element of retaliatory and punishment crimes against Dalit families.[63] India is also a party to the Convention on the Elimination of All Forms of Discrimination Against Women (see Chapter 4). Its monitoring body, the UN Committee on the Elimination of All Forms of Discrimination Against Women (CEDAW/C), has repeatedly addressed caste-based sexual violence against Dalit women and girls and the downplaying by the state of the grave nature of sexual violence, an egregious issue reiterated in 2013 in the report of the government-appointed Justice Verma Committee on sexual assault against women.[64]

Sexual violence against women and girls in India is systemic and widespread, underpinned by patriarchal social norms and social hierarchies and intersectional in nature.[65] Against this backdrop, attacks on Dalit women are on the increase.[66] However, to conceptualise caste-based sexual coercion and assault against Dalit women as semi-opportunistic acts of individual sexual exploitation would be to misunderstand the intersectional nature of caste/gender discrimination and the use of institutionalised sexual violence as a mechanism of social control and an exercise in power. Dalit women and girls are particularly vulnerable to violence when seeking access to "livelihood resources" such as water, firewood or wages. Nevertheless, a 2006 non-governmental organisation (NGO) study of violence against Dalit women found that only 15% of sexual crimes (barring forced prostitution) were being investigated by the police or pending hearing before the courts, and it accused the police of

---

61 Teltumbde (n 59). Gorringe found that caste violence in Tamilnadu is predominantly perpetrated against Dalits 'by insecure BC [Backward Class] groups'; Gorringe (n 57) 238, 24.

62 See CERD, Concluding observations on India's fifteenth to nineteenth reports; CERD/C/IND/CO/19, 5 May 2007, paras 13, 14, 26; E/C.12/IND/CO/5, 8 August 2008, paras 13, 14, 52, 53.

63 *See* A Irudayam s.j, J Mangubhai, and J Lee, *Dalit Women Speak Out: Violence Against Dalit Women in India, Volume I* (New Delhi: National Campaign on Dalit Human Rights, 2006); Saxena (n 57) 161; Rao (n 10) 237–240 (on the Khairlanji atrocity in Maharashtra in 2006); Teltumbde (n 59).

64 See CEDAW/C/IND/CO/4–5, 24 July 2014, para 10; Report, Justice Verma Committee on Amendments to Criminal Law (New Delhi: Government of India, 2013). The Committee's mandate was to recommend amendments to the criminal law so as to provide for quicker trial and enhanced punishment in cases of sexual assault against women.

65 Report of the Special Rapporteur on violence against women, its causes and consequences; mission to India; UN Doc. A/HRC/26/38/Add.1, 1 April 2014, para 7.

66 Ibid., para 15; 'Voices Against Caste Impunity; Narratives of Dalit Women in India' (All India Dalit Mahila Adhikar Manch/National Campaign for Dalit Human Rights, New Delhi, 2018); S Nigar, 'Violence Against India's Dalit Women on the Increase', *Asia Times* (23 July 2018).

wilful failure of enforcement, and collusion with dominant caste actors.[67] Dalit girls are also subject to the pseudo-religious practice of ritualised prostitution, known as *Devadasi* or *Jogini*, whereby pre-pubescent girls are dedicated to a temple or deity and condemned to a lifetime of sexual exploitation as temple prostitutes. The practice is illegal but remains widespread.[68] In 2007, CEDAW/C identified impunity for atrocities against Dalit women, bonded labour, manual scavenging (see more on that later in the chapter) and the *Devadasi* system as issues requiring India's 'priority attention'.[69] Seven years later, the UN Special Rapporteur on violence against women, during her 2014 mission to India, found consistent failures in the implementation of laws on bonded labour and manual scavenging, which particularly affect Dalit women, and a tendency to minimise the significance of the problem.[70]

3.3 Constitutional vision

In 1946, the Constituent Assembly was established by the British, under the presidency of Dr Rajendra Prasad, to draft a constitution for independent India and to act as an interim government pending its adoption, a process which took almost three years.[71] Jawaharlal Nehru became vice president of the interim government and then, from 15 August 1947, the first prime minister of independent India. On 29 August 1947, Dr Ambedkar, who had been elected as a member of the Constituent Assembly, was appointed Chairman of the Constitution Drafting Committee. According to its Preamble, the framers of India's 1950 Constitution aspired to achieve an end to poverty and a radical restructuring of Indian society, but as the late former Supreme Court Judge Chinnappa Reddy noted, given the make-up of the Constitution's drafting and steering committees, the Constitution which 'finally emerged' was 'property-oriented, not poverty-oriented', with the right to property enshrined as a justiciable Fundamental Right while the 'right to subsist, which was the most important requirement of the vast millions of Indians', became a non-justiciable Directive Principle of State Policy.[72]

In relation to the Scheduled Castes (Dalits), the Constitution embodies a three-pronged strategy which owes much to the legal and political vision of Dr Ambedkar and his skills as a legal negotiator and draftsman. The first legal scholar to conceptualise caste and untouchability-based exclusion as a civil and political *and* social and economic rights issue, not just a socio-religious matter, Ambedkar succeeded in transforming the "untouchables" into a pan-Indian social and political entity and securing their status as a *sui generis* legal

---

67 Irudayam et al. (n 63) 320; Nigar, ibid.
68 See, for example, Andhra Pradesh Devadasi (Prohibition of Dedication) Act 1988; Karnataka Devadasis (Prohibition of Dedication) Act 1982 (amended 2010). See also CERD, 5 May 2007 (n 62) para 18; A Shingal, 'The Devadasi System: Temple Prostitution in India', 22(1) *UCLA Women's Law Journal* (2015) 107–123; M-C Torri, 'Abuse of Lower Castes in South India: The Institution of Devadasi', 11(2) *Journal of International Women's Studies* (2009) 31–48; J Kothari et al., *Intersections of Caste and Gender: Implementation of Devadasi Prohibition Laws* (Bangalore: Centre for Law and Policy Research, 2019).
69 CEDAW/C/IND/CO/3, 27 February 2007, paras 7, 28, 29.
70 Special Rapporteur on VAW (2014) (n 65) para 15.
71 The Constitution of India was adopted on 29 November 1949, signed on 24 January 1950 and came into force on 26 January 1950.
72 See G Austin, *The Indian Constitution: Cornerstone of a Nation* (New Delhi: Oxford University Press, 2008) 26–27; O Chinnappa Reddy, *Summits and Shallows* (New Delhi: Oxford University Press, 2009) 14–15. Anand Teltumbde describes the Constitution as the product of the Congress Party which 'emphatically represented the ruling classes'; A Teltumbde, *Republic of Caste* (New Delhi: Navayana, 2018) 24–25.

category.[73] The constitutional framework consists of the following: first, legal protection from the ideology and practice of untouchability and from inequality and discrimination in the social and economic fields; second, affirmative action provisions or quotas (known as "reservations") in the spheres of political representation, government and public-sector employment and places in higher education institutions; and third, measures for socio-economic development. The purpose was to protect the Dalits from the imposition of untouchability-based disabilities (i.e. discrimination in the form of restrictions and exclusions), compensate them for the historical injustices and disadvantages inflicted by untouchability, increase their representation in the fields to which quotas apply and facilitate and promote their economic and social advancement.

3.4 Caste, equality and non-discrimination: the legal framework

The Constitution of India (COI) establishes India as a 'Sovereign, Socialist, Secular, Democratic Republic'.[74] Citizenship is guaranteed by Article 5 COI. Articles 14–31 COI guarantee to all citizens various individual fundamental rights, corresponding to civil and political rights, directly enforceable in the higher courts. Social and economic rights are incorporated in Part IV COI (Articles 36–51) as non-justiciable Directive Principles of State Policy (DPSPs), described in Article 37 as 'fundamental in the governance of the country' and which must be applied by the state in making laws.[75] Article 14 guarantees equality before the law, while Article 15(1) prohibits discrimination by the state 'against any citizen on grounds only of religion, race, caste, sex, place of birth or any of them'. Article 17 abolishes untouchability (although not the caste system per se), forbids its practice in any form and criminalises the enforcement of any disability arising out of 'untouchability' (which, however, is not defined). Articles 16(1) and 16(2), respectively, guarantee equality of opportunity and prohibit discrimination based on religion, race, caste, sex, descent, place of birth or residence in public employment or state office. Article 15(2) provides that

> [n]o citizen shall be subject, on grounds of religion, race, caste, sex or place of birth, to any disability, liability, restriction or condition with regard to access to shops, public restaurants, hotels or places of public entertainment, or the use of wells, tanks, bathing ghats, roads or places of public resort maintained out of state funds or for general public use

– these being the major forms in which untouchability is practiced by *private actors* in the public sphere. These provisions reflect Ambedkar's understanding of freedom and equality. He viewed discrimination, whether by public or private actors, as an invasion of and inimical to the fundamental rights of citizenship, accorded equal importance to economic and

73 This and the following section draw on A Waughray, 'Caste Discrimination and Minority Rights: The Case of India's Dalits', 17 *International Journal on Minority and Group Rights* (2010) 327–353, 342–344. See also C Jaffrelot, *Dr Ambedkar and Untouchability: Analysing and Fighting Caste* (New Delhi: Permanent Black, 2005); U Baxi, 'Emancipation as Justice: Babasaheb Ambedkar's Legacy and Vision', in U Baxi and B Parekh (eds.), *Crisis and Change in Contemporary India* (New Delhi: Sage Publications, 1995) 122–149.
74 COI, Preamble. The words 'Socialist, Secular' were added after 'Sovereign' by the Constitution (Forty-second) Amendment Act 1976, S.2.
75 A number of the DPSPs have been made justiciable by the Indian judiciary, for example the right to life and personal liberty (Article 21).

social and civil and political rights and conceived of rights generally as not merely imposing restrictions on state behaviour, but also as imposing obligations, or positive duties, on the state *and* wider civil society.[76]

3.4.1 *"Protective" legislation*

India's constitutional provisions relating to untouchability are given effect by criminal, or "protective," legislation designed to protect specific groups. Caste-based crimes, including untouchability, are punishable under the Indian Penal Code (IPC) and/or under special "hate crimes" legislation. The Protection of Civil Rights Act 1955 (PCRA) – formerly the Untouchability (Offences) Act 1955 – criminalises certain acts if committed 'on the ground of "untouchability."' Civil rights are defined in PCRA section 2(a) as 'any right accruing to a person by reason of the abolition of "untouchability" by Article 17 COI'. The PCRA defines "untouchability" by reference to its practice, including, for example, enforcing religious or social disabilities (such as refusing access to any shop, public restaurant, hotel or place of public entertainment, the use of utensils in public restaurants), refusing admission to a hospital, refusing to sell goods or render services on the same terms and conditions applicable to other persons, insulting a member of a Scheduled Caste on the ground of 'untouchability' and/or boycotting a person by reason of their exercise of their rights under Article 17 COI.[77]

The PCRA did not cover acts of gross violence or "hate crimes" against Dalits. Thirty years later, continuing anti-Dalit violence, combined with paltry punishments available under the PCRA, led to the enactment of the Scheduled Castes and Scheduled Tribes (Prevention of Atrocities) Act 1989 (POAA or "Atrocities Act"). The POAA defined "atrocity" by reference to a list of twenty-two acts, where the victim (but not the perpetrator) is a member of a Scheduled Caste or Scheduled Tribe.[78] The prohibited acts include forcing a Scheduled Caste or Scheduled Tribe person to drink or eat any inedible or obnoxious substance, corrupting or fouling water sources used by Scheduled Castes, forcibly dispossessing Scheduled Castes of their land or property and sexual assaults and sexual humiliation of Dalit women. The legislation also provided for Special Courts to hear trials relating to such offences, and for the relief and rehabilitation of victims. The very enactment of the POAA, and the nature of the offences it prohibits, is indicative of the persistence and severity of abuses suffered by Dalits in post-independence India; yet the POAA in turn has been heavily criticised for its ineffectiveness. It was amended by the Scheduled Castes and Scheduled Tribes (Prevention of Atrocities) Amendment Act 2015 together with the Scheduled Castes and Scheduled Tribes (Prevention of Atrocities) Amendment Rules 2016.[79] The amendment legislation strengthens the provisions on Special Courts and the rights of victims and witnesses, and adds fifteen new offences, such as abusing a Scheduled Caste person by their

---

76 BR Ambedkar, 'States and Minorities', in *BAWS Vol. 1* (n 5) 383–449, 395, 401, 406, 408–410.

77 See https://legislative.gov.in/sites/default/files/A1955-22_1.pdf. The Untouchability (Offences) Act 1955 was amended in 1976 and renamed the Protection of Civil Rights Act to enlarge its scope and to strengthen its penal provisions. See Rao (n 10) 173–175. On the use and meaning of the terms "Scheduled Caste," "Scheduled Tribe," "Dalit," "Adivasi" and "untouchability," see (n 8).

78 See https://tribal.nic.in/actRules/SCSTpoaact1989.pdf. Scheduled Castes are those castes notified as such by Presidential Order pursuant to COI Article 341. Castes are scheduled on a state-by-state basis; see Chapter 2.

79 See http://ncsk.nic.in/sites/default/files/POA_ACT_2016.01.pdf and http://ncsc.nic.in/files/PoA%20Amendment%20Rules,%202016.pdf (in Hindi).

caste name in public, imposing or threatening a social or an economic boycott, dedicating a Scheduled Caste woman as a *devadasi* to a temple, preventing Scheduled Castes from using common property resources, entering a place of worship that is open to the public or entering an education or health institution.[80] Sections 4(1) and (2) set out the duties of non-Scheduled Caste public servants (such as police officers) and introduce the possibility of prosecution under the POAA for 'wilful negligence', i.e. wilful neglect of duties, for example by refusing to register or pursue a complaint efficiently. There is also a new "presumption clause," whereby if the accused was acquainted with the victim or their family, the court will presume that the accused was aware of the caste or tribal identity of the victim unless proved otherwise (Section 6 (ii) (c)). This is intended to combat any denial by perpetrators of knowledge of the victim's identity and hence that they should not be prosecuted under the POAA. In March 2017, the Supreme Court, in its judgment in *Mahajan v State of Maharasthra*, issued guidelines limiting the operation of the new legislation, in response to arguments that it was being abused by individuals filing false accusations or mischievous claims in order to blackmail innocent public servants or to exact personal revenge. However, following protests that the guidelines diluted the legislation, Parliament passed an amendment Bill in August 2018 restoring the original provisions of the 2015 legislation.[81] The fact that it has been necessary to reinforce the constitutional prohibition of untouchability and the original (1955) criminal legislation operationalising it with additional legislation in 1976, 1989 and 2015 indicates that the practice of untouchability – and caste-related hate crime – remains a persistent problem in independent India.

3.4.2 Affirmative action: India's "reservations" policies

Although often thought of as an American phenomenon, India's affirmative action policies predate America's policies by many decades.[82] The COI provides for special measures of affirmative action – known as "reservations" – at national and regional levels, by way of quotas in electoral seats, public sector and government employment and places in higher education institutions, for three historically disadvantaged and under-represented groups: the Scheduled Castes (SCs) (officially considered the only group subjected to untouchability), Scheduled Tribes, or STs (*Adivasis*), and Other Backward Classes (OBCs).[83] Affirmative

---

80 See NCSC, 2015–16 (n 14) 265–271.

81 See *Subhash Kashinath Mahajan v State of Maharasthra*, Supreme Court of India, Criminal Appeal No.416/2018; Press Release, Press Information Bureau, GOI, MSJE, 9 August 2018 at http://pib.nic.in/newsite/PrintRelease.aspx?relid=181758.

82 See Deshpande (n 31); M Galanter, *Competing Equalities: Law and the Backward Classes in India* (Oakland: University of California Press, 1984); T Weisskopf, *Affirmative Action in the United States and India: A Comparative Perspective* (London: Routledge, 2004) 4; S Fredman, *Comparative Study of Anti-Discrimination and Equality Laws of the US, Canada, South Africa and India* (Luxembourg: European Commission, Directorate-General for Justice, 2012).

83 See Chapters 1 and 2. There is no definition of backward classes in the constitution, and no constitutional criteria for identifying OBCs. COI Article 340 provides for the appointment of a National Commission for Backward Classes (NCBC) to investigate the conditions of such groups and to make recommendations for their improvement. There have been two ad hoc commissions: the Kalelkar Commission, in 1953, and the Mandal Commission, in 1979. In 1992 the Supreme Court in *Indra Sawhney v Union of India* (the 'Mandal judgment) ruled in favour of national reservations at 27% in employment (but not education) for OBCs. In 1993, the NCBC was established as a statutory body responsible for determining the inclusion of groups in a central government list of backward classes (now around 2,300 castes and sub-castes) on the basis of published social, educational and economic indicators including caste. Unlike

action was not a new idea, since reservations in public employment and higher education in India originated prior to independence in special measures for non-Brahmins introduced by certain princely states and provinces in the early twentieth century.[84] In addition, in the Morley-Minto reforms of 1909, the British accorded reserved seats in the national and provincial legislatures to Muslims on the basis of their identity as a religious minority.[85] The COI mandates reservations for SCs and STs (but not OBCs) in political representation at local, provincial and national level on the basis of their population share.[86] Article 15(4)[87] authorises (but does not mandate) the reservation of seats in state higher education institutions for SCs and STs and, since 2006, for OBCs,[88] and in private educational institutions other than minority institutions covered by Article 30(1).[89] Article 16(4) authorises (but does not mandate) reserved posts in public-sector (but not private-sector) employment for SCs and STs in provincial and central government services[90] and for OBCs in provincial and (since 1993) central services.[91] In the absence of a constitutional ceiling on reservations in higher education and public employment, case law has established a 50% ceiling.[92] In appointments by direct recruitment to India-wide, open competition posts, the quota

---

SC status, OBC status is not defined by reference to religion; see 'Social, Economic and Educational Status of the Muslim Community of India: A Report' (GOI, Prime Minister's High-Level Committee, Cabinet Secretariat, 2006) ('Sachar Report'), 6, at https://minorityaffairs.gov.in/en/document/sachar-committee-report/complete-sachar-committee-reportenglish-2006-6655-kb.

84 Mendelsohn and Vicziany (n 16) 129–130; S Kumar, *Social Justice and the Politics of Reservation in India* (New Delhi: Mittal Publications, 2008) 61–63.

85 Galanter (n 82); 25; B Shiva Rao, *The Framing of India's Constitution: A Study* (New Delhi: Indian Institute of Public Administration, 1968) 3. Religious, linguistic and cultural minorities are guaranteed freedom of religion (COI Articles 25–28) and protection of their cultural, linguistic and educational rights (COI Articles 29 and 30) but are not eligible for the special measures afforded to the SCs and STs and, to a lesser extent, the OBCs. The draft constitution originally contained electoral and employment reservations for religious minorities (including Muslims who already benefitted pre-independence from electoral reservations) but in 1949 in the aftermath of the partition of India reservations for religious minorities were dropped; see Constituent Assembly Debates of India (CAD) VIII, 25 May 1949 (Lok Sabha Secretariat, New Delhi) 269–272; see also Z Hasan, *Politics of Inclusion: Castes, Minorities and Affirmative Action* (New Delhi: Oxford University Press, 2009). In 1992, a statutory body, the National Commission for Minorities (NCM), was established, minorities being defined by the National Commission for Minorities Act 1992 (NCMA) as 'a community notified as such by the Central government'. The minorities label has been accorded to religious minorities only. Six minorities have been notified – Muslims, Christians, Sikhs, Buddhists, Zoroastrians (Parsis) and (since 2014) Jains despite the fact that Article 25 COI subsumes Sikhs, Buddhists and Jains within Hinduism. While religious, linguistic and cultural minorities do not benefit from reservations as minorities, they may do as OBCs (for example about 40% of India's Muslims meet the criteria for notification as OBC communities). In January 2012 the government announced a 4.5% 'minorities sub-quota' within the 27% OBC quota for OBCs who are also minorities, but this was controversial and was not enacted.

86 COI, Articles 330, 332, 243-D(1)(a), and 243-T(1).

87 COI, Article 15(4) was inserted by the Constitution (First Amendment) Act 1951 S.2 following the Supreme Court's decision in *State of Madras* v *Champakam Dorairajan* AIR 1951 SC 226.

88 Central Educational Institutions (Reservations in Admissions) Act 2006, enacted pursuant to the Constitution (Ninety-third) Amendment Act 2005.

89 COI, Article 15(5), inserted by the Constitution (Ninety-third) Amendment Act 2005 S.2.

90 COI, Articles 335 and 16(4).

91 Prior to the Supreme Court decision in *Indra Sawhney* (n 83) states were free to grant state-wide backward class reservations in state sector employment at their discretion, but there were no Central OBC reservations.

92 *Devadasan* v *Union of India* AIR 1964 SC 179; *Indra Sawhney* (ibid.); *Balaji and Ors* v *State of Mysore* (1963) AIR SC 649.

for SCs is 15% and for STs 7.5%[93] (roughly their percentage of the overall population), and for OBCs 27%, such that the combined reservation quota for the three categories does not exceed 50%.[94]

3.4.3 Other measures

Legislation has also been introduced to protect Dalits, the majority of whom work in the unorganised sector, which in 2020–21 accounted for approximately 81% of all workers in India,[95] from degrading and humiliating customs and employment practices, and from economic exploitation. Manual scavenging – a grotesquely euphemistic term for unprotected, manual (i.e. un-mechanised) sanitation work – is a hereditary occupation carried out almost exclusively by Dalits (mostly women) involving the removal by hand of human waste from dry latrines, often using the most basic of tools and in the absence of protective clothing and equipment. The practice persists in India despite the availability of modern technology. The Employment of Manual Scavengers and Construction of Dry Latrines (Prohibition) Act 1993 prohibits manual scavenging and the construction of dry latrines, and it criminalises the employment of scavengers by public-sector actors. However, its adoption at state level was not compulsory and it resulted in no prosecutions.[96] Shah's 2006 study on untouchability found that there were still an estimated 1.2 million manual scavengers in India, many of whom were employed by local authorities and public bodies such as the railways.[97] It has been suggested that the legislation would have been more effective if framed as a caste issue rather than simply as a sanitation issue.[98] The Prohibition of Employment as Manual Scavengers and Their Rehabilitation Act 2013 extends the 1993 legislation by prohibiting manual cleaning of latrines and gutters, sewers and septic tanks without protective gear, as well as requiring the rehabilitation of scavengers through the provision of alternative employment, education and skills development.[99] That this legislation has not solved the problem is illustrated by a case brought against the central government by a non-governmental organisation supporting manual scavengers, resulting in a 2014 Supreme Court judgment that all state governments and Union Territories must implement the 2013 legislation immediately and take action against violators.[100] Yet the practice continues, in open sight but largely unaddressed by the authorities and civil society.[101]

The pseudo-religious practice of ritualised prostitution, known as *Devadasi* or *Jogini*, has also been the subject of legislation aimed at its abolition, as discussed earlier at 3.2.5. The

---

93 Galanter (n 82) 86.
94 *Indra Sawhney* (n 83) 93. The figures are very marginally different in the case of direct recruitment posts, other than by open competition.
95 See Ministry of Labour and Employment Annual Report 2020–21 (New Delhi: GOI, 2021) 84.
96 GOI, Ministry of Social Justice and Empowerment (MSJE), Report 2009–10, 47, at http://socialjus tice.nic.in/ar10eng.php. The adoption of manual scavenging legislation by states was not mandatory.
97 Shah et al. (n 18) 107–109. In contrast, the MSJE put the number of manual scavengers at 350,000 in January 2007 and 117, 000 in 2009; MSJE Report 2009–10, ibid., 48.
98 S Darokar, 'Manual Scavengers: A Blind Spot in Urban Development Discourse', *EPW* (2 June 2018), at www.epw.in/engage/article/manual-scavengers-blind-spot-urban-development-discourse.
99 See https://legislative.gov.in/sites/default/files/A2013-25.pdf.
100 *Safai Karamchari Andolan & Ors v Union of India & Ors*, Writ Petition (Civil) No. 583/2003; Judgment, 27 March 2014.
101 Darokar (n 98); G Singh, 'The Caste of Sanitation', *Democracy News Live*, 2 November 2017, at www. democracynewslive.com/asia/the-caste-of-sanitation-438130.

Bonded Labour System (Abolition) Act 1976 abolishes and criminalises bonded labour, while the Child Labour (Prohibition and Regulation) Act 1986 prohibits child labour in certain employments and regulates it in others. These statutes do not specifically mention Dalits, but since the majority of bonded labourers and many child labourers are Dalits, the provisions are particularly relevant to them. The Minimum Wage Act 1948 prevents employers appropriating the fruits of labour of the poor. Finally, laws have been introduced to reduce the concentration of productive assets and economic resources in the hands of the higher castes and to secure more equitable distribution of economic assets, for example through land reform and debt relief legislation.[102]

3.5 India's policies assessed

3.5.1 Overview

Constitutional and legislative prohibitions of untouchability practices and caste discrimination have enshrined formal equality, but nevertheless caste identity 'continues to define access to food, jobs, education and marriage partners', and it 'shapes modern opportunity at every level'.[103] The Constitution guarantees Dalits formal equality, and yet substantive (de facto) equality remains elusive. Shah observes that since independence Dalits have become at one level more unified 'and at the same time more stratified than [in] the past'. Upward mobility (due to affirmative action in education and employment) has created hope for improvement, which in turn, combined with reservations in political representation, has created unprecedented political consciousness. Nevertheless, many Dalits continue to suffer from discrimination and exclusion in the public and private spheres and in the economic, occupational, educational and social fields, as well as from caste-based violence and gross human rights abuses.[104] Mosse explains this conundrum by arguing that while Indian and international social and development policy now recognises the significance of gender, race, age, religion and other identity characteristics, it has overlooked the importance of caste 'as a structure of advantage and of discrimination in the modern economy' and as a structural cause of inequality and poverty. Instead, Mosse notes, caste is treated as a static, historical problem to be addressed through remedial provisions such as affirmative action and other protections, 'rather than as a dynamic relational problem subject to the state's general duty to address inequality and discrimination in economy and society'.[105] Caste clearly features in policymaking directly affecting the Scheduled Castes but is strangely absent from the mainstream agenda as a source of inequality and discrimination.

3.5.2 Reservations

Despite the longevity of India's reservation policies, it has been difficult to assess their impact. Although information on the numbers of Dalits in government and public employment is available, quantitative data on educational reservations and subsequent employment are less readily available, and qualitative data in both fields are lacking. Empirical studies looking at

---

102 See Saxena (n 57) 17.
103 G Omvedt, 'Caste System and Hinduism', *EPW* (13 March 2004) 1179–1180, 1179; Mosse (n 15) 427.
104 Shah (n 17) 221, 227, 229. Rao describes caste as '*the* public secret of secular modernity'; (n 10) 267. Yet, often, Dalits are "allowed" only one identity – as Dalits; see Gorringe (n 10).
105 Mosse (n 15) 422, 423, 424.

the take-up of reserved posts or seats, the experience of beneficiaries, the long-term impact of reservations on individual socio-economic mobility, or on the families and communities of beneficiaries, or the broader social impact of the policies on reducing inequality and discrimination are very few in number. Surprisingly, for a programme of such size and duration, comprehensive monitoring and evaluation have been largely absent beyond the collection by the authorities of basic-level statistics.[106] In its 2009 General Recommendation (GR) on special measures (including affirmative action policies and quotas), CERD recommended that special measures should be temporary, fair and proportionate, designed and implemented on the basis of the current need of the individuals and communities concerned, and should be continually monitored.[107] Whilst employment reservations have opened up coveted government and public sector jobs previously barred to Dalits, in central services they remain clustered in lower-level jobs and under-represented in senior posts.[108] Moreover, employment reservations are restricted to the shrinking public sector, representing only a fraction of India's total economic activity.[109] Recent studies of the urban corporate labour market provide strong evidence of caste discrimination in hiring; in other words, labour market discrimination means that Dalits 'will face worse employment outcomes even if they were similarly qualified as the "Others" [non-Dalits]'.[110]

Opponents of affirmative action in India argue that reservations solidify caste boundaries, thereby creating or perpetuating the very problem they seek to solve, and that they discriminate against non-beneficiaries at the same time as promoting the "underserving," leading to inefficiency and reduced productivity.[111] In 2017, the Supreme Court made a similar argument in *Mahajan* when it stated that the POAA 'should not result in perpetuating casteism which can have an adverse impact on integration of the society and the constitutional values'.[112] The argument that legislation against caste discrimination causes or perpetuates caste boundaries and caste prejudice, has been made by opponents of caste discrimination legislation in the British context (see Chapters 8 and 9). Yet, a 2014 study by Weiskopf and Deshpande on the effects of reservations on the Indian Railways found that the presence of Scheduled Caste employees who have secured their posts through the quota system does not reduce productivity, as critics frequently argue. Rather, they found that increased numbers of Scheduled Caste employees in high-level posts is positively associated with productivity growth.[113]

106 See GOI, MJSE, Plan Division, List of Research/Evaluation Studies at http://socialjustice.nic.in/User View/index?mid=76633; Indian Institute of Dalit Studies, Completed Research Projects at http://www.dalitstudies.org.in/completed-programmes-projects.php.
107 CERD GR. No. 32 (2009), The meaning and scope of special measures in the International Convention on the Elimination of All Forms of Racial Discrimination.
108 NCSC Annual Report 2004–5 (New Delhi: GOI, 2005) 179–183. Challenges by Dalits to the administration of the reservations policy gave rise to a body of case law on the interpretation and application of the rules on reservations-related recruitment, employment conditions and promotion. These so-called service cases historically formed a significant part of many Dalit lawyers' caseloads.
109 Of 470 million people employed in India, 90 million work in the organised sector (including public and government services) and 380 million (81%) in the unorganised sector (see n 95).
110 A Deshpande, 'Caste and Diversity in India', in J Davis and W Dolfsma (eds.), *Elgar Companion to Social Economics* (Cheltenham: Edward Elgar, 2015) 198–212, 207.
111 See, for example, A Shourie, *Falling Over Backwards: An Essay on Reservations and on Judicial Populism* (New Delhi: ASA Publications, 2006) 350.
112 See *Mahajan* (n 81), para 42.
113 A Deshpande and T Weisskopf, 'Does Affirmative Action Reduce Productivity? A Case Study of the Indian Railways', 64 *World Development* (2014) 169–180, 176–177; Deshpande (n 31) 153–160.

In 2004, Weisskopf, comparing affirmative action policies in India and the US, observed that is was difficult to assess how much difference education reservations have made in India.[114] If they are understood as a strategy to increase the representation of specific communities in elite occupations and decision-making positions – rather than a mechanism for improving educational opportunities for the disadvantaged – effectiveness must be judged on whether reservation beneficiaries complete their programmes and achieve successful careers.[115] According to Deshpande, writing in 2013, a large majority of Dalit students in higher education owe their presence to reservations. Nevertheless, at least half the seats reserved for Dalits go unfilled due to attendance gaps, failure and drop-out rates, even before the students reach higher education, thus highlighting the problem of inadequate and poor-quality public education at the lower levels of the system as well as systemic discrimination within the system.[116] Deshpande cites three studies on the academic suitability of reservation beneficiaries for the courses on which they enrol, and whether reservations provide economic or other "life chance" benefits post-university. The findings are contradictory as to whether Dalit students "catch up" academically with non-Dalit students by graduation, but one study found that reservations could improve earning potential, job quality and career satisfaction. Although empirical studies of the performance of beneficiaries and their post-university careers remain limited, Deshpande's conclusion is that admission to prestigious courses would alter the lives of students who gain entry through reservations.[117]

The impact of political reservations in increasing Dalit political involvement does not seem to be in doubt, and commentators assert that political reservations have had 'a profound effect on the Indian political landscape'.[118] In Uttar Pradesh (UP), the 'representation of Dalits in bureaucracy, thanks to the reservation policy'[119] led in the 1980s to the emergence of the BSP (Bahujan Samaj Party, or "party of the majority"),[120] a Dalit-based political party whose leaders – themselves beneficiaries of affirmative action – became a new "counter-elite" responsible for leading political mobilisation.[121] In 2007, the BSP, under its female Dalit leader Mayawati, won a decisive electoral victory in the UP state elections, having previously held power three times in coalition governments in 1995, 1997 and 2003.[122] Nevertheless, the success of north India's Dalit "new politicians" in improving the economic position of the Dalits and effecting a fundamental shift in traditional social relations is questioned by some scholars.[123] According to Weiner, for instance, the increase in Dalit bureaucrats and

---

114 Weisskopf, Impact of Reservations (n 34) 4340.

115 Ibid., 4347–4348; Mohanty (n 27) 3787.

116 Deshpande (n 9) 160–161; Waughray (n 1) 449.

117 Deshpande, ibid., 166–169. Widespread institutionalised discrimination against Dalit students must be tackled urgently if Dalit students are to succeed. (see n 55).

118 R Pande, 'Can Mandated Political Representation Increase Policy Influence for Disadvantaged Minorities? Theory and Evidence from India', 93(4) *American Economic Review* (2003) 1132–1151, 1133, 1147.

119 P Kumar, 'Dalits and the BSP in Uttar Pradesh: Issues and Challenges', *EPW* (3 April 1999) 822–826, 824.

120 S Pai, *Dalit Assertion and the Unfinished Democratic Revolution: The Bahujan Samaj Party in Uttar Pradesh* (New Delhi: Sage, 2002) xi–xii.

121 A Varshney, 'Is India Becoming More Democratic?' 59(1) *Journal of Asian Studies* (2005) 3–25, 20.

122 See V Kumar, 'Behind the BSP Victory', *EPW* (15 June 2007) 2237–2239. The BSP lost power in 2012 to the rural Samajwadi Party. Mayawati resigned her party leadership and was elected to India's upper house, the Rajya Sabha.

123 For the "Dalit revolution" perspective see C Jaffrelot, *India's Silent Revolution: The Rise of the Low Castes in North Indian Politics* (New Delhi: Permanent Black, 2003); S Pai, 'New Social and Political Movements of Dalits: A Study of Meerut District', 34 *Contributions to Indian Sociology* (2000) 189–220. Conversely see C Jeffrey, P Jeffery, and R Jeffery, 'Dalit Revolution? New Politicians in Uttar Pradesh, India', 67(4) *Journal of Asian Studies* (2008) 1365–1396.

politicians has not led to more effective public policies for overcoming the immense poverty and deprivation persisting in India which disproportionately affects their communities.[124] Some commentators ask whether Dalit political power has reached an impasse, in that it is 'no panacea' for continued casteism and deprivation.[125] In 2006, Christophe Jaffrelot suggested that the biggest impact of affirmative action may be indirect rather than direct: 'socio-economic change may result from the rise to power of the lower castes in an indirect way'.[126] Other commentators and scholars, as Gorringe explains, see a relationship between the Dalit political mobilisation of the earlier generation and the current explosion of local, grassroots Dalit activism demanding dignity, civility and equality.[127] Amidst all this, CERD notes that in India generally, Dalits still find themselves denied the right to vote, and Dalit candidates, especially women, are frequently prevented from standing for election or, if elected, are pressured to resign.[128]

The impact of political reservations on Indian democracy, political development and social order is much debated and highly contested. On the one hand, the very scheme which was designed as part of a strategy to eliminate caste inequality, by bringing Dalits "into the fold," has played a major role in entrenching caste as a political as well as a social identity, and in institutionalising it in the political system.[129] On the other hand, argues Varshney, the political rise of the lower castes, deploying caste identity and a 'reinvented' caste history, is resulting in a 'caste-based restructuration' of power, such that it 'can paradoxically be an instrument of equalisation and dignity'.[130] Nonetheless, the articulation of caste in modern India as essentially about political or cultural identity ("difference"), and caste groups as simply interest groups, is dangerous, says Balmurli Natrajan, precisely because caste has not been 'defanged'; fundamentally, it remains about power and inequality, manifesting in all spheres of life, including India's modern economy.[131]

3.5.3 Legislation

India's legislation to tackle untouchability and discrimination on grounds of caste – as with legislation on caste violence and caste hate crimes – imposes criminal sanctions on those who violate the law. In 1999, Mendelsohn and Vicziany argued, based on the widespread continuing discrimination and violence against Dalits and the small number of cases registered by the police and disposed of by the courts, that 'very few Indians have been directly affected' by this legislation, and that the best that can be said is that '[legislation] has contributed to stripping away the legitimacy of untouchability, but it is difficult to measure such an effect'.[132] The periodic strengthening of existing legislation and/or the introduction of new legislation (see earlier) show that untouchability and caste-based violence remain a serious problem. Caste hate crimes continue to suffer low conviction rates and high year-on-year

124 Weiner (n 4) 211–213.
125 Gorringe (n 10) 124.
126 C Jaffrelot, 'The Impact of Affirmative Action in India: More Political Than Socioeconomic', 5(2) *India Review* (2006) 173–189, 188.
127 Ibid. See also S Waghmore, *Civility Against Caste: Dalit Politics and Citizenship in Western India* (New Delhi: Sage, 2013).
128 CERD, 5 May 2007 (n 62) para 17.
129 Weiner (n 4) 220. See also Gorringe (n 10); Rao (n 10) 277.
130 Varshney (n 121) 4, 19–20.
131 Natrajan (n 7) xiii; Mosse (n 35).
132 Mendelsohn and Vicziany (n 16) 128, 145.

pendency of cases. In 2019, over 127,000 cases involving atrocities against SCs were pending trial from the previous year, with 31,580 cases sent for trial. Of almost 11,000 completed trials, 3,580 cases resulted in conviction and almost 7,500 in acquittal or discharge with almost 147,600 cases pending trial at the end of 2019.[133] The 2019 conviction rate for POAA offences was 28.2%.[134] NGOs and academics found that the entire system 'worked to exclude Dalits'; charges were dismissed by the courts because the investigation was not carried out by the correct person (described by one NGO as tantamount to punishing the victim for a procedural error by the government machinery), while many cases were dropped because of the police's failure to obtain within the time limit the caste certificates attesting to the victim's identity (this being material to prosecution under the atrocities legislation).[135] In 2017, the NCSC noted frequent procedural lapses and delays in the judicial process in the handling of POAA cases, delays in registering First Information Reports (punishable under section 4 of the amended legislation), frequent registering of counter-cases, delays in police investigations and faulty prosecution procedures, including last-minute withdrawals of witnesses.[136] Many cases are closed by the police and never reach court, and cases filed under the POAA are 'more likely to be categorized as false'.[137] The role of the judiciary in caste crime cases has also been criticised, with the 1995 Bhanwari Devi case being a well-publicised example involving five dominant-caste men acquitted of the gang rape of a government-employed Dalit woman rural development worker. According to the judge, since the accused were "upper-caste" men, the rape could not have taken place, because Bhanwari was from a lower caste. At the time of writing, her appeal against the acquittal, supported by the National Commission for Women, still remains unresolved.[138]

National and international human rights bodies, activists and scholars have repeatedly highlighted the poor enforcement of existing legislation, including in cases where atrocities have been committed by the law enforcement agencies themselves.[139] The fundamental problem underlying this 'culture of under-enforcement' is that the legislation lacks social legitimacy with the majority – and hence majority public support. A disconnect exists between the content of the legislation and wider (majority) social values and attitudes. As

---

133 Ministry of Home Affairs, National Crime Records Bureau (NCRB), *Crime in India 2019*, Court Disposal of Crime/Atrocities against SCs Cases (Crime Head-wise) – 2019, 539–542.

134 Ibid. The PCRA has never been heavily invoked; in 2016, 549 cases were pending trial from the previous year, and sixty-one trials were completed, resulting in only one conviction; see *Crime in India 2016*, Court Disposal of Crime/Atrocities against SCs Cases (Crime Head-wise) 303.

135 A Waughray, 'India and the Paradox of Caste Discrimination', 8 *European Yearbook of Minority Issues* (2009) 440.

136 National Commission for Scheduled Castes (NCSC) Annual Report 2016–17 (New Delhi: GOI, 2017) 158–159. A First Information Report (FIR) is a document written by the police when a complaint is first lodged (usually orally) by the victim of a cognizable offence or by someone on his/her behalf.

137 'Why Do We Need a Specific Law to Safeguard Dalits Against Caste Violence?' *EPW Engage* (30 August 2018).

138 G Pandey, 'Bhanwari Devi: The Rape That Led to India's Sexual Harassment Law', *BBC News*, 17 March 2017, at www.bbc.co.uk/news/world-asia-india-39265653. Devi's case led to the introduction of the Sexual Harassment of Women at Workplace (Prevention, Prohibition and Redressal) Act 2013; R Shukla, 'To Remove Caste Bias from the Judicial System, Judges Need to Self-Correct', *The Wire*, 23 March 2017.

139 National Human Rights Commission (NHRC), *Report on Prevention of Atrocities Against Scheduled Castes: Policy and Performance: Suggested Interventions and Initiatives for NHRC* (New Delhi: NHRC, 2004) 47; S Narula, 'Equal by Law, Unequal by Caste: The "Untouchable" Condition in Critical Race Perspective', 26(2) *Wisconsin International Law Journal* (2008) 255–343, 296; CERD, 5 May 2007 (n 62) para 26; Human Rights Watch (n 57).

Galanter remarked in 1994, 'the law goes counter to perceived self-interest and valued sentiments and deeply ingrained behavioural patterns',[140] whilst CERD has noted 'with concern' the entrenched nature of 'caste bias' in India and the social acceptance of caste-based discrimination.[141]

In addition to an absence of widespread social and cultural consensus in favour of existing legislation, there is increasing recognition that the current legislative approach itself is too narrow in focus. Ambedkar conceptualised untouchability and caste discrimination in structural and institutional terms[142] (unlike Gandhi, for whom untouchability was an individual religious and moral issue).[143] Yet – like many countries – India's existing legislative framework is ill-suited to addressing institutionalised, structural discrimination. The PCR and the POAA, as criminal statutes, focus legal attention on individual, worst-case manifestations of caste-based discrimination and violence. While it is important that such behaviour is punished, criminal law treats each instance of discrimination or violence as a single, disaggregated act committed by an individual offender or offenders, "shorn" of its social and historical context. Moreover, conviction depends on the prosecution meeting the criminal standard of proof.[144] Recognising discrimination as problematic only in its most overt or violent manifestations[145] entails a dangerous 'conceptual disconnection between extremism and the general culture'.[146] India currently lacks broader civil equality legislation designed to address "everyday" acts of discrimination, for example in recruitment, which fall outside the ambit of existing criminal law.[147] Whereas criminal law gives control to the state to take action on behalf of the victim – whose role as victim/witness may quickly become peripheral – civil anti-discrimination legislation actively involves the victim in pursuing their case. The downside to the civil legislation model is that it is reactive not proactive; consequently, claims can only be brought once harm has actually occurred, and barriers unrelated to the merits of the claim, such as lack of access to funding or legal representation, must be overcome, as must the psychological and practical pressures and burdens on individuals to bring and then pursue a case. One civil option is the introduction of a proactive equality duty imposed on public bodies (such as that imposed on public authorities in the UK by the public sector equality duty in section 149 of the UK's Equality Act 2010). Without civil equality legislation to tackle discriminatory behaviour which falls short of the criminal threshold and/or the introduction of proactive equality duties, the goal of challenging entrenched

140 M Galanter, *Law and Society in Modern India* (New Delhi: Oxford University Press, 1994) 217.
141 CERD, 5 May 2007 (n 62) paras 14, 27.
142 'To say that [a form of discrimination] is "institutionalised" is to recognise that this systemic [discrimination] runs into and shapes the institutions governing society': M Davies, *Asking the Law Question* (Sydney: Thomson Law Book Co., 2008) 296–297.
143 E Zelliot, *From Untouchable to Dalit: Essays on the Ambedkar Movement* (New Delhi: Manohar, 1998).
144 L Lustgarten, *Legal Control of Racial Discrimination* (London: Macmillan Press, 1980) 8; J Downing, '"Hate Speech" and "First Amendment Absolutism" Discourses in the US' (10) *Discourse & Society* (1999) 175–189, 181.
145 P Essed, *Understanding Everyday Racism: An Interdisciplinary Theory* (Thousand Oaks, CA: Sage, 1991) 283, cited in Downing, ibid., 181.
146 Downing (n 148) 181.
147 An example of asymmetrical anti-discrimination legislation is The Sexual Harassment of Women at Workplace (Prevention, Prohibition and Redressal) Act 2013 (see n 138), which provides for civil remedies for workplace sexual harassment of women via a non-judicial mechanism (a Complaints Committee) rather than judicial proceedings in a court or tribunal; see Handbook on the Sexual Harassment of Women at Workplace (Prevention, Prohibition and Redressal) Act 2013 (New Delhi: Ministry of Women and Child Development, 2015).

beliefs and promoting changed behaviour and social norms through legal means, i.e. law, is unlikely to be realised. In March 2017, in a step in this direction, Dr Sashi Tharoor MP introduced to the Lok Sabha (the Lower House of India's Parliament) a private members' Bill, the Anti-Discrimination and Equality Bill 2016, which draws on civil equality and anti-discrimination legislation in jurisdictions such as Canada, the UK and South Africa. The Bill adopts the "protected characteristics" model of UK equality law (see Chapters 7–9). Unlike India's criminal anti-discrimination law, which is asymmetrical, i.e. designed to protect specific groups, the Equality Bill 2016 provides symmetrical protection to anyone discriminated against because of a protected characteristic, not just specified categories of victims. Furthermore, it protects against intersectional discrimination, contains proactive positive equality duties and proposes the establishment of a Central Equality Commission with powers of promotion, protection, education, investigation and enquiry.[148] Regardless of whether the Bill becomes law (at the time of writing it is being considered by India's Parliament), it has played an important role in generating public debate on discrimination and how to tackle it. Legislation aside, activists and scholars have stressed the importance of civic or citizenship education in schools and higher education institutions to educate against racism, casteism, sexism, heterosexism and all forms of discrimination and inequality.[149]

3.5.4 Scheduled castes and religious restrictions

Despite widespread recognition that the ideology and practice of caste, and the discrimination it engenders, is a 'general social characteristic',[150] India's constitutional framework treats caste as a Hindu phenomenon. Under the Constitution (Scheduled Castes) Order 1950, only Hindus, Sikhs or Buddhists can be classified as SCs.[151] As "minorities within minorities," Dalit Muslims and Christians are widely recognised to suffer greater socio-economic and educational disadvantages than their non-Dalit co-religionists while suffering discrimination on grounds of caste at the hands of both the wider community and their co-religionists.[152] Nevertheless, they are excluded on grounds of religion from the SC category and hence from accessing SC reservations. Lack of SC status also means that Dalit Muslims and Christians who are victims of atrocities cannot file complaints under the POAA, as the

---

148 See http://164.100.47.4/BillsTexts/LSBillTexts/Asintroduced/2991.pdf. The Bill was drafted in consultation with Dr Tarunabh Khaitan of Oxford University. In July 2019, the Bengaluru-based Centre for Law and Policy Research published the Equality Bill 2019 'as an over-arching legislation to prohibit discrimination on the basis of various characteristics and obligations to promote equality'; see https://clpr.org.in/blog/an-overview-of-the-equality-bill-2019/.

149 See, for example, Thorat (n 50).

150 Government of India Ministry of Minority Affairs, Report on the National Commission for Religious and Linguistic Minorities (New Delhi: NCRLM, 2009) 153–154.

151 '[N]o person who professes a religion different from the Hindu, the Sikh or the Buddhist religion shall be deemed to be a member of a Scheduled Caste'; see Constitution (Scheduled Castes) Order 1950 (C.O. 19) para 3. Sikhs and Buddhists were originally excluded from the SC category (apart from Sikh members of four specific castes; CAD Vol. VIII, 25 May 1949, 272, 311). Sikhs were included in 1956 and Buddhists in 1990, on the grounds that these were indigenous religions, essentially variants of Hinduism; see Scheduled Castes and Scheduled Tribes Orders (Amendment) Act 1956 and Constitution (Scheduled Castes) Orders (Amendment) Act 1990. The Constitution (Scheduled Tribes) Order 1950 (C.O. 22) is religion-neutral; it contains no provisions akin to C.O. 19 para 3. See also Waughray, 'Caste Discrimination and Minority Rights: The Case of India's Dalits', (n 73) 327–353.

152 See S Deshpande, *Dalits in the Muslim and Christian Communities: A Status Report on Current Social Scientific Knowledge* (New Delhi: GOI, National Commission for Minorities, 2008).

legislation requires the victim to be a member of a Scheduled Caste.[153] This anomaly has led to national and international calls to open up the SC category to Dalit Muslims and Christians and/or for the 1950 Order to be made religion-neutral.[154] As Galanter observed in 1984, the exclusion of non-Hindus from reservations 'appears to give expression to a view of caste that is at variance with the [post-independence] constitutional and statutory "disestablishment" of the sacral concept of caste'.[155] In 2007, the government-appointed Misra Commission for Religious and Linguistic Minorities recommended the total decoupling of SC status from religion and the classification as SCs of all those groups among the excluded religions whose counterparts among the Hindus, Sikhs and Buddhists are so classified.[156] In 2008, a report for the National Commission for Minorities (NCM) on Dalits in the Muslim and Christian communities concluded that Dalits, irrespective of religion, are much worse off than non-Dalits. Dalit Muslims and Christians are socially known and treated as distinct groups within their own religious communities and are invariably regarded as "socially inferior" by their co-religionists; in most social contexts they are Dalits first, and Muslims and Christians only second. The report concluded that the denial of SC status to these groups is a historical anomaly and that there is a strong case for according them SC status.[157] In 2007, CERD recommended that eligibility for affirmative action benefits be extended to SC and ST converts to religions other than Sikhism or Buddhism,[158] while in 2009 the then UN Special Rapporteur on the freedom of religion or belief, Asma Jahangir, reporting on her 2008 country visit to India, highlighted as 'problematic in terms of human rights standards' the legal link between SC status and religious affiliation.[159] Given that India has repeatedly insisted before CERD that caste is a social/class system, not a religious system,[160] it follows logically that SC status should be accorded to Dalit Muslims and Christians. Enlarging the SC net, however, is both a political decision and politically contentious, since, currently, reservations for all categories of beneficiaries cannot exceed 50%. If the existing SC reservation ceiling of 17.5% remains unchanged but is opened up to Dalit Muslims and Christians, this would increase the competition for SC reservation benefits, hence reducing their availability for existing beneficiaries. Hindu opponents of de-linking SC status and religious affiliation also claim that granting SC status to Dalit Christians would encourage large-scale religious conversion of Dalits from Hinduism to Christianity, driven by Christian proselytism inside and outside India and threatening the preservation of Hindu religious identity.[161]

3.6 Lessons learned: looking ahead

The lawyer and jurist Antony Allott identified four stages in the 'business of producing a major social transformation through law': (1) determine social (policy) goals, (2) consider

---

153 Unlike the POA, the Protection of Civil Rights Act 1955 prohibits specified acts committed on the ground of untouchability, with no requirement that the victim be Scheduled Caste; see GOI, Report of the National Commission for Religious and Linguistic Minorities ("Misra Report") (New Delhi: Ministry of Minority Affairs, 2007) 7.
154 Deshpande (n 152) 81, 83. CERD, 5 May 2007 (n 62) para 21.
155 Galanter (n 82) 324.
156 Misra Report (n 153) 149, 154.
157 Deshpande (n 152) 83.
158 See CERD, 5 May 2007 (n 62) para 21.
159 UN Doc. A/HRC/10/8/Add.3, summary and para 28.
160 See Mani (India); UN Doc. CERD/C/SR.141, 2 May 1973, 131; CERD/C/299/Add.3, 29 April 1996, para 6.
161 B Kolappan, 'Focus on Quota for Dalit Christians', *The Hindu*, 16 September 2016.

what legal and administrative means to use to attain these goals, (3) introduce the legal and administrative programme and (4) monitor performance and rectify failures in effectiveness. This fourth stage 'ought to follow but rarely does'.[162] Lustgarten, writing in 1980 on the legal regulation of racial discrimination, argued that the success of a law genuinely intended to achieve a certain (social) end depends inter alia on whether it contains well-designed, effective enforcement procedures and whether adequate resources are allocated to bringing about the desired end.[163] The beneficiaries also need to be clearly definable and identifiable, although, as Chapter 7 shows, a grounds-based or "protected categories" approach to anti-discrimination law will inevitably give rise to challenges to "category boundaries." India's current legislative approach – criminalising the most overt and extreme manifestations of caste discrimination and violence – is only a partial legal response to endemic, institutionalised discrimination and inequality. Criminal legislation is insufficiently enforced, and so disinterest and/or unwillingness within state institutions must be recognised and tackled by ongoing civic education and human rights training of law enforcement agents and the judiciary,[164] coupled with civic education and awareness-raising among the general public.[165] Moreover, cases should be monitored for progress by state or central monitoring commissions. The absence of civil discrimination legislation represents a gap. Civil equality law (if well-designed, implemented and enforced) can serve both as a coercive tool and as an educative device,[166] providing concrete protection and redress for victims of discrimination whilst redefining behaviour hitherto considered acceptable as socially unacceptable as well as actionable legally.[167] Imposing a legal obligation on public authorities (as proposed in the Tharoor Bill) to have due regard in the exercise of their functions in eliminating discrimination and disadvantage inter alia on grounds of caste, and to promote equality and diversity, can contribute to social change and the transformation of legal norms into social norms. In contrast, the POAA Amendment Act 2015 criminalises 'dereliction of duty', i.e. failure by individual public servants in the efficient pursuit of criminal prosecution of private individuals for hate crimes.

Legislation, while necessary, is not sufficient in itself to tackle deep-rooted social phenomena such as caste discrimination. The Indian experience shows that to produce effective social transformation, law must be accompanied by social policy, including civic education, and so a holistic approach is needed in order to compel social reform.[168] Additionally, detailed data collection and wide-ranging qualitative studies are necessary for the design of appropriate policy interventions, with both law and policy being adequately resourced, including (in the case of law) resources for enforcement. Legislative and policy programmes must be monitored for effectiveness, and effective mechanisms of government accountability must be introduced. Ambedkar's response to inequality and discrimination on grounds of caste was to tackle the problem simultaneously on multiple, interrelated fronts, namely legal, economic, political and social, and yet one technique, reservations, has become the primary

---

162 A Allott, *The Limits of Law* (London: Butterworths, 1980) 202.
163 Lustgarten (n 144) xii.
164 Special Rapporteur on Racism, interim report to UNGA; UN Doc. A/66/313, 19 August 2011, paras 71, 73.
165 Ibid., para 75; Special Rapporteur on racism, report to HRC; UN Doc. A/HRC/17/40, para 88.
166 A Lester and G Bindman, *Race and Law* (Harmondsworth: Penguin, 1972) 85–87.
167 N Lacey, 'From Individual to Group', in B Hepple and E Szyszczak (eds.), *Discrimination: The Limits of the Law* (London: Mansell, 1993) 99–124.
168 Special Rapporteur on Racism, interim report (n 164) paras 68, 71. See also J Goldston, 'The Struggle for Roma Rights: Arguments that Have Worked', 32(2) *Human Rights Quarterly* (2010) 311–335, 311.

terrain and political focus of caste equality activity. India's reservations regime was originally conceived as a short-term ten-year measure,[169] but it has been repeatedly extended every ten years.[170] The high political investment in reservations, and India's continuing social and economic disparities, has until recently diverted attention from the development of a broader national "equality debate" going beyond the operation of the reservations policy and the three questions of who benefits, and what, and how much, is reserved. A new approach to equality and non-discrimination was signalled by the Sachar Committee, which reported in 2006 to the Ministry of Minority Affairs on the social, economic and educational status of Muslims in India, acknowledged to be the country's most disadvantaged minority religious group.[171] Instead of proposing the extension of reservations to Muslims (as demanded by some), the Sachar Committee recommended the creation of a national Equal Opportunities Commission (EOC), the introduction of a "diversity index" to incentivise organisations and companies in the spheres of education, public and private employment and housing, to measure and improve their "diversity performance," and the establishment of a national data bank. In addition, the committee required an autonomous assessment and monitoring authority to provide a source of reliable data on discrimination against socio-religious groups, as well as the design and monitoring of policies, initiatives and programmes ensuring transparency – ideas applicable to other groups suffering from discrimination. The Ministry of Minority Affairs convened two Expert Groups to report on proposals for a diversity index, and on the structure and functions of an EOC;[172] however, their recommendations, to date, have not been implemented.[173]

A long-standing issue has been Dalit demands for control of the fruits of their labour and a share in the nation's assets commensurate with their economic contribution, as well as equality of access to capital, education and training, markets and other tools of wealth creation, thus reflecting a shift from an exclusive focus on reservations and a move towards full Dalit participation on equal terms in India's capitalist market economy. In 2002, the Bhopal Declaration set out a twenty-one-point agenda including land ownership, use of common property resources, wages and working conditions, the elimination of manual scavenging and bonded labour, reservations in the private sector, the democratisation of capital and the implementation of supplier diversity (SD), this latter element subsequently taken up by the then Chief Minister of Madhya Pradesh, Digvija Singh.[174] Increasingly for transnational,

169 See Constituent Assembly Debates of India (CAD) Vol. VIII (New Delhi: Lok Sabha Secretariat) 331; see also COI Article 334 which originally provided for reservations until 1960.
170 The Constitution (95th Amendment) Act 2009 extended the Article 334 reservations in parliamentary seats and state legislative assemblies until 25 January 2020. In December 2019, India's Parliament passed the Constitution (126th) Amendment Bill to extend reservations in legislatures for another ten years.
171 See Sachar Committee Report at www.minorityaffairs.gov.in/sites/default/files/sachar_comm.pdf. The Sachar Committee was led by Rajinder Sachar (1923–2018), former Delhi High Court Chief Justice, member of the former United Nations Sub-Commission on the Promotion and Protection of Human Rights and counsel for the People's Union for Civil Liberties, an Indian civil rights organisation.
172 See https://minorityaffairs.gov.in/reports/report-expert-group-diversity-index-complete-report-1 and https://www.minorityaffairs.gov.in/sites/default/files/eoc_wwh.pdf.
173 Ministry of Minority Affairs, Implementation of Sachar Committee Recommendations (Status up to 30.11.2018), 16, at www.minorityaffairs.gov.in/sites/default/files/Follow-up-Sachar.pdf. The Equal Opportunities Commission recommended in the Sachar Report is different from the Central Equalities Commission proposed in the Tharoor Anti-Discrimination Bill.
174 The Declaration was the outcome document of the 2002 Bhopal Conference: Charting a New Course for Dalits in the 21st Century; see www.digvijayasingh.in/Bhopal%20Declaration.PDF. See also S Pai,

internationalised Dalit organisations, it is not only reservation policies that matter but also securing Dalits' wider economic rights, in particular securing a fair share of the national wealth, which in turn requires a wider approach to legal strategies for equality.

Dalit demands for the extension of reservations to the private sector, voluntarily or by law, have intensified in line with the decline in the public sector. Opponents argue that reservations undermine the "merit" principle and reduce efficiency, by promoting ill-qualified, poor performers at the expense of the well-qualified and the competent, albeit "merit" is a murky concept everywhere. As Jodhka and Newman point out, it requires that institutional inequality, discrimination and disinvestment are 'subtracted from the conversation'.[175] The Confederation of Indian Industry (CII) remains opposed to compulsory private-sector reservations, but it (along with other industry associations) has adopted a voluntary Code of Conduct on Affirmative Action,[176] including measures such as promoting equal opportunities and removing bias in employment for all sections of society, scholarships, vocational and skills training, entrepreneurship development programmes and coaching.[177] In 2006, the government created a Coordination Committee for Affirmative Action for SCs & STs in the Private Sector, which to date has met eight times. Compulsory reservations in the private sector are not on its agenda; rather, its position is that voluntary action by industry is the best way to achieve progress on the issue of private-sector affirmative action.[178]

Ambedkar believed that caste discrimination posed a problem for Indian society as a whole; in particular, the contradiction between the political equality introduced by the Constitution and the reality of entrenched economic and social inequality posed a threat to the country's democracy. In November 1949, on the eve of the adoption of the Constitution, he famously told the Constituent Assembly:

> On the social plane, we have in India a society based on the principle of graded inequality which means elevation for some and degradation for others. On the economic plane, we have a society in which there are some who have immense wealth as against many who live in abject poverty. On 26th January 1950, we are going to enter a life of contradictions. [. . .] [H]ow long shall we continue to live this life of contradictions? How long shall we deny equality in our social and economic life? If we continue to deny it for long, we will do so only by putting our political democracy in peril.[179]

The Constitution, in its Preamble, promises to secure to all citizens justice, liberty and equality, and to promote among them all fraternity, therefore assuring the dignity of the individual and the unity and integrity of the nation. Without fraternity, said Ambedkar, liberty and equality 'are no deeper than coats of paint'.[180] In the absence of fraternity – in

'Dalit Question and Political Response: Comparative Study of Uttar Pradesh and Madhya Pradesh', 39(11) *EPW* (2004) 1141–1150.

175 Jodhka and Newman (n 27) 4127.

176 See www.cii.in/documents/Code%20of%20Conduct.pdf.

177 See Government of India, Ministry of Social Justice & Empowerment, 'Reservation in Private Sector', *Press Release*, 22 December 2015 at http://pib.nic.in/newsite/PrintRelease.aspx?relid=133739.

178 See Ministry of Commerce and Industry, Answer to Parliamentary Question on Affirmative Action in the Private Sector, 2 January 2019 at https://dipp.gov.in/sites/default/files/ru_2274.pdf.

179 CAD X, 25 November 1949, 972–981, cited in 'Dr Ambedkar: The Principal Architect of the Constitution of India', *BAWS*, Vol. 13 (Govt. of Maharasthra Education Dept., Mumbai, 1994) 1216.

180 *BAWS*, Vol. 13, ibid.

both its private and civic sense – individual dignity and national unity and integrity come loose from their moorings. There is still a significant gap between the legal status of Dalits in India and their sociological status.[181] Government policies 'have granted Dalits the right to [legal] equality but not necessarily the right to be *treated* as equals',[182] whilst legislation 'guarantees Dalits the right to touch' (for example, to enter temples, hotels and restaurants), but it cannot guarantee the right 'to be touched'.[183] Without a holistic, proactive approach to tackling caste discrimination, the possibility of domestic social unrest is increased and India risks being held back politically, economically and socially.

In 1936, Ambedkar observed:

> [U]nless you change your social order, you can achieve little by way of progress [. . .] you cannot build on the foundation of caste. You cannot build up a nation, you cannot build up a morality. Anything that you will build on the foundations of caste will crack and will never be whole.[184]

In an interesting twist, Ambedkar's analysis was echoed over seventy-five years later by Bollywood actor and social activist Aamir Khan in a 2012 column in *The Hindu* newspaper, in which he argued that India cannot be a superpower while untouchability and discrimination based on caste exist; instead, what is required is to implement the vision of 'shared social good' laid down in India's Constitution:

> Our forefathers [. . .] have laid down laws that tell us that discrimination based on caste and religion [is] illegal. Now, we have to find [a] place in our hearts to follow them. We also have to find [a] place in our hearts to accept that discrimination between people is against the very concept of humanity.[185]

This chapter has examined India's legal and policy framework for the elimination of caste discrimination, highlighting its successes as well as the problems with the SC category and the need for a wide-ranging, holistic approach involving law and policies geared to effecting socio-cultural and economic change. India has taken pioneering steps since its independence to tackle caste inequality and discrimination, and yet its persistence illustrates its deeply entrenched nature. The challenges India faces in countering entrenched discrimination are not unique but common to all democracies with plural societies. As the country with both the largest numbers of people subjected to caste discrimination and world-leading experience in addressing it, India is ideally placed to show leadership, if it chooses, on what is truly a global problem. Hope lies with the younger generation, the growth of the anti-caste movement in India and beyond, the focus on dignity and civility, the increase in Dalit web

---

181 On the distinction between legal and sociological status, see J Balkin, 'The Constitution of Status', 106 *Yale Law Journal* (1997) 2313–2374, 2324.

182 V Kumar, *India's Roaring Revolution: Dalit Assertion and New Horizons* (New Delhi: Gagandeep, 2006) 19 (emphasis added).

183 G Guru, 'Power of Touch', *Frontline*, 16–29 December 2006.

184 Ambedkar (n 5) 25–96, 66.

185 A Khan, 'Can't Be a Superpower as Long as Untouchability Exists', *The Hindu*, 9 July 2012; M Thekaekara, 'Can Bollywood Shatter India's Caste System?' *New Internationalist Blog*, 13 July 2012, at www.newint.org/blog/2012/07/13/bollywood-untouchable-force/ (visited 17 August 2015).

forums and online activism and the connections and alliances being made between activists and intellectuals in movements for race and caste equality and legal and social change around the world, such as between Dalits in India and the USA, and between Dalits and African American and African activists.[186]

---

186 See, for example, G Teodros, 'Connecting the Movements for Dalit and Black Lives', *The Seattle Globalist*, 22 October 2015; GV Bhatnagar, 'Black Lives Matter Influences a Similar Campaign for Dalits, Minorities and Tribals in India', *The Wire*, 2 July 2017; Boston Study Group, Dalit and Black Lives Matter Symposium, 15 July 2017, at www.facebook.com/BostonStudyGroup/photos/gm.14934979 37360553/640386402830661/?type=3&theater. See also AK Thakur, 'And the Dalit Counter-Public Sphere', *Television and New Media*, published online 3 September 2019, 1–16, 1. Thakur stresses that Dalit online activism consists of multiple narratives, and also that these multiple narratives 'are challenged by caste Hindu narratives online, leading to a complicated scenario for networked resistance and collective action'.

Part II

Caste and international human rights law

4 Caste discrimination and international human rights law standards

International Convention on the Elimination of All Forms of Racial Discrimination 1965 and the UN human rights treaties

4.1 Introduction

Until the mid-1990s, few human rights lawyers or activists outside South Asia were aware of caste discrimination, its nature or extent. The issue was conspicuous in international human rights law discourse only by its absence, while governments of South Asian states, where such discrimination occurred, treated it as a strictly internal social-cultural matter. From the early 1980s, frustration with the limited success of domestic measures to combat persistent and widespread caste-based discrimination and anti-Dalit violence led Dalit activists in India and the diaspora to turn to international NGOs and the UN human rights treaty bodies and charter mechanisms for an international response to caste discrimination as a human rights issue.[1] Of the UN bodies and mechanisms with which Dalit activists sought to engage, two were at the forefront of UN activity: the former UN Sub-Commission for the Promotion and Protection of Human Rights[2] and the UN Committee on the Elimination of Racial Discrimination (CERD),[3] the monitoring body of the UN International Convention on the Elimination of All Forms of Racial Discrimination 1965 (ICERD).[4] Of these, CERD has played a crucial role in the international recognition of caste discrimination as a human rights issue and as an international human rights treaty violation. This chapter examines the international legal framework for caste discrimination as it has developed under the UN human rights treaty regime, in particular under ICERD and its monitoring body, CERD. Chapter 5 will examine how caste discrimination has been addressed by the UN charter bodies and procedures.

The principal difficulty in the conceptualisation of caste discrimination as a violation of international human rights law is the absence of caste as a category in any international human rights treaty and, consequently, the lack of an international frame or category within

---

1 See B Joshi (ed.), *Untouchable: Voices of the Dalit Liberation Movement* (London: Zed Books, 1986); C Bob, 'Dalit Rights Are Human Rights: Caste Discrimination, International Activism and the Construction of a New Human Rights Issue', 29(1) *Human Rights Quarterly* (2007) 167–193; S Thorat and Umakant (eds.), *Caste, Race and Discrimination: Discourses in International Context* (Jaipur: Rawat Publications, 2004); C Lennox, 'Norm Entrepreneurship on Caste-Based Discrimination', in D Mosse and L Steur (eds.), *Caste out of Development? The Cultural Politics of Identity and Economy in India and Beyond* (London: Routledge, 2015); J Lerche, 'Transnational Advocacy Networks and Affirmative Action for *Dalits* in India', 39(2) *Development and Change* (2008) 239–261. See also Chapter 5.
2 See www.ohchr.org/EN/HRBodies/SC/Pages/SubCommission.aspx.
3 See www.ohchr.org/EN/HRBodies/CERD/Pages/CERDIndex.aspx.
4 Adopted 21 December 1965. In force 4 January 1969. 660 UNTS 195. As at September 2019 ICERD has been ratified or acceded to by 181 states, including Pakistan (21 September 1966); India (3 December 1968); United Kingdom (7 March 1969); Nepal (30 January 1971); Bangladesh (11 June 1979); Sri Lanka (18 February 1982).

DOI: 10.4324/9781315750934-7

which to locate it. This has led to the subsuming of caste within categories which do not completely overlap with it, the interpretation of existing treaty categories to cover caste and the creation of a new non-treaty category which includes – but is not limited to – caste, resulting in objections from states such as India and Japan, which do not accept this approach.[5] The legal source of CERD's engagement with caste is the category of descent in Article 1(1) of ICERD. Since 1996, caste discrimination has been affirmed by CERD as a form of descent-based racial discrimination prohibited by ICERD, subsequently captured in CERD's General Recommendation 29 (2002) on Article 1(1) (Descent) (GR 29),[6] while in 2000, the former UN Sub-Commission for the Promotion and Protection of Human Rights declared caste discrimination as a violation of international human rights law and as a subset of a new, wider category, i.e. discrimination based on work and descent (DWD).[7] Both categories, namely descent-based racial discrimination and discrimination based on work and descent, include – but are not limited to – caste-based discrimination. Caste has been deemed to fall within the protected categories of the UN International Covenant on Civil and Political Rights (ICCPR) and the UN International Covenant on Economic Social and Cultural Rights (ICESCR), while caste discrimination has been identified as an impediment to the enjoyment of rights under the ICCPR, the ICESCR, the UN Convention on the Elimination of All Forms of Discrimination Against Women (CEDAW) and the UN Convention on the Rights of the Child (CRC).

This chapter shows how the adoption of a dynamic approach to human rights treaty interpretation has enabled treaty bodies, in particular CERD, to address caste discrimination within the parameters of existing human rights treaties. In 2007, a UN experts' report on the gaps in the existing international instruments to combat racism, racial discrimination, xenophobia and related intolerance concluded that there were no substantive gaps in protection in the existing instruments as regards descent-based communities.[8] In contrast, Navi Pillay, former UN High Commissioner for Human Rights, is quoted as suggesting in 2009 that a new international convention on caste may be required, because governments 'have successfully argued in UN conferences that existing international conventions against human rights abuses do not apply'.[9] However, it is unlikely that India would support a caste-specific treaty if it considered this as targeting India alone. Meanwhile, ICERD remains the pre-eminent human rights treaty for addressing caste-based discrimination.

4.2 Caste in international human rights instruments: International Bill of Rights

4.2.1 Background

The period between the end of the Second World War in 1945 and the adoption of the Constitution of India in 1950 saw not only the emergence of the modern human rights

---

5 See, for example, CERD/C/JPN/CO/7–9, 29 August 2014, para 22; CERD/C/IND/CO/19, 5 May 2007, para 8.
6 CERD, Concluding Observations – India; UN Doc. A/51/18 (1996), para 352; CERD General Recommendation 29 (2002), Article 1, Paragraph 1 (Descent).
7 UN Sub-Commission, Resolution 2000/4, Discrimination based on work and descent, 11 August 2000; UN Doc. E/CN.4/Sub.2/2000/46, 23 November 2000, 25.
8 Report on the study by the five experts on the content and scope of substantive gaps in the existing international instruments to combat racism, racial discrimination, xenophobia and related intolerance; UN Doc. A/HRC/4/WG.3/6, 27 August 2007, paras 71–76, 76.
9 B Crossette, 'Putting Caste on Notice', *The Nation*, 9 November 2009.

movement and the start of decolonisation, but also the beginning of the Cold War and the formal establishment in South Africa of apartheid as a legal and political system. In June 1945, the United Nations Charter was signed by fifty founding member states in San Francisco (including India). The primary purpose of the new United Nations Organisation (UN) was the maintenance of international peace and security, but its purposes also included encouraging respect for human rights and for fundamental freedoms for all without distinction as to race, sex, language or religion.[10] In December 1946, India's Constituent Assembly – the body charged with drafting a new Constitution for independent India – met for the first time under the auspices of the interim government established in September of that year, and on 14/15 August 1947, India was freed from colonial rule, becoming at the same time formally independent and partitioned into two states, India and Pakistan. In 1948, the apartheid regime (1948–1991) came to power in South Africa. On 9 December 1948, the UN General Assembly adopted the Convention on the Prevention and Punishment of the Crime of Genocide, followed a day later by the Universal Declaration of Human Rights (UDHR).[11] In January 1950, India adopted a new Constitution which abolished "untouchability," making its practice a criminal offence and prohibiting discrimination on grounds of caste by public and private actors alike.

4.2.2 Caste in the Universal Declaration of Human Rights 1948 (UDHR)

The non-discrimination principle applies to all human rights:[12] 'non-discrimination, together with equality before the law and equal protection of the law without any discrimination, constitutes a basic principle in the protection of human rights'.[13] Caste is not included as a ground of discrimination in any international human rights treaty, and until the mid-1990s, it was not conceptualised as a violation of international human rights law. Nonetheless, caste has been present, implicitly and explicitly, in debates about protected characteristics, categories and grounds of discrimination from the start of the post-1945 human rights movement, beginning with the drafting of the UDHR.

The non-discrimination provision (Article 2) of the UDHR provides

> [e]veryone is entitled to all the rights and freedoms set forth in this Declaration, without distinction of any kind, such as race, colour, sex, language, religion, political or other opinion, national or social origin, property, birth or other status.

While Article 2 UDHR limits the general principle of non-discrimination to the rights enshrined in the UDHR,[14] the expression 'such as' indicates that the enumerated grounds of discrimination did not constitute an exhaustive list.[15] The UDHR was drafted by a subcommittee of the UN Commission on Human Rights.[16] The initial text of Article 2 prohibited discrimination in the enjoyment of UDHR rights on five grounds: race, sex, language,

10 United Nations, Charter of the United Nations, 24 October 1945, 1 UNTS XVI; Article 1(1).
11 UN Doc. A/RES/217 A (III), 10 December 1948.
12 S Skogly, 'Article 2', in A Eide and G Alfredsson (eds.), *The Universal Declaration of Human Rights: A Commentary* (Oslo: Scandinavian University Press, 1992) 57–72, 71.
13 CERD, General Recommendation (GR) No. 14 (1993), Definition of discrimination (Art. 1, par. 1), para 1.
14 Skogly (n 12).
15 UN Doc. E/CN.4/52, cited in Skogly (n 12) 62.
16 See J Morsink, *The Universal Declaration of Human Rights: Origins, Drafting and Intent* (Philadelphia: University of Pennsylvania Press, 1999).

religion or political belief.[17] These were amended by the then UN Sub-Commission on the Prevention of Discrimination and the Protection of Minorities (subsequently the UN Sub-Commission for the Promotion and Protection of Human Rights) to 'race, sex, language, religion, political or other opinion, property status, or national or social origin'.[18] "Colour" was not included, as the Sub-Commission considered it to be embodied in the word "race."[19] It was introduced, however, into Article 2 at the behest of Minochecher Masani (India) and Hansa Mehta (India), Sub-Commission and Human Rights Commission members, with the support of Commission member Charles Habib Malik (Lebanon), on the grounds that race and colour were separate concepts which did not necessarily cover one another or mean the same thing, and that the term "race" did not include the conception of "colour."[20]

The 'national origin' element of 'national or social origin' was proposed by the Sub-Commission's Soviet member as referring to 'national characteristics' rather than a citizen of a state – which, argues Morsink, links it to race and colour.[21] The Commission's acceptance of this 'gloss', he says, makes this an 'authoritative interpretation' of the term.[22] It was disagreement over the meaning of 'national origin' which led India in 1965 to propose adding "descent" to the definition of racial discrimination in ICERD. "Birth" was added to the draft text of UDHR Article 2 in October 1948 by the General Assembly's Third Committee, in lieu of the term "class" proposed by the Soviet delegate, which was aimed at 'the abolition of differences based on social conditions as well as the privileges enjoyed by certain groups in the economic and legal fields'.[23] The substitution of birth for class was accepted by the Soviet delegate because it was agreed that the Russian word *soslovie*, literally *etat* in French and *estate* in English – in modern parlance, *naissance* in French and *birth* in English –

> referred to a legally sanctioned inequality such as had existed in feudal Europe when different groups of people had, by reason of their birth, different rights and privileges. Although such inequalities no longer existed in most countries, there were still some

---

17 Ibid., 93.

18 Ibid.

19 Ibid., 102. See also Skogly (n 12) 61.

20 Ibid., 102, 103. Colour was initially added as a subset of race but later added as a separate, distinct category; J Morsink, 'World War Two and the Universal Declaration', 15(2) *Human Rights Quarterly* (1993) 357–405, 364; S Skogly, 'Article 2', in A Eide and G Alfredsson (eds.), *The Universal Declaration of Human Rights: A Common Standard of Achievement* (The Hague: Martinus Nijhoff, 1999) 75–87, 78. Despite this, colour was long neglected as a separate ground of racial discrimination, or treated as encompassed by race, but growing understanding of discrimination against Afro-descendant populations and people of African descent, and awareness of the significance of colour in intra-community discrimination (for example the socio-cultural privileging of fair skin), has led to greater recognition of colour as ground of discrimination separate from race; see CERD, General Recommendation No, 34, Racial discrimination against people of African descent; UN Doc. CERD/C/GC/34, 30 September 2011, para 38; A Guimaraes, 'Colour and Race in Brazil: From Whitening to the Search for Afro-Descent', in F Bethencourt and A Pearce (eds.), *Racism and Ethnic Relations in the Portuguese-Speaking World* (Oxford: Oxford University Press, 2012). CERD recommends the prohibition of colour-based discrimination in domestic legislation and has expressly identified colour as the discrimination ground in certain cases; see P Thornberry, *The International Convention on the Elimination of All Forms of Racial Discrimination: A Commentary* (Oxford: Oxford University Press, 2016) 119, 136.

21 Morsink (n 16) 103.

22 Ibid., 104.

23 Ibid., 114.

remnants of that social structure left; *and the fight against those remnants should be continued by a definite statement in the draft declaration.*[24]

'In other words', says Morsink, 'the meaning of . . . birth [in Article 2] is to prohibit discrimination on the basis of inherited legal, social and economic differences'.[25] On the inclusion of birth, Morsink mentions that Mohammed Habib (India) 'said he, "[F]avoured the use of the word 'caste' rather than 'birth' as the latter was already implied in the Article"'. Later, A Appadorai (India) explained 'that, "[H]is delegation had only proposed the word 'caste' because it objected to the word 'birth'.[26] The words 'other status' and 'social origin' were sufficiently broad to cover the whole field"'.[27] This suggests that while caste was not explicitly included in the UDHR, it was understood to be covered by birth and social origin (subsequently included in the ICCPR and the ICESCR).[28]

4.2.3 *Caste in the ICCPR 1966 and ICESCR 1966*

In the hierarchy of human rights norms, the principle of non-discrimination, together with equality before the law and equal protection of the law without any discrimination, is considered a peremptory norm of *jus cogens*.[29] It is elaborated internationally in legally binding form in Article 26 ICCPR:

> All persons are equal before the law and are entitled without any discrimination to the equal protection of the law. In this respect, the law shall prohibit any discrimination and guarantee to all persons equal and effective protection against discrimination on any ground such as race, colour, sex, language, religion, political or other opinion, national or social origin, property, birth or other status.

In contrast to Article 2 UDHR and Article 14 of the European Convention on Human Rights 1950 (which provides only an accessory right to non-discrimination),[30] Article 26

---

24 Ibid. (emphasis added).

25 Ibid.

26 In a footnote in his 1999 book on the UDHR, Morsink attributes Indian reluctance regarding the word "birth" to the Hindu doctrine of reincarnation: Morsink (n 16) 356, fn 46.

27 Ibid., 115. See also P Prove, 'Caste and the Universal Declaration of Human Rights', Lutheran World Foundation, unpublished paper (2003), copy on file with author; P Thornberry, 'CERD, Indigenous Peoples and Caste/Descent-based Discrimination', in J Castellino and N Walsh (eds.), *International Law and Indigenous Peoples* (Leiden: Martinus Nijhoff, 2005) 37, fn 107.

28 The interpretation of "birth" as covering legally sanctioned inequality by reason of birth accords with caste as well as other characteristics such as colour. The absence in the UDHR of an explicit reference to caste is perhaps because at the time discrimination and racism were understood in the context of the dismantling of European colonialism; the *internal* struggles of discriminated groups within the different colonies in Africa and Asia were overshadowed by the wider anti-colonialism struggle; see Thorat and Umakant (n 1), xxix.

29 Human Rights Committee (HRC), General Comment (GC) No. 18 (1989), Non-discrimination, para 1. See also HRC GC No. 31 (2004), The Nature of the General Legal Obligation Imposed on State Parties to the Covenant, para 2. See also Restatement of the Foreign Relations Law of the United States (Third), Part VII, Chapter 1, s 701, Reporters' Note 3 (St Paul, Minnesota: American Law Institute, 1987) 155. On the historical significance and development of the principle of equality, see M Nowak, *UN Covenant on Civil and Political Rights: CCPR Commentary* (Kehl: NP Engel, 2005, 2nd edition) 598–560.

30 Protocol 12 to the ECHR (in force 1 April 2005) extends the ECHR to provide a free-standing prohibition on discrimination beyond the limited guarantee in Article 14: 'The enjoyment of any right set forth

contains both an independent right to equality and an autonomous, free-standing guarantee of non-discrimination, not limited to ICCPR rights.[31] Subordinate provisions[32] are found in Article 2(1) ICCPR and Article 2(2) ICESCR, which obligate States parties to guarantee the rights recognised in the Covenants, without discrimination or distinction of any kind, *such as* (in the case of the ICCPR) and *as to* (in the case of the ICESCR) race, colour, sex, language, religion, political or other opinion, national or social origin, property, birth or other status.[33]

Most non-discrimination provisions (including the UK's Equality Act 2010) prohibit discrimination on specified grounds, known in the US as 'suspect classifications'.[34] Distinctions on these grounds will be *prima facie* discriminatory, absent a reasonable and objective justification.[35] The prohibited grounds of discrimination in Articles 2(1) and 26 ICCPR and Article 2(2) ICESCR replicate those in the UDHR. The lists are not exhaustive. Both the ICCPR and the ICESCR include "other status" as a prohibited ground of discrimination. The Human Rights Committee (HRC, the monitoring body of the ICCPR) treats "other status" as a residual category which captures grounds not expressly listed in Article 26 ICCPR,[36] while the Committee on Economic, Social and Cultural Rights (CESCR, the monitoring body of the ICESCR) expressly treats the "other status" category as open ended.[37] Article 26 omits discrimination grounds now accepted as deserving of scrutiny, for example sexual orientation, disability and age. Some non-enumerated grounds have been found by the HRC to constitute "other statuses" for the purposes of the admissibility of individual communications,[38] for example nationality[39] and marital status[40] – illustrating the HRC's application of the living instrument principle to interpreting the ICCPR.[41] Caste

---

by law shall be secured without discrimination on any ground such as sex, race, colour, language, religion, political or other opinion, national or social origin, association with a national minority, property, birth or other status'. It has been ratified by 20 Council of Europe member states but not the UK, although ratification has been recommended by the UK's Joint Committee on Human Rights.

31 HRC GC No. 18, ibid., para 12. See also Nowak (n 29) 604.

32 M Craven, *The International Covenant on Economic, Social and Cultural Rights: A Perspective on Its Development* (Oxford: Clarendon, 1995) 178.

33 Nowak (n 29) 604.

34 "Suspect classification" is a US judicial concept whereby certain groups are recognised as deserving special protection, due to past discriminatory treatment and political powerlessness. There is no fixed definition of which groups merit suspect or quasi-suspect status, but the US Supreme Court has afforded suspect classification to groups which have experienced a history of purposeful unequal treatment, or which have been relegated to a position of political powerlessness; see *Korematsu v United States*, 323 U.S. 214, 223–224 (1944). The principal suspect classifications in US law are race, nationality and alienage, but there are other contenders; see, for example, J Watson, 'When No Place Is Home: Why the Homeless Deserve Suspect Classification', 88 *Iowa Law Review* (2003) 502–537, 508–511.

35 See Craven (n 32) 167; Nowak (n 29) 629.

36 HRC GC No. 18 (n 31), para 7; Nowak (n 29) 618.

37 CESCR GC No. 20 (2009), Non-discrimination in economic, social and cultural rights, para 15. This was not always the case; see Craven (n 32) 168.

38 S Joseph, J Schulz, and M Castan, *The International Covenant on Civil and Political Rights: Cases, Materials and Commentary* (Oxford: Oxford University Press, 2000) 530.

39 *Gueye v France* (195/85).

40 *Danning v The Netherlands* (180/84). The HRC has included sexual orientation in sex rather than as a subcategory of other status; *Toonen v Australia* (488/92) para 8.7; see also D McGoldrick, 'The Development and Status of Sexual Orientation Discrimination Under International Human Rights Law', 16(4) *Human Rights Law Review* (2016) 613–668.

41 Nowak (n 29) 628. The living instrument principle is a notion first introduced by the European Court of Human Rights in 1978 in *Tyrer v United Kingdom*, in which the court stated that the Convention was a

discrimination, untouchability and all forms of discrimination against Dalit communities are treated by the HRC as contributing to violations of ICCPR rights and as an impediment to its implementation, suggesting that caste falls within the Article 26 "other status" category, attracting ICCPR non-discrimination protection.[42]

The CESCR has long scrutinised differential treatment on grounds other than those enumerated in Article 2(2) ICESCR – for example age, disability and sexual orientation[43] – by identifying other (implied) grounds within the "other status" category.[44] Its General Comment (GC) No. 20 on Article 2(2) ICESCR (2009), for instance, states that the prohibited ground of birth 'also includes descent, especially on the basis of caste and analogous systems of inherited status', while the prohibited ground of social origin 'refers to a person's inherited social status, which is discussed . . . in the context of "property" status, descent-based discrimination under "birth" and "economic and social status"',[45] the latter an "other status" category.[46]

Thus, although caste is not itself an express ground in the International Bill of Rights, it was implicitly included in the birth and social origin categories in the UDHR. Moreover, caste is implicitly included in the birth, social origin and "other status" categories of the ICCPR, and since 2009, it has been explicitly included by the CESCR in the birth and social origin categories of the ICESCR as well as within the "other status" implied ground of economic and social status.

4.3 Caste in ICERD: drafting and text

4.3.1 ICERD: context and background

ICERD was the first of the nine core UN human rights treaties to be adopted (in 1965) and to come into force (in 1969).[47] It is also one of the most widely ratified treaties, with 182 ratifications as at 31 August 2021.[48] The prohibition of racial discrimination is central to the development of international human rights law – the UN human rights regime 'originated in the search for an effective response to racism and racial discrimination'[49] – and is consid-

'living instrument which . . . must be interpreted in the light of present-day conditions'; *Tyrer v United Kingdom*, Application 5856/72, Judgment 25 April 1978, para 31. See also D Keane and A Waughray, 'Introduction', in D Keane and A Waughray (eds.), *The International Convention on the Elimination of All Forms of Racial Discrimination: A Living Instrument* (Manchester: Manchester University Press, 2017) 1–31.

42 This has been the case in relation to India since 1997; see Concluding Observations – India; CCPR, Report; A/52/40 (1997), paras 420, 430. For HRC caste-related concluding observations to India and other states such as Nepal, Bangladesh, Sri Lanka, Yemen, see International Dalit Solidarity Network, Compilation of UN references to caste discrimination, May 2018 at https://idsn.org/un-2/compilation-of-un-references-to-caste-discrimination/.

43 See Craven (n 32) 170.

44 CESCR GC No. 20 (n 37).

45 Ibid., paras 26 and 24.

46 Ibid., para 24. 'Individuals and groups of individuals must not be arbitrarily treated on account of belonging to a certain economic or social group or strata within society'; ibid., para 35.

47 See (n 4). For the first legal commentary on ICERD, see Thornberry (n 20). For the first edited collection on ICERD see Keane and Waughray (eds.) (n 41).

48 See http://indicators.ohchr.org/.

49 K Boyle and A Baldaccini, 'International Human Rights Approaches to Racism', in S Fredman (ed.), *Discrimination and Human Rights: The Case of Racism* (Oxford: Oxford University Press, 2001) 135–191, 141.

ered to have the status of a peremptory norm of international law.[50] Initially conceived as a response to post-war anti-Semitism, ICERD also reflected the desire of newly independent countries emerging from colonial rule for an 'international statement against apartheid and colonialism'.[51] Consequently, ICERD's initial concerns were primarily decolonisation, apartheid and self-determination. As former CERD member Patrick Thornberry explains, 'many states viewed racial discrimination as a problem of colonialism, including the "internal colonialism" of apartheid South Africa and South West Africa', and compliance with ICERD obligations was seen as primarily entailing public condemnation of apartheid.[52] By extension, many states were reluctant to acknowledge the existence of any racial discrimination 'at home'.[53] According to former CERD member Michael Banton, 'most states saw accession to the Convention as a matter of foreign policy. Many perceived it as a way of establishing their anti-apartheid credentials with but few implications for their internal affairs'.[54] As Banton remarked in 1996, '[h]ad the scope of [ICERD] been apparent to them at the outset, maybe fewer states would have acceded to it'.[55]

4.3.1.1 United Nations General Assembly Resolution 44(I) 1946: treatment of Indians in South Africa

In December 1946, India secured the adoption by the new UN General Assembly (UNGA) of Resolution 44(I), declaring that the treatment of Indians in South Africa 'should be in conformity with the international obligations under the agreements concluded between the two Governments and the relevant provisions of the [UN] Charter'.[56] This was the first dispute to come before the General Assembly, 'and it resulted in the UN's first challenge to South Africa'.[57] The resolution had been prompted by South Africa's enactment of the 1946 Asiatic Land Tenure and Indian Representation Act No. 28 (the "Ghetto Act") prohibiting the transfer of property to Indians in areas designated for Europeans.[58] India argued that South Africa's discriminatory treatment of its Indian population 'on ground of colour and race' was in violation of the human rights provisions in Article 1.3 and 55 of the UN Charter.[59] As historian Manu Bhagavan explains, India's leaders envisioned the newly created UN as a supranational body capable of acting beyond the limits of national sovereignty where human rights were at stake, its purpose to 'uphold and defend the fundamental rights

---

50 P Thornberry, 'Confronting Racial Discrimination: A CERD Perspective', 5(2) *Human Rights Law Review* (2005) 239–268, 240.
51 D Keane, *Caste-Based Discrimination in International Human Rights Law* (Aldershot: Ashgate, 2007) 161, 168.
52 Thornberry (n 50) 241.
53 'It has been a long labour to convince some States that racial discrimination is primarily a domestic issue'; Thornberry, ibid.
54 M Banton, *International Action Against Racial Discrimination* (Oxford: Oxford University Press, 1996) 99, 305.
55 Ibid., viii.
56 General Assembly Resolution (GAR) 44(1), Treatment of Indians in the Union of South Africa, 8 December 1946.
57 L Lloyd, ' "A Most Auspicious Beginning": The 1946 United Nations General Assembly and the Question of the Treatment of Indians in South Africa', 16(2) *Review of International Studies* (1990) 131–153, 131.
58 See ibid., 133; J Dugard, *Human Rights and the South African Legal Order* (Princeton: Princeton University Press, 1978) 80; International Commission of Jurists, *South Africa and the Rule of Law* (Geneva: International Commission of Jurists, 1960) 32; M Cornell, 'The Statutory Background of Apartheid: A Chronological Survey of South African Legislation', 16(5) *The World Today* (1960) 181–194, 188.
59 VL Pandit, *The Scope of Happiness: A Personal Memoir* (New York: Crown, 1979) 209.

and the common good of all humanity'.[60] In her memoirs, the Indian representative to the UN, Laxmi Pandit (sister of Jawaharlal Nehru, independent India's first prime minister), recounts that during the UNGA debate on Resolution 44(I), South Africa 'raised the plea of domestic jurisdiction under Article 2(7) of the Charter'. Pandit's response was that this was a moral, not simply a legal, issue. For India, South Africa's actions were primarily 'a challenge to our dignity and self-respect':

> India has resisted every attempt to divert the debate to a consideration of the legal aspects of the issue . . . what the world needs is not more charters, not more committees to define and courts of justice to interpret, *but a more willing implementation of the principles of the Charter by all governments.*[61]

In the General Assembly, Pandit argued against South Africa's claim that its treatment of Indians in South Africa was a domestic matter and therefore not amenable to UN interference, describing it as a human rights test case and calling on the UN to 'respond to the "millions of voiceless people who, because of their creed or colour, have been relegated to positions of inferiority, [who] are looking to us for justice"'.[62] Resolution 44(I) secured India's status as an anti-apartheid and anti-racism champion; yet, in a revealing aside, Pandit adds that the South African Law Minister apparently sought to 'humiliate India by accusations that *were entirely irrelevant to the matter under discussion* . . . treatment of our Harijans [Dalits] was of course emphasized'.[63]

4.3.2 ICERD Article 1(1): racial discrimination

Article 1(1) of ICERD defines racial discrimination as

> any distinction, exclusion, restriction or preference based on race, colour, descent, or national or ethnic origin which has the purpose or effect of nullifying or impairing the recognition, enjoyment or exercise, on an equal footing, of human rights and fundamental freedoms in the political, economic, social, cultural or any other field of public life.[64]

As Thornberry points out, racial discrimination is an 'umbrella term'[65] covering discrimination on five grounds – race, colour, descent, or national or ethnic origin – but these grounds are not defined in the Convention. In its General Recommendation No. 14 (1993) on the

---

60 M Bhagavan, 'A New Hope: India, the United Nations and the Making of the Universal Declaration of Human Rights', 44(2) *Modern Asian Studies* (2010) 311–347, 328. During the drafting of the UDHR, India had proposed that the UN Security Council be afforded extensive powers to investigate alleged human rights violations and enforce redress within the framework of the UN; ibid., 329; UN Doc E/CN.4/11, 2; 31 January 1947. India's proposal was not adopted.
61 Pandit (n 59) 209 (emphasis added).
62 Lloyd (n 57) 147.
63 Pandit (n 59) 210 (emphasis added). "Harijan" meaning "children of God" was a term popularised by Gandhi in the 1930s to refer to India's Dalits; see Chapters 1 and 3.
64 In a contemporaneous commentary on ICERD, Schwelb described the definition of racial discrimination in ICERD as a 'composite concept' requiring (1) a certain act or omission to take place, (2) based on certain grounds and (3) having a certain purpose or effect; E Schwelb, 'The International Convention on the Elimination of All Forms of Racial Discrimination', 15 *International and Comparative Law Quarterly* (1966) 996–1068, 1001.
65 Thornberry (n 50) 239, 250.

definition of racial discrimination, CERD explained that a distinction based on the these grounds 'is contrary to the Convention if it has either the purpose or the effect of impairing particular rights and freedoms'.[66] However, a differentiation of treatment will not constitute discrimination if the criteria for such differentiation, judged against the objectives and purposes of ICERD, are legitimate or fall within the scope of ICERD Article 1(4). In determining whether an action has an effect contrary to ICERD, CERD will consider whether that action 'has an unjustifiable disparate impact upon a group distinguished by race, colour, descent, or national or ethnic origin'.[67] In the absence of an express reference to caste as a ground of discrimination in ICERD, "descent" was the vehicle by which it entered international human rights discourse – an interpretation which India, since 1996, has explicitly rejected.

4.3.3 UN Declaration on the Elimination of Racial Discrimination 1963

ICERD was preceded in 1963 by a Declaration on the Elimination of Racial Discrimination,[68] which prohibited discrimination on grounds of race, colour or ethnic origin. During drafting, the Indian and Pakistani delegates explained that their respective Constitutions prohibited discrimination based on colour, religion and caste, and (in India) race.[69] In the general debate on manifestations of racial prejudice in the UNGA Third Committee, the Indian representative had argued for an expansive understanding of the concept of racial discrimination covering *'all manifestations* of racial prejudice', arguing that 'the youth of the world had to be taught that all forms of racism and discrimination were meaningless and dangerous'. India, he said, had legislation punishing any acts prejudicial to the maintenance of harmony between the different religions, racial and language groups, castes and communities, and it would therefore 'have no constitutional or legal difficulties in implementing such a convention'.[70] India also stressed that the goal of any convention should be de facto equality: '[T]he important thing was *not to delve into the origins of discrimination but to rid the body politic of its ill-effects*'.[71]

4.3.4 ICERD and the meaning of descent

ICERD was prepared by the UN Sub-Commission on the Prevention of Discrimination and the Protection of Minorities in January 1964.[72] The original definition of racial discrimination contained four grounds – 'race, colour, national or ethnic origin'.[73] Descent was introduced in October 1965 in an amendment originally proposed by India,[74] intended

---

66 See CERD GR 14 (1993) (n 13). All treaty bodies with competence to do so adopt general comments or recommendations on the interpretation of the provisions of their respective treaties. These range from the interpretation of substantive provisions, to general guidance on the content of state reports. They may also address wider, cross-cutting issues. As of July 2018, CERD had made 35 General Recommendations.
67 CERD, GR 14 (1993) (n 13), para 2.
68 GAR 1904 (XVIII), 20 November 1963.
69 India, UNGA Third Committee; UN Doc. A/C.3/SR.1215, 30 September 1963, para 14; Pakistan, UNGA Third Committee, A/C/SR.1171, 2 November 1962, para 6.
70 India, UNGA Third Committee; UN Doc. A/C.3/SR.1168, 31 October 1962, paras 29, 31.
71 Ibid., para 28 (emphasis added).
72 For a detailed account of the drafting of ICERD, see Keane (n 51), Chapter 4.
73 UN Doc. A/5921, 16 June 1965, Annex, 2.
74 UN Doc. A/C.3/L.1238, 15 October 1965.

to resolve disagreements over the meaning of "national origin."[75] India's amendment proposed to replace "national origin" with "descent" and "place of origin."[76] Four days later, this was withdrawn and replaced with an amendment proposed jointly by Ghana, India, Kuwait, Lebanon, Mauritania, Morocco, Nigeria, Poland and Senegal which omitted "place of origin" but retained "descent" and "national origin."[77] This second amendment was adopted unanimously in October 1965 to become Article 1(1) of the Convention.[78]

The meaning of "national origin" was extensively debated in the Third Committee of the General Assembly.[79] The United States representative distinguished national origin from nationality, in that national origin relates to previous or ancestral nationality and geographical origins, covering people residing in foreign countries which were not the countries of their ancestors. Ethnic origin, in contrast, relates to racial and cultural characteristics.[80] This interpretation of national origin was endorsed by the Ghanaian representative, who felt that these notions were 'adequately represented' by 'descent' and 'place of origin' in India's initial amendment.[81] The *travaux préparatoires* are silent on the intended meaning of "descent," however, and no discussion or debate on this point is recorded.[82] India denies that descent was intended to include caste.[83] CERD member Thornberry observes that descent is 'not employed in the key pre-ICERD texts on discrimination, and neither is caste'.[84] In his 1966 commentary on the then new Convention, Egon Schwelb noted the absence of descent in any of the other international instruments dealing with related subjects, and the lack of any indication of the distinction between the concept of descent and the concepts of national or ethnic origin.[85] Schwelb suggested that '[i]t is reasonable to assume that the term "descent" includes the notion of "caste" which is a prohibited

75 India, UNGA Third Committee; UN Doc. A/C.3/SR.1299, 11 October 1965, para 29; India, UNGA Third Committee; A/C.3/SR.1304, 14 October 1965, para 19.
76 UN Doc. A/C.3/L.1216, 11 October 1965.
77 See (n 74).
78 UN Doc. A/6181, 18 December 1965, paras 37, 41.
79 UN Doc. A/C.3/SR. 1304 (n 56).
80 UN Doc. A/C.3/SR.1304, ibid., para 23.
81 Ghana, UNGA Third Committee; UN Doc. A/C.3/SR.1306, 15 October 1965, para 12.
82 The term *travaux preparatiores* describes the documentary evidence of the negotiation, discussions and drafting of a final treaty text. There is a discrepancy between Article 1 of ICERD and Article 5 which guarantees the right of equality before the law, 'without distinction as to race, colour, national or ethnic origin', but omits descent; see Keane (n 51) 198, 199–201.
83 See UN Press Release, 'Committee on Elimination of Racial Discrimination Considers Report of India', 26 February 2007; see also Intervention by the Solicitor-General of India on specific issues raised by CERD at the presentation of India's fifteenth to nineteenth reports, 26 February 2007, paras 32, 33; copy on file with author.
84 P Thornberry, 'Race, Descent and Caste Under the Convention on the Elimination of All Forms of Racial Discrimination', in K Nakano, M Yutzis, and R Onoyama (eds.), *Peoples for Human Rights Vol. 9: Descent-Based Discrimination* (Tokyo: International Movement Against All Forms of Discrimination and Racism, 2004) 119–137, 124. Descent is used in ILO Convention 169 (1989) on Indigenous and Tribal Peoples to cover indigenous status on the grounds inter alia of descent from the populations which inhabited the country at the time of conquest or colonisation or the establishment of present state boundaries and who, irrespective of their legal status, retain some or all of their own social, economic, cultural and political institutions; Thornberry, ibid; see also C169 – Indigenous and Tribal Peoples Convention, 1989, at www.ilo.org/dyn/normlex/en/f?p=NORMLEXPUB:12100:0::NO::P12100_ILO_CODE:C169.
85 Schwelb (n 64) 1002–1003.

ground of discrimination in Indian Constitutional Law [sic] . . . which, however, also uses the expression "descent" side-by-side with "caste" '.[86]

Why Schwelb came to this conclusion is not clear. It is unlikely that the term "descent" was intended (or at least intended by India) at the time of its introduction into ICERD to include caste.[87] There is an alternative explanation for India's proposal. Descent originates in a provision in the Government of India Act 1833 (drafted by the British) prohibiting racial and religious discrimination against Indians ('natives') seeking employment in British India with the East India Company:

> No Native of the said Territories [British India], nor any natural-born subject of His Majesty resident therein, shall, by reason only of his Religion, Place of Birth, Descent, Colour, or any of them, be disabled from holding any Place, Office or Employment under the said Company.[88]

The characteristics by which Indians in British India were distinguished from Europeans, and hence the prohibited grounds of discrimination, were religion, place of birth, descent and colour. The Court of Directors of the East India Company interpreted the provision to mean that, whatever the other tests of qualification for employment, they were not to include distinctions of race or religion: 'no subject of the King, *whether of Indian or British or mixed descent*, shall be excluded [from the specified posts]'.[89] At the time ICERD was drafted, India's concerns were, first, the treatment of Indians (i.e. persons of Indian origin, irrespective of legal nationality) in the foreign land of South Africa, and second, the legacy of colonialism whereby Indians had suffered racial discrimination in their own land. The terms "place of origin" or "national origin" and "descent" were put forward by India in 1965 to meet these twin concerns.[90] However, this does not mean that caste was not in the minds of the drafters of ICERD. That it was in the minds of the Indian delegates, at least, is evident from the debates on the provision which became Article 1(4) on special measures.

4.3.5 ICERD Articles 1(4) and 2(2): special measures

The concept of "special measures" in international law includes domestic affirmative action policies.[91] Article 2(2) ICERD provides that States parties shall, when the circumstances so warrant,

---

86 Ibid., 1003, fn 43.
87 See D Keane, 'Descent-Based Discrimination in International Law: A Legal History', 11 *International Journal of Minority and Group Rights* (2005) 93–116; Keane (n 51) 236–237.
88 Section 87, Government of India Act 1833; see A Lester and G Bindman, *Race and Law* (Harmondsworth: Penguin Books, 1972) 384. Lester (later Lord Lester of Herne Hill) and Bindman describe section 87 as 'the first British anti-discrimination law', introduced at a time when Britain, influenced by the writings of Jeremy Bentham and his disciples, was increasingly receptive to reforms at home and abroad; ibid., 383.
89 Lester and Bindman, ibid., 386–387 (emphasis added).
90 That these were India's concerns is confirmed by statements made by the country during CERD's examination of India's fifteenth to nineteenth reports; see UN Doc. CERD/C/SR.1796, 2 March 2007, para 7. Patrick Thornberry notes the overlap between descent and other terms in ICERD Article 1, especially where they include "origin"; Thornberry (n 20) 119.
91 See CERD, General Recommendation 23 (2009), The meaning and scope of special measures in the International Convention on the Elimination of Racial Discrimination; CERD/C/GC/32, 24 September 2009.

take, in the social, economic, cultural and other fields, special and concrete measures to ensure the adequate development and protection of certain racial groups or individuals belonging to them, for the purpose of guaranteeing them the full and equal enjoyment of human rights and fundamental freedoms.[92]

Article 1(4) ICERD ensures that special measures taken in compliance with Article 2(2) shall not be deemed racial discrimination:

Special measures taken for the sole purpose of securing adequate advancement of certain racial or ethnic groups or individuals requiring such protection as may be necessary in order to ensure such groups or individuals equal enjoyment or exercise of human rights and fundamental freedoms shall not be deemed racial discrimination, provided, however, that such measures do not, as a consequence, lead to the maintenance of separate rights for different racial groups and that they shall not be continued after the objectives for which they were taken have been achieved.[93]

During discussions on the provision which was to become Article 1(4), the Scheduled Castes were clearly envisaged by the Indian representatives in the UNGA Third Committee, Saksena and Pant, as falling within its scope.[94] Both delegates, whilst acknowledging that the Scheduled Castes were 'of the same racial stock and ethnic origin as their fellow citizens',[95] explicitly identified them as groups to which Article 1(4) would apply.[96] The provision, said Saksena, had been included in the draft Convention,

in order to provide for special and temporary measures to help certain groups of people, including one in his country, *who, though of the same racial stock and ethnic origin as their fellow citizens, had for centuries been relegated by the caste system to a miserable and downtrodden condition.*[97]

Their concern was to ensure that India's constitutional special measures, or affirmative action policies, for the Scheduled Castes would not be condemned as discriminatory under ICERD. It is difficult to read this as anything other than an assumption of the reach of ICERD to caste issues, at least as regards Article 1(4), in which case it is difficult to reconcile this with India's subsequent insistence that the definition of racial discrimination in Article 1(1) of ICERD cannot be interpreted as including caste.[98]

---

92 Article 2(2) ICERD continues, 'These measures shall in no case entail as a consequence the maintenance of unequal or separate rights for different racial groups after the objectives for which they were taken have been achieved'.
93 The notion that special measures in favour of specific disadvantaged groups should not be regarded as violating the basic principle of equality had been acknowledged explicitly during India's Constituent Assembly debates; see Shah, Constituent Assembly Debates (CAD) Vol. VII, 29 November 1948 (New Delhi: Lok Sabha Secretariat) 655.
94 India, UNGA Third Committee, 14 October 1965 (n 75), para 20. 'Scheduled Caste' is the constitutional, legal and administrative term in India for Dalits; see the first three chapters of this book.
95 India, 15 October 1965 (n 74), para 25.
96 India, UNGA Third Committee, 14 October 1965 (n 75), paras 20, 33.
97 India, 15 October 1965 (n 74), para 25 (emphasis added).
98 Observes Thornberry, '[I]n the context of the convention as a whole and in the particular concept of special measures the redress of caste disabilities finds a place'; Thornberry (n 84) 124; see also Thornberry (n 20) 137.

Logically, India should have argued, both during the drafting of ICERD and later in its State Reports, that Article 1(4) had no application to its special measures for Scheduled Castes, on the grounds that caste was not covered by Article 1(1); however, it did not do so. Until 1987, its expressed position was that Scheduled Caste reservations fell within Article 1(4). By implication, then, caste must have been covered by Article 1(1). Conversely, since 1987, India's position has been that caste does not fall within Article 1(1) and that information on the situation of the Scheduled Castes would be provided only as 'a matter of courtesy'.[99] As CERD member Van Boven observed in 1996, there was 'some discrepancy' between the contribution of the Indian delegation during the ICERD drafting process to Article 1(4), 'which advocated affirmative action', and India's subsequent attitude that caste is not covered by ICERD Article 1(1).[100]

4.4 CERD and caste: interpretation and practice

4.4.1 *Caste discrimination in India as an emerging issue 1965–1986*

India has been a State party to ICERD since 1969.[101] Implementation by States parties of their treaty obligations under the nine core international human rights treaties is monitored by independent committees, or "treaty bodies," created under each treaty. States must submit periodic reports to the relevant treaty body, at specified intervals, detailing their compliance with their obligations under the treaty in question. The committee examines the state reports in a process which includes formal discussion of the report with state representatives. The committee then issues "concluding observations" and recommendations to the state concerned on how to improve their compliance with the treaty. India has submitted nineteen periodic reports to CERD pursuant to Article 9 of ICERD, the first seven individually between 1970 and 1982, the eighth and ninth combined in 1986, the tenth to fourteenth combined in 1996 and the fifteenth to nineteenth combined in 2006. At the time of writing, India has not reported since 2006.[102] In its reports, India has repeatedly maintained that it has no racial discrimination at home, because 'the issue of race does not impinge directly on the consciousness of Indian people' – a position it has also adopted before other treaty bodies.[103] Instead, successive Indian Governments have identified the

99 See, for example, India's tenth to fourteenth periodic report; UN Doc. CERD/C/299/Add.3, 29 April 1996, para 7.

100 UN Doc. CERD/C/SR.1162, 13 August 1996, para 15.

101 Indian ratification 3 December 1968. In force 4 January 1969.

102 India – initial report; UN Doc. CERD/C/R.3/Add.3/Rev.1, 30 March 1970; second report; CERD/C/R.30/Add.4, 28 June 1972; third report; CERD/C/R.70/Add.29, 18 November 1974; fourth report; CERD/C/R.90/Add.32, 27 July 1977; fifth report; CERD/C/20/Add.34, 8 March 1979; sixth report; CERD/C/66/Add.33, 16 June 1981; seventh report; CERD/C/91.Add.26, 19 October 1982; eighth to ninth report; CERD/C/149/Add.11, 4 September 1986; fourteenth report (1996) (n 99); fifteenth to nineteenth report; CERD/C/IND/19, 29 March 2006.

103 See, for example, India – fourteenth report (1996), ibid., paras 2 and 5; UN Doc. CERD/C/SR.1797, 26 March 2007, para 16 (original in French); 'Committee on Elimination of Racial Discrimination Considers Report of India'; UN Press Release, 26 February 2007. In 1991, India stated before the Human Rights Committee (the monitoring body of the International Covenant on Civil and Political Rights 1966) that 'although there were racial and religious minorities in India, the Indian people formed a composite whole racially, and hence the concept of ethnic minorities and ethnic majority did not apply'; UN Doc. CCPR A/46/40 (1991) para 307. Likewise, India does not accept that the principle of self-determination applies to its minority ethnic groups and has entered Reservation to Articles 1 of the

elimination of racial discrimination primarily with the fight against apartheid and the anti-colonial struggle.[104]

Article 17 of the Constitution of India 1950 abolishes untouchability and criminalises 'the enforcement of any disability arising out of Untouchability'. This provision is operationalised by criminal anti-discrimination legislation and by hate crime legislation.[105] India's Constitution also provides for special measures for the Scheduled Castes in the form of affirmative action policies (known as reservations) in higher education, state employment and political representation. From its initial report in 1970, until its combined eighth and ninth reports in 1986, successive Indian Governments provided CERD with detailed information on the special measures for the Scheduled Castes and Scheduled Tribes, which CERD repeatedly acknowledged as conforming with Article 1(4).[106] It was not until 1987, during the oral examination of its ninth report, that India first stated expressly that it did not consider caste to fall within ICERD Article 1(1). In its report, India had stated that 'measures in favour of the scheduled castes and scheduled tribes are in conformity with Article 1(4) of the Convention',[107] but during discussion, its representative stated that, in his view, 'Article 1 of the Convention did not apply to India' and that information in the report on Scheduled Castes had been provided solely in response to the many questions by CERD members on the issue of caste.[108]

4.4.2 CERD concluding observations on India's 1996 report

India's first categorical written denial of the application of Article 1(1) to caste came in its combined tenth to fourteenth reports in 1996, stating 'the policies of the Indian Government relating to the Scheduled Castes and Scheduled Tribes do not come under the purview of Article 1 of [ICERD]'.[109] According to India, 'the term "caste" denotes a "social" and "class" distinction and is not based on race but has its origins in the functional division of Indian society during ancient times'.[110] Noting that Article 1 of ICERD includes the term "descent" in the definition of racial discrimination, India argued that although both castes and tribes are systems based on descent, since people are normally born into a particular caste or a particular tribe, it was 'obvious' that the use of the term in ICERD 'clearly referred to race'. The Scheduled Castes and Scheduled Tribes were 'unique to Indian society and its historical process'. As conveyed to the Committee during the presentation of its last periodic report [in 1986], India's policies relating to the Scheduled Castes and Tribes therefore did

---

ICCPR and the ICESR declaring that 'the words "the right of self-determination" appearing in [this article] apply only to the peoples under foreign domination and that these words do not apply to sovereign independent States or to a section of a people or nation – which is the essence of national integrity'.

104 See, for example, India – fourteenth report (1996) (n 99), paras 9, 13, 16, 19, 21, 22; India – nineteenth report (2006) (n 102), paras 53–56.

105 Protection of Civil Rights Act 1955; Scheduled Castes and Scheduled Tribes (Prevention of Atrocities) Act 1989. See also Chapter 3.

106 See, for example, CERD/C/SR.33, 14 September 1970, 53; UN Doc. A/10018) (1975), para 91; India, fifth report (1979) (n 102), paras 28, 45–47, 49; CERD, Concluding Observations – India; CERD, Report; A/34/18 (1979), para 365; CERD/C/SR.535, 15 November 1983, para 29; CERD/C/91. Add.26, 19 October 1986, paras 15–16.

107 India – ninth report (1986) (n 102), para 8.

108 CERD/C/SR.797, 10 November 1987, para 61.

109 CERD/C/299/Add.3, 29 April 1996, para 6.

110 India – fourteenth report (1996) (n 99), para 6.

not come under the purview of ICERD Article 1(1).[111] During the dialogue with CERD, India reiterated that caste denoted a social or class distinction and was originally occupation-oriented; it was not a racial issue: while

> the notion of "race" was not entirely foreign to that of "caste," according to experts on such questions, racial differences were secondary compared to cultural ones (economic and occupational status, language and dynastic or national loyalties), and the principle of race had never really been a determinant for caste.[112]

Constitutionally (in India) the concept of race was distinct from caste.[113] Given that, in India's view, descent referred solely to race, and caste was not a racial issue, India's policies on caste discrimination therefore did not fall under descent or indeed under the ambit of ICERD at all.

India's interpretation of descent as excluding caste was rejected categorically by CERD during its examination of India's report as 'not acceptable'.[114] CERD asserted that the fact that castes and tribes were based on descent brought them strictly within the Convention, under the terms of Article 1.[115] If descent were indeed the equivalent of race, it would not have been necessary to include both concepts in the Convention.[116] Although the concept of Scheduled Castes and Tribes was not based on race, it did have an ethnic connotation, and discrimination against members of those groups was therefore within the purview of Article 1. Even if caste denoted a social distinction and was not based on race, it was unacceptable, said the Committee, to say that the serious discrimination against certain castes, especially the "untouchables", was not within the Committee's competence.[117]

In its concluding observations to India in 1996, CERD stated categorically

> [T]he term descent mentioned in Article 1 of the Convention does not solely refer to race. The Committee affirms that the situation of the scheduled castes and scheduled tribes falls within the scope of the Convention.[118]

What CERD could have made absolutely clear, but did not, was that the concept of *racial* discrimination is wider than race, that descent and race are not interchangeable but constitute complementary grounds of racial discrimination under Article 1(1) and that CERD considered caste to come within the descent limb – not the race limb – of racial discrimination. The issue was not whether the concepts of caste and race were synonymous; rather, it was that caste falls within a subcategory (descent) of *racial* discrimination as defined in ICERD Article 1(1). This was the first time that CERD had explicitly identified caste discrimination as coming within the purview of ICERD and, by extension, as an international human rights violation. CERD's concern with caste discrimination had been prompted by information and "shadow reports" provided by human rights NGOs in India and elsewhere,

---

111 Ibid., para 7.
112 CERD/C/SR.1163, 20 November 1996, para 3.
113 CERD/C/SR.1162, 13 August 1996, para 35.
114 CERD/C/SR. 1161, 1 November 1996, para 20; CERD/C/SR.1162, 13 August 1996, para 27.
115 CERD/C/SR.1162, 13 August 1996, para 22; CERD/C/SR.1161, 1 November 1996, para 20.
116 CERD/C/SR.1161, 1 November 1996, para 20.
117 Ibid., paras 20, 23, 32.
118 CERD/C/304/Add.13, 13 September 1996, para 14.

and by other non-state actors.[119] This was also the first time NGOs had submitted shadow reports on caste discrimination to a UN treaty body – an important move, says Corinne Lennox, as it 'pushed CERD into taking a juridical position on whether caste fell within the remit' of ICERD.[120]

CERD's dialogue with India during the presentation of its report did not result in India changing its position. Its government considered that CERD was guilty of a misinterpretation of the term descent, and it rejected the accusation of racial discrimination which CERD's concluding observations implied; in its report, India had stressed its role as both a victim and a key opponent of racial discrimination.[121]

4.4.3 CERD: competence to interpret

CERD's competence to interpret ICERD stems from Article 9, by which CERD is mandated to receive and consider State party reports on the legislative, judicial, administrative and other measures which they have adopted to give effect to ICERD, and is empowered to make suggestions and General Recommendations on examination of the reports and information received from the States parties. By asserting that India's interpretation of descent (as referring solely to race, and hence inapplicable to caste) was unacceptable, CERD assumed an unequivocal authority to interpret ICERD.

The Vienna Convention on the Law of Treaties 1969 provides:[122]

> A treaty shall be interpreted in good faith in accordance with the *ordinary meaning* to be given to the terms of the treaty *in their context* and *in the light of its object and purpose*.[123]

As a general principle of international law, a treaty in force is binding upon the parties and must be performed by them in good faith.[124] However, human rights treaties differ from traditional multilateral treaties, in that the object and purpose of human rights treaties is not the 'exchange of reciprocal rights between a limited number of States'[125] or the protection

---

119 CERD/C/SR.1161, 1 November 1996, paras 11, 22; CERD/C/SR. 1162, 13 August 1996, para 23. 'Shadow reports' can be presented by NGOs to all of the human rights treaty monitoring bodies. They enable NGOs to supplement or provide an alternative viewpoint to state reports, and to highlight issues not raised by their governments, or to point out where the government may be downplaying the real situation. Shadow reports may address specific treaty articles or mirror the state report.

120 C Lennox, 'Norm Entrepreneurship on Caste-Based Discrimination', in D Mosse and L Steur (eds.), *Caste Out of Development? The Cultural Politics of Identity and Economy in India and Beyond* (London: Routledge, 2015).

121 CERD/C/299/Add.3, 29 April 1996, para 13.

122 Adopted 22 May 1969. Entered into force 27 January 1980. 1155 UNTS 331.

123 Article 31(1) VCLT (emphasis added). Article 32 VCLT provides that "context" comprises, in addition to the text, any materials related to the conclusion of the treaty.

124 Article 26 VCLT; M Addo, *The Legal Nature of International Human Rights Law* (Lieden: Martinus Nijhoff, 2010) 215–240.

125 Inter-American Court of Human Rights (IACtHR), Advisory Opinion on the Effect of Reservations on the Entry into Force of the American Convention ('Effect of Reservations'), 22 *International Legal Materials* (1983) 37–50, para 27; A Orakhelashivili, 'Restrictive Interpretation of Human Rights Treaties in the Recent Jurisprudence of the European Court of Human Rights', 14(3) *European Journal of International Law* (2003) 529–568, 532.

or advancement of state interests[126] but 'the protection of the basic rights of individual human beings irrespective of their nationality, against the state of their nationality and all other contracting states'.[127] Thus, in interpreting human rights treaties, it is necessary 'to seek the interpretation that is most appropriate in order to realise the aim and achieve the object of the treaty, *not that which would restrict to the greatest possible degree the obligations undertaken by the Parties*'.[128]

ICERD is a treaty of a general nature, in that, aside from apartheid, it makes no reference to the specific groups or forms of racial discrimination which fall within its ambit, nor does it define racism, or race, colour, descent or national or ethnic origin.[129] In common with other UN treaty bodies, CERD has adopted a dynamic – or evolutive – approach to interpreting ICERD, treating it as a living instrument.[130] From its initial focus on apartheid and racial segregation, CERD has addressed issues of ethnic discrimination (e.g. in Rwanda and the former Yugoslavia), discrimination against Roma,[131] indigenous people's rights[132] and the right to self-determination.[133] More recently, it has tackled the rights of non-citizens, descent-based discrimination and racial discrimination against people of African descent.[134] CERD has also taken into account the evolution of "racial discrimination," from conceptualisations which emphasise biological features to contemporary forms justified by cultural difference ("cultural/difference racism").[135] Moreover, it has interpreted the definition of racial discrimination in ICERD, in order to address "double" or multiple (intersectional) racial discrimination and aggravated forms of racial discrimination.[136] CERD has repeatedly clarified the meaning of the grounds in Article 1, in concluding observations and in various General Recommendations, emphasising that the concept of racial discrimination 'is much

---

126 See ICJ, Advisory Opinion, Reservations to the Convention on Genocide, 28 May 1951, ICJ Reports 1951, 15–69, 23.
127 IACtHR (n 125), para 29. On the special character of human rights treaties, see also HRC GC No. 24 (1994), Issues relating to reservations to the Covenant, para 18; *Loizidou v Turkey*, Application 15318/89, Judgment 18 December 1996, para 43; S Mullally, *Gender, Culture and Human Rights: Reclaiming Universalism* (Oxford: Hart, 2006) 95.
128 *Wemhoff v Germany*, Application 2122/64, Judgment 27 June 1968, 19, para 8. Moreover, the legal rights and obligations enshrined in human rights treaties are widely considered to be rights and obligations erga *omnes* (obligations owed to the international community as a whole): *Barcelona Traction Case*, ICJ Reports (1970), para. 33. See also HRC GC No 31, n 29 above.
129 Intergovernmental Working Group on the Effective Implementation of the Durban Declaration and Programme of Action (IGWG); views of CERD on the implementation of ICERD; UN Doc. E/CN.4/2004/WG.21/10.Add.1, 17 September 2004, para 12.
130 Communication No. 26/2002, *Stephen Hagan v Australia*, UN Doc. CERD/C/62/D/26/2002, para 7.3. The living instrument principle is a notion first introduced by the European Court of Human Rights in 1978 in *Tyrer v United Kingdom*, in which the court stated that the Convention was 'a living instrument which . . . must be interpreted in the light of present-day conditions'; *Tyrer v United Kingdom*, Application 5856/72, Judgment 25 April 1978, para 31. On the core human rights treaties as living instruments, see Committee on the Rights of the Child (CRC/C), GC No. 8 (2006), para 20. On ICERD as a living instrument, see Keane and Waughray (n 41) 1–34.
131 CERD GR No. 27 (2000), Discrimination against Roma.
132 CERD GR. No. 23 (1997), Indigenous Peoples.
133 CERD GR. No. 21 (1996), Right to self-determination.
134 CERD GR. No. 30 (2004), Discrimination Against Non-Citizens; CERD GR No. 29 (2002), Article 1, Paragraph 1 (Descent); CERD GR. No. 34 (2011), Racial discrimination against people of African descent.
135 See Thornberry (n 52); Thornberry (n 20) 91.
136 Durban Review Conference Outcome Document, 24 April 2009, para 35. See also Durban Review Conference, Preparatory Committee, CERD Replies to OHCHR questionnaire; UN Doc. A/CONF.211/PC.2/CRP.5, 23 April 2008, 15. See also Thornberry (n 20) 126–128.

broader than that perceived by many States which argue that there is no racial discrimination on their territory'[137] and expressing regret at the

> limited understanding by many States parties regarding the meaning and scope of the definition of the concept of racial discrimination in Article 1 of the Convention . . . which may lead some States to deny or minimize the extent of racial discrimination in their territory.[138]

4.4.4 CERD and the meaning of racial discrimination: General Recommendation 14 (1993)

As of November 2021, CERD had made thirty-six general recommendations.[139] CERD's General Recommendation (GR) 14 (1993) sets out its interpretation of the definition of discrimination in ICERD Article 1(1). A distinction is contrary to the Convention if it has either the purpose or the effect of impairing particular rights and freedoms:

> In seeking to determine whether an action has an effect contrary to the Convention, [CERD] will look to see whether that action has an unjustifiable disparate impact upon a group distinguished by race, colour, descent, or national or ethnic origin.[140]

GR 14 was issued three years before CERD's 1996 concluding observations to India affirming that caste is included in the descent limb of racial discrimination, reaffirmed in GR 29 (2002) (see subsection 4.4.6). As CERD member Thornberry pointed out in 2001, during CERD's examination of Japan's initial and second reports, the expression "racial discrimination" in Article 1(1) of ICERD

> covered different categories of discrimination, including that based on descent, *in order to cover all cases and to apply to all countries no matter their specific cultural characteristics.*[141]

4.4.5 CERD and the meaning of racial segregation and apartheid: General Recommendation 19 (1995)

While in some countries government policies created conditions of complete or partial racial segregation, partial segregation may also arise as an 'unintended by-product' of private (non-state) actions:

> In many cities, residential patterns are influenced by group differences in income, which are sometimes combined with differences of race, colour, descent and national or ethnic origin, so that inhabitants can be stigmatised and individuals suffer a form of discrimination in which racial grounds are mixed with other grounds.[142]

137 CERD, Replies, ibid., 12.
138 Ibid., 3.
139 General recommendations or general comments are adopted and published by treaty bodies as authoritative interpretations or clarifications of the provisions in the treaty in question and are applicable to all States parties to the treaty. As this book went to press CERD had drafted but not yet adopted General Recommendation 36.
140 CERD GR No. 14 (1993) (n 13), para 2.
141 CERD/C/SR.1444, 11 June 2001, para 39 (emphasis added).
142 CERD GR No. 19 (1995), Racial segregation and apartheid (Art. 3), para 3.

Racial segregation can thus arise "at home," without any initiative or direct involvement by the public authorities, and racial grounds of discrimination may combine with economic inequality and give rise to multiple-level discrimination. In its concluding observations in May 2007 on India's fifteenth to nineteenth reports, CERD identified the persistence of the de facto segregation of Dalits[143] and urged India to enforce legislation prohibiting and punishing untouchability and to take effective measures against segregation.[144] Apartheid – a 'loaded term'[145] – had not been widely associated by international lawyers with caste and the Dalits, but in December 2006, India's then prime minister surprised many observers at home and abroad by likening untouchability to apartheid, and in 2007, Human Rights Watch (HRW) in a shadow report to CERD described caste discrimination in India as a 'hidden apartheid', a term subsequently adopted in a 2009 report on caste discrimination in the UK by the Anti Caste Discrimination Alliance.[146]

4.4.6 CERD and the meaning of descent: General Recommendation 29 (2002)

In August 2002, CERD adopted GR 29 on descent.[147] The Preamble confirms 'CERD's consistent view . . . that the term "descent" in Article 1 paragraph 1 of the Convention does not refer solely to "race" and has a meaning and application which complements the other prohibited grounds of discrimination'.[148] In addition, it 'strongly reaffirms that discrimination based on "descent" includes discrimination against members of communities based on forms of social stratification such as caste and analogous systems of inherited status which nullify or impair their equal enjoyment of human rights'[149] and 'strongly condemn[s] descent-based discrimination, such as discrimination on the basis of caste and analogous systems of inherited status, as a violation of the Convention'. In paragraph 1, States parties are recommended to take steps to identify 'descent-based communities under their jurisdiction . . . suffer[ing] from discrimination, especially on the basis of caste and analogous systems of inherited status',[150] inter alia to review and enact or amend legislation, in order to outlaw all forms of discrimination based on descent and to implement resolutely legislation and other measures already in force.[151] In addition, states should adopt special measures in favour of descent-based communities, in order to ensure their enjoyment of human rights and fundamental freedoms, and audit and provide disaggregated information on the de facto economic and social situation of descent-based communities, including a gender perspective.[152]

---

143   Concluding Observations – India; UN Doc. CERD/C/IND/CO/19, 5 May 2007, para 13.
144   Ibid., para 14. Segregation remains an issue in India; see S Desai and A Dubey, 'Caste in 21st Century India: Competing Narratives', *Economic and Political Weekly* (12 March 2011).
145   J Dugard and J Reynolds, 'Apartheid, International Law, and the Occupied Palestinian Territory', 24(3) *European Journal of International Law* (2013) 867–913, 867.
146   M Rahman, 'Indian Leader Likens Caste System to Apartheid Regime', *The Guardian*, 28 December 2006; Human Rights Watch, "Hidden Apartheid: Caste Discrimination Against India's 'Untouchables'" (2007); Anti Caste Discrimination Alliance, 'Hidden Apartheid – Voice of the Community: Caste and Caste Discrimination in the UK: A Scoping Study' (2009). The present author was an advisor on the study.
147   CERD GR 29 (2002) on article 1 paragraph 1 (descent). For a longer analysis of GR 29, see A Waughray and D Keane, 'CERD and Caste-Based Discrimination', in Keane and Waughray (eds.) (n 41) 121–149.
148   CERD GR 29, ibid., Preamble.
149   Ibid.
150   CERD GR 29, para 1(a).
151   Ibid., paras 1(c), 1(d).
152   Ibid., paras 1(f), 1(j). (n 13).

The opposition of states such as India to CERD's application of descent to caste stimulated CERD to explain its approach to descent in a General Recommendation.[153] GR 29 was adopted following the 2001 UN World Conference Against Racism, Racial Discrimination, Xenophobia and Related Intolerance (WCAR) in Durban[154] (discussed in Chapter 5), where Dalit activists sought to secure a provision on caste in the conference's final document.[155] They were unsuccessful, but in the process they raised international awareness of caste discrimination as a global human rights issue. Thornberry observes that the absence of reference to caste in the WCAR final document is compensated for by its inclusion in GR 29.[156] However, CERD had 'independent reasons' to explore descent:

> [T]o understand better a key term in the Convention; to understand better the contemporary scope of such discrimination; and, to respond to the victims who impressed the Committee so greatly. There are issues here: the target of the General Recommendation is not or should not be the caste system itself, but discrimination – although the distinction is a thin one. In the author's view, powerful victim perspectives greatly influenced the Committee.[157]

GR 29 was preceded by an informal discussion on the concept of descent with NGOs, UN experts and States parties (including India), followed by a thematic debate within CERD – only the second time this had happened.[158] It was modelled on CERD's General Recommendation 27 on discrimination against Roma, the subject of its first thematic discussion.[159] The thematic debate had been proposed by CERD in November 2001. Descent had not been studied by CERD in any depth, and it had received little attention to that point. A thematic debate, it was suggested, would also enable CERD to collaborate with the UN Sub-Commission, which was working on discrimination based on work and descent (see Chapter 5). Due to the complex nature of "descent," it was felt that CERD should study the concept carefully, in order to clarify the basic notion as well its scope.[160]

At the informal discussion, activists urged that "descent" should be interpreted broadly and that 'caste-based discrimination should not be merely equated with the Dalit issue in India' nor should caste discrimination against communities in other parts of the world be overlooked.[161] The Indian Government reiterated its constitutional prohibition of untouchability and its commitment to addressing the situation of the Dalits. Members of the UN

153 Thornberry (n 20) 119.
154 UN World Conference Against Racism, Racial Discrimination, Xenophobia and Related Intolerance – Declaration. The aim of the WCAR was to 'create a new world vision for the fight against racism in the twenty-first century'. The UN world conferences against racism in 1978 and 1983 had focused primarily on apartheid in South Africa; see UNGAR 32/129, 16 December 1977; UNGAR 335/33, 14 November 1980.
155 Thornberry (n 20) 120. See also Chapter 5.
156 Ibid.
157 Thornberry (2005) (n 50) 264.
158 'Thematic debates are not a departure from ICERD's formal structures and processes but a manifestation of members' desire to develop their expertise in a particular direction'; Thornberry (2004), 'Race, Descent and Caste under ICERD' (n 84) 126.
159 CERD/C/SR.1531, 16 August 2002, para 1.
160 CERD/C/SR.1493, 12 November 2002, paras 38–44.
161 S Prasad, Dalit Human Rights Watch, Transcript of contemporaneous unofficial notes of informal discussion, 8 August 2002 (copy on file with author). There is no formal record of the meeting on 8 August 2002.

Sub-Commission felt that the problem of caste, and the debate, should not focus only on one country.[162]

In the thematic debate, CERD members noted the wide scope of descent, which encompassed but was not restricted to caste.[163] Pillai stressed that 'the scope and meaning of [ICERD] must be seen as inclusive rather than exclusive'.[164] The terms "descent-based discrimination", "members of descent-based communities" and "analogous systems of inherited status" were chosen to avoid focusing solely on caste discrimination or on specific states. As a basis of discrimination, the term "descent" signified forms of inherited status, said Thornberry. Caste systems, he argued, represented hierarchy, not equality; segregation, not integration; bondage, not freedom; and value determined at birth without regard for morality, achievement, intelligence or character. The issue of descent was wider than the notion of caste, the evidence of such discrimination was a matter of fact, and final, strict definitions were not necessary. Rather than trying to find a definition for the concept, the general recommendation should identify a set of indicators which would be of assistance to governments.[165]

GR 29 paragraph 1 on general measures to be taken by States parties explains that descent-based communities

> are those who suffer from discrimination, especially on the basis of caste and analogous systems of inherited status, and whose existence may be recognized on the basis of various factors including some or all of the following: inability or restricted ability to alter inherited status; socially enforced restrictions on marriage outside the community; private and public segregation, including in housing and education, access to public spaces, places of worship and public sources of food and water; limitation of freedom to renounce inherited occupations or degrading or hazardous work; subjection to debt bondage; subjection to dehumanizing lack of respect for their human dignity and equality.[166]

On the use of ICERD to address caste discrimination, Thornberry explains that 'if the various "grounds" of discrimination in Article 1 do not immediately translate themselves into recognisable varieties of community vulnerable to discrimination, the practice of the Committee has served to put a human face to the targets of discriminatory practices'.[167] He argued that caste or analogous forms of social stratification are 'appropriately brought within the frame of Article 1', because they have 'a "race-like" quality on a par with the other descriptors in Article 1. . . even if the surest of the specific descriptors [in Article 1] remains that of "descent"'.[168] On the use of descent for capturing caste, Thornberry explains that descent is a term 'which suggests a wide span of possibilities',[169] i.e. it

> has the most open character, since all human beings have a "descent." However much it may shade into other concepts, it is an appropriate term to act as a normative safety net

---

162 Ibid.
163 CERD, Thematic Discussion on Discrimination based on Descent, 9 August 2002; UN Doc. CERD/C/ SR.1531, 16 August 2002. paras 3, 6, 13, 16, 17, 20, 33.
164 Ibid., paras 7, 8.
165 Ibid., paras 11, 13.
166 The following section on GR 29 paragraph 1 is drawn from Waughray and Keane (n 147).
167 Thornberry (n 50) 257–258.
168 Thornberry (n 84) 122.
169 Thornberry (n 27) 37.

for clear cases of group-based discrimination based on inherited characteristics which are not easily caught by other, narrower descriptors.[170]

In this respect, he writes,

[T]he thrust of the Convention towards the elimination of "all forms" of racial discrimination suggests that an expansive reading of its scope is not unreasonable. There are overlaps among the Article 1 descriptors, and the *travaux* suggest that not every descriptor was clearly understood as marking out a sharply defined conceptual space or class of victim.[171]

Through the "living instrument" principle, human rights protection can be, and has been, extended to groups who are not directly referred to in existing instruments. Thus, the 'normative quality of the step taken by CERD' should not be exaggerated; CERD has also elaborated 'recommendations on minorities and indigenous peoples which are also not referred to in the body of the Convention'.[172]

The perspectives of victims 'greatly' impressed CERD members, according to Thornberry;[173] the Preamble refers specifically to CERD's receipt of oral and written information from individuals and NGOs which provided further evidence of the extent and persistence of descent-based discrimination around the world. CERD considered the issue of cultural intrusion during the thematic debate, but ultimately CERD could not accept a 'cultural' defence of caste 'when there is massive disaffection and dissent, and group "membership" is heavily contested'.[174] While the target of GR 29 is discrimination on the basis of descent (including caste discrimination), rather than caste or any other particular cultural or social system, the distinction, as Thornberry readily acknowledges, is 'a thin one'.[175] His observation speaks to the paradox of attacking caste discrimination but not the concept of caste itself.

General Comments and General Recommendations are not formally binding on States parties, but the status of the treaty-monitoring committees gives them 'a special claim for attention'.[176] All treaty bodies with competence to adopt General Comments or Recommendations have used them to interpret the provisions of the treaties which they monitor despite the absence of explicit authority to do so.[177] On the one hand, governments have challenged them as 'representing an unwarranted and unacceptable attempt to attribute to

---

170 Thornberry (n 84) 123.

171 Thornberry (n 50) 258.

172 Thornberry (n 84) 119–120.

173 Thornberry (n 50) 264.

174 UN Doc. CERD/C/SR.1531 (n 159), paras 12, 30–31; Thornberry (n 27) 42–43; Thornberry (n 50) 264.

175 Thornberry, ibid.

176 H Steiner, 'Individual Claims in a World of Massive Violations: What Role for the Human Rights Committee?' in P Alston and J Crawford (eds.), *The Future of UN Human Rights Treaty Monitoring* (Cambridge: Cambridge University Press, 2000) 15–54, 52. See also P Alston, 'The Historical Origins of the Concept of "General Comments" in Human Rights Law', in L Boisson de Chazournes and V Gowlland-Debbas (eds.), *The International Legal System in Quest of Equity and Universality* (The Hague: Martinus Nijhoff, 2001) 763–776, 764.

177 See Steiner, ibid. See also I Boerefijn, *The Reporting Procedure Under the Covenant on Civil and Political Rights: Practice and Procedures of the Human Rights Committee* (Antwerp: Intersentia, 1999) 295, citing CCPR/C/133, Report on the informal meeting on procedures, para 57.

treaty provisions a meaning which they do not have';[178] on the other hand, such challenges serve to draw attention to the relevant interpretation and 'help to establish it as a benchmark against which alternative interpretations will be forced to compete at something of a disadvantage'.[179] While states generally concur with treaty bodies on questions of interpretation and 'rarely put forward their own interpretations of specific rights',[180] this is not always the case; India claims that CERD's interpretation of descent as covering caste amounts to 'a redefinition of its mandate'.[181] By refusing to accept CERD's interpretation, India has asserted a right to an equal interpretive role. Japan has also rejected CERD's interpretation of descent and its application to the nation's Buraku people, a group which CERD has repeatedly identified as falling within the ambit of ICERD.[182] By contrast, Pakistan, Nepal, Bangladesh and the UK have not challenged CERD's application of descent to caste.

4.4.7 Beyond General Recommendation 29

In 2006, in its fifteenth to nineteenth reports, India reiterated that "caste" could not be equated with ' "race" nor was it covered under "descent" under Article 1 of the Convention'.[183] During CERD's oral examination of India's report in February 2007, India again reiterated its position that caste-based discrimination was an issue outside the purview of racial discrimination under Article 1(1) of ICERD,[184] and since its Constitution distinguished between caste, race and descent as separate concepts, its government 'had no doubt that the ordinary meaning of the term "racial discrimination" did not include caste'.[185]

When questioned on its proposal to include descent on the grounds of prohibited discrimination during the *travaux préparatoires*, India stated that this 'had been based on concerns regarding discriminatory treatment against Indians in their own land while under colonial rule, and to persons of Indian descent in countries where they had settled in large numbers'; there was nothing that supported the contention that descent was intended to include caste as an aspect of racial discrimination.[186] The reference by Saksena (the Indian representative) to Scheduled Castes during the drafting of the *travaux préparatoires* was

> for the limited purpose of protecting the special measures constitutionally sanctioned in the Indian Constitution for the historically disadvantaged Scheduled Castes. It had

178 Alston (n 176) 764. For example, the Human Rights Committee's GC No. 24 (1994) on reservations provoked objections from the USA and the UK; see Mullally (n 127) 92.
179 Alston (n 176), ibid., 765; Boerefijn (n 177) 300. The development of Human Rights Committee General Comment No. 34 (2011) on article 19 (freedoms of opinion and expression) illustrates the value of state input for the success of general comments; see M O'Flaherty, 'International Covenant on Civil and Political Rights: Interpreting Freedom of Expression and Information Standards for the Present and the Future', in T McGonagle and Y Donders (ed.), *The United Nations and Freedom of Expression and Information: Critical Perspectives* (Cambridge: Cambridge University Press, 2015) 55–88.
180 K Mechlem, 'Treaty Bodies and the Interpretation of Human Rights', 42(3) *Vanderbilt Journal of Transnational Law* (2009) 905–948, 920.
181 India, Concluding Statement, CERD 70th session, 26 February 2007, para 6. Likewise, states have objected by reference to the doctrine of domestic jurisdiction where treaty bodies have asserted competence to determine the validity of reservations; Mullally (n 127) 92, 95.
182 See UN Doc. CERD/C/JPN/Q/3–6/Add.1/Rev.1, 8 February 2010, paras 9, 10; CERD/C/JPN/CO/3–6, 6 April 2010, para 8. On the Buraku, see RKW Goonesekere, Working Paper on the topic of discrimination based on work and descent; E/CN.4/Sub.2/2001/16, 14 June 2001, paras 40–42.
183 CERD/C/IND/19, 19 March 2006, para16.
184 UN Doc. CERD/C/SR.1796, 2 March 2007, para 3.
185 CERD/C/SR.1796, ibid., para 7.
186 Ibid., para 8.

no relation to the definition of racial discrimination nor did it have anything to do with the word "descent." In view of the above, the use of the expression "descent" cannot be used to assert that the term "descent" as used in Article 1 (1) has a special meaning and that it must be taken as including caste-based discrimination.[187]

Logically, however, if India's constitutional special measures for the Scheduled Castes had nothing to do with racial discrimination, there was no need to refer to them during the preparatory debates, and no need for protection for such measures 'in a future scenario' to be built in to ICERD. Put another way, Saksena's assertion in 1965, that Article 1(4) applied to India's system of reservations for the Scheduled Castes, makes no sense unless caste is included, expressly or impliedly, within the ambit of ICERD Article 1(1).[188]

In its concluding observations to India in 2007, CERD noted India's view but maintained its position as expressed in GR 29, i.e. that discrimination based on caste was fully covered by Article 1 of the Convention.[189] India argued that CERD had only raised the issue of caste-based discrimination as a form of discrimination based on descent some thirty years after ICERD's establishment,[190] suggesting that CERD had 'redefined' – and therefore acted outside – its mandate.[191]

Although India's domestic distinctions between caste, race and descent are not binding on CERD, and cannot relieve India of its obligations under ICERD, it asserted that all discussion on the concept of caste 'must be within the parameters set out by the [Indian] Constitution'. Consequently, India was 'not in a position to accept reporting obligations on that issue under the Convention'.[192] By not reporting to CERD since 2006, India has avoided scrutiny of its compliance with its obligations under ICERD, including its measures to eliminate caste discrimination.

4.5 Descent

4.5.1 Origins of descent as a legal category

As explained earlier, "descent" was introduced into ICERD by India, but it was probably not intended to include caste.[193] Descent appears in Article 16(2) of the Constitution of

---

187 CERD, A/62/18 (2007), Annex X. See also Solicitor General's intervention, 26 February 2007, n 83, paras 28, 30.

188 India may have assumed that its need for Article 1(4) protection for its reservations regime would be short-lived, because it believed that caste was a disappearing social institution and hence that the reservations regime would be of short duration.

189 UN Doc. CERD/C/IND/CO/19, 5 May 2007, para 8.

190 See UN Doc. CERD/C/SR.1796 (n 90).

191 India, Concluding Statement, CERD, 70th Session, consideration of India's nineteenth report, 26 February 2007.

192 CERD/C/SR.1796 (n 90), para 3. India also rejects the application of ICERD to its *Adivasis* or Scheduled Tribes – despite CERD General Recommendation No. 23 (1997) on indigenous peoples, which reaffirms ICERD's application to indigenous peoples – on the grounds that the Indian Government 'regarded the entire population of India at independence, with the departure of the colonizers, and their successors to be indigenous'; see 'Committee on Elimination of Racial Discrimination Considers Report of India', UN Press Release, 26 February 2007; CERD/C/SR.1797, 26 March 2007, para 15 (original in French). Indigenous people's rights in international law are applicable to groups deemed "indigenous peoples" in postcolonial contexts, according to the African Commission on Human Rights' decision in the "Endorois" case; see J Gilbert, 'Indigenous People's Human Rights in Africa: The Pragmatic Revolution of the African Commission on Human and People's Rights' (60) *International & Comparative Law Quarterly* (2011) 245–270.

193 See D Keane, 'Descent-Based Discrimination in International Law: A Legal History', 11 *International Journal of Minority and Group Rights* (2005) 93–116.

India 1950 (COI), which lists the prohibited grounds of discrimination in relation to public sector or state employment, where it is enumerated separately from caste.[194] It was inserted in order to cover discrimination 'in the matter of distribution of offices and appointments in the State' on account of descent,[195] by which was meant discrimination 'on account of dynasty or family status'.[196] As a social category in India, descent calls up notions of common ancestry, common blood and membership of closed, birth-status groups, whether based on caste, lineage affiliation, religion or language.[197] As a legal category, descent is of British origin, namely section 87 of the Government of India Act 1833,[198] the purpose of which was to prohibit racial and religious discrimination against Indians in employment under the East India Company (the forerunner of state employment), who at that time were employed almost exclusively in subordinate positions irrespective of ability or competence.[199] "Descent" connoted geographical origins and racial ancestry.[200] It appears again, a century later, in section 298(1) of the Government of India (GOI) Act 1935 – on which the Constitution of India 1950 was based – as a prohibited ground of discrimination in state employment, alongside religion, place of birth and colour.[201] The notion of descent as a domestic law characteristic distinct from caste is reinforced by section 298(2)(b) of the 1935 Act, which qualifies the prohibition of discrimination in section 298(1):

> Nothing in this section shall affect the operation of any law which recognizes the existence of some *right, privilege or disability attaching to members of a community by virtue of some personal law or custom.*[202]

The prohibition of discrimination on the basis of descent was thus subordinated in the GOI Act 1935 to any caste or religion-based ("community") disabilities – or privileges – deriving from personal or customary law in force at the time. In other words, while discrimination *between Europeans and Indians* in the fields of employment, trade and business was prohibited by the 1935 Act on grounds of religion, place of birth, descent or colour, discrimination *between Indians* in the same fields on *grounds of caste* was explicitly exempted.

4.5.2 Descent in Indian jurisprudence post-1947

In the 1948 Constituent Assembly debates, the prohibition of discrimination based on descent in Article 16(2) was explained as meaning a prohibition, in the context of state employment, of nepotism, favouritism or preferential treatment for those from a particular

---

194 COI Article 16(2) provides, 'No citizen shall, on grounds only of religion, race, caste, sex, descent, place of birth, residence or any of them, be ineligible for, or discriminated against in respect of, any employment or office under the State'. Descent does not appear in COI Articles 15(1) and (2), which respectively prohibit discrimination by the state and by public and private actors in legally regulated spheres on grounds of religion, race, caste, sex and place of birth.
195 Shri RajBahdur, CAD Vol. VII (n 93) 650.
196 Ibid. See also Keane (n 51) 235.
197 A Beteille, 'Race and Descent as Social Categories in India', 96(2) *Daedalus* (1967) 444–463, 454.
198 See Lester and Bindman (n 88).
199 Ibid., 384.
200 Ibid., 390.
201 See https://www.legislation.gov.uk/ukpga/1935/2/pdfs/ukpga_19350002_en.pdf. The rubric to s. 298 reads 'Persons not to be subjected to disability by reason of race, religion, etc.'.
202 GOI Act 1935 s. 298(2)(b) (emphasis added).

family or dynastic background.[203] Indian case law since 1950 indicates that the term has been applied in the context of public-sector employment to prohibit 'hereditary' appointments or appointments 'by succession'.[204] *Prima facie*, the appointment of a son, daughter, widow or near relative of a government employee to that employee's post, for example where the employee has retired, or to a post in the same department because of a familial connection to the employee, would be tantamount to an appointment on the basis of descent and therefore violative of Article 16(2) – unless an exception applies, for example in the event of an employee's death in service.[205] Descent in the Indian legal context has thus been a "chameleon" term whose meaning and usage have evolved over time to meet changing legal and social needs.

4.5.3 *Descent and evolutionary interpretation*

In 2007, in its dialogue with CERD, India asserted that the ordinary meaning of the term "racial discrimination" did not include caste, and that 'the Indian caste system was not racial in origin' but was 'an institution unique to India and had not entered into the considerations of those who drafted the Convention'. Additionally, caste could not be considered as descent, which signified 'genealogically demonstrable characteristics'.[206]

CERD, for its part, from the moment it first directed its attention to discrimination based on caste, has maintained that caste is captured by the concept of descent in ICERD. Thornberry explained,

> [i]n international law, an *evolutionary interpretation* of terms was common practice; [CERD] had, over time, developed a broad interpretation of the term "descent" and was of the view that the language contained in the Convention was adequate to capture the notion of caste-based discrimination. It was important to bear in mind the main purpose of investigating racial discrimination as practiced by institutions, individuals or organisations – namely, to engage in public reflection and dialogue and thereby address deep-rooted social patterns of discrimination.[207]

On the question of whether by addressing caste, CERD was 'intruding into historical, cultural or religious systems', Thornberry observed during the debate on GR 29 'it might equally be asked whose culture was involved and who spoke for that culture';[208] the 'overwhelming evidence of oppression' suffered by the Dalits as subjects of the caste system 'could hardly escape the attention of CERD in the light of its duty to be faithful to the norms of the Convention'. Descent is the 'closest descriptor' for caste and analogous forms of social stratification and it is

> an appropriate term to act as a normative safety net for clear cases of group-based discrimination based on inherited characteristics which are not easily caught by other, narrower descriptors.[209]

203 Shri Raj Bahadur, CAD Vol. VII (n 93).
204 *Yogender Pal Singh & Ors. v Union of India & Ors.*, 1987 AIR 1015.
205 *V Sivamurthy v State of Andhra Pradesh & Ors.*; Supreme Court of India, Civil Appeal No. 4210 (2003); *Auditor General of India v G Ananta Rajeswara Rao*, 1994 AIR 1521; *Rashmi Dwivedi v State of U.P. and Ors.* (2002) 94 AWC 3065.
206 CERD/C/SR.1796 (n 90), paras 7, 8, 13.
207 Ibid., (n 90), para 36.
208 CERD/C/SR.1531 (n 159), para 12.
209 Thornberry (n 84), 122, 123.

CERD's affirmation of the place of caste discrimination within the framework of ICERD through descent is an illustration of 'the possibilities inherent in elaborating existing instruments on human rights to benefit particular communities, even in the absence of direct reference to the community in question'.[210] Both CERD and India have called up the ICERD *travaux préparatoires* to support their understanding of descent. Treaty interpretation, contends Klabbers, is 'a highly political exercise, continuing the politics of negotiation after the treaty's entry into force'. *Travaux préparatoires* constitute a political and historical, as well as a legal, record, and yet they remain 'an elusive concept'. As Klabbers points out, the intentions of the drafters may not always be cognisable; indeed, there 'may not be much of a common intention among treaty drafters', and states may 'enter into negotiations with various, possibly widely diverging goals in mind'. Invoking the *travaux préparatoires* may 'introduc[e] a static element into a treaty' – undesirable in the context of human rights treaties but which for particular actors – usually states – may be a desirable outcome. Conversely, the *travaux préparatoires* may be invoked to show that the drafting history does not preclude a particular (often more teleological) interpretation of the text.[211] Either way, argues Klabbers, recourse to the *travaux préparatoires* is an acknowledgement of the political nature of treaties.

Faced with India and Japan's recourse to the ICERD *travaux préparatoires* in support of their interpretations of descent, CERD has sought to emphasise the text of ICERD and subsequent practice instead of the *travaux*. During CERD's examination of Japan's combined third to sixth reports in February 2010, Thornberry, referring to the debates in the *travaux préparatoires* on the substitution of descent for national origin,[212] stressed that the *travaux* were 'supplementary; *the text of the Convention and subsequent practice should be used as the primary means of interpretation*'.[213]

4.5.4 Domestic jurisdiction, sovereignty and caste

Eide and Alfredsson recount how, during the drafting of the UDHR, the US emphasised the non-binding nature of the Declaration and that, according to their interpretation of the UN Charter, treatment of their African American population 'involve[d] only issues which are matters "essentially within the domestic jurisdiction" of the United States'.[214] Likewise, India has construed enquiry by CERD into caste issues as an unlawful intervention in its internal affairs,[215] its approach to caste discrimination being that it is an internal matter

---

210 Ibid., 120.
211 J Klabbers, 'International Legal Histories: The Declining Importance of *Travaux Préparatoires* in Treaty Interpretation?' 50 *Netherlands International Law Review* (2003) 267–288, 271.
212 UN Doc. CERD/C/SR.1987, 4 March 2010, para 10.
213 Ibid. (emphasis added).
214 A Samnoy, 'The Origins of the Universal Declaration of Human Rights', in Eide and Alfredsson (eds.) (n 20) 3–25, 9. In 1936, Dr BR Ambedkar wrote to WEB Du Bois, the Black American scholar and race activist, regarding 'the similarity between the position of the Untouchables in India and the position of the Blacks in America', adding '[t]he Blacks of America have filed a petition to the UNO. The Untouchables of India are thinking of following suit'; S Thorat and Umakant, 'Introduction', in Thorat and Umakant (ed.) (n 1), xxix. See also Chapter 1.
215 UN Sub-Commission, Resolution 2004/17, Discrimination based on work and descent, 12 August 2004; UN Doc. E/CN.4/Sub.2/2004/48, 21 October 2004, 48; see Statement by India, 12 August 2004, at www.indianet.nl/r040812.html. India is not alone in its resistance to UN supervision; as regards factors limiting the impact of UN human rights treaties, '[t]here is ample evidence . . . that because governments guard jealously over their sovereignty, they resist international supervision and

beyond the scope of ICERD, and that domestic law is sufficient to deal with it.[216] In February 2007, before CERD, India stated that any dialogue and discussion with international bodies on caste discrimination issues must be 'within the parameters of the Constitution' and that therefore India was not in a position to accept reporting obligations under ICERD on the issue of caste discrimination.[217]

India also suggested that international scrutiny by CERD of caste discrimination may hinder domestic efforts to overcome the problem, referring to its 'impressive array of constitutional, legal and administrative measures' to 'empower the Scheduled Castes', which 'enjoyed broad political consensus'.[218] Given the 'impressive gains' since the Constitution, it was India's concern that 'nothing should be done to introduce elements *which can only detract from such endeavours*'.[219] Moreover, there were 'enormous political and social sensitivities involved'.[220] India's position, namely that its national Constitution – not its treaty obligations under ICERD – must form the sole legal basis for addressing caste discrimination,[221] is in marked contrast to its argument in 1946 that South Africa's 'domestic jurisdiction' defence of discrimination against persons of Indian origin was morally, as well as legally, untenable (see Chapter 2).

4.5.5 *Beyond India and beyond caste: CERD and descent-based discrimination worldwide*

CERD has repeatedly clarified the meaning of the grounds enumerated in Article 1, in concluding observations and in various General Recommendations, emphasising that the concept of racial discrimination is 'much broader than that perceived by many States which argue that there is no racial discrimination on their territory'[222] and expressing regret at the

> limited understanding by many States parties regarding the meaning and scope of the definition of the concept of racial discrimination in Article 1 of the Convention . . . which may lead some States to deny or minimize the extent of racial discrimination in their territory.[223]

Since 1996, CERD has repeatedly affirmed that descent has its own distinct meaning and should not be 'confused with race or ethnic or national origin'.[224] Using "descent", CERD

---

are reluctant to implement views and recommendations'; C Heyns and Frans Viljoen, 'The Impact of the United Nations Human Rights Treaties on the Domestic Level', 23(2) *Human Rights Quarterly* (2001) 483–535, 517.

216 See, for example, CERD/C/SR.1796 (n 90), para 3. India is accused by Dalit advocacy groups of branding Dalit activists as 'anti-national' and of 'seek[ing] to domesticate the problem as an internal affair'; Decade of Dalit Rights UN, Declaration, at http://idsn.org/fileadmin/user_folder/pdf/New_files/UN/Printer_Friendly_Declaration_Decade_Dalit_Rights.pdf.

217 India, Introductory Statement, CERD, 70th session, 23 February 2007, para 8.

218 India, Concluding Statement (n 191), para 2.

219 Ibid., para 3 (emphasis added).

220 Ibid.

221 India, Introductory Statement (n 217), paras 5–8.

222 See CERD Replies to OHCHR questionnaire (n 136) 12.

223 Ibid., 3.

224 Concluding Observations – Japan; CERD, Report; UN Doc. A/56/18 (2001), para 166; UN Doc. CERD/C/SR.1987, 4 March 2010, para 10.

has enquired into and commented on caste-based discriminatory practices in India,[225] Nepal,[226] Pakistan[227] and Bangladesh[228] and has raised the issue of caste-based discrimination occurring in countries with a significant South Asian diaspora population, such as the UK.[229] CERD has also used "descent" in its wider sense to enquire into discriminatory practices in countries outside South Asia (e.g. Japan and certain African states) based on analogous systems of inherited status, often related to inherited occupation.[230]

Caste exists in both Nepal and Pakistan, countries which have accepted (or at least have not objected to) CERD's interpretation of descent as including caste, and hence CERD's authority to enquire about and to scrutinise measures taken in their countries to prevent, prohibit and eliminate caste-based discrimination.[231] Yet, despite the existence of constitutional provisions in both countries prohibiting discrimination on grounds of caste,[232] and a constitutional provision in Nepal prohibiting and criminalising untouchability,[233] CERD, in its most recent concluding observations to both countries, expressed concern about continuing de facto discrimination against Dalits on grounds of caste, including de facto residential and occupational segregation and social exclusion and sexual and other forms of violence against Dalit women and girls.[234] In the case of Pakistan, the absence of legislation which defines racial discrimination in conformity with Articles 1 and 2 of ICERD was also raised.[235] In 2011, Nepal adopted the Caste-based Discrimination and Untouchability (Offence and Punishment) Act, a 'landmark law' which was welcomed by the then UN High Commissioner for Human Rights, Navi Pillay, as providing new remedies for victims, improving their access to justice and increasing public and civil society awareness of caste-based discrimination and the means to fight it.[236] Nevertheless, awareness of the legislation, even among the police, is low, victims are reluctant to use it, the police are reluctant to enforce it and, according to CERD, de facto discrimination against Dalits persists;[237] notwithstanding the legisla-

---

225 CERD, Concluding Observations – India (1996) (n 6). CERD, Concluding Observations – India (2007) (n 143), paras 8, 9, 13–15, 17, 18, 20–27.

226 Concluding Observations – Nepal; UN Doc. CERD/C/64/CO/5, 28 April 2004, paras 11, 12.

227 Concluding Observations – Pakistan; UN Doc. CERD/C/PAK/CO/20, 16 March 2009, para 12.

228 Concluding Observations – Bangladesh; UN Doc. CERD/C/304/Add.118, 27 April 2001, para 73. At the time of writing, Bangladesh's next report to CERD, due in 2002, has not been submitted.

229 Concluding Observations – UK; UN Doc. CERD/C/63/CO/11, 10 December 2003, para 25; Concluding Observations – UK; UN Doc. CERD/C/GBR/CO/18–20, 14 September 2011, para 30.

230 See section 4.5.5.

231 See Concluding Observations – Nepal; UN Doc. CERD/C/64/CO/5, 26 April 2004, paras 4, 5, 11, 12; Concluding Observations – Pakistan: UN Doc. CERD/C/PAK/CO/20, 16 March 2009, paras 11, 12, 19, 21.

232 Constitution of Pakistan 1973, Articles 26(1), 27(1); Constitution of Nepal 2015, Articles 17–19. In Nepal, Dalits constitute between 16 and 20% of the population, or almost five million people. In Pakistan, Dalits number approximately 330,000 (1998 census), but according to researchers the real figure may be two million, or even higher; International Dalit Solidarity Network, Caste-based discrimination in Pakistan: Briefing Note (2014) at https://idsn.org/wp-content/uploads/user_folder/pdf/New_files/Pakistan/Pakistan_briefing_note.pdf.

233 Constitution of Nepal 2015, ibid., Article 24.

234 CERD, Concluding Observations – Nepal; UN Doc. CERD/C/NPL/CO/17–23, 11 May 2018, paras 10–36; CERD, Concluding Observations – Pakistan; UN Doc. CERD/C/PAK/CO/21–23, 3 October 2016, paras 19–20, 27–28, 31–32.

235 CERD, Concluding Observations – Pakistan (2009), ibid., para 12.

236 See Navi Pillay, Statement, House of Lords, London, 6 November 2013 at https://newsarchive.ohchr.org/EN/NewsEvents/Pages/DisplayNews.aspx?NewsID=13973&LangID=E.

237 W Pun, 'Untouchability Crime: Many "Unaware" of Discrimination Law', *Kathmandu Post*, 1 June 2014; CERD, Concluding Observations – Nepal (n 234), paras 11–12; HRC, Concluding Observations – Nepal (2014); UN Doc. CCPR/C/NPL/CO/2, 15 April 2014, para 9.

tion, discrimination on grounds of caste was identified by activists, academics and CERD in the provision of disaster recovery assistance in the wake of Nepal's 2015 earthquake.[238]

Bangladesh is home to an estimated three and a half million to five and a half million Dalits (out of a population of 160 million).[239] The Constitution of Bangladesh forbids discrimination on the grounds of religion, race, caste, sex or place of birth.[240] Bangladesh has not objected to CERD's position that caste falls within the scope of ICERD via descent, claiming in its seventh to eleventh reports in 2000[241] to take a 'broad view of its obligations under the Convention', including pursuing positive discrimination policies in favour of the disadvantaged.[242] Nevertheless, CERD recommended that Bangladesh should include in its next report information about the enjoyment of the rights in Article 5 of ICERD by all groups, including castes.[243] In Sri Lanka, caste discrimination is estimated to affect around four to five million people, or 20–30% of the total population, but is described by the International Dalit Solidarity Network as relatively mild compared to India or Nepal. The Constitution of Sri Lanka lists caste as a non-discrimination ground alongside race, religion, language, sex, political opinion and place of birth, and it forbids restrictions on access to shops, restaurants and places of public worship and other services, on the ground, inter alia, of caste.[244] During CERD's examination of its second report in 1986,[245] Sri Lanka acknowledged the existence of a caste system in the country, explaining not only that it was 'a racial phenomenon not based on any religious factor and was to be found among Tamils and Sinhalese', but also that 'no racial distinction could be made between the Sinhalese and Tamil communities'.[246] Sri Lanka made no reference to caste discrimination in its reports in 1994 and 2000,[247] but its 2015 report did refer to the constitutional prohibition of caste discrimination, albeit no insight was provided into the existence or otherwise of caste discrimination, or of measures or policies to combat it.[248] Caste discrimination was first raised by CERD in its 2016 concluding observations, in the context of caste discrimination against Tamils of Indian origin.[249] CERD requested Sri Lanka to provide information in its next report on the impact of special measures for this community and, pursuant to GR 29, 'to undertake awareness-raising campaigns in the relevant communities, to change attitudes and reject caste'.[250]

Outside South Asia, the existence of descent-based discrimination in its wider sense has been raised by CERD in concluding observations to Japan,[251] Yemen,[252]

238 CERD, Concluding Observations – Nepal (n 234), paras 20–21; see also P Barron, 'Dalits Left Behind as Nepal Slowly Recovers', *Asia Foundation*, 9 April 2017.
239 See International Dalit Solidarity Network, Factsheet for the UPR of Bangladesh 2018.
240 Constitution of Bangladesh 1971, Article 28.
241 UN Doc. CERD/C/379/Add.1, 30 May 2000.
242 Ibid., para 5.
243 Concluding Observations – Bangladesh (n 228), para 11.
244 Constitution of Sri Lanka 1978, Article 12(2) and 12(3).
245 Sri Lanka, second report; CERD/C/126/Add.2, 12 September 1985.
246 CERD, Report; UN Doc. A/42/18 (1987), para 293.
247 Sri Lanka, third to sixth reports; UN Doc. CERD/C/234/Add.1, 13 September 1994; Sri Lanka, seventh to ninth reports; UN Doc. CERD/C/357/Add.3, 20 November 2000.
248 Sri Lanka, tenth to seventeenth reports; CERD/C/LKA/10–17, 7 December 2015, paras 13, 33, 36.
249 Concluding Observations – Sri Lanka; CERD/C/LKA/CO/10–17, 6 October 2016, paras 20–22. Sri Lanka's state report refers to caste only in the context of its constitutional provisions against caste discrimination; see Sri Lanka, tenth to seventeenth reports; CERD/C/LKA/10–17, 7 December 2015.
250 UN Doc. CERD/C/LKA/CO/10–17, ibid.
251 UN Doc. CERD/C/304/ADD.114, 27 April 2001, para 8; CERD/C/JPN/CO/3–6, 6 April 2010, para 8; CERD/C/JPN/CO/7–9, 29 August 2014, para 22.
252 UN Doc. CERD/C/YEM/CO/16, 19 October 2006, paras 8, 9, 15, 16; CERD/C/YEM/CO/17–18, 4 April 2011, para 15.

Nigeria,[253] Madagascar,[254] Mauritania,[255] Senegal,[256] Chad,[257] Mali,[258] Ethiopia,[259] Burkina Faso,[260] Suriname[261] and Ghana.[262] Japan rejects CERD's application of the ground of descent to 'persons belonging to or descending from the Buraku community',[263] a group which CERD had repeatedly identified as falling within the ambit of ICERD,[264] and argues that CERD had misunderstood the meaning of descent in the context of ICERD. In 2001 Japan contended that when descent (together with place of origin) was proposed as a replacement for national origin during the drafting of ICERD, it was not intended to cover social class or social origin[265] – it was proposed because of concerns that "national origin" could lead to a misunderstanding that the term included "nationality" (a concept based on legal status). CERD's response was to affirm that 'the term descent has its own meaning and is not to be confused with race or ethnic or national origin'.[266] In 2010, Japan reiterated its view, arguing that descent in ICERD was intended to 'indicate a concept focusing on the *race or skin colour* of a past generation, or the *national or ethnic origins* of a past generation',[267] prompting Thornberry to reaffirm CERD's position that descent as a ground for discrimination 'carried its own meaning, which was distinct from the other grounds set forth in the Convention'.[268] In its 2010 concluding observations to Japan, CERD reiterated that descent has a meaning and application 'which complement the other prohibited grounds of discrimination' and 'that discrimination based on "descent" includes discrimination against members of communities based on forms of social stratification . . . and analogous systems of inherited status which nullify or impair their equal enjoyment of human rights'.[269]

---

253 UN Doc. CERD/C/NGA/CO/18, 27 March 2007, paras 15, 18, 25.
254 UN Doc. CERD/C/65/CO/4, 10 December 2004, paras 12, 17.
255 CERD/C/65/CO/5, 10 December 2004, para 15.
256 Concluding Observations – Senegal; CERD, Report; UN Doc. A/57/18 (2002), para 445; CERD/C/SEN/CO/16–18, 24 October 2012, para 13.
257 CERD/C/TCD/CO/15, 21 September 2009, para 15; CERD/C/TCD/CO/16–18, 23 September 2013, para 12.
258 UN Doc. CERD A/57/18 (2002), para 406.
259 UN Doc. CERD/C/ETH/CO/7–16, 7 September 2009, para 15.
260 CERD/C/BFA/CO/12–19, 23 September 2013, para 8.
261 CERD/C/SUR/CO/13–15, 28 August 2015, paras 15–16.
262 CERD/C/62/CO/4, 2 June 2003, para 22. A caste-like, hereditary system of social stratification has been identified in North Korea; R Collins, *Marked for Life: Songbun – North Korea's Social Classification System* (Washington, DC: Committee for Human Rights in North Korea, 2012); 'North Korea Caste System "Underpins Human Rights Abuses"', *The Telegraph*, 6 June 2012.
263 Japan, third to sixth reports, Replies to List of Questions; UN Doc. CERD/C/JPN/Q/3–6/Add.1/Rev.1, 8 February 2010, para 10; see RKW Goonesekere, Working Paper on the topic of discrimination based on work and descent; E/CN.4/Sub.2/2001/16, 14 June 2001.
264 See UN Doc. CERD/C/JPN/Q/3–6/Add.1/Rev.1, 8 February 2010, paras 9, 10; CERD/C/JPN/CO/3–6, 6 April 2010, para 8. The Buraku (or Burakumin) are a class of people at the bottom of Japanese society, numbering between 1.2 million and 3 million people. Described as *eta* (extreme filth) and *hinin* (non-human), historically they have been subjected to intense prejudice and discrimination, forbidden to marry or have physical contact with common people, as such contact was seen as "polluting" the higher classes; Goonesekere, ibid., paras 40–42.
265 UN Doc. CERD/C/SR.1444, 11 June 2001, para 28.
266 CERD, Concluding Observations – Japan (n 264); CERD, Report; UN Doc. A/56/18 (2001), para 166.
267 Japan, Replies to List of Questions (n 263), paras 9, 10 (emphasis added).
268 UN Doc. CERD/C/SR.1987, 4 March 2010, para 10.
269 CERD, Concluding Observations – Japan (n 264), para 8.

Japan has responded by disengaging from dialogue with CERD on the meaning and application of descent. Its 2013 periodic report contains no references to descent or the Burakumin peoples (although the Ainu, another discriminated against group, are mentioned).[270] In its 2014 concluding observations, CERD stated its regret relating to Japan's position on the application of descent to the Burakumin, given CERD's general recommendation No. 29 (2002), and recommended that Japan revise its position.[271]

CERD has also raised descent-based discrimination with the UK. In 2003, recalling that descent-based discrimination, including discrimination on the basis of caste and analogous systems of inherited status, is a violation of the Convention, it recommended that the UK introduce in domestic legislation a prohibition of descent-based discrimination.[272] Unlike India, the UK has not objected to CERD's application of descent to caste, and yet it has resisted the Committee's call for legislative action. The UK's Equality Act 2010 contained a discretionary power allowing the government to add caste at a future date as 'an aspect of' the protected characteristic of race in the legislation.[273] In its 2010 report, the UK stated that it had 'seen no firm evidence' on whether caste-based discrimination existed in regulated fields 'to any significant extent in the UK' but intended to commission research on the question.[274] In its 2011 concluding observations, CERD challenged the UK's assertion that evidence of caste discrimination was lacking, pointing out that CERD had received information to the contrary, and recommended that the government amend the Equality Act 2010.[275] In 2013, the discretion to add caste to race was replaced by a duty, but the duty was not complied with. In its 2015 report, the UK Government accepted the need for legal protection against caste discrimination but argued that, based on an employment appeal tribunal decision earlier that year, existing provisions in the Equality Act 2010 (specifically the "ethnic origins" limb of "race") provided sufficient protection from caste discrimination (see Chapter 9). In July 2018, it announced its decision not to amend the Equality Act 2010 to add caste to the definition of race and to repeal the statutory duty to do so, although at the time of writing this has not happened.[276]

4.5.6 *Caste and descent-based discrimination: other treaty bodies*

The final section of this chapter outlines the engagement of other UN treaty bodies with caste discrimination. India is taken as the primary reference point, although Nepal, Pakistan, Bangladesh, Sri Lanka and Japan offer equally useful examples of treaty body engagement with caste and descent-based discrimination. In total, since 1996, twenty states have been addressed by CERD and other treaty bodies on caste-based and descent-based discrimination.[277]

---

270 UN Doc. CERD/C/JPN/7–9, 10 July 2013.
271 CERD CERD/C/JPN/CO/7–9, 26 September 2014, para 22.
272 CERD, Concluding Observations – UK; UN Doc. CERD/C/63/CO/11, 10 December 2003, para 25.
273 Section 9(5)(a) Equality Act 2010 (as enacted).
274 UN Doc. CERD/C/GBR/18–20, 13 August 2010, para 42.
275 CERD, Concluding Observations – UK; UN Doc. CERD/C/GBR/CO/18–20, 14 September 2011, para 30.
276 See Chapter 9. At the time of writing, the duty has not been repealed.
277 For a comprehensive compilation of how UN human rights bodies and mechanisms have addressed caste and descent-based discrimination worldwide, see International Dalit Solidarity Network (IDSN), Caste Discrimination and Human Rights, UN Compilation 17E (January 2022). Eleven states have been addressed solely by CERD; these are Nigeria, Mauritania, Madagascar, Chad, Mali, Ethiopia, Ghana,

India is a party to the International Covenant on Civil and Political Rights (ICCPR);[278] the International Covenant on Economic, Social and Cultural Rights (ICESCR);[279] the Convention for the Elimination of All Forms of Discrimination Against Women (CEDAW);[280] the Convention on the Rights of the Child (CRC)[281] and the Convention on the Rights of Persons with Disabilities (CRPD),[282] in addition to ICERD. It has not objected to addressing, or answering questions on, caste discrimination before the Human Rights Committee (HRC), the Committee on Economic, Social and Cultural Rights (CESCR), the Committee on the Elimination of Discrimination Against Women (CEDAW/C) or the Committee on the Rights of the Child (CRC/C) despite these bodies' characterisations of caste discrimination as an impediment to the enjoyment of treaty rights and, in the case of the HRC and the CESCR, the conceptualisation of caste as a characteristic attracting ICCPR and ICESCR non-discrimination protection. Rather, it is the accusation of *racial* discrimination entailed by CERD's conceptualisation of caste discrimination as a form of descent-based racial discrimination to which India objects, given its experience as both a victim and an opponent of colonialism and its historical role in the anti-colonialism, anti-apartheid and non-aligned movements. Approaches to caste discrimination via categories such as birth, social origin or social status appear to be politically more acceptable and could offer a route to meaningful dialogue and concrete change.

The HRC, CESCR, CEDAW/C and CRC/C have all identified caste discrimination as an impediment to effective implementation of the treaties they monitor.[283] All four treaty bodies have highlighted the persistence of de facto caste discrimination, non-implementation and non-enforcement of legislation and lack of mechanisms to monitor enforcement,[284] the need for greater efforts to eliminate discriminatory practices, including untouchability and caste-motivated violence, and the need to prosecute those responsible, i.e. both state and private actors.[285] CESCR General Comment (GC) No. 20 (2009) on non-discrimination

---

Mauritius, Burkina Faso, Suriname and United Kingdom. One state (Micronesia) has been addressed solely by the Committee on the Rights of the Child.

278 Adopted 16 December 1966. In force 23 March 1976. 999 UNTS 171. Indian ratification 10 April 1979. India has not ratified the ICCPR Optional Protocol allowing individual communications. State reports; UN Doc. CCPR/C/10/Add.8 (1983); CCPR/C/37/Add.13 (1989); CCPR/C/76/Add.6 (1996).

279 Adopted 16 December 1966. In force 3 January 1976. 993 UNTS 3. Indian ratification 10 April 1979. India has not ratified the ICESCR Optional Protocol allowing individual communications. State reports; UN Doc. E/1980/6/Add.34 (1983, Initial, Arts. 10–12); E/1988/5/Add.5 (1989, Initial, Arts. 13–15); E/1984/6/Add.13 (1985, Initial, Arts. 6–9); E/C.12/IND/5 (second to fifth, 2006). Until 1990, the ICESCR reporting procedure required three reports for three different sets of articles. From 1990, the procedure was consolidated; ECOSOC Resolution 1988/4, 24 May 1988.

280 Adopted 18 December 1979. In force 3 September 1981. 1249 UNTS 13. Indian ratification 9 July 1993. State reports; UN Doc. CEDAW/C/IND/1 (1999, Initial); CEDAW/C/IND/2–3 (2005, second and third); CEDAW/C/IND/SP.1 (2009, Special).

281 Adopted 20 November 1989. In force 2 September 1990. 1577 UNTS 3. Indian ratification 11 December 1992. **State reports; UN Doc.** CRC/C/28/Add.10 (1997, Initial); CRC/C/93/Add.5 (2001, second); CRC/C/IND/3–4 (2011, third and fourth). India has ratified Optional Protocols 1 and 2.

282 Adopted 13 December 2006. In force 3 May 2008. 2515 UNTS 3. Indian ratification 1 October 2007.

283 See HRC, Report; UN Doc. A/52/40 (1997) para 420; E/C.12/IND/CO/5 (2008) paras 13, 14, 40, 53; CEDAW/C, Report; A/55/38 (2000) para 52; CRC/C, Report; CRC/C/94, 3 March 2000, para 41.

284 See, for example, HRC, Report; UN Doc. A/52/40 (1997) paras 420, 430; CCPR/C/79/Add.81, 4 August 1997, para 15; CEDAW/C/IND/CO/3, 2 February 2007, paras 28–29; CRC/C, Report, 3 March 2000, ibid., **para 63;** CRC/C/15/Add.228, 26 February 2004, para 25.

285 See, for example, CRC/C, Report (2000), ibid.

in economic, social and cultural rights explicitly locates caste within the ICESCR protected categories of social origin and birth, and implicitly within the "other status" category of economic or social situation.[286] This opens up opportunities for Dalit advocacy groups, as well as the CESCR itself, to make greater use of the ICESCR in challenging the persistence of caste discrimination. Likewise, Dalit groups can also make use of the possibilities inherent in the ICCPR to challenge states on the persistence of de facto caste discrimination and the non-implementation of related legislation. The CESCR has highlighted India's lack of progress in combating bonded labour and the worst forms of child labour (which disproportionately affect Scheduled Caste children), its failure to eliminate harmful traditional practices such as *devadasi* and the problem of trafficking, which disproportionately affects women and children from Scheduled Caste and Scheduled Tribe backgrounds.[287] It has also identified continued discrimination against Dalits in Nepal – with Dalit women and girls suffering multiple forms of discrimination – despite the adoption in 2011 of the Caste Based Discrimination and Untouchability (Offence and Punishment) Act.[288] CRC/C has identified India's caste system as compounding 'poverty, illiteracy, child labour, child sexual exploitation and children living and/or working on the streets' and has expressed concern at the persisting discrimination against children from Scheduled Castes and Scheduled Tribes.[289] Furthermore, CEDAW/C has repeatedly highlighted the intersectional nature of the discrimination suffered by Dalit women (including physical and sexual violence and the institution of *devadasi*),[290] and CRC/C has stressed the importance of comprehensive public education campaigns to prevent and combat caste-based discrimination[291] and the need for disaggregated data relating to caste discrimination and violence.[292]

4.6 Conclusion

International scrutiny of caste discrimination by CERD as a form of descent-based racial discrimination has transformed it from a domestic issue into an international human rights issue. Yet, while CERD's examination of caste-based discrimination under the rubric of descent has not been challenged by states such as Pakistan, Bangladesh, Nepal and the UK, its framing as a form of descent-based racial discrimination covered by ICERD is categorically rejected by India, resulting in a stalemate between CERD and India and raising the question of what CERD can achieve with India on caste if it refuses to engage on the issue. After all, India undertook long ago many of the steps recommended in GR 29, such as legislation and special measures. CERD has examined the problem of descent-based discrimination in a range of countries outside South Asia, for example Japan, Yemen and Mauritania,

---

286 CESCR GC No. 20; UN Doc. E/C.12/GC/20, 2 July 2009, paras 24, 26.
287 See, for example, UN Doc. E/C.12/IND/CO/5, 8 August 2008, paras 13, 14, 19, 25, 27, 53. On the institution of *devadasi* see Chapter 3.
288 E/C.12/NPL/CO/3, 28 November 2014, para 11.
289 See CRC/C, Report (2000) (n 283), para 41. CRC GC No.7 (2005), Implementing child rights in early childhood, explicitly identifies caste as a prohibited ground of discrimination in the context of children's right to non-discrimination; CRC/C/GC/7/Rev.1, 20 September 2006, para 11(b)(iv); CRC/C/IND/CO/3–4, 7 July 2014, para 31.
290 CEDAW/C, Report (2000) (n 283), paras 43, 68, 69, 74, 75; CEDAW/C/IND/CO/3, 2 February 2007, paras 14, 15, 21, 26, 28, 29; CEDAW/C/IND/CO/4–5, 18 July 2014, paras 10, 11, 20, 34, 35.
291 CRC/C, para 63; Concluding Observations – India; CRC/C/15/Add.228, 26 February 2004, para 28.
292 CRC, Concluding Observations – India (2004), Report (2000) (n 283), ibid., para 22.

but India continues to provide the paradigmatic example of caste discrimination, which is the most recognised form of descent-based discrimination. In 2006, CERD member January-Bardill asked India why it regarded ICERD as a threat rather than an opportunity to challenge the caste system, and whether the government could not use ICERD as a tool to assist in the fraternity project aimed at building substantive citizenship. She also challenged the government's assertion that there was no discrimination in the country. While discrimination was not embedded in the law, social practice had discriminatory effects, and she urged the government to consider this point, in order to facilitate a more constructive dialogue with the Committee in future.[293] Human rights treaties with wider grounds, where caste discrimination can be expressed as an impediment to the enjoyment of particular rights rather than as a form of racial discrimination per se, offer an alternative to ICERD as a means of challenging persistent de facto caste discrimination. CERD has repeatedly emphasised that descent is a wider category than caste, and that descent-based discrimination of different types affects a wide range of countries.[294] Japan has also challenged the use of descent to capture discrimination on the basis of inherited status in its territory. The UK with a growing South Asian diaspora population and evidence suggesting the existence of caste discrimination, has failed to draft, implement and enforce domestic legislation explicitly prohibiting caste discrimination in accordance with CERD recommendations in 2003, 2011 and 2016. The UK's legal response to caste discrimination "at home" forms the third part of this book. First, though, Chapter 5 examines the application of other international human rights law standards to caste discrimination.

293 CERD member January-Bardill, CERD/C/SR.1796 (n 90) paras 47–50.
294 See, for example, CERD GR No. 34 (2011), racial discrimination against people of African descent.

5 Caste discrimination and international human rights law standards

UN Charter bodies

5.1 Introduction

Chapter 4 traced the development of the legal framework for capturing caste discrimination through the category of descent in the International Convention on the Elimination of All Forms of Racial Discrimination (ICERD) and the engagement with caste discrimination by other United Nations (UN) treaty bodies. This chapter examines the contribution of the UN Charter procedures and mechanisms to the development of international law standards on caste discrimination. Chief among these are the former UN Sub-Commission on the Promotion and Protection of Human Rights, the UN Special Procedures (Special Rapporteurs and Working Groups) and the UN Universal Periodic Review mechanism. The chapter also examines the part played by the 2001 UN World Conference Against Racism, Racial Discrimination, Xenophobia and Related Intolerance; the UN minority rights mechanisms; and International Labour Organisation conventions and mechanisms.

Successive post-independence governments in India treated the problem of discrimination against the Dalits as a rather "marginal issue," in that caste was seen as antithetical to modern India, and there was an assumption that discrimination on grounds of caste, untouchability and the problems faced by the Dalits would disappear as India modernised (see Chapter 3).[1] In the immediate post-war years, India's Congress Party sought and secured Dalit political support in return for promises of change, which did not materialise,[2] while for the Left, class (not caste) was the key political and social enemy. Meanwhile, Dalits continued to suffer egregious discrimination; for them, freedom from colonial rule did not mean freedom from caste oppression.

From the 1970s and 1980s onwards, 'new Dalit movements' in India challenged successive governments and Dalit politicians to bring about meaningful change.[3] By the early 1980s, Dalit activists in India and the diaspora, frustrated by the limited success of domestic measures to combat caste discrimination, had turned to the United Nations in an attempt to 'internationalise' their situation as a human rights issue.[4] Over the next decade, they sought

---

1 O Mendelsohn and M Vicziany, *The Untouchables: Subordination, Poverty and the State in Modern India* (Cambridge: Cambridge University Press, 1998) 44, 118.
2 Hugo Gorringe, 'Dalit Politics: Untouchability, Identity and Assertion', in Atul Kohli and Prerna Singh (eds.), *Routledge Handbook of Indian Politics* (London: Routledge, 2012) 119–128, 122; Mendelsohn and Vicziany (n 1) 118.
3 Gorringe (n 2) 122.
4 C Bob, '"Dalit Rights Are Human Rights": Caste Discrimination, International Activism and the Construction of a New Human Rights Issue', 29(1) *Human Rights Quarterly* (2007) 167–193, 175.

DOI: 10.4324/9781315750934-8

to secure international recognition of caste discrimination by lobbying and appearing before a wide variety of international human rights bodies, including the UN Commission on Human Rights, the UN Working Group on Indigenous Peoples, the UN Working Group on Minorities and the Committee on the Rights of the Child, and at the UN World Conference on Human Rights in Vienna in 1993.[5] Their aims were to raise international awareness of caste discrimination in India, to secure allies (governments and non-governmental organisations, or NGOs) to pressure India to implement existing domestic law and policies to protect Dalits from discrimination and violence, and to secure recognition of caste discrimination as a distinct human rights violation under international law.[6]

In 1982, an expatriate Dalit activist from North America, Dr Laxmi Berwa, spoke before the former UN Sub-Commission on the Prevention of Discrimination and Protection of Minorities (UN Sub-Commission) on the situation of India's Dalits, calling on the UN to help 'free them and restore their human rights'.[7] Similar testimony was presented before the UN Sub-Commission in 1983 by Baghwan Das, an Indian Supreme Court lawyer and Dalit writer, activist and publisher. Das explained that the first World Conference on Religion and Peace in 1969 in Kyoto had 'discussed the problem of discrimination including the practice of untouchability'.[8] Das made various recommendations, including, presciently, the establishment of a commission to investigate and report 'on the practice of Untouchability in the countries wherever it is practised', and the enactment of laws to discourage caste discrimination and untouchability by those countries with South Asian diaspora populations where caste discrimination occurs. The same year (1983), Minority Rights Group International (MRG), a London-based non-governmental organisation (NGO), established a Working Group on "untouchables" to inform and influence public opinion, with the aim of the 'total abolition of Untouchability',[9] co-sponsoring a conference in New York in November 1983, 'Minority Strategies: Comparative Perspectives', to 'examine and compare race relations in the West and the issue of Untouchability in Asia'.[10] However, it was not until 2000 that the UN Sub-Commission adopted a resolution on caste discrimination – not in direct terms but through the creation of a new legal category, discrimination based on work and descent.

---

5 Ibid., 175, 177; C Lennox, 'Norm-Entrepreneurship on Caste-Based Discrimination', in D Mosse and L Steur (eds.), *Caste Out of Development? The Cultural Politics of Identity and Economy in India and Beyond* (London: Routledge, 2015).

6 Bob (n 4) 175.

7 Testimony by Dr Laxmi Berwa to the UN Sub-Commission on the Prevention of Discrimination and Protection of Minorities, Geneva, 31 August 1982, in B Joshi (ed.), *Untouchable: Voices of the Dalit Liberation Movement* (London: Zed Books, 1986) 136–139, 137. In his speech, Berwa used the term "untouchable," not "Dalit." On Dalit international activism in the 1980s and 1990s, see C Bob (ed.), *The International Struggle for New Human Rights* (Philadelphia: University of Pennsylvania Press, 2009).

8 Testimony, Bhagwan Das, Chairman, All India Samata Sainik Dal, and Ambedkar Mission Society, UK, to the UN Sub-Commission on the Prevention of Discrimination and Protection of Minorities, 36th Session, Geneva, August 1983. Das was born into a sweeper community and was a key activist in, and scholar and chronicler of, the post-Independence Dalit movement in India until his death in 2010, aged 83.

9 See www.minorityrights.org/; Joshi (n 7) vii.

10 Ibid., ix; G Omvedt et al., 'Conference Features Untouchables in India and Western Minority Condition', 15(6) *The Black Scholar* (1984) 53–55, 53. Other sponsors included inter alia Columbia University, Ambedkar Mission Canada and Carleton College.

5.2 UN Charter mechanisms

5.2.1 *UN Sub-Commission on the Promotion and Protection of Human Rights: discrimination based on work and descent*

The UN Sub-Commission on the Promotion and Protection of Human Rights was established in 1947 as the main subsidiary body of the former UN Commission on Human Rights,[11] charged with undertaking studies on human rights issues and making recommendations concerning the prevention of discrimination of any kind relating to human rights and fundamental freedoms and the protection of racial, national, religious and linguistic minorities. In 2006, the UN Commission on Human Rights was replaced by the Human Rights Council[12] and the UN Sub-Commission by the Human Rights Council Advisory Committee in 2007.

On 11 August 2000, the UN Sub-Commission adopted Resolution 2000/4 declaring discrimination based on work and descent to be a form of discrimination prohibited by international human rights law,[13] against the backdrop of lobbying by Dalit activists prior to the 2001 UN World Conference Against Racism, Racial Discrimination, Xenophobia and Related Intolerance (WCAR) in Durban for caste discrimination to be included in the conference agenda (opposed by the Government of India). The ground for the resolution was laid by three developments: (1) CERD's affirmation in 1996 that caste discrimination falls within the scope of ICERD as a form of descent-based racial discrimination; (2) the publication in 1999 by the NGO Human Rights Watch (HRW) of 'Broken People: Caste Violence Against India's "Untouchables"', a report funded by the Ford Foundation, which had generated international awareness of the situation of India's Dalits;[14] and (3) the creation in 1998 of an India-wide Dalit network, the National Campaign on Dalit Human Rights (NCDHR). The NCDHR's first campaign was a petition demanding that India implement its constitutional abolition of untouchability and legislation prohibiting violence against Dalits, followed in 1999 by the publication of 'Broken Promises and Dalits Betrayed: A Black Paper on the Status of Dalit Human Rights'.[15] In 1998, the first World Dalit Convention was held in Malaysia, attracting Dalit activists from India, South Asia and the diaspora, as well as Buraku activists from Japan.[16] In 2000, the International Dalit Solidarity Network, a transnational Dalit advocacy network based in Copenhagen, was established.[17]

---

11 See www.ohchr.org/EN/HRBodies/SC/Pages/SubCommission.aspx. Until 1999, the Sub-Commission was known as the Sub-Commission on Prevention of Discrimination and Protection of Minorities.

12 The Human Rights Council was created by the UN General Assembly in March 2006 by Resolution 60/251.

13 UN Sub-Commission, Resolution 2000/4, Discrimination based on work and descent (DWD), 11 August 2000; UN Doc. E/CN.4/Sub.2/2000/46, 23 November 2000, 25.

14 See www.hrw.org/reports/1999/india/; Bob (n 4) 178. See also C Bob, '"Dalit Rights Are Human Rights": Untouchables, NGOs and the Indian State', in C Bob (ed.), *The International Struggle for New Human Rights* (Philadelphia: University of Pennsylvania Press, 2009) 30–51, 35–40.

15 See www.ncdhr.org.in/; Bob (n 4). Hard copy on file with author.

16 See www.ambedkar.org/Worldwide_Dalits/first_world_dalit_convention.htm. The Buraku (or Burakumin) are a class of people at the bottom of Japanese society, numbering between 1.2 million and 3 million people. Historically they have been subjected to intense prejudice and discrimination, forbidden to marry or have physical contact with others, as such contact was seen as "polluting" the higher classes; see RKW Goonesekere, Working Paper on the topic of discrimination based on work and descent; UN Doc. E/CN.4/Sub.2/2001/16, 14 June 2001, paras 40–42.

17 See http://idsn.org; Bob (n 1) 180.

UN Sub-Commission Resolution 2000/4 contains no definition of 'discrimination based on work and descent' but asserts the non-discrimination provision in Article 2 of the Universal Declaration of Human Rights (UDHR) as its legal source, noting that discrimination based on work and descent 'has historically been a feature of societies in different regions of the world and has affected a significant proportion overall of the world's population'. The title of the draft resolution (introduced by Sub-Commission member Dr Francoise Hampson of the UK) was 'Discrimination based on occupation and descent', a formulation which combined 'a prohibited ground of discrimination already known in international human rights law ("descent," in the definition of racial discrimination in Article 1 of ICERD) with one 'that was not ("occupation")'. Peter Prove, an NGO lawyer and activist present at the August 2000 meeting, comments that 'the nexus is not self-explanatory' and that

> it is helpful to know, and unlikely to be recorded elsewhere, that the formulation 'discrimination based on occupation and descent' was suggested in the course of an informal conversation by Mr Soli Sorabjee, Sub-Commission member and – incidentally – Indian Attorney General, as a means of avoiding explicit mention of [caste] [as politically unacceptable].[18]

Prove explains that discussion on the draft resolution centred on the French translation of "occupation." To achieve consensus, "occupation" was replaced by "work," in order to use the word *emploi* in the French text.[19] The "work and descent" terminology drew on CERD's application of descent in ICERD to caste and was adopted to avoid focusing on any one state or on caste discrimination alone, thereby locating caste discrimination as a global issue within a wider international human rights category. Resolution 2000/4 appointed RKW Goonesekere, a Sri Lankan jurist, to prepare a Working Paper on discrimination based on work and descent, to identify affected communities, examine existing measures for the abolition of such discrimination and make recommendations for its effective elimination.[20] Goonesekere's paper did not define discrimination based on work and descent, but it did identify the manifestations of such discrimination as commonly including

> prohibitions on intermarriage between socially or occupationally defined groups; physical segregation of communities; restrictions upon access to resources including land, water and other means of production; social prohibitions regarding physical contact such as sharing food or utensils; restrictions on access to education or segregation in educational facilities; restrictions on access to religious buildings and restrictions on participation in religious ceremonies. The most widespread discrimination on the basis

18 P Prove, 'Caste Wars at the Sub-Commission on the Promotion and Protection of Human Rights: A Commentary on the Sub-Commission's On-Going Examination of Discrimination Based on Work and Descent', in K Nakano, M Yutzis, and R Onoyama (eds.), *Peoples for Human Rights, Vol. 9, Descent-based Discrimination* (Tokyo: International Movement Against all Forms of Discrimination and Racism, 2004) 152–161, 152.
19 Ibid., 153.
20 The idea of a Sub-Commission study on discrimination based on caste or descent, or on caste-based and similar discrimination, was suggested by Peter Prove and Paul Diwaker, a Dalit activist with the NGO Anti-Slavery International, at the Sub-Commission meeting on 11 August 2000.

of work and descent occurs in societies in which at least a portion of the population is influenced by the tradition of caste, including the Asian countries of Bangladesh, India, Nepal, Pakistan and Sri Lanka.[21]

Although focused on South Asia (India, Pakistan, Nepal and Sri Lanka) and Japan, the report identified work and descent-based discrimination as a worldwide problem and recommended further study of the human rights violations associated therewith.[22] The reaction to Goonesekere's paper in the UN Sub-Commission was mixed and its findings were not endorsed by the representatives of Pakistan or India.[23] It was decided that an expanded Working Paper should be prepared to address discrimination based on work and descent in other parts of the world. Two subsequent Working Papers by Aisbjorn Eide and Yozo Yokota, in 2003 and 2004, detailed the extent of such discrimination outside South Asia, including in diaspora communities such as the UK, and urged greater national and international examination of the problem.[24] According to Prove, at the presentation of the 2003 expanded paper, India's representative suggested that Sub-Commission resources would be better deployed in addressing 'more egregious violations of human rights'.[25] In August 2004, the Sub-Commission appointed two Special Rapporteurs, Yozo Yokota and Chin-Sung Chung, to prepare a comprehensive study on discrimination based on work and descent and to produce a set of Draft Principles and Guidelines (DPGs) for its effective elimination.[26] India opposed their appointment, arguing that the third (2004) Working Paper had focused almost exclusively on caste, resulting in an artificially narrow interpretation of a very broad issue. Caste, it said, was 'a complex sociological issue' with its roots in the way Indian society had evolved since ancient times, to which there was no simplistic solution: its domestic measures were sufficiently robust, and outside guidance unnecessary,[27] and it would be 'a travesty to treat discrimination based on work and descent as a simple human rights issue'.[28] India argued further that it would be counterproductive for the Sub-Commission to develop a set of principles and guidelines on discrimination based on work and descent; moreover, by addressing issues already covered by other UN bodies, and by focusing almost entirely on one country, the Working Paper had failed to respect the mandate of the Sub-Commission.[29]

---

21 See Goonesekere, Working Paper (n 19), para 8.

22 Ibid., paras 7–8, 49–50.

23 See Prove (n 21) 155.

24 A Eide and Y Yokota, expanded Working Paper on discrimination based on work and descent, UN Sub-Commission; UN Doc. E/CN.4/Sub.2/2003/24, 26 June 2003; Eide and Yokota, further expanded Working Paper, UN Sub-Commission; UN Doc. E/CN.4/Sub.2/2004/31, 5 July 2004. For a discussion of the Sub-Commission reports on discrimination based on work and descent, see D Keane, *Caste-based Discrimination in International Human Rights Law* (Aldershot: Ashgate, 2007) 220–227.

25 See (n 21) 159.

26 UN Sub-Commission, Resolution 2004/17, DWD, 12 August 2004; UN Doc. E/CN.4/Sub.2/2004/48, 21 October 2004, 48. The appointment of the Special Rapporteurs was approved by the former UN Commission on Human Rights (UN Commission) in December 2005; UN Commission, Decision 2005/109; UN Doc. E/CN.4/2005/134 (Part I) (2005) 340.

27 India Committee of the Netherlands, Statement by India, 12 August 2004, to resolution "Discrimination based on work and descent" of the UN Sub-Commission at www.indianet.nl/r040812.html.

28 UN Doc. E/CN.4/Sub.2/2004/SR.8, 10 August 2004, paras 26–27.

29 Ibid.

5.2.2 *UN draft principles and guidelines for the effective elimination of discrimination based on work and descent*

The Special Rapporteurs were mandated to investigate the phenomenon of discrimination based on work and descent, its nature and extent, and to produce DPGs for its elimination. The definition of the phenomenon in the DPGs is modelled on the 'composite' definition of racial discrimination in Article 1(1) of ICERD:

> [A]ny distinction, exclusion, restriction, or preference based on inherited status such as caste, including present or ancestral occupation, family, community or social origin, name, birth place, place of residence, dialect and accent that has the purpose or effect of nullifying or impairing the recognition, enjoyment, or exercise, on an equal footing, of human rights and fundamental freedoms in the political, economic, social, cultural, or any other field of public life. This type of discrimination is typically associated with the notion of purity and pollution and practices of [U]ntouchability and is deeply rooted in societies and cultures where this discrimination is practiced.[30]

The DPGs affirm that discrimination based on work and descent is a form of discrimination prohibited by international human rights law and a major obstacle to achieving development, and they provide a framework for its elimination.[31] They set out the obligations of states to combat segregation; ensure physical security and protection against violence; ensure access to justice and equal political participation; ensure equal employment opportunities and free choice of occupation; eradicate forced, bonded and child labour; ensure equal access to health care, a safe environment, adequate food, water, housing and education and to raise public awareness; and to address specifically multiple/intersectional discrimination against women. The Guidelines are described as articulating specific measures in order to implement the Principles, providing a possible template for domestic legislation. The Special Rapporteurs' final report, including the DPGs, was published by the Human Rights Council in May 2009,[32] and the DPGs were endorsed by Navi Pillay, former UN High Commissioner for Human Rights,[33] the Office of the UN High Commissioner for Human Rights (OHCHR),[34] the UN Special Rapporteur on contemporary forms of racism,[35] the European

---

30 Final report containing draft principles and guidelines (DPGs) for the effective elimination of DWD; UN Doc. A/HRC/11/CRP.3, 18 May 2009, Chapter III, para 2. See also See Y Yokota and C Chung, preliminary report; UN Doc. E/CN.4/Sub.2/2005/30, 21 June 2005; progress report; UN Doc. A/HRC/Sub.1/58/CRP.2, 28 July 2006.

31 Ibid., paras 4, 5; Special Rapporteur on contemporary forms of racism, Interim Report; UN Doc. A/66/313, 19 August 2011, para 41.

32 Human Rights Council Decision 10/117 (27 March 2009); UN Doc. A/HRC/11/CRP.3, 18 May 2009.

33 See International Dalit Solidarity Network (IDSN), Report from Side Event on Draft UN Principles and Guidelines for the elimination of DWD, Geneva, 16 September 2009. See also N Pillay, 'Tearing Down the Wall of Caste', *The Nation*, 19 October 2009. Pillay called on the Human Rights Council to promote the DPGs which 'complement existing international standards of non-discrimination' and urged all states to 'rally round and endorse these norms'. The OHCHR identified countering caste discrimination in Asia and the Pacific as a thematic priority; OHCHR, Strategic Management Plan, 2010–11, 100–101.

34 Statement, Ms. M Kran, OHCHR, DPG Side Event, ibid. (copy on file with author).

35 Special Rapporteur on Racism, Statement, 64th Session, UNGA, 2 November 2009; see also International Dalit Solidarity Network (IDSN), Compilation on Caste Discrimination and Human Rights, 11/E (May 2018).

Union (EU)[36] and the Government of Nepal.[37] However, neither the report nor the DPGs were endorsed or formally adopted by the Human Rights Council.

In 2009, Navi Pillay suggested that a new international Convention on caste may be needed,[38] a call also made by some Dalit activists.[39] This raised the question of whether a declaration on the elimination of discrimination based on work and descent (the first step towards an international treaty) could be developed out of the DPGs. There are three reasons why this was unlikely. First, the definition of discrimination based on work and descent, indeed the concept itself, lacks precision. The term was devised as a way of avoiding focusing specifically on caste discrimination or on India, but the "work and descent" terminology is widely seen as a proxy for caste.[40] Second, state input into the drafting of the DPGs was solicited from all UN member states as well as national human rights institutions, UN bodies and specialised agencies and NGOs, but only Japan, Colombia, Croatia, Germany and Mauritius responded.[41] The lack of input from the main South Asian and African states, where caste and descent-based discrimination exists, weakens their authority. Third, it is questionable whether India would support a declaration on discrimination based on work and descent, given the close conceptual linkage with caste. Conversely, Dalits and transnational advocacy networks consider the DPGs as providing 'an international reference point for action', applicable in their existing format as a framework for the elimination of caste discrimination.[42]

5.2.3 UN Special Procedures

UN Special Procedures are appointed by and report to the Human Rights Council. They are independent human rights experts (Special Rapporteurs, Independent Experts or working groups) with mandates to report and advise on human rights from a thematic or a country-specific perspective.[43] Increasingly, the Special Procedures are involved in shaping international law through their contribution to the development of soft (non-legally binding) law within their mandates.[44] Since the late 1990s, caste discrimination has been taken up by a range of UN Special Procedure mandate-holders,[45] with some jointly addressing caste discrimination as a cross-cutting issue. In May 2013, seven Special Procedures issued a joint statement calling for caste-based discrimination to be addressed as a major structural factor underlying poverty.[46] Caste discrimination has also been acknowledged by the global

36 Statement, Swedish Presidency of the EU, DPG Side Event (n 33).
37 Statement, Government of Nepal, DPG Side Event, ibid.
38 B Crossette, 'Putting Caste on Notice', *The Nation*, 9 November 2009.
39 P Divaker and J Varghese, 'Towards a Unifying Global Identity: A Framework on Discrimination Based on Work and Descent, Including Caste', *Asia Dalit Human Rights Forum*, 42.
40 See, for example, UN Special Rapporteur on Racism, Statement (2009) (n 35). The International Dalit Solidarity Network describes 'work and descent' as 'UN terminology for caste'.
41 See UN Doc. A/HRC/11/CRP.3, 18 May 2009, Introduction, para 9.
42 See IDSN, UN Principles and Guidelines at https://idsn.org/un-2/un-principles-guidelines-on-caste/; Decade of Dalit Rights UN 2011–20, Strategy Building Conference, Report, 24–25 June 2011.
43 See www.ohchr.org/en/hrbodies/sp/pages/introduction.aspx. As of October 2021 there were forty-five thematic and thirteen country mandates.
44 SP Subedi, S Wheatley, A Mukherjee, and S Ngane, 'The Role of the Special Rapporteurs of the United Nations Human Rights Council in the Development and Promotion of International Human Rights Norms', 15(2) *International Journal of Human Rights* (2011) 155–161.
45 On UN Special Procedures see www.ohchr.org/EN/HRBodies/SP/Pages/Welcomepage.aspx.
46 'Continued plight of the "untouchables": UN experts call for strengthened protection of more than 260 million victims of caste-based discrimination', 24 May 2013. The seven experts were the Independent

consultation on the post-2015 development agenda as a source of inequality, with the Special Procedures stressing the need for action to close the inequality gap between Dalits and similar communities and the rest of society,[47] and calling on states to adopt legislation on caste discrimination or to implement it where it already exists.

5.2.3.1 UN Special Rapporteur on contemporary forms of racism, racial discrimination, xenophobia and related intolerance[48]

Caste discrimination in India first came to the attention of then Special Rapporteur on Racism, Glélé Ahanhanzo (1993–2002), in 1996,[49] but it was not until 1999 that he confirmed that India's caste system was within his mandate. He concluded that 'specific attention should be given to the situation of the untouchables in India' and proposed a field mission for that purpose, if the Indian Government agreed.[50] In 2004, mandate-holder Doudou Diène (2002–2008) highlighted the 'persistence and . . . aggravation of discrimination against castes' and recommended an appeal to the member states concerned 'for open and constructive cooperation with the Special Rapporteur for the recognition and treatment of the question of castes'.[51] Since then, Diène and subsequent mandate-holders have repeatedly affirmed that caste discrimination falls within their mandate.[52] The legal – and political – basis for their stance is CERD's General Recommendation (GR) 29 (2002), which affirms that discrimination based on descent under ICERD includes discrimination based on caste and analogous systems of inherited status.[53] By interpreting their mandate in alignment with CERD, successive mandate-holders have affirmed the framing of caste discrimination in international law as a form of racial discrimination. In 2011, mandate-holder Githu Muigai (2008–2011) highlighted discrimination based on caste and analogous systems of inherited

---

Expert on minority issues; Special Rapporteur on violence against women; Special Rapporteur on contemporary forms of slavery; Special Rapporteur on the sale of children, child prostitution and child pornography; Special Rapporteur on contemporary forms of racism, racial discrimination, xenophobia and related intolerance; Special Rapporteur on the human right to safe drinking water and sanitation; Special Rapporteur on extreme poverty and human rights.

47 See, for example, 'Addressing Inequalities: Synthesis Report of Global Thematic Public Consultation on the Post-2015 Development Agenda', February 2013.

48 Mandate created by the UN Human Rights Council in 2008; Human Rights Council resolution 7/34, 28 March 2008, replacing the previous mandate of the same name created by the UN Commission on Human Rights in 1993; Commission resolution 1993/20; see www.ohchr.org/EN/Issues/Racism/SRRacism/Pages/IndexSRRacism.aspx. The Special Rapporteur requested to visit India in 2004, 2006 and 2008, but as at the time of writing, no visit has taken place.

49 UN Doc. E/CN.4/1997/71, 16 January 1997, para 127: 'The attention of the Special Rapporteur has been drawn to the situation of the untouchables in India' (communications, 14 and 29 June and 9 August 1996 from the Ambedkar Centre for Justice and Peace; communication, 31 October 1996 from the World Council of Churches; communication, 1 November 1996 from the Dalit Liberation Education Trust).

50 UN Doc. E/CN.4/1999/15, 15 January 1999, paras 88, 100.

51 See E/CN.4/2004/18, 21 January 2004; summary; para 55.

52 See, for example, Interim Report; A/64/271, 10 August 2009, paras 54–58, 67; Report; A/HRC/7/19, 20 February 2008, paras 69–71; Report; A/HRC/11/36, 19 May 2009, paras 17, 31; Durban Review Conference, Preparatory Committee; UN Doc. A/CONF.211/PC/WG.1/5, 31 July 2008, paras 44–47; Report; A/HRC/17/40, 24 May 2011, paras 26–30; SRR Interim Report, 19 August 2011 (n 31), paras 10, 11, 38–42.

53 See CERD GR No. 29 (2002), Article 1, Paragraph 1 (Descent); SRR Interim Report, 19 August 2011 (n 31), paras 38, 41.

status as a manifestation of 'societal' structural racial discrimination,[54] reminding states of their obligation to recognise that discrimination based on descent, including caste discrimination, is prohibited by ICERD, and not to sidestep the question of caste discrimination by claiming that it does not fall under the scope of the Convention. He also noted the multiple and pervasive nature of caste- and descent-based discrimination, which he said remained 'deplorably widespread and deeply rooted', including in a number of African countries and the Yemen.[55] This understanding of caste and descent-based discrimination as a form of structural and cross-cutting discrimination is seen in the repeated emphasis by mandate-holder Mutuma Ruteere (2011–2017) on the strong correlation between socio-economic inequality and racial discrimination and the link between caste, disproportionate poverty and social, economic and political discrimination and exclusion. In 2018, at the conclusion of her mission to the UK, mandate-holder Tendayi Achiume (2017–) highlighted the legal status of caste-based discrimination in the UK as an 'exceptional concern'.[56]

5.2.3.2 *Other UN Special Procedures*

Caste discrimination has been taken up by other thematic Special Procedures as a root cause of violations of internationally recognised rights, as well as an impediment to accessing and enjoying a spectrum of human rights. Dalits in India, Nepal and Bangladesh have been identified by the Special Rapporteurs on contemporary forms of slavery,[57] adequate housing,[58] the right to food,[59] the right to education,[60] the situation of human rights defenders,[61] violence against women,[62] freedom of religion or belief,[63] the right of everyone to the enjoyment of the highest attainable standard of health,[64] minorities,[65] the

54 See Statement, Intergovernmental Working Group on the Effective Implementation of the Durban Declaration and Programme of Action, Thematic discussion on structural discrimination, 18 October 2010; Report; UN Doc. A/HRC/17/40, 24 May 2011, paras 25–68; SSR Interim Report, 19 August 2011, ibid., paras 10, 11.

55 SSR Interim Report, 19 August 2011, ibid.; Report: UN Doc. A/HRC/17/40, 24 May 2011, paras 56–65; see also Report; UN Doc. A/HRC/17/40, 24 May 2011, paras 3, 88–90.

56 Report; UN Doc. A/HRC/20/33, 15 May 2012, paras 12, 15–16; Report; UN Doc. A/68/333, 19 August 2013, paras 46, 63. On national and international development policy and caste see D Mosse, 'Caste and Development: Contemporary Perspectives on a Structure of Discrimination and Advantage', *World Development* (2018) 110, 422–436. On the Special Rapporteur's 2018 mission to the UK see End of Mission Statement, May 2018, at www.ohchr.org/EN/NewsEvents/Pages/DisplayNews.aspx?NewsID=23073&LangID=E.

57 UN Doc. A/HRC/15/20, paras 69, 72, 99; A/HRC/15/20/Add.2, paras 9, 10, 12, 17, 51; A/HRC/12/21, paras 51, 53.

58 UN Doc. A/HRC/16/42/Add.2, paras 34–39; A/HRC/13/20, paras 16–18; A/HRC/10/7/Add.1, 17 February 2009, paras 52, 54, 55; A/HRC/7/16, paras 39, 75; A/HRC/7/16/Add.1, paras 57, 58, 104; E/CN.4/2005/48, para F.

59 UN Doc. A/HRC/16/40, para 56; A/HRC/10/5/Add.1, paras 53, 54; A/HRC/4/30, para 34; E/CN.4/2006/44/Add.2, paras 11, 43.

60 UN Doc. E/CN.4/2006/45, 8 February 2006, paras 80–85, 140.

61 UN Doc. A/HRC/16/44/Add.1, paras 1094, 1095, 1099, 1100; A/HRC/10/12, para 74; A/HRC/10/12/Add.1; A/HRC/7/28/Add.1.

62 See, for example, UN Doc. A/HRC/20/16, 23 May 2012, para 39.

63 UN Doc. A/HRC/10/8.Add.3, paras 18, 19, 27, 28, 71.

64 UN Doc. A/HRC/14/20/Add.2, para 36.

65 Thematic analysis on the topic of minorities and discrimination based on caste and analogous systems of inherited status; UN Doc. A/HRC/31/56, 28 January 2016.

Independent Expert on water and sanitation[66] and the Independent Expert on human rights and extreme poverty[67] as vulnerable groups whose access to and enjoyment of a range of human rights is compromised because of discrimination on the basis of caste, itself a violation of international human rights law. Dalit women and girls particularly are singled out as suffering from multiple, intersecting and aggravated forms thereof.[68] In 2007, the mandate of the UN Special Rapporteur on contemporary forms of slavery was created pursuant to Human Rights Council resolution 6/14, replacing the former UN Working Group on Contemporary Forms of Slavery.[69] The principal focus of the mandate is those aspects of contemporary forms of slavery not covered by existing Human Rights Council mandates.[70] Gulnara Shahinian, Special Rapporteur on contemporary forms of slavery (2008–2014), repeatedly highlighted the 'intrinsic link' between caste and contemporary forms of slavery, such as domestic servitude and debt bondage,[71] identifying caste discrimination as a root cause of contemporary slavery. Her successor, Urmila Bhoolo (2014–2020), identified inter alia caste-based forms of slavery as deserving specific attention, and domestic servitude as a key priority, as it exists 'across both developed and developing countries' and its victims are often from marginalised and discriminated-against communities.[72]

5.2.3.3 Competence of the UN Human Rights Council and its Special Procedures to consider caste discrimination

India has charged both CERD and the former UN Sub-Commission with a lack of competence to address caste discrimination.[73] Based on Alston, Morgan-Foster and Abresch's examination of a similar charge of 'mandate breach' by the US and the UK against the Human Rights Council and its Special Procedures in relation to extrajudicial executions in armed conflicts, India might rely on three arguments. First, that Charter bodies, procedures and mechanisms are restricted in focus, which excludes caste and descent-based discrimination and precludes the creation of new mechanisms with this focus. Second, that the development by Charter bodies and mechanisms of a consistent practice of examining caste discrimination does not thereby give them the competence to address this issue. And third, that discrimination based on caste is an internal matter falling exclusively within domestic jurisdiction.[74]

These arguments are rebuttable. The Human Rights Council derives its mandate from the UN Charter and therefore covers all forms of human rights violations regardless of the

66 UN Doc. A/HRC/15/55, paras 25, 26, 58, 5, 76, 125; A/HRC/12/24, paras 53, 54.

67 UN Doc. A/HRC/15/55, paras 25, 75, 76.

68 See UN Doc. E/CN.4/2006/118, paras 30, 31; E/CN.4/2006/45, paras 80–85, 140; A/HRC/7/6/Add.1, paras 23–25.

69 See www.ohchr.org/EN/Issues/Slavery/SRSlavery/Pages/SRSlaveryIndex.aspx. The international prohibition of slavery and forced or compulsory labour is expressed in UDHR Article 4 and in legally binding form in ICCPR Article 8. ICESCR Article 6 guarantees the right of everyone 'to the opportunity to gain his living by work which he freely chooses or accepts'.

70 See UN Doc. A/HRC/RES/15/2, 5 October 2010, para 4(d).

71 See UN Doc. A/HRC/9/20, 28 July 2008, para 11; A/HRC/12/21, 10 July 2009, para 51; A/HRC/15/20, 18 June 2010, paras 69, 72, 99.

72 Report; UN Doc. A/HRC/27/53, 22 July 2014, paras 18, 20.

73 See Statement, India (n 27); see also Chapter 4.

74 P Alston, J Morgan-Foster, and W Abresch, 'The Competence of the UN Human Rights Council and Its Special Procedures in Relation to Armed Conflicts: Extrajudicial Executions in the "War on Terror"', 19(1) *European Journal of International Law* (2008) 183–209, 199–203.

treaty obligations of individual states. Thus, the role of the Human Rights Council (as also the former Commission on Human Rights) is to further the UN Charter's general commitment to promoting and encouraging respect for human rights through a range of activities, irrespective of states' obligations under human rights treaties. The former Human Rights Commission did not treat the principal human rights treaties 'as self-limitations on its competence' but worked to fulfil its mandate in a broad way regardless of whether human rights abuses violated the treaty obligations of individual states.[75]

This *droit de regard* ("right of inspection") 'has been firmly established in customary international law', say Simma and Alston.[76] The resolutions establishing the mandates of the Special Procedures – one of the most important means by which the Council exercises its *droit de regard* – 'have routinely laid out *droits de regard* that exceed the scope of legal obligations even for those states that have ratified all relevant treaties'.[77]

Importantly,

> the space between the Commission and Council's *droits de regard* and the legal obligations of States has proven to be a fertile zone for normative development, pushing forward that aspect of the Commission and Council's mandates and even resulting in the drafting of new normative instruments.[78]

Special Procedure mandates evolve in response to situations which originally were not explicitly envisaged, respond to new forms of violations and increase public demand for effective responses in specific contexts. Alston et al. argue that organic 'mandate evolution' is fully reported in the annual reports of the mandate-holders, which are subject to stakeholder debate, feedback and responses in the form of resolutions from the parent bodies, which, in the 'vast majority of cases', explicitly endorse the developments reported and often also request the mandate-holder 'to further develop or strengthen certain measures'.[79] Alston et al. also point out that the domestic understanding of *ultra vires* (i.e. a consistent pattern of *ultra vires* acts does not cure the original defect) cannot be applied to international law, because 'an integral part of the international legal framework is its dynamic nature'.[80] Mandates are elaborated and refined by the Human Rights Council which reviews, accepts, discourages or rejects the interpretations proposed by successive mandate-holders.[81] As to the domestic jurisdiction argument, a basic premise of international law and the international human rights regime is that the characterisation of an issue as an internal or domestic matter is not solely a matter for the state concerned; indeed, the fact that a particular state denies the application of the human rights label to a given issue, or resists international scrutiny

75 Ibid., 200–201.
76 B Simma and P Alston, 'The Sources of Human Rights Law: Custom, Jus Cogens, General Principles', 12 *Australian Year Book of International Law* (1992) 82–108, 99, cited in Alston et al., ibid.
77 Alston et al., ibid.
78 Ibid., 202.
79 Report of the UN Special Rapporteur on extrajudicial, summary or arbitrary executions; UN Doc. A/62/265, 16 August 2007, para 53.
80 Alston et al. (n 74) 203. *Ultra vires* ("beyond the powers") means that someone is acting beyond the scope of the authority or power granted to them by law, contract or agreement.
81 Ibid., 206.

thereof (e.g. by criticising Special Rapporteur reports with which it disagrees), does not deprive the issue of its international character.[82]

5.2.4 Universal Periodic Review

The Universal Periodic Review (UPR) process was established by the Human Rights Council in 2007[83] and involves state-led reviews of the human rights records of all UN member states.[84] According to the NGO International Dalit Solidarity Network, UPR has increased public attention on caste discrimination and the involvement of other states in the issue; however, they argue, it is only really useful with regard to countries that take a cooperative approach (such as Nepal and Pakistan).[85] During the first UPR cycle (2008–2011), forty-one observations and recommendations relating to caste discrimination were made in the outcome reports adopted by the UPR Working Group in relation to India, Pakistan, Sri Lanka, Mauritania, Madagascar and Nepal.[86] In the second and third cycles, Bangladesh, Japan, Senegal, Mauritania and the UK were also addressed on caste-related issues. In total, fifty-eight caste-specific UPR recommendations were made to these states between 2008 and 2016, of which thirty-five were accepted or partly accepted.

During India's first review in April 2008, two recommendations on caste discrimination were made: to maintain disaggregated data thereon and to strengthen human rights education in order to address caste-based discrimination effectively.[87] Both were rejected by India, which reiterated its position expressed to CERD in 2007 that while it 'recognise[d] that caste-based discrimination exists in India, since the caste system, which is unique to India, is not racial in origin, caste-based discrimination cannot be considered a form of racial discrimination'.[88] At India's second review in May 2012, the status of caste-based discrimination and efforts to stamp out discrimination in general was one of the main issues raised by the Working Group.[89] Twelve states made oral statements on caste discrimination and the situation of the Dalits, and three states submitted advance questions on caste discrimination (Germany) and manual scavenging (Denmark and Slovenia).[90] Fifty-one stakeholder submissions were made by NGOs, including calls for the implementation of treaty body recommendations on caste-based discrimination, the de facto abolition of untouchability, the extension of affirmative action to the mandatory acceptance of caste discrimination

---

82 See, for example, E Pilkington, 'Nikki Haley Attacks Damning UN Report on US Poverty Under Trump', *The Guardian*, 21 June 2018.
83 See UN Doc. A/RES/60/251, 3 April 2006, para 5(e).
84 Ibid. A Working Group of three states conducts the Review and prepares a report with the involvement of the state under review and assistance from the OHCHR, consisting of the questions, comments and recommendations made by states to the state under review, as well as the responses of the reviewed state.
85 See International Dalit Solidarity Network, Compilation of UN references to caste-based discrimination by UN treaty bodies, Universal Periodic Review, and UN Special Procedures, 11/E (May 2018).
86 Ibid.
87 UPR Working Group Report, India; UN Doc. A/HRC/8/26, 23 May 2008, 17.
88 Ibid., para74.
89 See UPR Media Briefing Note, India, 24 May 2012, at www.ohchr.org/EN/HRBodies/UPR/Pages/Highlights24May2012pm.aspx; see also UPR Working Group Report, India; A/HRC/WG.6/13/IND/2, 11 April 2012.
90 See www.upr-info.org/sites/default/files/document/india/session_13_-_may_2012/advance_questions_to_india.pdf; www.ohchr.org/EN/HRBodies/UPR/Pages/MeetingsHighlightsSession13.aspx (visited 14 August 2012).

complaints and the prevention of caste-motivated abuse.[91] The Working Group Report made ten recommendations on caste discrimination and Scheduled Castes, including better enforcement of existing law,[92] the implementation of effective monitoring mechanisms for special measures (reservations), including the collection of data disaggregated by caste,[93] and the promotion of women's rights to choice of marriage independent of caste.[94] Recommendations were also made that India enact comprehensive anti-discrimination legislation and ensure adequate means of redress,[95] as well as to strengthen human rights training of teachers to end caste discrimination in schools.[96] Two recommendations were accepted by India: to monitor policies and measures for the promotion and protection of the welfare and the rights of the scheduled castes and scheduled tribes, and to promote the rights of women in their choice of marriage and their equality of treatment independently of caste and tribe or other considerations.[97] India's third review in 2017 resulted in thirteen recommendations related to caste, of which nine were accepted.[98] Advance questions on caste and Dalits were submitted by Germany,[99] Czechia and Norway.[100]

The UK was reviewed in May 2012 for the second time, by coincidence on the same day as India.[101] The UPR Working Group recommended that the UK put in practice a national strategy to eliminate caste discrimination through the immediate adoption of the provision in the Equality Act 2010 prohibiting such discrimination, in conformity with its international human rights obligations, including CERD's General Recommendation 29.[102] The UK did not accept this recommendation,[103] but it was drawn upon by Dalit advocacy groups in Britain in their campaign for a statutory prohibition of caste discrimination.[104] By the time of the UPR mid-term report in July 2014, the Conservative-Liberal Democrat coalition government was under a statutory duty to make caste 'an aspect of' the protected

91 UPR Working Group, Stakeholder Submissions, India; A/HRC/WG.6/13/IND/3, 12 March 2012.
92 UPR Working Group Report, India; UN Doc. A/HRC/21/10, 9 July 2012, paras 138.47, 138.72, 138.118.
93 Ibid., paras 138.71, 138.73, 138.75.
94 Ibid., para 138.87.
95 Ibid., para 138.53.
96 Ibid., para 138.163.
97 See UN Doc. A/HRC/21/10/Add.1, 17 September 2012.
98 India: Views on conclusions and/or recommendations, voluntary commitments and replies presented by the state under review; A/HRC/36/10/Add.1, 6 September 2017.
99 www.upr-info.org/sites/default/files/document/india/session_27_-_may_2017/advance_questions_india_add2.pdf.
100 www.upr-info.org/sites/default/files/document/session_27_-_may_2017/advance_questions_india_add1.pdf.
101 See www.upr-info.org/en/review/United-Kingdom/Session-13-May-2012.
102 UPR Working Group Report; UK; UN Doc. A/HRC/21/9, 6 July 2012, para 110.61. The domestic provision in question was section 9(5)(a) of the Equality Act 2010, which contained a power to add caste by Ministerial Order, at a future date, to the protected characteristic of race in the Act. In April 2013, legislation was adopted which converted this power into a duty; see Chapter 9.
103 'Recommendations that do not enjoy the support of the United Kingdom are generally those where we are not able to commit to implementation at this stage, whether or not we agree with the principles behind the recommendation, or where we have recently reviewed our position on the issue in question; or where we reject the assertions being made'; UPR Working Group Report, Views on conclusions and/or recommendations, voluntary commitments and replies presented by the state under review; UN Doc. A/HRC/21/9/Add.1, 17 September 2012, para 6; Annex document, ibid., 30. See Chapter 9.
104 See, for example, Anti Caste Discrimination Alliance and others, 'Joint Statement to the Coalition Government demanding that it brings into force clause 9(5)(a) of the Equality Act 2010', 28 November 2012 (copy on file with author).

characteristic of race in the Equality Act 2010. It changed its position and accepted the recommendation, stating 'The UK Government intends to introduce legislation to make caste discrimination unlawful, as a specific aspect of race discrimination under s.9(5) Equality Act 2010. A public consultation process on the detail of the prospective legislation is expected later in 2014'.[105] A general election took place in May 2015 by which time the outgoing government had neither conducted a public consultation process nor introduced legislation to make caste discrimination unlawful. A public consultation – not, as expected, on the detail of the legislation, but on whether to introduce legislation at all – took place in 2017. In July 2018, Theresa May's Conservative Government announced its intention not to introduce legislation on caste discrimination and to repeal the statutory duty to do so. The engagement of successive UK Governments between 2010 and 2018 with the legal regulation of caste discrimination is discussed in detail in Chapter 9.

5.3 International Labour Organisation: discrimination on the basis of social origin

The International Labour Organisation (ILO) is a tripartite UN agency working with governments, employers and workers of UN member states to promote decent work worldwide via the adoption of international standards (conventions and recommendations), enforced inter alia via a Committee of Experts on the Application of Conventions and Recommendations (CEACR), which can issue individual observations and direct requests to UN member states. ILO Discrimination (Employment and Occupation) Convention 1958 (No. 111) (Convention 111) establishes as a core labour standard the principle of non-discrimination, defined in Article 1(1) as

> any distinction, excision or preference made on the basis of race, colour, sex, religion, political opinion, national extraction *or social origin*, which has the effect of nullifying or impairing equality of opportunity or treatment in employment or occupation.[106]

ILO jurisprudence and publications show that the ILO regards caste discrimination as falling within the "social origin" category. There is no precise definition of social origin, and, like caste, the concept is defined by reference to its manifestations. Social origin discrimination arises, according to the ILO's Global Report on Discrimination, 'Equality at Work',

> when an individual's membership of a class, socio-occupational category or caste determines or influences his or her occupational situation either by denying access to certain jobs or activities or, on the contrary, by assigning that person to certain jobs . . . prejudices and preferences based on social origin may persist even where rigid stratification has disappeared.[107]

---

105 See UN UPR Mid-Term Report of the UK, 2014, 7, 78–79. The UK's third review took place on 24 May 2017. No recommendations directly addressed caste discrimination.
106 ILO Discrimination (Employment and Occupation) Convention 1958 (No. 111), at www.ilo.org/dyn/normlex/en/f?p=1000:12100:0::NO::P12100_INSTRUMENT_ID:312256 (emphasis added). Indian ratification 3 June 1960.
107 'Equality at Work: The Continuing Challenge – Global Report under the follow-up to the ILO Declaration on Fundamental Principles and Rights at Work' (Geneva: ILO, 2011) para 167.

The same report identifies caste-based discrimination as a form of discrimination on the basis of social origin, most widespread 'in the case of the Dalit population of South Asia'. Caste discrimination is manifested by 'limited access to certain types of jobs and wage gaps in comparison with other population groups. There are also considerable differences between castes in terms of educational attainment'. Moreover, 'social perceptions about certain castes limit employment opportunities and subject members of those castes to humiliation in their everyday lives and at work'.[108] With this in mind, the ILO initiated a project working with the Government of India and social partners on the eradication of manual scavenging in India – the removal of human excreta by hand from public and private "dry" latrines – work carried out exclusively by Dalits. It is unlawful in India to employ manual scavengers, but the practice continues.[109] CEACR has used the social origin category to address, via Individual Observations and Direct Requests, the persistence of caste discrimination in employment in India.[110] Its use of the social origin category to address caste issues appears to have been accepted by India without challenge, and yet India has failed to provide the detailed information on Dalits and work-related issues that CEACR has repeatedly requested. The ILO also offers valuable analysis on the impact of caste inequalities on the economy; a 2014 Working Paper on employment patterns in India, for instance, describes the Indian experience as remarkable in the way inequalities have intertwined with the economic growth process, and it highlights how patterns of social discrimination along gender and caste lines, and a lack of structural change, have reinforced segmented labour markets and low productivity.[111] In 2014, the ILO adopted a Forced Labour Protocol to supplement the ILO Forced Labour Convention (No. 29) 1930 and the ILO Abolition of Forced Labour Convention (No. 105) 1957. Both of these, as well as the UN Convention on Slavery, have been ratified by India, Nepal, Bangladesh, Sri Lanka and Pakistan. In 2017, India ratified the ILO Minimum Age Convention 1973 (No. 138) and the Worst Forms of Child Labour Convention 1999 (No. 182), both of which will allow international scrutiny of the situation of Dalit child labourers.

5.4 UN World Conference Against Racism, Racial Discrimination, Xenophobia and Related Intolerance 2001

In 2001, the third UN World Conference Against Racism, Racial Discrimination, Xenophobia and Related Intolerance (WCAR) was held in Durban, South Africa, the two previous conferences having been held in Geneva in 1978 and 1983.[112] The WCAR agenda was based on a Draft Programme of Action (DPA) drawn up ahead of the conference.[113]

---

108 Ibid., paras 168–172.
109 See Chapter 3.
110 Since 2000, CEACR has published seven Individual Observations concerning India and Convention 111 and social origin; see, for example, ILOLEX 062006IND111, para 6; ILOLEX 062010IND111 on manual scavenging. Since 1990, CEACR has issued ten Individual Direct Requests to India concerning Convention 111 and social origin, asking for information inter alia on the promotion of equal access of Dalits to employment and occupation, measures taken to assist the socio-economic development of the Scheduled Castes and discrimination on the basis of social origin (untouchability); see, for example, ILOLEX 092003IND111; ILOLEX 092006IND111.
111 C Chandrasekhar and J Ghosh, *Growth, Employment Patterns and Inequality in Asia: A Case Study of India* (Bangkok: ILO, 2014).
112 See www.un.org/WCAR/e-kit/backgrounder1.htm.
113 WCAR DPA; UN Doc. A/CONF.189/5, 22 August 2001. See also Chapter 4.

Dalits sought the inclusion of caste discrimination as a form of racism or racial discrimination in the DPA,[114] specifically recommended by the WCAR Bellagio Consultation in January 2000.[115] This demand was vigorously opposed by India, on four grounds: (1) caste does not fall within the ambit of racism or racial discrimination, because it does not denote race or a racial grouping, and neither is it a subcategory of descent, because descent refers solely to racial descent; therefore, caste was not relevant to the conference;[116] (2) caste discrimination is an internal matter not susceptible to UN scrutiny; (3) India already has internal mechanisms for addressing caste-based discrimination and violence which are unparalleled in scale and scope; and (4) India is doing everything possible to address caste discrimination, but as a long-standing issue it would take time to resolve.[117] Conversely, India's National Human Rights Commission argued that the WCAR provided a 'singular opportunity' to the international community to deal 'openly and courageously' with issues of discrimination and inequality 'all over the world, in all of their variety, including the forms of discrimination that persist in India', observing that 'it is not so much the nomenclature of the form of discrimination that must engage our attention, but the fact of its persistence that must cause concern'.[118] Despite India's objections, Dalits succeeded in securing a "work and descent" provision in the draft DPA, urging all governments to put in place 'constitutional, legislative and administrative measures, including appropriate forms of affirmative action . . . to prohibit and redress *discrimination on the basis of work and descent*'.[119] However, discussion of this provision and its inclusion in the Final Programme of Action was resisted by India, and caste discrimination does not appear in the Durban Declaration and Programme of Action (DDPA), the conference's outcome document.[120] Nonetheless, Article 2 of the DDPA recognises that racism, racial discrimination, xenophobia and related intolerance occur on the grounds set out in ICERD Article 1(1), namely race, colour, descent or national or ethnic origin. Other provisions similarly recognise the problem of racism, discrimination and xenophobia based on descent – even though caste as such is not mentioned.[121]

Although the DDPA contains no explicit references to caste discrimination, Dalit presence at the WCAR process directly contributed to the rapid 'internationalisation' of caste which occurred from the end of the twentieth century.[122] The WCAR opened up international debate about whether discrimination based on caste was a form of racial discrimination

---

114 See DE Berg, 'Sovereignties, the World Conference against Racism 2001 and the Formation of a Dalit Human Rights Campaign', 20 *Questions de Recherche/Research in Question* (2007), Paris, Centre d'études et de recherches internationales. Caste discrimination was not addressed in either of the previous UN World Conferences on Racism (see Chapter 4) nor at the 1993 UN World Conference on Human Rights in Vienna, nor the 2000 UN Millennium Summit.

115 UN Doc. A/CONF.189/PC.1/10, 8 March 2000, para 50.

116 See A Beteille, 'Race and Caste', in S Thorat and Umakant (eds.), *Caste, Race and Discrimination: Discourses in International Context* (Jaipur: Rawat, 2004) 49–52, first published in *The Hindu*, 10 March 2001.

117 S Sorabjee, 'The Official Position', in S Thorat and Umakant (eds.), ibid., 43–48.

118 WCAR, Plenary Statement of the National Human Rights Commission of India, Dr Justice K Ramaswamy, Member.

119 WCAR DPA (n 113), para 73. See also P Prove, 'Caste at the World Conference Against Racism', in Thorat and Umakant (eds.) (n 116) 322–325.

120 Durban Declaration and Programme of Action (DDPA); M Thekaekara, 'What Next for India's Dalits?' in Thorat and Umakant (eds.) (n 116) 313–316.

121 See DDPA, ibid., Articles 111, 171.

122 Bob (n 4); J Lerche, 'Transnational Advocacy Networks and Affirmative Action for *Dalits* in India', 39(2) *Development and Change* (2008) 239–261; C Lennox, 'Reviewing Durban: Examining the

as internationally defined (the "caste as race" debate).[123] The creation of a rebuttable presumption that caste discrimination is located within the international framework on racial discrimination resulted in pressure being put on states where discrimination on grounds of caste persists, by UN bodies and mechanisms as well as by civil society organisations, to fulfil their international obligations on caste discrimination, as well as domestic constitutional and legislative obligations. However, as seen in Chapter 4, the framing of caste discrimination as a form of descent-based racial discrimination has provoked staunch resistance from India, while Japan has resisted the application of descent to its Buraku population. Conversely, according to Indian sociologist Gopal Guru, the WCAR was a missed opportunity to 'embark on and sustain a thoroughgoing critique of caste discrimination' by revisiting the categories 'through which discrimination is experienced and understood – colour in the case of race, but *touch* in the case of caste'.[124]

5.4.1 Durban Review Conference 2009

The purpose of the Durban Review Conference (DRC) was 'to assess and accelerate progress' on the implementation of measures adopted at the WCAR in 2001.[125] Discrimination based on caste was referred to repeatedly in the DRC preparatory sessions by CERD members and the UN Special Procedures, and yet the DRC outcome document contains no explicit reference to discrimination based on caste or on work and descent.[126] CERD members and the Special Rapporteur on Racism believe that ICERD, if genuinely adhered to by states, constitutes a sufficient normative standard for overcoming caste discrimination. In 2007, the UN Office of the High Commissioner for Human Rights (OHCHR) circulated a questionnaire on contemporary manifestations of racism and measures and activities taken to implement the DDPA to a range of non-state actors, including UN bodies and specialised agencies, CERD and other human rights mechanisms, together with Special Procedures.[127] In its response, CERD observed that, 'as is the case with all international normative standards', ICERD 'is very useful and effective for States that genuinely wish to abide by it'. The key reasons, according to CERD, for states' failure to implement ICERD effectively were lack of political will and lack of a clear understanding of the meaning and scope of the definition of the concept of racial discrimination in Article 1(1) of ICERD, 'which may lead some States to deny or minimise the extent of racial discrimination in their territory'.[128] The following year (2008), in a joint Special Procedures response to the OHCHR questionnaire,

---

Outputs and Review of the 2001 World Conference Against Racism', 27(2) *Netherlands Quarterly of Human Rights* (2009) 191–235.

123 See Special Rapporteur on Racism, Report; UN Doc. A/HRC/7/19, 20 February 2008, para 70: '[Since the WCAR], the issue of discrimination on grounds of caste has been on the international agenda. Despite the objection of some member States, the main human rights bodies working in the arena of racism and discrimination have stated clearly that prohibition of this type of discrimination falls within the scope of existing instruments, in particular the [ICERD]'.

124 G Guru, cited in K Kannabiren, 'Important Similarities, Strange Differences: Caste, Race and Durban', *Economic and Political Weekly* (10 July 2010) 38–41, 39.

125 See www.un.org/en/durbanreview2009/. See also Lennox (n 122).

126 See www.un.org/en/durbanreview2009/pdf/Durban_Review_outcome_document_En.pdf.

127 See Decisions of the Organizational Session of the Preparatory Committee of the Durban Review Conference 27–31 August 2007, Decision PC.1/10, para (b).

128 CERD, replies to questionnaire prepared by the OHCHR Office pursuant to decision PC.1/10 of the Preparatory Committee of the Durban Review Conference; UN Doc. A/CONF.211/PC.2/CRP.5, 23 April 2008, pages 3, 12.

the then Special Rapporteur on Racism reiterated that in the absence of recognition by states that discrimination based on caste and other systems of inherited status constituted a form of discrimination prohibited by [ICERD], '*it [would] not be possible to effectively address the serious human rights violations and discrimination suffered by individuals and groups on grounds of caste and other systems of inherited status*'. He stressed the responsibility of governments and political leaders for shaping public opinion 'to move towards fairer societies based on the equality of all human beings' alongside 'meaningful legislative amendments to ensure equality and prohibit caste-based discrimination'.[129]

5.5 Decade of Dalit rights UN 2011–2020, conference 24–28 June 2011: work and descent, not race

In 2011, a decade after the WCAR, Dalit activists, NGOs and academics at an international strategy conference on Dalit rights concluded that the best way forward was to stress that 'caste is not race[,] but that caste-based discrimination is nevertheless a violation of international human rights law'.[130] The preferred category endorsed by the conference was discrimination based on work and descent. The delegates argued for a re-strategising of the Dalit stand – 'without in any way deflecting the stand taken by CERD' – towards a discourse based on 'descent and work-based discrimination and violence'.[131] This was reflected in the Conference's choice of the discrimination based on work and descent terminology. It was also mirrored in the final Declaration, which lists as an international objective to 'move beyond the caste-race debate and apply a policy of human rights principles of non-discrimination, substantive equality and non-retrogression'.[132] The Declaration called for promotion of the 'discrimination based on work and descent agenda' as a global and intersectional agenda, the creation of a UN Special Rapporteur or Working Group on discrimination based on work and descent issues, a UN World Conference on discrimination based on work and descent and the wide endorsement and implementation of the UN Principles and Guidelines on discrimination based on work and descent. Significantly, the Declaration did not call for a new UN Convention on discrimination based on work and descent, instead reiterating that the practice is already prohibited by international human rights law, including ICERD.

5.6 Dalit rights as minority rights and indigenous people's rights[133]

Minority Rights Group International (MRG) was one of the first NGOs outside India to address caste discrimination. MRG describes its mission as 'to secure the rights of minorities and indigenous peoples around the world and to improve cooperation between communities'.[134] Yet, as Castellino and Redondo observe, victims of caste discrimination 'do not easily

129 UN Doc. A/CONF.211/PC/WG.1/5, 31 July 2008, paras 45–47
130 See http://idsn.org/wp-content/uploads/user_folder/pdf/New_files/UN/Report_DecadeDalit Rights.pdf.
131 Ibid.
132 Decade of Dalit Rights, Declaration, at https://idsn.org/wp-content/uploads/user_folder/pdf/New_ files/UN/Declaration_Decade_Dalit_Rights_UN.pdf.
133 For a discussion of Dalits as a minority in India, see A Waughray, 'Caste Discrimination and Minority Rights: The Case of India's Dalits', 17 *International Journal on Minority and Group Rights* (2010) 327–353.
134 See http://minorityrights.org/our-work/.

fit into the universally agreed category of a "minority",[135] and neither do they readily fit the international definition of an indigenous people. There is no legally binding definition of "minority". However, there is a general international consensus on a core definition based on the 1977 definition proffered by Francesco Capotorti in his study for the UN, subsequently captured in the UN Declaration on the Rights of Persons Belonging to National or Ethnic, Religious and Linguistic Minorities (1992) (Minorities Declaration). This definition embraces non-dominant groups possessing stable ethnic, religious or linguistic characteristics that differ sharply from those of the rest of the population, and which have been retained over time and which members of the group wish to preserve.[136] The key characteristics of the indigenous people's category derive from the definition in Martinez Cobo's 1983 UN study, subsequently captured in the UN Declaration on the Rights of Indigenous Peoples (2000). These characteristics are the historical or traditional occupation of lands or territories, the use of and control over resources, distinct cultural and religious traditions, customs and ceremonies and distinct histories, philosophies, languages and institutions.[137]

Although Dalits do not readily fulfil either the minority or indigenous people's criteria in international human rights law, nevertheless, from the mid-1990s, they have utilised minority and indigenous peoples' mechanisms to advance their claims at the UN. In 1995, the UN Working Group on Minorities was established, its primary concern being the promotion and practical realisation of the 1992 Minorities Declaration.[138] Between 1997 and its demise in 2006, Dalit organisations were represented by observers at seven of the annual sessions of the Minorities Working Group. Dalit issues were also raised by other organisations (including NGOs in consultative status), thereby aligning the Dalits with other groups categorised under international law as minorities.[139] In international law, the existence of a minority is a question of fact, to be established by a set of objective and subjective factors independent of a group's domestic status.[140] Non-recognition as a minority at the domestic level – as in the case of the Dalits – does not preclude a group's characterisation as a minority at the

---

135 J Castellino and E Dominguez-Redondo, *Minority Rights in Asia: A Comparative Legal Analysis* (Oxford: Oxford University Press, 2006) 58.

136 F Capotorti, *Study on the Rights of Persons Belonging to Ethnic, Religious and Linguistic Minorities* (New York: United Nations, 1981) 96; see also UN Declaration on the Rights of Persons Belonging to National or Ethnic, Religious and Linguistic Minorities (Minorities Declaration) (1992); GA Res. 47/135 (1992).

137 JM Cobo, Study of the Problem of Discrimination Against Indigenous Populations, 30 September 1983; UN Doc. E/CN.4 Sub.2 /1983/21/Add.8, para 379; see also UN Declaration on the Rights of Indigenous Peoples (UNDRIP) 2007; A/Res/61/295. Regarding membership of the indigenous category, Article 33 UNDRIP emphasises self-identification. On the distinction between minority rights and indigenous people's rights, see Working Paper on the relationship and distinction between the rights of persons belonging to minorities and those of indigenous peoples; E/CN.4/Sub.2/2000/10, 19 July 2000. Despite not constituting a coherent group defined by the characteristics of indigenous peoples listed, aspects of the criteria relating to cultural and religious traditions overlap with the experience of some Dalit religious communities; see, for example, R Lamb, *Rapt in the Name: The Ramnamis, Ramnam, and Untouchable Religion in Central India* (Berkeley: State University of New York Press, 2002).

138 See www.ohchr.org/EN/Issues/Minorities/Pages/TheformerWGonMinorities.aspx; Report of the Working Group on Minorities, 1st session; UN Doc. E/CN.4/Sub.2/1996/2, 30 November 1995, para 2.

139 See, for example, Report of the Working Group on Minorities, 3rd session; Report, 11th session; UN Doc. E/CN.4/Sub.2/2005/27, 8 July 2005, Annex I (VI), para 32; Report, 12th session; UN Doc. A/HRC/Sub.1/58/19, 24 August 2006, Annex I (VII), para 12.

140 See A Eide, Commentary to the Declaration on the Rights of Persons Belonging to National or Ethnic, Religious and Linguistic Minorities; UN Doc. E/CN.4/Sub.2/AC.5/1998/WP.1.

international level.[141] In a 1998 Working Paper on the Minorities Declaration, Asjborn Eide, then Chairman of the Minorities Working Group, identified the objective factors as potentially including questions of descent, the mother tongue spoken by the persons concerned and the religion they practiced, while the subjective factors referred to self-identification by the persons concerned.[142] In 2005, an Independent Expert on Minority Issues was appointed by the UN High Commissioner for Human Rights with a mandate to promote the implementation of the Minorities Declaration.[143] In her first report in 2006, the independent expert, Gay McDougall (2005–2011), endorsed and developed this approach, noting that

> minority status is closely tied to how a group defines itself. The principle that belonging to a minority group is a matter of a person's choice includes the right not to be treated as a minority.[144]

McDougall further noted that CERD, in its General Recommendation No. 8 (1991) on identification with a particular racial or ethnic group, endorsed the self-identification approach to minority identity;[145] as such, 'groups falling within the mandate of the independent expert [would] include those that self-identify as minority communities'.[146] MRG defines minorities as 'non-dominant ethnic, religious and linguistic communities' – groups who are smaller in number than the rest of the population and believe they have a common linguistic, religious, cultural or ethnic identity that is different to that of a majority group around them.[147] Under the MRG framework, 'what matters is whether the minorities lack power, i.e. the ability to affect the decisions that concern them. It is those minorities that minority rights are designed to protect'.[148] This is the basis on which MRG has described and categorised the Dalits as a minority.[149]

Since the mid-1990s, Dalits have also been represented from time to time at indigenous people's mechanisms such as the UN Working Group on Indigenous Peoples, established in 1982.[150] The sense of Dalits as indigenous peoples permeated eighteenth- and nineteenth-

141 HRC General Comment No. 23; UN Doc. CCPR/C/21/Rev.1/Add.5, 8 April 1994, paras 5.1, 5.2. See also Greco-Bulgarian Communities Case, PCIJ Series B, No. 17, 1930; Report of the Independent Expert on minority issues; UN Doc. E/CN.4/2006/74, 6 January 2006, para 23.
142 UN Doc. E/CN.4/Sub.2/AC.5/1998/WP.1; Report of the Working Group on Minorities, 4th session; UN Doc. E/CN.4/Sub.2/1998/18, 6 July 1998, paras 24, 46.
143 See http://www2.ohchr.org/english/issues/minorities/expert/. The name of the mandate changed in March 2014 to the UN Special Rapporteur on Minority Issues.
144 Report, Independent Expert on minority issues (2006) (n 141), paras 17, 23.
145 CERD General Recommendation (GR) No. 8 on identification with a particular racial or ethnic group (Article 1(1) and 1(4)); UN Doc. A/45/18, 79 (1991).
146 See Report, Independent Expert on minority issues (2006) (n 141), para 23.
147 See https://minorityrights.org/about-us/
148 Minority Rights Group International, Submission to CERD on India, 19 February 2007.
149 See Minority Rights Group, World Directory of Minorities and Indigenous Peoples – India: Dalits at http://minorityrights.org/minorities/dalits/.
150 Established by ECOSOC Res. 1982/34, Study of the problem of discrimination against indigenous populations, 7 May 1982. Dalits were represented at the fifteenth and twentieth sessions of the Working Group by the Ambedkar Centre for Justice and Peace; see Report of the Working Group on Indigenous Populations, 15th session; UN Doc. E/CN.4/Sub.2/1997/14, 13 August 1997; Report, 20th session; UN Doc. E/CN.4/Sub.2/2002/24, 8 August 2002, para 22.

century colonial writing on caste,[151] although Ambedkar himself was non-committal on the question of Dalit indigeneity. Giving evidence in 1928 before the Simon Commission – a Parliamentary Commission appointed by the British Government to formulate the next stage of Indian constitutional reforms[152] – Ambedkar had stated of the "untouchables", 'Really, we cannot be deemed to be part of the Hindu community'. He was then asked by the Commission Chairman, 'You come, I believe, from an earlier set of inhabitants of this continent?', to which he replied, 'That is one view, I think'. The Chairman responded, 'It is supposed . . . that you are pre-Aryan?' to which Ambedkar replied, 'Well, I do not know. That is a view'.[153] Nonetheless, aspects of the indigeneity criteria resonate strongly with some Dalit communities and movements,[154] and the concept of indigeneity has been utilised since the 1990s as part of the Dalits' international strategy,[155] reflecting the view of anthropologist Alan Barnard that it is not really an anthropological concept but rather an ideological and a social construct and, essentially, a legal concept, as well as a useful tool for political persuasion.[156]

Despite the restrictive nature of Capotorti's core definition of minority, which appears to refer only to 'voluntary minorities' and not to 'involuntary minorities',[157] and although it may not be accepted universally that Dalits strictly fall into the minority groups category,[158] the UN minorities mechanisms have adopted an inclusive approach in addressing discrimination based on caste and analogous systems of inherited status under the minority rights framework. In 2007, the Minorities Working Group was replaced by the UN Forum on Minority Issues (Minorities Forum).[159] In 2009, the Minorities Forum brought Dalits into the international minority category based on their status as a group protected by ICERD, stating that the term "minorities", as used in the Minorities Declaration, 'encompasses the persons and groups protected under the International Convention on the Elimination of All Forms of Racial Discrimination from discrimination based on race, colour, *descent (caste)*, national or ethnic origin, citizen or non-citizen'.[160] This illustrates how ICERD-protected status has acted as a "passport" to the take-up of Dalit/caste issues by other UN mechanisms

151 See S Bayly, *Caste, Society and Politics in India from the Eighteenth Century to the Modern Age* (Cambridge: Cambridge University Press, 1999) 97–186; D Keane, *Caste-Based Discrimination in International Human Rights Law* (Aldershot: Ashgate, 2007) 31–37.
152 See S Wolpert, *A New History of India* (Oxford: Oxford University Press, 2009, 8th edition) 326.
153 See BR Ambedkar, 'Evidence Before the Simon Commission', in *BAWS Vol. 2* (Bombay: The Education Dept, Govt. of Maharasthra, 2005) 465.
154 See Waughray (n 133) 334.
155 See P Thornberry, 'The Convention on the Elimination of Racial Discrimination, Indigenous Peoples and Caste/Descent-Based Discrimination', in J Castellino and N Walsh (eds.), *International Law and Indigenous Peoples* (Leiden: Koninklijke Brill, 2005) 17–52, 18. See also VT Rajshekar, *Dalit: The Black Untouchables of India* (Atlanta, GA: Clarity Press, 2003).
156 A Barnard, 'Kalahari Revisionism, Vienna and the "Indigenous Peoples" Debate', 44(1) *Social Anthropology* (2006) 1–16, 7.
157 P Thornberry, *International Law and the Rights of Minorities* (Oxford: Clarendon Press, 1991) 9–10.
158 Report of the Special Rapporteur on minority issues; A/HRC/31/56, 28 January 2016, para 21.
159 Established by Human Rights Council Resolution 6/15, 28 September 2007. The Forum's mandate is to provide thematic contributions and expertise to the work of the Special Rapporteur on Minority Issues (until 2014 the Independent Expert on Minority Issues) and to identify and analyse best practices, challenges, opportunities and initiatives for the further implementation of the Declaration on Minorities.
160 Report of the Independent Expert on minority issues: Recommendations of the Forum on Minority Issues; UN Doc. A/HRC/10/11/Add.1, 5 March 2009, para 2, fn 1 (emphasis added).

and procedures (including, for example, successive Special Rapporteurs on Racism). In 2006, the then UN Independent Expert on minority issues (since 2014 the Special Rapporteur on minority issues)[161] emphasised the number of minority rights communications regarding violations of human rights that have as their root cause discrimination, racism or xenophobia against a minority group and its members. Often, the minority rights component of such communications is hidden, so the wider context of issues arising out of the minority status of the victims may be neglected and even remain unaddressed.[162] The nature of caste discrimination as a global human rights concern, due to its 'unique, distinct and transnational nature', the dynamic nature of human rights law and 'rigid definitions' as the antithesis of the concept of human rights and the 'urgent need to move beyond the caste-race debate', were highlighted at a UN Experts' Workshop convened by the Independent Expert on minorities at the Decade of Dalit Rights conference in June 2011 (described earlier). In 2013, the UN Secretary-General consolidated the place of Dalits within the UN minorities category in a Guidance Note setting out a framework for UN regional and country action on racial discrimination and the protection of minorities, which explicitly highlighted the marginalised position of persons targeted for discrimination based on descent, in particular caste-based discrimination and related practices, and the need for UN action and policies to reflect this.[163] In 2016, the Special Rapporteur on minority issues, Rita Izsak, produced a thematic analysis on minorities and discrimination based on caste and analogous systems of inherited status (the terminology in CERD's General Recommendation 29 on Descent [2002]).[164] It identifies the distinguishing characteristics of 'caste and analogous systems' as hereditary nature, labour stratification and occupational segregation, untouchability practices and enforced endogamy. Further, the report notes that

> [T]he term "caste" refers to a strict hierarchical social system that is often based on the notions of purity and pollution, in which individuals placed at the bottom of the system may face exclusion and discrimination in a wide range of areas. The concept of "caste system" is primarily associated with the South Asian region, where its existence is linked to the religiously sanctioned social structure of Hinduism, which identified four original and endogamous groups, or castes, called varnas. At present, the term "caste" has broadened in meaning, transcending religious affiliation. Caste and caste-like systems may be based on either a religious or a secular background and can be found within diverse religious and/or ethnic groups in all geographical regions, including within diaspora communities.[165]

Importantly, it confirms that Dalits and similar groups affected by discrimination based on caste and analogous systems of inherited status reside firmly within the UN minorities mandate by virtue of their 'minority-like characteristics, particularly their non-dominant and often marginalised position, stigma, and the historic use of the minority rights framework to

161 See www.ohchr.org/EN/Issues/Minorities/SRMinorities/Pages/SRminorityissuesIndex.aspx.
162 Report of the Independent Expert on minority issues (2006); see (n 141), para 47.
163 Guidance Note of the Secretary General on Racial Discrimination and Protection of Minorities, March 2013, para 20.
164 Report of the Special Rapporteur on Minority Issues: Minorities and discrimination based on caste and analogous systems of inherited status; A/HRC/31/56, 28 January 2016.
165 Special Rapporteur on Minority Issues, Report (2016), ibid., paras 26–27.

claim their rights', even if they may belong 'to the same larger ethnic, religious or linguistic community'. Equally,

> minority groups who are characterized by their non-dominant position and whose members possess ethnic, religious or linguistic characteristics differing from those of the rest of the population are also, in many cases, caste-affected groups, and therefore face multiple and intersecting forms of discrimination on the grounds of both their minority status and descent.[166]

The descent category in Article 1 of ICERD is referenced as the international legal source of the prohibition of discrimination on the basis of caste and analogous systems of inherited status.[167] However, it is noted that because caste can be determinative of occupation, 'it is also referred to as "discrimination based on work and descent"',[168] a form of discrimination prohibited by international human rights law. The report describes CERD's GR 29 as consolidating CERD's interpretation of descent and formulating 'a global definition of caste-based discrimination: "discrimination based on caste and analogous systems of inherited status"',[169] while the UN draft principles and guidelines for the effective elimination of discrimination based on work and descent are described as a 'comprehensive framework' to assist stakeholders, including states, in identifying caste-based discrimination and in implementing measures to combat it.[170] The report provides an overview of the impact of discrimination 'in caste-based and analogous systems', with specific discussion of the situation of 'caste-affected women and girls'. It also highlights the causal relationship between caste and analogous forms of discrimination and poverty, and it recommends the use of caste-specific indicators in the implementation of the UN's Sustainable Development Goals (SDGs).[171] States are also recommended to adopt specific legislation prohibiting discrimination on grounds of caste and/or analogous systems and to implement existing legal frameworks fully, including penalties for acts of caste-based discrimination.

In 2017, the UN network on racial discrimination and the protection of minorities,[172] under the auspices of the UN OHCHR, published a guidance tool on descent-based discrimination to assist UN Country Teams in identifying the 'key challenges and strategic approaches to combat caste-based and analogous forms of discrimination'.[173] The choice of the formulation "descent-based discrimination" rather than "discrimination based on work and descent" followed a two-day technical consultation with UN experts and agencies,

---

166 Ibid., para 21.
167 Ibid., paras 48–49.
168 Ibid., para 25.
169 Ibid., para 104.
170 Ibid., para 52.
171 Ibid., paras 23, 126. See also N Saracini and M Shanmugavelan, *Caste and Development: Tackling Work and Descent-Based Discrimination to Achieve the SDGs for All* (London: Bond Network, 2018).
172 Established in 2012 to enhance dialogue and cooperation between relevant UN departments, agencies and programmes.
173 United Nations Network on Racial Discrimination and Protection of Minorities, Guidance Tool on Descent-Based Discrimination: Key Challenges and Strategic Approaches to Combat Caste-Based and Analogous Forms of Discrimination (2017).

academics and representatives from affected communities and international NGOs.[174] It confirms 'descent-based discrimination' as the UN umbrella category capturing caste discrimination, and 'discrimination on the basis of caste and analogous systems of inherited status' as its paradigmatic manifestation,[175] firmly tying caste discrimination to the treaty category of descent. The formulation 'discrimination based on work and descent' is mentioned in a footnote as a term that emerged in 2000 'reflecting the fact that a person's caste can also be determinative of his or her occupation'.[176] The Guidance Tool contains no definition of descent-based discrimination, instead stating that the existence of communities suffering from discrimination on the basis of caste and analogous systems of inherited status may be recognised on the basis of the factors listed in paragraph 1 of CERD's GR 29 (see Chapter 4). The Guidance Tool identifies concrete actions that can be taken by the UN system to address descent-based discrimination, with the collection of disaggregated data in order to diagnose and understand the ways in which affected communities experience discrimination being described as an essential first step.[177]

5.7 Conclusion

Caste discrimination 'is not a problem of the past but a contemporary human rights violation occurring every day across South Asia and its diaspora[,] albeit one which remains insufficiently recognised'.[178] CERD's deployment of descent in 1996 to address caste discrimination as a form of descent-based racial discrimination prohibited by ICERD pushed caste discrimination into international view. India's resistance to CERD's scrutiny of caste discrimination as a violation of ICERD propelled the creation by the UN Sub-Commission on the Promotion and Protection of Human Rights of the new, non-treaty category of discrimination based on work and descent which is not limited to caste and is applicable to all UN member states. It allowed the Sub-Commission to address caste-based discrimination whilst avoiding explicit reference to caste or India, and without a direct linkage to racial discrimination. This led to the first UN Working Papers examining discrimination based on work and descent (with caste discrimination its paradigmatic manifestation), and to the production by the two UN Special Rapporteurs on discrimination based on work and descent of draft principles and guidelines for its effective elimination.[179] Dalits, meanwhile, were also engaging with other, non-treaty bodies within the UN system. To date, they have accessed minority rights and indigenous people's mechanisms, and caste discrimination has been addressed by various UN Special Procedures, notably the Special Rapporteur on Racism and the Special Rapporteur on Minority Issues, and by the UPR mechanism. Yet states

174 UN Office of the High Commissioner for Human Rights, Geneva, 5–6 October 2015. The present author participated in the two-day technical consultation.
175 UN Guidance Tool (n 173). Caste and analogous systems of inherited status are defined as 'social hierarchies wherein certain groups are branded as inferior based on their birth into a particular social group. In such systems, the marginalized status so acquired cannot be removed simply by individual merit or achievement'; 11.
176 Guidance Tool, ibid., fn 7.
177 Ibid., 71–72.
178 A Waughray and D Keane, 'CERD and Caste-Based Discrimination', in D Keane and A Waughray (eds.), *Fifty Years of the International Convention on the Elimination of All Forms of Racial Discrimination* (Manchester: Manchester University Press, 2017) 146.
179 DWD became understood by activists as the UN terminology for caste discrimination; see https://idsn.org/terminology/.

such as India and Japan continue to reject the application of descent to groups discriminated against on the basis of inherited status or origin, arguing that descent refers to racial and ethnic characteristics and was never intended to cover inherited status, caste or social origin discrimination. The UK has not disputed the interpretation of descent as including caste, but it has rejected CERD's recommendations to introduce a statutory prohibition of related discrimination in domestic law, arguing that there is 'no consensus' on the need for legislation among 'affected communities' and, more recently, that judicial interpretation of existing statutory provisions provides sufficient protection from caste discrimination, making an explicit prohibition unnecessary.

Despite these challenges, the UN human rights regime's conceptualisation of caste discrimination as a violation of international human rights law, including treaty bodies and non-treaty mechanisms and procedures, has three important effects. First, the presumption that caste discrimination falls foul of international human rights standards, including the prohibition of racial discrimination, puts states under domestic and international legal and political pressure to act on the recommendations of the treaty bodies and UN mechanisms. This is an important point, because while compliance with treaty obligations is a legal obligation, there are political factors in its realisation, a point India made to CERD in 1996: '[T]o confer a racial character on the caste system *would create considerable political problems* which could not be the Committee's intention'.[180] Second, UN engagement with caste discrimination, particularly the promotion of tools, mechanisms and procedures, increases its visibility and boosts the morale and confidence of victims and activists to continue combating violations. Third, the construction of an international legal framework for combating caste discrimination provides a benchmark and template for new domestic legislation, which in turn reinforces the conceptualisation of caste discrimination as a human rights and a discrimination issue.

The Special Rapporteur on Racism has asserted that the legal framework on caste discrimination is 'unambiguous',[181] while a UN experts' study on international instruments to combat racial discrimination decided that there are 'no substantive gaps' regarding the protection of members of descent-based communities from racial discrimination. It further noted that the DPGs on discrimination based on work and descent and the recommendations in CERD GR No. 29, if implemented, would serve to alleviate both the problems resulting from discrimination based on descent and the development of existing standards, and that inadequate implementation and lack of political will remain among the basic barriers impeding the elimination of descent-based discrimination.[182] CERD has reiterated that the concept of racial discrimination is 'much broader than that perceived by many states which argue that there is no racial discrimination on their territory' and that

> shortcomings in the implementation by States of the Convention stem not only from a lack of political will, but also from a lack of a clear understanding by many States parties regarding the meaning and scope of the definition of the concept of racial discrimination.[183]

---

180 UN Doc. CERD/C/SR.1162, 13 August 1996, para 35 (emphasis added).
181 SRR, Interim Report; A/64/271, 10 August 2009, para 58.
182 Report, Complementary International Standards; UN Doc. A/HRC/4.WG.3/6, 27 August 2007, para 76.
183 CERD, replies to questionnaires. 23 April 2008 (n 128) pages 11–15.

The political reality, however, is that not all states accept that existing normative frameworks apply to caste discrimination, or that caste discrimination is a legitimate international human rights issue, or that the prohibition of descent-based discrimination (or discrimination based on work and descent) applies to their own state. Similar problems of equivocal and inconsistent state responses have been identified in relation to human rights violations based on sexual orientation and gender identity, with states refusing to acknowledge that this constitutes a legitimate area of international human rights concern.[184] The 2011 international strategy conference on Dalit rights (described earlier) advocated the de-linking of caste and race in favour of framing caste discrimination in the language of discrimination based on work and descent as a global human rights concern. However, at the UN level, "descent-based discrimination" has emerged as the umbrella category capturing discrimination based on caste and "analogous systems of inherited status," tying caste discrimination to the treaty category of descent. The challenge is political as well as legal, namely to engage states in acknowledging the legitimacy of UN involvement and, if they are 'truly committed to social cohesion and eliminating bigotry and prejudice', to regard mechanisms such as CERD – and the DPGs – not as a threat but as an opportunity to understand and counter better caste and discrimination based on work and descent.[185]

This chapter concludes Part 2 of the book. We now turn in Part 3 to the debates surrounding the prohibition of caste discrimination in British equality law.

184 M O'Flaherty and J Fisher, 'Sexual Orientation, Gender Identity and International Human Rights Law: Contextualising the Yogyakarta Principles', 8 *Human Rights Law Quarterly* (2008) 207–248, 227–228. The 2007 Yogyakarta Principles constitute 'a coherent and comprehensive identification of the obligation of States to respect, protect and fulfil the human rights of all persons regardless of their sexual orientation or gender identity'; ibid., 207.
185 CERD member January-Bardill, CERD/C/SR.1796, 2 March 2007, paras 47–50.

Part III

Legal regulation of caste discrimination in the UK

6   Caste in the UK 1950–2009*

6.1 Introduction

The presence of South Asians in the UK, and the story of their contribution to the nation, is well documented.[1] Research on South Asian communities in the UK shows that caste is a feature of diaspora society, regardless of religion, and that caste has played a role in the construction and maintenance of internal divisions among South Asian communities since the 1950s, despite insistence by some actors that neither caste nor caste discrimination exist in this country. This chapter discusses caste's history in the UK from 1950 to 2009 (the year of the Equality Bill) and places in context the demands of British Dalits for legal regulation of caste discrimination – demands which gathered momentum around the start of the new millennium.

6.2 The South Asian presence in the UK

There are over three million people of South Asian origin in the UK, according to the 2011 Census, comprising over one and a half million people of Pakistani and Bangladeshi origin (over 1.4 million of whom are Muslim) and almost one and a half million people of Indian origin.[2] In total, in England and Wales, there are 2.7 million Muslims, around 816,600 Hindus, 423,150 Sikhs and 247,700 Buddhists.[3] Large-scale South Asian migration to the UK took place primarily between the 1950s and 1970s in response to Britain's post-war labour shortage, although there has been a South Asian presence in the UK since the seventeenth century.[4] Between 1961 and 2001, the percentage of people of South Asian origin

---

* Parts of this chapter appeared previously in A. Waughray, 'Caste Discrimination: A Twenty-First-Century Challenge for UK Discrimination Law?' 72(2) *Modern Law Review* (2009) 182–219.

1 See, for example, Making Britain: Discover How South Asians Shaped the Nation, 1870–1950, The Open University, at www.open.ac.uk/makingbritain; R Visram, *Asians in Britain: 400 Years of History* (London: Pluto Press, 2002); R Visram, *Ayahs, Lascars and Princes: Indians in Britain 1700–1947* (London: Pluto Press, 1986); R Ballard (ed.), *Desh Pardesh: The South Asian Presence in Britain* (London: Hurst & Co, 1994); J Brown, *Global South Asians: Introducing the Modern Diaspora* (Cambridge: Cambridge University Press, 2006).

2 Census 2011, Office for National Statistics (ONS), UK population by ethnicity and identity. The terms "Asian" and "Asian British" include people of Indian, Pakistani, Bangladeshi, Chinese and Other Asian origin; ONS, Ethnicity and National Identity in England and Wales 2011 (see www.ons.gov.uk). Chinese people account for 0.7% of the UK population as a whole.

3 Census 2011, ONS, Largest religious ethnic groups; ONS, What does the Census tell us about religion in 2011?; ONS, What is your religion? (see www.ons.gov.uk). For 2001 data, see J Dobbs et al. (eds.), *Focus on Ethnicity and Religion* (Basingstoke: Palgrave Macmillan, 2006) 22.

4 Ballard (n 1); Visram (2002) (n 1); Visram (1986) (n 1); Brown (n 1).

DOI: 10.4324/9781315750934-10

in the UK population increased from 0.23% to 4%.[5] South Asian immigration to the UK has exhibited two important features: (1) immigrants have come from a relatively small number of geographical areas, but (2) they are nevertheless differentiated by language, region, caste and religion. The bulk of South Asian mass immigration to the UK has come from four main regions: Punjab, which on Partition in 1947 was divided between Pakistan and India, Gujarat on the western coast of India, Sylhet in northern Bangladesh and, in Pakistan, the Mirpur District in Azad ("free") Kashmir and the North West Frontier Province.[6] According to Talbot and Thandi, 'by the end of the 20th century, Punjabis accounted for well over half of the UK's South Asian Diaspora community'.[7] South Asian migrants have primarily been rural, peasant landowner-cultivators who have arrived not as lone, unconnected individuals but in 'cascading chains . . . of kinship and friendship'.[8]

Britain's South Asian communities are not homogenous. Among Asian Muslims (the largest religious group), 402,000 are Bangladeshis and 1,028,000 are Pakistanis,[9] around two-thirds of whom originate from Mirpur District.[10] Bangladeshi Sylhetis are almost exclusively Muslim, and of the Punjabis, under half are from India (and these are mostly Sikhs), while Pakistani Punjabis are mostly Muslims but include 'a small Christian minority, most of whom are of "untouchable" descent'.[11] The Gujarati community is 'fragmented by a large number of religious, sectarian and caste disjunctions'.[12] Moreover, many Gujaratis are 'twice migrants'[13] who arrived in the UK via a history of prior emigration to East Africa and the Middle East.[14] Indo-Caribbeans constitute a separate group – they are either the descendants of Indian indentured migrants to Britain's West Indian colonies (such as Trinidad, Mauritius, British Guiana and Fiji) who worked as plantation labourers, later as agricultural workers or peasant farmers,[15] or descendants of Indian indentured labour recruited to work in the French colonies following the abolition of slavery in France in 1848.[16]

5   Ballard (n 1) 7.
6   Ballard (n 1) 10; A Shaw, 'The Pakistani Community in Oxford', in Ballard (ed.) (n 1) 35–57, 37.
7   I Talbot and S Thandi (eds.), *People on the Move: Punjabi Colonial and Post-Colonial Migration* (Oxford: Oxford University Press, 2004) xvi.
8   Ballard (n 1) 11.
9   ONS, What does the Census tell us about religion in 2011? (n 3).
10   Ballard (n 1) 20; H Blakey, J Pearce, and G Chesters, *Minorities Within Minorities: Beneath the Surface of Community Participation* (York: Joseph Rowntree Foundation, 2006) 34–35; R Jones and G Welhengama, *Ethnic Minorities in English Law* (Stoke on Trent: Trentham, 2000) 53.
11   Ballard (n 1) 20. Sikh emigration also has a 'compact' geographical base, being originally mainly from villages in the Jalandhar Doaba (Indian Punjab); E Nesbitt, ' "We Are All Equal": Young British Punjabis' and Gujaratis' Perceptions of Caste', 4(2) *International Journal of Punjab Studies* (1997) 201–218, 214.
12   Ballard (n 1) 20.
13   P Bhachu, *The Twice Migrants* (London: Tavistock, 1986) cited in Ballard (n 1) 23.
14   Ballard (n 1) 20; Brown (n 1); C Clarke, C Peach, and S Vertovec (eds.), *South Asians Overseas: Migration and Ethnicity* (Cambridge: Cambridge University Press, 1990); C Bates (ed.), *Community, Empire and Migration* (Basingstoke: Palgrave, 2001). The trajectory for Asians from East Africa to the UK was not easy. Between 1965 and 1968, thousands of East African Asians exercised their rights to come to the UK, but in 1968, the introduction of the Commonwealth Immigrants Act imposed entry restrictions on UK passport holders, effectively depriving entry on racial grounds to British East African Asians. In 1971, the European Commission on Human Rights found the legislation to violate the UK's obligations under Articles 3 and 8 of the European Convention on Human Rights 1950. See Lord Lester of Herne Hill, 'Thirty Years On: The East African Asians Case Revisited', *Public Law* (Spring 2002) 52–72; *East African Asians v. UK*, 3 EHRR 76 (1973).
15   S Vertovec, 'Oil Boom and Recession in Trinidad Indian Villages', in Clarke et al. (eds.), ibid., 89–111, 89. See Brown (n 3) 30–31.
16   P Singaravelou, 'Indians in the French Overseas Departments: Guadeloupe, Martinique, Reunion', in Clarke et al. (eds.) (n 14) 75–87, 75–76.

6.3 Dalits in the UK

6.3.1 Numbers and groupings

Dalits are castes (*jatis*) formerly known in India as "untouchable". "Dalit" is not an official term in India, rather a political term of self-identification (see Chapter 1). As we have seen in Chapter 1, the constitutional, legal and administrative term for Dalits (subject to certain exceptions) is "Scheduled Castes," meaning those castes listed in a Schedule to the Constitution who are entitled to the benefit of constitutional affirmative action policies and other legal and administrative protections and measures. The Scheduled Caste (SC) category in India is constitutionally restricted to adherents of Indic religions (Hinduism, Sikhism and Buddhism): Muslim and Christian Dalits are excluded from the category. However, in both India and the UK, the term "Dalit" is used by Dalits of all religions and none. There are no accurate figures for the number of South Asians of Dalit origin in the UK, as caste identity is not recorded in any official statistics, but it has been estimated by Dalit organisations (such as Dalit Solidarity Network UK, Voice of Dalit International and the Anti Caste Discrimination Alliance) as anywhere between 50,000 and 200,000 people.[17] This population comprises members of anti-caste religious groupings such as Ravidassias,[18] Valmikis and Ambedkarite Buddhists, as well as Dalit Christians, secular Ambedkarites and Dalits of no religious or political affiliation.[19]

Dalit presence in the UK dates from the 1950s with the first Punjabi immigrants, around 10% of whom (according to Mark Juergensmeyer) were Scheduled Castes, especially Chamars (traditionally described as leather-working castes).[20] Dalit immigrants had differing geographical origins and religious affinities, and differing responses to caste discrimination and approaches to dealing with it. Many of the Punjabi Chamars were Ravidassias, adherents of Ad Dharm (meaning "original religion"), the north Indian anti-caste religious movement founded in the 1920s by Mangoo Ram, and followers of the sixteenth-century anti-caste

---

17 *No Escape: Caste Discrimination in the UK* (London: Dalit Solidarity Network UK, 2006) 4. See also *Dalits in the New Millennium: Report of the Proceedings of the International Conference on Dalit Human Rights, 16–17 September 2000* (London: Voice of Dalit International (VODI), 2000) 1; *Hidden Apartheid – Voice of the Community: Caste and Caste Discrimination in the UK – A Scoping Study* (Anti Caste Discrimination Alliance (ACDA): Derby, 2009) 3, 6. In February 2013, Dalit organisations revised their estimate to 860,000; letter, Dalit organisations to Helen Grant MP, Minister for Women and Equalities, 14 February 2013; copy on file with author. This figure was relied on in a government-commissioned report on caste discrimination; see H Metcalfe and H Rolfe, *Caste Discrimination and Harassment in Great Britain* (London: GEO, 2010) 20. See also Chapter 9.

18 The Ad-Dharm anti-caste movement emerged in northern India in the 1920s. Contemporary Ad-Dharm in India and the UK includes Valmikis and Ravidassias – anti-caste religious groupings comprising individuals from diverse religious traditions, including Hinduism and Sikhism, usually with shared "untouchable" origins. ACDA put the numbers of Ravidassias in the UK at 175,000; ACDA, ibid., 2.

19 Ambedkarites are followers of Dr BR Ambedkar; see C Jaffrelot, *Dr Ambedkar and Untouchability: Analysing and Fighting Caste* (New Delhi: Permanent Black, 2004). See also Chapters 1, 2 and 3.

20 M Juergensmeyer, *Religion as Social Vision: The Movement Against Untouchability in Twentieth-Century Punjab* (Berkeley: University of California Press, 1982) 245–246; E-M Hardtmann, *The Dalit Movement in India: Local Practices, Global Connections* (New Delhi: Oxford University Press, 2009) 161; E Nesbitt, 'Religion and Identity: The Valmiki Community in Coventry', 16(2) *Journal of Ethnic and Migration Studies* (1990) 261–274, 263. See also M Dhanda, 'Caste and International Migration, India to the UK', in I Ness (ed.), *The Encyclopaedia of Global Human Migration* (Oxford: Wiley-Blackwell, 2013).

poet-saint, or *sant*, Ravi Das.[21] The Valmikis, also Ad Dharmis from north India,[22] were devotees of Bhagwan Valmiki (author of the ancient Indian epic *The Ramayana*) and primarily from the Chuhra (sweeper/scavenger) castes.[23] By the 1950s, the distinction between these two Dalit groups – the mainly Ravidassia Chamars and the mainly Valmiki Churahs – had become a distinction between two separate religious groupings.[24]

In addition to racial tensions between South Asian immigrants and the white majority, caste-based tensions existed between the Dalits and so-called higher or dominant-caste immigrants (for example regarding access to temples).[25] Tensions also existed between the Dalit groups themselves.[26] In 1956, Ravi Das *sabhas*[27] were established in Birmingham and Wolverhampton, forerunners to the establishment of Ravidassia temples. Ravidassias decided to set up and run their own temples as a consequence of experiencing the same prejudice and caste-based discrimination as in India when they sought to worship at other (dominant-caste) holy places. Meanwhile, in 1962, Ambedkarite Buddhists formed the Indian Buddhist Society and, in 1965, the Indian Republican Group of Great Britain.[28] Ambedkar Memorial Committees, notes Juergensmeyer, were formed in Wolverhampton and London.[29] By the mid-1960s, there were several hundred active Ambedkarites in Britain,[30] but the relationship between the Ravidassias and the Ambedkarites became increasingly strained, and, in 1965, the Ravidassias set up the Indian Mutual Support and Social Association, which "specifically exclud[ed] the Ambedkarites."[31] In 1968, the first Ravi Das temple was opened in Wolverhampton,[32] while in 1971, the Ad Dharm Federation of the UK was formed.[33] The Ravidassias and Ambedkarites differed in terms of social vision and strategy: Ambedkarites sought a clean break from Hinduism and assimilation into 'a wider egalitarian culture', whereas Ravidassias sought to consolidate and unite behind a religious tradition with links to Hindu culture, albeit the radical, egalitarian "*sant*" tradition.[34] The Ad Dharm movement considered the Dalits to be the descendants of the original inhabitants of India, a theory rejected by Ambedkar.[35]

For many years, Valmikis and Ravidassias – anti-caste religious movements largely comprising people with shared Dalit origins, influenced by aspects of Sikh and Hindu tradition

21 Juergensmeyer, ibid., 83–91. See also M Juergensmeyer, *Religious Rebels in The Punjab – the Ad Dharm Challenge to Caste* (New Delhi: Nayanana, 2009).
22 J Leslie, *Authority and Meaning in Indian Religions: Hinduism and the Case of Valmiki* (Aldershot: Ashgate, 2003) 47 and Chapter 7; see also Nesbitt (1990) (n 20).
23 See Leslie, ibid., 49–50.
24 Ibid., 60, 63.
25 Nesbitt (1994), 'Valmikis in Coventry: The Revival and Reconstruction of a Community', in Ballard (ed.) (n 1) 117–141, 119, 127–128; Leslie (n 22) 67.
26 Ibid., 123.
27 *Sabha* means association, group, society; *gurdwara* means temple.
28 Juergensmeyer (n 20) 249. Shortly before his death in 1956 Ambedkar converted to Buddhism along with thousands of his followers; see Jaffrelot (n 19) 120–121.
29 Ibid.
30 Hardtmann (n 20) 166.
31 Juergensmeyer (n 20) 250.
32 Ibid.
33 Leslie (n 22) 66; Juergensmeyer, ibid., 256.
34 Juergensmeyer, ibid., 250, 274; Hardtmann (n 20) 172–173.
35 Leslie (n 22) 57.

but which cannot be conflated with either mainstream Hinduism or Sikhism[36] – were active in their local communities, focused primarily on providing support and places of worship, and maintaining links with their communities in India. They established their own associations and temples in response to the discrimination and exclusion they experienced when they sought to attend the places of worship established by the dominant castes,[37] such that there now exists in the UK a plethora of temples or gurdwaras distinguished along caste lines. There are twenty-four Ravidass temples and gurdwaras, including one in Scotland, under the auspices of the Shri Guru Ravidass Sabha UK.[38] Valmik Sabhas have been established in Southall, Birmingham, Bedford, Coventry, Oxford and Wolverhampton. These groups have become increasingly visible, due in part to the Ravidassias' campaign for those in England and Wales to record "Ravidassia" in response to the national identity, ethnicity and religion questions in the 2011 census.[39] Ambedkarite Buddhists in the UK have an umbrella organisation, the Federation of Ambedkarite Buddhist Organisations (FABO-UK), whose purpose is to 'propagate Ambedkar's thought and Buddhist ideas throughout the world'.[40]

6.3.2 *"New" Dalit organisations*

From the mid-1990s, Dalit activists in India and the South Asian diaspora sought to raise international awareness of caste discrimination in India. The "internationalisation" of caste and the concomitant development of transnational Dalit advocacy networks[41] prompted the emergence in the UK of new, secular Dalit organisations and solidarity networks concerned with Dalit rights domestically and internationally, with a UK-focused political and campaigning agenda. Dalit Solidarity Network UK (DSN-UK, founded in 1998 and subsequently affiliated to the Copenhagen-based International Dalit Solidarity Network [IDSN], founded in 2000), Voice of Dalit International (VODI, 1999), CasteWatch UK (CWUK, 2004) and Anti Caste Discrimination Alliance (ACDA, 2008) have adopted international discourses of human rights and equality in engaging with the domestic political process on an anti-caste discrimination and "Dalit rights" agenda.

36 Nesbitt (n 25) 123–124; E Nesbitt, 'Pitfalls in Religious Taxonomy: Hindus and Sikhs, Valmikis and Ravidasis', 6(1) *Religion Today* (1990) 9–12; E Nesbitt, 'My Dad's Hindu, My Mum's Side Are Sikhs: Issues in Religious Identity', University of Manchester, Faculty of Arts, 1991, at https://www.research gate.net/publication/242242139_My_Dad's_Hindu_my_Mum's_side_are_Sikhs_Issues_in_Religious_ Identity; Leslie (n 22), chapter 7.
37 Nesbitt (n 25); S Singh Kalsi, *The Evolution of a Sikh Community in Britain* (Leeds: University of Leeds, Community Religions Project, 1992) 129–131.
38 Shri Guru Ravidass temples are represented by the Shri Guru Ravidass Sabha UK; see https://ravidassia. wordpress.com/list-of-temples/.
39 See ONS, Third sector and community groups. In the 2011 Census, eleven thousand people recorded their religion as Ravidassia in the 'any other religion' category.
40 See http://ambedkar.nspire.in/about-fabo-uk.html. FABO have campaigned to memorialise Ambedkar in the UK, where he trained as lawyer and was called to the Bar in 1923; see 'Maharashtra to Buy Ambedkar's London House', *The Hindu*, 24 January 2015.
41 See C Bob, 'Dalit Rights Are Human Rights: Caste Discrimination, International Activism and the Construction of a New Human Rights Issue', 29(1) *Human Rights Quarterly* (2007) 167–193; J Lerche, 'Transnational Advocacy Networks and Affirmative Action for Dalits in India', 39(2) *Development and Change* (2008) 239–261.

6.4 Caste and caste discrimination in the UK

6.4.1 *Migration and caste: the early days*

'Caste exists in Britain: this is not in dispute', affirmed the first (and, to date, only) government-commissioned report on caste discrimination in Britain in December 2010.[42] Yet, for decades, the existence of caste structures and practices in the UK was largely overlooked or even denied by many actors. In 1916, Ambedkar had described caste as 'a local [i.e. subcontinental] problem but one capable of much wider mischief', observing that 'if Hindus migrate to other regions on earth, Indian caste would become a world problem'.[43] In the early days of mass migration to the UK, when numbers were small and the immigrants were predominantly single men, individuals came together in linguistic-regional groups which operated as unified communities cutting across caste distinctions.[44] In 1963, Indian anthropologist Rashmi Desai, in a study of Gujarati and Punjabi immigrant communities in the UK, asserted that although caste distinctions were present in the UK, they did not take the same oppressive form as in India; for example, the rules against eating together '[did] not apply in the United Kingdom'.[45] He did not suggest that this was due to a repudiation of caste and caste distinctions; rather (at that time), there was 'not a sufficient number of castes in the United Kingdom', and they were economically dependent on the host society, not each other.[46] However, caste remained 'very much alive' in immigrants' relationship with society back home in India.[47] Whether cross-caste linguistic-regional groupings were the norm experienced by Dalits, or whether they were excluded from such groupings, is hard to tell. While, generally, life was better for Scheduled Castes in England, 'in some ways it [was] disturbingly the same . . . the Jat Sikhs [did] not hesitate to remind the Chamars that they [were] still Chamars, even in England'.[48]

---

42 H Metcalfe and H Rolfe, *Caste Discrimination and Harassment in Great Britain* (London: Government Equalities Office, 2010) 14.

43 BR Ambedkar, 'Castes in India: Seminar Paper', Columbia University, NY, 9 May 1916 in V Moon (ed.), *Dr Babasaheb Ambedkar Writings and Speeches (BAWS) Vol. 1* (Bombay: The Education Dept., Govt. of Maharasthra, 1989) 6, citing V Shridhar and AM Ketkar, *The History of Castes in India* (Ithaca, NY: Taylor & Carpenter, 1909) 4.

44 R Desai, *Indian Immigrants in Britain* (London: Oxford University Press, 1963) 14–16, 15; A Shukra, 'Caste, a Personal Perspective', in M Searle-Chatterjee and U Sharma (eds.), *Contextualising Caste: Post-Dumontian Approaches* (Oxford: Blackwell, 1994) 169–178, 174. Sato reports mixed-caste Sikh congregations in Leicester in the early 1960s; K Sato, 'Divisions Among Sikh Communities in Britain and the Role of the Caste System: A Case Study of Four Gurdwaras in Multi-Ethnic Leicester', 19(1) *Journal of Punjab Studies* (2012) 1–25, 8. See also P Ghuman, *British Untouchables: A Study of Dalit Identity and Education* (Farnham: Ashgate, 2011) 97.

45 Desai, ibid., 14.

46 Ibid., 15.

47 Ibid., 15–16.

48 Juergensmeyer (n 20) 246–247; Nesbitt (n 25) 118–119. Jats are peasant farmers and landowners from Punjab who can be adherents of Hinduism or Islam as well as Sikhism, although most are Sikhs. They have traditionally been considered a dominant caste. Moldenhawer argues that instead of regarding migrants as agents moving between two or more bounded and separate worlds (as either 'sojourners' or 'settlers'), their social worlds are essentially different locations of the same society; B Moldenhawer, 'Transnational Migrant Communities and Education Strategies Among Pakistani Youngsters in Denmark', 31(1) *Journal of Ethnic and Migration Studies* (2005) 51–78, 58.

6.4.2 *"Chain migration" and caste*

As Britain increasingly became seen as a place to settle permanently, and with the arrival of wives and families, social, religious and cultural institutions – including caste – were re-established,[49] and new axes of 'community fission' emerged alongside the existing linguistic-regional divisions.[50] The importance of caste as one such axis was highlighted in 1986 by Robinson, citing Michaelson's analysis of caste identity among East African Gujaratis in Britain as 'institutionalised by the growth of associations and organisations for each of the major sub-castes . . . and by residential concentration'.[51] Similarly, Ballard's 1994 account of the settlement strategies of South Asian migrants in Britain argues that 'chain migration' – migrants with shared caste, language and region of origin joining 'equally specific' communities in Britain[52] – has resulted in caste remaining 'a crucial feature of social organisation in almost every settlement'. Whilst stressing that the caste system is more fluid than many Western observers realise, he observed that in Britain, as in urban India, despite the de-linking of caste and occupation, caste loyalties are as active as ever, and inter-caste competition for status has indeed intensified. The reason for this is that 'the rules of endogamy are followed just as strictly in the Diaspora as in the subcontinent', and as a result, 'all kinship networks remain firmly caste-specific'.[53] A study in 1972 of Indian students and professionals ("elite" Indians), who, unlike immigrant workers, were not generally coming to join an established community, likewise identified caste consciousness alongside regional and linguistic ties as the 'principal forces of division and cohesion' at work within the elite subgroup.[54] Ironically, '[d]espite the lack of interest in caste [on the part of the majority society], *or perhaps because of it*, the old caste divisions persisted in the new locations'.[55]

6.4.3 *Survival of caste awareness: critical factors*

Clarke, Peach and Vertovec contrast the Indo-Caribbeans – among whom the caste system is commonly believed to have evolved into ethnicised groupings bearing caste (*jati*) or *varna* names which have lost their original Indian meaning, or to have 'dissolved save for status attributions on the extreme ends of the Brahmin-Chamar scale', or even to have lost its significance entirely (although this is contested) – with the Indian 'urban-based merchants and civil servants' in Africa, among whom 'caste consciousness remained high, even though a system of caste-based interaction and exchange ceased to function'.[56] They cite Kuper, who, in 1961, argued that caste awareness can survive if members

> (1) can maintain a ritual exclusiveness from the time they leave India, (2) hold a privileged position in the economic organization and can avoid proletarianization, (3) retain

---

49 Ballard (n 1) 15–18.
50 V Robinson, *Transients and Settlers: Asians in Britain* (Oxford: Clarendon Press, 1986) 82; Ghuman (n 44).
51 Robinson, ibid., 82–83 citing M Michaelson, 'The Relevance of Caste Among East African Gujaratis in Britain', 7(3) *Journal of Ethnic and Migration Studies* (1979) 350–360.
52 Leslie (n 20) 65.
53 Ballard (ed.) (n 1) 11, 25, 26.
54 H Kanitkar, 'An Indian Elite in Britain', 1(5) *Journal of Ethnic and Migration Studies* (1972) 378–383, 378.
55 Leslie (n 20) 66 (emphasis added).
56 Clarke et al. (eds.) (n 14) 13. See also X Trnka 'Cleanliness in a Caste-Less Context: Collective Negotiations of Purity and Pollution Among Indo-Fijian Hindus', 22(1) *Anthropological Forum* (2012) 25–43, 28. For findings contesting the common perception that the caste system among Hindu Mauritians has

ties with a protected caste nucleus in India, (4) isolate their women from intimate cross-caste contact.[57]

Such conditions, say Clarke et al., 'apply equally for the South Asian migrants in the contemporary period'.[58] The historical, social and cultural particularities of mass South Asian migration to great Britain – "chain migration," shared geographical origins, the retention of close ties with "home," the persistence of endogamy and control of women's sexuality through a variety of methods – mean that for a significant proportion of the UK's South Asian population, Kuper's criteria for the survival of caste consciousness and caste hierarchies are met.[59] Given that caste is both a cohesive and a divisive force, this has implications not only for understandings of equality and 'community cohesion' (damage to community cohesion being an argument put forward *against* legislating to prohibit caste discrimination in the UK),[60] but also for the choice of legal and policy measures to enhance formal and substantive equality and to combat caste discrimination in the UK.

6.4.4 Caste and caste discrimination in the UK: evidence from 1950–2009

Between 1950 and 2009, caste in Britain attracted only sporadic media coverage.[61] It emerges incidentally in academic studies of South Asian communities and identity in Britain during this period, in references to the role of caste (or *biraderi* among British Muslims),[62] but there is little research from this period looking specifically at the role of or attitudes to caste, or caste-based discriminatory practices, in Britain. An important exception is Eleanor Nesbitt's work on attitudes to and perceptions of caste, religion and identity among Gujarati and Punjabi youth in Britain, particularly in relation to Ravidasis and Valmikis.[63] In the 1990s, Nesbitt highlighted the existence of caste and caste discrimination among Gujaratis and Punjabis in Britain.[64] Caste was 'an observable dynamic' among Sikhs,[65] and Sikh and

---

disappeared or lost its ideological relevance, see M Claveyrolas, 'The "Land of the Vaish"? Caste Structure and Ideology in Mauritius', *South Asia Multidisciplinary Academic Journal*, 2015 at http://samaj.revues.org/3886.

57 H Kuper, *Indian People in Natal* (Durban: Natal University Press, 1961) 30, cited in Clarke et al. (eds.) (n 14) 13.

58 Clarke et al. (eds.), ibid., 14.

59 As regards the avoidance of proletarianisation, Shukra refers to the best jobs in the engineering factories where he worked being 'zealously monopolised by the Punjabi *Jats*'; (n 44) 174.

60 The term "community" can be seen being used interchangeably in India and the UK with "caste" and also with "religion."

61 See, for example, D Clark, 'The Harijans of Britain', *New Society*, 26 June 1975; J Kelly, 'Apart and Hated?' *The Times*, 6 July 1990; C Aziz, 'The Untouchables of London's Suburbs', *The Independent*, 10 January 1991; S Cook, 'Caste Out', *The Guardian*, 11 May 1991.

62 See, for example, Michaelson (n 51); Ballard (n 1); Leslie (n 22) 64–73; A Shaw, *Kinship and Continuity: Pakistani Families in Britain* (Abingdon: Routledge, 2000); I Din, *The New British: The Impact of Culture and Community on Young Pakistanis* (Aldershot: Ashgate, 2006). *Biraderi* is a Punjabi term, in the UK mostly used by Pakistani Muslims, to denote a system of endogamous, hierarchically ranked kinship groups or clans, similar but not identical to caste. It is generally translated as a kinship group, clan or brotherhood, with implied descent from a common male ancestor and entailing complex dynamics of support, reciprocity, obligation and control; see Chapter 1.

63 See E Nesbitt, 'Religion and Identity: The Valmiki Community in Coventry', 16(2) *New Community* (1990) 261–274; Nesbitt (1990) (n 36) 9–12; Nesbitt (1991) (n 36); Nesbitt (n 25); Nesbitt (n 11).

64 Ibid.

65 Nesbitt (n 11) 203. See also Singh Kalsi (n 37), for a detailed account of the role of caste among Sikhs in Leeds and Bradford; Sato (n 44).

Hindu children, including those who had never lived in India, identified peers by their caste,[66] but for Ravidasis and Valmikis, such caste awareness was accompanied by experiences or fear of prejudice.[67] In 1994, a British-based Dalit suggested that caste was in some ways stronger in the UK than in India and that despite Britain's prevailing liberal democratic norms, casteism – particularly among schoolchildren – was worse than in the early days of South Asian migration, and yet Dalits remained invisible to wider society. Consequently, he predicted that many Dalit children born and brought up in the UK would face a more confusing, and hence psychologically more insidious, kind of casteism.[68] Julia Leslie, in her 2003 study of Valmiki, states that 'the importance of caste loyalties in the Diaspora cannot be overstressed'. She describes caste as affecting and internally dividing all South Asian communities in Britain.[69] In the context of ethnographic and religious approaches to intercultural education, Nesbitt highlighted in 2004 the importance of caste for South Asians as

> part of the lived experience of many millions of Hindus and Sikhs in India and elsewhere. *These millions include young people, parents, teachers and others involved in the UK education system*, as well as in North America and other parts of the diaspora.[70]

Three studies in 2006 attested to the reality of caste in contemporary Britain.[71] *Minorities within Minorities*, for instance, looking at barriers to community participation among South Asians in Bradford, predominantly Pakistani Muslims, found a fractured and divided community characterised by divisions and power hierarchies based on caste and *biraderi* as well as region of origin, gender, sexuality and religious affiliation.[72] A study by DSN-UK, looking specifically at discrimination based on caste, argued that such intolerance was part of the lived experience of many individuals of Dalit origin in the UK.[73] Lastly, a government-sponsored study of British Hindu identity, commissioned by the Hindu Forum of Britain (HFB) from the Runnymede Trust, confirmed the importance of caste as a form of social organisation and a source of subgroup identity among Hindus in Britain.[74] Although silent on the hierarchical nature of the *varna* system and those deemed to fall outside it, namely the Dalits, the study did identify caste as a meaningful aspect of contemporary British Hindu life, at least for some. Moreover, its recommendations stated, 'a key task for any Hindu leadership is to find ways of respecting traditions but *challenging discrimination based on family background, religious tradition or jaati (caste)* within a community'.[75] In 2009, ACDA published *Hidden Apartheid – Voice of the Community*, a study on caste discrimination. It reported widespread experience by UK Dalits of discrimination occurring in spheres of activity covered by discrimination law, concern about lack of legislation to protect

---

66 E Nesbitt, *Intercultural Education: Ethnographic and Religious Approaches* (Brighton: Sussex Academic Press, 2004) 107; Nesbitt (n 11) 212.
67 Nesbitt (n 11).
68 Shukra (n 44) 175–177.
69 Leslie (n 22) 68. Leslie's study was prompted by a dispute between Valmikis and Sikhs in 2000 in Birmingham concerning references to Valmiki in a Punjabi radio programme.
70 Nesbitt (n 66) 98 (emphasis added).
71 In Denmark, caste has been identified as a factor influencing the education strategies of South Asian migrants; Moldenhawer (n 48) 51–78.
72 Blakey et al. (n 10) 2.
73 DSN-UK (n 17) 14–15, 19.
74 R Berkeley, *Connecting British Hindus: An Enquiry into the Identity and Public Engagement of Hindus in Britain* (London: Hindu Forum of Britain, 2006) 59.
75 Ibid., 12 (emphasis added).

victims and significant experiences suffered by children involving inter-pupil verbal abuse or threatening behaviour.[76] A small-scale study in 2009 on caste boundaries in interpersonal relationships among young urban Punjabi Dalits in India and the UK found that the UK interviewees had all experienced caste-related bullying in school via exclusion or, more commonly, name-calling, resulting in 'a reluctance to work in an all-Indian environment for fear of caste discrimination'.[77] Paramjit Judge, researching Punjabis in the UK in 2002, found all aspects of the caste system in existence.[78] In certain situations, he says, caste considerations were more important than race.[79] Alongside these studies, "Jatt Pride" websites, internet chatrooms and the Bhangra music phenomenon testify to the existence of caste awareness, and sometimes prejudice, among sections of South Asian youth (in this case, Jatt Sikhs), many of whom have never lived on the subcontinent.[80]

6.4.5 *Caste and marriage in the UK*

Ghuman observes that there is no doubt that 'the institutions of family and marriage are the bastions of caste retention and divisions' in the UK,[81] and that a vast amount of research 'affirms that most marriages among first- and second-generation Indians are arranged on caste and religious lines'.[82] It is clear that caste continues to be an important factor in marriage for many people of South Asian origin in the UK. Endogamy was identified by Ambedkar as the vehicle by which caste is maintained and replicated (and inter-caste marriage as the 'solvent of caste'),[83] but family and community disapproval of inter-caste marriages remains strong, and many such couples in the UK continue to experience hostility and even violence. Marriage "within caste" still appears to be the expected or preferred norm, at least among the older generation, while for many younger people caste seems to acquire salience when it comes to marriage, whether they like it or not, including for those who claim indifference to it in daily life.[84] The preference for marriage within caste extends to Dalits.[85] Asian matrimonial websites in the UK continue to advertise candidates on the basis of caste

76 ACDA (n 17) 2.

77 M Dhanda, 'Punjabi *Dalit* Youth and Dynamics of Transitions in Identity', 17(1) *Contemporary South Asia* (2009) 47–64, 57.

78 P Judge, 'Punjabis in England: The Ad-Dharmi Experience', *Economic and Political Weekly* (3 August 2002) 3244–3250, 3247.

79 Ibid., 3249.

80 See, for example, D Kennedy, 'Young Generation Keeps Old Identities Alive with Bhangra Music and Tradition', *The Times*, 5 July 2010.

81 Ghuman (n 44) 99. The literature on caste and marriage cited in this chapter invariably refers to marriage (or relationships) between opposite-sex couples. There is an urgent need for research on the role of caste in same-sex relationships.

82 Ibid.

83 Ambedkar (n 46) 289.

84 Nesbitt (n 66) 109–110; R Kallidai, *Caste in the UK: A Summary of the Consultation with the Hindu Community in Britain* (London: Hindu Forum of Britain, 2008) 14; R Jaspal and O Thakar, 'Caste and Identity Processes Among British Sikhs in the Midlands', *Sikh Formations Religion, Culture, Theory* (2016) 1–16; R Arya, 'Inter-Generational Perspectives on Caste: A Hindu Punjabi Study', 25(3) *Contemporary South Asia* (2017) 285–300; P Chandra, 'Why Is Inter-Caste Marriage a Problem?' *DesiBlitz*, 22 June 2017; M Bassi, 'The Views of British Asians on Inter-Caste marriage', *DesiBlitz*, 29 June 2020, both at www.desiblitz.com.

85 Judge (n 78) 3248; Dhanda (n 77). See also www.ravidasiamatrimony.com/ (matrimonial website exclusively for Ravidassias).

(including 'scheduled caste') and community alongside religion and other characteristics,[86] although inter-caste marriages also appear to be rising.[87] Caste has been identified by the police and the Crown Prosecution Service, as well as by academics, activists and civil society organisations, as a factor in sexual violence and so-called honour crimes in Britain (marriages or relationships which transgress caste boundaries being unacceptable to some families)[88] and also as a driver for forced marriage, where individuals are compelled to marry within caste.[89] Although endogamy practiced by choice is not a matter for the law – unless the marriage contravenes legislation restricting marriages within prohibited degrees[90] – any marriage involving force or coercion will contravene the Forced Marriage (Civil Protection) Act 2007 under which civil forced marriage Protection Orders can be sought; and since 2014, it is a criminal offence in England and Wales to force someone to marry, or to breach a forced marriage Protection Order.[91]

6.4.6 *Caste and education*

According to Eleanor Nesbitt, caste in the context of education 'impacts on pupils' relationships and self-esteem in subtle and powerful ways' and hence concerns 'not only religious educationists but all who are concerned with the welfare of South Asian pupils'.[92] ACDA's 2009 report highlighted experiences of caste discrimination during childhood (aged up to twelve) and in schools: 47% of respondents reported being treated differently as children or being on the receiving end of comments based on their caste, while 7% claimed to have been subjected to verbal abuse (for example being insulted through the use of caste names) and 16% to threatening behaviour, predominantly by other pupils but to a lesser extent by teaching staff.[93] Similar findings emerged from Ghuman's research on Dalits and education in the

---

86 See, for example, Jeevansathi.com and MatrimonialsIndia.com.

87 See Kallidai (n 84) 17; Nesbitt (n 66) 106; J Jacobson, *Islam in Transition: Religion and Identity Among British Pakistani Youth* (London: Routledge, 1998) 90–93.

88 J Brandon and S Hafez, *Crimes of the Community: Honour-Based Violence in the UK* (London: The Centre for Social Cohesion, 2010, 2nd edition); S Bird, 'Sister Is Stabbed to Death for Loving the Wrong Man', *The Times*, 17 June 2006; see also Karma Nirvana at www.karmanirvana.org.uk/; 'Why Is Inter-Caste Marriage a Problem?' *DesiBlitz*, 20 January 2017; P Solanki, 'Is Caste Still an Issue for Marriage?' *DesiBlitz*, 20 January 2017, both at https://desiblitz.com; A Waughray, 'Honour-Based Violence and Caste', presentation at HBV and Forced Marriage National Roadshow Launch Event, 17 May 2018, Manchester Metropolitan University at https://www2.mmu.ac.uk/business-school/research/research-centres/national-hbv/ examining the role of caste in honour-based violence in opposite-sex relationships against males deemed unsuitable by the female's family on grounds of caste. See also CPS, Sexual Offences, Legal Guidance, 21 May 2021 at https://www.cps.gov.uk/legal-guidance/rape-and-sexual-offences-chapter-5-issues-relevant-particular-groups-people

89 Brandon and Hafez, ibid.; Southall Black Sisters, *Forced Marriage: An Abuse of Human Rights* (London: Southall Black Sisters, 2001). Forced marriage is distinguished from approved marriage and consensual arranged marriage; see UK Home Office Forced Marriage Unit Statistics 2020, 16 July 2021, para 2.

90 Marriage Act 1949, Part I s 1 and Sched. 1, Part 1; Marriage Act 1949 (Remedial Order) 2007 (S.I. 438/2007).

91 Forced Marriage (Civil Protection) Act 2007 c 20, inserted as Part 4A s 63A(4) Family Law Act 1996 c 27; Anti-social Behaviour, Crime and Policing Act 2014 c 12, ss. 120–121. See also UN Convention on Consent to Marriage, Minimum Age for Marriage and Registration of Marriages 1962, Article 1; Treaty Series No. 102/1970: Cm 4538; UK ratification 9 July 1970.

92 Nesbitt (n 66) 98, 107–109; Moldenhawer (n 48). See also Ghuman (n 44).

93 ACDA (n 17) 25. In total, 300 adults took part in the research, and 101 completed an online questionnaire which included three questions about their experiences of caste discrimination during childhood and adolescence; ibid., 41–42.

UK.[94] In contrast, the Hindu Forum of Britain in 2008, while recognising the occurrence in schools and universities of caste-based insults, name-calling and derogatory remarks, dismissed such incidents as rare and no more than 'a lighter form of bullying [sic]'. Similarly, casteist behaviour in temples and community centres was characterised as '[a way] of social interaction that could be improved, rather than actual discrimination about provision of goods and services at community centres'.[95]

6.4.7 Caste in the UK disputed

As the issue of caste and caste discrimination increased in visibility throughout the 2000s, so did opposition from certain parliamentary and civil society actors to the idea that it actually exists in the UK, let alone that caste discrimination occurs. The 2006 DSN study was reportedly challenged as exaggerated by the late Piara Khabra, former MP for Ealing Southall.[96] In 2008, the Hindu Forum of Britain (HFB) published a report in response to a government questionnaire on caste discrimination, circulated to twenty-one religious and civil society organisations, which argued that 'caste discrimination is not endemic in British society and there is no role for caste in the provision of education, employment or goods and services' (an ambiguous statement which could be understood as condemning caste discrimination in these fields, alternatively as refuting its occurrence). The report also identified what it called the 'Dalit-Christian link', arguing that 'Christian' support (from British parliamentarians and civil society organisations) for Dalit campaigns in Britain and India was a cover for proseletysm, evangelism and the conversion of Dalits in India ('the most "promising" target group for conversions'), and that this was 'one of the main reasons why Christian groups [were] involved in Dalit rights'[97] (a theme which has been taken up vociferously by some opponents of caste discrimination legislation in the UK).[98] In the same year (2008), the Hindu Council UK (HCUK) declared itself 'not aware of caste discrimination here in the UK';[99] indeed, according to its director in 2007, the caste system itself had been 'demolished' in the UK in one generation by 'a change in the socio-economic landscape'.[100]

In 1978, Indian sociologist CT Kannan argued that, just as the caste system in India had been 'severely modified',[101] so in the UK 'immigrant young people in particular and their parents in general' were 'not bothered about the caste system here'. Kannan did concede that 'among the parental generation there may be a little awareness left of the caste tradition, *but these are never shown outside, and as a result free mixing is a general pattern in Britain*'.[102] Such comments underestimated the resilience of caste as an institution and failed to engage with the critical factors identified by Kuper as sustaining caste in the diaspora. Although studies suggest that the younger generation attaches less importance to caste in day-to-day life than their parents, Nesbitt's work in the late 1990s showed nevertheless that young

---

94 Ghuman (n 44).
95 Kallidai (n 84) 17–18.
96 H Muir, 'Caste Divide Is Blighting Indian Communities in UK, Claims Report', *The Guardian*, 4 July 2006.
97 Kallidai (n 84) 22–23, 27, 28.
98 See Chapter 9; D Mosse, 'Outside Caste? The Enclosure of Caste and Claims to Castelessness in India and the United Kingdom', 62(1) *Comparative Studies in Society and History* (2020) 1–31.
99 RP Sharma, *The Caste System* (London: Hindu Council UK, 2008) 3.
100 J Lakhani, 'Caste and Conversion', 14 May 2007, at www.hindujagruti.org/news/2128.html.
101 CT Kannan, *Cultural Adaptation of Asian Immigrants: First and Second Generation* (Greenford: CT Kannan, 1978) 23.
102 Ibid., 156 (emphasis added).

Gujaratis and Punjabis at that time understood caste as a hereditary form of vertical hierarchical ranking, and they were aware of the expectation of endogamy.[103] More recently, the continued relevance of caste is apparent from a variety of sources, including the Equality and Human Rights Commission, the British Sikh Report and academic work by Meena Dhanda, Paul Ghuman, Eleanor Nesbitt, Rusi Jaspal and Opinderjit Thakar (among others).[104] Repudiation of caste among the young appears to vary according to sphere of activity, and the extent to which it is subject to class, religion, education and caste and regional background is unclear.[105] Various studies assert the continuance of caste consciousness – and discrimination – among Punjabis and Sikhs in Britain, while in 2017, a government-commissioned study on the feasibility of conducting a national survey on the extent of caste discrimination found that 'regardless of whether they identified with the caste system or not, there was a strong understanding about caste and how it worked across Hindu and Sikh respondents'.[106]

6.5 Awareness of caste discrimination prior to the Equality Bill 2009[107]

6.5.1 *Caste discrimination as an overseas issue*

To the extent that caste discrimination was addressed in parliamentary and government circles in the UK prior to the Equality Bill 2009, it was as an "overseas" issue rather than a domestic problem.[108] The context was India's emergence, following its 1991 economic liberalisation, as an aspiring global economic power, and expanding British-India trade and business interaction.[109] Caste inequality in India 'was perceived as being out of step with modern ideas about human rights and a limitation on India's economic development and global political aspirations'.[110] British concern with caste in India was explained on two grounds. The "business case" highlighted the threat to India's social stability and economic growth – and by extension British business interests – which caste discrimination was perceived to pose.[111] The "moral case," or "human rights case," emphasised untouchability and

---

103 See Nesbitt (n 11) 205–206.
104 M Dhanda et al., *Caste in Britain* Research Reports 91 and 92 (Equality and Human Rights Commission, 2014); British Sikh Report 2016, 18; M Dhanda, 'Casteism Amongst Punjabis in Britain', *Economic and Political Weekly* (21 January 2017); Ghuman (n 44); Jaspal and Thakar (n 84).
105 See Dhanda (n 77); Judge (n 78); Din (n 62) 101–117; Jacobson (n 87) 85; N Meer, 'The Politics of Voluntary and Involuntary Identities: Are Muslims in Britain an Ethnic, Racial or Religious Minority?' 42(1) *Patterns of Prejudice* (2008) 61–81, 66.
106 Sato (n 44) 17; Dhanda (n 77). Jaspal and Thakar (n 84); see also the British Sikh Report 2013 and 2016; N Howatt et al., 'Measuring Caste Discrimination in Britain – a Feasibility Study', at www.gov.uk/government/publications/measuring-caste-discrimination-in-britain-a-feasibility-study, 5.
107 This section draws on A Waughray, 'Caste Discrimination: A Twenty-First-Century Challenge for UK Discrimination Law?' 72(2) *Modern Law Review* (2009) 182–219.
108 See, for example, T Harrison et al., 'A Political Introduction to India', House of Commons Library, International Affairs and Defence Section, Research Paper 07/41 (2007) 43–47.
109 See G Das, *India Unbound* (New Delhi: Penguin Books India, 2000); 'Trade and Investment Opportunities with India: Third Report of Session 2005–06, Volume I'; House of Commons Trade and Industry Committee, HC 881-I (2006) 21.
110 Waughray, 'Caste Discrimination: A Twenty-First-Century Challenge for UK Discrimination Law?' (n 107) 194.
111 House of Commons Foreign Affairs Committee, South Asia: Fourth Report of Session 2006–07 (London: The Stationery Office Ltd); HC 55 (2007) 260–262.

caste discrimination as human rights violations.[112] In both cases, Britain's role as a friend of India was stressed.[113] For British companies operating in India, caste surfaces primarily in human resources and decision-making, although British staff may be oblivious to its manifestations.[114] In 2006, the House of Commons Trade and Industry Committee described it as 'a trap for the unwary',[115] advising UK companies not to break the letter or spirit of Indian law, to take note of the "Ambedkar Principles" (a voluntary code of practice for national and multinational companies and foreign investors addressing caste discrimination in the private sector, drafted by the transnational advocacy organisation International Dalit Solidarity Network)[116] and to monitor their recruitment and employment policies in India. In response, the then Labour Government reiterated its support for the Ambedkar Principles and the commitment of the Department for International Development (DfID) to address caste-based discrimination through its various programmes.[117] Moreover, it urged UK businesses to comply with the laws of the countries in which they operate, noting that 'discrimination on the grounds of caste is inconsistent with the standards that the UK applies and is illegal in India'.[118] There is an obvious irony in these denouncements of caste discrimination in India, given Britain's contribution to the "construction" of caste and its embedding in the administrative structures, law and legal system of British India.

6.5.2 *Caste discrimination as a domestic issue*

The readiness of UK parliamentary and governmental actors from the late 1990s onwards to condemn caste discrimination in India was matched by reluctance to acknowledge it as a domestic issue. British Dalits struggled to convince the political establishment of its existence closer to home.[119] Between 2000 and 2009, personal experience of casteism in Britain was voiced more publicly than before in oral testimonies,[120] on radio[121] and through

---

112 See, for example, Early Day Motion 1604, Violence with Impunity Against Dalits in India, 5 June 2007, Stunnell, Andrew.

113 H L Deb vol 690 col 1434–1436, 26 March 2007.

114 O Morgan, 'British "Failing India's Lowest Caste Workers"', *The Observer*, 24 June 2007; E Wilson, 'Managing Diversity: Caste and Gender Issues in Organisations in India', in M Davidson and S Fielden (eds.), *Individual Diversity and Psychology in Organisations* (Oxford: Wiley, 2003) 149–172.

115 Trade and Investment Opportunities with India: Third Report of Session 2005–06, Volume I, House of Commons Trade and Industry Committee, HC 881-I (2006) 21.

116 The Ambedkar Principles: Employment and Additional Principles on Economic and Social Exclusion Formulated to Assist All Foreign Investors in South Asia to Address Caste Discrimination', at http://idsn.org/key-issues/caste-business/ambedkar-principles/.

117 E Stott, House of Lords Library Note, 'Government Proposals for International Development Policy, Including Proposals on the Situation of the Dalits', LLN 2011/037, 28 November 2011.

118 'Trade and Investment Opportunities with India: Government Response to the House of Commons Trade and Industry Committee's Third Report of Session 2005–06, Fifteenth Special Report of Session 2005–06', HC 1671 (2006) 29.

119 Similarly, in the early 1970s, the UK's Trades Union Congress (TUC) saw racial discrimination as an international rather than a domestic issue. Race relations 'was handled by the TUC's International Committee, though clearly this was a home economic and manpower question'; I MacDonald, *Race Relations and the Law* (London: Butterworths, 1977) 6. Many States parties to ICERD initially saw racial discrimination as a foreign policy rather than a domestic issue; see Chapter 4.

120 See S Muman, 'Caste in Britain', in *Report of the Proceedings of International Conference on Dalit Human Rights* (London: Voice of Dalit International, 2000) 71–79, 76.

121 For example, N Puri, 'The Caste Divide', broadcast on BBC Radio 4, April 2003, transcript at www.countercurrents.org/dalit-puri050704.htm (visited 7 September 2012).

theatre.[122] In 2004, the UN identified caste discrimination as continuing to affect diaspora communities (including the UK) 'whose original cultures and traditions include aspects of inherited social exclusion'.[123] In 2003, the UN Committee on the Elimination of Racial Discrimination (CERD) recommended that the UK introduce legislation prohibiting descent-based discrimination (including caste-based discrimination).[124] While some respondents cited in the 2006 HFB report saw *jati* and *varna* as 'an expression of tradition and positive familial and community links', others referred to intra-community prejudice, division and barriers based on caste, and the study highlights as a 'particular issue for people of Hindu backgrounds' the question of whether caste 'operates to exclude people from full participation in Hindu communities'.[125] In 2008, the HFB asserted that while 'most people in the UK do not experience caste discrimination, it could still be a purely cultural issue based on personal choices and social interaction in three broad areas', i.e. temples and community centres, schools and marriage.[126] Convincing the political establishment to acknowledge certain casteist behaviours as discrimination amenable to and justifying legal regulation, rather than as merely a cultural issue based on "personal choices" and social interaction, was to prove (and still proves) a huge challenge for Dalit activists.

6.6 Conclusion

Caste has been a feature of the South Asian presence in the UK since the 1950s, but it has remained largely hidden, due partly to ignorance and a lack of interest on the part of society at large. For some, it has been a force for cohesion, but it has also been a significant force for division. Caste-based tensions between Dalit and dominant caste communities resulted, from the late 1960s onwards, in the establishment of separate social and religious facilities distinguished along caste lines. Dalits, too, are divided amongst themselves, but the primary division remains between Dalits and the dominant castes. Unless these fractures within Britain's South Asian communities are addressed as the population expands, the risk is that further social disunity, tensions and frustrations will follow. In 2000, at an international conference on Dalit human rights in London, Dalit activist Satpal Muman called explicitly for UK discrimination law to be 'amended and brought up to date', to address caste discrimination. He argued that, in the context of 'an ever-increasing Asian population in Britain', the matter was likely to play 'a key role' in the future. For these reasons, he argued, '*British law will need to be brought into line with an emerging new social order in Britain*'.[127] The remaining chapters interrogate and then examine progress towards, and setbacks to, this goal.

---

122 See A Waughray and N Weichgennant-Thiara, 'Challenging Caste Discrimination in Britain with Literature and Law: An Interdisciplinary Study of British Dalit Writing', 21(2) *Contemporary South Asia* (2013) 116–132; E Nesbitt, 'Ethnography, Religious Education and *The Fifth Cup*', in J Miller, K O'Grady, and U McKenna (eds.), *Religion in Education, Innovation in International Research* (London: Routledge, 2013) 11–25.
123 UN Doc. E/CN.4/Sub.2/2004/31, para 35.
124 UN Doc. CERD A/58/18 (2003) para 544.
125 See Berkeley (n 74) 58–60.
126 Kallidai (n 84) 14.
127 Muman (n 120) 78 (emphasis added).

7 British discrimination law and caste[*]

From the Race Relations Act 1965 to the Equality Bill 2009

7.1 Introduction

Prior to the enactment of the Equality Act 2010 (EA), British discrimination law had developed in an ad hoc fashion since the Race Relations Act 1965 first prohibited direct discrimination on racial grounds in places of public resort.[1] The Race Relations Act 1968 extended the prohibition of direct discrimination on racial grounds to employment, the provision of goods, facilities and services and the disposal of business premises and housing accommodation.[2] Between 1968 and 2007, successive pieces of legislation increased the prohibited grounds of discrimination from one (racial grounds) to six: sex (Equal Pay Act 1970 and Sex Discrimination Act 1975); disability (Disability Discrimination Act 1995); religion or belief (Employment Equality (Religion or Belief) Regulations 2003); sexual orientation (Employment Equality (Sexual Orientation) Regulations 2003 and Equality Act (Sexual Orientation) Regulations 2007) and age (Employment Equality (Age) Regulations 2007).[3] Meanwhile, the Race Relations Act 1976 (discussed later) had replaced the 1965 and 1968 legislation. In 2010, the EA increased the prohibited grounds of discrimination (referred to in the EA as 'protected characteristics') from six to nine by separating out, from the existing six grounds, gender reassignment, pregnancy and maternity and marital or civil partnership status as free-standing characteristics.[4]

Until its inclusion in an enabling provision in the EA, the word "caste" was not found in any anti-discrimination legislation – and there is still no express statutory prohibition of caste discrimination in British law. Of the six prohibited grounds of discrimination before 2010, only "racial grounds" (replaced by "race" in the EA) or religion or belief contend

---

[*] Parts of this chapter have previously been published in A Waughray, 'Caste Discrimination: A Twenty-First-Century Challenge for UK Discrimination Law?' 72(2) *Modern Law Review* (2009) 182–219.

1 See B Hepple, 'Race Relations Act 1965', 29(3) *The Modern Law Review* (1966) 306–314. Initially, racial discrimination was seen as a public order problem to be dealt with by criminal law, but the then Labour Government was persuaded that civil measures were likely to be more effective than criminal sanctions in enforcing anti-discrimination law; see A Lester and G Bindman, *Race and Law* (Harmondsworth: Penguin, 1972) 112–116.

2 B Hepple, *Equality: The New Legal Framework* (Oxford: Hart, 2/E, 2014) 11–12.

3 Hepple, ibid.; A McColgan, *Discrimination, Equality and the Law* (Oxford: Hart, 2014). Protection against sexual orientation, religion or belief and age discrimination was introduced in order to implement EU law obligations; see Council Directive 2000/78/EC establishing a general framework for equal treatment in employment and occupation; OJ L 303/16, 2 December 2000.

4 See Equality Act 2010. These nine characteristics are the same as those protected by the anti-discrimination legislation in place prior to the entry into force of the EA on 1 October 2010. The umbrella category "racial grounds" in the RRA was replaced by "race" in the EA.

DOI: 10.4324/9781315750934-11

as possible "legal homes" for caste. This chapter explains the limitations of these categories in relation to caste and discusses some of the implications of using race or religion or belief provisions to address caste discrimination. The perceived inadequacy of existing law for capturing caste discrimination, coupled with the Labour Government's announcement in 2005 of its intention to introduce a new, single Equality Act to modernise and simplify equality legislation, led British Dalit campaigners to step up their calls for caste to be added to anti-discrimination legislation as an express category or ground of discrimination.[5] The inadequacy of discrimination legislation in relation to caste is the consequence of a discrimination law model which uses a fixed list of closed categories to identify the beneficiaries of protection – a point which has been made in relation to other categories previously excluded from the list, such as religion, sexual orientation and gender identity.[6]

7.2 UK discrimination law model

7.2.1 Purpose of discrimination law

The primary liberal justification for discrimination law is the principle of equality,[7] now understood in terms of substantive equality (equality of results or outcomes and respect for human dignity and worth), rather than simply equality of opportunity or formal equality.[8] From a liberal perspective, discrimination legislation is both a coercive tool and an educative device,[9] providing concrete protection and redress for victims of discrimination whilst playing an important political and symbolic role in the 'shaping and expressing of social messages'.[10] Legal regulation of discrimination serves both functions, redefining as socially unacceptable, and actionable legally, behaviour hitherto considered acceptable.[11]

7.2.2 Meaning of discrimination

Discrimination has both ordinary and legal meanings; behaviour labelled discriminatory in ordinary language is not necessarily recognised as discrimination in legal terms. UK discrimination law is limited in scope and contains no general guarantee of equality: there is no general right not to be discriminated against, whatever the reason. Discrimination is prohibited in a limited range of specific areas of activity only, and 'outside these areas, discrimination

---

5 The Labour Party committed to introduce a Single Equality Act in its 2005 General Election manifesto.

6 A McColgan, 'Reconfiguring Discrimination Law', *Public Law* (Spring 2007) 74–94, 75; S Fredman, *Discrimination Law* (Oxford: Oxford University Press, 2011) 73–92; A McColgan (n 3), Chapter 2; N Busby and S Middlemiss, 'The Equality Deficit: Legal Protection for Homosexuals and Lesbians in Employment?' 8(4) *Gender, Work and Organisation* (2001) 387–410.

7 Lester and Bindman (n 1) 73; N Bamforth, M Malik, and C O'Cinneide, *Discrimination Law: Theory and Context* (London: Sweet and Maxwell, 2008) 167.

8 A large body of scholarship exists on the justifications and foundational values of discrimination law. On equality, see Hepple (n 2) 12–26; McColgan (n 3); Fredman (n 6) 4–33. See also T Khaitan, *A Theory of Discrimination Law* (Oxford: Oxford University Press, 2015) 91, 113, 130–132.

9 Lester and Bindman (n 1) 85–87.

10 M Burton, *Legal Responses to Domestic Violence* (Abingdon: Routledge-Cavendish, 2008) 7. For a discussion of the argument that 'law will not itself be formative of the progressive argument', see B Hudson, 'Beyond White Man's Justice: Race, Gender and Justice in Late Modernity', 10(1) *Theoretical Criminology* (2006) 29–47.

11 N Lacey, 'From Individual to Group', in B Hepple and E Szyszczak (eds.), *Discrimination: The Limits of the Law* (London: Mansell, 1993) 99–124, 108.

is not unlawful'.[12] This reflects a tension between two distinct approaches to discrimination law say O'Cinneide and Lui: the principled and the pragmatic. The principled approach demands the maximisation of protection against all forms of discrimination while "minimising exceptions to its reach"; in contrast, the pragmatic approach places more emphasis on considerations weighing against the expansion of discrimination law.[13] British discrimination law is designed largely to respond with individual remedies to individual claims made on the basis of legally defined grounds, in relation to certain types of regulated behaviour and social goods.[14] The Public Sector Equality Duty (PSED) contained in section 149 EA extends this by imposing a proactive equality promotion duty on public bodies, while the Equalities and Human Rights Commission (EHRC), established by the Equality Act 2006 (EA 2006), has a broad general duty to protect and promote equality, as well as enforcement powers to conduct enquiries and formal investigations into discriminatory practices perpetrated by organisations.[15]

To amount to unlawful discrimination, behaviour must meet three criteria. First, the behaviour must be because of a protected characteristic. Second, it must occur in a legally regulated field such as employment, the provision of goods, facilities and services, education and vocational training, management or the disposal of premises or the exercise of public functions. Discriminatory behaviour occurring in non-regulated fields (e.g. social, private or intimate relations) is outwith the law. Third, it must amount to a prohibited type of conduct (namely direct or indirect discrimination, harassment or victimisation). Behaviour which does not meet these criteria may be objectionable, but it is not unlawful. To convince governmental and parliamentary actors of the need for an express prohibition of caste discrimination in the Equality Bill, supporters of caste discrimination legislation first had to show the existence of a problem in regulated fields and, second, show that existing grounds of discrimination did not cover, or did not fully cover, caste.

7.2.3 Regulated fields and the "public-private" divide

Opponents of caste discrimination legislation have argued that such discrimination occurs only in non-regulated fields (if it exists at all) and is therefore outside the ambit of the law.[16] British discrimination law targets behaviour or conduct in particular sectors only, irrespective of motivation; opinions, beliefs, preferences and choices are not unlawful unless

---

12 J Spencer and M Spencer, 'International Law and Discrimination', in M Sargeant (ed.), *Discrimination Law* (Harlow: Pearson, 2004) 46. Also see Hepple (n 2) 1, 14–15, on the history of equality legislation in Britain and, with the Equality Act 2010, a shift towards a regime based on a 'unitary human rights perspective' shifting focus from negative duties not to discriminate, to positive duties to advance equality (although see Khaitan (n 8) 130–133). On the limited nature of UK discrimination law, see C O'Cinneide and K Lui, 'Defining the Limits of Discrimination Law in the United Kingdom: Principle and Pragmatism in Tension', 15(1–2) *International Journal of Discrimination Law* (2014) 80–100.

13 O'Cinneide and Lui, ibid., 81.

14 Bamforth et al. (n 7) 18.

15 Part 1 of the EA 2006 establishes the EHRC and sets out its duties and powers; see also www.equality-humanrights.com/en/our-legal-action/our-powers. Section 149 EA requires public authorities in the exercise of their functions to have due regard to the need to eliminate prohibited discrimination, advance equality of opportunity and foster good relations; Hepple (n 2) 12 on the general duty of the EHRC, 134–140 on the PSED, and 149–154 on EHRC enforcement powers; *Review of the Public Sector Equality Duty: Report of the Independent Steering Group* (London: Government Equalities Office, 2013) 11.

16 See, for example, R Kallidai, *Caste in the UK: A Summary of the Consultation with the Hindu Community in Britain* (London: Hindu Forum of Britain, 2008) 16.

they give rise to prohibited conduct or impacts.[17] Legal regulation does not extend to discriminatory behaviour deemed to be in the private or intimate spheres (for example associational preferences, intimate social interactions, marriage), and it is the '"privacy barrier" which was – and still is – called up to exclude caste from the reach of discrimination law.[18] However, the boundary between associational preferences and discrimination in regulated fields, for example between 'personal choices' in 'business networks' (the example given by the Hindu Forum of Britain in 2006)[19] and discrimination in the provision of goods and services, is not always clear-cut.[20] The notion of a separation between public and private spheres is a predominant organising principle of liberal legal discourse, with the "private" not considered to be a proper subject of state regulation.[21] Nevertheless, as critical theorists argue, the boundary between private and "non-private" behaviour is not immutable but is open to contestation and legal revision (after all, the concept of "private" behaviour is itself a socio-political-legal construct: 'All struggles against oppression in the modern world begin by re-defining what had previously been considered "private," non-public and non-political issues as matters of public concern').[22] Over time, the spheres deemed "private" and beyond the reach of the law have shrunk, while those within the law's ambit have increased. Examples of "private" behaviour which have been brought within the ambit of the law include racial discrimination in private contractual relationships,[23] domestic violence;[24] rape within marriage[25] and forced marriage.[26] The public-private distinction, and the separation between public and private spheres, has been challenged, particularly by feminist legal theorists,[27] while the exclusion of "private contact discrimination" from legal regulation remains a key criticism of liberal discrimination law.[28]

17 Discrimination law recognises beliefs, choices and preferences as such in very limited circumstances only, by the granting of exemptions or exceptions to its application; see Hepple (n 2) 136–149.

18 Kallidai (n 16) 16.

19 R Berkeley, *Connecting British Hindus: An Enquiry into the Identity and Public Engagement of Hindus in Britain* (London: Hindu Forum of Britain, 2006) 12; Kallidai (n 16) 11.

20 Kalsi argued in 1989 that among Sikhs in the UK, endogamous groups organise their relationships with one another, *both social and economic*, 'through idioms of ritual purity and avoidance behaviour'; S Singh Kalsi, 'The Sikhs and Caste: A Study of the Sikh Community in Leeds and Bradford', PhD thesis, University of Leeds, 1989, 71; published as S Singh Kalsi, *The Evolution of a Sikh Community in Britain; Religion and Social Change Among the Sikhs of Leeds and Bradford* (Leeds: University of Leeds, Community Religions Project, 1992).

21 M Thornton, 'The Cartography of Public and Private', in M Thornton (ed.), *Public and Private: Feminist Legal Debates* (Oxford: Oxford University Press, 1995) 2–16, 5; Preface, ibid., xiii.

22 S Benhabib, *Situating the Self: Gender, Community and Post-modernism in Contemporary Ethics* (Cambridge: Polity Press, 1992) 100, cited in Hudson (n 10) 35. Privacy is nevertheless recognised as serving important functions; K Kelly, *Domestic Violence and the Politics of Privacy* (New York: Cornell University Press, 2003) 3–6; Burton (n 10) 140–141.

23 Race Relations Act 1968.

24 Kelly (n 22); Burton (n 10); C Smart, *Feminism and the Power of Law* (London: Routledge, 1989); E Schneider, *Battered Women and Feminist Lawmaking* (New Haven: Yale University Press, 2000) 87–97.

25 *R v R* [1992] 1 AC 599.

26 The Anti-social Behaviour, Crime and Policing Act 2014 made it a criminal offence in England, Wales and Scotland to force someone to marry. Violation of a civil Forced Marriage Protection Order – made under the Forced Marriage (Civil Protection) Act 2007, inserted as Part 4A s 63A(4) Family Law Act 1996 – became a criminal offence in 2014; see Anti-social Behaviour, Crime and Policing Act 2014 s 120.

27 See Smart (n 24); Thornton (ed.) (n 21); S Boyd (ed.), *Challenging the Public/Private Divide: Feminism, Law, and Public Policy* (Toronto: University of Toronto Press, 1997).

28 Bamforth et al. (n 7) 857.

7.2.4 Discrimination: grounds-based approach

The grounds-based approach to discrimination, whereby legislation affords protection on specified grounds (known in the EA as 'protected characteristics', because they derive from personal attributes or characteristics), is 'common to many anti-discrimination regimes'.[29] In UK (and EU) discrimination legislation, the prohibited grounds of discrimination are enumerated in a closed and exhaustive list; this is in contrast, for example, to the more open formulation in the International Covenant on Civil and Political Rights 1966 (ICCPR) Articles 2(1) and 26, which qualify an enumerated list of characteristics or grounds with the words 'such as', to indicate that the list is not exhaustive, and which include the category "other status" as a residual category which can capture grounds not expressly enumerated.[30]

As McColgan explains, the grounds-based approach gives rise to 'two obvious questions', namely which grounds are regulated, and how the grounds are defined, as well as to calls to extend the list.[31] Although 'there is no inherent reason why legal protection from discrimination is organised on the basis of categories', says Solanke,[32] McColgan points out that a grounds-based approach is 'inevitable where discrimination is addressed by a detailed statutory scheme such as the Equality Act 2010'.[33] Moreover, she says, it is inevitable that such a model will give rise to demands for the list of grounds or categories to be extended by legislation, or for existing categories to be interpreted expansively as forms of discrimination not covered by existing categories or interpretations emerge.[34] It has also been pointed out that, while 'not preordained',[35] categorisation 'may have been inevitable given the nature of political campaigns for discrimination law'.[36] However, the addition of new categories has been resisted historically by the legislature, for instance, it took years of campaigning and sixteen unsuccessful private members' bills before the Disability Discrimination Act 1995 was passed. Categories such as sexual orientation, age and religion or belief were introduced in order to comply with EU law obligations, as was the Sex Discrimination Act 1975. In the absence of caste as a statutory protected characteristic in its own right or as a statutory subset of an existing characteristic, legal protection against caste discrimination in the UK depends on establishing in the courts that caste is subsumed within an existing characteristic such as race or religion or belief.

---

29 McColgan (n 6) 75.
30 On the ICCPR grounds and caste, see Chapter 4. In contrast to the UK, section 15 of the 1982 Canadian Charter of Rights and Freedoms contains a non-exhaustive list of grounds; see G Moon, 'From Equal Treatment to Appropriate Treatment: What Lessons Can Canadian Equality Law on Dignity and on Reasonable Accommodation Teach the United Kingdom?' 6 *European Human Rights Law Review* (2006) 695–721, 697. On discrimination grounds generally see Fredman (n 6) 110–143.
31 McColgan (n 6), 75.
32 I Solanke, 'Putting Race and Gender Together: A New Approach to Intersectionality', 72(5) *Modern Law Review* (2009) 723–749, 723. Khaitan, conversely, describes "personal grounds" (i.e. personal attributes or characteristics that persons have) as a key defining feature or condition which must be satisfied if a duty-imposing legal norm is to be characterised as a norm of discrimination law; see Khaitan (n 8) 42.
33 McColgan (n 3) 59.
34 McColgan (n 6) 75–76.
35 Ibid., 86.
36 Solanke (n 32) 723; O'Cinneide and Lui (n 12). Race and disability discrimination legislation was introduced following political and activist campaigning; see Lester and Bindman (n 1) 107–149; Hepple (n 2) 9–10.

7.3 Caste and racial discrimination

7.3.1 *Race Relations Act 1976*

Prior to the EA, protection against racial discrimination was provided by the Race Relations Act 1976 (RRA),[37] as amended by the Race Relations (Amendment) Act 2000[38] and the Race Relations Act 1976 (Amendment) Regulations 2003,[39] which implemented the EC Race Directive 2000.[40] The RRA introduced a prohibition of indirect discrimination (a concept imported from US civil rights legislation) and stronger enforcement provisions.[41] Specifically, it prohibited direct[42] and indirect discrimination,[43] harassment[44] and victimisation[45] on 'racial grounds'[46] or by reference to members of a 'racial group'.[47] By 1969, the UK was a party to the International Convention on the Elimination of All Forms of Racial Discrimination 1965 (ICERD), which in Article 1(1) defines racial discrimination as any distinction, exclusion, restriction or preference based on race, colour, descent or national or ethnic origin. ICERD was implemented in the UK by the RRA, which defined 'racial grounds' as 'colour, race, nationality or ethnic or national origins'[48] – but not descent. Notably, there was no reference to the international legal definition of racial discrimination in the 1975 White Paper *Racial Discrimination*. Neither was there any reference to the international definition in the 1976 Parliamentary Committee debates on the interpretation clause of the draft legislation.[49] As a State party to ICERD, the UK has an obligation to implement the Convention fully and in good faith, including a duty to prohibit and punish, within its jurisdiction, those forms of discrimination within the Convention's

---

37 The RRA replaced the 1965 and 1968 legislation.
38 Race Relations (Amendment) Act 2000, introduced following the Macpherson Report into the 1993 murder of the black teenager Stephen Lawrence and the charge of institutional racism against the Metropolitan Police. It imposed a general duty on all public authorities to promote race equality.
39 Race Relations Act 1976 (Amendment) Regulations 2003; SI 2003/1626.
40 Council Directive 2000/43/EC implementing the principle of equal treatment between persons irrespective of racial or ethnic origin; OJ L180/22, 7 July 2000. Recital 3 of the Directive refers to the right to equality before the law and protection against discrimination as a universal right recognised inter alia by the International Convention on the Elimination of All Forms of Racial Discrimination 1965 (ICERD), to which all EU member states are signatories.
41 *Racial Discrimination* White Paper Cm 6234 (1975) 25–27.
42 S 1(1)(a) RRA 1976.
43 Indirect discrimination on grounds of colour, race, nationality, ethnic or national origins was prohibited by RRA s 1(1)(b).
44 RRA 1976 s 3A prohibiting harassment on grounds of race, ethnic or national origins Race Relations (Amendment) Regulations 2003, reg. 5; S.I. 2003/1626.
45 RRA 1976 s 2(1).
46 RRA 1976 s 1(1)(a) and s 3.
47 RRA 1976 s 1(1)(b) and s 3. "Racial grounds" is replaced by the umbrella term "race" in the EA, defined as including colour, nationality or ethnic or national origins.
48 RRA s 3(1). Nationality was introduced following the House of Lords decision in *Ealing London Borough Council v Race Relations Board* [1972] 1 All ER 105: "national" in the term "national origins" means national only in the sense of race, not nationality or citizenship.
49 1975–1976 Race Relations Bill, HC Standing Committee A col 83–130 29 April – 4 May 1976. During the 2010 parliamentary debates on the Equality Bill, Lord Lester of Herne Hill QC explained that the RRA drafters had regard to the ICERD definition of racial discrimination, but they did not include descent because it was assumed that the concept of ethnicity included the notion of descent and origins; Lord Lester, HL Deb vol 716 col 336–337, 11 January 2010. See also Chapter 8.

ambit. In the absence of the descent category in the RRA – the meaning of which has been affirmed as including caste by ICERD's monitoring body, the UN Committee on the Elimination of Racial Discrimination (CERD) – application of the RRA to caste discrimination depended on whether caste was deemed subsumed by race, colour, national or ethnic origins or nationality. This remains the case under the EA, unless or until caste – or descent – is expressly added to the legislation. There is no link between caste and nationality or national origins, and the connection between caste and colour is not sufficient to argue that caste membership or identity can be defined by reference to this ground.[50] Historically, however, there has long been an overlap in the usage and application of race and caste.[51] Discourses of ethnicity are also applied to caste. For these reasons, as the Dalit campaign for statutory protection from caste discrimination gained momentum in the run-up to the publication of the Equality Bill 2009, the question of whether caste identity can be defined by reference to race or ethnic origins for the purposes of British discrimination law acquired greater urgency.

7.3.2 *Caste and race*

Race, in common with the other RRA subcategories or grounds, was not defined in the legislation, and there is no RRA case law on the specific meaning of "race,"[52] a notoriously imprecise term. In 1980, Lustgarten observed that the only way in which the distinction between race and colour in the RRA formula made any sense was if race were understood as meaning 'what might more appropriately have been called "ethnic group" – Scottish, Polish, West Indian and so forth'.[53] From the eighteenth century, Western ideas about race were dominated by "scientific" arguments for race and racial difference as innate biological categories and for the biological superiority of white people, thereby underpinning the colonial project with its utilisation of "objective" racial classifications to justify economic exploitation.[54] In the early twentieth century, new analyses emerged of race as a sociopolitical construct, a product of power relations, real in terms of its impact on people's lives and sense of self, 'but devoid of inherent scientific meaning'.[55] More recently, academic analysis of the constructed nature of race and the racialisation of new social groups has sparked debate about legal protection against emerging forms of racial discrimination such

---

50 Zinkin points out that while 'most upper-caste people are fairer than most lower-caste people of their region', one cannot tell caste from skin colour; T Zinkin, *Caste Today* (London: Oxford University Press, 1962) 1.

51 S Bayly, *Caste, Society and Politics in Modern India from the Eighteenth Century to the Modern Age* (Cambridge: Cambridge University Press, 1999) 103–138; P Thornberry, 'Race, Descent and Caste Under the Convention on the Elimination of All Forms of Racial Discrimination', in K Nakano, M Yutzis and R Onoyama (eds.), *Peoples for Human Rights Vol. 9: Descent-Based Discrimination* (Tokyo: International Movement Against All Forms of Discrimination and Racism, 2004) 119–137, 123.

52 M Connolly, *Townshend-Smith on Discrimination Law: Text, Cases and Materials* (London: Cavendish, 2004) 139; IDS, Employment Law Handbooks, *Vol. 4: Discrimination at Work* (Thompson Reuters, 2018) 10.10.

53 L Lustgarten, *Legal Control of Racial Discrimination* (London: MacMillan Press, 1980) 76.

54 D Ingram, *Rights, Democracy, and Fulfilment in the Era of Identity Politics: Principled Compromises in a Compromised World* (Lanham: Rowman and Littlefield Publishers, 2004) 54.

55 R Frankenburg, *White Women, Race Matters: The Social Construction of Whiteness* (Minneapolis: University of Minnesota Press, 1993) 11, 11–13; R Miles and M Brown, *Racism* (London: Routledge, 2003) 39–50.

as cultural racism.[56] According to Lord Fraser of Tullybelton in *Mandla v Dowell Lee* (1983), the leading case on the definition of racial group under the RRA (discussed later), Parliament cannot have intended that membership of a particular racial group should depend on scientific proof that a person possessed the relevant distinctive biological characteristics (assuming that such characteristics exist), as the practical difficulties of such proof would be prohibitive. Moreover, within the human race, there are very few, if any, distinctions which are scientifically recognised as racial.[57] Race in the popular sense calls up wider markers such as culture, language and political and economic power, or lack thereof,[58] and yet the term nevertheless also encompassed shared geographical origins and hereditary, immutable physical traits such as skin colour and physical or outward appearance, irrespective of linguistic, cultural, national or religious factors.[59] While caste possesses features associated with race in its wider sense, this does not mean that it is the same as race.[60] In the nineteenth century, scholars searching for a scientific "racial" explanation for the caste system failed to identify pan-Indian or regional phenotypical profiles of "untouchable" groups.[61]

7.3.3 *Caste and ethnic origins*

7.3.3.1 *Content of "ethnic origins"*

Like race, the term "ethnic origins" was not defined in the RRA, nor is it defined in the EA; the meaning of ethnic origins or ethnicity is elusive, but the term has been understood in a culturally oriented, not just a purely physical, sense[62] as '[acknowledging] the place of history, language and culture in the construction of subjectivity and identity'.[63] According to Capotorti, in his landmark 1991 UN study on minorities, the UN Sub-Commission for the Promotion and Protection of Human Rights, in its 1950 draft resolution on the definition of minorities, decided to replace the word "racial" with "ethnic" in all references to minority groups described by ethnic origin, because so-called racial groupings were not based on scientific facts; the word "ethnic" referred to all biological, cultural and historical characteristics, whereas 'racial referred only to inherited physical characteristics'.[64] Reference was made to the Convention on the Prevention and Punishment of the Crime of Genocide 1948,[65]

---

56 N Meer, 'The Politics of Voluntary and Involuntary Identities: Are Muslims in Britain an Ethnic, Racial or Religious Minority?' 42 *Patterns of Prejudice* (2008) 61–81; Bamforth et al. (n 7) 822–832.

57 *Mandla v Dowell Lee* [1983] 1 All ER 1062, 1066; [1983] 2 AC 548, 561.

58 W Felice, 'The UN Committee on the Elimination of Racial Discrimination: Race, and Economic and Social Human Rights', 24(1) *Human Rights Quarterly* (2002) 205–236, 205–207.

59 See, for example, *Prosecutor v Akayesu*, Case ICTR-96-4-T, Judgment, 2 September 1998, 514. The Macpherson Report defined racism as consisting of conduct or words or practices which advantage or disadvantage people because of their colour, culture or ethnic origin; *The Stephen Lawrence Enquiry: Report of an Enquiry by Sir William MacPherson of Cluny* (London: HMSO, 1999) 6.4.

60 See S Sabir, 'Chimerical Categories: Caste, Race and Genetics', 3(2) *Developing World Bioethics* (2003) 170–177.

61 Bayly (n 51) 126–138.

62 S Poulter, *Ethnicity, Law and Human Rights* (Oxford: Clarendon Press, 1998) 4.

63 S Hall, 'New Ethnicities', in J Donald and A Rattansi (eds.), *'Race', Culture and Difference* (London: Sage, 1992) 252–259, 257. McColgan has described ethnic origins as 'the most problematic sub-category' of racial grounds/racial group; A McColgan, *Discrimination Law: Text, Cases and Materials* (Oxford: Hart, 2005) 534.

64 F Capotorti, *Study on the Rights of Persons Belonging to Ethnic, Religious and Linguistic Minorities* (New York: United Nations, 1991) 34.

65 Adopted 9 December 1948. In force 12 January 1951. 78 UNTS 277.

where "ethnic" had been used to cover cultural, physical and historical characteristics of a group.[66] Reference was also made to a 1970 UN-sponsored research conference on race relations and the observation of one scholar that whereas 'in the most common usage race refers to aggregates of people based upon physical differences, particularly skin colour', ethnic groups 'may be defined as peoples who conceive of themselves as one kind by virtue of their common ancestry (real or imagined) who are united by emotional bonds, a common culture, and by concern with preservation of their group'.[67] According to Capotorti, the substitution of 'ethnic minorities' for 'racial minorities' in Article 27 ICCPR 'reflect[ed] a wish to use the broadest expression and to imply that racial and national minorities should therefore be regarded as included in the [wider] category of ethnic minorities'.[68]

7.3.3.2 Mandla v Dowell Lee *(1983): wide interpretation of "ethnic origins"*

In *Mandla v Dowell Lee*[69] (*Mandla*), a Sikh schoolboy brought a claim of indirect racial discrimination against an independent school which refused to admit him unless he complied with school uniform rules, which required him to remove his turban. The case was brought under the RRA because at that time there was no statutory protection against religious discrimination. The Court of Appeal (CA), upholding the earlier decision in the Birmingham County Court, dismissed the claim of racial discrimination, because Sikhs were not a racial group with a common ethnic origin as defined by the RRA; rather, they were a group defined by religion, and therefore discrimination against them was not contrary to the RRA.[70] The question facing the House of Lords on appeal was whether Sikhs were a racial group for the purposes of the RRA. It was not suggested that Sikhs were a group defined by reference to colour, race, nationality or national origins; in none of these respects were they distinguishable from other groups living, like most Sikhs, in the Punjab. The argument turned upon whether they were a group defined by ethnic origins. It was therefore necessary to ascertain the sense in which the word "ethnic" was used in the RRA.[71] Lord Fraser rejected meanings which treated it as synonymous with race in the narrow, biological sense. While recognising that ethnic 'conveyed a flavour of race', he held that it could not have been used in the RRA 'in a strictly racial or biological sense' and that Parliament 'must have used the word in some more popular sense'; indeed, 'the word is used nowadays in an extended sense to include other characteristics which may be commonly thought of as being associated with common racial origin'. He therefore held that the term "ethnic" was to be construed 'relatively widely' in a broad cultural/historic sense.[72] Citing Richardson J. in *King-Ansell v Police* (New Zealand),[73] Lord Fraser held that for a group to constitute an ethnic group, it must regard itself, and be regarded by others, as a distinct community by virtue of two essential

66 Capotorti (n 64) 34.
67 R Burkey, 'Discrimination and Racial Relations', in *Report on the International Research Conference on Race Relations, Aspen, Colorado, 7–9 June 1970*, 62, cited in Capotorti (n 64) 34.
68 Capotorti, ibid., 35. Article 27 ICCPR provides: 'In those States in which ethnic, religious or linguistic minorities exist, persons belonging to such minorities shall not be denied the right, in community with the other members of their group, to enjoy their own culture, to profess and practise their own religion, or to use their own language'.
69 *Mandla* (n 57).
70 [1982] 3 All E.R. 1108.
71 *Mandla* (n 57) 560.
72 Ibid., 563.
73 *King-Ansell v Police* [1979] 2 NZLR 531.

characteristics: (1) a distinct, living and long-shared history as a group and (2) a cultural tradition of its own, including family and social customs, often but not necessarily associated with religious observance. Additional but non-essential characteristics include: (3) common geographical origins or descent, (4) a common language (although not necessarily peculiar to the group), (5) common literature peculiar to the group, (6) a common religion different from that of neighbouring groups or the surrounding community and (7) being a minority or an oppressed or dominant group within a larger community.[74]

The House of Lords, reversing the Court of Appeal's decision, found that Sikhs were a group defined by reference to ethnic origins, because they possessed 'a sufficient combination of shared customs, beliefs, traditions and characteristics derived from a common or presumed common past' such as to give them 'an historically determined social identity in their own eyes and in the eyes of those outside the group', even though they were not biologically distinguishable from other people in the Punjab.[75] Jews,[76] Gypsies (in the narrow sense of Romany Gypsies rather than the wider sense of New Age travellers)[77] and Irish travellers[78] – but not Rastafarians[79] or Muslims[80] – have also been held by the courts to fall within the purview of ethnic origins.[81]

7.3.3.3 *Caste and the* Mandla *criteria*

Caste as ethnicity or ethnic identity, and castes as ethnic groups, is a familiar topic among caste scholars, while the question of Dalits as an ethnic group has also been raised within CERD.[82] *Mandla* identified an ethnic group, within the meaning of the RRA, as one which

---

74 *Mandla* (n 57) 562.
75 Ibid., 564–565. Ian McKenna explains that it was the intention of the then government that the Sikhs would be protected by the RRA on grounds of ethnic origin; I McKenna, 'Racial Discrimination', 46(6) *Modern Law Review* (1983) 759–770, 760–761, cited in McColgan (n 63) 535.
76 *Seide v Gillette Industries* [1980] IRLR 427 (EAT).
77 *Commission for Racial Equality v Dutton* [1990] QB 783; [1989] 1 All ER 306; [1989] IRLR 8, CA; decided that a sign in a pub saying "No Travellers" was discriminatory, as Romany Gypsies are an ethnic group.
78 *O'Leary & Others v Punch Retail & Others* (Westminster County Court 29 August 2000) (unreported); see C Gray, 'Irish Travellers Gain Legal Status of Ethnic Minority', *The Independent*, 30 August 2000.
79 *Crown Suppliers v Dawkins* [1993] ICR 517; the Court of Appeal, applying Lord Fraser's test, held that Rastafarians lacked a sufficiently long-shared group history for the purposes of s 3(1) RRA.
80 *Nyazi v Rymans*, EAT 6/88 (unreported); Muslims were held to be a group defined by reference to religion, not ethnic origins, and hence outside the purview of the RRA. Contrast *CRE v Precision Manufacturing Services Ltd* (1991) reported in *Equal Opportunities Review*, Discrimination Case Law Digest No. 12, where an employer who had refused to hire Muslims (at a time when religious discrimination was not unlawful) had not directly discriminated against Muslims on grounds of race, as "Muslims" were not a race, but he was guilty of indirect race discrimination on grounds of national origins, because Muslim-majority national-origins groups' [such as Pakistanis and Bengalis] 'were disproportionately affected by the jobs ban on Muslims'. Thus, Pakistani and Bengali Muslims were indirectly protected under the RRA; C Joppke, *Immigration and the Nation-state: The United States, Germany, and Great Britain* (Oxford: Oxford University Press, 1999) 250. On Muslims as an ethnic group, see Meer (n 56); K Dobe and S Chhokar, 'Muslims, Ethnicity and the Law', 4 *International Journal of Discrimination and the Law* (2000) 369–386.
81 In *Dhinsa v Serco* ET Case No. 07/08/2018, an employment tribunal held that Amritdhari Sikhs are not a distinct and different racial group separate from Sikhs generally.
82 See, for example, D Reddy, 'The Ethnicity of Caste', 78(3) *Anthropological Quarterly* (2005) 543–584. See CERD member Mr Prosper, CERD, Summary Records, 2 March 2007; UN Doc CERD/C/ SR.1796, 38. Guha argues for an understanding of caste as 'a highly involuted and politicised form of

'regard(s) itself and [is] regarded by others as a distinct community by virtue of certain characteristics', including, at a minimum, a distinct and long-shared history and its own cultural tradition. The question was whether this *legal* – rather than *anthropological* – definition of "ethnic" could be applied to Dalits as a broad category, to individual caste or *jati* groups, or to both – or neither. A fundamental element of caste is the separateness of caste (*jati*) groups. Dalits in India are not a culturally, linguistically or historically homogenous group; indeed, for centuries, they were separated from each other geographically, regionally, linguistically and culturally, the distinctions and hierarchies between Dalit *jatis* sometimes enforced almost as rigorously as those between Dalit and non-Dalit *jatis*.[83] It was not until the early twentieth century that Dalits emerged as a nationally identifiable political and social entity, linked by a common experience of oppression and untouchability. Although Dalits in India have become an increasingly important political category, it was not clear whether collectively they could fulfil the *Mandla* criteria.[84] In *Nyazi v Rymans*, Muslims were denied ethnic group status, due to their linguistic, geographical and racial heterogeneity.[85] While individual *jatis* could perhaps fulfil the *Mandla* criteria, collectively, Dalits as a "universal" category might struggle to demonstrate sufficient commonality in terms of geography, language, religion and culture and a sufficiently distinct, long-shared history as a group.

7.3.3.4 *Revisiting* Mandla: R (E) v Governing Body of JFS *(2009)*

In *R (E) v Governing Body of JFS and the Admissions Appeal Panel of JFS* (2009),[86] the UK Supreme Court, in its first case, revisited the *Mandla* interpretation of ethnic origins. JFS (Jewish Free School) was a designated "faith" school[87] which benefitted from an exception to the obligation not to discriminate based on religion or belief in the admission and treatment of pupils.[88] The JFS policy was to admit children who were recognised by the Office of the Chief Rabbi (OCR) as being Jewish. The extent of religious observance actually practiced by a family was irrelevant. The only consideration was whether the child was Jewish within the OCR's understanding of the Halakah (Jewish law). The OCR recognised as Jewish those born of an Orthodox Jewish mother or grandmother, or those born of female converts whose conversion was recognised by an Orthodox synagogue. E challenged JFS's refusal to admit his son, M, to the school on the grounds that M did not satisfy the admission requirement of descent in the matrilineal line from a woman recognised by the OCR as Jewish. M's mother was an Italian Catholic convert who had converted in a Reform – not

---

ethnic ranking', and castes as 'bounded ethnic groups'; S Guha, *Beyond Caste: Identity and Power in South Asia, Past and Present* (Leiden: Brill, 2013) 5, 7.

83 O Mendelsohn and M Vicziany, *The Untouchables: Subordination, Poverty and the State in Modern India* (Cambridge: Cambridge University Press, 1998) 2.

84 On the *Mandla* criteria and caste, see K MacPherson and K Shaw, 'Is It Time to Legislate on Caste?' *Employment Law Journal* (February 2012) 12–15, 14. On Dalit cultural tradition, Deliège argues (controversially) that the "untouchables" [in India] 'know perfectly well that . . . they have no culture of their own'; R Deliège, 'Introduction: Is There Still Untouchability in India?' in M Aktor and R Deliège (eds.), *From Stigma to Assertion: Untouchability, Identity and Politics in Early and Modern India* (Copenhagen: Museum Tusculanum Press, 2010) 13–30, 28. For the converse argument, see, for example, E Zelliot, *From Untouchable to Dalit: Essays on the Ambedkar Movement* (New Delhi: Manohar, 1998).

85 See *Nyazi v Rymans* (n 80); Meer (n 56) 67–71.

86 *R (on the application of E) v The Governing Body of JFS and the Admissions Appeal Panel of JFS* [2009] UKSC 15 (*JFS*).

87 For the definition of a "faith" school, see EA Schedule 11 s 5(a)-(g).

88 See EA Schedule 11 s 5.

an Orthodox – synagogue. E alleged that the refusal constituted direct racial discrimination based on M's ethnic origins, while JFS argued that the refusal to admit M was made purely on religious grounds. The question to be determined was whether in being denied admission to JFS, M was disadvantaged based on his ethnic origins.[89] The Supreme Court, by five to four, held that the JFS/OCR matrilineal descent admission test focused on genealogical descent. Such a test was one based on ethnic origins. The reason M was denied admission was because of his mother's ethnic origins, which were not halachically Jewish, and so treating an individual less favourably because of his ancestry amounted to discrimination based on ethnic origin; the refusal to admit M thus constituted direct discrimination on racial grounds. The fact that the discrimination was based upon a devout, venerable and sincerely held religious belief or conviction could not excuse such conduct from liability under the law.[90]

7.3.3.5 *Caste and* JFS

The Supreme Court in *JFS* held that the RRA prohibited discrimination based on ethnic origin not only as defined by the wide *Mandla* test but also in the narrower, more traditional sense of a person's lineage or descent. Indeed, prior to *Mandla*, 'a narrow test based on birth or descent would have been regarded as required in order for there to be discrimination based on ethnic origin'.[91] The Court referred to statements in *Ealing London Borough Council v Race Relations Board* (1972)[92] that discrimination on account of race or ethnic or national origins involved consideration of a person's antecedents and that "origin" signified a source, or someone or something, from which someone or something has descended. In *JFS*, M was at a disadvantage because of his descent.[93] On the meaning of descent, Lord Mance referred, *obiter*,[94] to the ICERD definition of "racial discrimination," and CERD's interpretation of the descent limb of "racial discrimination," as including 'descent-based communities . . . who suffer from discrimination . . . on the basis of caste and analogous systems of inherited status'.[95]

Lord Mance was not declaring that the term "ethnic origins" in domestic law included caste; rather, in international law, descent was a wide enough concept to cover the situation in *JFS*, and therefore the concept of discrimination on grounds of ethnic origins (in domestic law) should also be widely rather than narrowly interpreted. In this way, *JFS* opened up arguments that caste is or could be covered within ethnic origins – and hence under "racial grounds" (now "race"' in the EA) – by virtue of the "descent" aspect of "ethnic". This argument, i.e. that ethnic origins in domestic law can be interpreted as including caste, has

---

89 *JFS* (n 86); Lord Kerr, paras 116, 117, 122; Lady Hale, para 54. Lord Phillips and Lady Hale stressed that it was not suggested or implied that JFS or the OCR were accused of being 'racist' in the 'popular sense of the term' as 'generally understood'; paras 9, 54.

90 Lord Kerr, ibid., paras 113, 119, 120; Lord Phillips, ibid., para 35; Lady Hale, ibid., paras 61, 71.

91 Lord Mance, ibid., para 82.

92 Ibid.; *Ealing London Borough Council v Race Relations Board* [1972] AC 342.

93 Ibid., para 89.

94 *Obiter dicta*: made or said by a judge in passing but not essential to the decision and not forming part of the *ratio decidendi* (the legal principle, rationale or authority on which the decision is based). Unlike *obiter dicta*, which do not possess binding authority, the *ratio* of a case is binding on inferior courts, by reason of the doctrine of precedent.

95 Ibid., para 81. The development of ICERD's interpretation of "descent" to include caste is discussed in detail in Chapter 4.

been made in three cases since the introduction of the EA, with differing outcomes (*Naveed v Aslam, Tirkey v Chandhok* and *Meshram v Tata Consultancy Services*); these cases are discussed in Chapter 9.

Caste not only has flavours of both race and ethnicity – "ethnic origins" in British law – but also distinct features such as endogamy (socially enforced restrictions on marriage outside the community); inability or restricted ability to alter inherited status; the link between caste identity and status and inherited occupation; the notion of hierarchy and graded inequality; the notion of untouchability; social stratification and segregation and (in the case of Hindus) scriptural sanction of the social hierarchy. "Ethnicising" caste under British law might lead to the legal elevation of *jati* identities into separate "free-standing" ethnic identities – the antithesis of Ambedkar's 'annihilation of caste', or indeed successive governments' stated desire to eradicate caste from British life (see Chapters 8 and 9); alternatively, conceptualising caste as a distinct ground of discrimination, or characteristic, entails the acknowledgement, but not the reification or essentialisation, of caste/*jati* identity. These two legal approaches, namely subsuming caste (*jati*) into ethnicity, or conversely making it a distinct ground of discrimination, correspond broadly to the two divergent political strategies which have emerged in the Dalits' struggle against casteism in Britain. One strategy advocates the embracing and assertion by Dalits of caste (*jati*) identities, alternatively of anti-caste religious identities (e.g. Ravidassia, Valmiki), as the means for resisting casteism. The other rejects caste in its totality and, with it, caste as a form or source of personal identity.[96] Until discrimination legislation is extended to explicitly cover caste, whether as a new characteristic or an explicit aspect of an existing characteristic, or until discrimination is regulated in a different way, in those cases where religion is not available as a characteristic or ground of discrimination, lawyers will argue that caste is subsumed within the ethnic origins element of race.

7.4 Caste and discrimination based on religion or belief

7.4.1 Religion or belief as a ground of discrimination

Proposals to include religion as a ground of discrimination in the RRA were debated but rejected in Parliament in 1976,[97] and it was not until 2003 that religion or belief discrimination legislation was introduced in Britain in compliance with EU obligations.[98] Prior to that point, protection from religious discrimination was potentially covered in certain circumstances by Articles 9 and 14 of the European Convention on Human Rights (ECHR) on freedom of religion and non-discrimination in the enjoyment of ECHR rights.[99] Separately,

---

96 See I Ansari (ed.), *Readings on Minorities: Perspectives and Documents Vol. 1* (New Delhi: Institute of Objective Studies, 1996) xviii; L Dudley Jenkins, *Identity and Identification in India: Defining the Disadvantaged* (London: Routledge Curzon, 2003) 110; P Thornberry, *International Law and the Rights of Minorities* (Oxford: Clarendon Press, 1991) 9–10; S Morton, *Gayatri Chakravorty Spivak* (London: Routledge, 2003) 73–75.

97 See 1975–1976 Race Relations Bill, HC Standing Committee A cols 84–85, 96–118, 29 April 1976. An international instrument prohibiting both racial and religious discrimination was proposed when ICERD was drafted, but it was agreed to focus only on racial discrimination; see D Keane, *Caste-Based Discrimination in International Human Rights Law* (Aldershot: Ashgate, 2007) 168–169.

98 Contrast Northern Ireland which had legislation outlawing discrimination on grounds of religion or political opinion from 1976 onwards.

99 Treaty Series No. 071/1953: Cm 8969. UK Ratification 8 March 1951. On the distinction between Article 9 ECHR (freedom of thought, conscience and religion) and the statutory prohibition of religious discrimination, see Bamforth et al. (n 7) 866–874.

RRA case law had established that protection from indirect racial discrimination might be available to members of religious groups who also shared a common nationality or colour, or national or ethnic origins.[100] From 2003, two instruments on religious discrimination were in force: the Employment Equality (Religion or Belief) Regulations 2003,[101] which implemented the UK's obligations under the religion and belief strand of the EC Employment Equality Directive 2000,[102] and Part 2 of the Equality Act 2006 (EA 2006). Both instruments defined religion or belief as any religion or religious or philosophical belief, or lack of religion or belief.[103] 'Any religion' is 'a broad definition in line with Article 9 ECHR', including

> those religions widely recognised in this country such as Christianity, Islam, Hinduism, Judaism, Buddhism, Sikhism, Rastafarianism, Baha'is, Zoroastrians and Jains. Equally, denominations or sects within a religion can be considered as a religion or religious belief, such as Catholics or Protestants within Christianity.[104]

The main limitation is that the religion must have a clear structure and belief system[105] (this being ultimately a matter for the courts to decide). The definition of philosophical belief, and what it constitutes for the purposes of the legislation, was considered in a number of cases prior to the EA.[106] *Grainger plc v Nicholson*, for instance, identified five criteria for a philosophical belief to qualify for protection: it must (1) be genuinely held; (2) be a belief and not an opinion or viewpoint based on the present state of information available; (3) concern a weighty and substantial aspect of human life and behaviour; (4) attain a certain level of cogency, seriousness, cohesion and importance; and (5) be worthy of respect in a democratic society and compatible with human dignity and not conflict with the fundamental rights of others.[107] These criteria are contained in the EA Explanatory Notes on belief.[108]

7.4.2 Meaning of direct discrimination based on religion or belief

The UK's 2003 Regulations (as amended) and the EA 2006 provided that direct discrimination occurs where, because of the religion or belief of B or of any other person except A (whether or not it is also A's religion or belief), A treats B less favourably than he [sic] treats or would treat others.[109] Direct discrimination could therefore occur if it were not B's religion or belief but the religion or belief of another person which motivated the less favourable

---

100 See, for example, *CRE v Precision Manufacturing Services Ltd* (n 81).
101 Employment Equality (Religion or Belief) Regulations 2003; S.I. 2003/1660.
102 Council Directive 2000/78/EC of 27 November 2000 establishing a general framework for equal treatment in employment and occupation.
103 EA 2006 s 44(a), s 44(b); EA 2006 s 77(1) 1, which replaced the original definition of religion or belief in reg. 2(1) of the 2003 Regulations.
104 Explanatory Notes to the Equality Act 2006 para 170.
105 Ibid., Explanatory Notes to the Equality Act 2010 para 51.
106 See L Vickers, 'Religious Discrimination in the Workplace: An Emerging Hierarchy?' 12(3) *Ecclesiastical Law Journal* (2009) 280–303, 282. Section 10(1) EA retains the definition of religion as 'any religion', and section 10(2) EA retains the definition of belief as 'any religious or philosophical belief'.
107 UKEAT/02/19/09. Grainger relied on *Campbell and Cosans v UK* (1982) 4 EHRR 293, para 33. In *Grainger*, a belief in climate change was found to be protected philosophical belief. Ethical veganism and anti-fox hunting views have also been held to be protected beliefs.
108 Explanatory Notes to the Equality Act 2010 paras 51–52.
109 Equality Act 2006 s 45(1); Equality Act 2006 s 77(2), which replaced regulation 3(1)a of the 2003 Regulations.

treatment by A – and regardless of whether A was of the same religion or belief as B.[110] The legislation excluded from the ambit of direct discrimination less favourable treatment of B occurring *solely because of A's religion or belief*, for example 'where A feels motivated to take particular action because of what his [sic] religion or belief requires'.[111] For religious discrimination to have occurred, the less favourable treatment of B must have occurred because of the actual or perceived religion or belief of B or of another person. Less favourable treatment of B motivated by A's own religious beliefs would not amount to *religious* discrimination, although it might amount to discrimination on another ground, e.g. sex or sexual orientation. The EA formulation, on the other hand, is simpler: direct discrimination occurs if, because of a protected characteristic (e.g. religion or belief), A treats B less favourably than A treats or would treat others.[112]

7.4.3 Caste discrimination as religious discrimination

Caste discrimination is captured by religious discrimination provisions only if the victim's ascribed caste status can be considered "part of" or integral to their religion or belief. However, the concept of caste is distinct from the characteristic of religion or belief; it is misconceived to conflate caste status or identity with religion, and caste discrimination with religious discrimination.[113] The conflation of caste with religion in British legal discourse has deep roots, because of the scriptural association between caste and classical Hinduism, the mistaken view that caste and caste discrimination is solely a Hindu phenomenon and because of the colonial approach to caste and caste-based inequalities as essentially "religious" matters (and hence outside the ambit of state interference).[114] Caste status is not solely a religious identity. Discrimination based on caste and discrimination based on religion are not the same, because, by definition, *caste* discrimination is motivated by an individual's known, perceived or assumed *caste status/identity*, not the religion or belief to which they are known or thought to subscribe or belong. Thus, for example, "low-caste Hindu" is an ascribed socio-religious status rather than a distinct religion or belief within the meaning of discrimination legislation.[115] Indeed, because of their caste, Dalits have not always been included in the Hindu fold; in the early twentieth century, the proposal that for political reasons the so-called Depressed Classes should be counted as Hindus was highly controversial among some Hindus.[116] It is on the basis of caste, not religion, that Dalits have been and continue to be denied entry to temples and public places.[117] By collapsing religion and caste into each other, the distinct nature of each is lost.

---

110 Equality Act 2006 s 45(2). The EA retains association and perception discrimination in relation to religion or belief.
111 Explanatory Notes to the Equality Act 2006, para 173. See also Equality Act 2006 s 45(1).
112 EA s 13(1).
113 See, for example, N Addison, *Religious Discrimination and Hatred Law* (London: Routledge Cavendish, 2007) 64.
114 R Viswanath, *The Pariah Problem: Caste, Religion and the Social in Modern India* (New York: Columbia University Press, 2014) 6–7. See also Chapter 2.
115 A similar mis-conceptualisation of caste status as a purely religious identity occurred during debates on the 1975 *Racial Discrimination* White Paper on the inclusion of religion as a subset of racial grounds; see *Racial Discrimination* White Paper, Cm 6234 (1975) 23.
116 M Galanter, *Competing Equalities: Law and the Backward Classes in India* (Berkeley: University of California Press, 1984) 25–26.
117 See *Suntharalingham v Inspector of Police, Kankesanturai* [1971] 3 WLR. 896, on appeal to the Privy Council from the (then) Supreme Court of Ceylon, whereby the appellant appealed unsuccessfully

7.4.4 *Where caste and religion overlap*

Historically, and particularly for Dalits, religion has been a means to escape from caste identity via conversion to a religion other than Hinduism, or via adherence to anti-caste religious
movements.[118] For some members of anti-caste religious groups or movements (e.g. Valmikis, Ravidassias, Ambedkarite Buddhists), religious identity may overlap completely with
caste status, meaning that discrimination based on caste could be captured by provisions
on religious discrimination. If a court found that such a group is a distinct sect within a
broader religious category (such as Hinduism or Sikhism), or alternatively an independent
religion with clear structures and belief systems, caste discrimination against members of
such groups, although motivated in whole or in part by caste rather than religious affiliation, could theoretically be captured by religious discrimination provisions – subject to the
evidence – as caste and religious identity are sufficiently conflated.[119] However, using religious discrimination provisions in such cases would mask rather than expose the caste-based
nature of the discrimination. For example, someone who discriminates against an Ambedkarite Buddhist may not discriminate against a Sri Lankan Buddhist, the underlying reason for
the discrimination being caste, not Buddhism.[120] Relying on religious discrimination provisions to address caste discrimination creates a divide whereby victims who are members of
anti-caste religious groups can in certain circumstances call up a prohibited ground which is
not available to non-members of such groups. Alternatively, where discrimination is because
of religion *and* caste, the religion or belief provisions may be relied on where religion is a
significant, even if not the only, reason for the discriminatory treatment.[121]

Two pre-EA reported cases, one in the UK and one in Canada, illustrate the use of
religious discrimination provisions where caste might also be at play. In *Saini v All Saints
Haque Centre* (2009)[122] the employment appeals tribunal (EAT) found that the claimant,
Mr Saini, had been subjected to discriminatory harassment based on religion. The employment tribunal (ET) had found that Mr Saini and his manager, Mr Chandel, who were
both Hindu, had been unfairly dismissed from their posts at the All Saints Haque Centre, an advice centre in Wolverhampton, by the Ravidassi-controlled management board.
Mr Chandel's Hindu faith was the effective cause of his dismissal, but Mr Saini's claim of
harassment on grounds of religion was rejected on the basis that although he had been
harassed, it was not because of his Hindu faith. He appealed, submitting that the tribunal
should have considered whether he had been harassed because of Mr Chandel's religion.[123]

---

against his conviction under the (Ceylonese) Prevention of Social Disabilities Act 1957 for preventing a
"low-caste Hindu" from entering the inner courtyard of a temple by reason of his *caste*.

118 See Chapter 1.

119 See Waughray (n 1) 214; H Metcalfe and H Rolfe, *Caste Discrimination and Harassment in Great
Britain* (London: Government Equalities Office, 2010) 60.

120 I am grateful to Professor Patrick Olivelle for this example.

121 Where a protected characteristic (for example religion) is a significant but not sole reason for the discriminatory treatment, a claimant may proceed on the grounds of that characteristic alone; see *O'Reilly
v BBC* case no. 2200432/2010 (2010) and *MoD v DeBlique* [2010] IRLR 471 at 165. This is not the
same as a "multiple discrimination" or "combined discrimination" provision.

122 [2009] 1 CMLR 38, 1060–1070; UKEAT/0227/08/ZT.

123 This is known as "association discrimination," where discrimination occurs because of a person's association with someone who has a protected characteristic. The Employment Equality (Religion or Belief)
Regulations 2003 – the legislation in force at the time – prohibited harassment because someone else
held certain religious beliefs. Where – as in this case – an employee established that he had been subjected to prohibited conduct (harassment) because of his employer pursuing a discriminatory policy

The EAT noted the tribunal's conclusions that Mr Saini had been mistreated because of the desire to get rid of Mr Chandel for the sole reason that he (Mr Chandel) was a Hindu; thus, if Mr Saini was harassed because of the wish to remove Mr Chandel on grounds of his religion, it followed that the mistreatment of Mr Saini was on grounds of religion. Ravidassias 'form a distinct group with distinctive religious beliefs that distinguish them from both the Sikh and Hindu communities'.[124] Caste was not brought up explicitly before the EAT, but was referred to in the earlier, unreported tribunal hearing, by way of evidence concerning discriminatory treatment meted out in parts of medieval India to "lower castes" such as Ravidassias by "higher-caste" Hindus.[125] Had caste been a protected characteristic, the claimants might have alleged discrimination on grounds of caste as well as – or instead of – religion.

The Canadian case of *Sahota & Shergill v Shri Guru Ravidass Sabha Temple (Vancouver)* (2008)[126] involved a complaint brought before the British Columbia Human Rights Tribunal (BCHRT) by two Jat Sikhs alleging discrimination contrary to the British Columbia Human Rights Code 1996 (the Code) based on ancestry, race and religion in the provision of an accommodation, service or facility customarily available to the public by the Shri Guru Ravidass Sabha Temple of Vancouver (the Sabha). They claimed that although the Sabha is predominantly Ravidassia, it advertised for new members who did not have to be Ravidassia. They applied but were told three or four weeks later that they would not be accepted because of their caste.[127] The Sabha had denied them membership, they said, because they were not Ravidassias of the Chamar caste (a Dalit caste). The complainants claimed that the discrimination against them was inter alia discrimination based on religion – a form of discrimination covered by the Code, whereas discrimination based on caste was not. Specifically, they complained that they were refused membership because of their caste 'and the religious background of the caste'.[128] The respondents argued that membership of the Sabha was restricted to the Ravidassia community, who by definition were members of the Chamar caste. They also argued that the Code did not apply to membership of the Sabha, because it was a private, purely social, religious and cultural organisation.[129] The BCHRT concurred with the latter argument and dismissed the complaint as lying outside the tribunal's jurisdiction, finding that the organisation was a result of a private selection process based on attributes personal to the members,[130] and as a purely private organisation it had chosen to restrict its membership to persons in the Ravidassi community and had defined that community to include only those of the Chamar caste.[131]

These two cases both feature caste dimensions and might have been brought under caste discrimination provisions, had they been in place.

---

against the religious beliefs of another employee, that amounted to a violation of the legislation; [2009] 1 CMLR 38, 1060–1070, para 29.
124 [2009] 1 CMLR 38, 1060–1070, para 2.
125 *Mr J Chandel v All Saints Haque Centre* ET Case No. 1306296/2006 (unreported).
126 *Gurshiner Sahota & Sohan Shergill v Shri Guru Ravidass Sabha Temple (Vancouver) (Sahota)* 2008 BCHRT 269.
127 Ibid., para 5.
128 Ibid.
129 Ibid., para 16.
130 Per *Marine Drive Golf Club v Buntain* (2007 BCCA 17); ibid., para 34.
131 Ibid.

7.4.5 *Religion or belief as a defence to discrimination*

Article 9(2) ECHR provides that the right to manifest religion or belief 'shall be subject only to such limitations as are prescribed by law and are necessary in a democratic society' for inter alia 'the protection of the rights and freedoms of others'. British courts have emphasised the qualified nature of Article 9 protection and have been unwilling to allow individuals to manifest their beliefs in a way which involves 'discriminating on grounds which Parliament has provided to be unlawful'.[132] The courts have not allowed protection from discrimination based on religion or belief, or the right to freedom of religion, to be called up in defence of behaviour which, albeit motivated by religious belief, is itself discriminatory on grounds of another protected characteristic, for example, ethnic origin[133] or sexual orientation.[134] In *JFS*, Munby J. explained that while

> the civil courts must be slow to interfere in the life of any religious minority or to become involved in adjudicating on purely religious issues . . . it is important to realise that reliance on religious belief, however conscientious the belief and however ancient and respectable the religion, can never of itself immunise the believer from the reach of the secular law. And invocation of religious belief does not necessarily provide a defence to what is otherwise a valid claim.[135]

It has been suggested by some scholars that a hierarchy of protection is developing whereby religion or belief is protected to a lesser extent than other protected characteristics[136] and that the right to hold and express beliefs freely is illusory if 'citizens are not also free to conduct themselves in accordance with those beliefs'.[137] There are also arguments for a 'reasonable accommodation' approach to religious belief and general legislative provisions on discrimination, i.e. certain beliefs should be tolerated to some extent, even if they are out of step with equality law.[138] Against this backdrop, McColgan argues that it is a mistake to protect religion or belief in the same way as sex, race, sexual orientation and disability, and warns against accommodating practices or beliefs categorised as religious, because often they are problematic on equality grounds.[139]

---

132 *Ladele v London Borough of Islington, Liberty intervening* [2008] UKEAT/0453/08/RN, 127.

133 *JFS* (n 86).

134 *Ladele v Borough of Islington* [2009] EWCA Civ 1357; *McFarlane v Relate Avon Ltd* [2010] EWCA Civ 880; *Bull & Bull v Hall & Preddy* [2012] EWCA Civ 83.

135 See *JFS* (n 86); *Ladele v Borough of Islington* [2009] EWCA Civ 1357; *McFarlane v Relate Avon Ltd* [2010] EWCA Civ 880; *Bull & Bull v Hall & Preddy* [2012] EWCA Civ 83. See also *Lee v Ashers Baking Company Ltd and others* [2018] UKSC 49, where the Supreme Court held that the refusal of a Christian bakery to make a cake for a gay customer with a message supporting same-sex marriage was not discriminatory on grounds of sexual orientation, because its objection was to the message, not the customer. The Court held that the message was not (as the claimants argued) indissociable from the sexual orientation of the customer, as support for gay marriage was not a proxy for any particular sexual orientation.

136 Vickers (n 106).

137 L West, 'These Judgments Restrict Freedom', *Church Times*, Issue 7679, 21 May 2010.

138 See R Sandberg, 'The Right to Discriminate', 13(2) *Ecclesiastical Law Journal* (2011) 157–181; R Sandberg, 'Laws and Religion: Unravelling *McFarlane v Avon Relate Ltd*', 12(3) *Ecclesiastical Law Journal* (2010) 361–370.

139 A McColgan, 'Class Wars? Religion and (In)Equality in the Workplace', 38(1) *Industrial Law Journal* (2009) 1–29, 1; McColgan (n 3), Chapter 5.

From the preceding, it follows that if caste is brought within an existing protected characteristic, such as race, a defence that the maintenance of "caste boundaries" should not be captured by race discrimination provisions, for example, because such behaviour flows from a genuine religious (or philosophical) belief, should not succeed. The argument that legislation against caste discrimination is itself a form of religious discrimination against Hindus is discussed in Chapters 8 and 9.

7.5 Conclusion

The legal capture of caste, and discrimination based thereon, presents as much of a theoretical and practical challenge to domestic discrimination lawyers as it does to international lawyers. UK discrimination law provides protection from discrimination occurring in specific sectors and on particular grounds only. The "grounds-based" approach to discrimination, one of the fundamental concepts underpinning the UK's anti-discrimination regime, is vulnerable to two related pressures: first, calls to expand the list of protected characteristics by adding more characteristics, adding an open "other status" category, or making the list non-exhaustive, and second, calls for expansive approaches to interpreting the existing list.[140] Groups suffering from hitherto unrecognised forms of discrimination (such as caste discrimination) may be denied legal protection because they are not explicitly included in the list, or, says McColgan, because courts 'may be unwilling, or perceive themselves as unable, to shape interpretive outcomes so as to make legislation fit for current purpose'.[141] Caste did not easily "fit" into the pre-EA grounds of discrimination and the EA protected characteristics still do not adequately capture caste. Only in certain circumstances can religious discrimination provisions capture caste discrimination, and only by successfully and definitively bringing caste within race, specifically within ethnic origins, can caste discrimination be caught by race discrimination provisions. The 1975 Racial Discrimination White Paper stated:

> To fail to provide a remedy against an injustice strikes at the rule of law. To abandon a whole group of people in society without legal redress against unfair discrimination is to leave them with no option but to find their own redress.[142]

In 2003, 2011 and 2016, the UN Committee on the Elimination of Racial Discrimination (CERD) recommended that the UK introduce a domestic prohibition of discrimination on grounds of descent, including caste-based discrimination.[143] The next chapter charts the passage of the Equality Bill 2009 through Parliament, the debates on the inclusion of an express prohibition of caste discrimination in domestic legislation and the last-minute amendment to the Equality Bill adding an enabling provision (in the form of a ministerial power) allowing caste to be added to the definition of the protected characteristic of race at a future date.

---

140 McColgan (n 6) 75.
141 Ibid., 75–76; section 3 of the Human Rights Act 1998 has provided British courts with an additional interpretive tool.
142 See *Racial Discrimination* White Paper (n 41) 23.
143 Concluding Observations – UK; UN Doc. CERD/C/63/CO/11, 10 December 2003, para 25; Concluding Observations – UK; UN Doc. CERD/C/GBR/CO/18–20, 14 September 2011, para 30.

8 Caste discrimination and the making of the Equality Act 2010

8.1 Introduction

When the Equality Bill was introduced to Parliament in April 2009, no mention was made of caste;[1] yet, by the time the Bill received Royal Assent in April 2010, an enabling provision had been added containing a ministerial power to introduce secondary legislation at a future date, to make caste 'an aspect of' the protected characteristic of race.[2] The provision was celebrated as a victory by Dalit organisations in the UK and abroad, who hoped that the power to make caste 'an aspect of' race would quickly be exercised, but its inclusion was condemned by various governmental, parliamentary and civil society actors who would go on, over the next three years, to oppose its exercise vigorously. There were four main objections to the legal regulation of caste discrimination: (1) lack of evidence of a problem requiring a legislative solution; (2) legislation was unnecessary, because caste discrimination, if it occurred, was already covered by existing law; (3) 'proliferation of the protectorate' – the unjustifiable extension of the list of prohibited grounds of discrimination – and (4) undesirable socio-political consequences, including negative impacts on community cohesion. This chapter charts the passage of the Equality Bill through Parliament and explains and analyses these objections, and the circumstances which led to the last-minute inclusion of the "caste power." In doing so, the chapter looks ahead to the post-Equality Act 2010 developments, discussed in Chapter 9. Opposition to the legal regulation of caste discrimination has not diminished since the enactment of the Equality Act in 2010. On the contrary, the legal, political and ideological arguments against caste discrimination legislation in the UK identified in this chapter have been pursued with increasing vigour.

In 2001, the UN World Conference Against Racism, Racial Discrimination, Xenophobia and Related Intolerance (WCAR) in Durban provided a springboard for the transformation of caste discrimination from domestic grievance into an international human rights issue.[3] From 2006 onwards, the prospect of an Equality Bill provided a rallying point for British Dalit organisations and activists, an opportunity to make the strategic and rhetorical shifts necessary to take their claims to the highest governmental level and a catalyst for debate on

---

1 See https://publications.parliament.uk/pa/cm200809/cmbills/085/voli/2009085i.pdf.
2 Equality Act 2010, s 9(5)(a). An enabling provision in a statute gives the entity to which it is addressed (e.g. government officials) the power to take certain actions. For example, section 81 of the Equality Act 2006 gave the Secretary of State power to make regulations concerning 'discrimination or harassment on grounds of sexual orientation', which was exercised by the introduction of the Equality Act (Sexual Orientation) Regulations 2007.
3 C Bob, ' "Dalit Rights Are Human Rights": Caste Discrimination, International Activism and the Construction of a New Human Rights Issue', 29(1) *Human Rights Quarterly* (2007) 167–193.

DOI: 10.4324/9781315750934-12

the inclusion of caste in domestic discrimination legislation. The strategic projection of caste discrimination as a human rights and discrimination issue challenged the conceptualisation of caste as a purely social, cultural or religious matter. Critical to the campaign for domestic legal regulation of caste discrimination was, first, the resources of key activists;[4] second, the willingness of individuals to provide personal testimony of caste discrimination; third, the willingness of Dalit organisations to work together; fourth, the support of a handful of parliamentarians and academics; and finally, the role of national non-governmental organisations (NGOs) such as Anti Caste Discrimination Alliance (ACDA, formed in 2008), Dalit Solidarity Network UK (DSN-UK) and the National Secular Society, and transnational advocacy networks such as International Dalit Solidarity Network (IDSN). Two "key moments" can be identified as turning points at this stage of the campaign for legal change. The first was the publication in November 2009 of ACDA's study on caste discrimination in the UK, written with academic collaboration.[5] This study proved instrumental in securing official acknowledgement that caste discrimination might exist in the UK. The second was a meeting on 4 February 2010 in the House of Lords on caste and the Equality Bill, called by Baroness Thornton, the government minister responsible for the passage of the Bill through the Lords, for the purpose of hearing from Dalit organisations, community representatives and individuals with direct experience of caste discrimination. At this meeting "behind the scenes", government support (or at least non-opposition) was secured for an amendment to the Bill adding an enabling provision allowing for the future inclusion of caste in the definition of race.

This chapter starts with an examination of the Labour Government's Equalities Review, followed by an explanation and analysis of the first three objections to the legal regulation of caste discrimination just identified as they developed at the time, and their impact on the present-day debate. There follows a brief account of the meeting on caste and the Equality Bill at the House of Lords on 4 February 2010. Lastly, the fourth objection is explained, and its significance is dissected.

8.2 Equalities Review and Discrimination Law Review

By the time Tony Blair's Labour Government came to power in 1997, reform of the UK's anti-discrimination regime – described by McColgan as 'a tangle of acts and regulations whose variety [owed] little to principle and much to happenstance'[6] – was long overdue. In February 2005, the Labour Government announced a two-stage overhaul of the UK's equality framework, leading to a new, comprehensive, single Equality Act.[7] The first stage, the Equalities Review (to investigate the causes of persistent discrimination and inequality in British society), was completed in February 2007.[8] In October 2007, the Equality and Human Rights Commission (EHRC) was established by the Equality Act 2006.[9] The second

---

4 In social movement discourse, resources are defined as including the professional and educational background of movement personnel; C Hilson, 'New Social Movements: The Role of Legal Opportunity', 9(2) *Journal of European Public Policy* (2002) 238–255, 240.

5 ACDA, *Hidden Apartheid – Voice of the Community: Caste and Caste Discrimination in the UK – A Scoping Study* (Derby: ACDA, 2009). The academic collaborators were Professor Stephen Whittle; Dr. Roger Green; Dr. Gurharpal Singh; the present author.

6 A McColgan, *Discrimination Law: Text, Cases and Materials* (Oxford: Hart, 2005) 9.

7 The Labour Party committed to introduce a Single Equality Act in its 2005 General Election manifesto.

8 *Fairness and Freedom: The Final Report of the Equalities Review* (Norwich: HMSO, 2007).

9 Equality Act 2006. The EHRC merged the Commission for Racial Equality (CRE), the Equal Opportunities Commission and the Disability Rights Commission; Equality Act 2006 Part 1 section 1.

stage, the Discrimination Law Review (DLR),[10] was intended to culminate in the drafting of new equality legislation to replace the plethora of existing anti-discrimination statutes and statutory instruments. A Consultation on the new legislation was launched in June 2007.[11] In June 2008, the Labour Government announced its intention to proceed with a Bill[12] with the publication of its key proposals,[13] followed in July 2008 with its written response to the Consultation.[14]

The DLR provided an ideal opportunity to examine the existence, forms and extent of caste discrimination in Great Britain and to bring caste within the new legislative framework. The 2007 Consultation paper did not mention caste but – partly in response to a 2006 study by the non-governmental organisation Dalit Solidarity Network UK on caste discrimination in the UK[15] – the government in August 2007 conducted 'an informal survey of around 20 [sic] key stakeholders to determine whether they were aware of any evidence that individuals or communities had been discriminated against, based on caste, in the UK'.[16] In July and August 2009, two Freedom of Information Act (FOIA) requests submitted to the Department for Communities and Local Government (DCLG) by the Anti Caste Discrimination Alliance (ACDA) revealed that the DCLG sent a questionnaire on caste and caste discrimination on 15 August 2007 to twenty-three organisations – of which only two were Dalit groups – asking for replies within two weeks. Nineteen organisations responded.[17] Based on this limited evidence, the government concluded:

> We have decided . . . not to extend protection against caste discrimination. While recognising that caste discrimination is unacceptable, we have found no strong evidence of such discrimination in Britain, in the context of employment or the provision of goods, facilities or services. We would, however, consult the [EHRC] about monitoring the position.[18]

---

10 The Department of Trade and Industry was charged with developing a simpler, fairer legal framework, informed by the findings of the Equalities Review. In 2007, the remit moved to the Government Equalities Office (GEO), a department created in October 2007.

11 'A Framework for Fairness: Proposals for a Single Equality Bill for Great Britain – a consultation paper' (London: HMS0, 2007).

12 HC Deb vol 478 col 499 26 June 2008.

13 'Framework for a Fairer Future: The Equality Bill' (Norwich: The Stationery Office, 2008).

14 *The Equality Bill – Government response to the Consultation* Cm 7454 (2008).

15 DSN-UK, *No Escape: Caste Discrimination in the UK* (London: DSN-UK, 2006); see Chapter 6.

16 Cm 7454 (2008) (n 14) 177, 183–184. The organisations consulted by the DCLG in August 2007 included the Hindu Council UK; Hindu Forum of Britain; National Council of Hindu Temples; Ahmaddiyya Muslim Community UK; British Muslim Forum; League of British Muslims; Muslim Council of Britain; Sufi Muslim Council; British Sikh Consultative Forum; Jain Samaj Europe; National Council of British Indians; Network of Buddhist Organisations (UK); Network of Sikh Organisations; Zoroastrian Trust Funds of Europe; Caste Watch UK; Dalit Solidarity Network; as well as various women's organisations, ACAS and the TUC and the Aga Khan Foundation; see ACDA, Hidden Apartheid (n 5) 55.

17 DCLG provided a list of the twenty-three organisations surveyed and confirmed that nineteen responses were received but were unable to say which organisations did not respond. None of the organisations which responded was willing to make its responses public. No report was produced following the survey. See A Ahmed (DCLG), emails to P Lal (ACDA), 2 July 2009 and 14 August 2009, in *Hidden Apartheid* (n 5) 53–57.

18 Cm 7454 (2008) (n 14) 177. See also V Keter, 'Equality Bill: Bill 85 of 2008–9', House of Commons Library Research Paper 09/42, 7 May 2009, 20. The government also decided not to introduce protection from (among others) discrimination for Welsh speakers, for carers, on grounds of genetic predisposition; Cm 7454, ibid., 9.

8.3 Equality Bill 2009

8.3.1 Organisation of the legislation

The Bill was introduced in the House of Commons on 24 April 2009 and received Royal Assent on 8 April 2010. It had two stated purposes: to harmonise and in some areas extend existing discrimination law, and to 'strengthen the law to support progress on equality'.[19] Its successful passage through Parliament was of crucial political importance to the Labour Government in what were to prove its final months in office. It occurred against the backdrop of an impending General Election of uncertain outcome and government anxiety to ensure that the Bill received Royal Assent before time ran out and Parliament was dissolved.

Part 1 of the Equality Act 2010 (EA), in section 1, imposed on certain public authorities a new (and controversial) public sector duty regarding socio-economic inequalities, which the subsequent Conservative-Liberal Democrat coalition government did not bring into force in England.[20] Part 2 establishes the key concepts on which the EA is based, including protected characteristics and prohibited conduct (direct and indirect discrimination, harassment and victimisation). Nine protected characteristics, i.e. the grounds on which discrimination is prohibited, are listed in section 4 and elaborated in sections 5–11: age, disability, gender reassignment, marriage and civil partnership, pregnancy and maternity, race (which includes colour, nationality and ethnic or national origin), religion or belief, sex and sexual orientation.[21] A provision on combined discrimination because of 'dual characteristics', i.e. a combination of two relevant protected characteristics (section 14), was not brought into force by the subsequent Conservative-Liberal Democrat coalition government.[22]

8.3.2 The "caste amendment"

At Lords' Report stage on 2 March 2010, a highly significant amendment (unopposed by the government) was agreed. Lords Amendment 1, which became EA section 9(5)(a), provided for caste to be added to the legislation at a future date, by ministerial order, 'as an aspect of' the protected characteristic of race.[23] This meant that it could be brought within the EA protected characteristics via secondary legislation, without the need for further primary legislation. It was agreed in the House of Commons on 6 April 2010,[24] just two days before Royal Assent and six days before Parliament was dissolved. In bringing the term "caste" into domestic discrimination legislation for the first time, the so-called caste amendment was of huge significance for Dalit activists. However, it was not the outcome they originally hoped for. The goal of the Dalit organisations had been to secure an immediate,

---

19 Keter, ibid., 11. The Bill consolidated and updated existing legislation which treated the protected characteristics separately and differently.

20 Section 1(1) provides 'An authority to which this section applies must, when making decisions of a strategic nature about how to exercise its functions, have due regard to the desirability of exercising them in a way that is designed to reduce the inequalities of outcome which result from socio-economic disadvantage'. See B Hepple, *Equality: The New Legal Framework* (Oxford: Hart, 2/E, 2014) 163–175. Section 1 was brought into force for Scotland by the Scottish Government in 2018 as the 'fairer Scotland duty', imposing a requirement on relevant public authorities to actively address persistent inequalities in outcomes caused by socio-economic disadvantage.

21 These are the same characteristics as protected by pre-EA legislation.

22 See *The Plan for Growth* (Dept. for Business, Innovation and Skills, March 2011) para 2.51.

23 HL Deb vol 717 col 1350 2 March 2010.

24 HC Deb vol 508 col 942 6 April 2010.

express prohibition of caste discrimination in the new legislation via the addition of caste as a new (tenth) protected characteristic. Instead, the amendment was a "halfway house" providing government with a power to amend the legislation to cover caste at a future date rather than legislating immediately. Second, caste was conceptualised not as a new characteristic but, in a novel formulation, 'as an aspect of' the existing protected characteristic of race. In the circumstances, the Dalit groups had little option but to accept a compromise solution or lose the possibility of any reference to caste being included in the Bill. Exercise of the power in section 9(5)(a) was linked by the government to the outcome of independent research on caste discrimination, which was commissioned in March 2010 and published in December 2010. The provision contained no timeframe or deadline for the exercise of the power. The four main objections to an explicit statutory prohibition of caste discrimination, noted earlier, were raised by the government and other actors. These are examined in the following sections.

8.4 Objections to caste discrimination legislation (1): no evidence of a problem

8.4.1 *Context*

A key objection to proposals for the legal regulation of caste discrimination was lack of evidence of discrimination sufficient to justify a legislative response. The arguments were (1) the absence of any evidence of caste discrimination in the UK, (2) the absence of evidence of caste discrimination in spheres regulated by discrimination law and (3) what little evidence was available was merely "anecdotal" and hence insufficiently credible to justify a change in the law. The government stressed its willingness to consider any evidence that became available, and to legislate, but only if there were 'sufficient evidence of a real problem that can be rectified by discrimination legislation'.[25] In 2003, in its concluding observations on the UK's 16th–17th periodic reports, the UN Committee on the Elimination of Racial Discrimination (CERD), recalling its General Recommendation 29 (2002) on descent-based discrimination,[26] recommended that a prohibition against such discrimination be included in domestic legislation and asked for information on this issue in the UK's next periodic report.[27] In response, the government declared that it had seen no evidence that there was a particular problem with discriminatory practices against the Dalit community[28] or of descent-based discrimination, although it was happy to consider any evidence that was available.[29] However, it did not propose to initiate an investigation into caste discrimination in the UK.

---

25 HL Deb vol 716 col 345 11 January 2010.
26 CERD General Recommendation 29 (2002), Article 1, Paragraph 1 (Descent); see Chapter 4.
27 CERD, concluding observations, UK; CERD/C/63/CO/11, 10 December 2003, para 25.
28 Fiona MacTaggart, Parliamentary Under-Secretary for the Home Office; HC Deb vol 419 col 1602–1603W 1April 2004.
29 See CERD, concluding observations on the UK's sixteenth and seventeenth reports; UN Doc. CERD A/58/18 (2003) para 544; Fiona MacTaggart, Parliamentary Under-Secretary of State, Home Office, letter and memorandum to the Joint Committee on Human Rights on the International Convention on the Elimination of all Forms of Racial Discrimination, 13 January 2005, reproduced in 'The Convention on the Elimination of Racial Discrimination: Fourteenth Report of Session 2004–05', Joint Committee on Human Rights; HL 88 (2005), HC 471 (2005) 42.

8.4.2 Evidence-based policymaking

The "evidence" objection was premised on the principle of 'evidence-based policy-making (EBPM) – an ideological position, central to the Labour Government's political strategy',[30] which asserted that policymaking should be driven by information and knowledge of 'what works'.[31] Despite claims to objectivity and neutrality, the term "EBPM" is used in different ways in the policy and academic worlds and with 'varying degrees of rigour'.[32] Greg Marston and Rob Watts point out that, while the idea that policy should be based on evidence is not new or particularly controversial, what counts as valid knowledge or evidence in policymaking processes *is* contentious; further, the framing of policy problems and solutions is subject to factors such as institutional political interests and the status of the policy or decision maker. They identify a hierarchy of what counts as 'valid knowledge', with 'lay forms of evidence' being placed lower down the hierarchy, and formal hierarchies in policy communities which frame policy problems and solutions.[33]

Dalit activists challenged the assumptions underpinning EBPM by questioning what counts as evidence, namely which evidence is deemed to constitute the "truth," and who is considered to be in a position to speak the truth or to judge what is or is not the "truth". It was not clear at what point evidence of caste discrimination would cease to be "merely anecdotal," or how much evidence was necessary to establish a problem requiring policy change and a legislative solution. In practice, there seemed to be little difference between the Labour party's EBPM approach and the Conservatives' approach in the 1990s requiring discriminated-against groups to 'make their case' for legislation by providing (unspecified) 'strong and compelling evidence'.[34]

8.4.3 Equality Bill Consultation

The Equality Bill Consultation was launched in June 2007,[35] and various Dalit groups submitted written representations.[36] In July 2008, in its formal written response to the Consultation, the government insisted that it had found '*no strong evidence* of [caste] discrimination in Britain, in the context of employment or the provision of goods, facilities or services',[37] but it would consult the [EHRC] about monitoring the position. Referring to the results of the government's August 2007 survey, the Consultation response asserted that, to the extent that caste was a factor in individual decision-making, 'some anecdotal

---

30 P Wells, 'New Labour and Evidence-Based Policymaking: 1997–2007', 1(1) *People, Place and Policy Online* (2007) 22–29, 23.

31 D Blunkett, Speech to the Economic and Social Research Council, 2 February 2002, cited in Wells, ibid., 22.

32 Wells (n 30) 23, citing W Parsons, 'From Muddling Through to Muddling Up – Evidence Based Policy Making and the Modernisation of British Government', 17(3) *Public Policy and Administration* (2002) 43–60.

33 G Marston and R Watts, 'Tampering with the Evidence: A Critical Appraisal of Evidence-Based Policymaking', 3(3) *The Drawing Board: An Australian Review of Public Affairs* (2003) 143–163, 146.

34 See, for example, Baroness Miller HL Deb vol 565 cols 2004–2022 14 July 1995 (debate on Private Members' Bill to add protection against sexual orientation discrimination to the Sex Discrimination Act 1975).

35 Discrimination Law Review – A Framework for Fairness: Proposals for a Single Equality Bill for Great Britain; A consultation paper (Department for Communities and Local Government: London, June 2007).

36 See, for example, DSN-UK, *Submission to the Equalities Review* (London: DSN-UK, 2006); DSN-UK, *Submission to the Discrimination Law Review 2007* (London: DSN-UK, 2007).

37 Cm 7454 (2008) (n 14) 177 (emphasis added).

evidence suggests that this would appear to be a reflection of social or cultural considerations', for example choice of marriage partner, which is not a matter for discrimination law.[38]

8.4.4 Commons Committee stage: June–July 2009

At Commons Committee stage,[39] Amendment 111 was moved to outlaw discrimination based on a person's caste by adding caste as a new protected characteristic to the list of characteristics in what became EA section 4.[40] The government's claim that it had found no evidence of caste discrimination was challenged on the ground that government engagement with established lobby groups might not have included those who experience caste discrimination.[41] At the very least, the Bill should include an enabling clause to 'protect against a future where we discover the evidence', 'rather than miss the opportunity of a generation to outlaw a potential form of discrimination that flies in the face of everything that the Bill tries to do'.[42] The government's response was dismissive. It was not 'a claim' but 'the fact' that there was no evidence of caste discrimination occurring in any regulated fields; while government was willing to keep an open mind, there was insufficient evidence to suggest that it was a significant problem domestically or to justify protection against such discrimination.[43]

The Solicitor-General explained that the government's 'scoping survey' in August 2007 was carried out 'by contacting a number of Hindu, Sikh and Muslim organisations to ask whether they were aware of any evidence that individuals or communities had been discriminated against on the ground of caste in Great Britain' and that it was designed to pave the way for a formal consultation if the evidence came up in the survey, but no evidence appeared. She stated that the government would have followed the survey with a 'real investigation if there was the evidence to justify such a step'; moreover, officials from the DCLG and the Government Equalities Office (GEO) (the department sponsoring the Bill) were continuing to monitor the situation and to meet representatives of interested parties. She added: '[T]he concern was rightly raised, *but I hope that it has now been put to rest*'.[44] On assurance that government was actively monitoring the situation, Amendment 111 was withdrawn.[45]

---

38 Ibid., 183–184.

39 Commons Committee stage ran over twenty sittings between 2 June and 7 July 2009. Committee Stage involves line-by-line scrutiny by a Bill Committee (a smaller group of MPs), following which government may decide to introduce amendments at Report stage.

40 HC Equality Bill Committee Deb col 176 11 June 2009.

41 Lynne Featherstone; HC Equality Bill Committee Deb col 177 11 June 2009.

42 Ibid. See also Mark Harper, ibid., col 178, who proposed that if evidence became available, caste could be subsumed in the protected characteristic of race as a new dimension, rather than create another protected characteristic.

43 Vera Baird, Solicitor-General; HC Equality Bill Committee Deb col 178 11 June 2009.

44 Ibid., col 179 (emphasis added).

45 In June 2009, GEO and DCLG officials, including the DCLG's Head of Faith Engagement, met with Bharti Tailor, Secretary-General of the Hindu Forum of Britain (HFB), and Dr Gautam Sen of the Hindu Dharma Acharya Sabha. The HFB expressed their opposition to the inclusion of caste as a ground of discrimination in the Equality Bill as they said they had not encountered caste discrimination. They did concede that there might be some prejudice in the area of marriage and relationships but argued that that was no different to a person stipulating in a matrimonial advertisement that they sought someone who was the same race as themselves; see A Ahmed (DCLG), emails to P Lal (ACDA), 2 July 2009 and

In November 2009, ACDA published *Hidden Apartheid – Voice of the Community*, based on research conducted between August and October 2009.[46] A total of 58% of respondents (71% of whom self-identified as Dalits) claimed to have experienced caste discrimination in a regulated field, and 37% stated that this had occurred on several occasions.[47] A further 85% believed there was no legislation in place to protect victims of caste discrimination, while 28% said that as children (defined as under twelve years of age) they had been subjected to verbal abuse or threatening behaviour based on caste. The study received wide publicity.[48] However, the government was not convinced of the need to legislate immediately, and it did not consider the ACDA study to warrant amending the Bill, arguing that it indicated that 'caste prejudice' occurred predominantly in marriage and social and personal interactions, rather than in areas covered by the Bill, such as employment and the provision of goods and services.[49]

8.4.5 Commons Report stage and Third Reading: December 2009

By the time the Bill reached Commons Report stage on 2 December 2009,[50] three new amendments on caste had been tabled. Two added caste as a new characteristic to the list of protected characteristics.[51] The lengthier of these was the first attempt to define caste for legislative purposes in the UK.[52] Sub-clause (1) defined caste as including *jati* and *biraderi* (the original draft commenced with *varna* but this was dropped as being too complex) and a person having the protected characteristic of caste as a 'member of a caste group found within a hierarchical group-based system of social stratification, where both membership and group and individual status are hereditary, ascribed and permanent'.[53] The third amendment was an enabling provision for the characteristic of caste to be added to the legislation by ministerial order at a future date as a new protected characteristic.[54] The common feature of these amendments was the formulation of caste as a separate protected characteristic. It was government's rejection of this approach which resulted in the subsuming of caste within the protected characteristic of race, as this chapter shows later.

---

14 August 2009 (n 17). Two MPs supportive of caste discrimination legislation had met with the then Government Equalities Office Minister 18 months earlier, in January 2008, but there were no meetings between GEO and DCLG officials and Dalit groups.

46 ACDA, *Hidden Apartheid* (n 65).

47 Ibid., 2.

48 See, for example, S Jones, 'Asian Caste Discrimination Rife in UK, Says Report', *The Guardian*, 11 November 2009; 'Dalits Facing Caste Discrimination in UK: Study', *The Indian Express*, 12 November 2009.

49 See Baroness Thornton; HL Deb vol 717 col 1349 2 March 2010; Vera Baird; HC Deb vol 508 col 928 6 April 2010.

50 Commons Report stage and Third Reading took place on 2 December 2009; HC Deb vol 501 col 1111–1233 2 December 2009. Report stage gives MPs an opportunity, on the floor of the House, to consider further amendments to a Bill which has been examined in Committee. At Report stage, the government may introduce amendments, issues not voted on at Committee Stage are returned for discussion, and the whole of the House may table further amendments.

51 The shorter amendment read as follows: 'In relation to the protected characteristic of caste (a) a reference to a person who has a particular protected characteristic is a reference to a person of a particular caste (b) a reference to persons who share a protected characteristic is a reference to a person of the same caste'; HC Deb (n 51) 1176–1177.

52 Drafted with input from the present author.

53 New clause 43 – Caste (No.3); HC Deb vol 501 col 1178 2 December 2009. For the meaning of the terms *varna, jati* and *biraderi*, see Chapter 1.

54 New clause 30 – Caste (No.2); HC Deb vol 501 col 1177, ibid.

Sceptics questioned the number of victims of caste discrimination cited by ACDA and the robustness of their claims.[55] Others were not surprised that the government had found no problem with caste discrimination, because they only consulted nineteen organisations in August 2007, none of which were anti-caste organisations.[56] It was argued that caste-based discrimination was wrong, and 'if we recognise it as such, we should legislate; we should not wait for the evidence'. Supporters of caste discrimination legislation argued that it should 'form a tenth strand under the Bill' and the government was asked to confirm that, if research demonstrated a problem of such discrimination in the UK, it would introduce legislation promptly.[57]

8.4.6 Enter the Equality and Human Rights Commission

At Commons Third Reading on the same day (2 December 2009), the Solicitor-General made an unexpected announcement: if necessary, caste discrimination could be banned via an amendment in the House of Lords, if the research commissioned by government from the Equality and Human Rights Commission (EHRC) could be 'completed quickly'.[58] The announcement that research had been commissioned from the EHRC came as a surprise, given the government's insistence that there was no evidence to justify expanding its 2007 survey. FOIA requests to the DCLG in summer 2009 revealed that no research had been carried out by government on caste discrimination since its August 2007 'scoping survey'.[59] Responding to a further request to the EHRC in December 2009 the EHRC stated:

> The Commission has not been commissioned to carry out any research on caste and discrimination in the UK by the Solicitor-General or any Government Department in the last five years. The Commission is not currently undertaking work on this issue and is not currently proposing to undertake research on this issue in future. Consequently, we do not have a scope nor response time for such a research [. . .].[60]

The EHRC explained that it understood caste discrimination to be based on descent, occurring in African communities as well as in the Hindu community, but that there was limited evidence of caste discrimination in regulated fields or its effects on equality of opportunity and it appeared reluctant to treat caste discrimination as a domestic issue.[61] It believed that caste discrimination was already covered as descent-based discrimination by existing international, European and UK law concerning race and religious discrimination, and that

---

55 Mark Harper; HC Deb vol 501 col 1185–1186 2 December 2009.
56 Dr Harris; HC Deb, ibid., col 1196; Jeremy Corbyn; HC Deb, ibid., col 1185.
57 Marris, ibid., col 1203.
58 HC Deb, ibid., col 1226.
59 A Ahmed (DCLG), email to P Lal (ACDA), 14 August 2009 (n 18) 57; letter, P Lal (ACDA) to EHRC, 5 December 2009; copy on file with author.
60 Letter, O Varney (EHRC) to P Lal (ACDA), 6 January 2010; copy on file with author.
61 Despite its recognition since 1996 as a form of racial discrimination in international human rights law, caste discrimination was not taken up by the former Commission for Racial Equality (CRE). Caste was not addressed at the CRE Race Convention 2006 despite General Recommendation 29 (2002) of the UN Committee on the Elimination of Racial Discrimination (see Chapter 4), which affirmed that discrimination on the basis of caste and analogous systems of inherited status is a violation of the UN International Convention on the Elimination of all Forms of Racial Discrimination.

including a specific clause on caste discrimination may have (unspecified) 'unintended impacts' on (unspecified) 'other groups'.[62]

8.4.7 Lords Second Reading: December 2009

At Lords Second Reading,[63] Baroness Flather (Cross Bench) argued that caste discrimination 'blights people's lives in the UK in the same way as all other discrimination' and called for the Bill to address the issue in the UK.[64] The Labour Government reiterated that much of ACDA's 2009 study relied on 'anecdotal evidence', so further work was needed to test the study's assertions.[65]

8.4.8 Lords Committee stage: January–February 2010

At Lords Committee stage,[66] seven amendments on caste were submitted.[67] Amendment 5 sought to add caste to the list of protected characteristics in clause 4. Amendment 17 sought to define caste as a new protected characteristic, but minus the references to *jati* and *biraderi*, which were considered unnecessarily legalistic. Amendment 18 provided an enabling clause to be inserted, allowing caste to be added to the list of protected characteristics in the future, by ministerial order. The remaining amendments sought to include it as a relevant protected characteristic for combined discrimination claims, indirect discrimination claims, to prohibit direct and indirect discrimination based thereon and to prohibit harassment based on caste.

8.4.8.1 Lord Lester's amendment – "descent" as an additional limb of "race": January 2010

In an important development, Lord Lester of Herne Hill QC (Liberal Democrat) tabled Amendment 16 at the same time, which instead of formulating caste as a new protected characteristic, sought to add the term "descent" to the definition of the protected characteristic of race in clause 9. As such, under the rubric of race, the Bill would prohibit unlawful discrimination, harassment and victimisation based on descent as well as colour, nationality and ethnic or national origin.[68] This represented a departure from the amendments seeking to add caste as a new protected characteristic, and it opened the door for the

---

62 Letter, 6 January 2010 (n 60).
63 Lords First Reading was on 3 December 2009 and Second Reading on 15 December 2009; HL Deb vol 715 col 842 3 December 2009; HL Deb vol 715 col 1404–1418; 1432–1516 15 December 2009.
64 HL Deb vol 715 col 1458, 1460 15 December 2009. It was added that discrimination against trans people had been prohibited on the basis of similar evidence. Lord Harries; HL Deb vol 715 col 1453 15 December 2009. Protection against discrimination on grounds of gender reassignment was required by EU law; see Directive 2006/54 (EC), 5 July 2006, on the implementation of the principle of equal opportunities and equal treatment of men and women in matters of employment and occupation (recast). The principle had already been established in English common law; see *P v S and Cornwall County Council*, Case C-13-94 (1994); *Sarah Margaret Richards v Secretary of State for Work and Pensions* 6 Case C-423/04 (2006).
65 Baroness Royall; HL Deb vol 715 1514 15 December 2009 (emphasis added).
66 Lords Committee stage ran over six sittings between 11 January and 9 February 2010.
67 House of Lords, Revised Marshalled List of Amendments to be Moved in Committee as at 8 January 2010 at https://publications.parliament.uk/pa/ld200910/ldbills/020/amend/ml020-i.htm.
68 Amendment 16; Revised Marshalled List of Amendments, ibid.

formulation which was eventually adopted, which provides for caste to be 'an aspect of' race. This amendment is discussed in further detail later in the chapter.

8.4.8.2 *Lords Committee stage, January–February 2010: debate on caste 11 January 2010*

On 11 January 2010, the first day of Lords Committee stage, a Joint Statement signed by fourteen groups and organisations working with or representing Dalits called on the government to provide protection for victims and future victims of caste discrimination in the UK.[69] An extensive debate took place, focusing particularly on the lack of evidence argument.[70] Lord Avebury referred to the government's consultations with the Hindu Forum of Britain (HFB) and the Hindu Council UK (HCUK), arguing that these organisations '[did] not speak for the lower castes and the Dalits'.[71] It became apparent that, contrary to the Solicitor-General's announcement, the government had not yet commissioned any research.[72] The government reiterated that it was not opposed to legislating but would not do so 'without sufficient evidence of a real problem that can be rectified by discrimination legislation'.[73]

Lord Lester challenged this approach, arguing that even if there was just one case of caste discrimination, it should be unlawful because it was wrong in principle. Why, he asked, was research needed 'into the scientific extent of the problem, when all we are talking about is one or two words in the Bill?'[74] Baroness Thornton responded that Lord Lester was 'too much of an experienced lawyer to say that one or two words in a Bill are insignificant. These words are very significant'.[75] Lord Avebury lamented that time had been wasted, but nevertheless he was prepared to give the government 'the benefit of good faith', and he therefore withdrew his amendment seeking to add caste to the list of protected characteristics (Amendment 5).[76] The other amendments on caste – including Lord Lester's – were not moved.

8.5 Objections to caste discrimination legislation (2): existing law already covers caste discrimination

8.5.1 *Commons Second Reading, May 2009: caste discrimination already unlawful*

At Commons Second Reading, Harriet Harman MP (Leader of the House and Minister for Women and Equality) was asked whether it was possible that, under the Bill, 'discrimination by caste and descent would be absolutely illegal'.[77] She thought that such discrimination was already 'outwith the law'[78] – although she did not explain how. It was

69 ACDA, Demonstration Flyer, 11 January 2010; Joint Statement, 11 January 2010 (copies on file with author).
70 See, for example, Lord Harries, HL Deb vol 716 col 335 11 January 2010.
71 Lord Avebury, HL Deb vol 716 col 332 11 January 2010.
72 Baroness Thornton, ibid., col 344.
73 Ibid., col 345.
74 Lord Lester, ibid., col 344.
75 Baroness Thornton, ibid., col 344.
76 Lord Avebury, ibid., col 348.
77 Jeremy Corbyn; HC Deb vol 492 col 562 11 May 2009.
78 Harriet Harman, ibid., col 562.

pointed out that existing UK law is not as explicit as Australian law, which defines racial discrimination in identical terms to ICERD, and therefore UK law did not provide adequate protection.[79]

8.5.2 *Lord Lester and descent*

The possibility of addressing caste discrimination by reference to ICERD was first raised by Lord Lester during Second Reading in the Lords on 15 December 2009. He argued that race should be 'interpreted and applied in accordance with ICERD, by which the UK is internationally bound'.[80] On the following day, 16 December 2009, the UK Supreme Court delivered its judgment in the *JFS* case (discussed in Chapter 7), in which the notions of descent, ancestry and antecedents were identified as components of the concept of ethnic origins. This opened the door to the argument that caste is subsumed within ethnic origins (and hence within race) for the purposes of UK discrimination law by virtue of the descent aspect of "ethnic", given CERD's interpretation of descent in ICERD as including caste.[81] By the time the Bill reached Lords Committee stage in January 2010, Lord Lester had tabled his amendment adding descent to the definition of race in the Bill,[82] stating his belief that 'transnational caste discrimination' applies in this country as well as elsewhere and 'it needs to be covered by a measure dealing with racial discrimination'.[83]

Explaining the omission of descent in 1976 from the RRA definition of racial grounds – defined in RRA section 3(1) as meaning any of the following: colour, race, nationality or ethnic or national origins – Lord Lester (an architect of the 1976 legislation) stated that the drafters had regard to the definition in ICERD which was the source of the phrase 'colour, race or ethnic or national origins' (nationality was added later). Descent was not included, but it was 'perfectly plain' that 'ethnic descent was included within the concept of ethnicity, because the concept of ethnicity is about your birthright, where you have come from and who your parents and grandparents were', i.e. 'what your origins were and what your descent was'. Although the inclusion of descent as a separate category was deemed unnecessary in 1976, now, however, Lord Lester asked the government to clarify whether and to what extent it considered caste discrimination 'capable of falling within the concept of race as it stands'.[84] Calling up the principle of the presumption of compatibility,[85] he argued that if the question were to be litigated, English courts would necessarily have to have regard to ICERD and the descent category, because the UK is bound by ICERD 'and by an

---

79 Patricia Hewitt, ibid., col 577; see Racial Discrimination Act 1975 (Australia), section 9(1). Hewitt cited CasteWatch UK's belief that 'current law does not adequately protect those in South Asian, or indeed, other communities who find themselves discriminated against on those grounds'.

80 Lord Lester; HL Deb vol 715 col 1418 15 December 2009. This was a reference to CERD's interpretation of descent in the definition of racial discrimination in Article 1(1) of ICERD as including caste and analogous systems of inherited status.

81 *R (on the application of E) (Respondent) v The Governing Body of JFS and the Admissions Appeal Panel of JFS and others (Appellant)* [2009] UKSC 15; see Chapter 7.

82 Revised Marshalled List of Amendments (n 67).

83 Lord Lester; HL Deb vol 716 col 336 11 January 2010.

84 Ibid., cols 336–337.

85 Legislation which postdates the ratification of an unincorporated Treaty, where the meaning is ambiguous (i.e. capable of a meaning which either conforms or conflicts with the Treaty obligation), should be construed consistently with the Treaty if it is reasonably capable of bearing such a meaning; see *Garland v British Rail* [1983] 2 AC 751 (HL) 771A-C; S Fatima, *Using International Law in Domestic Courts* (Oxford: Hart, 2005) 296–307.

obligation to give effect in domestic law to the definition in the Convention'. He called on the government to include, for the sake of clarity, either caste or descent in the Bill, to avoid litigation 'up to the Supreme Court to decide a fairly obvious question'.[86] He also called on the government to make a *Pepper v Hart* statement[87] to the effect that descent and, through descent, caste are subsumed within the ethnic origins aspect of race, in which case, 'there should be no problem' in embodying this understanding in statutory language and accepting either his own or Lord Avebury's amendment.[88]

The Labour Government was reluctant to entertain new categories. Its view was that 'current discrimination law may already cover some aspects of caste discrimination where it can be shown that the active discrimination was grounded in race or religious discrimination', and therefore 'some victims of caste discrimination may already be able to seek redress under existing laws'. Nonetheless, the government did acknowledge that 'the extent to which caste-related issues are covered by existing laws' had not been tested in the courts.[89]

8.5.3 Equality and Human Rights Commission – support for descent but opposition to caste: January 2010

By early January 2010, the EHRC's position was that caste discrimination was based on descent, which it considered was already covered by existing international, European and UK law on race and religious discrimination.[90] In a Briefing dated 11 January 2010, produced for Lords Committee stage, the EHRC opposed Lord Avebury's Amendment 5 to include an express prohibition of caste discrimination, because it considered that existing provisions in the Bill on discrimination on the basis of religion or belief were sufficient to prohibit such discrimination; however, it did support Lord Lester's Amendment 16, to include descent in the definition of race, for two reasons.[91] First, caste discrimination was a form of descent-based discrimination prohibited by ICERD, to which the UK has been a signatory since 1969. Following *JFS*, descent fell within the definition of race in existing UK law as an element of "ethnic" (although the point in *JFS* was *obiter*),[92] and while descent was not expressly included in the definition of race in the Bill, race must be interpreted so as to prohibit discrimination based on descent, including caste. Descent was also 'more consistent with international human rights law and jurisprudence'. Second, descent was 'broader, neutral and sufficiently flexible' to include other (unspecified) 'new and emerging characteristics on which discrimination may be based'. Unlike the government, which was concerned about

---

86 Lord Lester, HL Deb vol 716 cols 337–338, 11 January 2010.
87 Lord Lester, ibid., col 338. In *Pepper v Hart* [1993] AC 593, the House of Lords held that (1) the rule whereby reference to parliamentary material is prohibited in questions of statutory interpretation would be overturned (2) where legislation is obscure or ambiguous, reference to statements by a minister would be allowed, where such statements were sufficiently clear, and (3) this did not constitute a breach of parliamentary procedure – and thus did not infringe the Bill of Rights 1688.
88 Lord Lester; HL Deb vol 716 cols 338, 347 11 January 2010.
89 Baroness Thornton; HL Deb vol 716 col 344–345 11 January 2010.
90 Letter, 6 January 2010 (n 60).
91 EHRC, *Lords Committee Stage Briefing*, 11 January 2010, paras 19, 32; copy on file with author. The EHRC stressed that its primary aim was that the Equality Bill should succeed, and further amendments that would delay it should be avoided; ibid., page 6. Lord Avebury's amendment was withdrawn on 11 January 2010.
92 See Chapter 7.

'social or class-based elements' getting into the protected characteristics, the EHRC saw this broader feature as an advantage, not a disadvantage.[93]

8.5.4 *Race, caste, descent and the Equality Act 2010*

In international law, ICERD prohibits *racial discrimination*, defined as discrimination based on race, colour, descent or national or ethnic origin. In domestic law, RRA 1976 prohibited discrimination on *racial grounds*, defined as discrimination based on race, colour, nationality or national or ethnic origin (but not descent). In both these cases, race is a subset of a wider umbrella category. In contrast, the umbrella term in the EA is race, and section 9(5)(a) provides for caste to be 'an aspect' (i.e. a subset) thereof. The argument that ICERD prohibits caste discrimination as a form of descent-based discrimination was correct insofar as CERD has interpreted descent to include caste, but ICERD contains no express reference to caste and no express prohibition of caste-based discrimination. Under ICERD, descent is not a subset of race; instead, both descent and race are subsets of racial discrimination – and it is under descent, rather than race (or ethnic origin), that CERD has addressed caste. However, the pragmatic approach – expressed by certain parliamentarians – to obtaining an enabling provision on caste in the Bill was to agree for it to be subsumed as a subset of race, without entering into theoretical arguments about whether caste was or was not a form of racial discrimination as interpreted by CERD.

8.5.5 *Leaving the matter to the courts*

The logical consequence of arguing that caste was already covered by existing discrimination law was the requirement for a test case to establish the principle in the courts – and thereby its practical deterrent effect. The first UK case involving caste discrimination allegations, *Begraj and Begraj v Heer Manak Solicitors and others*, was a pre-EA case which came before an employment tribunal in August 2011. The claimants submitted that caste discrimination fell within the existing provisions of the RRA (specifically ethnic origins) and the existing provision on religious discrimination, a claim which the respondents disputed. However, its potential as a test case was lost when, after thirty days of hearing, and before judgment was reached, the judge recused herself and the case collapsed.[94] The lack of cases reaching the courts prior to *Begraj* alleging caste discrimination might indicate an absence of such discrimination, but there are other possible reasons, including the non-existence of an express prohibition of caste discrimination in discrimination legislation which may have deterred complainants from coming forward and advisors from taking on cases, as there were no obvious grounds on which to base a claim.[95] The difficulty in testing allegations of caste discrimination in the courts, 'if there is no [legal] basis on which to do so', was raised in December 2009 at Commons Report stage,[96] while in January 2010, at Lords

---

93 See EHRC Briefing, 11 January 2010 (n 91), paras 30–33.
94 See *Begraj and another v Heer Manak Solicitors and others* [2014] *Industrial Relations Law Reports* 689–696. *Begraj* is discussed in greater detail in Chapter 9. A judge must recuse themselves (step down) in circumstances where there appears to be bias or "apparent bias", and may step down if it is not appropriate for them to hear a case on their list; M Ahmed, 'Judicial Recusal', *Law Society Gazette*, 14 October 2013.
95 See A Waughray, 'Caste Discrimination: A Twenty-First-Century Challenge for UK Discrimination Law?' 72(2) *Modern Law Review* (2009) 182–219, 201.
96 Dr Harris; HC Deb vol 501 col 1196 2 December 2009.

Committee stage, the lack of a 'clear remedy in law' was suggested as one reason why caste discrimination cases had not been brought to the attention of the 'proper authorities'.[97] In November 2009, Robin Allen QC argued that it would be unlikely for a caste discrimination case to be defended on the basis that caste-based distinctions were lawful and were outside existing law on race and religious discrimination; therefore, advisors 'should be confident in characterising [caste discrimination] as merely [sic] a specific form of race and religious discrimination'.[98] Yet the problem remained that 'since there is no specific mention of caste in our law, it would be a chancy and expensive business for anybody to try this out in the courts':[99]

These concerns were not fanciful. In the first two post-EA caste discrimination cases to come to court to date (discussed in Chapter 9), the respondents – as in *Begraj* – vigorously disputed that caste discrimination is captured by existing provisions on race or religion discrimination.[100]

In early 2010, while the idea of a test case to establish the application of existing law to caste discrimination was supported by Dalit activists, their primary demand was for the express inclusion of its prohibition in the new legislation.

8.6 Objections to caste discrimination legislation (3): "proliferation of the protectorate"

8.6.1 *Rationing protection*

Grounds-based models of discrimination law, as McColgan points out, involve rationing protection from discrimination to members of groups defined along grounds-related lines, yet 'the categories to which things, or people, are assigned for the purposes of social or, indeed, legal organisation' are not pre-ordained.[101] As Chapter 7 explains, this inevitably results in calls to expand the "protectorate" (those protected by reason of possessing a specific characteristic) by adding more characteristics, or by making the list non-exhaustive, as well as for expansive interpretation of the existing list. In the UK, for example, prior to 2003, sex and race discrimination legislation, as McColgan puts it, 'came under pressure to accommodate' discrimination based on sexual orientation and religion – characteristics not protected by legislation at that time.[102]

---

97 Lord Harries; HL Deb vol 716 col 334 11 January 2010.

98 R Allen, 'Tackling Caste and Descent-Based Discrimination – Jews, Hindus and Others', 38 *Discrimination Law Association Briefing* (November 2009) 10–12, 12.

99 Lord Avebury; HL Deb vol 717 col 1345 2 March 2010.

100 In *Naveed v Aslam* (November 2012) a complaint of caste-based racial (ethnic origins) discrimination failed in part because no order had yet been made extending s 9 EA so as to provide for caste to be an aspect of race. *Naveed v Aslam*, ET Case No. 1603968/2011 (unreported). Conversely, in *Chandhok v Tirkey* (December 2014), the Employment Appeal Tribunal held that the fact that caste did not exist as a separate strand in the definition of race discrimination did not exclude the possibility that some situations which would fall within an acceptable definition of caste would fall within the scope of "ethnic origins"; *Chandhok & Anor v Tirkey*, UKEAT/0190/14/KN, paras 44–45. In *Agarwal and Meshram v Tata Consultancy Services Ltd* (ET case no. 2202616/2018 and no. 22025035/2018, unreported), a claim of race/caste discrimination failed because there was insufficient evidence that caste as a category met the *Mandla* test for ethnic group.

101 A McColgan, 'Reconfiguring Discrimination Law', *Public Law* (Spring 2007) 74–94, 86.

102 Ibid., 75.

8.6.2 *Caste as a new protected characteristic*

One explanation for legislative and judicial reluctance to admit claims based on "new" grounds was that this would lead to what Owen Fiss famously termed the 'proliferation of the protectorate'[103] – the creation of ever more classes of protected groups 'governed only by the mathematical principles of permutation and combination'.[104] In its response to the Equality Bill consultation, the government had declined to extend protection from discrimination to Welsh speakers, carers or on grounds of genetic predisposition. Proliferation was raised several times during the Bill's passage through Parliament. In June 2009, at Commons Committee stage, the case was made for including caste as a new protected characteristic:

> My understanding is that the caste system makes distinctions between different sections of society by dividing communities into rigid social groups determined by birth and/ or occupation. That type of behaviour is exactly what the Bill . . . seeks to outlaw, so we ought to give serious consideration to whether caste-based discrimination should be specifically outlawed by making caste a protected characteristic.[105]

The Solicitor-General dismissed this as an invitation to add caste to the list of characteristics 'speculatively', to which she did not propose to accede.[106]

The case for adding caste was always going to be compounded by a lack of familiarity with the issue as both an ideological construct and as a *sui generis* ground of discrimination. It was suggested that if the evidence became available, caste could be subsumed within race, rather than creating 'yet another protected characteristic'.[107]

At Commons Report stage in December 2009, the proliferation argument resurfaced. Three amendments tabled at this stage sought to add caste as a new, separate protected characteristic. It was suggested that it would help if those making the proposals '*explained what other type of discrimination caste discrimination is most akin to*'. One of the central purposes of the Bill, it was argued, was to bring together a number of strands of discrimination and simplify the legislation so that it could be enforced more effectively in practice; there may be a good case for including caste as a protected characteristic, but this could apply to a lot of other characteristics, in which case the law would become ever more complex.[108]

8.6.3 *New characteristic, new subset, or neither: Lords Committee stage, January 2010*

In January 2010, at Lords Committee stage, amendments were tabled to add caste as a new protected characteristic, and to add descent to race. During the debate on caste as a new

---

103 O Fiss, 'The Fate of an Idea Whose Time Has Come: Antidiscrimination Law in the Second Decade After *Brown v Board of Education*', 41 *University of Chicago Law Review* (1974) 742–773, 748.
104 *Degraffenreid v General Motors*, 413 F Supp. 142 (1976), cited in McColgan (n 103) 80; N Lacey, 'From Individual to Group', in B Hepple and E Szyszczak (eds.), *Discrimination: The Limits of the Law* (London: Mansell, 1992) 99–124, 118.
105 Lynne Featherstone; HC Deb vol 493 col 177 11 June 2009.
106 Vera Baird, ibid., col 178.
107 Mark Harper: HC Deb vol 493 col 177–178 11 June 2009.
108 Mark Harper: HC Deb vol 501 col 1185 2 December 2009. The Equality Bill included no characteristics not already protected under existing legislation. On the unfamiliarity of caste, there is no intrinsic reason why caste as a ground of discrimination could not be understood and enter into the mainstream in the same way as previously "challenging" characteristics such as sexual orientation or gender re-assignment.

characteristic, the House was reminded that the intention of the legislation was to simplify and consolidate equality law and that any decision to extend the list of protected characteristics must be taken seriously. If there were indeed a good case for caste and descent, they should be taken into consideration, but the list could not be extended indefinitely, and other characteristics might also have a good case.[109] The government objected to the descent amendment, because it would have added a new ground to the list. Moreover, through judicial interpretation, descent might cover characteristics not hitherto considered for protection. It could 'amount to a significant addition to the strand-based structure of equality law and . . . introduce *social or class-based elements* directly into protected characteristics', and therefore it 'may be an unacceptably high-risk way of dealing with the issue without proper examination of all its implications'.[110] The government also opposed the inclusion of caste as a new characteristic on the grounds that many people would not know what it means, or may have different understandings of the concept.[111]

Dismissing the wording of Amendment 17 (which, as explained earlier, sought to define caste as a new protected characteristic), Baroness Thornton argued that if caste were to be a protected characteristic in discrimination legislation, its definition would require great thought, to ensure that it was correct and that the coverage was appropriate. She objected to the description of caste status as permanent, arguing that 'for a woman, it can change on marriage to someone of a different caste. The amendment would not cover such people'.[112] However, there was insufficient time to arrive at what, to government, would be a suitable definition of caste as a new characteristic. For these reasons, she was also opposed to committing (via an enabling power) to add it as a new, separate and protected characteristic in the future.[113] This argument – that caste was 'somehow more fluid than other protected categories' – was dismissed as 'specious' by Priyamvada Gopal: 'Race is not a biologically fixed category either, but likewise a historically constructed and shaped construct', and yet it is 'rightly seen as a category to be protected from discrimination'. Caste as a category, argued Gopal, is not 'somehow less recognisable' because a woman's caste can (sometimes) change upon marriage.[114]

8.6.4 The solution: caste as a subset rather than a new characteristic

The idea of incorporating caste as a subset of another characteristic, rather than as a new protected ground, took root following the debate on caste at Lords Committee stage on

---

109 Lord Mackay; HL Deb vol 716 col 341 11 January 2010.

110 Baroness Thornton: HL Deb vol 716 col 345 11 January 2010 (emphasis added).

111 Baroness Thornton, ibid. There is no intrinsic reason why caste as a ground of discrimination could not be understood and enter into the mainstream in the same way as previously "challenging" characteristics such as sexual orientation or gender re-assignment. A government study published in March 2017, on the feasibility of conducting a national survey on the extent of caste discrimination in Britain, found that 'there was a strong understanding about caste and how it worked across Hindu and Sikh respondents' and that 'misunderstanding of the concept of caste would not be a barrier to a national survey being conducted'; see Howat et al., 'Measuring caste discrimination in Britain – a feasibility study', at www.gov. uk/government/publications/measuring-caste-discrimination-in-britain-a-feasibility-study. Wider public awareness can be raised through education and information via governmental and non-governmental actors including the media.

112 Baroness Thornton; 11 January 2010 (n 110). Alteration of caste status for women pursuant to intercaste marriage is not automatic; see Chapter 1.

113 Ibid., cols 345–346.

114 P Gopal, 'Dominating the Diaspora', *Himal Southasian*, April 2010, at https://www.himalmag.com/ dominating-the-diaspora/.

11 January 2010. At the meeting on 4 February 2010 (see the following section), although the inclusion of caste as an independent characteristic was raised, debate coalesced around the formulation of caste (or descent) as a subcategory of race, which was attractive to the government and to some of the parliamentarians present. This was the approach adopted in the amendment tabled at Lords Report stage on 2 March 2010. By the time the Commons came to consider the Lords' amendments, the government had abandoned any idea of adding caste as a new, protected ground. Rather than 'inventing a new protected characteristic', the categorisation of caste as a subset of another characteristic was established as the acceptable solution – and race was seen as the only viable 'legal home' for caste.[115]

8.7 Meeting on caste and the Equality Bill, House of Lords: 4 February 2010

8.7.1 *Background*

On 4 February 2010, an important meeting on caste and the Equality Bill took place in the House of Lords.[116] This meeting (described at the time as evoking the passion of the early days of race relations legislation)[117] marked a turning point in the Labour Government's attitude to the legal regulation of caste discrimination at that time, and led to the inclusion of the word "caste" in the EA. It was called by Baroness Thornton, the Labour Minister steering the Bill through the Lords, who requested to meet with representatives of Dalit organisations in response to caste amendments to the Bill.[118] The meeting was attended by representatives from sixteen organisations working with or representing Dalits in the UK; Lord Avebury; Lord Lester QC; Lord Harries; Baroness Northover (Liberal Democrat); Rodney Bickerstaffe (General Secretary of the trade union UNISON); the present author, speaking to the applicability of UK discrimination law and international law to caste discrimination; one of the academics who had collaborated with ACDA on Voice of the Community; officials from the GEO; representatives from the Bill drafting team and individual victims of caste discrimination.[119] The purpose of the meeting was for the government to hear direct testimony from individual victims and organisations dealing with caste discrimination, to hear arguments as to the adequacy or inadequacy of existing law for caste discrimination and, if appropriate, to consider what form a provision on caste discrimination might take in the Bill.

8.7.2 *The research conundrum*

The Dalit organisations questioned the need for further research. How much discrimination did victims need to demonstrate, they asked, in order to persuade the government that a legislative solution was appropriate? The parliamentarians pointed out that no research

---

115 See Harper; HC Deb vol 508 col 931 6 April 2010; Baird; HC Deb vol 508 col 927–928 6 April 2010.
116 HL Deb vol 717 col 1346 2 March 2010. See also blogpost, Lord Avebury, 'Equality Bill: Caste' at http://ericavebury.blogspot.co.uk/2010/02/equality-bill-caste.html.
117 HL Deb vol 717 col 1346–1347 2 March 2010.
118 See HL Deb vol 715 col 342 11 January 2010; blogpost, Lord Avebury (n 116).
119 The organisations included ACDA; CWUK; DSN-UK; Catholic Association for Racial Justice; Coalition Against Caste Discrimination; British Asian Christian Council; Asian Christian Association; VODI; Central Valmik Sabha International UK; Shri Guru Ravidass Temple (Coventry); Federation of Ambedkarite and Buddhist Organisations and International Humanist and Ethical Alliance.

was carried out before the 1965, 1968 and 1976 race discrimination legislation, or before the Race Relations (Amendment) Act 2000, and that it would be unacceptable if a lack of research was used as an excuse for a delay in acting. The Labour Government representatives took a different view. The government, they said, was committed to evidence-based legislation. It therefore intended to commission 'robust research' to examine the nature and extent of caste discrimination in the UK in legally regulated fields, to assess what public policy and legislation was already in place and, in the light of this information, to assess the implications for government policy of any mismatch between existing discrimination, policy and legislation, including identifying the necessary government response. The government conceded that although debate on caste in the Commons had been concerned with the lack of an evidence base, evidence had been emerging, such that the government now accepted that a more substantial issue existed. It was unfortunate, given the stage of the Bill and the forthcoming General Election and dissolution of Parliament, that ACDA's November 2009 report had not been available in 2008, because the government research necessary to inform its response would now not be available until after the election. Nevertheless, the government representatives assured the meeting that discrimination on grounds of caste was very much within its sights: it was 'an issue whose time had come', those at the meeting were 'pushing at an open door', the government was convinced by what it was hearing and its response was a matter of "how" not "whether, and "when" not "if"; in other words, a government response would be forthcoming.[120]

8.7.3 Wording the provision

Regarding the form of a provision on caste discrimination, the options of caste or descent as a new category, or alternatively as a subset of race, were discussed. The present author explained that under international law, descent was a wider legal category which included but was not limited to caste. Concern was expressed that descent might be too inclusive a category, and therefore caste would be preferable. Arguments were also made by some of those present in favour of putting caste under the definition of race, which already had multiple components, and that it would be consonant with the definition of race to include it (or descent) as an expansion or a component thereof.[121]

8.7.4 Dalits faced with a compromise

The Dalit organisations' preferred option was an immediate and express prohibition of caste discrimination in the Bill. Against this backdrop, government representatives and parliamentarians emphasised the time constraints and the need to get the Bill through Parliament, to avoid it going into 'wash-up'.[122] The GEO representatives explained that it would be very difficult for government to table its own amendment at Lords Report stage in the time available, as the agreement of all the other ministries and departments would have to be sought. The alternative was for peers to table an amendment which was acceptable to – and

---

120 See blogpost, Lord Avebury (n 116); 'Equality Bill: Caste'; author's personal contemporaneous notes, 4 February 2010, on file with author.
121 See Lord Lester's amendment at Committee stage to add descent to the definition of "race" (n 68).
122 "Wash-up" is the period of the last few days of a Parliament, after an election has been announced, but before the formal dissolution of Parliament. During this period, Bills which have not yet completed their passage will only be passed if there is agreement between the parties. This means that opposition parties, particularly in the Lords, effectively have a veto.

therefore would not be opposed by – government. Given the overriding need to get the Bill through Parliament before the election, the question was what provision could be put into the Bill that (1) would not jeopardise the Bill's progress and (2) would be compatible with the findings of the government's future research. The government's proposed solution was to include an enabling power allowing descent or caste to be added to the legislation at a future date by ministerial order, as a component of race, on completion of government-commissioned research. The Dalit organisations were asked for their views on an amendment along these lines. It was suggested that this would be similar to section 81(1) of the Equality Act 2006, which conferred a ministerial power to make provision, by regulations, about discrimination or harassment on grounds of sexual orientation, once the legislation came into force.[123] It would be an acknowledgement that the Bill as currently drafted did not adequately cover caste, and, if the research indicated that there was a problem, the new government would, so it was implied, have no choice but to trigger the power. The inclusion of an enabling power was recommended to the Dalit groups by the government representatives and the parliamentarians as the best they could expect, given the timing.[124]

8.7.5 *The twin-track approach*

The Dalit organisations expressed concern (rightly, as it transpired) about whether the power would actually be triggered if there were a change of government following the forthcoming General Election, so they were reluctant to sacrifice the chance of an amendment adding caste (or descent) directly to the Bill. A "twin-track" approach was therefore mooted, whereby government would pursue speedy consultation with ministries and departments regarding two government amendments – one to add caste to the Bill immediately as a protected characteristic, and the other to include a power to add it by ministerial order at a future date. There was unanimity on the adoption of the twin-track approach, but the government representatives immediately stressed that no guarantees could be given regarding either amendment. If it was decided to include a power in the Bill to introduce caste at a later stage, once the legislation was enacted, the necessary additional legislation would have to be prepared, and issues such as the possible burdens on employers and the private sector would have to be addressed. In the event, the twin-track approach was dropped and government did not table its own amendment, instead accepting (i.e. not opposing) the amendment at Lords Report stage providing for the inclusion of a ministerial power to add caste "as an aspect of race" at a future date.

8.8 Finalising the Equality Act: an "intermediate solution"

8.8.1 *Lords Report stage and Third Reading*

At Lords Report stage on 2 March 2010, Amendment 10 was moved, which provided for the definition of race in clause 9 of the Bill to be amended by ministerial order, so as to provide for caste to be "an aspect of race:"

---

123 See www.legislation.gov.uk/ukpga/2006/3/section/81 (visited 3 December 2021); Equality Act (Sexual Orientation) Regulations 2007; S.I. 2007 No. 1263. The enabling power allowed for extension of the prohibition of discrimination on grounds of sexual orientation to the provision of goods and services.

124 GEO informal list of key points from the meeting; email on file with author. The meeting was not officially minuted.

(5) A Minister of the Crown may by order

    (a) amend this section [section 9] so as to provide for caste to be an aspect of race;

    (b) amend this Act so as to provide for an exception to a provision of this Act to apply, or not to apply, to caste or to apply, or not to apply, to caste in specified circumstances.

(6) The power under section 205(4)(b), in its application to subsection (5), includes power to amend this Act.[125]

The unusual formulation "as an aspect of" was suggested by the GEO.[126] Amendment 10 was accepted by the government as a 'proportionate approach' which would allow it 'to act in an appropriate way in response to the research evidence and any subsequent public consultation'.[127] The government would consider whether exercising the power was a proportionate response, if and when the research showed evidence of caste discrimination in Great Britain.[128]

The amendment was a disappointment to the Dalit organisations, who believed that the ACDA study contained ample evidence of a problem requiring a legislative solution, and who wanted an immediate and express prohibition of caste discrimination. Lord Avebury described the amendment as an 'intermediate solution' whilst remaining optimistic that it would soon be 'conclusively proved that caste discrimination occurs in the fields covered by the Bill'.[129] Final amendments were made to the Bill during the Third Reading in the Lords on 23 March 2010, whereupon the Bill was passed and returned to the Commons. Before that, however, the government had announced at Report Stage on 2 March 2010 that it had commissioned the National Institute for Economic and Social Research (NIESR) to conduct wide-ranging research on the nature, extent and severity of caste prejudice and discrimination in Britain and its associated implications for future government policy.[130] The outcome would come too late for inclusion in the Bill of a specific provision prohibiting caste discrimination, but Baroness Thornton reiterated that legislating immediately was not the only option – on the contrary, the government was unwilling to legislate unless evidence of caste discrimination was produced. In a sense, the Labour Government's own delay in commissioning research had provided it with a reason for not legislating immediately against caste discrimination.

8.8.2 *Consideration of Lords amendments and Royal Assent: 6 and 8 April 2010*

Commons consideration of Lords amendments took place on 6 April 2010. The "caste amendment" – now Lords Amendment 1 – was agreed by the House as section 9(5)(a) of the new legislation.[131] The Solicitor-General defended the government's handling of caste discrimination on the grounds that the ACDA report contained only a 'small amount of

---

125 HL Deb vol 717 col 1345 2 March 2010.

126 Baroness Thornton had previously described Lord Lester's amendment to add descent to the protected characteristic of race in similar language as a proposal to add descent 'as a further aspect' of race; HL Deb vol 715 col 341 11 January 2010.

127 HL Deb vol 717 col 1349 2 March 2010.

128 Baroness Thornton; HL Deb vol 717 col 1346 2 March 2010.

129 Lord Avebury; HL Deb vol 717 col 1350 2 March 2010.

130 HL Deb vol 717 col 1349 2 March 2010.

131 HC Deb vol 508 col 927 6 April 2010.

mainly anecdotal evidence' primarily covering discrimination in relation to personal or social situations beyond the scope of discrimination law. Any evidence found of caste discrimination would be disclosed and discussed with all the stakeholders who had brought the issue to government's attention. Amendment 1 was described as 'a precautionary measure . . . because we do not yet know what the research will show'.[132] It was suggested that whoever formed a government after the election should look very clearly at the evidence and make a decision 'depending on whether there is evidence of harm'.[133] Two days later, on 8 April 2010, the Bill received Royal Assent.

8.9 Objections to caste discrimination legislation (4): political and ideological objections

During the passage of the Equality Bill through parliament, alongside legal and technical arguments about lack of evidence, extending the protected grounds and the scope of existing law, a further set of political, ideological and policy objections to caste discrimination legislation emerged on the part of various government, parliamentary and civil society actors, including organisations such as the Hindu Forum of Britain (HFB) and the Hindu Council UK (HCUK). Objectors characterised legislation as 'cultural intrusion', damaging to community cohesion and anti-Hindu. They also argued that it was not government's role to interfere with minority religious or cultural practices except when unlawful, and that legal regulation of caste discrimination might have unintended impacts or unexpected effects on 'other groups'. In June 2009, at Commons Committee stage, the Solicitor General stressed that the Hindu Council UK (HCUK) and the Hindu Forum of Britain (HFB), described as 'the two largest and the best we could do in terms of representative organisations in [the] field', were and remain 'totally against the introduction of caste legislation'.[134] The Hindu organisations consulted by the government considered that proposals for caste discrimination legislation denigrated Hinduism and presented Hindus as a "problem," wrongly labelled as discrimination personal choices and associational preferences in spheres outside the ambit of discrimination law and amounted to an attack on the fundamental freedom of Hindus to retain their intra-group identities. For these organisations, caste was a positive source of social or corporate identity and social cohesion. Furthermore, they argued that caste discrimination did not occur in the UK, at least not in the fields regulated by discrimination law, and that legislation was inappropriate, unnecessary and an attack on Hinduism. These arguments are discussed briefly below.

8.9.1 *Cultural intrusion and the "privacy barrier"*

In 2004, in a statement which echoed the colonial policy of non-interference in "personal law" (i.e. religious) matters, the Secretary of State for the Home Department, in response to a parliamentary question about government measures taken to tackle discriminatory practices against the UK's Dalit community, had said:

132 Vera Baird; ibid., col 928.
133 Mark Harper; HC Deb vol 508 col 931 6 April 2010.
134 Vera Baird; HC Equality Bill Committee Deb col 179 11 June 2009 at https://publications.parliament. uk/pa/cm200809/cmpublic/equality/090611/pm/90611s06.htm. The government had 'consulted a variety of predominantly Hindu groups and some Sikh and Muslim groups as well'; ibid.

We acknowledge that there have been criticisms levelled at the Hindu caste system with regards to the treatment of Dalits. *However, it is not the role of Government to take a position on the rites, beliefs or practices of any particular religious faith, other than where these give rise to conflict with the law.*[135]

This statement reflects policymakers' fears that caste legislation could be characterised either as unfairly targeting a specific minority population (South Asians or, specifically, Hindus) or as interference by (white) policymakers in minority religious and cultural matters ("cultural intrusion"). It also reveals a misunderstanding of caste as a purely religious and Hindu phenomenon. During the Equality Bill debates, the government repeated this stance, pointing out in January 2010 that the HFB and the HCUK also considered legislation 'the wrong option to cure what they primarily see as a cultural matter'.[136] In 2008, the HFB, while accepting that due to 'cultural practices and tradition' caste 'can play a role in social interactions and personal choices like marriages, conversations and friendships', asserted that there was no evidence that it was 'endemic' in British society, nor did it affect 'the provision of education, employment or goods and services'. Moreover, it was not for government '[to] interfere in personal choices and . . . social interaction'. Instead, community organisations should be empowered to 'break any existing barriers to promote *further intra-community integration and cohesion*'. Moreover, rather than becoming 'directly involved in legislating caste in the UK', government should 'facilitate and encourage community organisations and individuals to play a greater role in building programmes of awareness and education'.[137]

In its 2008 report 'The Caste System', the HCUK defended the maintenance of caste distinctions in the private and social spheres, using the language of identity and fundamental rights:

Hindus too wish to preserve their core beliefs and identities. How can this not be allowed to extend to who they wish to socialise with or whom they choose as a life partner? This is surely a fundamental freedom for each and every one of us, one in which there is no harm per se and which enables Hindus to maintain their distinct identities while simultaneously enriching the diverse cultural milieu.[138]

Of course, one may lawfully choose who to marry and who to associate privately with, or not, (although, as Nicolas Jaoul points out,

even though who you marry and who you are willing to share your meal with is a private matter, the question of inter-dining can become a public issue leading to the institutionalisation of caste once it is introduced in public places,

for example workplace or school canteens).[139] However, the HCUK's 2008 report appeared to suggest that calling for a prohibition of caste discrimination in domestic discrimination

135 HC Deb vol 419 col 1602W 1 April 2004 (emphasis added).
136 Baroness Thornton; HL Deb vol 716 col 343 11 January 2010.
137 R Kallidai, *Caste in the UK: A Summary of the Consultation with the Hindu Community in Britain* (London: Hindu Forum of Britain, 2008) 26–28 (emphasis added).
138 RP Sharma, *The Caste System* (London: Hindu Council UK, 2008) 28.
139 N Jaoul, 'Caste Discrimination and the Challenge of Multiculturalism', paper delivered at CasteWatch UK conference, Sandwell, 15 July 2007, unpublished; copy on file with author; see www.castewatchuk.org/conf07_1130.html.

law was opposed to the fundamental human right of Hindus to preserve their 'core beliefs' and 'distinct identities' – despite such discrimination being unlawful in India.[140]

8.9.2 *Community cohesion and "divisive" legislation*

The claim that caste discrimination legislation was "divisive" was raised again on 11 June 2009 by the Solicitor-General during the passage of the Equality Bill through Commons Committee stage. Baird argued that it was 'socially divisive to have legislation against something that is not happening and is needed by no one', and introducing 'a new characteristic when there was no evidence that protection was needed' was 'hardly going to contribute to community cohesion', she said. Additionally, the HFB and HCUK were 'very sensible' in opposing caste discrimination legislation, 'having, we are satisfied, conscientiously sought what we asked for' (i.e. evidence of discrimination).[141] It was not clear whether by 'community cohesion' the government meant *inter-* or *intra-*community cohesion, i.e. between South Asians and other communities, or internally among South Asian communities. Six months later (January 2010), in a sharp exchange during Lords Committee stage, Baroness Flather (cross-bench) referred to a claim by the National Hindu Students Forum that caste was not an issue in Britain, suggesting that this was because it had no 'non-caste Hindus' among its members.[142] Baroness Thornton replied that the case for legislation on caste discrimination was 'not so clear-cut that it universally unites the community it is alleged to affect'.[143] Among the organisations consulted by the government, she said there 'was not a consensus' on caste discrimination, while the HFB and the HCUK remained of the opinion that legislation was inappropriate.[144] In answer, Baroness Flather retorted that these organisations felt that 'to consult them about caste discrimination is to cast aspersions on them', tantamount to accusing them 'of discriminating on the basis of caste . . . they are not going to admit that they discriminate: no-one does'.[145]

The Labour Government's position during the 2009–2010 parliamentary debates on the Equality Bill, namely that caste discrimination legislation would be divisive and damaging to community cohesion, and that the case for legislation did not enjoy universal support in 'the community it is alleged to affect', made sense only if there is an underlying cultural and social homogeneity within the South Asian community – which is not supported by the evidence.[146]

---

140 Dhanda describes as disingenuous 'defending as freedom of choice the practice of keeping within caste borders'; M Dhanda, 'Punjabi *Dalit* Youth: Social Dynamics of Transitions in Identity', 17(1) *Contemporary South Asia* (2009) 47–64, 57.

141 Vera Baird; HC Equality Bill Committee (n 134). Officials from the DCLG and the GEO met representatives of the Hindu Forum of Britain and Dr Gautam Sen (Hindu Dharma Acharya Sabha) in June 2009 to discuss the issue of caste in relation to the Equality Bill, but it is not clear if this was before or after Baird's intervention on 11 June 2009; see *Hidden Apartheid* (n 5) 54.

142 Baroness Flather; HL Deb vol 716 col 339 11 January 2010. Baroness Flather is Britain's first Asian woman peer, formerly a Conservative but now a cross-bencher, and a Patron of the British Humanist Association. It is not clear whether by 'non-caste Hindus' she was referring to those outside the four Hindu *varna* groups, i.e. Dalits, because later on she refers to 'the three upper castes', presumably excluding both Shudras and Dalits.

143 Baroness Thornton, 11 January 2010 (n 110).

144 Ibid. The list of organisations consulted includes several Dalit organisations, all of them pro-legislation, in addition to Hindu, Sikh and Muslim organisations (n 12).

145 Baroness Flather, 11 January 2010 (n 142) col 343.

146 See H Blakey, J Pearce, and G Chesters, *Minorities within Minorities: Beneath the Surface of Community Participation* (York: Joseph Rowntree Foundation, 2006) 2; E Nesbitt, *Intercultural Education:*

An extensive body of literature exists on the phenomenon of internal (intra-community) discrimination experienced by so-called minorities within minorities. Scholars argue that such discrimination is often invisible to the majority community or is concealed by state policies of multicultural accommodation of wider minority group identity, norms and practices.[147] The problem of internal minorities was alluded to in the Equalities Review Interim Report (although not in its Final Report), which noted that 'analysis [of equality] by characteristics such as gender and ethnicity can conceal considerable variation within sub-groups'.[148] As regards anti-legislation arguments based on culture and community cohesion, whether state intervention is perceived (or construed) as an attack on minority culture or religion depends on whose voices are considered as representative of the group in question, the extent to which existing intra-group diversity, power hierarchies and division are acknowledged and recognised[149] and the willingness of the wider minority group to countenance challenges from among its members to its power hierarchies and dominant norms.

8.9.3 An anti-Hindu conspiracy?

The HFB and the HCUK linked efforts to outlaw caste discrimination to a Christian/Western anti-Hindu, pro-Christian conspiracy. Many Dalit campaigners and organisations, according to the HFB, had 'substantial backing from Christian groups', the reason being that the majority of Indian converts to Christianity were Dalits, traditionally 'the largest target group for evangelical groups operating in India'.[150] Caste, said the HCUK, 'was used to justify Christian proselytising and domination over the Indian population by Europeans, an excuse that persists today',[151] while Christian missionary attacks on the institution of caste and the 'Brahmin priestly caste' were 'full-fledged anti-Brahmanism, *the Indian equivalent of anti-Semitism*'.[152] Support for caste discrimination legislation was thus characterised as anti-Hindu and as discrimination against Hindus. This was noted at Lords Committee stage by Baroness Flather, who referred to an article in *Asian Voice* by the National Hindu Students Forum which, she said, accused organisations working for Dalits of attacking Hinduism.[153]

Ethnographic and Religious Approaches (Brighton: Sussex Academic Press, 2004); J Leslie, *Authority and Meaning in Indian Religions: Hinduism and the Case of Valmiki* (Aldershot: Ashgate, 2003); I Din, *The New British: The Impact of Culture and Community on Young Pakistanis* (Aldershot: Ashgate, 2006).

147 L Volpp, 'Feminism Versus Multiculturalism', 105(5) *Columbia Law Review* (2001) 1181–1218; A Shachar, 'On Citizenship and Multicultural Vulnerability', 28(1) *Political Theory* (2000) 64–89, 65–68; G Mahajan, 'Can Intra-Group Equality Co-Exist with Cultural Diversity?' in A Eisenberg and J Spinner-Halev (eds.), *Minorities Within Minorities: Equality, Rights and Diversity* (Cambridge: Cambridge University Press, 2004) 91–95.

148 See Equalities Review (n 8) 76.

149 Mahajan (n 147) 91; A Eisenberg, 'Identity and Liberal Politics: The Problem of Minorities Within Minorities', in Eisenberg and Spinner-Halev (eds.) (n 147) 249–270.

150 Kallidai (n 137) 20.

151 Sharma (n 138) 21. Religious conversion (specifically conversion to Christianity) is a highly politicised and controversial phenomenon in India. Several Indian states have enacted anti-conversion laws particularly targeting conversion by force or allurement of individuals or groups deemed vulnerable; see for example A Misra, 'The Missionary Position: Christianity and Politics of Religious Conversion in India', 17 *Nationalism and Ethnic Politics* (2011) 361–381; J Huff, 'Religious Freedom in India and Analysis of the Constitutionality of Anti-Conversion Laws', 10(2) *Rutgers Journal of Law and Religion* (2009) 1–36. See also D Sutton, ' "So-Called Caste": SN Balagangadhara, the Ghent School and the Politics of Grievance', 26(3) *Contemporary South Asia* (2018) 336–349.

152 Sharma (n 138) 21 (emphasis added).

153 Baroness Flather, 11 January 2020 (n 142), col 339.

The accusation of proselytism and "Hindu-phobia" was to become a key plank of UK Hindu organisations' ongoing campaign against caste discrimination legislation, and from 2013, it was also taken up by a small but vocal group of lobbyists and academics opposed to such legislation.

8.10 Conclusion

The objections to legislating against caste discrimination, detailed earlier, were not new or unique to the issue of caste discrimination; similar arguments were made by both Conservative and Labour Governments and politicians in the 1990s against the introduction of legislation prohibiting sexual orientation discrimination.[154] The presumption against the use of legislation to deal with new and emerging grounds of discrimination – even in the face of evidence of discrimination – is a feature of what has been termed the UK's "pragmatic" approach to anti-discrimination legislation. While social action in favour of discrimination legislation is an important driver for legislative change, the reverse is also true, say O'Cinneide and Liu, i.e. governments already disinclined to legislate may accord more weight to the anti-legislation arguments of social actors opposed to legislation, including arguments that are primarily ideological in nature.[155]

Caste presents a challenge to Britain's discrimination law framework. In 2010, the concept of caste had yet to permeate mainstream social, political and legal discourse in the UK. As debates on the Equality Bill progressed throughout 2009 and 2010, legislators remained unconvinced of the need for an immediate statutory prohibition of caste discrimination. There was also disagreement as to how to conceptualise caste legally. Many difficulties were experienced by government, parliamentarians, equality actors and activists in their efforts to locate caste within existing classificatory categories which were not designed with caste in mind. The fact is that caste does not fit easily into any of the legal categories currently available under UK discrimination law. At different times, different actors advanced opposing and sometimes contradictory arguments regarding the most appropriate "legal home" for caste. Moreover, for government, it seemed to be a "Pandora's box," with the possibility of caste discrimination legislation generating unwelcome political opposition from some sectors of the South Asian community – a response presciently anticipated by Dalit activist Satpal Muman in 2000:

> Asians are already victims of racism in Britain. There may be a curious effect whereby the indigenous community may use the Caste divisions amongst the Asians as a weapon of further oppression. The Asians could be accused of in-fighting, and those Asians who are fighting against Racism may see their work being undermined by our outcry against Caste. Some thought ought to be given as to how best we can achieve our goals notwithstanding the fact there will certainly be a backlash at least from the conservative elements of the Indian community for placing Caste System [sic] in the public domain.[156]

---

154 See N Busby and S Middlemiss, 'The Equality Deficit: Protection Against Discrimination on the Grounds of Sexual Orientation in Employment', 8(4) *Gender, Work and Organization* (2001) 387–410.

155 C O'Cinneide and K Liu, 'Defining the Limits of Discrimination Law in the United Kingdom: Principle and Pragmatism in Tension', 15(1–2) *International Journal of Discrimination and the Law* (2015) 80–100.

156 S Muman, 'Caste in Britain', in *Report of the Proceedings of International Conference on Dalit Human Rights* (London: Voice of Dalit International, 2000) 71–79, 78.

The Equality Bill presented an historic opportunity to secure a statutory prohibition of caste discrimination as a protected characteristic in domestic law. While the EA acknowledged caste as a potential ground of discrimination in the UK, it fell short of including an immediate, express prohibition of discrimination on this ground. Moreover, it envisaged caste as "an aspect of race" rather than as a new characteristic. Yet, the inclusion of section 9(5)(a) in the EA was nevertheless a major advance for those campaigning for caste discrimination legislation, and it represented an important stage in the development of British equality legislation. In May 2010, a Conservative-Liberal Democrat coalition government came to power, replacing the Labour Government which had overseen the enactment of the EA. In December 2010, the research on caste discrimination in Britain, commissioned from the National Institute for Economic and Social Research (NIESR) by the former Labour Government, was published by the GEO.[157] It affirmed that caste indisputably exists in Britain, it found evidence suggesting the occurrence of caste discrimination and harassment and it identified legislation as the most useful response.[158] Chapter 9 picks up the story.

---

157 H Metcalfe and H Rolfe, *Caste Discrimination and Harassment in Great Britain* (London: GEO, 2010).
158 Metcalfe and Rolfe, ibid., 14, 22, 63–65.

9 Caste discrimination in the UK

Beyond the Equality Act 2010

9.1 Introduction

The first part of this chapter examines the developments in the legal regulation of caste discrimination in the period from April 2010 to the government's announcement in July 2018 of its intention to repeal the duty to add caste to race in the EA. The inconsistent and contradictory positions and responses of successive governments, and their prevarication and obfuscation on the question of legal protection from caste discrimination, are laid bare. The second part of the chapter explains and examines the interlocking domestic and international legal and socio-political factors affecting the legal regulation of caste discrimination in domestic law. At the international level, two factors are highlighted: the UK's interaction with the UN Committee on the Elimination of Racial Discrimination (CERD), and the UK's economic and political relationship with India. At the domestic level, the socio-political context, including the shifting views and positions of the various institutional and legal actors and civil society protagonists, is examined. The significance of the inclusion of the word "caste" in the EA – even if it is ultimately removed by repealing EA section 9(5)(a) – is also addressed.

9.2 From the Equality Act 2010 to the public consultation on caste and equality law in Great Britain, 2017–2018

9.2.1 NIESR study: 'Caste discrimination and harassment in Great Britain'

'Caste discrimination and harassment in Great Britain' ('NIESR study') is to date the only government-commissioned study on manifestations of caste discrimination in the UK. Conducted on a limited budget, it did not purport to be a wide-ranging quantitative study;[1] rather, the aim was to interview individuals who perceived themselves to have suffered from, and could provide an account of, caste discrimination in regulated fields, and to assess its nature and severity, the need for a public policy response and the form this might take.[2]

---

1 H Metcalfe and H Rolfe, *Caste Discrimination and Harassment in Great Britain* (London: GEO, 2010) 63.
2 'Research into caste systems and the existence and nature of caste prejudice and discrimination in Great Britain', NIESR, March 2010 (copy on file with author). The study used the EA Explanatory Notes definition of caste; see Equality Act 2010, Explanatory Notes (revised edition August 2010); Section 9, Race; para 49; ibid., 3.

DOI: 10.4324/9781315750934-13

Thirty-two interviews were conducted.[3] The study relied on existing estimates of anything between 50,000 and 200,000 people of "low-caste" (i.e. Dalit) origin in Britain,[4] the population most likely to experience caste discrimination'. Contradictory views were noted as to whether caste consciousness and discrimination in Britain were in decline, making legislation unnecessary, but this could only be established by a major programme of research. Despite the need for such research, it has yet to be undertaken.

Despite its small scale, the NIESR study was important because it categorically affirmed that caste exists in Britain[5] and that discrimination and harassment on grounds of caste is likely to occur. It also found that, as in India, caste in Britain is not religion-specific. Evidence was found suggesting caste discrimination and harassment in employment and the provision of services, caste-related inter-pupil bullying in schools, which was differently and inadequately dealt with compared to bullying related to protected strands, and caste discrimination and harassment falling outside the EA in relation to voluntary work, demeaning behaviour and violence.[6] The discrimination identified in the study was found to be perpetrated by 'higher castes' against 'lower castes'. Potential social consequences included reduced confidence and self-esteem, depression, anger, social isolation, reduced access to care and social provision and detrimental effects on employment (e.g. reduced career prospects) and education. Potential public consequences ranged from civic violence through to a reduction in community cohesion. The study acknowledged the difficulty (common to all discrimination strands) inherent in proving workplace caste discrimination and in under-reporting perceived incidents, explained partly by a lack of knowledge of the issue among those unfamiliar with caste, and partly by victims' reluctance to challenge perceived discrimination, because they would need to complain to the perpetrators themselves, or to people of a "higher caste."

In the absence of caste-specific legislation, possible responses to alleged caste discrimination included going to the authorities (police, employer, school, service provider), speaking to the perpetrators, bringing a claim based on existing law, doing nothing or taking the law into one's own hands. In cases where religious identity, correctly or incorrectly, is taken as an indicator or a "proxy" for caste status (for example, in the case of anti-caste religious groups), individuals may be able to rely on existing protection against religion or belief discrimination, but this does not make protection against caste discrimination unnecessary, as religion or belief provisions would not cover all such cases.[7]

The NIESR study concluded that to reduce caste discrimination, the government could take educative or legislative approaches; either would be useful in the public sector, but non-legislative approaches were less likely to be effective in the private sector and would

---

3 Metcalfe and Rolfe (n 1) 7, 9.

4 Ibid., 20. The study explains that a variety of terms are used to identify the castes 'perceived to be the lowest, i.e. those termed "untouchable" or "Dalit" in the Explanatory Notes to the [EA]', each of which in their own way is 'problematic'. The terms "low caste" or "lowest caste" were used in the Report 'to indicate this group'. The authors chose not to use the term "Dalit" because it carries specific political connotations; ibid., 3.

5 The existence of caste in the UK has been and continues to be denied by certain civil society actors; see Chapter 6.

6 Metcalfe and Rolfe (n 1) 22, 63, vi. An educational institution may contravene the EA if it treats inter-pupil bullying based on one protected characteristic less seriously than similar behaviour based on another protected characteristic, where the reason for the difference in treatment is a pupil's protected characteristic. Additionally, the Education and Inspections Act 2006 s. 89(1)(b) imposes a duty on schools to prevent all forms of bullying among pupils.

7 'Caste Discrimination and Harassment in Great Britain', GEO, Research Findings No. 2010/8, 1.

not assist where the authorities themselves were discriminating.[8] Additionally, relying on South Asian communities to take action to reduce caste discrimination was problematic, and EA provisions on religion and belief discrimination could not cover all cases. If caste discrimination was considered an issue which needed to be tackled, and legislation was an appropriate means to achieve this, then reliance on religious discrimination legislation would be inadequate; without legislation specifically prohibiting caste discrimination, it would only be partially reduced by existing law.

Sikh and Hindu organisations criticised the NIESR study for failing to take into account (unspecified) 'cutting-edge real field research' on caste,[9] providing no evidence 'that caste discrimination is a widespread issue within the UK', and neglecting to identify the size of the UK population belonging to the so-called lower castes.[10] In response, the study's authors acknowledged that it was impossible to identify caste discrimination with absolute certainty from a statement made by a person who felt they had suffered discrimination; nevertheless, it was possible to determine the likelihood of caste discrimination where factors 'strongly suggestive' of such discrimination occurred.[11] Problems included the possible reluctance of Dalits in the UK to open up about caste and caste discrimination, especially to a stranger. Moreover, individuals are not well positioned to identify patterns of institutional or systemic discrimination where it exists. Yet despite its acknowledged weaknesses and limitations, the NIESR report was important because it provided independent evidence of the likely existence of caste discrimination in the UK, corroborating earlier studies by Dalit organisations.[12]

9.2.2 Government response to the NIESR study

No official response was issued by the coalition government. The most detailed reaction was from Baroness Verma (spokesperson for Women and Equalities) in the House of Lords on 22 December 2010. Stressing that the study had been commissioned by 'a different government', she stated that law had not eradicated caste discrimination in India, and whilst the government had not ruled out a legislative response, the only way to change individual attitudes in the UK – if caste discrimination did indeed exist – was through existing legislation. Moreover, unless the communities practicing such discrimination dealt with the problem themselves through self-education, legislation would not help.[13] Dalit organisations in the UK pointed to the UK's strong rule-of-law culture and the influence of civil equality legislation on behaviour, citing the examples of changed attitudes on race and sex equality in areas

---

8 Metcalfe and Rolfe (n 1) 65, 66.
9 Letter, P McGhan (Department for Communities and Local Government) to L Pall (ACDA), 3 August 2011, in response to Freedom of Information Act Request dated 4 July 2011; Attachment D (email from the British Sikh Consultative Forum (BSCF) to Lynne Featherstone MP, 11 January 2011); copy on file with author.
10 Ibid., Attachment E (letter from National Hindu Students Forum to Theresa May MP, 2 March 2011).
11 Metcalfe and Rolfe (n 1) 11. These issues also arise with other discrimination grounds.
12 See, for example, Dalit Solidarity Network, 'No Escape: Caste Discrimination in the UK' (2006); Anti Caste Discrimination Alliance, 'Hidden Apartheid – Voice of the Community: Caste and Caste Discrimination in the UK – A Scoping Study' (2009).
13 Baroness Verma; HL Deb vol 723 col 1098–1100 22 December 2010 cols 1099–1100. In contrast, Baroness Verma strongly supported legislation against forced marriage and female genital mutilation; HL Deb vol 723 col 1604–1609 13 January 2011. The NIESR did not consider self-education alone to be a sufficient solution; see (n 1) 60, 65, 66.

covered by discrimination legislation.[14] Baroness Verma also reprised the proliferation and community cohesion arguments discussed in Chapter 8, saying,

> As one who has always supported equality through integration, I think we need to come away from the idea that constantly supporting people to be separate is an easier form of dealing with the problem now. *The big picture should be that we can get on with our lives and treat people without having to worry that we will offend them in some way because of one issue or another.* The law will not cover every possibility of discrimination, even if we are constantly legislating to bring in more and more groups to protect.[15]

This statement confused domestic measures enabling minorities to preserve their distinct identities (associated in the UK with state policies of "multiculturalism," which many minority religious organisations have supported), and anti-discrimination law designed to protect people from discrimination. It also implied that caste was a "lesser" ground of discrimination and that victims are over-sensitive and too easily offended by casteist behaviour. By May 2012, the government's position was that while the NIESR study identified evidence suggesting the existence of caste discrimination in the UK, it also noted that it was 'impossible to determine categorically that discrimination within the meaning of the [Equality Act] has occurred'.[16] The government therefore took on board representations from both 'those who want the government to legislate and those who are opposed to such legislation'.[17]

9.2.2.1 *The coalition equality agenda: reducing "red tape" and costs*

The potential cost of putting certain EA provisions into effect was cited by the coalition government as a reason for not enacting them, as part of its 'Red Tape Challenge' following the Conservative Party election manifesto commitment to reduce the regulatory burden on business.[18] The government's Equality Act Impact Assessment (EAIA) – published before the NIESR study – had identified three options for addressing caste discrimination: do nothing (i.e. rely on existing law), legislate immediately or include an enabling power to add caste in the future as a subset of race.[19] Doing nothing was rejected at the time as potentially more costly than introducing caste-specific legislation, because the cost of processing caste discrimination cases based on the existing race or religious discrimination provisions might be greater than through a specific statutory route.[20] Legislating immediately was considered premature in the absence of independent evidence on the extent of discrimination and the

14 Letter, Dalit organisations to Helen Grant MP, Minister for Women and Equalities, 14 February 2013; copy on file with author.
15 Baroness Verma; (n 13) (emphasis added).
16 Lynne Featherstone; HC Deb vol 545 cols 432–433W 21 May 2012.
17 Ibid.
18 This was the reason given for not enacting the EA dual discrimination provisions; see Department for Business Innovation and Skills, 'The Plan for Growth' (March 2011) 7.
19 Equality Act Impact Assessment (EAIA), Final Version (London: GEO, 2010) 249–250. Impact Assessments assist policymakers in identifying the need for legislative or other intervention and proposals 'that best achieve the policy objectives while minimising the costs and burdens imposed in achieving the objectives'; Impact Assessment Guidance (London: Department for Business, Innovation and Skills, 2011) 4–5.
20 EAIA, ibid., 250. The "do nothing" option relied on judicial interpretation of the existing protected characteristics of race and/or religion to extend them to caste.

numbers affected, especially as adding caste to "race" would extend the Public Sector Equality Duty in EA section 149 to caste, affecting public bodies and government departments.[21] An enabling power was considered the least risky option, because a decision could be made at a future date in the light of the evidence.[22] However, the secondary legislation was not introduced, and in the Conservative Government's March 2017 Public Consultation 'Caste in Great Britain and Equality Law', the "do nothing" option was re-packaged as Option 1, 'Prohibiting caste discrimination through developing case law' (discussed later).[23]

9.2.2.2 Government regard for anti-legislation views

Between December 2010 and April 2013, the government repeatedly referred to the need to take into account the views of 'people right across the caste system' and those who opposed legislation to ensure that 'both sides of the argument [were] put'.[24] In November 2011 the House was told that during CERD's examination in August 2011 of the UK's 20th state report submitted under the International Convention on the Elimination of All Forms of Racial Discrimination (ICERD), the UK delegation had informed CERD that there was '*no consensus of opinion* with regards to the need for legislative protection against caste discrimination, *even among those communities potentially most affected by it*' – a reference not only to those identified by the NIESR as being most vulnerable to caste discrimination (i.e. Dalits) but also self-identified Hindu and Sikh communities generally.

In July 2012, following the UN Human Rights Council's examination of the UK under the Universal Periodic Review (UPR) mechanism, the immediate implementation of EA section 9(5)(a) was recommended in order to eliminate caste discrimination.[25] The government rejected the recommendation, reiterating that it was still 'considering' the available evidence, together with representations from both those 'who want the government to legislate *and those who are opposed to such legislation being introduced*', before reaching any conclusion.[26]

The government's argument, namely that legislation was problematic because it could affect Hindus and Sikhs generally, not just individuals of specific castes, missed the point that protection against direct discrimination is symmetrical for most protected characteristics.[27] Protection against race and sex discrimination, for example, is available to anyone, irrespective of sex or race, who is a victim of discrimination on these grounds. Similarly, any person who believes they have suffered discrimination because of caste could rely on caste provisions in UK discrimination legislation to seek redress, were such provisions introduced. The purpose of anti-discrimination legislation is to safeguard the fundamental right to equality

---

21 EAIA, ibid., 251. Section 149 EA requires public bodies to have due regard to the need to eliminate discrimination, advance equality of opportunity, and foster good relations between groups when carrying out their activities. On EA section 149, see L Vickers, 'Promoting Equality or Fostering Resentment? The Public Sector Equality Duty and Religion or Belief', 31(1) *Legal Studies* (2011) 135–158, 156.

22 EAIA, ibid., 247, 245.

23 See https://assets.publishing.service.gov.uk/government/uploads/system/uploads/attachment_data/file/609641/170419_-_Caste_condoc_-_Final.pdf, 13.

24 Baroness Verma (n 13).

25 Report of the Working Group on the UPR (United Kingdom of Great Britain and Northern Ireland), UN Doc. A/HRC/21/9, 6 July 2012, para 110.61.

26 UN Doc. A/HRC/21/9/Add.1, 17 September 2012, para 21 and Annexe document, 30 (emphasis added).

27 An exception to this rule is the asymmetric protection against disability discrimination, which is only available to those who are disabled within the meaning of the legislation.

and non-discrimination; for this reason the inclusion of equalities in the Red Tape Challenge was itself controversial. Unlike other (e.g. technical) legislation, where there may be good grounds for consulting those likely to be affected by its introduction, anti-discrimination legislation has moral, ethical and social policy dimensions. Its form should be discussed with those considered the most likely "primary beneficiaries," but its introduction should not be contingent on the support of those identified by independent research as least likely to need its protection.

9.2.3 *Dalit and anti-caste activism in response to the NIESR study*

Following publication of the NIESR study, Dalit organisations and anti-caste activists continued to lobby the government and other actors such as CERD,[28] calling for legal protection for victims of caste discrimination similar to that afforded to other British citizens experiencing discrimination in the UK and for the government to treat caste discrimination 'like any other form of unacceptable discrimination'.[29] In May 2012, they engaged with the All-Party Parliamentary Group on Dalits (APPGD),[30] resulting in an Equality and Human Rights Commission (EHRC) policy statement in support of 'the enactment [sic] of s. 9(5)(a) Equality Act 2010', thus reversing the EHRC's previous opposition to caste-specific legislation and recommending that in light of the NIESR study, legal protection under the Equality Act 2010 for those experiencing discrimination in Britain should be 'as comprehensive as possible'.[31]

Two meetings in January 2011 and November 2012 in the House of Lords, chaired by Lord Avebury, called on the government to exercise the 'caste power' to make caste an aspect of race. At the first meeting, Lynne Featherstone, then Minister for Women and Equalities (who had supported the introduction of caste legislation in 2010), declined to indicate when, or even whether, the government would make a decision, repeating simply that it was 'considering' the NIESR report.[32] By 2012, government responsibility for equalities had moved from the Home Office to the Department of Culture, Media and Sport (DCMS)

---

28 During its examination of the UK's 20th report in August 2011, CERD recalled its 2003 Concluding Observations recommending that the UK introduce a prohibition of descent-based discrimination into domestic law, and its General Recommendation No. 29 (2002) on descent, and recommended that the UK invoke EQA s 9(5)(a) to 'provide for "caste to be an aspect of race" in order to provide remedies to victims of this form of discrimination'; UN Doc. CERD/C/GBR/CO/18–20, 1 September 2011, para 30.

29 'Evidence of Caste discrimination and harassment in the UK confirmed in independent research commissioned by Government'; ACDA Press Release, 16 December 2010; copy on file with author; 'Caste Discrimination in the UK: Joint Statement calling on the Government to enact clause 9(5)(a) of the Equality Act 2010 [sic]'; 23 December 2010; copy on file with author.

30 All-Party Parliamentary Groups are informal, cross-party interest groups run by and for Members of the House of Commons and House of Lords; they have no official status and are not accorded any powers or funding. The APPGD was formed in October 2010 to draw attention to discrimination against Dalits wherever it occurs and to support attempts to eliminate it; www.publications.parliament.uk/pa/cm/cmallparty/register/dalits.htm.

31 See HL Deb vol 742 col GC85 9 January 2013; Anti Caste Discrimination Alliance, Alternative Report to the UN Committee on the Elimination of Racial Discrimination in review of the 21–23 periodic reports of the United Kingdom, 7, at https://tbinternet.ohchr.org/Treaties/CERD/Shared%20Documents/GBR/INT_CERD_NGO_GBR_24636_E.pdf; EHRC policy statement on caste discrimination; copy on file with author.

32 Meeting, 17 January 2011, unofficial transcript, copy on file with author; 'Joint Statement calling for enactment of clause 9(5)(a) of the Equality Act for caste to be an aspect of race', 17 January 2011, signed

under Maria Miller MP, but the DCMS did not attend the second meeting.[33] Afterwards, Lord Avebury sent a Joint Statement signed by thirty-six organisations to the Minister for Equalities, stressing the 'moral importance of legislative equality for Dalits',[34] and he wrote to the Prime Minister, berating the government for its inaction on caste discrimination.[35] At the meetings in 2011 and 2012 it was suggested that a court might interpret the inclusion of section 9(5)(a) in the EA as meaning that Parliament intended to exclude caste from statutory protection unless and until the section 9(5)(a) power was exercised, because it would not have included the power if it thought caste was already covered by other provisions; therefore, unless the power was invoked, claimants would be deprived of a remedy. The absence of an order extending section 9 EA by making caste an aspect of race was one reason why an employment tribunal in the unreported case of *Naveed v Aslam* in November 2012 (discussed later) considered a claim of caste discrimination 'doomed to fail'.[36]

9.2.4 Enterprise and Regulatory Reform Act 2013

9.2.4.1 Enterprise and Regulatory Reform Bill: Thornton amendment 9 January 2013

In an ironic twist, it was the Enterprise and Regulatory Reform Bill 2012, which was intended inter alia to 'cut unnecessary red tape for businesses' by repealing 'unnecessary legislation', that provided the vehicle for the next stage in the attempt to secure a statutory prohibition of caste discrimination.[37] The Enterprise and Regulatory Reform Bill 2012 as originally introduced contained no provision on caste. At Lords Grand Committee stage on 9 January 2013,[38] a novel amendment to the Bill was moved by Baroness Thornton and others to convert the *power* in EA section 9(5)(a) to make caste an aspect of race into a *duty* to do so, by replacing the word "may" with the word "shall."[39] The debate concluded without a vote.

9.2.4.2 Government decision not to exercise the "caste power": 1 March 2013

A direct appeal during this debate by Baroness Thornton to the Equalities Minister led to a meeting on 6 February 2013 between Helen Grant, junior Minister for Women and Equalities, Baroness Northover and representatives from five Dalit organisations.[40] This was the first meeting between the government and Dalit organisations since publication of the

---

by 23 organisations; copy on file with author; letter, ACDA to Lynne Featherstone, 31 January 2011; copy on file with author.
33 The director of the NIESR study and the present author attended both meetings.
34 Letter, Lord Avebury to Maria Miller MP, 29 November 2012; copy on file with author.
35 Letter, Lord Avebury to the prime minister, 24 December 2012; copy on file with author. See also S Jones, 'Campaigners Urge Government to Tackle Caste Discrimination in the UK: Politicians and Human Rights Groups Say People from Traditionally Lower Status Asian Backgrounds Need Legal Protection', *The Guardian*, 30 November 2012.
36 Meeting, 17 January 2011, unofficial transcript; (n 32); *Naveed v Aslam & Anor*, UKET /1603968/2011.
37 The Bill was presented in the House of Commons on 23 May 2012; see HC Deb vol 545 col 1171 23 May 2012.
38 Lords Committee stage ran over ten sittings between 3 December 2012 and 31 January 2013.
39 HL Deb vol 742 col GC85 9 January 2013.
40 Ibid., col GC87. Lord Avebury, Baroness Thornton and three GEO officials were also present.

NIESR study in 2010, despite repeated requests by Dalit groups. Afterwards, they sent a joint letter to the minister stressing Dalit organisations' agreement on the need for legislative protection from caste discrimination and its condemnation in international human rights law, with information on the likely numbers affected, examples of approaches to caste discrimination in other countries and examples of the benefits of statutory protection in Britain.[41] They argued that lack of legal redress violated all principles of equality and non-discrimination. However, on 1 March 2013, Helen Grant issued a Written Statement announcing that the government had decided 'not to exercise the caste power' at that time.[42] Stating that 'absolutely no-one should suffer prejudice because of caste', she instead announced an educational programme run by the organisation Talk For A Change targeted at Sikh and Hindu communities – even though the NIESR had stressed that caste discrimination was not religion-specific.[43] In a letter to the Anti Caste Discrimination Alliance (ACDA) on the same day, the minister declared herself unconvinced that caste-specific legislation was the best or most proportionate way of tackling the issue, despite the NIESR's contrary finding.[44]

9.2.4.3 *Enterprise and Regulatory Reform Bill: Harries amendment*

On 4 March 2013, at Lords Report stage, Lord Harries moved Amendment 73 to add a new subsection, 9(1)(d) "caste", to the definition of race in EA section 9(1) after subsections 9(1)(a)-(c) (colour, nationality and national or ethnic origins).[45] The amendment, which had cross-party, cross-bench support, was agreed by a majority of 103.[46] Its supporters rejected the need for further review of the evidence on caste discrimination, arguing that there is rarely a consensus for legal measures against certain kinds of discrimination, that absence of consensus was not used to block legislation protecting other discriminated groups and that the real reason for not legislating was not that legislation was disproportionate or that education would work better but that the government had been swayed by the argument that legislation labelled Hindus and Sikhs as discriminatory.[47] Lord Lester, who was instrumental in the adoption of race relations legislation in the 1960s, argued that legislation would provide legal certainty and concrete protection and redress. Contrasting the legal protection from race discrimination for Jews and Sikhs through judicial interpretation of ethnic origins, he suggested that 'it would take a case all the way to the Supreme Court [for Dalits] to prevail in the way that Sikhs and Jews have done'.[48]

41 Letter, Dalit organisations to Helen Grant MP, Minister for Women and Equalities, 14 February 2013; copy on file with author.
42 Ministerial Written Statement, Caste, 1 March 2013, at www.parliament.uk/documents/commons-vote-office/March-2013/1st-March/1.DCMS-Caste.pdf. See also Department for Culture, Media & Sport and Helen Grant, Press Release, 'New Education Package to Help Stamp Out Caste Discrimination in Communities', 4 March 2013.
43 Ibid.
44 Letter, Helen Grant MP to ACDA, 1 March 2013; copy on file with author.
45 See Enterprise and Regulatory Reform Bill, Second Marshalled List of Amendments to be moved on Report.
46 HL Deb vol 743 cols 1295–1319 4 March 2013.
47 Ibid., cols 1295–1302.
48 Ibid., cols 1307–1308.

When the Bill returned to the Commons on 16 April 2013, the Harries amendment (now Amendment 37) was rejected on the ground that further consultation was needed.[49] Jo Swinson, Under-Secretary for Women and Equalities, explained that the government recognised the existence of caste prejudice in the UK but distinguished it from other forms of prejudice and discrimination as being 'entirely contained within Hindu and Sikh communities', hence the focus on changing attitudes in these communities through education. The government also argued that the lack of evidence on the extent of caste discrimination in the UK meant there was a low likelihood of cases coming to court. Some cases, she said, could be brought under existing 'employment law or constructive dismissal legislation', but many instances of caste prejudice were outside the scope of discrimination law. In addition, the 'communities affected' had different views on legislation: some were concerned that legislation would increase stigma and undo years of work 'to remove the differentiation by caste in all aspects of life'. The government was therefore not convinced legislation was necessary but would keep an open mind subject to EHRC advice.[50]

On the Bill's return to the Lords on 22 April 2013, Amendment 37 was adopted by a majority of 181 to 168.[51] Baroness Stowell, for the government, warned the House against taking action which might create 'new, unintended consequences which could make it harder for people to seek redress'. There remained 'genuine uncertainty' over the definition of caste and concerns as to whether descent would be more appropriate than caste as a ground of discrimination. The government also insisted that there was a 'fundamental difference' between caste and the 'other protected characteristics such as colour or ethnic origin', declaring that 'not only do we wish to get rid of caste prejudice from British society, *we actually see no useful value in caste itself, or of anyone defining themselves by their caste*' and warning of the danger of '*embedding caste as a concept in domestic law*'.[52]

Lord Parekh, an expert on multiculturalism, opposed legislation, but for different reasons. He accepted that untouchability still existed 'in a small way in Indian society in Britain' but said that this was 'the extreme form' of the 'caste system' and there was no evidence of any (other) kind of caste discrimination in the UK. Caste as a category of discrimination, he declared, was 'not in the same league as race, religion or any of the other protected categories'. Contrary to the government's position – and those who denied the existence of caste in the UK – he thought it would be 'extremely problematic' to get rid of caste categories, the hierarchy amongst these categories or the principle of heredity, because the system 'covers everybody' and affects all interactions. Legislation would therefore only lead to 'frivolous complaints' (although he offered no evidence for this assertion).[53] Yet, as Baroness Flather explained, caste is not solely about untouchability but about treating people differently because of caste.[54] Lord Dholakia, agreeing with Parekh, claimed that caste was of little

---

49 HC Deb vol 561 col 221 16 April 2013; see also Enterprise and Regulatory Reform Bill, 37A at https:// publications.parliament.uk/pa/bills/cbill/2012-2013/0163/13163.1-2.html.

50 HC Deb vol 561 cols 219–221 16 April 2013.

51 HL Deb vol 744 col 1320 22 April 2013.

52 Ibid., cols 1298, 1299 (emphasis added).

53 Lord Parekh; HL Deb vol 744 col 1305 22 April 2013. 'Multiculturalism' evades easy definition, but Ashcroft and Bevir cite as its features a challenge by a minority to the norms and practices of a majority and the supposed neutrality of the state, the idea of distinctive rights and 'a desire for societal recognition of the existence and value of minority cultures'; R Ashcroft and M Bevir, 'Multiculturalism in Contemporary Britain: Policy, Law and Theory', 21(1) *Critical Review of International Social and Political Philosophy* (2017) 1–21.

54 Baroness Flather; HL Deb vol 744 col 1314 22 April 2013.

significance in the UK, there was no substantive evidence of associated discrimination and legislating without evidence would revive a dying issue – but he did not provide any evidence for his assertions.[55]

9.2.4.4 *Enterprise and Regulatory Reform Bill: government amendment in lieu – from caste "power" to "duty"*

Faced with the loss of the Bill if agreement could not be reached between the Houses before the end of the parliamentary session on 25 April 2013, the government proposed on 23 April 2013 its own amendment in lieu which, rather than adding caste immediately as a subset of race in the EA, converted the *power* in EA section 9(5)(a) to make caste an aspect of race into a *duty* to do so.[56] This would require the government to draw up secondary legislation making caste discrimination illegal.[57] This amendment was agreed by the House of Lords on 24 April 2013 to become section 97(3) of the ERRA.[58]

Introducing the amendment in the House of Commons, Swinson insisted that the government was not averse in principle to legislating and that converting the 'caste power' in the EA into a duty 'w[ould] ensure that the government legislate to incorporate caste protection into discrimination law'.[59] However, section 97(3) ERRA was a minimalist provision. It imposed no deadline for compliance with the new duty in EA section 9(5)(a). It required that caste be made an aspect of race but did not specify how this was to be done – whether via an interpretative approach, where caste is read into the existing subsets of race, in particular ethnic origins, or via an iterative approach, whereby it is named as an additional, fifth, subset of race.

9.2.4.5 *Enterprise and Regulatory Reform Bill: the "sunset clause"*

ERRA section 97(5) provided for a "sunset clause" – a ministerial power to review 'the effect of section 9(5) of the Equality Act 2010 (and orders made under it) and whether it remains appropriate' while ERRA section 97(7) included a power to repeal or otherwise amend EA section 9(5)(a) if a minister considered it no longer appropriate.[60] The sunset clause was unprecedented for an anti-discrimination provision. Specific timeframes are generally used for affirmative action policies (for example India's reservation policies) but not anti-discrimination provisions, and no other protected characteristic in the EA has been subject to a similar review power. The government described the review power as a safeguard to prevent caste becoming – through its inclusion in legislation – a 'permanent feature of British society', because it did not 'believe or accept that caste and caste divisions should

---

55 Lord Dholakia, ibid., col 1311. See also A Waughray, 'Caste in Britain; Public Consultation on Caste and Equality Law', 53(10) *Economic and Political Weekly* (*EPW*) (10 March 2018).
56 HC Deb vol 561 cols 789–790 23 April 2013; Amendment No 37.
57 Jo Swinson, HC Deb vol 561 col 794 23 April 2013.
58 HL Deb, Vol 744, cols 1470–1476, 24 April 2013. See also Enterprise and Regulatory Reform Act 2013 s 97, Equality Act 2010: caste as an aspect of race; A Waughray, 'Capturing Caste in Law: Caste Discrimination and the Equality Act 2010', 14(2) *Human Rights Law Review* (2014) 359–379.
59 Jo Swinson; HC Deb vol 561 col 789 23 April 2013 cols 789–790.
60 Under section 97(6) the review power could not be exercised until the end of a five-year period beginning on the date the ERRA was passed, i.e. not before 25 April 2018, but could be exercised more than once thereafter.

have any long-term future in Britain',[61] suggesting that the government opposed caste as a form of social organisation and individual and group identity as well as discrimination on grounds of caste. Opposition MPs in favour of legal protection from caste discrimination supported the sunset clause for similar reasons to those stated by the government.[62] Yet, as later research explained, the spirit of the EA is to 'combat specific instances of discrimination as it arises', to generate attitudinal change and to 'guard against future practices'. In distinguishing caste from other protected characteristics in the EA by allowing a review and repeal of its inclusion in the legislation, the sunset clause was inconsistent with the spirit of UK equality and non-discrimination law.[63]

9.2.4.6 *Enterprise and Regulatory Reform Act 2013: expectation, opposition and prevarication*

By requiring secondary legislation rather than adding caste to the EA immediately, the government bought itself time to conduct a lengthy public consultation – an approach supported by opposition MPs, and by the Alliance of Hindu Organisations (AHO) – a lobby group – and the Sikh Federation UK (SFUK), who also supported the sunset clause.[64] In July 2013, the government published a timetable for a two-stage public consultation in 2014–2015, leading to the introduction of secondary legislation during summer 2015;[65] but the consultation was never issued. Whether the government genuinely intended to enact the secondary legislation is questionable. Helen Grant, Minister for Women and Equalities, wrote to the AHO in May 2013 stating that she had 'made no secret' of her disappointment that the government had been obliged, in order to avoid losing the Enterprise and Regulatory Reform Bill, to make an order to include caste as an element of race in the EA 'following the further defeat in the House of Lords'.[66]

Despite its limitations, section 97(3) ERRA was welcomed by Dalit and anti-caste organisations.[67] In contrast, British Hindu Voice and the Anti-Caste Legislation Committee declared that, if adopted, the new legislation would create long-term [unspecified] problems 'for the Hindu and Jain communities in the UK', while the Hindu Forum of Britain (HFB) simply denied the existence of caste discrimination 'within the Hindu and other Dharmic communities in any significant measure' and declared itself 'deeply insulted' by the inclusion of caste in legislation, a move which it deemed a form of racial discrimination.[68] The AHO

---

61 Letter, H Grant, Minister for Women and Equalities, to G Das, AHO, 9 May 2013; formerly at www.mycasteishindu.org/images/pdfs/Helen_Grant_Letter_to_AHO.pdf (expired domain name) (copy on file with author).

62 HC Deb vol 561 col 792 April 2013.

63 M Dhanda, A Waughray, D Mosse, D Keane, and S Whittle, *Caste in Britain: Socio-legal Review, Equality and Human Rights Commission Research Report no. 91* (Manchester: Equality and Human Rights Commission, 2014) 36.

64 AHO Press Release, 22 May 2013, at www.hinducounciluk.org/2013/05/22/alliance-of-hindu-organisations-aho-press-release/; Sikh Siyasat News, 24 April 2013, at https://sikhsiyasat.net/caste-discrimination-set-to-become-unlawful-in-the-united-kingdom/

65 'Caste legislation introduction – programme and timetable' (Government Equalities Office, July 2013).

66 See (n 61).

67 Letter, ACDA to Helen Grant MP, Minister for Women and Equalities, 24 April 2013 (copy on file with author).

68 Hindu Forum of Britain, Joint Statement on the issue of caste legislation, 27 March 2013 (copy on file with author).

initially acknowledged that caste discrimination exists and should be eradicated,[69] but saw legislation as an affront to the Hindu community, claiming (incorrectly) that it would 'result in individuals . . . having to identify themselves by caste' for equal opportunities purposes and would label the Hindu community as being institutionally discriminatory.[70] By 2014, its language had hardened, ridiculing the idea that there is 'a terrible phenomenon called "caste discrimination"' in the UK, arguing that existing legislation was sufficient, demanding the removal of the 'negatively charged and inherently racist' word "caste" from the legislation and describing its 'continued use' as 'an act of anti-Hindu racial and religious violence and prejudice of the highest order'.[71] From 2013 onwards, a series of anti-legislation online articles and blogposts (later a book) by a UK academic, Prakash Shah, emerged, claiming that caste legislation was a plot driven by Christian (Protestant) churches to damage the UK's 'Dharmic [i.e. Hindu, Sikh and Jain] communities'. Shah postulated that adding caste as a ground of discrimination in legislation amounted to a 'planned attack against Indian communities in Britain and elsewhere'.[72]

The SFUK and the Sikh Council UK (SCUK) also opposed section 97(3) ERRA, but for different reasons. They reiterated Sikhism's ideological rejection of the caste system and ritual purity, and its opposition to all discrimination including based on caste, contrasting their position with anti-legislation Hindu groups which 'refuse to condemn caste and wrongly believe caste discrimination does not exist'.[73] They supported the 'underlying spirit' of the legislation but questioned its desirability, arguing that legislation would lead to the increased use of caste as an identifier contrary to the objectives of the legislation. Primarily, they objected to the association of Sikhs with caste in the Equality Act Explanatory Notes as 'offensive and inaccurate', and opposed the introduction of legislation unless the reference to Sikhs in the Explanatory Notes was removed.[74] Meena Dhanda points to a 'split consciousness amongst Sikhs with regard to caste, owing to a gap between Sikhism's proclaimed anti-casteist religious ideology and its erosion in practice.[75] Caste identity remains culturally important to many young Sikhs, according to Jaspal and Takhar, and it also influences their views about others' 'social status, character, and competence'.[76] Sikh opposition to

69 AHO Press Release, 'Let's Solve This Problem Together', 21 April 2013, at www.hinducounciluk.org/2013/04/21/aho-press-release-lets-solve-this-problem-together/.
70 AHO Press Release, 12 April 2013, 'Don't take us back to the caste system' (copy on file with author); Press Release, 22 May 2013, 'Hindu Community Called to Action' (copy on file with author).
71 AHO Briefing for the APPG on British Hindus, 20 March 2014 (copy on file with author).
72 See P Shah. 'Caste Discrimination: Reflection Needed, Not Legislation', 9 April 2013 (copy on file with author); P Shah, *Against Caste in British Law: A Critical Perspective on the Caste Discrimination Provision in the Equality Act 2010* (Basingstoke: Palgrave MacMillan, 2015). Shah is associated with the "Ghent School," which rejects the existence of caste and, by extension, caste discrimination; see D Sutton, ' "So-Called Caste': SN Balagangadhara, the Ghent School and the Politics of Grievance', 26(3) *Contemporary South Asia* (2018) 336–349. See also National Council of Hindu Temples UK, 'Caste, Conversion and a "Thoroughly Colonial Conspiracy" (2017), at www.nchtuk.org/index.php?option=com_acymailing&ctrl=archive&task=view&mailid=148&key=OhzS64K1&subid=7465-fzDzWStW5b6eX4&tmpl=component.
73 See www.facebook.com/SikhFederationUK/posts/443577599063798.
74 Ibid.
75 M Dhanda, 'Casteism Amongst Punjabis in Britain', *Economic and Political Weekly*, 21 January 2017, 62–65, 63.
76 See R Jaspal, 'Caste, Social Stigma and Identity Processes', 23(1) *Psychology and Developing Societies* (2011) 27–62; R Jaspal and O Takhar, 'Caste and Identity Processes Among British Sikhs in the Midlands', 12(1) *Sikh Formations* (2016) 87–102.

legislation, suggests Dhanda, was driven partly by fear that community organisations based on caste identity would be outlawed.[77]

9.2.4.7 *Equality and Human Rights Commission:* Caste in Britain

In September 2013, the Equality and Human Rights Commission appointed a team of academic researchers (including the present author) to conduct socio-legal research on British equality law and caste, in order to identify and address the legal issues, to consider how best to insert the new provisions on caste agreed by parliament into the UK's existing legal framework, and to engage with experts and stakeholders to capture views and experiences relevant to implementing the legislation. Two *Caste in Britain* research reports were published in February 2014.[78] In the absence of an agreed legal definition of caste in domestic or international law, the reports proposed a definition for EA purposes in terms of endogamy, inherited status and social stratification. They presented testimonies of caste discrimination and the various views on legislation and, given the existing legal duty to make caste an aspect of race in the EA, recommended including it as a distinct fifth subset of race.[79] However, the expected government action did not follow. The EHRC had intended to commission research to establish baseline data on the extent of caste discrimination in Britain (necessary as a starting point for a "sunset clause" assessment), but instead it argued that research 'would not be possible' and might be intrusive and damaging to community relations.[80] The government subsequently commissioned its own independent study on the feasibility of measuring caste discrimination, completed in October 2014 but not published until March 2017.[81] Contrary to anti-legislation assertions, the study concluded that 'there was a strong understanding about caste and how it worked across Hindu and Sikh respondents [who] were often able to identify their own caste or at least how they would be perceived by those who did observe castes if they did not: '*Misunderstanding of the concept of caste would not be a barrier to a national survey being conducted*'.[82]

9.2.5 *Case law on caste*

In the absence of caste as an autonomous concept in the EA, claimants in three employment cases between 2011 and 2013 sought to argue that caste discrimination was already prohibited by existing provisions on race and religion or belief discrimination. The first case, *Begraj and Begraj v Heer Manak Solicitors,* collapsed in February 2013 due to judicial recusal while substantive issues were still being heard.[83] Amardeep and Vijay Begraj alleged

---

77 Dhanda (n 75).
78 Dhanda et al. (n 63); M Dhanda, D Mosse, A Waughray et al., *Caste in Britain: Experts' Seminar and Stakeholders' Workshop, Equality and Human Rights Commission Research Report no. 92* (Manchester: Equality and Human Rights Commission, 2014).
79 *Caste in Britain: Socio-legal Review* (n 63) 36.
80 HC Deb vol 584 col 140WH 9 July 2014.
81 See, for example, HL Deb vol 766 No 41 Written Answers: Castes; Discrimination, 21 December 2015.
82 N Howat, A Ryley, J Williams, R Mcleod, A Busby, and H Metcalfe, 'Measuring Caste Discrimination in Britain – a Feasibility Study', 5, at www.gov.uk/government/publications/measuring-caste-discrimina tion-in-britain-a-feasibility-study (emphasis added).
83 *Begraj v Heer Manak Solicitors* [2014] *Industrial Relations Law Reports* 689–696; S Jones, 'Employment Tribunal Hearing First Claim for Caste Discrimination Collapses: Judge Recuses Herself After Visit by Police Officers', *The Guardian*, 14 February 2013.

unfair dismissal, caste discrimination and race and religious discrimination. Amardeep Begraj also alleged sex discrimination.[84] Vijay Begraj was a Dalit (he asserted Valmiki identity after the claim was lodged), and his wife, Amardeep, was from a Jat Sikh (dominant) background, as were their mutual (former) employers, Heer Manak Solicitors. The couple claimed that they suffered discrimination following their inter-caste marriage, which occurred during the course of their employment with the respondents and of which the respondents disapproved. In the absence of caste as a statutory protected characteristic, they argued that the discrimination they suffered was because of race or religion or belief. Since the case predated the EA, the claimants argued that caste fell within race or ethnic origins under the Race Relations Act 1976, following *R (on the application of E) v Governing Body of JFS*, which opened up arguments that caste is subsumed within ethnic origins by virtue of the 'descent' element of 'ethnic' – descent being the category which captures caste in international human rights law.[85] Moreover, in 2011, the High Court held that being a minority group within a larger community can also be a 'part of ethnicity' within the meaning of the EA.[86]

The EA implements the EU Race Directive (2000) and the principle of equal treatment irrespective of racial or ethnic origin,[87] which in Recital 3 refers to protection against discrimination for all persons as a universal right recognised inter alia in the International Convention on the Elimination of All Forms of Racial Discrimination (ICERD).[88] Racial and ethnic origin are not defined in the Directive, but the reference to ICERD suggests that it seeks to give effect to the principle of non-discrimination as understood in ICERD. It would therefore have been open to the tribunal in *Begraj* to request the Court of Justice of the European Union (CJEU) for an Article 267 TFEU preliminary ruling on the question of whether racial and/or ethnic origin in the Race Directive – and hence race and ethnic origins in domestic legislation – should be interpreted as including caste.[89]

The collapse of the *Begraj* case was disappointing not only for the claimants, but also for UK Dalit organisations, since a successful argument that caste was captured by race or ethnic origins would have been an important step in acknowledging both the existence of caste discrimination in the UK and its unacceptability, as well as benefitting the individual claimants. Conversely, a finding in *Begraj* that caste was captured by existing provisions on race/ethnic origins would have strengthened arguments that a statutory prohibition of caste discrimination was unnecessary. However, consistency of outcome in the lower courts is not guaranteed, and the principle will remain precarious unless and until a binding precedent is established by a superior court, or until a body of case law emerges such that caste becomes

---

84 The relevant forms of legislation at the time the facts arose were the Race Relations Act 1976 (RRA) and the Employment Equality (Religion or Belief) Regulations 2003; SI No. 2003/1660.

85 *R (on the application of E) v The Governing Body of JFS and the Admissions Appeal Panel of JFS* [2009] UKSC 15. See also Chapter 7.

86 *G (by his litigation friend) v The Head Teacher and Governors of St Gregory's Catholic Science College* [2011] EWHC 1452, paras 40–41.

87 Council Directive 2000/43/EC of 29 June 2000 implementing the principle of equal treatment between persons, irrespective of racial or ethnic origin.

88 On ICERD, see Chapter 4. Recitals contain the statement of reasons for the act and its aims and objectives, rather than normative provisions. They do not have an independent legal value but can be used to determine the nature of a provision; see T Klimas and J Vaiciukaite, 'The Law of Recitals in European Community Legislation', 15(1) *ILSA Journal of International and Comparative Law* (2008) 1–33.

89 Article 267 TFEU: 'Where such a question is raised before any court or tribunal of a Member State, that court may, if it considers that a decision on the question is necessary to enable it to give judgment, require the Court of Justice to give a ruling thereon'. See, for example, *P v (1) S and (2) Cornwall County Council* (1996) IRLR 347.

treated in Britain as simply another aspect of race/ethnic origins, both sociologically and in law. For this reason, it remains the case that a statutory prohibition of caste discrimination is desirable, irrespective of the outcome of future cases.

In *Naveed v Aslam* (2011, unreported), the claimant alleged that he had suffered racial discrimination in the form of ridicule and abuse because of his membership of the Pakistani Arain caste.[90] The employment tribunal found that his claim was 'doomed to fail' for two reasons: (1) no order had yet been made extending section 9 of the EA, so as to provide for caste to amount of itself to an aspect of race, and (2) it was 'quite impossible' for the claimant's caste to fall under the existing definition of ethnic origins, because he accepted that movement within the Arain caste was possible and that it was his status within the same caste as the respondents (also members of the Arain caste, but, according to the claimant, of a higher subcategory) which he claimed led to his treatment. Consequently, the tribunal judged that he was being treated differently on account of his 'class',[91] but what it did not consider were the various meanings ascribed to the word "caste," in that the claimant and the respondents may have been of different sub-castes or *jatis* – with ensuing differences in status – within the wider Arain group. It therefore attributed the discrimination to being class- rather than caste-based.[92] *Naveed* illustrates the difficulty of bringing a caste discrimination claim in the absence of an explicit statutory prohibition, as well as the need for 'caste literacy' on the part of all those involved in bringing or defending or deciding caste discrimination claims.

In *Tirkey v Chandhok* (2015), the employment tribunal held that in certain situations caste can fall within the scope of the ethnic origins subset of race.[93] *Tirkey* was the first case involving caste as an element of a successful race discrimination claim. The tribunal held that the claimant had suffered unlawful harassment on grounds of race because of her ethnic origins, defined by reference to her inherited position in society (in whole or in part on the basis of her caste), her birth and her upbringing.[94] The judgment was immediately hailed in the media as a legal landmark.[95] The claimant, Permila Tirkey, was a domestic servant from India employed by the respondents, Mr and Mrs Chandhok, in their home in Britain. She claimed breaches of employment law and damages under the EA for direct or indirect discrimination on grounds of religion or belief, and direct discrimination or harassment on grounds of race, which she alleged had occurred for reasons related to her ethnic origins, including her perceived status in the caste system.[96] There were three judgments in the case. Ms Tirkey had amended her original race discrimination claim by adding ethnic origins to nationality and national origins as a further or alternative ground of alleged mistreatment. She averred that her ethnic or national origins included but were not limited to her status

90 *Naveed v Aslam* (n 36).
91 Ibid., para 27. On the Arain, see A Shaw, *Kinship and Continuity: Pakistani Families in Britain* (London: Routledge, 2000), Chapter 4.
92 This section appears in A Waughray 'Capturing Caste in Law: Caste Discrimination and the Equality Act 2010', 14(2) *Human Rights Law Review* (2014) 359–379, 376; *Caste in Britain: Socio-legal Review* (n 69) 14.
93 *Tirkey v Chandhok & Anor* [2015] UKET/3400174/2013, 199.
94 *Tirkey v Chandhok*, ibid., 205–207.
95 For example, see O Bowcott, 'Woman Awarded £184,000 in UK's First Caste Discrimination Case', *The Guardian*, 22 September 2015.
96 *Tirkey v Chandhok* [2015] (n 93). See also A Waughray, 'Is Caste Discrimination in the UK Prohibited by the Equality Act 2010?' 2 *International Labor Rights Case Law* (2016) 70–76; A Waughray and M Dhanda, 'Ensuring Protection Against Caste Discrimination in Britain: Should the Equality Act 2010 Be Extended?' 16(2–3) *International Journal of Discrimination and the Law* (2016) 177–196.

in the caste system as perceived by the respondents. There was no specific claim of caste discrimination as such. The respondents applied to strike out the amendment, claiming that caste did not fall within the definition of race in the EA, and that the enactment of EA section 9(5) both initially and as subsequently amended demonstrated that Parliament recognised that caste was excluded from the current definition of race (the argument in *Naveed*). The tribunal rejected the argument that it had no jurisdiction to consider the amended claim and refused to strike out the amended pleading. The obligation to legislate to make caste an aspect of race did not preclude an interpretation of ethnic origins as including caste.[97] The respondents appealed. In December 2014, Judge Langstaff in the employment appeal tribunal refused the appeal and upheld the tribunal's decision, ruling that though "caste" as an autonomous concept did not come within EA section 9(1) at that time, 'many of the facts relevant in considering caste in many of its forms might be capable of doing so'.[98] He did not accept that EA section 9(5) limited the scope to which the statutory definition of race extends,[99] instead determining by reference to *Mandla* and *JFS* (discussed in Chapter 7) that since ' "ethnic origins" is a wide and flexible phrase and covers questions of descent, at least some of those situations which would fall within an acceptable definition of caste would fall within it'.[100] However, he emphasised that this was not a definitive decision in principle that discrimination on grounds of caste was or was not within the scope of the EA; rather, his decision was based on the facts in the particular case.[101] In the merits judgment in September 2015, the employment tribunal determined that the Chandhoks had brought a servant from India to the UK because they wanted a "low-caste," servile person of Indian descent who would not be aware of her rights and who would work in conditions unacceptable to a UK-based employee.[102] Ms Tirkey was ideal because, by virtue of birth, her inherited position in society or caste and her upbringing, namely because of her ethnic origins, she would have expected to be no more than a domestic servant.[103] In fact, Ms Tirkey was not a member of a Scheduled Caste in India (see Chapter 3); instead, she was an Adivasi – a person of tribal heritage. Despite being categorised differently, legally and administratively, from Scheduled Castes, Adivasis (Scheduled Tribes) in India share a common experience of inferiorisation and discrimination on the basis of inherited status. Ms Tirkey 'used the term "caste" to capture this experience, describing herself both as an "Adivasi" and "low-caste" '.[104]

The judgment provides an insight into how caste discrimination manifests in the UK through behaviours of control, humiliation and the negation of personal autonomy. It does not establish a binding precedent that caste is captured by "ethnic origins," and yet the governments of David Cameron and Theresa May both relied on *Tirkey* to justify non-compliance with the duty to add caste to the EA by arguing that, because of that case, 'anyone who feels that they have been discriminated against because of caste' can potentially bring a discrimination claim under the 'existing ethnic origins limb of the race provisions

97 *Tirkey v Chandhok* [2013] UKET/3400174/2013.
98 *Chandhok and Anor v Tirkey* [2014] UKEAT/0190/14/KN, Summary.
99 *Chandhok v Tirkey* [2014], ibid., 52.
100 Ibid., 42, 44.
101 Ibid., 55.
102 *Tirkey v Chandhok* [2015] (n 93) 202.
103 Ibid., 206.
104 See Waughray and Dhanda (n 96) 188.

in the Equality Act 2010'.[105] In July 2015, in its periodic report to CERD, the government agreed that 'legal protection against caste discrimination [was] appropriate' and that it was considering the implications for legislation of the *Tirkey* judgment before deciding how to proceed. By August 2016, when it appeared before CERD for examination of its report, it asserted categorically (but incorrectly) that 'the Equality Act 2010 offered legal protection against discrimination on grounds of ethnic origin, which included caste'; moreover, 'since there was no unanimous agreement on what constituted caste, it was unclear whether adding the term to the Equality Act would help clarify the situation'.[106] This directly contradicted the EHRC's recommendation to CERD in July 2016 to ask the UK to amend the statutory definition of race in the EA to include caste, as required by amended EA section 9(5)(a). In its 2016 concluding observations to the UK, CERD, referring to its general recommendation No. 29 (2002) on descent, recommended the government invoke EA section 9(5)(a) immediately to ensure an explicit legal prohibition of caste-based discrimination access to effective remedies for victims.[107]

9.2.6 Public consultation on caste and equality law 2017–2018

On 2 September 2016, the government (possibly fearing a judicial review application by anti-caste organisations) announced its intention to issue a public consultation on caste and equality law – not on *how* to introduce the required secondary legislation but *whether* legislation should be introduced, and whether the duty to legislate should be repealed.[108] The consultation ran between 28 March 2017 and 18 September 2018. Respondents were asked to choose between two competing "options" for protection from caste discrimination: "case law" (Option 1), meaning judicial interpretation of existing law, treating caste as related to ethnic origins as a subset of race in the EA; and "legislation" (Option 2), i.e. explicit statutory protection by making caste an aspect of race in the EA. Repealing the duty to legislate was not offered as an option. The consultation document rehearsed the familiar arguments against legislation: the danger of 'socially divisive consequences such as promoting, creating or entrenching ideas of caste or heightening caste consciousness where they do not previously exist', the lack of a 'universally accepted functional definition' of caste, its 'controversial and sensitive' nature, the danger of stereotyping it as 'a discriminatory practice of certain ethnic groups' and the potential problems this would create for social harmony in modern British society. However, it failed to identify the arguments against the "case law" ("do nothing") option, and it did not explain that the EAT judgment in *Tirkey* was 'not an authority for the proposition that caste will fall within the definition of ethnic origins or race in the EA', merely that it might be capable of doing so, 'provided that the case law tests are

---

105 See, for example, HL Deb vol 764 col 572 15 July 2015; HL Deb vol 774 11 July 2016, Caste-based discrimination.

106 CERD/C/GBR/21–23, 6 July 2015, para 8; CERD/C/SR.2455, 12 August 2016; para 25.

107 See EHRC, 'Race Rights in the UK', Submission to the UN Committee on the Elimination of Racial Discrimination in advance of the public examination of the UK's implementation of ICERD, July 2016, 10, 83–85, 114; EHRC, 'Commission Policy Statement on Caste Discrimination', 14 June 2016, copy on file with author. See also CERD/C/GBR/CO/21-23, 3 October 2016, paras. 7–8.

108 Caste in Great Britain and equality law: a public consultation, 28 March 2017, paras 1.8, 1.9. On the threat of judicial review, see P Shah, 'What Lies Behind the Inclusion of Caste in the UK Equality Act?' 11 October 2016 at https://blogs.lse.ac.uk/religionglobalsociety/2016/10/what-lies-behind-the-inclusion-of-caste-in-the-uk-equality-act/.

satisfied'.[109] Additionally, it did not explain that cases can only be brought once harm has occurred, and that it may take many years for a sufficient body of case law to emerge or for a binding appellate decision to provide effective protection, if ever: '[w]hile some groups have achieved protection by case law without specific mention, the protection has been secured only after many years of actual harm'.[110]

The consultation's terms directly contravened Parliament's decision to introduce statutory protection against caste discrimination via secondary legislation. It also contravened the EHRC's call for immediate implementation of the secondary legislation, and CERD's repeated recommendations to the UK to introduce statutory protection from descent-based discrimination, including caste discrimination. In an open letter to the government, British Dalit and anti-caste organisations questioned why it was consulting on whether to implement legislation which was already agreed by Parliament in 2013. They described the consultation as misleading, biased in favour of Option 1 ("case law") and against Option 2 ("legislation"), impenetrable, over-technical, unclear, and that it omitted crucial information and fell short of government consultation principles.[111] In contrast, the National Council of Hindu Temples UK, which opposed legislation, initially praised the consultation as 'wonderful news for the British Hindu community,'[112] but by May 2017, a number of Hindu organisations had condemned it as 'misguided' for presuming that caste discrimination exists in Britain, rejecting both options and demanding repeal of the duty in section 9(5)(a) EA.[113] The Sikh Federation UK opposed legislation as 'totally unnecessary', claiming it would 'entrench caste consciousness in legislation, have unintended consequences and pose significant additional burdens for employers, providers of goods and services and individuals'. It demanded repeal of the duty to legislate at the same time as supporting the "case law" approach, on condition that the 'erroneous and offensive' reference to Sikhs in the Equality Act Explanatory Notes on caste was removed.[114]

The government concluded in July 2018 that 53% of the 16,000-plus respondents preferred Option 1 ("case law").[115] In a written statement, Penny Mordaunt, Minister for Women and Equalities, announced the government's intention to repeal the duty to make caste an aspect of race, once a suitable legislative vehicle became available 'because it is now sufficiently clear that the Equality Act provides this protection'.[116]

109 Public Consultation, ibid.; Law Society of Scotland, Consultation Response: Caste in Great Britain and Equality Law (September 2017) 2.
110 Law Society of Scotland, ibid., 3.
111 Letter to Justine Greening, Minister for Equalities and Women, signed by seven anti-caste organisations, 19 April 2017; copy on file with author.
112 Shubh Sandesh ('Hindu Good News'), 'PM Theresa May Announces "Caste" Public Consultation', 2 September 2016 at http://nchtuk.org/index.php?option=com_acymailing&ctrl=archive&task=view&mailid=143&key=2zoZBs5v&subid=7465-fzDzWStW5b6cX4&tmpl=component.
113 Waughray (n 55); K Purohit, 'Hindu Groups in UK Hit Back at British Government's Plans to Ban Caste-Based Discrimination', *The Wire*, 11 July 2017.
114 Sikh Federation UK, Annual Report 2017–18, 17–19, at www.sikhfeduk.com/assets/files/SFUK-2017-18-FINAL-PROOF-compressed.pdf; Y Rana, 'UK Sikhs Hail Government Backing Off on Anti Caste Discrimination Legislation', *Times of India*, 25 July 2018. See also P Sonwalkar, 'UK Government Decides not to Enact Law on Caste Discrimination Among Indians, Community Divided', *Hindustan Times*, 24 July 2018.
115 See https://assets.publishing.service.gov.uk/government/uploads/system/uploads/attachment_data/file/727790/Caste_in_Great_Britain_and_equality_law-consultation_response.pdf.
116 HC Deb Vol 645 HCWS898, 23 July 2018.

The government promised to produce short guidance before introducing the repeal legislation, explaining what sort of conduct could be unlawful under the EA. In a briefing note to the All Party Parliamentary Group on Dalits, Professor David Mosse (co-author of the EHRC *Caste in Britain* research reports) described both the consultation and the government's analysis as flawed.[117] Mosse found that over 60% of those who answered the specific question on whether legislation or relying on case law was the preferable option responded 'don't know', while a significant number failed to express a preference, instead questioning whether caste or caste discrimination exists, or demanding that the word "caste" be expunged from legislation.[118] The EHRC also questioned the government's conclusion, stating that legal protection from caste discrimination would continue to be limited by the government ruling out a change in the law, contrary to the UK's international obligations to provide distinct protection in domestic legislation, restricting the scope of protection to what can be interpreted through case law.[119]

At the time of writing, the guidance on caste and the Equality Act has not been published, but it cannot replace caste-specific legislation. The value of discrimination legislation lies in its capacity to name and tackle the harm to be addressed and to create social change, rather than simply in the number of cases coming to court. When a principle is embodied in legislation, the words and language start to enter public consciousness and usage. Public bodies are obliged to take the issue seriously and to change policy and practice in line with specific legislative requirements, and guidance will be taken seriously when it relates to a principle captured in legislation. However, if the word "caste" were removed from the legislation, it would become easier to claim that related discrimination does not exist, and any guidance would be less likely to give rise to concrete changes in policy and practice, because there is no specific obligation to do so. Legislation is almost immediate, but the trajectory of case law cannot be guaranteed; it could take many years to establish with certainty through case law the principle that caste is covered by ethnic origins, and that caste discrimination is unlawful, and doing so is likely to be a costly process, as the 2010 Equality Act Impact Assessment noted.

9.3 Factors bearing on the legal regulation of caste discrimination in British law

A decade after the enactment of the EA, caste has been recognised politically as a ground of prejudice, discrimination and mistreatment, but legal recognition remains incomplete, and legal regulation of caste discrimination remains unsecured. Figure 9.1 brings together the multiplicity of factors in the domestic and international arenas affecting both negatively and positively the legal regulation of caste discrimination in the UK. These factors are now assessed.

The prospect of a single Equality Act in the mid-2000s created the "opportunity space" for Dalit activists and their supporters to advance demands for explicit statutory protection from caste discrimination within the context of a broader national debate about rights

---

117 D Mosse, Consultation Analysis, presented to the APPG on Dalits, Westminster, 5 November 2018 (unpublished), copy on file with author. I thank David Mosse for permission to cite his analysis. See also D Mosse, 'Outside Caste? The Enclosure of Caste and Claims to Castelessness in India and the United Kingdom', 62(1) *Comparative Studies in Society and History* (2020) 1–31.

118 Ibid.

119 EHRC, 'Caste Consultation: Our Response to the Government Statement', 23 July 2018, at www.equalityhumanrights.com/en/our-work/news/caste-consultation-our-response-government-statement.

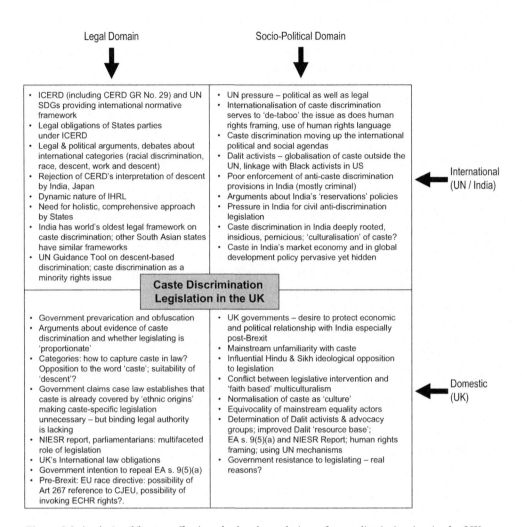

Figure 9.1 Analysis of factors affecting the legal regulation of caste discrimination in the UK

and equality. Yet, throughout the Equality Bill debates, the capture of caste in law presented a problem. The formulation of race in the EA differs from racial discrimination in ICERD. Although successive UK governments have not challenged CERD's use of descent to address caste under ICERD, Parliament chose "caste," not "descent," to capture caste in domestic law, but it chose to formulate it as a subset of race rather than as a separate new category. Descent was considered too broad, risking the possibility of claims of discrimination based on social class, while the creation of a tenth protected characteristic was politically unacceptable.[120] Internationally, many Dalit and anti-caste activists favoured the broader category of discrimination based on work and descent, but this did not gain traction with UK parliamentarians in 2010. Yet, despite the recommendations made by CERD and the UPR, successive governments have rejected calls for an explicit statutory prohibition of caste

120 See Chapter 8.

discrimination, claiming that case law developments mean that legislation is unnecessary and unjustified.

Since 2013, the word "caste" has emerged as a specific site of contestation. Parliamentary opponents of caste legislation argued against its inclusion in statute because there is no consensus on its definition (an argument that could apply equally to race and ethnic origins).[121] The Alliance of Hindu Organisations (AHO) distinguished caste from supposedly 'easy-to-define' categories of discrimination such as race and gender, on the basis that there is no 'objective assessment' of caste.[122] From 2013, the word itself has been denounced by certain Hindu groups as negatively charged, inflammatory, offensive, discriminatory, racist, its continued use in legislation an 'act of anti-Hindu racial and religious violence and prejudice of the highest order' and caste discrimination legislation as a '250-year old hate crime against Hindus'.[123] The concept of caste, and therefore caste as a ground of discrimination, asserts Prakash Shah, does not exist but is, rather, a racist orientalist/Christian confection designed to denigrate Indian culture. Thus, says David Mosse, caste becomes 'externalised as a racist misinterpretation' and delegitimised as an idea and as 'a mistaken and offensive category of description'.[124]

Other underlying, socio-political factors influencing successive governments' decisions on legislation exist. First, in the context of contemporary globalisation and India's emergence as a major economic power, competition amongst Western nations to establish and maintain a "special relationship" with India is intense. In 2013, India was the UK's largest non-EU market and the third largest investor in the country. Of the twelve hundred Indian companies in the EU, seven hundred were in the UK, and Tata was one of the UK's largest manufacturing employers – but this relationship is not guaranteed.[125] It is unsurprising that successive UK governments have not wished to alienate Indian business and the political establishment by introducing caste discrimination legislation in the UK, especially in the context of Brexit.[126]

Second, for many years, British Dalits struggled to make their case. Dalits, wrote a UK-based Dalit in 1994, are an 'invisible community' in the UK. Among South Asians in Britain, the issue of caste was marginalised and denied politically and intellectually. To the wider community, Dalits did not even exist in the UK, and their history, culture and traditions are not covered in the textbooks: 'There are Hindus, Sikhs, Jains, but no Dalits'. Historically, non-Dalits tended to be dominant among South Asians in Britain, he wrote, monopolising the jobs 'that require interfacing with the host English community'.[127] The anti-caste

121 See, for example, HL Deb vol 774, Caste-based discrimination, 11 July 2016.

122 See, for example, AHO Press Release (n 69).

123 See letter, Vivek Sharma on behalf of the Alliance of Hindu Organisations (AHO) to Rt Hon Bob Blackman, Chair APPG for British Hindus, Response to EHRC Report on Caste Prejudice in the UK, 19 March 2014, cited in Mosse (2020) (n 117) 12; see also 'Caste, Conversion and a "Thoroughly Colonial Conspiracy"' (n 72).

124 See, for example, P Shah, 'Intellectuals and the Indian Traditions', 20 December 2014 at https://ary-alegal.wordpress.com/2014/12/20/intellectuals-and-the-indian-traditions/; Mosse (n 117) 12–14.

125 See Foreign and Commonwealth Office, UK-India Relations (2013), at www.gov.uk/government/publications/india-uk-relations; House of Commons Foreign Affairs Committee, 'Building Bridges: Reawakening UK-India Ties', Eighteenth Report of Session 2017–19 (2019) at https://publications.parliament.uk/pa/cm201719/cmselect/cmfaff/1465/1465.pdf.

126 See, for example, M Mitta, 'UK Bill Links Caste to Race, India Red-Faced', *Times of India*, 31 March 2010.

127 A Shukra, 'Caste, a Personal Perspective', in M Searle-Chatterjee and U Sharma (eds.), *Contextualising Caste: Post-Dumontian Approaches* (Oxford: Blackwell, 1994) 169–178, 170, 177.

cause is not well-understood by the mainstream British public. Historically, Dalits have had only limited access to key political actors and decision-makers. In contrast, organisations opposed to caste discrimination legislation, such as the HFB and the HCUK, have long benefitted from close links with senior South Asian parliamentarians who as South Asians are familiar with caste, but who as non-Dalits may not conceptualise caste discrimination in Britain as a form of discrimination requiring the same legal treatment as other forms of discrimination (despite it being unlawful in India).[128] In the past, Dalit groups have been insufficiently united – like other social movements they have suffered from ideological divisions and factionalism, and the campaign for caste discrimination legislation initially suffered from insufficient involvement among women and young Dalits, although this is changing.[129] Nevertheless, Dalit and anti-caste organisations were remarkably united in their campaign for the inclusion of EA section 9(5)(a) and for its activation.

Third, for many years, caste discrimination was not taken up by mainstream UK equality actors.[130] In 2010, the EHRC supported a prohibition of descent-based discrimination in the EA but was opposed to the inclusion of caste, arguing at the time that caste discrimination was covered by existing provisions. It declined to support *Begraj* as a test case but subsequently changed its position to support explicit statutory protection from caste discrimination.[131] Various factors account for the initial reluctance of equality actors to associate themselves with the legal regulation of caste discrimination: first, insufficient awareness and understanding of caste and discrimination based thereon, second, the reluctance of victims to come forward and third, the historical inability of small, voluntary associations and interest groups to capture the attention of anti-discrimination actors.[132]

Lastly, the political cost of introducing caste discrimination legislation was seen as too high. During its first two years, the coalition government was under pressure to present a united front given the unpopularity of many of its policies, and there may have been a fear of accusations of "cultural intrusion" and of losing Asian (Indian) votes. Opposition to caste legislation has been consistently strong among certain Hindu, Sikh and Jain organisations who argue that legislation is racist, "Hinduphobic," denigratory and an attack on "Dharmic communities." Moreover, they argue that any legislation would reinforce or reignite 'long-abandoned' caste distinctions and discrimination and result in caste labelling, despite the supposed disinterest in caste identity other than among the elderly, and that there is no valid evidence of the existence of caste discrimination in spheres covered by equality law.[133] Conservative prime minister David Cameron (2010–2016) reportedly vetoed a proposal by ministers to make caste discrimination unlawful, to avoid legislating on the issue ahead of the

---

128 For example, Baroness Verma was the keynote speaker at the HFB AGM on 17 June 2012.
129 See M Dhanda, 'Certain Allegiances, Uncertain Identities: The Fraught Struggles of Dalits in Britain', in Om Prakash Dwivedi (ed.), *Tracing the New Indian Diaspora* (New York: Editions Rodopi, 2014) 99–119.
130 A search in October 2019 for "caste" and "Dalit" on the Liberty Human Rights website produced no results; see www.libertyhumanrights.org.uk/search?query=caste. The former Commission for Racial Equality declined to engage with caste discrimination despite its categorisation in international human rights law from 1996 as a form of racial discrimination; see Chapter 6.
131 Letter, T Phillips (EHRC) to L Pal (ACDA), 3 October 2011; copy on file with author.
132 In contrast, Press For Change (PFC) raised awareness of discrimination against trans people and achieved legislative change through pro-active use of domestic and European legal mechanisms; see www.pfc.org.uk/.
133 'Anti Caste Legislation Committee' Briefing Paper, 2 April 2013; copy on file with author. Theresa May's reluctance to "take on" vocal Hindu opponents of caste discrimination legislation is cited as the reason for issuing a consultation on whether legislation was even required; see Purohit (n 113).

2015 general election (the government denied this).[134] In the run-up to the 2015 general election, "Dharmic voters" were seemingly encouraged to vote Conservative because of the party's opposition to caste legislation, in contrast to the pro-legislation stance of Labour and the Liberal Democrats; the National Council of Hindu Temples UK (a charity) was reprimanded by the Charity Commission for publishing an online open letter extolling the Conservative Party for its commitment to repealing the caste amendment, and for agreeing with a third-party statement deriding British Hindu, Sikh and Jain Labour Party supporters.[135]

9.3.1 Caste and the multicultural conundrum

There is a link between state policies on multiculturalism and "faith communities" in the 2000s, and government reluctance to legislate for caste discrimination. In 1972, Anthony (later, Lord) Lester and Geoffrey Bindman, in their book 'Race and Law', anticipated the challenge of 'minorities within minorities', warning that, in a society which is culturally as well as racially plural, 'cultural tolerance must not become a cloak' for intra-community oppression and injustice.[136] Nicolas Jaoul argues that British policies of multiculturalism have favoured the development of a British form of caste discrimination which,

> even though it is a by-product of caste in India, needs to be dealt with as a British phe-nomenon that has much to do with existing British policies and that therefore needs to be addressed by British law on discrimination.[137]

British multiculturalism, argues Jaoul, corresponds to a view that accepts such discrimina-tion as being 'an internal matter to Indian communities' and in which the state has no right to interfere.[138] Further, because multicultural policies 'boast of being progressive and anti-racist', they give a 'new legitimacy' to tolerance of casteism in British society. However, notes Jaoul, modern multiculturalism cannot be blamed alone. The tendency to 'accommodate caste in the name of cultural adaptation' is not new: the British Raj incorporated caste as a convenient building block of the colonial order, because it 'could be an effective warrant of social order in a country divided in a multitude of castes and communities'.[139]

Pragna Patel argues that the problem lies more in the shift in state social policy in the late 1990s from liberal multiculturalism to 'faith-based multiculturalism',[140] bolstered by the inclusion of religion as a category for the first time in the 2001 Census, alongside

---

134 M Woolf, 'Cameron "Blocks Ban on Caste Bias"', *Sunday Times*, 21 December 2014.
135 See Mosse (n 117).
136 A Lester and G Bindman, *Race and Law* (Harmondsworth: Penguin, 1972) 18.
137 N Jaoul, 'Multiculturalism and Caste in Britain', paper delivered at CasteWatch UK conference, Sandwell, 15 July 2007, unpublished; copy on file with author.
138 Liberal multiculturalism as it developed in the 1970s and 1980s in the UK was underpinned by the principle of universal individual rights and individual citizenship in the public sphere alongside toler-ance in private of 'particularistic cultural practices'; S Hall, 'Conclusions: The Multicultural Question', in B Hesse (ed.), *Un/Settled Multiculturalisms: Diasporas, Entanglements, Transruptions* (London: Zed Books, 2000) 209–241, 210. On the contested meanings of the term "multiculturalism," see D McGol-drick, 'Multiculturalism and Its Discontents', 5(1) *Human Rights Law Review* (2005) 27–56, 31–39; A Xanthakis, 'Multiculturalism and International Law: Discussing Universal Standards', 23(1) *Human Rights Quarterly* (2010) 21–48, 23; B Parekh, *Rethinking Multiculturalism: Cultural Diversity and Political Theory* (Basingstoke: Palgrave MacMillan, 2006) 2–11.
139 Jaoul (n 137).
140 P Patel, 'Asian Women's Struggles for Human Rights in the UK', 16 *Feminist Legal Studies* (2008) 9–36.

'increasing self-identification in terms of religion [and] demands that the public space should recognise religious claims and religious differences'.[141] In the 'movement from race to religion' in the 2000s,[142] ethnic minority communities became reframed as 'faith communities',[143] and religion emerged as the 'main badge' of minority identity.[144] Underpinning this approach is the idea of religion as a 'common value'.[145] However, this is not necessarily positive or benign. According to Patel – a founder of Southall Black Sisters, a non-profit Asian women's domestic violence organisation – it has provided an opportunity for certain ' "faith groups" to use the terrain of multiculturalism to further an 'authoritarian and patriarchal agenda' which poses a threat to human rights.[146] The danger, concurs Kundnani, is a 'tokenistic and unthinking approach to minority representation', whereby – in the case of South Asian communities – 'under the guise of multiculturalism, leaders of communalist [sectarian] groups can easily become accepted as authentic representatives of Asian "culture" ', giving undue influence to the most reactionary elements in the community.[147]

9.3.2 *"Community cohesion" and "faith communities"*

"Community cohesion" (damage to which has been cited by successive governments as a reason for *not* legislating against caste discrimination) was the Labour Government's policy response to the 2001 civil disturbances in northern England – widely understood as resulting from a decline in, or a lack of, social (or community) cohesion.[148] The main theme of community cohesion was the compatibility of cultural pluralism and integration.[149] Religion was central to this vision, in that ethnic minority communities, re-labelled 'faith communities', were identified as 'important sources of social capital' with a key role to play in urban regeneration and tackling antisocial behaviour.[150] However, social or community cohesion in caste societies, historically, has often meant intra-caste or intra-group, rather than inter-caste or inter-group, cohesion or solidarity. The terms "community" and "caste"

---

141 G Singh, *The Adab 'Respect' Programme: A Perspective on Muslim-Sikh Relations in the UK and Causes of Tensions and Mistrust between the two Communities* (London: Faith Matters, 2010) 34.

142 C Allen, 'From Race to Religion: The New Face of Discrimination', in T Abbas (ed.), *Muslim Britain: Communities Under Pressure* (London: Zed Books, 2005) 49–65, cited in J Zavos, 'Negotiating Multiculturalism: Religion and the Organisation of Hindu Identity in Contemporary Britain', 35(6) *Journal of Ethnic and Migration Studies* (2009) 881–900, 882.

143 Zavos, ibid., 890.

144 Patel (n 140) 11, 14–15.

145 Zavos (n 142) 890.

146 Patel (n 140) 15; Zavos, ibid.

147 A Kundnani, 'Racism, Religion and Communalism', 44(2) *Race and Class* (2002) 71–80, 79; K Malik, 'The Failure of Multiculturalism: Community versus Society in Europe', 94(2) *Foreign Affairs* (2015) 21–32, 29. For a discussion of the relationship between multiculturalism and international law standards, see Xanthakis (n 138).

148 C Worley, ' "It's Not About Race. It's About the Community": New Labour and "Community Cohesion" ', 25 *Critical Social Policy* (2005) 483–496, 483, 485.

149 D McGhee, 'Moving to "Our" Common Ground – a Critical Examination of Community Cohesion Discourse in Twenty-First-Century Britain', 51(3) *Sociological Review* (2003) 376–404, 387; Local Government Association (LGA), *The Local Government Association's Guidance on Community Cohesion* (London: LGA, 2002); D Robinson, 'The Search for Community Cohesion: Key Themes and Dominant Concepts of the Public Policy Agenda', 42(8) *Urban Studies* (2005) 1411–1427.

150 See Patel (n 140); Kundnani (n 147) 79.

are frequently used interchangeably in India, and Ambedkar described caste as antisocial, anti-cohesive and divisive.[151]

9.3.3 Caste and the "Hindu community"

British Hindu organisations opposed to caste discrimination legislation on the grounds that it is an attack on Hindus have sought to present the "Hindu community" as a "clearly articulated group" – and themselves as its representatives. But there are problems with this approach. The Christian theological model, says Searle-Chatterjee, addresses religion as 'a separable and definable phenomenon which has crystallised into six or so distinct "major" faiths'.[152] Within this "world religions" paradigm, Hinduism is seen as a distinct religion and "Hindu" as a distinct and "bounded" religious identity, 'to which other identities of class, caste, gender, etc. are subordinate'.[153] However, such a view of Hinduism is neither historically, geographically nor culturally accurate.[154] Searle-Chatterjee explains that in the [Indian] subcontinent, it was not religion but caste which more frequently provided a basis for identification, even though the institution of caste was, historically, more fluid and segmental than the British realised; hence, '[*i*]*t is not surprising that in Britain many Indian organisations, including 'religious' ones, are caste-based*'.[155] The word "Hindu", explains Searle-Chatterjee, is used differently depending on the individual's caste status and identity: "lower" castes have traditionally used "Hindu" to refer to "upper" castes but not to themselves, while "high" castes often used it 'to refer to those who were seen as truly Indian' i.e. 'not having any religious link or allegiance to "foreign" traditions' (such as Christianity or Islam).[156] Lack of awareness of popular religious practices on the subcontinent, combined with the idea that religions are 'bounded unities', has resulted in the use of "Hindu" as an identity label in the UK.[157] This has made it possible for organisations such as the Hindu Forum of Britain to 'construct a monolithic "Hindu" voice and community in the UK', despite the deeply contested nature of the word, and to promote themselves as the institutional face of a homogenised Hinduism, representative of all Hindus in the UK and thereby enabling them – along with certain other minority religious organisations – to exert 'an unprecedented influence on state policy towards minorities'.[158] Furthermore, Searle-Chatterjee argues that Western academic accounts of Hindus in Britain promote a monolithic picture of Hinduism 'suffused uncritically' with positive images, partly due to sensitivity to accusations of ethnocentricity

---

151 BR Ambedkar, 'Annihilation of Caste', in V Moon (ed.), *Babasaheb Ambedkar Writings and Speeches Vol. 1* (Bombay: Education Dept., Govt. of Maharasthra, 1989) 25–96, 50–52, 56.

152 M Searle-Chatterjee, ' "World Religions" and "Ethnic Groups": Do These Paradigms Lend Themselves to the Cause of Hindu Nationalism?' 23(3) *Ethnic and Racial Studies* (2000) 497–515, 500.

153 Ibid., 498.

154 On the vagueness of the term "Hindoo" and the 'blurred boundary between Hinduism and animism' encountered by colonial administrators, see J Zavos, *The Emergence of Hindu Nationalism in India* (New Delhi: Oxford University Press, 2000) 74–77. For a contrary argument, see D Lorenzen, 'Who Invented Hinduism?' *Society for Comparative Study of Society and History* (1999) 630–659.

155 Searle-Chatterjee (n 152) 519–500 (emphasis added).

156 Ibid., 504. See also M Searle-Chatterjee, 'Caste, Religion and Other Identities', in M Searle-Chatterjee and U Sharma (eds.) (n 127) 147–168, 159–162. The rise of Hindu nationalism in India, and the labelling as "anti-nationals" of its critics and those deemed outside the "Hindu fold" is intimately linked to the politics of national identity.

157 Searle-Chatterjee (n 152) 503, 506.

158 Patel (n 140) 15–17. The tagline of the HCUK's website is 'For a unified Hindu voice'.

or racism, and partly to the view that religion generally is 'primarily benign and positive, with socially integrative functions'. The result, she writes, is that 'many kinds of social and cultural contradictions disappear from [Western academic] writing [on Hinduism]'.[159] Kundnani argues that the reputation of Hinduism as inherently tolerant, humane and peaceful has meant that fundamentalists within UK Hindu communities often escape scrutiny. For too long, he claims, communalism (sectarianism) in British Asian communities has escaped discussion, while fundamentalism is a charge levelled only at Muslims.[160] Concurring, Priyamvada Gopal argues that, in the current climate of pre-occupation with Islam, 'British Hindu and Sikh communities have become even less accountable for some of the more unsavoury features of their collective existence', in particular as 'some of their high-profile spokespeople have made concerted attempts to distance both communities from Muslims, arguing that they are better assimilated and make a more positive contribution to the "host" community'.[161]

There is an associated issue here. Chetan Bhatt is particularly critical of what he calls the 'disingenuous humanism' of Hindutva discourse. He stresses that an 'important attempt' is being made by Hindutva organisations in the West to rearticulate the concept of *dharma* as a 'universal human philosophy, a natural law for the whole of humanity', inherently tolerant and open. In this conceptualisation of Hinduism, *varna* is considered an essential aspect of natural law which recognises equality of soul as well as hierarchical classification based on personal qualities; conversely, *jati* is conceived as a 'false system of classification and division that was imposed by foreign imperialists'.[162] Hindutva is a religio-political ideology propagated and promoted by the Hindu nationalist movement in India, whose agenda is increasingly reflected in certain aspects of Hinduism in the UK.[163] The movement consists of three organisations based in India[164] which, in the UK, says John Zavos, 'present themselves as cultural and social organisations and downplay their political agenda', emphasising cultural and charitable work and distancing themselves from [right-wing Hindu] organisations in India.[165] Parita Mukta argues that the tenets of Hindu nationalism 'are being disseminated and made acceptable' within British politics via the construction of a 'monolithic (and seemingly innocent) "religious" community which British politicians support in the name of cultural plurality and diversity', insufficiently attentive to its hostility to minorities in India, and to the failure of [British] multiculturalism to take account of international human rights. Meanwhile, the 'prominent space carved out by Hindutva forces within

159 Searle-Chatterjee (n 152) 507–509.
160 Kundnani (n 147) 71. See also C Bhatt, 'Dharmo rakshati rakshitah: Hindutva movements in the UK', 23(3) *Ethnic and Racial Studies* (2000) 559–593.
161 P Gopal, 'Dominating the Diaspora', *Himal Southasia*, April 2010; Kundnani (n 147) 72.
162 C Bhatt, *Hindu Nationalism: Origins, Ideologies and Modern Myths* (Oxford: Berg, 2001) 568–570, 587.
163 See Zavos (n 154): C Jaffrelot (ed.), *Hindu Nationalism: A Reader* (Princeton: Princeton University Press, 2007); Bhatt, ibid. Shani describes Hindu nationalism as 'ethno-Hinduism', illustrated by its hostility to 'outsiders' and adherents of 'non-Indic' religions such as Islam and Christianity; O Shani, *Communalism, Caste and Hindu Nationalism: The Violence in Gujarat* (Cambridge: Cambridge University Press, 2007).
164 Known collectively as the Sangh Parivar (family). The umbrella political organisation is Rashtriya Swayamsevak Sangh (RSS or National Volunteer Corps, modelled on Mussolini's Brownshirts, with a presence in 150 countries); Bharatiya Janata Party (BJP), a political party, and Vishwa Hindu Parishad (VHP), a cultural organisation which has a strong presence in the UK.
165 J Zavos, 'Situating Hindu Nationalism in the UK: Vishwa Hindu Parishad and the Development of British Hindu Identity', 48(1) *Commonwealth & Comparative Politics* (2010) 2–22, 3–4.

British politics' is overriding democratic movements which organise 'outside the boundaries of religion and caste'.[166]

Against this backdrop, caste discrimination legislation is framed by some of its opponents as "anti-Hindu" and "anti-Indian," a form of legal violence against Indians – the position of Hindu organisations such as the NCHTUK and the academic Prakash Shah.[167] Drawing on the ideas of SN Balagangadhara, and in contrast to Lord Parekh, Shah's overarching argument is that "caste" is a Western concept which does not reflect the reality of Indian society, and that the "Indian caste system" is an idea propagated by European colonialists who labelled and denigrated Indian culture and religion as morally backward and corrupt, thereby justifying Christian proselytism in India. The demand for caste legislation in the UK is portrayed as a project of the Christian church (aided by the UN and the EU), part of a campaign of transnational proselytism and interference in India's internal affairs aimed at boosting conversions to Christianity and pressuring India to extend its caste-based affirmative action ('reservations') policies to Dalit Christians.[168] Those who fail to see this – including Indian intellectuals – are accused of suffering from what Balagangadhara calls colonial consciousness – a 'crude derivative' of Edward Said's concept of orientalism.[169] An extreme version of this position was articulated by the NCHTUK in a 2017 report which accused Lord Harries and the Church of England, by promoting caste legislation, of inflicting a hate crime 'upon the Dharmic community . . . and other communities of non-Abrahamic Indian origin in the UK'.[170]

The DIPF has itself used the word "caste" when describing organisations 'primarily based on caste membership (e.g. a *jati* or *gnati* belonging)'[171] – despite Shah's own condemnation of the word as an insult to Indians.[172] The UK has many "caste associations" representing different *jati* groups. Under the EA's present provisions on exceptions, 'single-characteristic associations' (as defined for EA purposes) are permitted to restrict membership to people sharing a protected characteristic, for example religion or belief, or race (including nationality and national or ethnic origins, but not colour).[173] Contrary to the DIPF's assertions, associations for particular castes would be permissible under the EA's present provisions if caste were made an aspect of race or captured by ethnic origins. Nevertheless, Shah depicts Indian organisations, businesses, employers and service providers as victims of caste legislation, at risk of spurious allegations of discrimination and malicious threats of litigation.[174] Legislation

---

166 P Mukta, 'The Public Face of Hindu Nationalism', 23(3) *Ethnic and Racial Studies* (2000) 442–466, 453. See also S Narula, 'Overlooked Danger: The Security and Rights Implications of Hindu Nationalism in India', 16 *Harvard Human Rights Journal* (2003) 41–68; F Raj, 'More Dangerous Than Shariah: Hindutva', *Washington Times*, 8 September 2011.

167 See the Dharmic Ideas Policy Foundation (DIPF), created in 2015, which describes itself as a think-tank and a forum 'for public and private discussion of issues concerning the British Dharmic communities'; see https://dharmicideas.wordpress.com/about/.

168 See Shah (n 72). For a detailed critique of Shah's position, see A Waughray, review of P Shah, *Against Caste in British Law*, 36(3) *South Asia Research* (2016) 409–413; Sutton (n 72).

169 Sutton (n 72) 336.

170 'Caste, Conversion and a "Thoroughly Colonial Conspiracy" ' (n 72) 9.

171 See, for example, DIPF, open letter to voluntary and community organisations (signed by Prakash Shah), 24 May 2016 at https://dharmicideas.files.wordpress.com/2016/08/caste-discrimination-letter-to-voluntary-organisatiop-ns.pdf.

172 Shah (n 72).

173 Equality Act 2010, Schedule 16. For a full discussion of caste and exceptions to the EA, see M Dhanda et al., *Caste in Britain: Socio-legal Review*, Equality and Human Rights Commission (n 63) 20–24.

174 Shah (n 72) 71.

is framed not as a source of protection from caste discrimination but as a source of insult, intimidation and offence to 'Indian communities' and which threatens their very existence.[175] Nowhere in this literature is there any acknowledgement that discrimination or exclusion on grounds of caste might be a problem for anyone in India or the diaspora, or that being a Dalit – whether in India or as a 'minority within a minority' in the diaspora – might be a very different experience from not being a Dalit.[176]

9.4 The legal regulation of caste discrimination in the UK: lessons learned

As UK citizens, British Dalits are entitled to protection from discrimination based on caste – a principle recognised in India since 1950 (even if not fully realised). Moreover, Dalits are entitled to core basic rights, namely equality of treatment and equality of opportunity to lead an unimpaired and peaceful life. Caste discrimination is a social problem in the diaspora as well as in the subcontinent, and it affects not only Dalits; it can occur regardless of the perceived, known or imagined caste identity of the victim and regardless of the victim's known or perceived religion or belief (or lack thereof). Domestic legislation is an essential, albeit not the sole, element in addressing caste discrimination in the UK, as CERD and the EHRC have made clear. Yet, following the 2017 public consultation on caste and equality law, the government decided not to add caste to race in the EA and instead to repeal the statutory duty to do so. Opponents of caste legislation argue that it is unnecessary and unjustified, because there is insufficient evidence of a problem, its occurrence is difficult to prove and there is no consensus for legislation among those of South Asian origin. Moreover, legislating on such a 'sensitive and controversial' issue would, they claim, damage community cohesion and community relations, re-introduce or entrench the idea of caste in British society and be viewed by some as inherently racist, anti-Hindu and anti-Indian; in any case, the existing prohibition of discrimination on grounds of ethnic origins provides sufficient protection against caste discrimination. Legislation has also been criticised on grounds of cost, despite the Equality Act Impact Assessment advice that the "case law" route, namely judicial interpretation of existing anti-discrimination law, would be more costly (due to legal uncertainty) than introducing specific statutory protection against caste discrimination.

Although caste-specific legislation would indeed involve initial "familiarisation" costs, these would diminish as the concepts of caste and caste discrimination become more familiar. Discrimination legislation not only provides a vital route to redress, but it also serves a wider educational purpose. This is particularly important in the case of caste discrimination, because much of the population lacks sufficient understanding of caste issues. Successive governments have now acknowledged the existence of caste-based prejudice and discrimination; legislation would name the problem and send an important public policy message, creating the climate in which compliance with the law becomes accepted and expected.[177]

---

175 Ibid., 80–81; Waughray (n 55).
176 Waughray (n 96) 410.
177 This is not a new argument. In 1966, during parliamentary debates on the Race Relations Act 1965 (Amendment) Bill, Maurice Orbach MP argued that legislation not only provides a means of redress but 'serves to set standards of decent human behaviour to which the citizen can conform'; the effect of legislation is to 'prevent habits of discrimination by actively promoting equality of treatment', because 'the dignity of the individual is struck at' whether 'a score, 200, or 2000' people suffer this kind of discrimination; HC Deb vol 738 cols 897–905 16 December 1966.

Legislation would push employers, educators and providers of goods and services to develop non-discrimination and anti-harassment policies, which in turn would reduce the acceptability of caste discrimination and harassment and lead to greater understanding of the issues, thereby making it easier for victims to raise problems. It has been claimed that this could be achieved through education alone. While policies to combat caste discrimination could be introduced in the public sector without legislation, the NIESR was doubtful whether, without specific legislation, such policies would be properly implemented, while the private sector 'would be largely untouched'.[178] Legislation is a necessary but not sufficient condition for achieving rights and equalities; nevertheless, effecting a culture shift is largely dependent on having legislation in place. In 2010 the NIESR recommended extending equality legislation to cover caste, and extending criminal law on race hate crime to address caste-motivated harassment and violence, as being more effective than education in providing redress for victims.[179] There is emerging recognition in the UK of the link between caste, forced marriage and honour-based violence and abuse.[180] Consequently, bringing caste hate crime within the ambit of race hate crime would open up the possibility of prosecuting caste-motivated honour crimes perpetrated against males as well as females, particularly males in heterosexual relationships where the female's family deems the male "undesirable" on grounds of his caste – with the potential for sentence uplift.[181,182]

At the EHRC *Caste in Britain* Experts' Seminar and Stakeholders' Workshop in November 2013, experts and stakeholder groups agreed on the importance of education, training and sensitisation for professionals and the wider public on caste discrimination and the law, whilst also reiterating the need to bring caste within the ambit of legislation. Caste is listed as an 'irrelevant ground' of difference and differentiation and a recognised source of prejudice and unequal treatment in the Bangalore Principles of Judicial Conduct (2002), the internationally agreed standard for judges which applies to the judiciary in the UK.[183] Legal education, training and familiarisation on caste discrimination for actors such as the judiciary, police, the legal profession, social services, employers, trades unions, education and services providers is essential, but it is unclear whether the government would make resources available for such programmes. A particularly valuable feature of the EA in addressing casteist behaviour is the provision on harassment in section 26, which covers unwanted conduct related to a relevant protected characteristic that has the purpose or effect of violating the complainant's dignity or creating an intimidating, hostile, degrading, humiliating or offensive environment for the complainant. If caste discrimination is to recede, a combination of awareness training, education and legislation is required in order to generate attitudinal change and to combat discrimination as it arises.[184]

178 Hilary Metcalfe (NIESR), meeting 17 January 2011 (n 32).
179 Metcalfe and Rolfe (n 1) 65.
180 See A Waughray, 'Honour-Based Violence and Caste', presentation, National Honour-Based Violence Roadshow 2018, House of Commons, 24 January 2019 (unpublished, copy on file with author).
181 See A Waughray, 'Honour-Based Violence and Caste', presentation, National Honour-Based Violence Roadshow 2018, House of Commons, 24 January 2019 (unpublished, copy on file with author).
182 The Law Commission's 2021 review of hate crime law recognises the occurrence of caste-based violence but it does not recommend explicitly including caste in race hate crime unless it is explicitly included in race in the Equality Act 2010.
183 Dhanda et al. (n 78). Bangalore Principles of Judicial Conduct (2002), at www.unodc.org/res/ji/ import/international_standards/bangalore_principles/bangaloreprinciples.pdf.
184 See Dhanda et al. (n 63) 36.

The EHRC, as the UK's UN Paris Principles national human rights institution (NHRI), is the regulatory body responsible for enforcing the EA.[185] Under the Equality Act 2006 it has a range of litigation powers, including the power to intervene in human rights and equality cases initiated by others, where this will strengthen equality and human rights.[186] In November 2014, the EHRC intervened in *Chandhok v Tirkey* (the Chandhoks' appeal against Ms Tirkey's amendment of her race discrimination claim to argue that her caste was a factor in the way she was perceived by them). It contended that her amended claim fell within direct race discrimination 'as a matter of domestic law and EU law', while simultaneously noting the UK's international law obligations to legislate against caste discrimination.[187] Afterwards, the EHRC confirmed its view that, while the EAT's decision that caste discrimination is capable of being covered by the EA was 'helpful', this would not necessarily be so in all cases, and so each case must be considered on its own facts and therefore an express provision in the EA is desirable for legal clarity.[188] In July 2018, the EHRC reiterated its unequivocal support for separate and distinct legislative protection against caste discrimination in its statement following the government's consultation response:

> Victims of caste discrimination will continue to have limited legal protection by the government ruling out a change in the law and restricting the scope of protection to what can be interpreted through case law. The government has missed a crucial opportunity to improve legal clarity and has taken a step back by looking to repeal the duty to include caste as an aspect of race in the Equality Act 2010. This is inconsistent with the UK's international obligations to provide for separate and distinct protection for caste in our legislation.[189]

The ICERD regime and the Geneva mechanisms have been important tools in British anti-caste activists' efforts to put caste discrimination onto the domestic equality agenda.[190] At

---

185 In 2012, following a government review, the EHRC's functions and budget were reduced and it was re-conceived as a strategic body; see D Barratt, 'The Regulatory Space of Equality and Human Rights in Britain: The Role of the Equality and Human Rights Commission', 39(2) Legal Studies (2019) 247–265, 249.

186 See www.equalityhumanrights.com/en/court-action. Other enforcement mechanisms include the power to undertake enquiries (for example, the 2019 enquiry into racial harassment in universities), although the threshold for enquiries is high; see www.equalityhumanrights.com/en/publication-download/tackling-racial-harassment-universities-challenged; Barratt, ibid., 257.

187 See www.equalityhumanrights.com/en/legal-casework/legal-cases; *Chandhok v Tirkey* [2014] UKEAT/0190/14/KN (n 98), skeleton argument on behalf of the EHRC, copy on file with author.

188 Letter, EHRC to Anti Caste Discrimination Alliance (subject: Chandok [sic] v Tirkey), 25 February 2015, copy on file with author.

189 See EHRC, Caste consultation: our response to the government statement, 23 July 2018 (n 119).
     The pitfalls of the judicial interpretation ("case law") approach, particularly for litigants in person, were apparent in *Agarwal and Meshram v Tata Consultancy Services Ltd* (ET case no. 2202616/2018 and 22025035/2018) in which Mr Meshram – representing himself – claimed race/caste discrimination and harassment. He asserted that "caste," "lower caste" and "upper caste" are each an ethnic origin and a protected characteristic; likewise that "Shudra" and "Brahmin" are ethnic origins. The Employment Tribunal held that, while it was possible that members of a particular caste might constitute an ethnic group per *Mandla*, Mr Meshram did not provide evidence to enable it to find that they did so, or to find that he was a member of a different ethnic group to that of the Respondents or his comparators.

190 See, for example, on the relationship between UN human rights treaties and domestic law and policy, C Heyns and F Viljoen, 'The Impact of the United Nations Human Rights Treaties on the Domestic Level', 23(2) *Human Rights Quarterly* (2001) 483–535, 48. See also A Waughray and D Keane, 'CERD

the same time as transnational Dalit advocacy networks were reorienting the framing of caste discrimination towards discrimination based on work and descent, British Dalits were turning to ICERD and CERD's affirmation that it is a violation of ICERD as a form of descent-based racial discrimination. The UK's international law obligations require it to ensure domestic compliance with ICERD. CERD's recommendations to the UK to introduce legislation prohibiting descent-based and caste-based discrimination in 2003, 2011 and 2016 – when CERD recommended the immediate addition of caste 'as an aspect of race' as required by EA section 9(5)(a) – were relied upon by British Dalit activists and their supporters in their campaign for domestic legislative reform.

The *process* of achieving social change is as important as securing legislation and case law developments. Increasing "caste literacy" (knowledge and understanding of caste and prejudice and discrimination on grounds thereof) among the wider UK population is critical, particularly among young people, in schools and universities and via mainstream and social media.[191] The importance of caste-aware teaching in religious education has been highlighted by Nesbitt.[192] The research by ACDA and the NIESR revealed the existence of caste-related harassment and bullying between pupils and students in schools and universities, which must be addressed institutionally as well as by organisations such as students' unions. Dalit voices on caste discrimination must be taken seriously at local, regional and national levels, especially those of "least heard" groups such as women and the young.

A far more sophisticated approach to multiculturalism is called for in the UK. Minorities are not homogenous entities; decisions need to be made and policies developed in full knowledge and understanding of their internal workings and heterogeneity. In respecting and protecting cultural diversity in compliance with international law, when protection is demanded for an aspect of "culture" or cultural identity which is violative of the core rights of others, culture (or religion) should not constitute a shield to scrutiny.[193] In the context of domestic policies on "multiculturalism", the question of whether caste groups should be treated as "cultural groups" from an international human rights law cultural rights perspective is critical.[194] The idea that castes (*jatis*) were distinct "cultural groups" was argued by caste groups wishing to protect their caste-related rights and privileges before colonial courts in British India. In contrast, Natrajan argues that conceptualising caste purely as "cultural identity" and caste groups as 'communities of identity seeking recognition for their cultural differences in a multicultural society' – in other words treating caste as 'an "internal" matter of heritage and culture'[195] – promotes a view of it as "natural" and benign rather than 'socio-culturally constructed relations' of ascribed status and inequality.[196] The

---

and Caste-based Discrimination', in D Keane and A Waughray (eds.), *Fifty Years of the International Convention on the Elimination of All Forms of Racial Discrimination (ICERD): A Living Instrument* (Manchester: Manchester University Press, 2017) 121–149.

191 See, for example, 'Hindus: Do We Have a Caste Problem?' *BBC One*, 13 October 2019.

192 See E Nesbitt, *Intercultural Education: Ethnographic and Religious Approaches* (Brighton: Sussex Academic Press, 2004). See also Chapter 6.

193 See Xanthakis (n 138) 47: 'International instruments "stress the need for equal respect to every culture, be it the national, sub-national, or regional, and urge states to protect such cultural loyalties. Also, States are strongly encouraged to take positive measures in order to ensure the effective protection of sub-national groups and their cultures'".

194 See Xanthakis (n 138) 47.

195 D Mosse, 'Caste and Development: Contemporary Perspectives on a Structure of Discrimination and Advantage', 110 *World Development* (2018) 422–436, 423.

196 See Chapters 1 and 2; B Natrajan, *The Culturalisation of Caste in India: Identity and Inequality in a Multicultural Age* (Abingdon: Routledge, 2012) xiii, 5.

focus on religion as the 'main badge' of minority identity in the 2000s contributed to a 'religious rites and practices' (i.e. 'internal') conceptualisation of caste and caste discrimination in the UK,[197] in contrast to the UN (and anti-caste) framing of caste discrimination as a discrimination and human rights issue. Hence, it was primarily the views of the spokespeople of established minority religious organisations which were sought by government on the legal regulation of caste discrimination, but their views were not necessarily the same as the views of those on the receiving end of such discrimination.[198] Moreover, successive governments have lacked sufficient critical awareness of the influence of political and religious actors and political developments and events overseas on political developments and actors in the UK, and vice versa.

As regards international policy, British businesses operating abroad in India, Nepal, Pakistan and other states where caste discrimination occurs – both in their own operations and among their suppliers – must comply with national and international law obligations on caste discrimination and should be encouraged to comply with the Ambedkar Principles and UK discrimination law on caste, and to cooperate with compliance monitoring and auditing.[199] According to the former director of Anti-Slavery International, a UK-based NGO, 'caste discrimination is the single biggest enabler of labour exploitation and modern slavery in all of South Asia and arguably the single largest human and civil rights issue in the contemporary world'.[200] British businesses in India should be encouraged to adopt British diversity approaches to caste as well as being reminded of India's national laws on caste discrimination; government should fund familiarisation, training and advice on caste, rewarding those businesses which comply. Indian businesses and investors operating in the UK should be monitored for compliance with both Indian law on caste discrimination and relevant UK equality law and equal opportunities best practice.[201]

In relations with India, UK Governments must adopt an open and yet robust approach to caste discrimination, acknowledge that it is an equality and human rights issue in the UK as well as India and elsewhere and be open to the need for global solutions. In other words, caste discrimination should be treated with the same seriousness as other forms of discrimination, rather than as a taboo issue. A bi- or multi-lateral government-level working group on caste discrimination could be established, so that other countries can learn from India as the state with the greatest experience in countering it, while India could gain insights from the successes and weaknesses of other states' anti-discrimination legislation models and equal opportunities practices.

Caste and caste discrimination are not yet sufficiently familiar concepts in the UK's political, diplomatic, development, aid and international trade and business relations. Mosse observes that despite the importance of inherited caste identity as 'a determinant of life opportunity for a fifth of the world's population', it does not feature in global development policy debates in the way that gender, race, religion, age or other identity characteristics do, nor does caste-based discrimination and inequality feature in international commitments

---

197 See HC Deb vol 419 col 1603W 1 April 2004; Mosse (n 117).

198 The government's August 2007 "scoping study" focused on religious groups, predominantly Hindu, although some Sikh and Muslim groups were also consulted; see HC Deb vol 493 col 179 11 June 2009.

199 The Ambedkar Principles: Principles and Guidelines to address Caste Discrimination in the Private Sector at https://idsn.org/wp-content/uploads/user_folder/pdf/New_files/IDSN/Ambedkar_Principles_brochure.pdf. See also Ethical Trading Initiative (ETI), *Base Code Guidance: Caste in Global Supply Chains* (London: ETI, 2019).

200 ETI, ibid., 6.

201 See *Agarwal and Meshram v Tata Consultancy Services Ltd.* (n 188).

such as the Sustainable Development Goals.[202] Given its global significance, and the commitment of successive UK Governments to overseas aid and development, the UK is ideally placed to show leadership (alongside India) by explicitly introducing the issue of caste-based discrimination and inequality into debates about aid and development policies and planning.

9.5 Conclusion

The UK is the first European country to introduce the word "caste" into equality legislation and to legislate for the introduction of a prohibition of caste discrimination despite the reluctance of successive governments and in the face of concerted opposition, primarily from religious organisations and those who portray anti-discrimination legislation as a cultural and religious attack. The existing prohibited grounds of discrimination in British law were not adopted with caste discrimination in mind and do not easily capture it. Only in a limited number of cases can religious discrimination provisions capture caste discrimination. *Tirkey* (2015) held that in certain circumstances caste will fall within the definition of race (specifically, the ethnic origins subset), but it is not an authority for this proposition and does not set a binding precedent that ethnic origins (or race) covers caste. In 1975, the racial discrimination White Paper stated:

> To fail to provide a remedy against an injustice strikes at the rule of law. To abandon a whole group of people in society without legal redress against unfair discrimination is to leave them with no option but to find their own redress.[203]

In 2007, the Discrimination Law Review acknowledged that discrimination law 'needs to keep pace with and reflect the changes in our society'.[204] To this end, its Consultation Paper accepted that it is necessary to review who is protected from discrimination and to consider the case for updating the grounds or personal characteristics protected under discrimination law, 'in order to ensure that the law remains a dynamic reflection of our society's attitudes' – where this is both 'necessary and proportionate and once any additional regulatory burden has been considered'.[205] While legislation alone cannot 'untwist the mind',[206] it can act as a disincentive to discriminatory behaviour, challenge the cultural consensus, lead to the development of new social norms and provide legal redress for discrimination.[207] Over the past fifteen years, caste as a ground of discrimination has risen in legal and wider public awareness, and its traction as a ground of discrimination has increased, but the process of embedding legal protection against caste discrimination in the UK is unfinished. It has been found to occur but is yet to be brought explicitly within the ambit of discrimination legislation; however, doing so would be acknowledging such discrimination as unacceptable and unlawful, wherever it occurs, as well as providing a clear and direct route for legal redress for those in the UK who are or have been subject to discrimination on grounds of caste.

---

202 Mosse (n 194). See also N Saracini and M Shanmugavelan, *Caste and Development: Tackling Work and Descent-Based Discrimination to Achieve the SDGs for All* (London: Bond, 2019), at www.bond.org.uk/sites/default/files/resource-documents/bond_caste_reportscreen.pdf.

203 See *Racial Discrimination* White Paper, Cm 6234 (1975) 23.

204 See *A Framework for Fairness: Proposals for a Single Equality Bill for Great Britain – A Consultation Paper* (London: Department for Communities and Local Government, 2007) 15.

205 Ibid., 127.

206 See BR Ambedkar, 'The Real Issue', in V Moon (ed.), *What Congress and Gandhi Have Done to the Untouchables: Dr Babasaheb Ambedkar Writings and Speeches (BAWS) Vol. 9* (Bombay: Education Dept., Govt. of Maharasthra, 1991) 197.

207 See Lester and Bindman (n 136) 85–87.

Conclusion

The persistence of caste

As this book has explained, caste is a distinct form of hereditary social identity, differentiation and stratification associated primarily with South Asia and its diaspora.[1] It has existed in changing forms for many hundreds of years, and it is complex, deep-rooted and difficult to understand and to theorise. It is distinguished by its theoretical and historical underpinnings in certain Hindu texts, and by the concept of untouchability. Central to the ideology of caste is the presupposition that individuals are not empirically equal at birth, that inequality is the result of freely chosen behaviour in this life and previous lives and, hence, that a person's caste in this life is of their own making.[2] Classical Hindu law was instrumental in constructing and maintaining the ideology of caste and its normative framework, which naturalises a hierarchical system of "graded inequality" entailing increasing rights for the so-called higher castes and increasing civil, political, social and economic disabilities and discrimination for those at the bottom of the hierarchy.[3] The lot of the Dalits is the threat – even if it is not a present danger – of untouchability, the ultimate denial of rights and dignity. Caste and caste-based discrimination can be found among South Asian followers of Hinduism, Sikhism, Islam and Christianity as well as adherents of other religions and none. In India, Dalits (numbering around 201 million people, over 16% of India's population) have historically been kept "outside the fold" by the "dominant" castes' exercise of social, economic and political power, both individual and systemic. Caste-based discrimination, marginalisation and exclusion have been a reality for many hundreds of years in South Asia, and they continue despite the assumption that India's post-1991 economic liberalisation would bring about the dissolution of caste. More recently, in Britain, the existence of caste and the occurrence of caste discrimination have been identified in government-commissioned research in 2010 and in research from the UK's Equality and Human Rights Commission (EHRC) in 2014; however, large-scale research on its nature, extent and manifestations is still lacking.[4] In 2011, there were over three million people of South Asian origin in the UK (nearly 5% of the total population), while the number of people of Dalit origin is estimated at between 50,000 to 200,000 or more (there are no official statistics).[5] In 2015, the Conservative-

---

1 See Chapters 1 and 2.
2 See Chapter 2.
3 BR Ambedkar, 'Who Were the Shudras?' in V Rodrigues (ed.), *The Essential Writings of B.R. Ambedkar* (New Delhi: Oxford University Press, 2002) 385–395, 385–386.
4 See Chapter 9. The present author is a member of the EHRC *Caste in Britain* research team.
5 H Metcalfe and H Rolfe, *Caste Discrimination and Harassment in Great Britain* (London: Government Equalities Office, 2010) 20; Census 2011, Office for National Statistics (ONS), UK population by ethnicity and identity.

DOI: 10.4324/9781315750934-14

Liberal Democrat coalition government (2010–2015) conceded the existence of domestic caste discrimination in its 2015 periodic report to CERD (UN Committee on the Elimination of Racial Discrimination – the monitoring body of ICERD, the UN Convention on the Elimination of All Forms of Racial Discrimination)[6] and agreed that legal protection was needed.[7] In April 2013, Parliament decided that statutory protection against caste discrimination must be added to the UK's Equality Act 2010 (EA) by making caste 'an aspect of' the protected characteristic of race. After five years of prevarication by successive governments, in July 2018, amid denials that caste discrimination occurs in the UK and vigorous resistance to legislation by Dharmic (Hindu, Sikh and Jain) activists, the Conservative Government of Theresa May – following a much delayed and highly criticised public consultation on caste and equality law – acknowledged the existence of caste discrimination and declared the government's concern to ensure 'sufficient, appropriate and proportionate' legal protection against such discrimination. However, it also announced its intention not to legislate on the issue but instead to leave it to the courts to decide on a case-by-case basis whether caste as a ground of discrimination is captured by the characteristic of race as currently defined in the EA, specifically by the concept of ethnic origins, claiming (incorrectly) that the case of *Tirkey v Chandhok* (2015) provides an authority for this proposition.[8]

Caste in India

In 1945, Ambedkar described the caste system as 'a legal system maintained at the point of a bayonet'.[9] On gaining independence in 1947, India legally abolished untouchability and criminalised its practice, and it introduced constitutional affirmative action policies in favour of the Scheduled Castes (those Dalit castes identified in a Schedule to the Constitution) in political representation, public employment and higher education.[10] Yet, de facto, Dalits in India continue to suffer from untouchability and caste-related social, economic, occupational and educational inequality, discrimination and violence.[11] This book has sought to explain why that is the case despite the constitutional, legislative and policy measures referred to herein. The gap between the legal status and sociological status of India's Dalits remains vast, and casteism remains entrenched in the country, ideologically, materially and psychologically. Paradoxically, caste in contemporary India has become institutionalised as a tool of political mobilisation – even as a depoliticised, benign view of caste as cultural or ethnic identity, or cultural "difference," in a diverse and multicultural modern India is promoted (termed by Balmurli Natrajan the 'culturalisation' of caste).[12] Meanwhile, argues David Mosse, there is a societal, business and bureaucratic failure – or refusal – to recognise

6 ICERD; Adopted 21 December 1965. In force 4 January 1969. 660 UNTS 195. As at November 2021, ICERD has been ratified or acceded to by 182 states, including India (3 December 1968) and the United Kingdom (7 March 1969). CERD.
7 UK's 21st-23rd reports to CERD; CERD/C/GBR/21–23, 16 July 2015, para 8.
8 Penny Mordaunt, Minister for Women and Equalities, Government Response to Caste Consultation: Written statement – HCWS898, 23 July 2018; *Tirkey v Chandhok & Anor* [2015] UKET/3400174/2013.
9 BR Ambedkar, 'What Congress and Gandhi Have Done to the Untouchables', in V Moon (ed.), *Babasaheb Ambedkar Writings and Speeches Vol. 9* (Bombay: Education Dept., Govt. of Maharasthra, 1991) 1–387, 289.
10 Muslim and Christian Dalits are constitutionally excluded from categorisation as Scheduled Castes; see Chapter 3.
11 See Chapter 3.
12 B Natrajan, *The Culturalization of Caste in India: Identity and Inequality in a Multicultural Age* (Abingdon and New York: Routledge, 2012).

and address the way caste as a resource or positive property for the advantaged and a negative property for the disadvantaged is embedded, concealed, disguised and rendered invisible in India's supposedly caste-free modern market economy.[13]

India's reliance on criminal legislation to address caste discrimination has proven insufficient.[14] Criminal law is not designed to address institutional or systemic discrimination, or casteist behaviour by individuals or organisations which falls short of the criminal standard of proof; rather, it suggests that casteist behaviour is "abnormal" or "exceptional" rather than something "everyday." Moreover, enforcement is weak, and in some cases, those responsible for enforcement of the law are themselves perpetrators. Alongside criminal law, India needs civil anti-discrimination legislation to protect individuals from unfair treatment, to provide remedies for discrimination which fall short of the criminal threshold and to promote equality, together with economic initiatives and a large-scale civic education programme designed to tackle deep-rooted, entrenched attitudes (a need shared by countries around the world).[15] India has the world's oldest and most extensive measures on caste discrimination.[16] Rather than seeing UN mechanisms as a threat, India should use these as tools to hone its law, policies and practices, and to disseminate its valuable experience worldwide.

Criminal law aside, since 1950, affirmative action policies, known as "reservations," have been the principal vehicle for achieving caste equality, to the exclusion of a broader debate on caste discrimination as a human rights violation, equality, its meaning and how to achieve it. Yet, despite being the world's oldest and most extensive affirmative action scheme, the effectiveness of India's reservations policy has never been adequately monitored. CERD General Recommendation No. 32 (2009) on special measures (e.g. affirmative action policies) provides a template for an affirmative action monitoring regime which India could adopt and develop as a best practice model to disseminate among other countries. A wide-ranging public debate at all levels of civil society needs to be initiated which challenges caste, untouchability and caste discrimination, and interrogates and examines the kind of society India wants to be in the twenty-first century. This is already taking place to some extent, driven by activists, civil society organisations, academics, theorists and public intellectuals with radical visions inspired by the social and political ideas and anti-caste agenda of Dr Ambedkar, by a deep historical understanding of the centrality of Dalits and Dalit experience to India's future[17] and by the development of critical alliances with African American and African activists and intellectuals beyond India's borders.[18]

Capturing caste in law

As this book has shown, caste is an elusive concept that is difficult to define and categorise legally. A key theme that emerges from this book is the challenge of capturing caste in law. It appears in no international instrument and has proved challenging to capture under

---

13 D Mosse, 'The Modernity of Caste and the Market Economy', *Modern Asian Studies* (2019) (online) 1–47.
14 See Chapter 3.
15 In March 2017, the Anti-Discrimination and Equality Bill was introduced in the Lok Sabha by Shashi Tharoor MP. As a Private Members' Bill, it remains to be seen whether the Bill will ever become law and, if so, whether it can become a tool or, if not, a catalyst for deeper change.
16 See Chapter 3.
17 See, for example, A Singh Rathore, 'Dalit Svaraj: The Precondition for Authentic Indian Political Theory', in *Indian Political Theory: Laying the Groundwork for Svaraj* (London: Routledge, 2018) 192–206.
18 See, for example, International Conference on Caste and Race: Reconfiguring Solidarities – The Unfinished Legacy of Dr BR Ambedkar at http://engagement.umass.edu/crrs/node/36.

conventional international grounds of discrimination. Following independence, India's fail-ure to eradicate untouchability and caste discrimination using domestic law led Dalits to take their grievances to the UN human rights bodies. In 1996, in response to the realities of caste discrimination brought to its attention by Dalit activists, CERD, in its conclud-ing observations to India's ninth to fourteenth periodic reports, addressed the issue under "descent" in Article 1(1) of ICERD, thereby formalising caste discrimination as a form of descent-based racial discrimination and affirming that States parties are under internationally binding obligations to work for its elimination.[19] In 2002, in its General Recommendation 29, CERD affirmed that descent-based discrimination 'includes members of communities based on forms of social stratification such as caste and analogous systems of inherited sta-tus'.[20] India, however, has consistently rejected CERD's application of descent, as a form of racial discrimination, to caste. Descent is also rejected by Japan as a category for captur-ing discrimination against its Burakumin population.[21] Discrimination based on work and descent (DWD) emerged in 2000 as an alternative, non-treaty category to CERD's applica-tion of the descent category to caste, but India opposed the appointment in 2005 of two UN Special Rapporteurs on DWD – on the grounds that caste, and by extension India, was really the intended target of scrutiny – and did not engage with the subsequent drafting of the UN Draft Principles and Guidelines (DPGs) on the subject.

India has not opposed the identification of caste by other international human rights treaty bodies as an impediment to the enjoyment of other rights, and other treaty bodies and Charter body mechanisms have raised caste discrimination with a range of other states, with-out formal or legal objections. However, India has resisted international scrutiny of caste discrimination by CERD, arguing that descent does not cover caste and that it is an internal matter which is being addressed by domestic measures.[22] The result is that the primary source for the prohibition of caste-based discrimination in international human rights law – descent, a form of racial discrimination under Article 1(1) of ICERD – is disputed by the state most associated with caste. The question that arises is whether the solution is a caste-specific instrument (such as a Declaration or, eventually, an international convention) which would target caste directly. However, support from India is highly unlikely. In 2017, the UN OHCHR Network on Racial Discrimination and Protection of Minorities published a guidance tool for UN country teams on the key challenges and strategic approaches to combat descent-based discrimination which could possibly lead to a free-standing Declara-tion on descent-based discrimination, including on the basis of caste and analogous systems of inherited status. As the international understanding of descent-based discrimination and caste evolves, it is possible in the future that a relevant instrument will emerge.

Meanwhile, international human rights law imposes clear obligations on states to pro-hibit descent-based discrimination (including caste discrimination) as a form of racial dis-crimination, and it also prohibits discrimination based on work and descent (DWD). Some Dalit activists and transnational advocacy groups, stressing the distinct, transnational and global nature of caste discrimination, have argued for a move away from a 'caste as racial

19 CERD, Concluding Observations – India; UN Doc. A/51/18 (1996), para 352.
20 CERD, General Recommendation 29 on Article 1(1) of ICERD (2002); see Chapter 4.
21 The Burakumin are a group at the bottom of Japanese society, numbering between 1.2 million and 3 mil-lion people, historically subject to intense prejudice and discrimination and considered "polluting" to higher groups; see Chapter 4.
22 See Chapter 4.

discrimination' perspective towards a discourse based on 'descent and work-based discrimination and violence'.[23] However, there are practical and policy problems with the DWD approach.[24] First, the concept and definition of DWD lacks precision. Second, the lack of input into the UN Draft Principles and Guidelines for the Elimination of Work and Descent Discrimination from South Asian states where caste discrimination is prevalent, or from African states affected by DWD, weakens the credibility of the DPGs. Third, a Declaration on the elimination of DWD is unlikely to secure Indian support unless the conceptual linkage between DWD and caste discrimination is removed. That said, Dalits and transnational advocacy networks see value in promoting the UN DPGs as a tool which provides 'an international reference point for action' and which can be applied in their existing format as a framework for the elimination of caste discrimination.[25] Yet, caste – unlike identity characteristics such as gender, race, religion, age, sexual orientation and gender identity and expression – has been identified as being largely absent from global development policy debates and from international commitments such as the Sustainable Development Goals.[26] Caste-based discrimination and inequality must be explicitly introduced into national, regional and global debates about development, and caste must also find a place in debates on combating systemic inequality and discrimination and strategies for social and economic transformation, in the same way as other identity characteristics.[27]

Caste in the United Kingdom

The United Kingdom has stepped back from becoming the first non-South Asian country to introduce into domestic legislation a statutory prohibition of caste discrimination and harassment, although, unlike India, it has not challenged CERD's categorisation of caste discrimination as a form of descent-based racial discrimination. However, despite government acknowledgement that caste discrimination occurs in the UK, the legislative process initiated in 2010, when the outgoing Labour Government reluctantly introduced a provision into the Equality Act 2010 (EA) enabling caste to be added to race at a future date by secondary legislation, has stalled under successive governments. Parliament's 2013 imposition of a duty on government to add caste to the EA 'as an aspect of race' was not complied with. This stalled legislative process culminated in July 2018 when Theresa May's Conservative Government announced that the duty to legislate against caste discrimination would be repealed at the next available legislative opportunity, arguing that the EA already provided appropriate protection against such discrimination under existing provisions on race discrimination.

---

23 See Chapter 5.
24 Ibid.
25 The UN Guidance Tool on Descent-Based Discrimination refers to the DPGs, explaining that because a person's caste can also be determinative of his or her occupation, caste-based discrimination is also addressed under the title 'discrimination based on work and descent'; see Guidance Tool on Descent-Based Discrimination; Key Challenges and Strategic Approaches to Combat Caste-Based and Analogous Forms of Discrimination (UN Network on Racial Discrimination and Protection of Minorities, 2017) 2.
26 See D Mosse, 'Caste and Development: Contemporary Perspectives on a Structure of Discrimination and Advantage', 110 *World Development* (2018) 422–436; N Saracini and M Shanmugavelan, *Caste and Development: Tackling Work and Descent-Based Discrimination to Achieve the SDGs for All* (London: Bond, 2019).
27 See Mosse, ibid.

Various reasons explain the stance of successive governments and their persistent refusal to legislate against caste discrimination, while governments themselves have put forward a variety of justifications. These include: unwillingness to accept that caste discrimination occurs in the fields regulated by the EA, coupled with conflicting claims about the numbers potentially affected (i.e. legislation is a disproportionate response to a small or non-existent problem) – arguments which reinforce the urgent need for further independent research on the phenomenon of domestic caste discrimination; the argument that caste discrimination is already prohibited under existing law on religious and racial discrimination, particularly under the ethnic origins subset of race (although there is no binding authority to this effect);[28] governmental aversion to the 'proliferation' of protected characteristics in anti-discrimination legislation, coupled with the belief that introducing statutory protection runs counter to the ideological imperative to reduce the 'legislative burden' on the private and public sector;[29] the argument that statutory references to caste will perpetuate, entrench or revitalise it as an undesirable social identifier which is of decreasing relevance to South Asians in the UK and, conversely, the influence of certain diaspora-based opponents of legislation who deny that caste discrimination occurs and have promoted an argument that related legislation amounts to an attack against a minority community, i.e. British Hindus (and British Indians more generally), because it labels them as discriminators. A radical version of this argument holds that the very idea of caste, and by extension the existence of caste discrimination, both in India and the diaspora, is a product of the European Christian colonial imagination, and that the demand for legislation is motivated by Protestant-Christian hostility to Hinduism and a desire to further conversions to Christianity in India and to pressurise India to extend constitutional affirmative action policies for the Scheduled Castes to Dalit Christians.[30]

This book shows that caste discrimination in the UK is not readily captured by existing religious discrimination provisions, and there is still no binding authority for its capture by existing provisions on race or ethnic origins; moreover, categorising caste as a form of ethnic origin under British law might result in the elevation of *jati* identities into legally recognised "free-standing" ethnic identities – the antithesis of Ambedkar's call for the 'annihilation of caste' or of Dalit identity as an anti-caste identity.[31] UK Governments must take the issue of caste discrimination seriously, since acquiescing to caste-based factionalism and fracture among a growing South Asian-origin population is damaging to intra- and inter-community cohesion and stores up long-term problems for the future. Caste discrimination is unlawful under international human rights law, and the UK's international obligations require it to be addressed by law, which for CERD and the UK's Equality and Human Rights Commission means an express legislative provision. Legislating would improve legal clarity and send a clear message that this type of discrimination is not acceptable, either socially or legally.

28 See Chapter 9.
29 See Chapter 8 and Chapter 9.
30 See P Shah, *Against Caste in British Law: A Critical Perspective on the Caste Discrimination Provision in the Equality Act 2010* (Basingstoke: Palgrave MacMillan, 2015). For an analysis and critique of this argument see D Mosse, 'Outside Caste? The Enclosure of Caste and Claims to Caste-Lessness in India and the United Kingdom', 62(1) *Comparative Studies in Society and History* (2020) 1–31; D Sutton ' "So-Called Caste": SN Balagangadhara, the Ghent School and the Politics of Grievance', 26(3) *Contemporary South Asia* (2018) 336–349.
31 See A Waughray, 'Caste Discrimination: A Twenty-First Century Challenge for UK Discrimination Law', 72(2) *Modern Law Review* (2009) 182–219.

Looking ahead

A crucial question is whether the problem to be addressed is caste discrimination or caste – and caste identity – per se, and whether caste discrimination is severable from caste and from caste identity. In the UK, it is too early to tell what effect Dalit political mobilisation and the assertion of Dalit and anti-caste identity (including anti-caste religious identities) will have on caste as a social phenomenon and/or the discrimination and casteist practices associated with caste divisions, or whether it is even possible to "retain" caste as an aspect of "cultural diversity", somehow de-coupled from casteist practices and discrimination.[32] In 2013, the UK Government justified its opposition to caste discrimination legislation by describing caste as 'inherently an undesirable concept',[33] which it did not want to perpetuate by enshrining in law, stating elsewhere 'we do not believe or accept that caste and caste divisions should have any long-term future in Britain'.[34] Conversely, a strand of opposition to caste discrimination legislation claims that it would threaten the existence of Indian *jati*-based (i.e. caste-based) organisations and 'associational life' (despite also arguing that neither caste nor caste discrimination exist in India or the UK).[35] The problem of what Balmurli Natrajan terms 'the culturalisation of caste', namely the promotion and valorisation of caste identity, including Dalit identity, as benign "cultural" identity in a multicultural society in the context of the promotion and protection of diversity, has been highlighted in this book.[36] Further studies are needed on this question in the UK context. Research suggests that the younger generation of British Dalits, while supporting the legal prohibition of caste discrimination in the UK, 'are less affected by ascriptions of caste inferiority because they identify less with caste hierarchy', even 'embrac[ing] caste difference and assert[ing] a separate identity, freed from the yoke of inferiority'.[37] However, older research suggests that notions of caste hierarchy, untouchability and inferiority underpin caste-based bullying among the young, for example

---

32 See Chapters 6 and 7. It is well-documented that migration and settlement in the UK invigorated and solidified caste identities (despite some examples of the subordination of caste identity to religious or anti-caste solidarity). The importance of caste identity for many dominant-caste Gujarati Hindus and Punjabis, whether Sikh or Muslim, and the role of caste organisations and associations in cementing communal identity in the UK, is also well-documented; M Dhanda, 'Caste and International Migration, India to the UK', in I Ness (ed.), *The Encyclopaedia of Global Human Migration* (Wiley Blackwell Online, 2013); M Dhanda, 'Casteism Amongst Punjabis in Britain', *Economic and Political Weekly* (21 January 2017) 62–65, 63. In 2014, the Liberal Democrats published an Equalities policy paper which juxtaposed recognition/celebration of caste identity with the promotion of an inclusive environment and community diversity. However, this stance is potentially in conflict with the assertion of Dalit identity as a radical anti-caste identity; see B Natrajan, 'Cultural Identity and Beef Festivals: Toward a "Multiculturalism Against Caste"', *Contemporary South Asia* (published online 25 July 2018).
33 HC Deb Vol 561 col 790 23 April 2013. The desire not to 'perpetuate caste' or to 'entrench caste as an identifier' by statutory references to it was given by the government as a reason for *not* legislating against caste discrimination.
34 Grant, Helen, Letter to the AHO dated 9 May 2013 (copy on file with author).
35 See P Shah, 'Caste Discrimination: Reflection Needed, not Legislation', *Law, Culture, Religion Blog*, 9 April 2013; copy on file with author. See also P Shah, *Against Caste in British Law: A Critical Perspective on the Caste Discrimination Provision in the Equality Act 2010* (Basingstoke: Palgrave Macmillan, 2015) 65. In fact, specifying caste as an aspect of race in the Equality Act 2010 would not prohibit organisations and associations based on a shared caste or *jati* identity.
36 See Natrajan (n 12).
37 M Dhanda. 'Held Back by In-Fighting: The Fraught Struggles for Recognition of Dalits in Wolverhampton', paper presented at the international conference 'The Internationalisation of Dalit and Adivasi Activism', University of London, 26 June 2012. Unpublished.

in schools.[38] Further research is required on the complex relationship between caste (and religious) identity and caste discrimination in the UK, as well as on its forms, manifestations and extent and its increase, decline or diversification. Regardless of whether the Equality Act 2010 is amended to prohibit caste discrimination, there is a great need for awareness-raising, education and training for employers, in the workplace, in the justice system, for young people, in schools and universities and for the general public. The onus of challenging caste and casteist practices must not fall on Dalits alone; the commitment of anti-caste non-Dalits from both South Asian and wider communities is essential. If equality legislation is amended to include caste as an aspect of race, the Public Sector Equality Duty in section 149 will apply to caste (unless an exception is introduced), requiring public bodies to exercise greater sophistication in dealing with South Asian minority groups by not treating such parties as homogenous, undifferentiated entities. The PSED duty could likewise come into play if caste is brought within the ambit of race via judicial interpretation (case law), as would the positive action provision in section 158. A return to the pre-2010 demand for caste to be added to equality legislation as a new, free-standing characteristic is also conceivable. At the same time, Dalit groups must grapple with the paradox of promoting an anti-caste identity or caste (*jati*) identities – or both – in challenging caste discrimination.

Caste discrimination as a global issue: the necessity and limits of law

Law is one of the primary means by which states and the international community identify, address and seek to rectify discrimination and inequality. Non-discrimination and equality have become fundamental normative elements of national, regional and international legal systems. This book highlights the difficulty in capturing caste in international and domestic law and has suggested some solutions. It also highlights the dynamic relationship between universal human rights standards and domestic protection from human rights violations, and the importance of connecting UN standards to national law, especially where national law has not succeeded in eradicating deep-rooted forms of discrimination, marginalisation and exclusion. The book calls for creative, holistic responses to the problem of caste discrimination, driven by a human rights approach, which include and yet go beyond legislative reform. It also highlights the importance of activism (social and civic action) in securing legal, political and social change. There has been a great deal of focus on formal transnational advocacy networks in recent years, but the case of British Dalits shows that domestic, grassroots activism by determined activists on a low budget, aligned with the right skills and strategy, can succeed in pushing caste into the political and legal mainstream, while in India there has been a surge in Dalit web forums and online activism which reference activists around the globe, including the Black Lives Matter movement in the USA.[39] Finally, the book is about the relationship between law and society as manifested in the case of caste.

---

38 See Chapter 6.
39 See AK Thakur, 'New Media and the Dalit Counter-Public Sphere', *Television and New Media*, published online 3 September 2019, 1–16, 1. As this book was being edited, a caste discrimination case brought by California's state civil rights agency, the California Department of Fair Employment and Housing, against CISCO, a California-based tech company employing a predominantly South Asian workforce, thrust caste and caste discrimination in the US into the mainstream media; see T Soundararajan, 'A New Lawsuit Shines a Light on Caste Discrimination in the U.S. and Around the World', *The Washington Post*, 13 July 2020; Y Raj, 'California State Sues Cisco for Caste-Based Workplace Bias', *Hindustan Times*, 2 July

Although the UK Government's 2018 announcement of its intention to repeal the statutory duty to add caste to race in the Equality Act 2010 is a setback for anti-caste activists, the failure of successive UK Governments hitherto to legislate against caste discrimination is not the final word on the subject, in the diaspora or elsewhere. There continues to be a need for education and legal training and development so that when suitable cases arise, judges are prepared and can develop the law accordingly, in line with the UK's international obligations under ICERD. Developments in common law protection, however, do not replace the need for distinct legislative protection against caste discrimination. Inequality and discrimination on grounds of caste are an affront to civilised society and have no place in twenty-first-century democracies, whether India, the UK or elsewhere. As the challenge to annihilate caste continues, effective legal protection and effective enforcement of the law in countries where caste discrimination occurs is essential if it is to be combated definitively and successfully.

2020. A civil claim filed in 2003 alleging *inter alia* discrimination on grounds of caste was dismissed on appeal when the applicant failed to establish a prima facie case of discrimination: *Mazumder v. University of Michigan* [2006] WL 2310822 (6th Cir.(Mich.)), [2006] Fed. App. 0570N; S. Roy, 'Indian American Files Lawsuit Alleging Caste Bias'; *Pacific News Service Civil Liberties Digest*, 9 July 2003.

Bibliography

Books

Abbas, T. (2005), *Muslim Britain: Communities under Pressure* (London: Zed Books)

Acharyya, B.K. (1914), *Codification in British India* (Calcutta: S.K. Banerji & Sons)

Addison, N. (2007), *Religious Discrimination and Hatred Law* (London: Routledge-Cavendish)

Addo, M. (2010), *The Legal Nature of International Human Rights Law* (The Hague: Martinus Nijhoff Publishers)

Ahmed, I. (1978), *Caste and Social Stratification Among Muslims in India* (New Delhi: Manohar)

Ajnat, S. (ed.) (1993), *Letters of Ambedkar* (Jalandhar: Bheem Patrika Publications)

Aktor, M. & Deliège, R. (eds.) (2010), *From Stigma to Assertion: Untouchability, Identity and Politics in Early Modern India* (Copenhagen: Museum Tusculanum Press)

Allott, A. (1980), *The Limits of Law* (London: Butterworths)

Alston, P. & Crawford, J. (eds.) (2000), *The Future of UN Human Rights Treaty Monitoring* (Cambridge: Cambridge University Press)

Ansari, I. (ed.) (1996), *Readings on Minorities: Perspectives and Documents Vol. 1* (New Delhi: Institute of Objective Studies)

Ansari, I. (ed.) (1996), *Readings on Minorities: Perspectives and Documents Vol. II* (New Delhi: Institute of Objective Studies)

Atal, Y. (1968), *The Changing Frontiers of Caste* (New Delhi: National Publishing House)

Austin, G. (1966), *The Indian Constitution: Cornerstone of a Nation* (New Delhi: Thirteenth Impression 2008, Oxford University Press)

Austin, G. (1999), *Working a Democratic Constitution: The Indian Experience* (New Delhi: Oxford University Press)

Avari, B. (2007), *India: The Ancient Past: A History of the Indian Sub-Continent from c.7000 BC to AD 1200* (Abingdon: Routledge)

Bahadur, G. (2017), *Ants Among Elephants: An Untouchable Family and the Making of Modern India* (New York: North Point Press)

Bailey, F.G. (1964), *Caste and the Economic Frontier* (Manchester: Manchester University Press)

Baird, R. (ed.) (1993), *Religion and Law in Independent India* (New Delhi: Manohar)

Ballard, R. (ed.) (1994), *Desh Pardesh: The South Asian Presence in Britain* (London: Hurst & Co)

Bamforth, N., Malik, M. & O'Cinneide, C. (2008), *Discrimination Law: Theory and Context* (London: Sweet and Maxwell)

Banton, M. (1996), *International Action Against Racial Discrimination* (Oxford: Oxford University Press)

Baxi, U. & Parekh, B. (eds.) (1995), *Crisis and Change in Contemporary India* (New Delhi: Sage)

Bayly, S. (1999), *Caste, Society and Politics in India from the Eighteenth Century to the Modern Age* (Cambridge: Cambridge University Press)

Benhabib, S. (1992), *Situating the Self: Gender, Community and Post-modernism in Contemporary Ethics* (Cambridge: Polity Press)

Berreman, G. (1979), *Caste and Other Inequalities: Essays on Inequality* (Meerut: Folklore Institute)

Bhachu, P. (1986), *The Twice Migrants* (London: Tavistock)

Bhatia (ed.) (1976), *Origin and Development of Legal and Political System in India, Vol. II* (New Delhi: Deep and Deep Publications)

Bhatt, C. (2001), *Hindu Nationalism: Origins, Ideologies and Modern Myths* (Oxford: Berg)

Boerefijn, I. (1999), *The Reporting Procedure Under the Covenant on Civil and Political Rights: Practice and Procedures of the Human Rights Committee* (Antwerp: Intersentia)

Boisson de Chazournes, L. & Gowlland-Debbas, V. (eds.) (2001), *The International Legal System in Quest of Equity and Universality* (The Hague: Martinus Nijhoff)

Bouglé, C. (1971), *Essais sur le régime des castes* (English translation. First published 1908, Cambridge: Cambridge University Press)

Bressey, C. (2013), *Empire, Race and the Politics of* Anti-Caste (London: Bloomsbury)

Brown, J. (2006), *Global South Asians: Introducing the Modern Diaspora* (Cambridge: Cambridge University Press)

Burton, M. (2008), *Legal Responses to Domestic Violence* (Abingdon: Routledge-Cavendish)

Castellino, J. & Dominguez-Redondo, E. (2006), *Minority Rights in Asia: A Comparative Analysis* (New Delhi: Oxford University Press)

Castellino, J. & Walsh, N. (eds.) (2005), *International Law and Indigenous Peoples* (Leiden: Martinus Nijhoff Publishers)

Clarke, C., Peach, C. & Vertovec, S. (eds.) (1990), *South Asians Overseas: Migration and Ethnicity* (Cambridge: Cambridge University Press)

Cohn, B. (2012), *An Anthropologist Among the Historians and Other Essays* (First published 1987. New Delhi: Oxford University Press)

Cowell, H. (1936), *History and Constitution of the Courts and Legislative Authorities in India*, 6th Edition (Calcutta: Thacker, Spink & Co.)

Craven, M. (1995), *The International Covenant on Economic, Social and Cultural Rights: A Perspective on Its Development* (Oxford: Clarendon)

Das, G. (2000), *India Unbound* (New Delhi: Penguin Books India)

Davidson, M. & Fielden, S. (eds.) (2003), *Individual Diversity and Psychology in Organisations* (Oxford: Wiley)

Davies, M. (2008), *Asking the Law Question* (Pyrmont: Thomson Lawbook Co.)

de Reuck, A. & Knight, J. (eds.) (1967), *Caste and Race: Comparative Approaches* (London: J. & A. Churchill Ltd.)

Derrett, J.D.M. (1968), *Religion, Law and the State in India* (London: Faber & Faber)

Derrett, J.D.M. (1973), *Dharmasastra and Juridical Literature* (Wiesbaden: Otto Harrassowitz)

Desai, R. (1963), *Indian Immigrants in Britain* (Oxford: Oxford University Press)

Deshpande, A. (2011), *The Grammar of Caste: Economic Discrimination in Contemporary India* (New Delhi: Oxford University Press)

Deshpande, A. (2016), *Affirmative Action in India* (New Delhi: Oxford University Press)

Desika Char, S.V. (1963), *Centralised Legislation: A History of the Legislative System of British India from 1843 to 1861* (London: Asia Publishing House)

Desika Char, S.V. (1983), *Readings in the Constitutional History of India 1957–1947* (New Delhi: Oxford University Press)

Desika Char, S.V. (1997), *Hinduism and Islam in India: Caste, Religion and Society from Antiquity to Early Modern Times* (Princeton: Markus Wiener Publishers)

Din, I. (2006), *The New British: The Impact of Culture and Community on Young Pakistanis* (Aldershot: Ashgate)

Dirks, N.B. (2002), *Castes of Mind: Colonialism and the Making of Modern India* (New Delhi: Permanent Black)

Donald, J. & Rattansi, A. (eds.) (1992), *'Race', Culture and Difference* (London: Sage)

Doniger, W. (trans.) (1981), *The Rig Veda* (London: Penguin Books)

Doniger, W. (2010), *The Hindus: An Alternative History* (Oxford: Oxford University Press)

Donnelly, J. (2003), *Universal Human Rights in Theory and Practice* (New York: Cornell University Press)

Douglas, M. (2002), *Purity and Danger* (First published 1966. London: Routledge)

Dudley Jenkins, L. (2003), *Identity and Identification in India; Defining the Disadvantaged* (New York: RoutledgeCurzon)

Dugard, J. (1978), *Human Rights and the South African Legal Order* (Princeton: Princeton University Press)

Dumont, L. (1980), *Homo Hierarchicus: The Caste System and its Implications* (Chicago: University of Chicago Press)

Edwardes, M. (1967), *British India 1772–1947* (London: Sidgewick & Jackson)

Eide, A. & Alfredsson, G. (1992), *The Universal Declaration of Human Rights: A Commentary* (Oslo: Scandinavian University Press)

Eide, A. & Alfredsson, G. (1999), *The Universal Declaration of Human Rights: A Common Standard of Achievement* (The Hague: Martinus Nijhoff Publishers)

Eisenberg, A. & Spinner-Haley, J. (eds.) (2004), *Minorities within Minorities: Equality, Rights and Diversity* (Cambridge: Cambridge University Press)

Essed, P. (1991), *Understanding Everyday Racism: An Interdisciplinary Theory* (Thousand Oaks, CA: Sage)

Fatima, S. (2005), *Using International Law in Domestic Courts* (Oxford: Hart)

Flood, G. (1998), *An Introduction to Hinduism* (Cambridge: Cambridge University Press)

Flood, G. (ed.) (2005), *The Blackwell Companion to Hinduism* (Oxford: Blackwell)

Frankenburg, R. (1993), *White Women, Race Matters: The Social Construction of Whiteness* (Minneapolis: University of Minnesota Press)

Fraser, N. (2010), *Scales of Justice: Reimagining Political Space in a Globalised World* (New York: Columbia University Press)

Fraser, N. & Honneth, A. (2003), *Redistribution or Recognition? A Political-Philosophical Exchange* (London: Verso)

Fredman, S. (ed.) (2001), *Discrimination and Human Rights: The Case of Racism* (Oxford: Oxford University Press)

Fredman, S. (2011a), *Discrimination Law* (Oxford: Oxford University Press)

Fredman, S. (2011b), *Comparative Study of Anti-Discrimination and Equality Laws of the US, Canada, South Africa and India* (Luxembourg: European Commission, Directorate-General for Justice)

Galanter, M. (1984), *Competing Equalities: Law and the Backward Classes in India* (Berkeley: University of California Press)

Galanter, M. (1994), *Law and Society in Modern India* (First published 1989, New Delhi; Berkeley: University of California Press)

Gardner Cassels, N. (2010), *Social Legislation of the East India Company* (New Delhi: Sage)

Ghuriye, G.S. (1969), *Caste and Race in India* (Mumbai: Popular Prakashan Pvt. Ltd.)

Gupta, D. (ed.) (2004), *Caste in Question: Identity or Hierarchy?* (New Delhi: Sage)

Guru, G. (ed.) (2011), *Humiliation: Claims and Context* (First published 2009. New Delhi: Oxford University Press)

Hardtmann, E.-M. (2009), *The Dalit Movement in India: Local Practices, Global Connections* (New Delhi: Oxford University Press)

Hasan, Z. (2009), *Politics of Inclusion: Castes, Minorities and Affirmative Action* (New Delhi: Oxford University Press)

Hepple, B. (2011), *Equality: The New Legal Framework* (Oxford: Hart)

Hepple, B. & Szyszczak, E. (eds.) (1993), *Discrimination: The Limits of the Law* (London: Mansell)

Hess, B. (2000), *Un/Settled Multiculturalisms: Diasporas, Entanglements, Transruptions* (London: Zed Books)

Hofer, A. (1979), *The Caste Hierarchy and the State in Nepal: A Study of the Muluki Ain of 1858* (Innsbruck: Universitatsverlag Wagner)

Hutton, J.H. (1946), *Caste in India: Its Nature, Function and Origins* (Cambridge: Cambridge University Press)

Inden, R.B. (2000), *Imagining India* (London: Hurst & Co.)

Ingram, D. (2004), *Rights, Democracy and Fulfilment in the Era of Identity Politics: Principled Compromises in a Compromised World* (Lanham: Rowman and Littlefield Publishers)

Jacobsen, K. & Raj, S. (2008), *South Asian Christian Diaspora: Invisible Diaspora in Europe and North America* (Farnham: Ashgate)

Jacobson, J. (2004), *Islam in Transition: Religion and Identity Among British Pakistani Youth* (Abingdon: Routledge)

Jaffrelot, C. (2003), *India's Silent Revolution: The Rise of the Low Castes in North Indian Politics* (New Delhi: Permanent Black)

Jaffrelot, C. (2005), *Dr Ambedkar and Untouchability: Analysing and Fighting Caste* (New Delhi: Permanent Black)

Jaffrelot, C. (2007), *Hindu Nationalism: A Reader* (Princeton: Princeton University Press)

Jayal, N.G. & Pai, S. (2001), *Democratic Governance in India: Challenges of Poverty, Development and Identity* (New Delhi: Sage)

Jones, H. (1930), *The Geography of Strabo (Vol. 7)* (Reprint, Loeb Classical Library. Cambridge, MA: Harvard University Press)

Jones, R. & Welhengama, G. (2000), *Ethnic Minorities in English Law* (Stoke-on-Trent: Trentham)

Joseph, S., Schulz, J. & Castan, M. (2000), *The International Covenant on Civil and Political Rights: Cases, Materials and Commentary* (Oxford: Oxford University Press)

Joshi, B. (ed.) (1986), *Untouchable: Voices of the Dalit Liberation Movement* (London: Zed Books)

Juergensmeyer, M. (1982), *Religion as Social Vision: The Movement Against Untouchability in 20th Century Punjab* (Berkeley: University of California Press)

Kane, P.V. (1930), *History of Dharmasastra (Ancient and Medieval Religion and Civil Law) Vol. 1* (Poona: Bhandarkar Oriental Research Institute)

Kannan, C.T. (1978), *Cultural Adaptation of Asian Immigrants: First and Second Generation* (Greenford: C.T. Kannan)

Keane, D. (2007), *Caste-Based Discrimination in International Human Rights Law* (Aldershot: Ashgate)

Keane, D. & Waughray, A. (eds.) (2017), *The International Convention on the Elimination of All Forms of Racial Discrimination: A Living Instrument* (Manchester: Manchester University Press)

Kelly, K. (2003), *Domestic Violence and the Politics of Privacy* (New York: Cornell University Press)

Ketkar, S.V. & Sridhar, V. (2010), *History of Caste in India* (First published 1909, New Delhi: Low Price Publications)

Killingley, D. (ed.) (1991), *The Sanskritic Tradition in the Modern World (2): Hindu Ritual and Society* (Newcastle-upon-Tyne: S.Y. Killingley)

Kothari, R. (ed.) (1995), *Caste in Indian Politics* (Hyderabad: Orient Longman)

Kumar, D. (1965), *Land and Caste in South India: Agricultural Labour in the Madras Presidency During the Nineteenth Century* (Cambridge: Cambridge University Press)

Kumar, V.S. (2006), *India's Roaring Revolution: Dalit Assertion and New Horizons* (New Delhi: Gagandeep)

Kumar, V.S. (2008), *Social Justice and the Politics of Reservation in India* (New Delhi: Mittal Publications)

Kuper, H. (1961), *Indian People in Natal* (Durban: Natal University Press)

Lamb, R. (2002), *Rapt in the Name: The Ramnamis, Ramnam, and Untouchable Religion in Central India* (Berkeley: State University of New York Press)

Lapierre, D. & Collins, L. (1997), *Freedom at Midnight* (New Delhi: Vikas Publishing House Pvt. Ltd.)

Law, N. (1914), *Studies in Ancient Hindu Polity Vol. I* (London: Longmans, Green & Co.)

Lawson, P. (1987), *The East India Company: A History* (London: Longman)

Leslie, J. (2003), *Authority and Meaning in Indian Religions: Hinduism and the Case of Valmiki* (Aldershot: Ashgate)

Lester, A. & Bindman, G. (1972), *Race and Law* (London: Penguin/Longman)

Lingat, R. (2004), *The Classical Law of India* (First published 1973. Oxford: Oxford University Press)

Lipner, J. (1994), *Hindus: Their Religious Beliefs and Practices* (London: Routledge)

Lok Sabha Secretariat. (2000), *50th Anniversary of the Republic of India* (New Delhi: Lok Sabha Secretariat)

Lubin, T., Davis, D. & Krishnan, J. (eds.) (2010), *Hinduism and Law: An Introduction* (Cambridge: Cambridge University Press)

Lustgarten, L. (1980), *Legal Control of Racial Discrimination* (London: MacMillan Press)

MacDonald, I. (1977), *Race Relations and the Law* (London: Butterworths)

Maisels, C. (2010), *Archaeology of Politics and Power: When, Where and Why the First States Formed* (Oxford: Oxbow Books)

Majumdar, R.C. (ed.) (1960), *The History and Culture of the Indian People: Vol. VI The Delhi Sultanate* (Bombay: Bharatiya Vidya Bhavan)

Majumdar, R.C. (ed.) (1974), *The History and Culture of the Indian People: Vol. VII The Mughal Empire* (Bombay: Bharatiya Vidya Bhavan)

Mandelbaum, D. (1970), *Society in India, Vol. 2: Change and Continuity* (Berkeley: University of California Press)

Mander, H. (2001), *Unheard Voices: Stories of Forgotten Lives* (New Delhi: Penguin)

McColgan, A. (2005), *Discrimination Law: Texts, Cases and Materials* (Oxford: Hart)

McConville, M. & Hong Chui, W. (eds.) (2007), *Research Methods for Law* (Edinburgh: Edinburgh University Press)

Mendelsohn, O. & Vicziany, M. (1998), *The Untouchables: Subordination and Poverty and the State in Modern India* (Cambridge: Cambridge University Press)

Menski, W. (2006), *Comparative Law in a Global Context: The Legal Systems of Asia and Africa* (Cambridge: Cambridge University Press)

Michael, S.M. (ed.) (2007), *Dalits in Modern India: Vision and Values* (New Delhi: Sage)

Mittal, S. & Thursby, G. (eds.) (2007), *The Hindu World* (Abingdon: Routledge)

Moffat, M. (1979), *An Untouchable Community of South India* (Princeton: Princeton University Press)

Moon, V. (ed.) (1979), *Dr Babasaheb Ambedkar Writings and Speeches, Vol. 1* (Bombay: Education Dept., Govt. of Maharasthra)

Moon, V. (ed.) (1989), *Dr Babasaheb Ambedkar Writings and Speeches, Vol. 5* (Bombay: Education Dept., Govt. of Maharasthra)

Moon, V. (ed.) (1991), *Dr Babasaheb Ambedkar Writings and Speeches, Vol. 9* (Bombay: Education Dept., Govt. of Maharasthra)

Moon, V. (ed.) (1993), *Dr Babasaheb Ambedkar Writings and Speeches, Vol. 12* (Bombay: Education Dept., Govt. of Maharasthra)

Moon, V. (ed.) (1994), *Dr Babasaheb Ambedkar Writings and Speeches, Vol. 13* (Bombay: Education Dept., Govt. of Maharasthra)

Morsink, J. (1999), *The Universal Declaration of Human Rights: Origins, Drafting and Intent* (Philadelphia: University of Pennsylvania Press)

Morton, S. (2003), *Gayatri Chakravorty Spivak* (Abingdon: Routledge)

Mosse, D. (2012), *The Saint in the Banyan Tree: Christianity and Caste Society in India* (Berkeley: University of California Press)

Mullally, S. (2006), *Gender, Culture and Human Rights* (Oxford: Hart)

Nakano, K., Yutzis, M. & Onoyama, R. (eds.) (2004), *Peoples for Human Rights Vol. 9: Descent-Based Discrimination* (Tokyo: International Movement Against All Forms of Discrimination and Racism)

Narke, H. (ed.) (2005), *Dr Babasaheb Ambedkar Writings and Speeches Vol. 2* (Bombay: Education Dept., Govt. of Maharasthra)

Natrajan, B. (2010), *The Culturalization of Caste in India: Identity and Inequality in a Multicultural Age* (Abingdon: Routledge)

Natrajan, B. & Greenough, P. (eds.) (2009), *Against Stigma: Studies in Caste, Race and Justice Since Durban* (Hyderabad: Orient Blackswan)

Nesbitt, E. (2004), *Intercultural Education: Ethnographic and Religious Approaches* (Brighton: Sussex Academic Press)

Nowak, M. (2005), *UN Covenant on Civil and Political Rights: CCPR Commentary* (Kehl: N.P. Engel)

O'Hanlon, R. (1985), *Caste, Conflict and Ideology: Mahatma Jotirao Phule and Low Caste Protest in the Nineteenth-Century Western India* (Cambridge: Cambridge University Press)

Olivelle, P. (1999), *Dharmasutras: The Law Codes of Ancient India* (New Delhi: Oxford University Press)

Olivelle, P. (2004), *The Law Code of Manu* (Oxford: Oxford University Press)

Olivelle, P. (2012), *The Arthasastra: Selections from the Classic Indian Work on Statecraft* (Indianapolis: Hackett)

Olivelle, P. (2013), *King, Governance, and Law in Ancient India: Kautilya's Arthasastra* (New York: Oxford University Press)

Olivelle, P. (2016), *A Dharma Reader: Classical Indian Law* (New York: Columbia University Press)

Omvedt, G. (1994), *Dalits and the Democratic Revolution: Dr Ambedkar and the Dalit Movement in Colonial India* (New Delhi: Sage)

Omvedt, G. (2004), *Ambedkar: Towards an Enlightened India* (New Delhi: Penguin Books)

Omvedt, G. (2008), *Seeking Begumpura: The Social Vision of Anti-Caste Intellectuals* (New Delhi: Navayana Publishing)

Omvedt, G. (2011), *Understanding Caste: From Buddha to Ambedkar and Beyond* (Hyderabad: Orient Blackswan)

Ovichegen, S. (2015), *Faces of Discrimination in Higher Education in India: Quota Policy, Social Justice and the Dalits* (London: Routledge)

Pai, S. (2002), *Dalit Assertion and the Unfinished Democratic Revolution: The Bahujan Samaj Party in Uttar Pradesh* (New Delhi: Sage)

Pandit, V.L. (1979), *The Scope of Happiness: A Personal Memoir* (New York: Crown)

Parasher-Sen, A. (ed.) (2004), *Subordinate and Marginal Groups in Early India* (New Delhi: Oxford University Press)

Parekh, B. (2006), *Rethinking Multiculturalism: Cultural Diversity and Political Theory* (Basingstoke: Palgrave MacMillan)

Poulter, S. (1998), *Ethnicity, Law and Human Rights: The English Experience* (Oxford: Clarendon Press)

Prakash, A. (2015), *Dalit Capital: State, Markets and Civil Society in Urban India* (New Delhi: Routledge)

Rajkumar, P. (2010), *Dalit Theology and Dalit Liberation: Problems, Paradigms and Possibilities* (Aldershot: Ashgate)

Rajshekar, V.T. (1995), *Dalits: The Black Untouchables of India* (Atlanta: Clarity Press)

Ramaswamy, G. (2005), *India Stinking: Manual Scavengers in Andhra Pradesh and Their Work* (Pondicherry: Navayana Publishing)

Rao, A. (ed.) (2006), *Gender and Caste* (New Delhi: Kali for Women)

Rao, A. (2009), *The Caste Question: Dalits and the Politics of Modern India* (Berkeley: University of California Press)

Risley, H.H. (2003), *The People of India* (Reprint, first published in 1915, New Delhi: Low Price Publications)

Robb, P. (ed.) (1997), *The Concept of Race in South Asia* (New Delhi: Oxford University Press)

Robinson, V. (1986), *Transients and Settlers: Asians in Britain* (Oxford: Clarendon Press)

Robinson, R. & Kujur, J.M. (eds.) (2010), *Margins of Faith: Dalit and Tribal Christianity in India* (New Delhi: Sage)

Rodrigues, V. (ed.) (2002), *The Essential Writings of B.R. Ambedkar* (New Delhi: Oxford University Press)

Said, E. (2003), *Orientalism* (London: Penguin)

Sainath, P. (1996), *Everyone Loves a Good Drought: Stories from India's Poorest Districts* (London: Review)

Sargeant, M. (ed.) (2004), *Discrimination Law* (Harlow: Pearson Education Ltd.)

Schneider, E. (2000), *Battered Women and Feminist Lawmaking* (New Haven: Yale University Press)

Searle-Chatterjee, M. & Sharma, U. (1994), *Contextualising Caste: Post-Dumontian Approaches* (Oxford: Blackwell Publishers)

Seneviratne, H.I. (ed.) (1999), *Identity, Consciousness and the Past: Forging of Caste and Community in India and Sri Lanka* (New Delhi: Oxford University Press)

Shah, A., Lerche, J., et al. (2018), *Ground Down by Growth: Tribe, Caste, Class and Inequality in Twenty-First-Century India* (London: Pluto Press)

Shah, G. (ed.) (2001), *Dalit Identity and Politics* (New Delhi: Sage)

Shah, G. (2002), *Caste and Democratic Politics in India* (New Delhi: Permanent Black)

Shah, G., Mander, H., Thorat, S. et al. (2006), *Untouchability in Rural India* (New Delhi: Sage)

Shah, P. (2015), *Against Caste in British Law: A Critical Perspective on the Caste Discrimination Provision in the Equality Act 2010* (Basingstoke: Palgrave MacMillan)

Shani, O. (2007), *Communalism, Caste and Hindu Nationalism: The Violence in Gujarat* (Cambridge: Cambridge University Press)

Sharma, A. (2003), *Hinduism and Human Rights: A Conceptual Approach* (New Delhi: Oxford University Press)

Sharma, G. (2004), *Human Rights and Social Justice* (New Delhi: Deep & Deep Publications Pvt. Ltd.)

Sharma, U. (2002), *Caste* (New Delhi: 'Viva Books)

Shaw, A. (2000), *Kinship and Continuity: Pakistani Families in Britain* (Abingdon: Routledge)

Shiva Rao, B. (1966), *The Framing of India's Constitution, Select Documents Vol. 1* (New Delhi: The Indian Institute of Public Administration)

Shiva Rao, B. (1968), *The Framing of India's Constitution: A Study* (New Delhi: The Indian Institute of Public Administration)

Shridhar, V. & Ketkar, A.M. (1909), *The History of Castes in India* (Ithaca, NY: Taylor and Carpenter)

Singh, U. (2015), *A History of Ancient and Early Medieval India* (New Delhi: Pearson)

Singh Kalsi, S. (1989), *The Sikhs and Caste: A Study of the Sikh Community in Leeds and Bradford. PhD Thesis, University of Leeds* (Leeds: University of Leeds)

Singh Kalsi, S. (1992), *The Evolution of a Sikh Community in Britain* (Leeds: University of Leeds, Department of Theology and Religious Studies)

Smart, C. (1989), *Feminism and the Power of Law* (London: Routledge)

Smith, B. (1994), *Classifying the Universe: The Ancient Indian Varna System and the Origins of Caste* (New York: Oxford University Press)

Subramanian, A. (2019), *The Caste of Merit: Engineering Education in India* (Cambridge, MA: Harvard University Press)

Talbot, C. (2001), *Precolonial India in Practice; Society Region, and Identity in Medieval Andhra* (Oxford: Oxford University Press)

Teltumbde, A. (2008), *Khairlanji: A Strange and Bitter Crop* (New Delhi: Navayana Publishing)

Teltumbde, A. (2018), *Republic of Caste* (New Delhi: Navayana)

Thalbot, I. & Thandi, S. (eds.) (2004), *People on the Move: Punjabi Colonial and Post-Colonial Migration* (Oxford: Oxford University Press)

Thapar, R. (2002), *The Penguin History of Early India from the Origins to AD 1300* (New Delhi: Penguin Books)

Thapar, R. (2009), *Ancient Indian Social History: Some Interpretations* (Reprint, first published 1978. Hyderabad: Orient BlackSwan/Orient Longman)

Thorat, S. & Kumar, N. (eds.) (2008a), *In Search of Inclusive Policy: Addressing Graded Inequality* (Jaipur: Rawat)

Thorat, S. & Kumar, N. (eds.) (2008b), *B.R. Ambedkar: Perspectives on Social Exclusion and Inclusive Policies* (New Delhi: Oxford University Press)

Thorat, S. & Newman, K. (2011), *Blocked by Caste: Economic Discrimination in Modern India* (New Delhi: Oxford University Press)

Thorat, S. & Umakant (eds.) (2004), *Caste, Race and Discrimination: Discourses in an International Context* (New Delhi/Jaipur: Rawat/Indian Institute of Dalit Studies)

Thornberry, P. (1991), *International Law and the Rights of Minorities* (Oxford: Clarendon Press)

Thornberry, P. (2002), *Indigenous Peoples and Human Rights* (Manchester: Manchester University Press)

Thornberry, P. (2016), *The International Convention on the Elimination of All Forms of Racial Discrimination: A Commentary* (Oxford: Oxford University Press)

Thornton, M. (1995), *Public and Private: Feminist Legal Debates* (Oxford: Oxford University Press)

Visram, R. (2002), *Asians in Britain: 400 Years of History* (London: Pluto Press)

Viswanath, R. (2014), *The Pariah Problem: Caste, Religion and the Social in Modern India* (New York: Columbia University Press)

Waghmore, S. (2013), *Civility Against Caste: Dalit Politics and Citizenship in Western India* (New Delhi: Sage)

Wakaner, C. (2010), *Subalternity and Religion: The Prehistory of Dalit Empowerment in South Asia* (Abingdon: Routledge)

Weisskopf, T. (2004), *Affirmative Action in the United States and India: A Comparative Perspective* (London: Routledge)

Wilkerson, I. (2020), *Caste: The Lies That Divide Us* (London: Allen Lane)

Wolpert, S. (2000), *A New History of India*, 6th edition (Oxford: Oxford University Press)

Wolpert, S. (2009), *A New History of India*, 8th edition (Oxford: Oxford University Press)

Zavos, J. (2000), *The Emergence of Hindu Nationalism in India* (New Delhi: Oxford University Press)

Zelliot, E. (1998), *From Untouchable to Dalit: Essays on the Ambedkar Movement* (New Delhi: Manohar)

Zinkin, T. (1962), *Caste Today* (London: Oxford University Press)

Chapters in books

Allen, C. (2005), 'From Race to Religion: The New Face of Discrimination' in Abbas, T. (ed.), *Muslim Britain: Communities Under Pressure* (London: Zed Books)

Alston, P. (2001), 'The Historical Origins of the Concept of "General Comments" in Human Rights Law' in Boisson de Chazournes, L. & Gowlland-Debbas, V. (eds.), *The International Legal System in Question of Equity and Universality* (The Hague: Martinus Nijhoff Publishing)

Ambedkar, B.R. (1989a), 'Annihilation of Caste' in Moon, V. (ed.), *Dr Babasaheb Ambedkar Writings and Speeches, Vol. 1* (Bombay: Education Dept., Govt. of Maharasthra)

Ambedkar, B.R. (1989b), 'Castes in India: Seminar Paper' in Moon, V. (ed.), *Dr Babasaheb Ambedkar Writings and Speeches, Vol. 1* (Reprint, Bombay: Education Dept., Govt. of Maharasthra)

Ambedkar, B.R. (1989c), 'Outside the Fold' in Moon, V. (ed.), *Dr Babasaheb Ambedkar Writings and Speeches, Vol. 5* (Bombay: Education Dept., Govt. of Maharasthra)

Ambedkar, B.R. (1991a), 'The Real Issue' in Moon, V. (ed.), *Dr Babasaheb Ambedkar Writings and Speeches, Vol. 9* (Bombay: Education Dept., Govt. of Maharasthra)

Ambedkar, B.R. (1991b), 'What Congress and Gandhi Have Done to Untouchables' in Moon, V. (ed.), *Dr Babasaheb Ambedkar Writings and Speeches, Vol. 9* (Bombay: Education Dept., Govt. of Maharasthra)

Ambedkar, B.R. (1993), 'The Untouchables and the Pax Britannica' in Moon, V. (ed.), *Dr Babasaheb Ambedkar Writings and Speeches, Vol. 12* (Bombay: Education Dept., Govt. of Maharasthra)

Ballard, R. (1994a), 'Differentiation and Disjunction Among the Sikhs' in Ballard, R. (ed.), *Desh Pardesh: The South Asian Presence in Britain* (London: Hurst & Co.)

Ballard, R. (1994b), 'The Emergence of Desh Pardesh' in Ballard, R. (ed.), *Desh Pardesh: The South Asian Presence in Britain* (London: Hurst & Co.)

Banks, M. (1994), 'Jain Ways of Being' in Ballard, R. (ed.), *Desh Pardesh: The South Asian Presence in Britain* (London: Hurst & Co.)

Bates, C. (1997), 'Race, Caste and Tribe in Central India: The Early Origins of Indian Anthropometry' in Robb, P, (ed.), *The Concept of Race in South Asia* (New Delhi: Oxford University Press)

Baxi, U. (1995), 'Emancipation as Justice: Babasaheb Ambedkar's Legacy and Vision' in Baxi, U. & Parekh, B. (eds.), *Crisis and Change in Contemporary India* (New Delhi: Sage Publications)

Bayly, S. (1997), 'Caste and "Race" in the Colonial Ethnography of India' in Robb, P. (ed.), *The Concept of Race in South Asia* (New Delhi: Oxford University Press)

Beteille, A. (2004), 'Race and Caste' in Thorat, S. & Umakant (eds.), *Caste, Race and Discrimination: Discourses in International Context* (New Delhi/Jaipur: Rawat)

Bhatty, Z. (1996), 'Social Stratification Among Muslims in India' in Srinivas, M.N. (ed.), *Caste: Its Twentieth Century Avatar* (New Delhi: Penguin)

Boyle, K. & Baldaccini, A. (2001), 'International Human Rights Approaches to Racism' in Fredman, S. (ed.), *Discrimination and Human Rights: The Case of Racism* (Oxford: Oxford University Press)

Coward, H. (1993), 'India's Constitution and Traditional Presuppositions Regarding Human Nature' in Baird, R. (ed.), *Religion and the Law in Independent India* (New Delhi: Manohar)

Davis, D. (2010), 'A Historical Overview of Hindu Law' in Lubin, T., Davis, D. & Krishnan, J. (eds.), *Hinduism and Law: An Introduction* (Cambridge: Cambridge University Press)

Deliege, R. (2010), 'Introduction: Is There Still Untouchability in India?' in Aktor, M. & Deliege, R. (eds.), *From Stigma to Assertion: Untouchability, Identity and Politics in Early and Modern India* (Copenhagen: Museum Tusculanum Press)

Deshpande, S. (2008a), 'Exclusive Inequalities' in Thorat, S. & Kumar, N. (eds.), *In Search of Inclusive Policy: Addressing Graded Inequality* (Jaipur: Rawat Publications)

Deshpande, S. (2008b), 'Caste and Diversity in India' in Davis, J. & Dolfsma, W. (eds.), *Elgar Companion to Social Economics* (Cheltenham: Edward Elgar, 2015)

deSouza, P. (2011), 'Humiliation in a Crematorium' in Guru, G. (ed.), *Humiliation: Claims and Context* (New Delhi: Oxford University Press India)

Dirks, N. (1999), 'The Invention of Caste: Civil Society in Colonial India' in Seneviratne, H.L. (ed.), *Identity, Consciousness and the Past: Forging of Caste and Community in India and Sri Lanka* (New Delhi: Oxford University Press)

Dube, C.S. (1968), 'Foreword' in Atal, Y. (ed.), *The Changing Frontiers of Caste* (New Delhi: National Publishing House)

Eisenberg, A. (2004), 'Identity and Liberal Politics: The Problem of Minorities Within Minorities' in Eisenberg, A. & Spinner-Haley, J. (eds.), *Minorities Within Minorities: Equality, Rights and Racial Diversity* (Cambridge: Cambridge University Press)

Fell McDermott, R. (2008), 'From Hinduism to Christianity, from India to New York: Bondage and Exodus Experiences in the Lives of Indian Dalit Christians in the Diaspora' in Jacobson, J. & Raj, S. (eds.), *South Asian Christian Diaspora: Invisible Diaspora in Europe and North America* (Farnham: Ashgate)

Geetha, V. (2011), 'The Humiliation of Untouchability' in G. Guru (ed.), *Humiliation: Claims and Context* (New Delhi: Oxford University Press)

Gorringe, H. (2013), 'Dalit Politics: Untouchability, Identity and Assertion' in Kohli, A. & Singh, P. (eds.), *Routledge Handbook of Indian Politics* (Abingdon: Routledge)

Guru, G. (2009), 'What It Means to Be an Indian Dalit: Dalit Responses to the Durban Conference' in Natrajan, B. & Greenough, P. (eds.), *Against Stigma: Studies in Caste, Race and Justice Since Durban* (Hyderabad: Orient Blackswan)

Hall, S. (1992), 'New Ethnicities' in Donald, J. & Rattansi A. (eds.), *Race, Culture and Difference* (London: Sage)

Hall, S. (2000), 'Conclusions: The Multicultural Question' in Hess, B. (ed.), *Un/Settled Multiculturalisms: Diasporas, Entanglements, Transruptions* (London: Zed Books)

Hanumanthan, K.R. (2004), 'Evolution of Untouchability in Tamil Nadu up to AD 1600' in Parasher-Sen (ed.), *Subordinate and Marginal Groups in Early India* (New Delhi: Oxford University Press)

Hinnells, J. (1994), 'Parsi Zoroastrians in London' in Ballard, R. (ed.), *Desh Pardesh: The South Asian Presence in Britain* (London: Hurst & Co.)

Holdrege, B. (2007), 'Dharma' in Mittal, S. & Thursby, G. (eds.), *The Hindu World* (Abingdon: Routledge)

Jha, V. (2004), 'Candala and the Origin of Untouchability' in Parasher-Sen (ed.), *Subordinate and Marginal Groups in Early India* (New Delhi: Oxford University Press)

Killingley, D. (1991), 'Varna and Caste in Hindu Apologetic' in Killingley, D. (ed.), *The Sanskritic Tradition in the Modern World (2): Hindu Ritual and Society* (Newcastle upon Tyne: S.Y. Killingley)

Lacey, N. (1993), 'From Individual to Group' in Hepple, B. & Szyszczak, E. (eds.), *Discrimination: The Limits of the Law* (London: Mansell)

Leach, E. (1967), 'The Taxonomic Problem' in de Reuck, A. & Knight, J. (eds.), *Caste and Race: Comparative Approaches* (London: J. & A. Churchill Ltd.)

Mahajan, G. (2004), 'Can Intra-Group Equality Co-Exist with Cultural Diversity?' in Eisenberg, A. & Spinner-Haley, J. (eds.), *Minorities with Minorities: Equality, Rights and Racial Diversity* (Cambridge: Cambridge University Press)

Marriot, M. (2007), 'Varna and Jati' in Mittal, S. & Thursby, G. (eds.), *The Hindu World* (Abingdon: Routledge)

McGee, M. (2007), 'Samskara' in Mittal, S. & Thursby, G. (eds.), *The Hindu World* (Abingdon: Routledge)

Menski, W. (1993), 'The Indian Experience and Its Lessons for Britain' in Hepple, B. & Szyszczak, E. (eds.), *Discrimination: The Limits of the Law* (London: Mansell)

Michaels, A. (2010), 'The Practices of Classical Hindu Law' in Lubin, T., Davis, D. & Krishnan, J. (eds.), *Hinduism and Law: An Introduction* (Cambridge: Cambridge University Press)

Mitra, S.K. (1994), 'Caste, Democracy and the Politics of Community Formation in India' in Sharma, U. & Searle-Chatterjee, M. (eds.), *Contextualising Caste: Post-Dumontian Approaches* (Oxford: Blackwell)

Nesbitt, E. (1994), 'Valmikis in Coventry: The Revival and Reconstruction of a Community' in Ballard, R. (ed.), *Desh Pardesh: The South Asian Presence in Britain* (London: Hurst & Co.)

Panini, M. (1996), 'The Political Economy of Caste' in Srinivas, M.N. (ed.), *Caste: Its Twentieth Century Avatar* (New Delhi: Penguin)

Parasher-Sen, A. (2004), 'Introduction' in Parasher-Sen (ed.), *Subordinate and Marginal Groups in Early India* (New Delhi: Oxford University Press)

Patton, L. (2007), 'Veda and Upanishad' in Mittal, S. & Thursby, G. (eds.), *The Hindu World* (Abingdon: Routledge)

Prove, P. (2004a), 'Caste at the World Conference Against Racism' in Thorat, S. & Umakant (eds.), *Caste, Race and Discrimination: Discourses in International Context* (New Delhi/ Jaipur: Rawat)

Prove, P. (2004b), 'Caste Wars at the Sub-Commission on the Promotion and Protection of Human Rights: A Commentary on the Sub-Commission's On-Going Examination of Discrimination Based on Work and Descent' in Nakano, K., Yutzis, M. & Onoyama, R. (eds.), *Peoples for Human Rights, Vol. 9, Descent-based Discrimination* (Tokyo: International Movement Against all Forms of Discrimination and Racism, 2004)

Quigley, D. (1994), 'Is a Theory of Caste Still Possible' in Sharma, U. & Searle-Chatterjee, M. (eds.), *Contextualising Caste: Post-Dumontian Approaches* (Oxford: Blackwell)

Rao, A. (2006), 'Introduction' in Rao, A. (ed.), *Gender and Caste* (New Delhi: Kali for Women)

Rocher, L. (2005), 'The Dharmasatras' in Flood, G. (ed.), *The Blackwell Companion to Hinduism* (Oxford: Blackwell)

Rocher, R. (2010), 'The Creation of Anglo-Hindu Law' in Lubin, T., Davis, D. & Krishnan, J. (eds.), *Hinduism and Law: An Introduction* (Cambridge: Cambridge University Press)

Schwartz, M. (1999), 'Indian Untouchable Texts of Resistance: Symbolic Domination and Historical Knowledge' in Seneviratne, H.L. (ed.), *Identity, Consciousness and the Past: Forging of Caste and Community in India and Sri Lanka* (New Delhi: Oxford University Press)

Shah, G. (2001), 'Dalit Politics: Has It Reached an Impasse?' in Jayal, N. & Pai, S. (eds.), *Democratic Governance in India: Challenges of Poverty, Development and Identity* (New Delhi: Sage)

Shaw, A. (1994), 'The Pakistani Community in Oxford' in Ballard, R. (ed.), *Desh Pardesh: The South Asian Presence in Britain* (London: Hurst & Co.)

Shukra, A. (1994), 'Caste, a Personal Perspective' in Searle-Chatterjee, M. & Sharma, U. (eds.), *Contextualising Caste: Post-Dumontian Approaches* (London: Oxford University Press)

Singaravelou, P. (1990), 'Indians in the French Overseas Departments: Guadeloupe, Martinique, Reunion' in Clarke, C., Peach, C. & Vertovec, S. (eds.), *South Asians Overseas: Migration and Ethnicity* (Cambridge: Cambridge University Press)

Skogly, S. (1992), 'Article 2' in Eide, A. & Alfredsson, G. (ed.), *The Universal Declaration of Human Rights: A Commentary* (Oslo: Scandinavian University Press)

Skogly, S. (1999), 'Article 2' in Eide, A. & Alfredsson, G. (ed.), *The Universal Declaration of Human Rights: A Common Standard of Achievement* (The Hague: Martinus Nijhoff Publishing)

Sorabjee, S.J. (2004), 'The Official Position' in Thorat, S. & Umakant (eds.), *Caste, Race and Discrimination: Discourses in International Context* (New Delhi/Jaipur: Rawat)

Spencer, J. & Spencer, M. (2004), 'International Law and Discrimination' in Sargeant, M. (ed.), *Discrimination Law* (Harlow: Pearson)

Srivastava, A. (1974), 'Law and Legal Institutions' in Majumdar, R.C. (ed.), *The History and Culture of the Indian People: Vol VII the Mughal Empire* (Bombay: Bharatiya Vidya Bhavan)

Steiner, H. (2000), 'Individual Claims in a World of Massive Violations: What Role for the Human Rights Committee?' in Alston, P. & Crawford, J. (eds.), *The Future of UN Human Rights Treaty Monitoring* (Cambridge: Cambridge University Press)

Sturman, R. (2010), 'Marriage and Family in Colonial Hindu Law' in Lubin, T., Davis, D. & Krishnan, J. (eds.), *Hinduism and Law: An Introduction* (Cambridge: Cambridge University Press)

Tharamangalam, J. (1996), 'Caste Among Christians in India' in Srinivas, M.N. (ed.), *Caste: Its Twentieth Century Avatar* (New Delhi: Penguin)

Thekaekara, M.M. (2004), 'What Next for India's Dalits' in Thorat, S. & Umakant (eds.), *Caste, Race and Discrimination: Discourses in International Context* (New Delhi/Jaipur: Rawat)

Thorat, S. & Umakant. (2004), 'Introduction' in Thorat S. & Umakant (eds.), *Caste, Race and Discrimination: Discourses in International Context* (New Delhi: Rawat/ Indian Institute of Dalit Studies)

Thornberry, P. (2004), 'Race, Descent and Caste under the Convention on the Elimination of All Forms of Racial Discrimination' in Nakano, K., Yutzis, M. & Onoyana, R. (eds.), *Peoples for Human Rights Vol. 9: Descent-Based Discrimination* (Tokyo: International Movement Against All Forms of Discrimination and Racism)

Thornberry, P. (2005), 'CERD, Indigenous Peoples and Caste/Descent-Based Discrimination' in Castellino, J. & Walsh, N. (eds.), *International Law and Indigenous Peoples* (Leiden: Martinus Nijhoff Publishing)

Thornton, M. (1995), 'The Cartography of Public and Private' in Thornton, M. (ed.), *Public and Private: Feminist Legal Debates* (Oxford: Oxford University Press)

Tull, H. (2007), 'Karma' in Mittal, S. & Thursby, G. (eds.), *The Hindu World* (Abingdon: Routledge)

Vajpeyi, A. (2010), 'Sudradharma and Legal Treatments of Caste' in Lubin, T., Davis, D. & Krishnan, J. (eds.), *Hinduism and Law: An Introduction* (Cambridge: Cambridge University Press)

Vertovec, S. (1990), 'Oil Boom and Recession in Trinidad Indian Villages' in Clarke, C., Peach, C. & Vertovec, S. (eds.), *South Asians Overseas: Migration and Ethnicity* (Cambridge: Cambridge University Press)

Visweswaran, K. (2009), 'India in South Africa: Counter-Genealogies for a Subaltern Sociology?' in Natrajan, B. & Greenough, P. (eds.), *Against Stigma: Studies in Caste, Race and Justice Since Durban* (Hyderabad: Orient Blackswan)

Webster, J. (2007), 'Who Is a Dalit?' in Michael, S. (ed.), *Dalits in Modern India: Vision and Values* (New Delhi: Sage)

Weiner, M. (2001), 'The Struggle for Equality: Caste in Indian Politics' in Kohli, A. (ed.), *The Success of India's Democracy* (Cambridge: Cambridge University Press)

Wilson, E. (2003), 'Managing Diversity: Caste and Gender Issues in Organisations in India' in Davidson, M. & Fielden, S. (eds.), *Individual Diversity and Psychology in Organisations* (Oxford: Wiley)

Witzl, M. (2005), 'Vedas and Upanishads' in G. Flood (ed.), *The Blackwell Companion to Hinduism* (Oxford: Blackwell)

Zelliot, E. (1998), 'Dalit – New Cultural Context for an Old Marathi World' in Zelliot, E. (ed.), *From Untouchable to Dalit: Essays on the Ambedkar Movement* (New Delhi: Manohar)

Journal articles

Ajit, H., Donker, H. & Saxena, R., 'Corporate Boards in India: Blocked by Caste?' (11 August 2012) *Economic and Political Weekly* 39–43

Allen, R., 'Tackling Caste and Descent-Based Discrimination – Jews, Hindus and Others' (2009) 38 *Discrimination Law Association Briefings* 10–12

Alston, P., Morgan-Foster, J. & Abresch, W., 'The Competence of the UN Human Rights Council and Its Special Procedures in Relation to Armed Conflicts: Extrajudicial Executions in the "War on Terror"' (2008) 19(1) *European Journal of International Law* 183–209

Alston, P. & Simma, B., 'The Sources of Human Rights Law: Custom, Jus Cogens, General Principles' (1992) 12 *Australian Year Book of International Law* 82–108

Anandan, P.I., 'The Coronation and the Depressed Classes' (1911) 24 *Hindustan Review* 529–532

Ashcroft, R. & Bevir, M., 'Multiculturalism in Contemporary Britain: Policy, Law and Theory' (2017) 21(1) *Critical Review of International Social and Political Philosophy* 1–21

Balkin, J., 'The Constitution of Status' (1997) 106 *Yale Law Journal* 2313–2374

Bamshad, M. et al., 'Genetic Evidence on the Origins of Indian Caste Populations' (2001) 11 *Genome Research* 994–1004

Barnard, A., 'Kalahari Revisionism, Vienna and the "Indigenous Peoples" Debate' (2006) 14(1) *Social Anthropology* 1–16

Basu, A. et al., 'Ethnic India: A Genomic View, With Special Reference to Peopling and Structure' (2003) 13 *Genome Research* 2277–2290

Berg, D.E., 'Sovereignties, the World Conference Against Racism 2001 and the Formation of a Dalit Human Rights Campaign' (2001) 20 *Questions de Recherche/Research Questions* 2–66

Berreman, G., 'Caste and India in the United States' (1960) 66(2) *American Journal of Sociology* 120–127

Berreman, G., 'The Study of Caste Ranking in India' (1965) 21(2) *South Western Journal of Anthropology* 115–129

Berreman, G., 'Caste as Social Process' (1967) 23(4) *South Western Journal of Anthropology* 351–370

Berreman, G., 'The Brahminical View of Caste in "On the Nature of Caste in India: A Review Symposium"' (1971) 5 *Contributions to Indian Sociology* 16–23

Berreman, G., 'Social Categories and Social Interaction in Urban India' (1972) 74(3) *American Anthropologist* 567–586

Beteille, A., 'Race and Descent as Social Categories in India' (1967) 96(2) *Daedalus* 444–463

Beteille, A., 'The Peculiar Tenacity of Caste' (31 March 2012) *Economic and Political Weekly*

Bhatia, B., 'Dalit Rebellion Against Untouchability in Chakwada Rajasthan' (2006) 40 *Contributions to Indian Sociology* 29–61

Bhatt, C., 'Dharmo Rakshati Rakshitah: Hindutva Movements in the UK' (2000) 23(3) *Ethnic and Racial Studies* 559–593

Bidner, C. & Eswaran, M., 'A Gender-Based Theory of the Origin of the Caste System in India' (2015) 114 *Journal of Development Economics* 142–158, 154, 156

Bob, C., ' "Dalit Rights Are Human Rights": Caste Discrimination, International Activism, and the Construction of a New Human Rights Issue' (2007) 29(1) *Human Rights Quarterly* 167–193

Cameron, M., 'Considering Dalits and Political Identity in Imagining a New Nepal' (2007) *Himalaya* XXVII

Chakravarti, U., 'Conceptualising Brahmanical Patriarchy in Early India: Gender, Caste, Class and State' (3 April 1993) *Economic and Political Weekly* 579–583, 579

Charsley, S., 'Untouchable: What Is in a Name?' (1996) 2(1) *Journal of the Royal Anthropological Institute* 1–23

Clark, D., 'The Harijans of Britain' (26 June 1975) *New Society*

Claveyrolas, M., 'The "Land of the Vaish"? Caste Structure and Ideology in Mauritius' (2015) *South Asia Multidisciplinary Academic Journal*

Cornell, M., 'The Statutory Background of Apartheid: Chronological Survey of South African Legislation' (1960) 16(5) *The World Today* 181–194

Cox, O., 'Race and Caste: A Distinction' (1945) 50(5) *American Journal of Sociology* 360–363

Davis, D., 'Hinduism as a Legal Tradition' (2007) 75(2) *Journal of the American Academy of Religion* 241–267

Deliege, R., 'Replication and Consensus: Untouchability, Caste and Ideology in India' (1992) 27(1) *Man* 155–173

Deliege, R., 'The Myths of Origin of the Indian Untouchables' (1993) NS 28(3) *Man* 533–549

Desai, S. & Dubey, A., 'Caste in 21st Century India: Competing Narratives' (12 March 2011) *Economic and Political Weekly* 40–49

Deshpande, S., 'Caste and Castelessness' (13 April 2013) *Economic and Political Weekly (EPW)* 32–39

Dhanda, M., 'Punjabi Dalit Youth: Social Dynamics of Transitions in Identity' (2009) 17(1) *Contemporary South Asia* 47–64

Dhanda, M., 'Casteism Amongst Punjabis in Britain' (21 January 2017) *EPW*

Dhavan, R., 'Dhamasastra and Modern Indian Society: A Preliminary Exploration' (1992) 34(4) *Journal of the Indian Law Institute* 515–540

Dirks, N., 'The Invention of Caste: Civil Society in Colonial India' (1989) 25 *Social Analysis* 42–52

Dobe, K. & Chhokar, S., 'Muslims, Ethnicity and the Law' (2000) 4 *International Journal of Discrimination and the Law* 369–386

Downing, J., ' "Hate Speech" and "First Amendment Absolutism" Discourses in the US' (1999) (1) *Discourse and Society* 175–198

Dumont, L. et al., 'On the Nature of Caste in India: A Review Symposium' (1971) Vol. 5, *Contributions to Indian Sociology* 58–78

Felice, W., 'UN Committee on the Elimination of All Forms of Racial Discrimination: Race and Economic and Social Human Rights' (2002) 24(1) *Human Rights Quarterly* 205–236

Fiss, O., 'The Fate of an Idea Whose Time Has Come: Antidiscrimination Law in the Second Decade After *Brown v Board of Education*' (1974) 41 *University of Chicago Law Review* 742–773

Folmer, S., 'Identity Politics Among Dalits in Nepal' (2007) *Himalaya* XXVII (1–2) 41–53

Fredman, S., 'Reversing Discrimination' (1997) 113 *Law Quarterly Review* 575–600

Gellner, D., 'Caste, Ethnicity and Inequality in Nepal' (19 May 2007) 42(20) *Economic and Political Weekly* 1823–1828

Gilbert, J., 'Indigenous People's Human Rights in Africa: The Pragmatic Revolution of the African Commission on Human and People's Rights' (2011) (60) *International and Comparative Law Quarterly* 245–270

Goldston, J., 'The Struggle for Roma Rights: Arguments That Have Worked' (2010) 32(2) *Human Rights Quarterly* 311–335

Goodman, R. & Jinks, D., 'Measuring the Effects of Human Rights Treaties' (2003) 14(1) *European Journal of International Law* 171–183

Gopal, P., 'Dominating the Diaspora' (April 2010) *Himal Southasia*

Gorringe, H., ''You Build Your House, We'll Build Ours': The Attractions and Pitfalls of Dalit Identity Politics' (2005) 11(6) *Social Identities: Journal for the Study of Race, Nation and Culture* 653–672

Gorringe, H., 'Banal Violence? The Everyday Underpinnings of Collective Violence' (2006) 13 *Identities: Global Studies in Culture and Power* 237–260

Gorringe, H. & Rafanell, I., 'The Embodiment of Caste: Oppression, Protest and Social Change' (2007) 41(1) *Sociology* 97–114

Gorringe, H. 'Afterword: Gendering Caste: Honor, Patriarchy and Violence' (2018) 19 *South Asia Multidisciplinary Journal* 1–11

Gupta, D., 'The Certitudes of Caste: When Identity Trumps Hierarchy' (2004) 38(1/2) *Contributions to Indian Sociology* v–xv

Gupta, D., 'Caste and Politics: Identity Over System' (2005) 34 *Annual Review of Anthropology* 409–427

Guru, G., 'Power of Touch' (16–29 December 2006) *Frontline*

Guru, G, 'Archaeology of Untouchability' (12 September 2009) *EPW* 49–56

Hasan, R. & Mehta, A., 'Under-Representation of Disadvantaged Classes in Colleges: What Do the Data Tell Us?' (2 September 2006) *Economic and Political Weekly* 3791–3796

Heyns, C. & Viljoen, F., 'The Impact of the United Nations Human Rights Treaties on the Domestic Level' (2001) 23(2) *Human Rights Quarterly* 483–535

Hilson, C., 'New Social Movements: The Role of Legal Opportunity' (2002) 9(2) *Journal of European Public Policy* 238–255

Hudson, B., 'Beyond White Man's Justice: Race, Gender and Justice in Late Modernity' (2006) 10(1) *Theoretical Criminology* 29–47

Huff, J., 'Religious Freedom in India and Analysis of the Constitutionality of Anti-Conversion Laws' (2009) 10(2) *Rutgers Journal of Law and Religion* 1–36

Iyer, L., Khanna, T. & Varshney, A., 'Caste and Entrepreneurship in India' (9 February 2013) *EPW* 52–60, 52, 56, 58

Jain, H. & Venkata Ratnam, C.S., 'Affirmative Action in Employment for the Scheduled Castes and the Scheduled Tribes in India' (1994)15(7) *International Journal of Manpower* 6–25

Jaiswal, S., 'Studies in Early Indian Social History: Trends and Possibilities' (1979–80) 6(1–2) *Indian Historical Review* 1–63

Jaspal, R., 'Caste, Social Stigma and Identity Processes' (2001) 23(1) *Psychology and Developing Societies* 27–62

Jaspal, R. & Thakhar, O., 'Caste and Identity Processes Among British Sikhs in the Midlands' (2016) 12(1) *Sikh Formations; Religion, Culture, Theory* 187–102

Jeffrey, C., Jefferey, P. & Jeffery, R., 'Dalit Revolution? New Politicians in Uttar Pradesh India' (2008) 67(4) *Journal of Asian Studies* 1365–1396

Jha, V., 'Stages in the History of Untouchables' (1975) II(I) *Indian Historical Review* 14–31

Jha, V., 'Social Stratification in Ancient India: Some Reflections' (1991) 13(3–4) *Social Sciences* 19–40

Jodhka, S., 'Dalits in Business: Self-Employed Scheduled Castes in Northwest India' (13 March 2010) *Economic & Political Weekly*

Jodhka, S. & Kumar, A., 'Internal Classification of Scheduled Castes: The Punjab Story' (27 October 2007) *Economic and Political Weekly* 20–23

Jodhka, S. & Newman, K., 'In the Name of Globalisation: Meritocracy, Productivity and the Hidden Language of Caste' (13 October 2007) *Economic and Political Weekly* 4125–4132

Jodhka, S. & Shah, G., 'Comparative Contexts of |Discrimination: Caste and Untouchability in South Asia' (27 November 2010) *EPW* 99–106

Judge, P., 'Hierarchical Differentiation Among Dalits' (12 July 2003) *Economic and Political Weekly* 2990–2991

Judge, P., 'Punjabis in England: The Ad-Dharmi Experience' (3 August 2002) *Economic and Political Weekly* 3244–3250

Juegensmeyer, M., 'What If the Untouchables Don't Believe in Untouchability?' (1980) 12(1) *Bulletin of Concerned Asian Scholars* 23–28

Kannabiren, K.G., 'Important Similarities, Strange Differences: Caste, Race and Durban' (10 July 2010) *Economic and Political Weekly* 38–41

Keane, D., 'Descent-Based Discrimination in International Law: A Legal History' (2005) 12(1) *International Journal on Minority and Group Rights* 93–116

Kenoyer, J.M., et al., 'A New Approach to Tracking Connections Between the Indus Valley and Mesopotamia' (2013) 40(5) *Journal of Archaeological Science* 2286–2297

Klabbers, J., 'International Legal Histories: The Declining Importance of Travaux Préparatoires in Treaty Interpretation?' (2003) 50 *Netherlands International Law Review* 267–288

Klimas, T. & Vaiciukaite, J., 'The Law of Recitals in European Community Legislation' (2008) 15(1) *ILSA Journal of International and Comparative Law* 1–33

Kothari, R., 'Rise of the Dalits and the Renewed Debate on Caste' (25 June 1994) *Economic and Political Weekly* 1589–1594

Kumar, P., 'Dalits and the BSP in Uttar Pradesh: Issues and Challenges' (3 April 1999) *Economic and Political Weekly* 822–826

Kumar, V., 'Behind the BSP Victory' (15 June 2007) *Economic and Political Weekly* 2237–2239

Kumar, V., 'Discrimination on Campuses of Higher Learning: A Perspective from Below' (6 February 2016) *EPW* 12–15

Kundnani, A., 'Racism, Religion and Communalism' (2002) 44(2) *Race and Class* 71–80

Lariviere, R., 'Dharmasastra, Custom, "Real Law: and "Apocryphal" Smritis' (2004) 32 *Journal of Indian Philosophy* 611–662

Lennox, C., 'Reviewing Durban: Examining the Outputs and Review of the 2001 World Conference Against Racism' (2009) 27(2) *Netherlands Quarterly of Human Rights* 191–235

Lerche, J., 'Transnational Advocacy Networks and Affirmative Action for Dalits in India' (2008) *Development and Change* 39(2) 239–261

Lorenzen, D., 'Who Invented Hinduism?' (1999) 41(4) *Comparative Studies in Society and History* 630–659

Louis, P., 'Dalit Christians: Betrayed by State and Church' (21 April 2007) *Economic and Political Weekly* 1404–1408

Marston, G. & Watts, R., 'Tampering with the Evidence: A Critical Appraisal of Evidence-Based Policy-Making' (2003) 3(3) *The Drawing Board: An Australian Review of Public Affairs* 143–163

McColgan, A., 'Reconfiguring Discrimination Law' (Spring 2007) *Public Law* 74–94

McColgan, A., 'Class Wars? Religion and (In)equality in the Workplace' (2009) 38(1) *Industrial Law Journal* 1–29

McCormack, W., 'Caste and the British Administration of Hindu Law' (1966) 1(1) *Journal of African and Asian Studies* 25–32

McGhee, D., 'Moving to "Our" Common Ground – a Critical Examination of Community Cohesion Discourse in Twenty-First Century Britain' (2003) 51(3) *Sociological Review* 376–404

McGoldrick, D., 'Multiculturalism and Its Discontents' (2005) 5(1) *Human Rights Law Review* 27–56

Mechlem, K., 'Treaty Bodies and the Interpretation of Human Rights' (2009) 42(3) *Vanderbilt Journal of Transnational Law* 905–948

Meer, N., 'Politics of Voluntary and Involuntary Identities: Are Muslims in Britain an Ethnic, Racial or Religious Minority?' (2008) 42(1) *The Patterns of Prejudice* 61–81

Mencher, J., 'The Caste System Upside Down, or The Not-So-Mysterious East' (1974) 15(4) *Current Anthropology* 469–493

Meron, T., 'The Meaning and Reach of the International Convention on the Elimination of All Forms of Racial Discrimination' (1985) 79 *American Journal of International Law* 283–318

Michaelson, M., 'The Relevance of Caste Among East African Gujuratis in Britain' (1979) 7(3) *Journal of Ethnic and Migration Studies* 350–360

Misra, A., 'The Missionary Position: Christianity and Politics of Religious Conversion in India' (2011) 17 *Nationalism and Ethnic Politics* 361–381

Mohanty, M., 'Social Inequality, Labour Market Dynamics and Reservation' (2 September 2006) *Economic and Political Weekly* 3777–3789

Moldernhawer, B., 'Transnational Migrant Communities and Education Strategies Among Pakistani Youngsters in Denmark' (2005) 31(1) *Journal of Ethnic and Migration Studies* 51–78

Moon, G., 'From Equal Treatment to Appropriate Treatment: What Lessons Can Canadian Equality Law on Dignity and on Reasonable Accommodation Teach the United Kingdom?' (2006) 6 *European Human Rights Law Review* 695–721

Mosse, D., 'Replication and Consensus Among Indian Untouchable (Harijan) Castes' (1994) 29(2) *Man* 457–461

Mosse, D., 'Caste and Development: Contemporary Perspectives on a Structure of Discrimination and Advantage' (2018) 110 *World Development* 422–436, 423

Mosse, D., 'The Modernity of Caste and the Market Economy' (2019) *Modern Asian Studies* (online), 1–47, 1, 37

Mosse, D., 'Outside Caste? The Enclosure of Caste and Claims to Castelessness in India and the United Kingdom' (2020) 62(1) *Comparative Studies in Society and History* (2020) 1–31

Mukta, P., 'The Public Face of Hindu Nationalism' (2000) 23(3) *Ethnic and Racial Studies* 442–466

Narula, S., 'Overlooked Danger: The Security and Rights Implications of Hindu Nationalism in India' (2003) 16 *Harvard Human Rights Journal* 41–68

Narula, S., 'Equal by Law, Unequal by Caste: The 'Untouchable' Condition in Critical Race Perspective' (2008) 26(2) *Wisconsin International Law Journal* 255–343

Natrajan, B., 'Cultural Identity and Beef Festivals: Toward a "Multiculturalism Against Caste"' *Contemporary South Asia*, published online 25 Jul 2018

Nesbitt, E., 'Pitfalls in Religious Taxonomy: Hindus and Sikhs, Valmikis and Ravidasis' (1990) 6(1) *Religion Today* 9–12

Nesbitt, E., 'Religion and Identity: The Valmiki Community in Coventry' (1990) 16(2) *New Community* 261–274

Nesbitt, E., '"We Are All Equal": Young British Punjabis' and Gujuratis' Perceptions of Caste' (1997) 4(2) *International Journal of Punjab Studies* 201–218

Obinna, E., 'Contesting Identity: The Osu Caste System Among Igbo of Nigeria' (2012) 10(1) *African Identities* 111–121

O'Flaherty, M. & Fisher, J., 'Sexual Orientation, Gender Identity and International Human Rights Law: Contextualising the Yogyakarta Principles' (2008) 8 *Human Rights Law Quarterly* 207–248

O'Hanlon, R., 'Caste and Its Histories in Colonial India: A Reappraisal' (2017) 51(2) *Modern Asian Studies* 432–461, 438–439

O'Hanlon, R., et al., 'Discourses of Caste Over the Longue Duree: Gopinatha and Social Classification in India, ca. 1400–1900' (2015) 6(1) *South Asian History and Culture* 102–129, 118

Omvedt, G., 'Caste System and Hinduism' (13 March 2004) *Economic and Political Weekly* 1179–1180

Omvedt, G., et al., 'Conference Features Untouchables in India and Western Minority Condition' (1984) 15(6) *The Black Scholar* 53–55, 53

Orakhelashivili, A., 'Restrictive Interpretation of Human Rights Treaties in the Recent Jurisprudence of the European Court of Human Rights' (2003) 14(3) *European Journal of International Law* 529–568

Pai, S., 'New Social and Political Movements of Dalits: A Study of Meerut District' (2000) 34 *Contributions to Indian Sociology* 189–220

Paik, S., 'Mahar-Dalit-Buddhism: The History and Politics of Naming in Maharasthra' (2011) 45(2) *Contributions to Indian Sociology* 217–241

Paik, S., 'Building Bridges: Articulating Dalit and African American Women's Solidarity' (2014) 42(3/4) *Women's Studies Quarterly* 74–96

Pande, R., 'Can Mandated Political Representation Increase Policy Influence for Disadvantaged Minorities? Theory and Evidence from India' (2006) 93(4) *American Economic Review* 1132–1151

Parsons, W., 'From Muddling Through to Muddling Up – Evidence-Based Policy-Making and the Modernisation of British Government' (2002) 17(3) *Public Policy and Administration* 43–60

Patel, P., 'Faith in the State? Asian Women's Struggles for Human Rights in the UK' (2008) 16 *Feminist Legal Studies* 9–36

Peabody, N., 'Cents, Sense, Census: Human Inventories in Late Precolonial and Early Colonial India' (2001) 43(4) *Comparative Studies in Society and History* 819–850

Piliavsky, A., 'The "Criminal Tribes" in India Before the British' (2015) 57(2) *Comparative Studies in Society and History* 323–354, 325

Reber, E., 'Buraku Mondai in Japan: Historical and Modern Perspectives and Directions for the Future' (1999) 12 *Harvard Human Rights Journal* 297–359

Reddy, D., 'The Ethnicity of Caste' (2005) 78(3) *Anthropological Quarterly* 543–584

Ritter, M., 'Human Rights: The Universalist Controversy, a Response to Surya Subedi' (1999) 30 *California Western International Law Journal* 71–90

Robinson, D., 'The Search for Community Cohesion: Key Themes and Dominant Concepts of the Public Policy Agenda' (2005) 42(8) *Urban Studies* 1411–1427

Rocher, L., 'Hindu Conceptions of Law' (1978) 29(6) *Hastings Law Journal* 1283–1305

Rocher, L., 'Law Books in an Oral Culture' (1993) 137(2) *Proceedings of the American Philosophical Society* 254–267

Sabir, S., 'Chimerical Categories: Caste, Race and Genetics' (2003) 3(2) *Developing World Bioethics* 170–177

Samarendra, P., 'Census in Colonial India and the Birth of Caste' (13 August 2011) *Economic and Political Weekly* 51–58

Sandberg, R., 'Laws and Religion: Unravelling *McFarlane v Avon Relate Ltd.*' (2010) 12(3) *Ecclesiastical Law Journal* 361–370

Sandberg, R., 'The Right to Discriminate' (2011) 13(2) *Ecclesiastical Law Journal* 157–181

Sarukkai, S., 'Phenomenology of Untouchability' (12 September 2009) *Economic and Political Weekly* 39–48

Sato, K., 'Divisions Among Sikh Communities in Britain and the Role of the Caste System: A Case Study of Four Gurdwaras in Multi-Ethnic Leicester' (2012) 19(1) *Journal of Punjab Studies* 1–25

Schwelb, E., 'The International Convention on the Elimination of all Forms of Racial Discrimination' (1966) 15 *International and Comparative Law Quarterly* 996–1068

Searle-Chatterjee, M., 'World Religions and "Ethnic Groups": Do These Paradigms Lend Themselves to the Cause of Hindu Nationalism?' (2000) 23(3) *Ethnic and Racial Studies* 497–515

Shachar, A., 'On Citizenship and Multicultural Vulnerability' (2000) 28(1) *Political Theory* 64–89

Sharma, S., 'Caste-Based Crimes and Economic Status: Evidence from India' (2015) 43(1) *Journal of Comparative Economics* 204–226

Shukla, R., 'To Remove Caste Bias from the Judicial System, Judges Need to Self-Correct' *The Wire*, 23 March 2017

Shyam Babu, D. & Prasad, C.B., 'Six Dalit Paradoxes' (6 June 2009) *Economic and Political Weekly* 22–25

Sitlhou, M., 'India's Universities are Falling Terribly Short on Addressing Caste Discrimination' *The Wire*, 21 November 2017

Solanke, I., 'Putting Race and Gender Together: A New Approach to Intersectionality' (2009) 72(5) *Modern Law Review* 723–749

Subedi, S., 'Are the Principles of Human Rights "Western" Ideas? An Analysis of the Claim of the "Asian" Concept of Human Rights from the Perspectives of Hinduism' (1999) *California Western International Law Journal* 45–69

Subramanian, A., *The Caste of Merit: Engineering Education in India* (Cambridge, MA: Harvard University Press, 2019)

Tahkur, R. et al., 'Mitochondrial DNA Variation in Ranked Caste Groups of Maharashtra (India) and Its Implications on Genetic Relationships and Origins' (July–August 2003) 30(4) *Annual of Human Biology* 443–454

Talbot, C., 'A Revised View of "Traditional" India: Caste, Status, and Social Mobility in Medieval Andhra' (1992) 15(1) *South Asia: Journal of South Asian Studies* 17–52

Tamari, T., 'The Development of Caste Systems in West Africa' (1991) 32(2) *The Journal of African History* 221–250

Thakur, A.K., 'New Media and the Dalit Counter-Public Sphere' *Television and New Media*, published online 3 September 2019, 1–16

Thorat, S. & Attewell, P., 'The Legacy of Social Exclusion: A Correspondence Study of Job Discrimination in India' (13 October 2007) *Economic and Political Weekly* 4141–4145

Thorat, S. & Newman, K., 'Caste and Economic Discrimination: Causes, Consequences and Remedies' (13 October 2007) *Economic and Political Weekly* 4121–4124

Thornberry, P., 'Confronting Racial Discrimination: A CERD Perspective' (2005) 5(2) *Human Rights Law Review* 239–269

Tomotsune, T., 'Nakagami Kenji and the Buraku Issue in Post-War Japan' (2003) 4(2) *Inter-Asia Cultural Studies* 220–231

Torri, M-C., 'Abuse of Lower Castes in South India: The Institution of Devadasi' (2009) 11(2) *Journal of International Women's Studies* 31–48

Trinka, S., 'Cleanliness in a Caste-less Context: Collective Negotiations of Purity and Pollution among Indo-Fijian Hindus' (2012) 22(1) *Anthropological Forum* 25–43

Varshney, A., 'Is India Becoming More Democratic?' (2005) 59(1) *Journal of Asian Studies* 3–25

Vickers, L., 'Religious Discrimination in the Workplace: An Emerging Hierarchy?' (2009) 12(3) *Ecclesiastical Law Journal* 280–303

Vickers, L., 'Promoting Equality or Fostering Resentment? The Public Sector Equality Duty and Religion or Belief' (2011) 31(1) *Legal Studies* 135–158

Volpp, L., 'Feminism Versus Multiculturalism' (2001) 101(5) *Columbia Law Review* 1182–1218

Warner, L., 'American Caste and Class' (1936) 42(2) *American Journal of Sociology* 234–237

Watson, J., 'When No Place Is Home: Why the Homeless Deserve Suspect Classification' (2003) 88 *Iowa Law Review* 515–533

Waughray, A., 'Caste Discrimination: A 21st Century Challenge for UK Discrimination Law?' (2009) 72(2) *Modern Law Review* 182–219

Waughray, A., 'India and the Paradox of Caste Discrimination' (2009) 8 *European Yearbook of Minority Issues* 413–452

Waughray, A., 'Caste Discrimination and Minority Rights: The Case of India's Dalits' (2010) 17 *International Journal on Minority and Group Rights* 327–353

Waughray, A. & Weickgennant Thiara, N., 'Challenging Caste Discrimination in Britain with Literature and Law: An Interdisciplinary Study of British Dalit Writing' (forthcoming) *Contemporary South Asia*

Waughray, A. 'Capturing Caste in Law: Caste Discrimination and the Equality Act 2010' (2014) 14(2) *Human Rights Law Review*

Waughray, A., review of P. Shah, *Against Caste in British Law*, 36(3) *South Asia Research* (2016)

Waughray, A. and Dhanda, M., 'Ensuring Protection Against Caste Discrimination in Britain: Should the Equality Act 2010 Be Extended?' (2016) 16(2–3) *International Journal of Discrimination and the Law*

Waughray, A., 'Is Caste Discrimination in the UK Prohibited by the Equality Act 2010?' (2016) 2 *International Labor Rights Case Law*

Waughray, A., 'Caste in Britain; Public Consultation on Caste and Equality Law' (10 March 2018) 53(10) *Economic and Political Weekly (EPW)*

Wells, P., 'New Labour and Evidence-Based Policy-Making: 1997–2007' (2007) 1(1) *People, Place and Policy Online* 22–29

Worley, C., ' "It's not About Race. It's About the Community": New Labour and "Community Cohesion" ' (2005) 25 *Critical Social Policy* 483–496

Xanthakis, A., 'Multiculturalism and International Law: Discussing Universal Standards' (2010) 23(1) *Human Rights Quarterly* 21–48

Zavos, J., 'Negotiating Multiculturalism: Religion and the Organisation of Hindu Identity in Contemporary Britain' (2009) 35(6) *Journal of Ethnic and Migration Studies* 881–900

Zavos, J., 'Situating Hindu Nationalism in the UK: Vishwa Hindu Parishad and the Development of British Hindu Identity' (2010) 48(1) *Commonwealth and Comparative Politics* 2–22

Reports and newspaper articles

Anti Caste Discrimination Alliance. (2009), *Hidden Apartheid – Voice of the Community: Caste and Caste Discrimination in the UK – A Scoping Study* (ACDA, Derby)

Berkeley, R. (Hindu Forum of Britain) (2006), *Connecting British Hindus: An Enquiry into the Identity and Public Engagement of Hindus in Britain* (Hindu Forum of Britain, London)

Blakey, H., Pearce, J. & Chesters, G. (2006), *Minorities Within Minorities: Beneath the Surface of Community Participation* (Joseph Rowntree Foundation, York)

Brandon, J. & Hafez, S. (2008), *Crimes of the Community: Honour-Based Violence in the UK* (Centre for Social Cohesion, London)

Burkey, R. (1970), 'Discrimination and Racial Relations' in *Report on the International Research Conference on Race Relations, Aspen, Colorado, 7–9 June 1970* (Aspen, Colorado)

Church Times. (2010), West, L., 'These Judgments Restrict Freedoms' 21 May 2010

Dalit Solidarity Network UK. (2006a), *No Escape: Caste Discrimination in the UK* (Dalit Solidarity Network UK, London)

Dalit Solidarity Network UK. (2006b), 'Submission to the Equalities Review' (Dalit Solidarity Network UK, London)

Dalit Solidarity Network UK. (2007), 'Submission to the Discrimination Law Review' (Dalit Solidarity Network UK, London)

Deshpande, A. (2016), 'Contours of Caste Disadvantage' *The Hindu*, 25 September 2014

Deshpande, S. (2008), *Dalits in the Muslim and Christian Communities: A Status Report on Current Social Scientific Knowledge* (Government of India, National Commission for Minorities, New Delhi)

Dhanda, M., Waughray, A., Mosse, D., Keane, D. and S. Whittle, *Caste in Britain: Socio-legal Review, Equality and Human Rights Commission Research Report no. 91* (Manchester: Equality and Human Rights Commission 2014)

Dhanda, M., Mosse, D., Waughray, A. et al., *Caste in Britain: Experts' Seminar and Stakeholders' Workshop, Equality and Human Rights Commission Research Report no. 92* (Manchester: Equality and Human Rights Commission, 2014)

Government of India, Ministry of Labour. (2008), *Annual Report 2008* (Government of India, New Delhi)

Government of India, Ministry of Minority Affairs. (2009), *Report of the National Commission for Religious and Linguistic Minorities* (Government of India, New Delhi)

Government of India, Ministry of Social Justice and Empowerment. (2009), *Annual Report 2009–10* (Government of India, New Delhi)

Government of India, National Commission for Scheduled Castes. (2005), *Annual Report 2004–5* (Government of India, New Delhi)

Government of India, Ministry of Home Affairs, National Crime Records Bureau, Crime in India 2016, Court Disposal of Crime/Atrocities against SCs Cases (Crime Head-wise) at https://ncrb.gov.in/sites/default/files/crime_in_india_table_additional_table_chapter_reports/Table%207A.5.pdf

Government of India, Ministry of Home Affairs, National Crime Records Bureau, Crime in India 2019, Court Disposal of Crime/Atrocities against SCs Cases (Crime Head-wise) at https://ncrb.gov.in/sites/default/files/crime_in_india_table_additional_table_chapter_reports/Table%207A.5_2.pdf

The Guardian. (1991), Cook, S., 'Caste Out' 11 May 1991

The Guardian. (2000), Singh, J., 'Court Rules Out Caste Differences' 7 March 2000

The Guardian. (2006), Muir, H., 'Caste Divide Is Blighting Indian Communities in UK, Claims Report' 4 July 2006

The Guardian. (2009), Jones, S., 'Asian Caste Discrimination Rife in UK, Says Report' 11 November 2009

The Guardian. (2010), Sparrow, A. & Wintour, P., 'Coalition Reconsidering Tory Plan to Scrap Human Rights Act' 19 May 2010

The Guardian. (2011), Kidron, B., 'Devadasis Are a Cursed Community' 21 January 2011

The Guardian. (2012), Jones, S., 'Campaigners Urge Government to Tackle Caste Discrimination in the UK: Politicians and Human Rights Groups Say People from Traditionally Lower Status Asian Backgrounds Need Legal Protection' 30 November 2012

The Guardian. (2013), Jones, S., 'Employment Tribunal Hearing First Claim for Caste Discrimination Collapses: Judge Recuses Herself After Visit by Police Officers' 14 February 2013

Harrison, T. et al. (2007), *A Political Introduction to India, House of Commons Library Research Paper 07/41* (House of Commons, London)

The Hindu. (2012a), Karthikeyan, D., 'Madurai Villages Still Practising the Two-Tumbler System' 24 May 2012

The Hindu. (2012b), Khan, A., 'Can't Be a Superpower as Long as Untouchability Exists' 9 July 2012

House of Commons Foreign Affairs Committee. (2007), *South Asia: Fourth Report of Session 2006–2007* (The Stationary Office Ltd., London)

House of Commons Trade and Industry Committee. (2006a), *Trade and Investment Opportunities with India: Fifteenth Special Report of Session 2005–2006* (House of Commons Trade and Industry Committee, London)

House of Commons Trade and Industry Committee. (2006b), *Trade and Investment Opportunities with India: Third Report of Session 2005–2006* (House of Commons Trade and Industry Committee, Vol. 1, London)

Human Rights Watch. (1999), *Broken People: Caste Violence Against India's Untouchables* at https://www.hrw.org/reports/1999/india/India994.htm

Human Rights Watch. (2001), *Caste Discrimination: A Global Concern* at www.hrw.org/news/2001/08/29/global-caste-discrimination

The Independent. (1991), Aziz, C., 'The Untouchables of London's Suburbs' 10 January 1991

The Indian Express. (2009), 'Dalits Facing Caste Discrimination in UK: Study' 12 November 2009

International Dalit Solidarity Network. (2009), *Report from Side Event on Draft UN Principles and Guidelines for the Elimination of Discrimination based on Work and Descent* at https://idsn.org/report-from-hrc12-side-event/

International Dalit Solidarity Network, *The Ambedkar Principles: Employment and Additional Principles on Economic and Social Exclusion Formulated to Assist All Foreign Investors in South Asia to Address Caste Discrimination* at http://idsn.org/business-csr/ambedkar-principles/

International Dalit Solidarity Network, *Decade of Dalit Rights, Declaration* at http://idsn.org/fileadmin/user_folder/pdf/New_files/UN/Printer_Friendly_Declaration_Decade_Dalit_Rights.pdf

International Dalit Solidarity Network, *Decade of Dalit Rights UN 2011–20, Strategy Building Conference, Report* at www.idsn.org/fileadmin/user_folder/pdf/New_files/UN/Report_DecadeDalitRights.pdf

International Dalit Solidarity Network, 'UN Principles and Guidelines' at http://idsn.org/international-advocacy/un/un-principles-guidelines/

Joint Committee on Human Rights. (2005), *The Convention on the Elimination of Racial Discrimination: Fourteenth Report of Session 2004–05*

Justice Verma Committee, Report on Amendments to Criminal Law (New Delhi: Government of India, 2013)

Kallidai, R. (Hindu Forum of Britain) (2008), *Caste in the UK: A Summary of the Consultation with the Hindu Community in Britain* (Hindu Forum of Britain, London)

Keter, V. (2009), *Equality Bill: Bill 85 of 2008–9*, House of Commons Library Research Paper 09/42 (House of Commons, London)

Lankesh, G. (2015), 'Dalits and African Americans: Struggles and Solidarity' *Bangalore Mirror*, 14 July 2015

Local Government Association. (2002), *The Local Government Association's Guidance on Community Cohesion* (LGA, London)

Metcalf, H. & Rolfe, H. (UK Government Equalities Office) (2010), *Caste Discrimination and Harassment in Great Britain* (Government Equalities Office, London)

The Nation. (2009a), Crossette, B., 'Putting Caste on Notice' 9 November 2009

The Nation. (2009b), Pilay, N., 'Tearing Down the Walls of Caste' 19 October 2009

National Council for Teacher Education. (2003), *Addressing Discrimination Based on Sex, Caste and Religion and Disability Through Educational Intervention: A Handbook for Sensitising Teachers and Teacher Education* (NCTE, New Delhi)

Nigar, S., 'Violence Against India's Dalit Women on the Increase' *Asia Times*, 23 July 2018

The Observer. (2007), Morgan, O., 'British "Failing India's Lowest Caste Workers"' 24 June 2007

Outlook India. (2010), 'Abusing Dalit by Caste in Private Not an Offence' 15 October 2010

Outlook India. (2011), Dogra, C., 'The First Law: Sing My Name' 11 July 2011

Roy, S. (2003), 'Indian American Files Lawsuit Alleging Caste Bias' *Pacific News Service Civil Liberties Digest*, 9 July 2003

Sachar, R. (Government of India) (2006), *Social, Economic and Educational Status of the Muslim Community of India: A Report* (Government of India, New Delhi)

Sakshi Human Rights Watch. (2003), *Dalit Human Rights Monitor, Ahdhra Pradesh 2000–2003* (Sakshi Human Rights Watch, Secunderabad)

Saracini, N., and Shanmugavelan, M., *Caste and Development: Tackling Work and Descent-Based Discrimination to Achieve the SDGs for All* (London: Bond Network, 2018)

Saxena, K.B. (2004), *Report on Prevention of Atrocities Against Scheduled Castes: Policy and Performance: Suggested Interventions and Initiatives for National Human Rights Commission* (Government of India, National Human Rights Commission, New Delhi)

Sharma R.P. (2008), *The Caste System* (Hindu Council UK, London)

Soundararajan, T. (2020), 'A New Lawsuit Shines a Light on Caste Discrimination in the U.S. and Around the World' *The Washington Post*, 13 July 2020

Southall Black Sisters. (2001), *Forced Marriage: An Abuse of Human Rights* (Southall Black Sisters, London)

The Telegraph. (2012), 'North Korea Caste System "Underpins Human Rights Abuses"' 6 June 2012

Thorat, S., 'Discrimination on the Campus' *The Hindu*, 26 January 2016

The Times. (1990), Kelly, J., 'Apart and Hated' 6 July 1990

The Times. (2006), Bird, S., 'Sister Is Stabbed to Death for Loving the Wrong Man' 17 June 2006

The Times. (2010), Kennedy, D., 'Young Generation Keeps Old Identities Alive with Bhangra Music and Tradition' 5 July 2010

Times of India. (2010), Mittra, M., 'UK Bill Links Caste to Race, India Red-Faced' 31 March 2010

UK Government. (1999), *The Stephen Lawrence Enquiry: Report of an Enquiry by Sir William McPherson of Cluny* (HMSO, London)

UK Government. (2006), *Interim Report for Consultation* (The Equalities Review, London) at https://eurogender.eige.europa.eu/system/files/Equalities_Review_interim_report.pdf

UK Government. (2007a), *A Framework for Fairness: Proposals for a Single Equality Bill for Great Britain – A Consultation Paper* (HMSO, London)

UK Government. (2007b), *Fairness and Freedom: The Final Report of the Equalities Review* (HMSO, Norwich)

UK Government. (2008a), *Framework for a Fairer Future: The Equality Bill* (HMSO, Norwich)

UK Government. (2008b), *The Equality Bill – Government Response to the Consultation*, CM 7454

UK Government, Department for Business Innovation and Skills. (2011), *The Plan for Growth* (HM Treasury, London)

Vadlapatla, S., 'Devadasi System Still Exists in Telangana, AP, Says Report' *Times of India*, 23 February 2015

Voice of Dalit International. (2000), *Dalits in the New Millennium: Report of the Proceedings of the International Conference on Dalit Human Rights, 16–17 September 2000* (Voice of Dalit International, London)

Washington Times. (2011), Raj, F., 'More Dangerous Than Shariah: Hindutva' 8 September 2011

Other

Alkire, S. & Santos, M. (2010), *Acute Multidimensional Poverty: A New Index for Developing Countries*, Oxford Poverty & Human Development Initiative Working Paper No. 38 (University of Oxford Press, Oxford)

American Law Institute. (1987), 'Restatement of the Foreign Relations Law of the United States' (Third), Part VII, Chapter 1, s 701, Reporters' Note 3 (American Law Institute, St Paul, Minnesota)

The Anthropological Survey of India, People of India Project at www.ansi.gov.in

Anti Caste Discrimination Alliance. (2010), *Demonstration Flyer, Joint Statement* (copy on file with author) 11 January 2010

Anti Caste Discrimination Alliance and Others. (2010), *Caste Discrimination in the UK – Joint Statement Calling on the Coalition Government to Enact Clause 9(5)(a) of the Equality Act 2010* 23 December 2010 (copy on file with author)

Anti Caste Discrimination Alliance and Others. (2011), *Joint Statement Calling for Enactment of Clause 9(5)(a) of the Equality Act 2010 for Caste to Be an Aspect of Race* 17 January 2011 (copy on file with author)

Anti Caste Discrimination Alliance and Others. (2012), *Joint Statement to the Coalition Government Demanding That It Brings into Force Clause 9(5)(a) of the Equality Act 2010*, 28 November 2012

Anti Caste Discrimination Alliance, Press Release. (2010), *Evidence of Caste Discrimination and Harassment in the UK Confirmed in Independent Research Commissioned by Government* (copy on file with author) 16 December 2010

Anti Caste Legislation Committee Briefing Paper. (2013), 2 April 2013 (copy on file with author)

Asian Legal Resource Centre, India: *Manual scavenging, a shame on the nation*, Human Rights Council 9th Session, www.alrc.net

Avebury, Lord E. (2010), Blogpost, *Equality Bill – Caste* at http://ericavebury.blogspot.co.uk/2010/02/equality-bill-caste.html

Bates, C. (1995), 'Race, Caste and Tribes in Central India: The Early Origins of Indian Anthropometry' Edinburgh Papers in South Asian Studies Number 3

British Columbia Human Rights Code at www.bclaws.ca/EPLibraries/bclaws_new/document/ID/freeside/00_96210_01

British Columbia Human Rights Tribunal at www.bchrt.bc.ca

British High Commission New Delhi, India-UK Relations at http://ukinindia.fco.gov.uk/en/about-us/working-with-india/india-uk-relations

Caste Away Arts at http://casteawayarts.com

Conservative Party UK. (2010a), *Contract for Equalities, Conservative Party Equalities Manifesto* at https://issuu.com/conservatives/docs/equalities_manifesto

Conservative Party UK. (2010b), *Conservative Party Manifesto* at http://media.conservatives.s3.amazonaws.com/manifesto/cpmanifesto2010_easyread.pdf

Constituent Assembly Debates of India. (1947), CAD Vol. III 29 April 1947

Council of Valmik Sabhas, United Kingdom at https://www.facebook.com/Central-Valmiki-Sabha-International-Uk-165721326935165/

Countercurrents. (2003), Puri, N., *The Caste Divide*, Broadcast on BBC Radio 4 April 2003 at www.countercurrents.org/dalit-puri050704.htm

Decade of Dalit Rights UN, Declaration. (2011), at http://idsn.org/fileadmin/user_folder/pdf/New_files/UN/Printer_Friendly_Declaration_Decade_Dalit_Rights.pdf (visited 2 January 2013)

Dhanda, M. (2012), 'Held Back by In-Fighting: The Fraught Struggles for Recognition of Dalits in Wolverhampton' paper presented at the international conference 'The Internationalisation of Dalit and Adivasi Activism' University of London, 26 June 2012. Unpublished

Durban Review Conference. (2009), *Durban Review Conference Outcome Document* at www.unhcr.org/refworld/docid/49f584682.html 24 April 2009

Equality Act Impact Assessment, Final Version. (2010) (Government Equalities Office, London)

Equality and Human Rights Commission at www.equalityhumanrights.com

Equality and Human Rights Commission. (2010), *Lords Committee Stage Briefing*

Equality and Human Rights Commission. (2012), *Commission Policy Statement on Caste Discrimination*

European Union. (2003), *Guide of the European Parliament, the Council and the Commission for Persons Involved in the Drafting of Legislation Within the Community Institutions* at http://eur-lex.europa.eu/en/techleg/index.htm

Explanatory Notes to the Equality Act 2006. (Crown Copyright, 2006)

Explanatory Notes to the Equality Act 2010. (Crown Copyright, 2010)

Government of India. (2001), Census of India at www.censusindia.gov.in

Government of India, Ministry of Human Resource Development, Department of Higher Education. (2005), Selected Educational Statistics 2005–6, Gross Enrolment Rates

Government of India, Ministry of Labour, New Delhi, Annual Report 2017–18, 94

Government of India, MJSE, Planning, Research, Evaluation and Monitoring Division at http://socialjustice.nic.in/aboutdivision5.php

Government of Nepal. (1990), Constitution of Nepal at https://www.mohp.gov.np/downloads/Constitution%20of%20Nepal%202072_full_english.pdf

Government of Pakistan. (1973), Constitution of Pakistan at http://www.na.gov.pk/uploads/documents/1333523681_951.pdf

Government of Sri Lanka. (1978), Constitution of Sri Lanka at https://www.parliament.lk/files/pdf/constitution.pdf

GuruRavidassBhawan.org, History at http://gururavidassbhawan.org/history

Handbook on the Sexual Harassment of Women at Workplace (Prevention, Prohibition and Redressal) Act 2013 (New Delhi; Ministry of Women and Child Development, 2015)

Harris-White, B. & Prakash, A. (2011–12) 'Social Discrimination in India: A Case for Economic Citizenship' University of Oxford South Asia Work in Progress Research Papers No. 5

Himal Southasia. (2010), Gopal, P., *Dominating the Diaspora* at http://himalmag.com/compo nent/content/article/135-.html 01 April 2010

Hindu Forum of Britain. (2012), Results of AGM at www.hfb.org.uk/Default.aspx?sID=45& cID=508&ctID=43&lID=0 26 June 2012

Hindujagruti.org, Caste and Conversion at www.hindujagruti.org/news/2128.html

House of Commons. (1966), Debate vol 738 16 December 1966

House of Commons. (1976), 1975–1976 Race Relations Bill, HC Standing Committee a col 83–130, 29 April-4 May 1976

House of Commons. (2004), Debate vol 419 1 April 2004

House of Commons. (2007), Stunnell, A., *Early Day Motion 1604, Violence with Impunity Against Dalits in India* 5 June 2007

House of Commons. (2008), Debate vol 478 26 June 2008

House of Commons. (2009a), Equality Bill Committee Debate col 176 at www.publications.par liament.uk/pa/cm200809/cmbills/085/amend/pbc0851106m.91-97.html 11 June 2009

House of Commons. (2009b), Debate vol 492 11 May 2009

House of Commons. (2009c), Debate vol 493 11 June 2009

House of Commons. (2009d), Debate vol 501 2 December 2009

House of Commons. (2009e), Consideration of Equality Bill as at 2 Dec 2009 at www.publica tions.parliament.uk/pa/cm200910/cmbills/005/amend/pbc0050212m.106-112.html

House of Commons. (2010), Debate vol 508 6 April 2010

House of Commons. (2012), Debate vol 545 1 May 2012

House of Commons Equality Bill Committee. (2009), Debate col 179 at www.publications. parliament.uk/pa/cm200809/cmpublic/cmpbequality.htm 11 June 2009

House of Commons Library Note. (2011), Stott, E., *Government Proposals for International Development Policy, Including Proposals on the Situation of the Dalits* LNN 2001/037, 28 November 2011

House of Lords. (2007), Debate vol 690 26 March 2007

House of Lords. (2009), Debate vol 715 15 December 2009

House of Lords. (2010a), Debate vol 716 11 January 2010

House of Lords. (2010b), Debate vol 717 2 March 2010

House of Lords. (2010c), Debate vol 723 22 December 2010

House of Lords. (2010d), Revised Marshalled List of Amendments to be Moved in Committee as at 8 January 2010 at www.publications.parliament.uk/pa/ld200910/ldbills/020/amend/ ml020-ir.htm

House of Lords. (2010e), Revised Marshalled List of Amendments to Be Moved on Report as at 1 March 2010 at www.publications.parliament.uk/pa/ld200910/ldbills/035/amend/ ml035-ir.htm

House of Lords. (2011a), Debate vol 732 23 November 2011

House of Lords. (2011b), Debate vol 733 28 November 2011

House of Lords. (2013a), Debate vol 742 9 January 2013

House of Lords. (2013b), Debate vol 743 4 March 2013

House of Lords. (2013c), Sixth Marshalled List of Amendments to Be Moved in Grand Commit tee as at 8 January 2013 at www.publications.parliament.uk/pa/bills/lbill/2012-2013/0045/ amend/ml045-vi.htm

Indian Institute of Dalit Studies. (2009), *Caste-Based Discrimination in Nepal*, Working Paper Series Vol. 3, No. 8 (2009) at https://idsn.org/wp-content/uploads/user_folder/pdf/New_ files/Nepal/Caste-based_Discrimination_in_Nepal.pdf

Indian Institute of Dalit Studies, Completed Research Projects at www.dalitstudies.org.in/index. php?option=com_content&view=article&id=101&Itemid=109

International Dalit Solidarity Network at http://idsn.org/front-page

Jaoul, N. (2007), 'Multiculturalism and Caste in Britain' paper presented at the Caste-Watch UK conference, Sandwell, 15 July 2007. Unpublished. See http://castewatchuk.org/archives/castewatch-orig/sandwellconference.htm and www.castewatchuk.org/conf07_1130.html

Jeevansathi.com at https://www.jeevansathi.com/matrimonials/uk-matrimonial/

Jorde, L. (1999), Transcript of Conference paper presented at Anthropology, Genetic Diversity and Ethics: A Workshop at the Center for Twentieth Century Studies, University of Wisconsin-Milwaukee, 12–13 Feb 1999

Kannabiren, K. (People's Union for Civil Liberties) (2001), 'Race and Caste: A Response to Andre Beteille' at http://www.doccentre.net/docsweb/CasteRace/documents_caste/beteille_response.htm

Karma Nirvana at https://karmanirvana.org.uk/

Letter. (2009a), Ahmed, A. (DCLG), Letter to P. Lal (ACDA) (Copy on file with author) 14 August 2009

Letter. (2009b), Lal, P. (ACDA), Letter EHRC (Copy on file with author) 5 December 2009

Letter. (2010), Varney, O. (EHRC), Letter to P. Lal (ACDA) (Copy on file with author) 6 January 2010

Letter. (2011a), British Sikh Consultative Forum, Email to Lynne Featherstone MP (copy on file with author) 11 January 2011

Letter. (2011b), McGhan, P. (Department for Communities and Local Government), Letter to L. Pall (ACDA) (copy on file with author) 3 August 2011

Letter. (2011c), Phillips, T. (EHRC), Letter to L. Pal (ACDA) (copy on file with author) 31 October 2011

Letter. (2011d), Lord Avebury, Letter to Baroness Verma (copy on file with author) 4 December 2011 (P1104122)

Letter. (2011e), Lord Avebury, Letter to Baroness Verma (copy on file with author) 4 December 2011 (P1104126)

Letter. (2011f), ACDA, Letter to Lynne Featherstone MP (copy on file with author) 31 January 2011

Letter. (2012a), Government Equalities Office, Letter to Lord Avebury (copy on file with author) 19 January 2012

Letter. (2012b), Baroness Verma, Letter to Lord Avebury (copy on file with author) 2 February 2012

Letter. (2012c), Lord McNally, Letter to Dr Francis (JCHR) (copy on file with author) 20 September 2012

Letter. (2012d), Lord Avebury to Maria Miller MP (copy on file with author) 29 November 2012

Letter. (2012f), Lord Avebury, Letter to the Prime Minister (copy on file with author) 24 December 2012

Letter. (2013a), Metcalfe, H. (NIESR), Letter to Lord McNally (copy on file with author) 6 February 2013

Letter. (2013b), Dalit organisations to Helen Grant MP, Minister for Women and Equalities, 14 February 2013 (copy on file with author)

Letter. (2013c), Helen Grant MP to ACDA, 1 March 2013 (copy on file with author)

Liberty, Search Results at www.liberty-human-rights.org.uk/search.php?q=caste

Muman, S. (2000), 'Caste in Britain' in *Dalits in the New Millennium: Report of the Proceedings of the International Conference on Dalit Human Rights 16–17 September 2000* (Voice of Dalit International, London)

National Archives, Commission for Racial Equality at http://webarchive.nationalarchives.gov.uk/20060820160817/cre.gov.uk

National Institute of Economic and Social Research. (2010), 'Research into Caste Systems and the Existence and Nature of Caste Prejudice and Discrimination in Britain' (copy on file with author)

Nesbitt, E. (1991), ' "My Dad's Hindu, My Mum's Side Are Sikhs": Issues in Religious Identity' University of Manchester, Centre for Applied South Asian Studies at http://casas.org.uk/papers/pdfpapers/identity.pdf

Notorious Jatt at www.notorious-jatt.com/#/Home-01-00

Office of the United Nations High Commissioner for Human Rights, Committee on Eliminating Racial Discrimination at https://www2.ohchr.org/english/bodies/cerd/

O'Hanlon, R. (2010), 'Lineages of Non-Brahman Thought in Western India c. 1600–1850' Mahatma Phule Memorial Lecture, University of Calcutta, 3 December 2010

Olivelle, P. (2000), *From the Rg-Veda to Asoka: A Brief History of Dharma*, conference paper presented at the University of California, Santa Barbara Dept. of Religious Studies, 31 May 2000. Unpublished

Press for Change at www.pfc.org.uk

Prove, P. (2003), 'Caste and the Universal Declaration of Human Rights' *Lutheran World Foundation*. Unpublished paper (copy on file with author)

Racial Discrimination White Paper, Cm 6234 (1975)

Raghavan, V. (2017), 'B R Ambedkar: Perspectives on International Law and Foreign Policy' paper presented to the Ambedkar International Conference, Bangalore, India, June 2017 (unpublished; copy on file with author)

Rajgopal, B. (2004), 'Limits of Law in Counter-Hegemonic Globalisation: The Indian Supreme Court and the Narmada Valley Struggle' *JNU CSLG Working Paper Series* 04/04

Ramaswamy, Dr Justice K., National Human Rights Commission (India), Statement (2001) at www.unhchr.ch/huricane/huricane.nsf/view01/C0D479DFDCB0275941256AC0003637 5C?opendocument (visited 2 January 2013)

Ravidassiauk.co.uk at www.ravidassiauk.co.uk/content/new-identity-our-community

Ravidassia Matrimonials at https://www.facebook.com/Ravidassia-Matrimonials-269151143143216/

Shaadi.com at https://www.shaadi.com/matrimony/united-kingdom-nri-matrimony

Shri Guru Ravi Dass Sabha at www.gururavidas.org

Shri Guru Ravidas Ji at www.shrigururavidasji.com/index.html

Stott, E. (2011), House of Lords Library Note, 'Government Proposals for International Development Policy, Including Proposals on the Situation of the Dalits' LLN 2011/037, 28 November 2011

Tantriclub.co.uk, To C-A-S-T-E aspersions or not at www.tantriclub.co.uk/asian-dating-blog-caste-system-and-dating.php

Thekaekara, M. (2012), *Can Bollywood Shatter India's Caste System?* New Internationalist Blog, at www.newint.org/blog/2012/07/13/bollywood-untouchable-force 13 July 2012

Thorat, A. & Joshi, O. (2015), 'The Continuing Practice of Untouchability in India: Patterns and Mitigating Influences' India Human Development Survey Working Paper No. 2015–2, National Council of Applied Economic Research and University of Maryland, 13

UK Government. (2011), Red Tape Challenge https://www.gov.uk/government/news/red-tape-challenge

UK Government. (2012), The Queen's Speech 2012 at www.gov.uk/government/news/the-queens-speech-2012

UK Government, Department for Business Innovation and Skills. (2011), Impact Assessment Guidance

UK Government, DLR Terms of Reference at http://archive.cabinetoffice.gov.uk/equalities review/reference_grp/rg_terms_ref.html

UK Government Equalities Office, 'Caste Discrimination and Harassment in Great Britain' Research Findings No 2010/8 at www.homeoffice.gov.uk/publications/equalities/research/caste-discrimination/caste-discrimination-summary?view=Binary

UK Government, Equality Bill Committee, Debates and Bill Committee Members at www.pub lications.parliament.uk/pa/cm200809/cmpublic/cmpbequality.htm

UK Government, Home Office, Equality Duty Review, Terms of Reference https://www.gov.uk/government/groups/review-of-public-sector-equality-duty-steering-group#terms-of-reference

UK Government, Home Office, Equalities Move to Department for Culture, Media and Sport at http://homeoffice.gov.uk/equalities

UK Government, Office of National Statistics. (2001), Census 2001, Largest Ethno-Religious Groups at www.ons.gov.uk/ons/taxonomy/index.html?nscl=Identity

UK Government, Treasury. (2011), Plan for Growth at http://cdn.hmtreasury.gov.uk/2011budget_growth.pdf

UK Parliament. (2012), Bill Stages – Enterprise and Regulatory Reform Bill 2012–2013 at http://services.parliament.uk/bills/2012-13/enterpriseandregulatoryreform/stages.html

UK Parliament. (2013a), Enterprise and Regulatory Reform Bill, Amendments to be moved on Report at www.publications.parliament.uk/pa/bills/lbill/2012-2013/0083/amend/am083-e.htm

UK Parliament. (2013b), Enterprise and Regulatory Reform Bill, Sixth Marshalled List of Amendments to Be Moved in Grand Committee at www.publications.parliament.uk/pa/bills/lbill/2012-2013/0045/amend/ml045-vi.htm

UK Parliament at https://www.parliament.uk/about/how/laws/passage-bill/commons/coms-commons-first-reading/

UK Parliament, Register of All Party Parliamentary Groups at www.publications.parliament.uk/pa/cm/cmallparty/register/dalits.htm

UK Trade and Investment, Foreign and Commonwealth Office Country Profile: India at www.ukti.gov.uk/export/countries/asiapacific/southasia/india.html

UN Doc. A/HRC/26/38/Add.1, 1 April 2014

UN News. (2011), 'Nepal: UN Welcomes New Law on Caste-Based Discrimination' at www.un.org/apps/news/story.asp?newsid=38496

UN Press Release. (2007), 'Committee on Elimination of Racial Discrimination Considers Report of India' 26 February 2007

University of Massachusetts Amherst. (2018), Caste and Race: Reconfiguring Solidarities, Conference on Caste in India and Race Relations in the US, 4–6 May 2018

World Directory of Minorities and Indigenous Peoples at www.minorityrights.org/5652/india/dalits.html

United Nations Documents

Caportorti, F. (1981), *United Nations Study on the Rights of Persons Belonging to Ethnic, Religious and Linguistic Minorities* (UN, New York)

Cobo, J.R.M. (1983), 'Study of the Problem of Discrimination Against Indigenous Populations' 30 September 1983; UN Doc. E/CN.4 Sub.2/1983/21/Add.8 (1983)

Declaration on the Elimination of Racial Discrimination, GA Resolution 1904 (XVIII), 20 November 1963

Durban Review Conference, Preparatory Committee, CERD Replies to OHCHR Questionnaire (2008); UN Doc. A/CONF.211/PC.2/CRP.5, 23 April 2008

Durban Review Conference, Preparatory Committee, Joint Special Procedures Response to OHCHR Questionnaire (2008); UN Doc. A/CONF.211/PC/WG.1/5, 31 July 2008

Durban Review Outcome Document at http://www.un.org/durbanreview2009/pdf/Durban_Review_outcome_document_En.pdf (visited 2 January 2013)

Eide, A. and Daes, E.I. (2000), 'Working Paper on the Relationship and Distinction between the Rights of Persons Belonging to Minorities and those of Indigenous Peoples' (2000); UN Doc. E/CN.4/Sub.2/2000/10, 19 July 2000

Eide, A. and Yokota, Y. (2003), 'UN Sub-Commission on the Promotion and Protection of Human Rights'; expanded working paper on discrimination based on work and descent; UN Doc. E/CN.4/Sub.2/2003/24, 26 June 2003

Eide, A. and Yokota, Y. (2004), 'UN Sub-Commission on the Promotion and Protection of Human Rights'; further expanded working paper on discrimination based on work and descent; UN Doc. E/CN.4/Sub.2/2004/31, 5 July 2004

General Assembly (GA) Resolution 44(1), Treatment of Indians in the Union of South Africa, 8 December 1946

Goonesekere, R.K.W. (2001), 'UN Sub-Commission on the Promotion and Protection of Human Rights' working paper on discrimination based on work and descent; UN Doc. E/CN.4/ Sub.2/2001/16, 14 June 2001

Independent Expert on minority issues, Report (2006); UN Doc. E/CN.4/2006/74, 6 January 2006

Independent Expert on minority issues, Report (Recommendations of the Forum on Minority Issues) (2009); UN Doc. A/HRC/10/11/Add.1, 5 March 2009

Independent Expert on the Question of Human Rights and Extreme Poverty and Independent Expert on the Issue of Human Rights Obligations Related to Access to Safe Drinking Water and Sanitation, Joint Report (2010); UN Doc. UN Doc. A/HRC/15/55, 22 July 2010

Intergovernmental Working Group on the Effective Implementation of the Durban Declaration and Programme of Action, Thematic discussion on structural discrimination (2010) *in* UN Special Rapporteur on Racism, Report (2011); UN Doc. A/ HRC/17/40, 24 May 2011

OHCHR Questionnaire on Contemporary Manifestations of Racism and Measures and Activities Taken to Implement the DDPA (2007) at http://www.un.org/durbanreview2009/pdf/questionnaire1st.pdf (visited 2 January 2013)

Report on the study by the five experts on the content and scope of substantive gaps in the existing international instruments to combat racism, racial discrimination, xenophobia and related intolerance ('Report on Complementary International Standards') (2007); UN Doc. A/HRC/4/WG.3/6, 27 August 2007

Special Rapporteur on adequate housing as a component of the right to an adequate standard of living, Report (2005); UN Doc. E/CN.4/2005/48, 3 March 2005.

Special Rapporteur on adequate housing as a component of the right to an adequate standard of living, Report (2008); UN Doc. A/HRC/7/16, 13 February 2008

Special Rapporteur on adequate housing as a component of the right to an adequate standard of living, Report (2008); UN Doc. A/HRC/7/16/Add.1, 4 March 2008

Special Rapporteur on adequate housing as a component of the right to an adequate standard of living, Report (2009); UN Doc. A/HRC/13/20, 18 December 2009

Special Rapporteur on contemporary forms of slavery, including its causes and consequences, Report (2009); UN Doc. A/HRC/12/21, 10 July 2009

Special Rapporteur on contemporary forms of slavery, including its causes and consequences, Report (2010); UN Doc. A/HRC/15/20, 28 June 2010

Special Rapporteur on contemporary forms of slavery, including its causes and consequences, Report (2010); UN Doc. A/HRC/15/20/Add.2, 24 August 2010

Special Rapporteur on extrajudicial, summary or arbitrary executions, Report (2007); UN Doc. A/62/265, 16 August 2007

Special Rapporteur on freedom of religion or belief (2009); Country visit report on India; UN Doc. A/HRC/10/8/Add.3, 26 January 2009

Special Rapporteur on Racism (2011a), Interim Report; UN Doc. A/66/313, 19 August 2011

Special Rapporteur on Racism (2011b); Interim Report to UNGA; UN Doc. A/66/313, 19 August 2011

Special Rapporteur on Racism (2011c), Report; UN Doc. A/HRC/17/40, 24 May 2011

Special Rapporteur on Racism, Interim Report (2009); UN Doc. A/64/271, 10 August 2009

Special Rapporteur on Racism, Report (1997); UN Doc. E/CN.4/1997/71, 16 January 1997

Special Rapporteur on Racism, Report (1999); UN Doc. UN Doc. E/CN.4/1999/15, 15 January 1999

Special Rapporteur on Racism, Report (2004); E/CN.4/2004/18, 21 January 2004

Special Rapporteur on Racism, Report (2008); UN Doc. A/HRC/7/19, 20 February 2008

Special Rapporteur on Racism, Report (2009); UN Doc. A/HRC/11/36, 19 May 2009

Special Rapporteur on Racism, Report (2011); UN Doc. A/ HRC/17/40, 24 May 2011

Special Rapporteur on the right of everyone to the enjoyment of the highest attainable standard of physical and mental health, Report (2010); UN Doc. A/HRC/14/20/Add.2, 15 April 2010

Special Rapporteur on the right to adequate housing, Report (2009); UN Doc. A/HRC/10/7/Add. 1, 17 February 2009

Special Rapporteur on the right to education, Report (2006); UN Doc. E/CN.4/2006/45, 8 February 2006

Special Rapporteur on the right to food, Report (2007); UN Doc. A/HRC/4/30, 19 January 2007

Special Rapporteur on the right to food, Report (2009); UN Doc. A/HRC/10/5/Add.2, 4 February 2009

Special Rapporteur on the situation of human rights defenders, Report (2008); UN Doc. A/HRC/7/28, 31 January 2008

Special Rapporteur on the situation of human rights defenders, Report (2009); UN Doc. A/HRC/10/12, 12 February 2009

Special Rapporteur on the situation of human rights defenders, Report (2009); UN Doc. A/HRC/10/12/Add.1, 4 March 2009

Special Rapporteur on the situation of human rights defenders, Report (2011); UN Doc. A/HRC/16/44/Add.1, 28 February 2011

Special Rapporteur on the situation of human rights defenders, Report (2012); UN Doc. A/HRC/22/47/Add.1, 13 December 2012 Universal Periodic Review Working Group Report, India (2012); UN Doc. A/HRC/21/10, 9 July 2012

Special Rapporteur on Violence Against Women, Report (2012); UN Doc. A/HRC/20/16, 23 May 2012

Study of the Human Rights Council Advisory Committee on discrimination in the context of the right to food (2011); UN Doc. A/HRC/16/40, 16 February 2011

UN Commission on Human Rights, Decision 2005/109; UN Doc. E/CN.4/2005/134 (Part I) (2005)

UN Declaration on the Rights of Indigenous Peoples (2007); UN Doc. A/Res/61/295.

UN Declaration on the Rights of Persons Belonging to National or Ethnic, Religious and Linguistic Minorities (1992); GA Res. 47/135 (1992)

UN Information Note, Durban Review Conference (2009) at http://www.un.org/durban review2009/pdf/InfoNote_04_BasicFacts_En.pdf (visited 2 January 2013

Universal Periodic Review Working Group Report, India (2008); UN Doc. A/HRC/8/26, 23 May 2008

Universal Periodic Review Working Group Report Report, United Kingdom (2012); UN Doc. A/HRC/21/9, 6 July 2012

Universal Periodic Review Working Group Report, Views on conclusions and/or recommendations, voluntary commitments and replies presented by the state under review (United Kingdom) (2012); UN Doc. A/HRC/21/9/Add.1, 17 September 2012

UN Sub-Commission on the Promotion and Protection of Human Rights (2000); Resolution 2000/4 on discrimination based on work and descent, 11 August 2000; UN Doc. E/CN.4/Sub.2/2000/46, 23 November 2000

UN Sub-Commission on the Promotion and Protection of Human Rights (2004); Resolution 2004/17, Discrimination based on work and descent, 12 August 2004; UN Doc. E/CN.4/Sub.2/2004/48, 21 October 2004

World Conference Against Racism Racial Discrimination, Xenophobia and Other Related Forms of Intolerance, Bellagio Consultation (2000); UN Doc. A/CONF.189/PC.1/10, 8 March 2000

World Conference Against Racism Racial Discrimination, Xenophobia and Other Related Forms of Intolerance, Draft Programme Of Action (2001); UN Doc. A/CONF.189/5, 22 August 2001

Yokota, Y. and Chung, C. (2005), Preliminary Report on discrimination based on work and descent; UN Doc. E/CN.4/Sub.2/2005/30, 21 June 2005

Yokota, Y. and Chung, C. (2006); Progress Report on discrimination based on work and descent; UN Doc. A/HRC/Sub.1/58/CRP.2, 28 July 2006

Yokota, Y. and Chung, C. (2009), Final Report on discrimination based on work and descent; Human Rights Council; UN Doc. A/HRC/11/CRP.3, 18 May 2009

Committee on the Elimination of Racial Discrimination (CERD)

Intergovernmental Working Group on the Effective Implementation of the Durban Declaration and Programme of Action (IGWG); views of CERD on the implementation of ICERD (2004); UN Doc. E/CN.4/2004/WG.21/10.Add.1, 17 September 2004

Replies to the Office of the High Commissioner for Human Rights (OHCHR) Questionnaire; UN Doc. A/CONF.211/PC.2/CRP.5, 23 April 2008

Thematic Discussion on Discrimination Based on Descent (2002); UN Doc. CERD/C/SR. 1531, 16 August 2002

UN Press Release (2007), 'Committee on Elimination of Racial Discrimination Considers Report of India', 26 February 2007

Selected State Reports to CERD

Bangladesh: Eleventh report (2000); UN Doc. CERD/C/379/Add.1, 30 May 2000

Concluding observations – Bangladesh (2001); UN Doc. A/56/18 (2001)

Concluding observations – Burkina Faso (2013): CERD/C/BFA/CO/12–19, 23 September 2013

Concluding observations – Chad (2009): UN Doc. CERD/C/TCD/CO/15, 21 September 2009

Concluding observations – Ethiopia (2009); UN Doc. CERD/C/ETH/CO/7-16, 7 September 2009

Concluding observations – Ghana (2003); UN Doc. CERD/C/62/CO/4, 2 June 2003

Concluding observations – India (1979); UN Doc. A/34/18 (1979)

Concluding observations – India (1996); CERD; Report; UN Doc. A/51/18 (1996)

Concluding observations – India (2007); UN Doc. CERD/C/IND/CO/19, 5 May 2007

Concluding observations – Japan (2001); UN Doc. A/56/18 (2001)

Concluding observations – Japan (2001); UN Doc. CERD/C/304/ADD.114, 27 April 2001

Concluding observations – Japan (2010); UN Doc. CERD/C/JPN/CO/3-6, 6 April 2010

Concluding observations – Japan (2014): CERD CERD/C/JPN/CO/7–9, 26 September 2014

Concluding observations – Madagascar (2004): UN Doc. CERD/C/65/CO/4, 10 December 2004

Concluding observations – Mali (2002); CERD, Report; UN Doc. A/57/18 (2002)

Concluding observations – Mauritania (2004): UN Doc. CERD/C/65/CO/5, 10 December 2004

Concluding observations - Nepal (2004); UN Doc. CERD/C/64/CO/5, 26 April 2004

Concluding observations – Nigeria (2007): UN Doc. CERD/C/NGA/CO/18, 27 March 2007

Concluding observations – Pakistan (2009); UN Doc. CERD/C/PAK/CO/20, 16 March 2009

Concluding observations – Senegal (2002); CERD, Report; UN Doc. A/57/18 (2002)

Concluding observations – Suriname (2015); CERD/C/SUR/CO/13–15, 28 August 2015

Concluding observations – UK (2003); UN Doc. CERD/C/63/CO/11, 10 December 2003

Concluding observations – UK (2011); UN Doc. CERD/C/GBR/CO/18-20, 14 September 2011

Concluding observations – UK (2016); CERD/C/GBR/CO/21-23, 3 October 2016

Concluding observations - Yemen (2006); UN Doc. CERD/C/YEM/CO/16, 19 October 2006
Concluding observations - Yemen (2011); UN Doc. CERD/C/YEM/CO/17-18, 4 April 2011
India, Concluding Statement, CERD, '70th Session, Consideration of India's Nineteenth Report' 26 February 2007 at http://www2.ohchr.org/english/bodies/cerd/docs/statements/No.8 India26Feb2007.pdf
India: Eighth to ninth reports (1986); UN Doc. CERD/C/149/Add.11, 4 September 1986
India: Fifteenth to nineteenth reports (2006); UN Doc. CERD/C/IND/19, 29 March 2006
India: Fifth report (1979); UN Doc. CERD/C/20/Add.34, 8 March 1979
India: Fourth report (1977); UN Doc. CERD/C/R.90/Add.32, 27 July 1977
India: Initial report (1970); UN Doc. CERD/C/R.3/Add.3/Rev.1, 30 March 1970
India, Introductory Statement, CERD, 70th session, 23 February 2007
India: Second report (1972); UN Doc. CERD/C/R.30/Add.4, 28 June 1972
India: Seventh report (1982); UN Doc. CERD/C/91.Add.26, 19 October 1982
India: Sixth report (1981); UN Doc. CERD/C/66/Add.33, 16 June 1981
India: Tenth to fourteenth periodic reports (1996); UN Doc. CERD/C/299/Add.3, 29 April 1996
India: Third report (1974); UN Doc. CERD/C/R.70/Add.29, 18 November 1974
Intervention by the Solicitor-General of India on specific issues raised by CERD at the presentation of India's fifteenth to nineteenth report, 26 February 2007; copy on file with author
Japan, seventh to ninth reports (2013); UN Doc. CERD/C/JPN/7-9, 10 July 2013
Japan, third to sixth reports, Replies to List of Questions (2010); UN Doc. CERD/C/JPN/Q/3-6/Add.1/Rev.1, 8 February 2010
Sri Lanka: Second report (1985); UN Doc. CERD/C/126/Add.2., 12 September 1985
Sri Lanka: Seventh to ninth reports (2000); UN Doc. CERD/C/357/Add.3, 20 November 2000
Sri Lanka: Third to sixth reports (1994); UN Doc. CERD/C/234/Add.1, 13 September 1994
United Kingdom: 21st to 23rd reports (2015); CERD/C/GBR/21–23, 16 July 2015
United Kingdom: Eighteenth to twentieth reports (2010); UN Doc. CERD/C/GBR/18-20, 13 August 2010

CERD General Recommendations

General Recommendation No. 14 (1993), Definition of discrimination, 22 March 1993
General Recommendation No. 19 (1995), Racial segregation and apartheid (Art. 3), 18 August 1995
General Recommendation No. 21 (1996), Right to self-determination, 23 August 1996
General Recommendation No. 23 (1997), Indigenous Peoples, 18 August 1997
General Recommendation No. 27 (2000), Discrimination against Roma, 16 August 2000
General Recommendation No. 29 (2002), Article 1, Paragraph 1 (Descent), 22 August 2002
General Recommendation No. 30 (2004), Discrimination Against Non-Citizens, 1 October 2004
General Recommendation No. 32 (2009), The meaning and scope of special measures, 24 September 2009; UN Doc. CERD/C/GC/32
General Recommendation No. 34 (2011), Racial discrimination against people of African descent, 3 October 2011: UN Doc. CERD/C/GC/34

Other Treaty-monitoring Bodies

Human Rights Committee

Concluding observations – India (1997); UN Doc. A/52/40 (1997)
General Comment No. 18 (1989), Non-discrimination, 10 November 1989
General Comment No. 31 (2004), The Nature of the General Legal Obligation Imposed on State Parties to the Covenant, 26 May 2004; UN Doc. CCPR/C/21/Rev.1/Add. 13
India: Initial report (1983); UN Doc. CCPR/C/10/Add.8 (1983)

India: Second report (1989); UN Doc. CCPR/C/37/Add.13 (1989)
India: Third report (1996); UN Doc. CCPR/C/76/Add.6 (1996)

Committee on Economic, Social and Cultural Rights

Concluding observations – India (2008); UN Doc. E/C.12/IND/CO/5, 8 August 2008
General Comment No. 20 (2009), 'Non-discrimination in Economic, Social and Cultural Rights'
   2 July 2009: UN Doc. E/C.12/GC/20
India: Initial report (Arts. 10–12) (1983); UN Doc. E/1980/6/Add.34 (1983)
India: Initial report (Arts. 13–15) (1989); UN Doc. E/1988/5/Add.5 (1989)
India: Second to fifth reports (2006); UN Doc. E/C.12/IND/5 (2006)

Committee on the Elimination of Discrimination Against Women

Concluding observations – India (2014); CEDAW/C/IND/CO/4–5, 24 July 2014
India: Initial report (1999); UN Doc. CEDAW/C/IND/1 (1999)
India: Second and third reports (2005); UN Doc. CEDAW/C/IND/2-3
India: Special report (2009); UN Doc. CEDAW/C/IND/SP.1

Committee on the Rights of the Child

Concluding observations – India (2004); CRC/C/15/Add. 228, 26 February 2004.
Concluding observations – India (2014); CRC/C/IND/CO/3–4, 7 July 2014.
General Comment No. 7 (2005), Implementing child rights in early childhood, 20 September
   2006; UN Doc. CRC/C/GC/7/Rev.1
General Comment No. 8 (2006), 'The Right of the Child to Protection from Corporal Punish-
   ment and other Cruel or Degrading Forms of Punishment' 2 March 2007: UN Doc. CRC/
   C/GC/8
India: Initial report (1997); UN Doc. CRC/C/28/Add.10 (1997)
India: Second report (2001); UN Doc. CRC/C/93/Add.5 (2001)
India: Third and fourth reports (2011); UN Doc. CRC/C/IND/3-4 (2011)

Index

Note: page numbers in *italics* indicate a figure.

ACDA *see* Anti-Caste Discrimination Alliance
Achiume, Tendayi 143
activism: on caste as human rights issue 2–3,
  6, 99, 135–137, 260; on Equality Act caste
  inclusion 197–198, 200–202, 204, 214;
  on legalised caste inequality in India prior
  to independence 62–68; online 95–96,
  264; and sociological theories of caste 39;
  transnational 167, 264; in UK 2, 167, 179,
  184, 190, 197–198, 200–202, 204, 214,
  229–231, 242–243, 244–245, 253–254;
  and UN Charter bodies' standards
  135–137, 141, 150, 152, 158; and US
  racial discrimination 23; at WCAR 150
Ad Dharm Federation of the UK 166
Ad-Dharm movement 22, 64, 165–166
affirmative action (India): assessment of
  effectiveness of 84–87, 259; and beyond
  in India 92–94, 259; ceiling on 82–83;
  challenges to 68, 85; Code of Conduct on
  94; Constitutional provisions 79, 81–83,
  113, 258; for Dalits 2, 15, 20, 22, 65,
  68, 73, 79, 81–83, 84–87, 92–94, 113,
  258, 259; educational opportunities and
  79, 81–82, 84, 86; for OBCs 81–83;
  occupation opportunities and 20, 73,
  81–83, 84–87; political participation
  and 86–87; private sector extension of
  94; religious restrictions on 90–91; for
  Scheduled Tribes 81–83; social mobility
  and 84
age, UK discrimination law on 178, 182, 200
agrarian slavery 20, 40, 59
Ahanhanzo, Glélé 142
Alliance of Hindu Organisations (AHO)
  234–235, 244
All-India Census 35, 40, 62
All-India Scheduled Castes Federation 23
Allott, Antony 91–92
All-Party Parliamentary Group on Dalits
  (APPGD) 229, 242

Ambedkar, Bhimrao Ramji ("Babasaheb"):
  'Annihilation of Caste' by 18, 69; Buddhist
  conversion of 21, 64, 67, 166n28; caste
  scholarship of 3, 15, 18, 258; as Constitution
  drafter 3, 15, 65, 78–80; as Dalit 15, 63–64;
  on Dalit indigeneity 155, 166; on endogamy
  172; and graded inequality 37, 38, 94, 259;
  legalised caste inequality opposition by 44,
  63–67; on migration of caste 168; multifaceted response to caste discrimination
  92, 95; on racial theories of caste 36; on
  societal effects of caste 94–95, 248; theory
  of caste of 37–38, 41; UN petition of 23; on
  untouchability 25, 28–29, 33n165, 63–66,
  89; on *varna* 37–38
Ambedkar Memorial Committees 166
Ambedkar Principles 176, 255
Anti-Caste Discrimination Alliance (ACDA):
  activism of 167, 198, 214, 231; on caste
  as hidden apartheid 118, 171, 204; on
  caste discrimination in education 172, 173;
  FOIA requests by 199; research findings of
  165, 171–172, 204, 205, 215, 254
Anti-Discrimination and Equality Bill (India)
  90, 259n15
Anti-Slavery International 255
Anti-social Behaviour, Crime and Policing Act
  (2014), UK 181n26
apartheid 101, 106, 117–118; hidden 118,
  171, 204
APPGD (All-Party Parliamentary Group on
  Dalits) 229, 242
Aranyakas 47–48
Arthasasthra (Kautilya) 49
Aryans 29–30, 31–32, 35–36, 48
Asiatic Land Tenure and Indian
  Representation Act No. 28 ('Ghetto Act,'
  1946), South Africa 106
association discrimination 193n123
Atharva Veda 47
Atlee, Clement 67

20–21n62; law and 38, 44–53, 56, 57–60, 62–68, 218–222, 235, 244, 248–251; nationalism and 248n156, 249; as neologism 20n62, 248; reform of 63–64; untouchability and 27–29, 63–67
Hindutva 249–250
historical origins of caste society: in Ancient India 29–31; commensality in 32; endogamy in 32–33; hierarchy and heredity in 32–33, 257; *jati* origins in 31–32; legalised caste inequality in (*see* India: legalised caste inequality); religious foundations in (*see* religion); untouchability origins in 32, 33; *varna* origins in 30–31, 32
honour-based abuse and violence: and caste 173, 252
HRC (Human Rights Committee), UN 104–105, 132
human rights, law on *see* international human rights law
Human Rights Committee (HRC), UN 104–105, 132
Human Rights Council, UN 137, 140–141, 144–146, 228
Human Rights Council Advisory Committee, UN 137; *see also* Sub-Commission on the Promotion and Protection of Human Rights, UN
Human Rights Watch 118, 137

ICCPR *see* International Covenant on Civil and Political Rights
ICERD *see* International Convention on the Elimination of All Forms of Racial Discrimination
ICESCR *see* International Covenant on Economic, Social and Cultural Rights
IDSN (International Dalit Solidarity Network) 137, 146, 167, 176, 198
India: and caste discrimination: CERD observations on 112–123, 133–134, 260; contemporary context for 71–78, 258–259; Dalits in (*see* Dalits); descent and (*see* descent; heredity); embeddedness of 1–2, 69–71; historical origins of 29–33; *jati* and (*see jati*); law addressing (*see* India: law; international human rights law); overview of 258–259; poverty and 71; racial segregation and 118; religion and (*see* religion); scholarship, research, and study of 3–6; sociological theories of 34–43; tenacity of 41–43, 257; UK migration of (*see* United Kingdom and caste); untouchability in (*see* untouchability); *varna* in (*see varna*); violence in (*see* caste-based violence); *see also* caste
India: law: activism on caste in 2–3, 62–68; caste discrimination illegality

in 2 (*see also* India: legal regulation of caste discrimination); Constitution (*see* Constitution (1950, India)); descent in 124–125; domestic jurisdiction 126–127; Indian Penal Code and 59, 60, 64, 80; legalised caste inequality with (*see* India: legalised caste inequality); legal regulation of caste discrimination with (*see* India: legal regulation of caste discrimination); personal law and 58–59, 60; Universal Periodic Review of 146–147; untouchability criminalisation in 2, 27, 28, 66, 79–81, 101, 113, 258; *see also specific laws*
India: legalised caste inequality 44–68; in 1500–500 BCE 45–48; in 500 BCE–700 CE 48–52; in 800–1200 CE 52; in 1206–1707 CE 53–55; in 1600–1772 CE 55–56; in 1772–1857 CE 56–59, 61–62; in 1858–1947 CE 60–61, 62–68; Ambedkar's opposition to 44, 63–67; in Anglo-Hindu law 57–59; in British India 55–61, 62–68; in colonial era 44, 55–61, 62–68; Dalits and 44–68; *dharma* and 44, 45–47, 48–52, 54; in early Vedic texts 47–48; in feudal era 52; *karma* and 47; Kautilya's *Arthasasthra* and 49; in medieval/Islamic India 53–55; in Nepal vs. 44, 61–62; overview of 44, 68; *panchayats* and 53, 56, 59, 60; personal law and 58–59, 60; in post-Vedi and classical period 48–52; reform of 44, 62–68; Scheduled Caste identity and 65–68; slavery and 59; *smrti* commentaries and 53–55; social mobility and 52, 55; untouchability and 58, 63–67; *varna* and 45, 48, 50–51, 58; in Vedic period 45–48
India: legal regulation of caste discrimination 69–96; affirmative action in 79, 81–83, 84–87, 92–94, 258, 259; assessment of policies and legislation 84–91; civil anti-discrimination and equality laws and 89–90, 92; Constitutional rights 78–84 (*see also* Constitution (1950, India)); contemporary context for caste discrimination and 71–78, 258–259; de facto situation vs. 71, 95; framework for equality and non-discrimination 79–84; future developments and opportunities for 91–96; lessons learned from 91–96; other provisions for 83–84; overview of 69–71; "protective" legislation and 80–81; religious restrictions and 90–91; social transformation through 91–92
Indian Buddhist Society 166
Indian Mutual Support and Social Association 166
Indian Penal Code 59, 60, 64, 80
Indian Republican Group of Great Britain 166

Printed in Great Britain
by Amazon

37233285R00185